Understanding Canadian
Public Administration

SECOND EDITION

Understanding Canadian Public Administration

AN INTRODUCTION TO THEORY AND PRACTICE ✦ **GREGORY J. INWOOD**

PEARSON

Prentice Hall

Toronto

Canadian Cataloguing in Publication Data

Inwood, Gregory J.

    Understanding Canadian public administration: an introduction to theory and practice / Gregory J. Inwood. –2nd ed.

Includes bibliographic references and index.
ISBN 0-13-008153-1

1. Public administration—Canada—Textbooks. 2. Canada—Politics and government—Textbooks. I. Title.

JL108.I58 2003   351.71   C2003-900440-6

ISBN 0-13-008153-1

Vice President, Editorial Director: Michael J. Young
Acquisitions Editor: Lori Will
Marketing Manager: Christine Cozens
Developmental Editor: John Polanszky
Production Editor: Charlotte Morrison-Reed
Copy Editor: Nadia Halim
Production Coordinator: Wendy Moran
Page Layout: Heidi Palfrey
Art Director: Mary Opper
Cover and Interior Design: Michelle Bellemare
Cover Image: Getty Images

1 2 3 4 5   08 07 06 05 04

Printed and bound in Canada.

For Alison and Matthew

Brief Contents

Chapter 1   Introduction: The Nature of Public Administration   1

Chapter 2   Theories of Organization   27

Chapter 3   Organization Theory and Canadian
Public Administration   63

Chapter 4   Public Administration and Democracy   77

Chapter 5   Public Administration and Institutions: The Real World
of Organizations and the Machinery of Government   115

Chapter 6   Public Administration and Law   163

Chapter 7   Public Administration and Public Policy   199

Chapter 8   Public Administration and Evaluation   237

Chapter 9   Public Administration and the Management
of Human Resources   259

Chapter 10 Public Administration, Management Reform and Financial
Management   305

Chapter 11 Public Administration and Ethics   337

Chapter 12 Public Administration and Accountability   363

Chapter 13 Public Administration and the Post-Deficit World:
Surpluses and Security   395

Contents

Preface   xv

Chapter 1   Introduction: The Nature of Public Administration   1

What You Will Learn   1

What Is Public Administration?   2

Public Administration and Democratic Government   5

Bureaucracy   7
    Personnel   7
    Formal Rules   8
    Policy Instruments   8
    Conventions of Behaviour   8
    Institutions   8

Comparing Public and Private Sectors   9
    Mandate and Goals   10
    Efficiency and Service   13
    Professionalism and Ethics   14

Restructuring the Public Sector and the Role of the State   18
    The Minimalist State   18
    The Keynesian Welfare State   18
    The Neoconservative State   19

What You Have Learned   21

Chapter 2   Theories of Organization   27

What You Will Learn   27

Perspectives on Bureaucratic Organization   28
    The Neo-Marxists   32
    Criticisms of Marxist Theory   32
    Max Weber   33
    Criticisms of the Weberian Model   35

Structuralist and Humanist Theories   41
    Scientific Management   42
    Criticisms of Scientific Management   47
    The Human Relations Approach   48
    Criticisms of the Human Relations School   54
Other Theoretical Approaches   56
What You Have Learned   59

**Chapter 3   Organization Theory and Canadian
                 Public Administration   63**

What You Will Learn   63
The Impact of Organization Theory   64
Contemporary Developments   67
    Participatory Management   67
    The New Public Management   69
What You Have Learned   74

Chapter 4   Public Administration and Democracy   77

What You Will Learn   77
Power, Politics and Public Administration   79
What Is Democracy?   83
    Direct Democracy   84
    Representative Democracy   85
    Political Democracy   86
    Economic Democracy   87
State and Government   89
Political Culture   92
    Geography   94
    Demography   94
    Three Founding Cultures   94
    Continentalism   95
    Interpretations of Canadian Political Culture   95
The Interplay of Democracy, Political Culture, and the Institutions of Public
Administration   101
    The Canadian Constitution   101

The North American Free Trade Agreement   103
Federalism   103
The Parliamentary Actors   104
The Extra-Parliamentary Actors   108
What You Have Learned   110

**Chapter 5   Public Administration and Institutions: The Real World
of Organizations and the Machinery of Government   115**

What You Will Learn   115
Factors Influencing Organizational Structure   116
Capitalist Democracy   116
Federalism   117
Cabinet-Parliamentary Government   119
Political-Administrative Relationships   125
Departmental Organizations   126
Central Agencies   133
Alternative Service Delivery   137
Ministerial Responsibility   140
The Deputy Minister   140
Regulatory Agencies   144
Crown Corporations   149
What You Have Learned   153

Chapter 6   Public Administration and Law   163

What You Will Learn   163
The Law and the Courts   164
What Is a Constitution?   166
A History of Canada's Constitution   168
Federalism and the Constitution   174
Federal versus Provincial Rights   177
Federal-Provincial Bargaining   181
Administrative Law   186
What You Have Learned   194

Chapter 7   Public Administration and Public Policy   199

What You Will Learn   199

Defining Public Policy   200
    Scope   201
    Means   202
    Resources   204

Formulating Public Policy   207
    Environmental Factors   208
    Distribution of Power   209
    Social Attitudes and Ideas   209
    Institutional Structure   210
    Procedural Factors   210
    The Rational-Comprehensive Theory   210
    The Incremental Theory   212
    The Mixed-Scanning Theory   214
    Pluralism   214
    Marxist Analysis   215
    Public Choice Theory   217

Implementing Public Policy   218
    The Process of Implementation: How Does Anything Get Done?   218
    Choice of Governing Instrument   222
    Recent Developments in Policy Implementation   227

Evaluating Public Policy   229

What You Have Learned   230

Chapter 8   Public Administration and Evaluation   237

What You Will Learn   237

The Development of Evaluation   238

Problems of Evaluation   243

Evaluation in Action   246

Contemporary Evaluation Practices   248

What You Have Learned   255

Chapter 9 Public Administration and the Management of Human Resources 259

What You Will Learn 259

A Brief History of the Public Service: Who Works There, Anyway? 260

The Public Service Today: An Overview 272

    The Theory of Representativeness 276

    Region 277

    Language 277

    Equity 278

    Unionization of the Public Service 286

    Public Servants and Politics 288

Human Resources Management 290

What You Have Learned 298

Chapter 10 Public Administration, Management Reform and Financial Management 305

What You Will Learn 305

Restructuring the Public Service: The Management View 306

    The Productivity Improvement Program 310

    The Ministerial Task Force on Program Review 310

    Increased Ministerial Authority and Accountability 311

    PS2000 312

    Program Review 314

    La Relève 316

Financial Management 321

    The State and Economy 321

    Managing Government Fiscal Resources 325

    The Budgetary Cycle 329

What You Have Learned 332

Chapter 11 Public Administration and Ethics 337

What You Will Learn 337

Ethical Dilemmas in the Public Service 338

    Discretion 345

    Partisanship 345

Public Comment   346
Conflict of Interest   347
Lying for the Public Good   347
Public Sector versus Private Sector Ethics   348
Codes of Conduct   350
Do Codes of Conduct Work?   351
Training and Education   355
Role Models   356
An Attentive Public   357
What You Have Learned   358

Chapter 12 Public Administration and Accountability   363

What You Will Learn   363
Accountability and Democracy   364
Ministerial Responsibility   370
Accountability and Public Servants   377
Accountability in Action: The Role of the Office of the Auditor General   381
Contemporary Issues of Accountability and Control   384
What You Have Learned   389

Chapter 13 Public Administration and the Post-Deficit World:
             Surpluses and Security   395

What You Will Learn   395
The Politics of Deficits   396
Toward a Post-Deficit Future and the New Security Agenda   406
What You Have Learned   419

Glossary   423

Index   432

PREFACE

This second edition of *Understanding Canadian Public Administration: An Introduction to Theory and Practice* builds on the main purposes for which the original was conceived and executed. It addresses the need for an introductory text in the theory and practice of public administration in Canada. As with the first edition, this edition provides an overview of the essential theoretical issues in the field, and then uses that theoretical grounding to examine the actual practice of public administration. As an introduction to public administration, both in it's historical context, and in the contemporary context of rapid change, the goal of this work is to foster an understanding of the basic elements of public administration, leaving detailed analysis of specific sub-fields to more specialized sources. As such, this text is geared to undergraduate university and college students, as well as public servants, who require a clear and concise introduction to the topic. It is meant to be used as the primary text for courses in public administration.

One of the striking features of public administration is that it is constantly in a state of flux. As this edition goes to press, the Chretien government has introduced a sweeping omnibus bill that sets the stage for the largest reform of the federal public service in years. The proposed legislation is intended to modernize the public service, alter the relationship between the government and its unions, change the definition of merit, reform the process of hiring, firing and managing federal public servants, adapt a new code of conduct and rules for ethical behaviour, introduce a new accountability framework for senior public servants, and make numerous other changes. It even proposes changing the name of the federal public service to the "federal public administration". Part of the goal is to effect a cultural transformation in the institutions of government, as well as attend to the basic "plumbing." What, if anything, will come of these reforms remains to be seen – there have been approximately 37 inquiries into the state of the public service in the past 40 years, after all. However, the fact that these reforms are being mandated in law will make a difference which students of public administration will be able to observe.

Understanding Canadian Public Administration begins with an introduction to the basic elements of public administration and explains the field in the context of democratic government. It also focuses on the impact of recent developments, such as restructuring. In particular, it compares the roles of the private and public sectors, and examines the impact that the latter has had on the former. The text then examines theories of public administration, grouping them broadly into three categories: classic, structuralist and humanist. It critically analyses the impact of each category on public administration in Canada and concludes with an assessment of how recent theoretical innovations, such as the New Public Management and Participatory Management, have reshaped our thinking.

The real world of government organizations is examined as well, allowing students to see how theoretical ideas are translated into practice in the Canadian government. Here, the student learns about the executive, legislative and judicial branches of government, as well as the nature of bureaucratic organizations. The relationship between democracy and bureaucracy is a recurring theme, illustrated with real life examples.

This introductory material sets the stage for an analysis of how public policy is actually set within the context of a federal state. Policy outcomes and processes are also considered in the context of the roles of key government players: the executive, legislative and judicial branches of government, the bureaucracy, the central agencies. Outside government, other actors are examined, such as political parties, interest groups and social movements, and the media. The text explains policy formulation, implementation and evaluation, and examines the issue of choosing governing instruments. Specific key issues such as financial and personnel management are also considered. Finally, the text concludes with a speculative chapter on the future of public administration in a world dominated by surpluses and security issues.

Understanding Canadian Public Administration addresses the outstanding need and demand for an easily accessible introductory text in the field that is neither encyclopedic nor esoteric. It is meant to be a simple (though not simplistic) explanation of the basics of Canadian public administration. The narrative is in an interrogative style that can be easily understood by undergraduate students. In addition, the text provides real-life examples that are relevant to students' experiences, and incorporates these examples into the analysis of public administration. In this way the topic is brought to life and made immediately relevant. The text invites students to examine the issues of public administration from their own viewpoints, through their own experiences, by posing questions about day-to-day issues that they may not have realized relate to the way public administration affects them.

A variety of pedagogical features in *Understanding Canadian Public Administration* enhance the student's learning experience. These include sections at the beginning and end of each chapter entitled *What You Will Learn* and *What You Have Learned*, which clarify learning objectives through brief introductory and concluding passages. There is a list of *Key Words and Concepts* (boldfaced within the text), and suggested lists for *Further Reading* and useful *Weblinks*. Each chapter also contains summary questions with which the instructor can test the student's understanding of the material, or generate essay questions; students can use these questions to self-test their comprehension of the material. Sidebars complement the main text; these short asides illuminate issues with supplementary information that might otherwise interrupt the flow of the narrative. Occasional editorial cartoons highlight points in a humorous, but effective, manner. This second edition features many updates on topical issues and new developments in the field of public administration. While retaining the intention of providing a solid grounding in the basics, this edition also addresses issues and themes which have emerged since the first edition was published. In particular, the chapters on human resource and financial management have been substantially restructured. Throughout the text, updated data, statistical information and policy issues have been introduced as well.

Understanding Canadian Public Administration is divided into 13 chapters. Chapter 1 provides an overview of some central issues of public administration. It defines the field, examines what bureaucracy means, and compares the public sector with the private sector. As well, it introduces the concept of the role of the state, a central notion that is returned to in the final chapter.

Chapter 2 deals with organization theory, and is divided into two broad sections. The first critically examines classic theories and theorists; the second assesses structuralist and humanist theories and theorists. In this chapter, students are introduced to Weber, Marx, Taylor, and many other key actors in the development of public administration as both theory and practice.

Chapter 3 applies organization theory to the Canadian experience. It explores the impact of various approaches to public administration on Canadian thinking and practice, and examines the most recent trends and developments affecting the organization of the Canadian government, including emerging post- New Public Management issues.

Chapter 4 explores the link between public administration and democracy by illuminating the meaning of concepts such as responsible and representative government.

Chapter 5 turns to the "real world" of public administration by examining the actual organizations and machinery of governing in Canada. It does so within a framework of factors that influence the organizational structure of government.

Chapter 6 discusses the relationship between public administration and law—both constitutional and administrative.

In Chapter 7, the wide-ranging issue of public policy is explored. The term is defined and placed within the context of the policy cycle, which involves the formulation, implementation and evaluation of public policy. Various theoretical perspectives on public policy decision-making are also surveyed.

Chapter 8 builds on the insights provided in the prior chapter by focusing in more detail on the increasingly important concept of policy evaluation.

Public administration is nothing without the people who make up the public service, and so Chapter 9 has been reworked to focus more sharply on the key elements that shape the world of those who work in government administration. Merit and patronage, equity and collective bargaining, and recruitment and retention are all considered. So, too, are the many issues surrounding the recent restructuring of the public service.

This leads us to consider the role of management in public administration, which is the topic of Chapter 10. Specifically, management reform and management of financial resources are explored in the context of current restraints on the public service.

The ethical dilemmas confronting public administrators are many, and are of a different nature than those facing private sector administrators. Chapter 11 explains why this is so, and explores various public administration issues related to ethics and morality.

This chapter is followed by one on accountability, a fundamental issues of public administration. Chapter 12 assesses the ways in which accountability is maintained in the public sector by looking at issues such as ministerial and Cabinet responsibility. It also explores the structures of accountability, while revealing the inherent tensions among democracy, bureaucracy, efficiency and other important values within public administration.

Finally, Chapter 13 ties together several of the main themes by speculating on what governing in Canada will look like under the newly emerging conditions of the "post-deficit era." As Canadian governments get their fiscal houses in order, the rationale that has underpinned Canadian public administration has changed. In addition, this chapter considers the impact of security issues on public administration in the wake of Septmber 11, 2001. How these issues might play out, and why they are important to both students and practitioners of public administration and the public, are the subjects of this last chapter.

No text on a topic as broad as public administration is going to cover every possible issue and development in the depth each deserves. No attempt has been made to do so in *Understanding Canadian Public Administration*. Rather, an overview is provided, recognizing that the literature is both rich and deep, and that students with particular interests not covered explicitly here can pursue them through the Further Readings or Weblinks listed herein. As well, it should be admitted that the focus is unabashedly federal, which is not to suggest that provincial and municipal public administration are not worthy of attention. Certainly they are, but space and time are cruel masters for those writing about so complex a matter as the public administration of this country, necessitating a sharper focus than we might otherwise prefer.

It is extremely gratifying to be asked to produce a second edition of this book. Doing so simply reminds me that a text such as *Understanding Canadian Public Administration* is the product of the distillation of years of reading and thinking about the topic at hand inspired by countless intellectual contributions from others too numerous to list. As such, my debts are many, but must mainly go unnamed. Still, happily, there are those whose direct contribution to this text I can acknowledge. The reviews and comments supplied by Geoffrey Booth (Georgian College), Lloyd Brown-John (University of Windsor), Ken Gibbons (University of Winnipeg), Ross Gibbons (King's College, University of Western Ontario), Dennis Roughley (Georgian College), and Bruce Smardon (York University) were helpful in the genesis of the text. My own public administration students at Ryerson University—many of them practising civil servants—have provided invaluable feedback as I field-tested my ideas on them. Many of my colleagues in the Department of Politics and School of Public Administration have provided unstinting support and encouragement for which I am very grateful. The team at Pearson Education Canada has been extraordinarily patient with me, and understanding of the pressures on my time. I particularly want to thank John Polanszky, Nadia Halim and Charlotte Morrison Reed.

All of the above made important contributions to the writing of this book. Of course, responsibility for whatever errors and defects appear in the text is mine alone.

Gregory J. Inwood

Chapter ①

Introduction: *The* Nature *of* Public Administration

WHAT YOU WILL LEARN

Your study of public administration will require you to canvass many issues from a variety of perspectives. You will discover that the theory and practice of the field range across a surprisingly broad spectrum. This first chapter introduces the topic by addressing some basic issues related to the nature of public administration in Canada. By the end of the chapter, you will be able to answer the following questions: How has the field of public administration been defined? What is the relationship between public administration and democratic government? What are some of the common assumptions about bureaucratic organizations, and how do these assumptions influence how we view public sector organization and management in Canada? What are the major differences and similarities between public and private sector administration? How can the growth and ongoing restructuring of the bureaucratic state be explained, and what are the implications for democracy? The discussion highlights five central issues:

1. *What Is Public Administration?*

   This introductory section will briefly address the following questions: How do we define public administration, and what key terms and concepts are used in the study and practice of public administration? The intent is to familiarize you with the basic jargon employed in this area, to lay the basis for an understanding of later material.

2. *Public Administration and Democratic Government*

   The second section concerns the tensions between democratic representation and bureaucracy. You will consider the following question: If elected officials as representatives of the people are responsible for government policy, how do nonelected bureaucrats influence the policy agenda, policy decisions and the way in which policies are implemented? In short, is the will of the people realized through the bureaucratic institutions of our political system?

3. Bureaucracy

This section focuses on the nature of bureaucracy by briefly examining its component parts: personnel, formal rules, policy instruments, conventions of behaviour and institutions. It also asks you to consider the question of what happens when the values of democracy and efficiency clash within the organizational structure of bureaucracy.

4. Comparing Public and Private Sectors

The fourth section compares the public and private sectors. You will note important differences between the two with regard to the following questions: What are the mandates and goals of the public sector compared to the private sector? How do the issues of efficiency and service differ in each? What roles do professionalism and ethics play in the one compared to the other?

5. Restructuring the Public Sector and the Role of the State

The fifth section looks at the extent, significance and consequences of government restructuring. It asks the following: Why is organizational change taking place? What forms does it take? How has organizational change redefined the nature and scope of public administration?

The five sections cited above are followed by a section that summarizes 10 of the concepts most vital to the study of public administration. After reading this chapter, you should be able to explain what is meant by the following: public administration; the politics-administration dichotomy; public versus private sector management; and bureaucracy. The terms and concepts introduced in this chapter are revisited elsewhere in the book and are analyzed in more detail.

What Is Public Administration?

So, you have embarked on the study (and perhaps career) of **public administration**. When you excitedly told your family and friends the news, though, you were probably greeted with polite but quizzical looks. They may not have said it aloud, but many were probably thinking to themselves, "What the heck is that?" Perhaps you yourself are a little unsure of what direction your studies in this area will take you. This is not unusual. As one author puts it,

To the practitioner seeking a bit of advice or the student trying to understand the operation of government, a journey into the literature of public administration can be a bewildering experience. The collective wisdom of public administration emerges from at least six separate fields and disciplines; bits of knowledge sought by one set of experts may be hidden behind another's disciplinary boundary; principles drawn from one field have a tendency to contradict lessons drawn from additional sources; no unifying theory exists to help guide the investigator. Experts frequently cannot agree on a definition of public administration. Some view the subject broadly so as to include the entire process of running a modern government, while others view it as narrowly confined to the administrative policies that governments formulate, such as laws regulating the hiring and firing of personnel. The field comes from so many places—and leads to so many subjects—that even people who make a profession out of studying the subject have trouble keeping up with it all.[1]

However, the depth and breadth of the field, though they may seem intimidating to those who seek to understand public administration, are precisely the features that make it such an interesting study, as well as such a challenging career.

While the systematic and organized academic study of public administration is relatively young (dating from around the start of the 1900s), the practice of public administration is ancient. Author E.N. Gladden presents an extremely detailed history of public administration that discusses the administrative practices of every civilization in recorded history.[2] He shows that by the era of ancient China and Egypt, there were incredible feats of organization (think of the construction of the pyramids, for example) as well as massive public bureaucracies, red tape, and corruption of the sort we often associate with contemporary bureaucracy. Many characteristics of present-day public bureaucracy also existed during the period of the Roman Empire. The Roman Catholic church kept many of the Roman administrative practices alive during the Dark Ages, and the rise of the Enlightenment from the 17th century in Western Europe, as well as the emergence of the modern nation-state beginning in Germany shortly thereafter, contained the seeds of modern public administration. By the 1800s the characteristics of contemporary systems of bureaucracy were emerging in Europe, Great Britain, the United States and Canada. But what exactly is public administration? Defining the term is a challenge, since there are many conceptions.

Rather than get bogged down in a definitional quagmire, we will dispense with the traditional list of definitions, the presentation of which would likely only lead to a certain confusion.[3] For our purposes, public administration will be viewed from two perspectives. It is a field of academic study derived from several disciplines, including political science, business administration, sociology, psychology, law and economics. But it is also a set of administrative practices and institutional arrangements geared toward the provision of public services and regulations as realized through the public bureaucracy. The knowledge derived from the academic side of public administration supports the practices of the field, while, at the same time, the practices continuously feed academic study, requiring a constant reviewing and updating of findings in light of the increasingly professionalized real world of government.

The relationship between study and practice, then, is mutually reinforcing. Education for public administration careers can be eclectic in nature, based as it is on several different disciplines. Professor of public administration Dwight Waldo draws an analogy between the study of public administration and that of medicine: aspiring doctors must draw on a variety of sciences to prepare themselves for their careers.[4] Similarly, practitioners of public administration educate themselves by drawing on a range of academic literatures.

Writings on public administration go back thousands of years. But it is generally acknowledged that the first modern statement that public administration was a distinct professional field came in an essay written in 1887 by Woodrow Wilson, later a president of the United States (see Box 1-1).[5] Wilson argued that political scientists had ignored the fundamental question of how governments are administered, and thought they ought to refocus their attention on precisely that issue. He advocated a focus on personnel, organization and management of the public sector in the interest of discovering ways in which public administration could achieve greater organizational efficiency and economy. These are concerns that animate the field to this day. But overlaying these concerns are ones about the democratic nature of governing.

BOX 1-1

Woodrow Wilson on "The Study of Administration"

Woodrow Wilson (1856–1924) made an important contribution to the understanding of public administration in an essay he wrote in 1887 for the journal *Political Science Quarterly*. Wilson would later become president of the United States, but at the time he was an instructor at a college for women. He wrote, "It is the object of administrative study to discover, first, what government can properly and successfully do, and secondly, how it can do these proper things with the utmost possible efficiency and at the least possible cost either of money or of energy." Wilson also pointed out that an important distinction needed to be made between "politics" and "administration." This observation served as the underpinning for the important theory of the politics-administration dichotomy, discussed below.

The American influence on Canadian public administration is indisputable. Indeed, in Chapter 2 we will examine some of the most influential thinkers in the field, and the majority of them are American. The original concerns were with corruption and the party "bosses" who tended to rule local politics with iron fists. Thus, administrative reform became an early concern of theorists there. So, too, did management issues. Early writers were concerned with the management of personnel and budgets, and with finding the "one best way" of administratively organizing the workplace. Moreover, they were concerned with finding this "one best way" through the systematic adoption and application of scientific theory and rationalism. As we will see later, the assumptions of these approaches came under attack in the United States by the middle part of the century, fuelling debates about the theory and practice of public administration that continue today.

These types of issues spilled over the border into Canada (as well as elsewhere in the world).[6] But in Canada, public administration was long regarded as the poor cousin to political science, with its teachers and students buried somewhere in the recesses of political science departments. For several generations, R. MacGregor Dawson's book *The Government of Canada* (1947) served as the main (and indeed only) text for students studying Canadian political science. But Dawson was also to publish the first two Canadian books in the field now known as public administration. The first was *The Principle of Official Independence* in 1922, and the second was *The Civil Service of Canada* in 1929.[7] A number of universities began to offer degrees in public administration, starting with Dalhousie University in 1936 and Carleton College (now Carleton University) in 1946. In 1957 the Institute of Public Administration of Canada (IPAC) was formed, and a year later the journal *Canadian Public Administration* was launched, dedicated to disseminating the views and experiences of both practitioners and scholars in the field of public administration. Debates about the purpose of the institute, the journal, and indeed the field of Canadian public administration revealed a belief that educational training in public administration should not simply be restricted to learning the administrative techniques necessary to run a government department. Rather, it should be tied to the broader social sciences and should draw on them to produce a well-rounded approach based on a broader conception of the management of the state.[8] From about the 1960s, there were increased efforts to position public administration as a more distinct field of study. A rapid growth in the size of the public service contributed to this trend by fuelling the need for highly trained professionals versed in the art of public administration. Today, there are 16 universities in Canada with programs in public administration, several of which also offer master's degrees in public administration.[9]

A recent study commissioned by the Canadian Association of Programs in Public Administration (CAPPA) and the Canadian Centre for Management Development (CCMD) uncovered some interesting aspects of public administration courses and programs in Canada.[10] These included the fact that there is no single model for the location of public administration within universities. About an equal number of programs are located in faculties of social science or faculties of administrative and business studies (44% each). Only about 8% are located in separate schools of public administration and management, with the remainder scattered in a variety of other places. The orphan-like character of the discipline reflects its hybrid nature as the product of a variety of academic influences.

Public Administration and Democratic Government

Since public administration is about the public provision of services and regulations, we necessarily are talking about politics. Politics is about who gets what, when and how; or how the state responds to the demands and wants of the public. Public administration, then, is about how the state answers the question of who gets what, when and how (which will be different from, for instance, how the private-sector marketplace answers this question through the law of supply and demand). State action involves a myriad of complex decisions and actions by various actors and institutions in what we call the public sector.

We will explore these issues in more detail in Chapter 4, on democracy. For now, we will briefly consider that for the purpose of carrying out decisions and actions, a handy but somewhat artificial division of labour exists in the practice of public administration between those who make the decisions, and those who carry out the decision-makers' wishes. In a **democratic society** such as Canada, these roles fall into the hands of **elected representatives** (the decision-makers) and **bureaucrats** (who carry out their political masters' wishes) respectively. This neat little division of labour is referred to as the **politics-administration dichotomy** (see Box 1-2). In this sense, then, public administration is the process of (bureaucrats) carrying out (politicians') public decisions. There is a division or dichotomy between politics and administration.

— CANADA —
elected   Bureaucrats
reps

BOX 1-2

The Politics-Administration Dichotomy

The politics-administration dichotomy reflects the notion that "politics" is about deciding what government should do, while "administration" is about how to do it, and thus there should be clearly defined responsibilities that differentiate the roles of politicians and bureaucrats. The concept manifests itself in several ways. For instance, it is reflected in the desire to find the "one best way" of administering public affairs. It reflects the desire to achieve the ultimate in efficiency in the provision of public services and the business of government by putting public administration on the most rational basis possible. This means, for example, hiring and promoting the best possible candidate for a job (the **merit principle**) rather than a political supporter of the minister (patronage). The political neutrality of public servants is vital to the realization of the politics-administration dichotomy. Public servants should serve the *government* of the day, not the political party that happens to hold power.

In reality, of course, the politics-administration dichotomy is less straightforward than theory implies. Not only do bureaucrats respond to orders from politicians, but they also sometimes initiate action on their own. In other words, the traditional role of bureaucrats, which is implementation of policy following the instructions of their political masters, is accompanied by the role they play in policy formulation. This is because bureaucrats enjoy a fair amount of discretionary power. After all, no elected official who is given the job of heading up as large and complex an institution as a government department or ministry can know absolutely everything that goes on therein. So in aiding the elected representatives, bureaucrats engage in policy formulation as well as implementation.

Indeed, during the 1960s and 1970s, it became fashionable to assert that bureaucrats were highly trained technocratic experts who knew and understood the "ins and outs" of government, and ought to have a more responsible role in the areas traditionally left up to politicians. Some theorists and practitioners went so far as to suggest that since frontline bureaucratic workers (i.e., those who dealt directly with members of the public) had firsthand and intimate experience with the needs of their clients, they ought to have a more hands-on role in formulating and implementing policy. In the 1980s and 1990s, however, the view emerged that the bureaucracy had usurped too much power from the politicians, and reforms were enacted by many governments to restore the proper relationship between the two sets of actors. These views represent some of the many attempts to sort out the proper balance between the power of public servants and elected representatives in a democratic society.

Bureaucracy

The public provision of services and regulations, the political question of who gets what, when and how, and the issue of how the state responds to the demands and wants of the public take place within a structure known generically as a **bureaucracy**. We have all encountered bureaucracy. When you go to renew your driver's licence, file your income tax, register in a program at a community centre, go to court, apply for a passport or a parking permit, etc., you are involved in a relationship with a bureaucracy whose job it is to satisfy your needs and wants as a citizen.

The term *bureaucracy* comes from a combination of the French word *bureau,* which means "desk" and a Greek word meaning "rule." Given the remarkable accomplishments of human societies that have emerged from bureaucratic organizations in both the public and private sector through the ages, it is striking that the term carries such pejorative connotations. It is negatively associated with red tape, inefficiency, rigid lines of control, corruption, petty officiousness, delay and so on. How many times have you stood in a line or waited patiently on the phone— while being tortured by Muzak—for service from some bureaucratic institution? But this is nothing new.

Bureaucracies are made up of a mixture of elements. Personnel, of course, is a key component of bureaucracies. But bureaucracies also include a set of formal rules, policy instruments, conventions of behaviour and institutions, all of which affect the manner in which services are provided for citizens. Each of these factors is important in any political system. But in a democracy there are particular issues in terms of the relationship of these components to how citizens hold their governments accountable for their actions. Thus, each of these components of bureaucracy is considered below in relation to democracy.

Personnel

Behind the clerk you meet face-to-face when you seek a government service stands a veritable army of people, usually arranged in a hierarchical relationship characterized by a division of labour. The public bureaucracy in Canada employs hundreds of thousands of people at all three levels of government (federal, provincial and municipal) in an array of professions. From firefighters to diplomats, from judges to environmental scientists, from presidents of Crown corporations to street sweepers—all serve in bureaucracies dedicated to providing services, enforcing regulations and formulating, implementing and evaluating policies for citizens. None of these people are elected, yet together they wield a tremendous amount of influence and power over the citizens of Canada. This raises the issue of whom they are accountable to and how that accountability is realized. This is discussed below.

Formal Rules

Bureaucracy is notorious for its "red tape." But in reality, it must have clearly laid out, if somewhat time-consuming and onerous, rules that must be followed to ensure that all services are provided equally to all citizens, and that all regulations are fairly enforced. This is due to the requirement of **accountability** in public bureaucracies. After all, the money spent to support the services and regulations being provided is *your* money—i.e., taxpayers' money—and so must be accounted for very thoroughly. This results in the buildup of formal rules that must be followed to promote accountability, sometimes at the expense of efficiency. This implies that at times the value of efficiency comes into conflict with the value of democracy, and this is an important ongoing public administration conundrum, which we will consider in more detail later.

Policy Instruments

Policy instruments are the means by which services are provided and regulations enforced. The government has at its disposal a vast array of tools to ensure that citizen needs and wants are satisfied.[11] These range from instruments that rely on voluntary compliance on the part of citizens all the way to those that use coercion or even violence. Laws, regulations, Crown corporations, expenditures, taxes, and the *War Measures Act* are but a few examples of different types of policy instruments.

Conventions of Behaviour

Bureaucracies often appear to develop their own internal logic and way of doing things. An emphasis is often placed on formal rules, hierarchies of power, divisions of labour and accountability. In a perfect world, there would always be "one right way" of doing something. Bureaucracies often behave as though they believe we live in such a world, when they develop codes of conduct and conventions of behaviour about how to fulfill their mandates based on the "one right way" of doing things. Bureaucracies must not, in serving the people, appear to be arbitrary and unfair, but must treat each citizen equally. This is why elaborate conventions of behaviour exist, even though such conventions sometimes make institutions appear hidebound and inflexible.

Institutions

This term refers to the complex of government ministries and departments, regulatory bodies, Crown corporations and other institutions responsible for translating the will of the people into action. One response to the democratization of modern society has been to construct ever more elaborate structures to ensure that all voices and interests in society are accommodated within the institutions of the state. But some critics charge that, ironically, as the bureaucracy has increased in size, the level of responsiveness to citizens' needs has declined due to the growth of red tape and bureaucratic procedure within those institutions.

All five of these components of bureaucracy—personnel, formal rules, policy instruments, conventions of behaviour and institutions—profoundly affect the type and quality of public administration we get. In a democratic society, there is the expectation that each component will contribute to a system of administration that is fair and equitable in its treatment of citizens. The key problem is that in fulfilling this mandate, bureaucracies often appear to lack efficiency. Thus, there is a real tension in society between those who hold the value of democracy as paramount and those who regard efficient provision of service as most important.

Some of the actions of the Mike Harris government in Ontario illustrate how this tension can play out. The Harris Conservatives initiated a number of steps designed to enhance efficiency in the provision of government services. This included cutting back on the number of politicians from 130 to 103. It also included reducing the personnel within the public service by about 12 000, reducing and eliminating regulations and red tape, streamlining the delivery of services, or, in some cases, turning them over entirely to the private sector, and reengineering the institutions of government to make them more lean and efficient. But critics of this process allege that democratic accountability was trampled on in the rush to create a more efficient public administration. They suggest that reducing the number of politicians results in a government that may indeed save money, but one in which citizens will get less representation from their elected officials. Fewer elected officials also means centralizing power in the hands of the premier and cabinet, which may reduce the democratic quality of debate and discussion within government. Reduction of personnel, privatization and deregulation are all recipes for diminishing the quality of democratic life—a process that leaves ordinary citizens with fewer avenues through which to force the government to explain itself.

But this debate about efficiency versus democracy is neither new nor particular to Ontario. It is part of the larger ongoing debate that all democracies have about the values appropriate in guiding and informing the administration of the public will. Indeed, an important part of that debate revolves around the increasingly contentious issue of what the role of government (i.e., the public sector) ought to be. Are there some things that the marketplace (i.e., the private sector) can better attend to? These questions are considered in the next section.

Comparing Public and Private Sectors

While the categories discussed above (personnel, formal rules, policy instruments, conventions of behaviour and institutions) help us understand what bureaucracy is, it is apparent that they apply in many regards to what goes on in the private sector as well as in the state (or public sector). The question of the differences between public and private administration goes back a long way in both the study and practice of the field.

Since Woodrow Wilson wrote his classic essay exhorting reformers to help make the business of government "less unbusinesslike," the field of public administration has been seeking to differentiate itself from business administration. But comparisons between business and government are inevitable. In fact, they are important to understanding how management ideas from the private sector have been imposed on public administration and how this process affects what is actually done in public organizations. A key question is, how appropriate are these ideas, and how well has the transfer worked?[12]

Especially since the 1980s, the line between public and private administration has become increasingly blurred. As the role of government has changed, steps have been taken to place public administration on a more businesslike footing and to use modern business techniques, theories and methods to run government. Furthermore, there has been an increase in contracting out to the private sector, and more and more services are being privatized outright. And there has been increased interaction between public managers and private managers, and a good deal more crossover between the two in terms of career paths.

In Canada, the career of public servant was once held in high esteem. It was seen as a noble calling in which individuals dedicated themselves to the service of their country.[13] But recently, this attitude has changed. Now, private sector managers are often seen as inherently superior, more intelligent, industrious and efficient than their public sector counterparts, who are disdained as incompetent, lazy and wasteful.[14] This view is simplistic, patently unfair and inaccurate. Still, you may have heard the following popular refrain: "If only they would run the government like a business, then things would get done!" And in fact, at least superficially, public and private administration are alike in that they share many of the same basic functions. Both engage in the management of complex organizations of people through planning, organizing, staffing and budgeting.

But this ignores the underlying differences between business and government operations. As public administration theorist Wallace Sayre once noted, "Business and public administration are alike only in all unimportant respects."[15] After all, we refer to the "business of business" but to the "art of government." So how do we distinguish between private and public administration? By examining the mandate and goals, efficiency and service, and professionalism and ethics of both, differences between public and private administration should become clear. As you read the next subsections, ask yourself how public and private administration are alike and how they are different.

Mandate and Goals

It may be easiest to grasp these differences by referring to what public administration is not. It is not the same as organizations and institutions dedicated to the pursuit of private profit. Public administration is geared toward the provision of services, not the "bottom line." This has important implications for the way bureaucracies function in the private and public sectors.

According to political scientist Graham Allison, the first difference is related to the amount of time government managers have compared to their private sector counterparts.[16] The former tend to work with relatively shorter time horizons dictated by the political calendar. Second, duration of service is a factor. Top level public sector managers usually serve for a relatively short time before moving to another position within or outside government, while private sector managers seem to hold tenure for longer periods on average.

Third, goal measurement distinguishes the public from the private sector. This can be further complicated when multiple or contradictory ends are sought by governments. For example, the mandate of the Ministry of Finance may be to reduce the deficit by reducing government spending. But it may simultaneously be the mandate of another department to reduce child poverty, a goal that may require the expenditure of more money. Moreover, certain intangible goals unique to government are impossible to measure. For instance, how can you establish whether an increased "quality of life" has been achieved through the implementation of family service policies? This stands in contrast to the relatively straightforward measurement of goals in the private sector in terms of market share, financial performance and so on. In the face of intangible or contradictory goals, it is sometimes argued that public sector managers actually have to be more creative and imaginative than their private sector counterparts.

A fourth factor relates to the problems associated with human resource management in the public sector.[17] It is a much more complicated process to hire or fire someone in the public service. Consider the merit principle, which essentially suggests that all Canadian citizens should have a reasonable opportunity to be considered for employment in the public sector and that selections and promotion must be based exclusively on fitness to do the job.[18] The strict application of this principle means that a detailed, time-consuming and thorough process must be initiated to ensure that every hiring in the public service has been done fairly and equitably. Firings, too, must be carefully justified by extensive documentation of failure to perform or malfeasance in duty. In addition, provisions such as bilingualism and employment equity may mean that in some cases, extra effort must be put into recruiting and training candidates for positions. These steps guide (some would say constrain) the public sector manager through a maze of regulations and rules intended to ensure that human resource management is scrupulously fair and equitable. Overlying the entire process is the requirement that the public sector be somehow representative of the population it serves (i.e., all of Canada). The private sector manager has few such requirements.

Fifth, equity and efficiency concerns are different in the public and private sectors. Public sector managers tend to emphasize providing equity among various constituents. The private sector, on the other hand, tends to be more oriented toward concerns about efficiency and competitiveness.

Sixth, whatever service the public sector provides, it is open to scrutiny by the attentive public and the media in a way that private business is not. Looking over the shoulder of every senior public sector manager is a reporter. Watching the actions of every government member are the opposition parties. The public scrutinizes the actions of every frontline clerk. Service to the public is the raison d'être of the public service, but along with this mandate comes a level of attention that simply is not present in the private sector. Corporate executives operate in relative obscurity, but the limelight frequently shines on public sector managers and especially on their political masters. Success seems to be downplayed, while errors are often magnified out of proportion by a media looking for that juicy lead story for the front page or six-o'clock news. As a result, public administrators are invariably plunged into the political process—a point made more than 50 years ago by Paul Appleby, journalist turned administrator turned academic, who said administrators live in a goldfish bowl where "each employee hired, each one demoted, transferred, or discharged, every efficiency rating, every assignment of responsibility, each change in administrative structure, each conversation, each letter, has to be thought about in terms of possible public agitation, investigation, or judgement."[19]

A seventh aspect of the difference between public and private administration with regard to mandate and goals is the provision of what are called *public goods*. These are goods provided for the benefit of all members of society, such as national defence or roads and bridges. Sometimes these services are inherently unprofitable, but they must be provided nonetheless. So the state assumes responsibility for doing so. In any event, the value of the provision of some goods is often intangible. How, for instance, does one measure the efficient production of national defence?

An eighth factor is accountability. According to the Office of the Auditor General, the watchdog agency that conducts audits and examinations of government programs and departments,

Parliament, the government and the public service are the guardians of public funds entrusted to them for delivering programs and services to benefit Canadians. An important part of the confidence that people have in our democratic institutions is their belief that public funds are spent wisely and effectively. There must be, and there must be seen to be, value from money spent, compliance with authority and environmental stewardship. In a significant way, then, confidence in our national government depends upon clear and timely accountability by the government for its performance.[20]

The public sector faces standards of accountability that are simply absent in the private sector. The public sector is mandated to ensure that its actions are available to public scrutiny, that there is a "paper trail" documenting every step in the delivery of services, and that its actions are transparent and aboveboard. Lines of authority and responsibility are complex, and rules and regulations can impede speedy decision-making. The private sector does not labour under these types of standards because strict rules of accountability are absent there. Public sector managers are scrutinized in their performance by legislatures and the courts. Parliament oversees the actions of the bureaucracy through a variety of watchdog agencies such as the Office of the Auditor General and the Canadian Human Rights Commission. Moreover, a whole body of administrative law has built up that is overseen by the courts, adjudicating disputes between the bureaucracy and the public. Such scrutiny, both legislative and judicial, tends to constrain public sector managers, whereas their private sector equivalents enjoy more freedom from this kind of probing into their actions.

Finally, in the private sector, efficient operation leads to enhanced profitability. There is a clear and sobering focus on the "bottom line" in private business, which is often absent in the public sector. Thus, private businesses will shy away from operations that provide a service or good in an inefficient manner and from which a profit cannot be derived. The private sector, in effect, receives its mandate from the marketplace. The law of supply and demand determines when and where a private sector actor will take action. But where do public sector managers get their mandate? From their political masters who, theoretically, are seeking to express the broadly understood will of the people. And that will must be turned into action through legislative or regulatory means—that is, by the passing of laws and regulations—which may or may not result in profitable activities by government.

Efficiency and Service

Notwithstanding the differences noted above, there has been an increasing trend to impose ever greater efficiencies on the functions of the public sector, such that efficiency has become one of the most dominant values of our time.[21] Indeed, the "three Es" of *efficiency, economy* and *effectiveness* have acquired a place of prominence in the minds of many public sector managers, and a major aspect of holding public servants accountable has been in determining the extent to which they have provided efficient, economical and effective service. As a result, a series of government institutions have evolved which try to ascertain whether or not the public is getting the biggest bang for its buck, so to speak. The Treasury Board, one of the central agencies of government mentioned in Chapter 5, is mandated to ensure that the public service as a whole is run efficiently and effectively. To this end, it has introduced a series of sophisticated innovations over the years to ensure that "the managers are being managed properly." Other government institutions, such as the Office of the Comptroller General and the Office of the Auditor General, have been created or enhanced to assist and cajole public sector managers into performing their jobs more efficiently, economically and effectively. The impact of each of these innovations has varied. But there can be no doubt about the emphasis on the three Es in today's public sector.

But how does one "measure" success in the three Es? How, for instance, does a public sector manager who has been given the job of implementing programs to enhance the "quality of life" of a group of citizens determine if he has been successful? How can increased national security be measured? Or how can it be determined that preventive policies have been effective? Even defining the service provided can be a challenge. If the Ministry of Health has a mandate of securing the mental health of citizens, what is "mental health"? Without this basic information, how can you determine whether it has been efficiently, economically and effectively increased? To further complicate matters, along with the three Es, government has the responsibility of providing services to citizens equitably and fairly. For instance, subsidizing air or rail links to remote communities may not be economical, but may be undertaken in the interests of fairness for all citizens. Thus, the three Es alone cannot be the guiding principle of public administration in the same way that they are in the private sector. In any event, as noted above, the public sector lacks the motivation for efficiency that is present in the private sector: compete efficiently or perish. Indeed, many times governments make decisions that are patently inefficient in a strict economic sense. For instance, it may not be cost-effective to decentralize the delivery of a particular program by setting up regional offices across the country. But it may make good political sense to do so, as it will make the government appear responsive to regional needs. Political scientist James John Guy suggests that "a government service is an activity or benefit directly produced by the government and usually made available to people free of charge, or below or at cost."[22] Indeed, many government services are monopolistic; that is, they have no competition. For instance, there is only one police force, and it does not need to be as conscious of the efficient provision of services as does a private corporation. This does not mean that it should not be as efficient as possible. But the standard of efficiency is different from that applied to the private sector, since there is no competition. And in cases in which government activities do generate a profit against which efficiency can be measured, some people argue that those activities should be turned over to the private sector.

There are, however, certain kinds of incentives for governments to provide services efficiently. While they do not compete in the free market to make a profit, government departments do compete with one another for public funds. This form of competition can be especially tough during periods of reduced government revenues and expenditures. This has led many government institutions to pay more attention to imposing efficiency on their internal operations, including reducing staff, introducing performance measurement, rationalizing program delivery, contracting out, and operating programs on a cost-recovery basis. These developments will be explored later.

Another important incentive in the public realm is the fact that politicians must seek reelection. Part of doing so means running an efficient government, so that voters do not withdraw their support. But in reality, the public pays little attention to the nuts-and-bolts of effective public sector management unless a scandal of large proportions develops. Thus, this incentive for efficient management is a relatively weak one.

Professionalism and Ethics

When Sir John A. Macdonald and the Fathers of Confederation founded Canada in 1867, there was little need for a large, sophisticated professional civil service.[23] The activities of government were extremely limited compared to today, and the art of governing could be accomplished with a ratio of about 100 public servants per politician. Today there are several thousand public servants per politician, since government has become involved in so many more aspects of life than was common in Macdonald's day.

But there is more to the differences than simply numbers of public servants. Back then, many bureaucrats owed their positions to **patronage**—the practice of rewarding loyal supporters, friends and relatives with government positions. Today, however, most jobs in the public service are based on merit.

A patronage-based public service is by definition amateurish and unprofessional. The office-holders are not hired for *what* they know, but rather *who* they know. The result is a lack of skills and ability, compounded by a high turnover rate, since every time a new government is elected, the old government's supporters get fired from their positions and are replaced by the new government's supporters. Thus, the capability of developing a professional, well-trained and dedicated civil service is undermined. As well, service to the public is compromised, since the best person for a job is not always hired.

As governing Canada became much more complicated than in the days of Macdonald, the need for a well-trained, skilled, educated and professional civil service became more and more apparent. Indeed, calls for reform of the patronage-based system of appointments actually started as soon as the new Dominion was created. In 1911, a group of important Ontario businessmen made a proposal to the leader of the opposition, Robert Borden. They promised their support for him and his Conservative Party in the next election if he promised to initiate a merit system of appointment to the civil service. "Since they also wanted a stronger role for the federal government in promoting Canadian trade around the world," according to political scientist Reginald Whitaker, "they obviously saw a merit-based administration as the prerequisite to a more effective government that could act in their interests."[24]

Borden did win the subsequent election, and reforms were implemented after the First World War when the *Civil Service Act,* 1918 was passed. The Act called for the Civil Service Commission (later the Public Service Commission) to oversee all appointments to the public service, rather than leave them in the hands of the politicians. As well, competitive exams were initiated as the basis of appointments, political activity by civil servants was prohibited, the civil service was reorganized, and a new job classification system was introduced. (At this stage you may ask yourself, In what way do these steps reflect the principles of the politics-administration dichotomy?) In addition, special provisions were included in the reforms to favour returning war veterans, setting a precedent as an early form of affirmative action.

The long-term result of these changes was to usher in an era of professionalism within the public service. Further reforms followed that reinforced the competency and ability of the public service, particularly with regard to ongoing training and education. As new technological, economic and social developments shaped modern Canada, the government responded by improving the operation and organization of the civil service. For instance, the Royal Commission on Government Organization, known as the Glassco Commission after its chairperson, determined that by the 1960s, the rules used to enforce the merit system had become too cumbersome and complicated. So it sought to hand the recruiting and hiring functions, held by the Civil Service Commission, to individual departments for jobs above a certain salary level. This would expedite the filling of positions and give managers more direct responsibility in staffing senior positions in their departments, while the Civil Service Commission retained responsibility for filling junior positions and all initial appointments across the public service. This reflected a general growing desire then current in government to "let the managers manage" by decentralizing certain personnel functions. In 1967, the government passed the *Public Service Employment Act*, which incorporated many of the Glassco Commission's recommendations.

Subsequent developments affecting the professionalism of the public service included affirmative action programs related to language, gender, ethnicity and disability (discussed in Chapter 9). While controversy has often dogged these steps, the program's intent was to create a professional civil service that was more representative of the public it served.

Most recently, the professionalism of the public service has been under attack for a new set of reasons. From the mid-1970s onward, a fiscal crisis engulfed Canadian governments, as rising expenditures and declining revenues resulted in ever higher deficits. Some of the blame for this situation was placed at the doorstep of the public service, which, it was argued, had grown too large, inefficient and expensive. Bureaucrats were increasingly seen as self-interested "empire builders" to whom no program initiative or expenditure was resistible. These attitudes spurred the call for further reforms, this time in the direction of downsizing and restructuring the civil service to make it leaner and more efficient.

But one result of this trend has been to severely undermine the morale of a once-proud profession, since it appeared that the blame for every problem in Canadian society was being laid on the public service, while few were crediting it for the good work it was doing under trying circumstances. It became increasingly difficult to draw good young people to a career in a public service that was increasingly denigrated in the public's mind.

One result was that the federal government launched a substantial internal review in 1989 called PS2000.[25] Led by the clerk of the Privy Council (the top public servant in the government) and involving the participation of about 120 deputy and assistant-deputy ministers and other senior bureaucrats, the central goal of PS2000 was ostensibly to make government organizations more "client-centred." As the minister responsible for the public service, Marcel Masse, explained, this involved making organizations more open and consultative; greater accountability for results at all levels, particularly at the top; the importance of effective management of people; the value of continuous learning; the need to eradicate silly rules and red tape; greater delegation of authority; more scope for initiative and innovation; public reporting on performance; and the like.[26]

The results of PS2000 were mixed, but the scope of the exercise indicated the level of concern about the professionalism of the public service under contemporary conditions. So too did subsequent exercises. La Relève, initiated in 1997, addressed the low morale and "quiet crisis" among public servants after years of downsizing and pay freezes, criticism, insufficient renewal and the premature departure of experienced bureaucrats.[27] Meanwhile, the massive Program Review, which began in 1994, required each department of the federal government to conduct an internal review of its programs to determine where cuts should be made.[28] All of this added up to an enormous rethinking about the government's role, and, more particularly, the place of the public service as the new millennium approached.

Related to professionalism is the issue of ethics, which raises particular concerns in the context of government bureaucracies. Governments are entrusted with a special responsibility to act in the best interests of the society as a whole. Thus, the personnel of governments are held up to the highest standards of ethical behaviour. But governments are composed of individuals, and individuals are susceptible to temptation. As two theorists of Canadian public administration put it, "Nothing is more dangerous than a public servant who is technically fit but ethically flabby."[29] To prevent individuals from succumbing to that temptation, elaborate systems of checks and balances are built into government bureaucracy.

Ethics involves the study, implementation and enforcement of codes of behaviour designed to promote "proper" governmental behaviour and to punish "improper" behaviour. Various formal methods of promoting ethics within government have emerged in recent times, and are applied both to politicians and bureaucrats. In general, the stipulation exists that public office is not to be used for private gain. For instance, information gained in confidence in the performance of one's duties should not be used for financial advantage. Thus, an official in the Department of Finance must not use her knowledge of the contents of an upcoming budget—regarding changes to regulations of a particular sector of the economy, for example—to make money on the stock market. Related to this, conflicts of interest, both real and perceived, must be avoided, as must enriching one's relatives or friends by sharing insider knowledge with them.

Of course, the concern not to overstep the bounds of ethical behaviour sometimes means that extraordinary steps must be taken by high-ranking public servants. "It's no wonder that to be a senior public servant these days is to live constantly on your guard," according to a former deputy minister in the Ontario government. "If someone sends you flowers for any reason, you immediately give them away. You politely decline an offer of free baseball tickets, no matter who is giving them to you and regardless of the fact that the person offering them has nothing to do with your job."[30]

To enforce ethical behaviour on the part of government personnel, a complex set of cumbersome rules has been built up over the years. This often results in delays in the development or implementation of a policy, but it also ensures that taxpayers know that decisions are being taken on their behalf on the merits of a particular issue, and not because of the material self-interest of particular government officials. Public servants are guardians of the public interest. Ethical codes and rules ensure that there is some way of guarding the guardians. Comparing the issues of mandate and goals, efficiency and service, and professionalism and ethics between the private and public sectors reveals some important distinctions. The issues are complex, yet we frequently hear the rather simplistic and dogmatic call for government to somehow achieve businesslike standards in what it does. What this ignores are the profound differences between public and private administration.

Restructuring the Public Sector and the Role of the State

As alluded to above, recent reforms to the public service have focused on downsizing and restructuring, as the value of efficiency has taken precedence in the public sector. But to place these developments in context requires understanding the evolution of the public sector in the longer term. This evolution can, for convenience's sake, be divided into three eras: the minimalist state from roughly 1867 to the 1930s; the Keynesian welfare state from the 1930s to the late 1970s; and the neoconservative state from the 1970s to the present.

The Minimalist State

It has already been suggested that Confederation in 1867 was accompanied by a state with minimal responsibilities. The prevailing ideology of the time was based on a laissez-faire attitude that suggested the role of the state should essentially be limited to national defense and the provision of infrastructure (roads, canals, railways) to help facilitate the expansion of business in the interests of the capitalist (or business) class. There was little or no role for government in the provision of welfare and social services, which were regarded as private matters to be attended to by the family, the church or charitable organizations. Even the state's role in education was relatively limited by today's standards. Consequently, the bureaucracy was small.

This is not to suggest that it was nonexistent, of course. The early Canadian state played an important role in building the national economy, for instance, through the three planks of Sir John A. Macdonald's 1878 National Policy. This consisted of a system of tariffs to protect infant Canadian industries from foreign (i.e., American) competition; an aggressive immigration policy to settle the great Western prairies, which supplied raw materials and markets for central Canadian industry; and a transcontinental railway to further assist in the creation of a national economy. Thus from early on, the Canadian state established a presence in the economic life of the nation. But apart from this area, the provision of law and order, national defense, the post office and a handful of other areas, the role of the state was minimal.

The Keynesian Welfare State

The middle part of the twentieth century witnessed the emergence of a much more activist, interventionist state in areas beyond economic matters. The horrors of the Great Depression of the 1930s revealed starkly that laissez-faire capitalism could not function unregulated, as hundreds of thousands of Canadians were thrown out of work without means of support. The strain this placed on private charities, the church and families proved unbearable. Thus, gradually and reluctantly, the Canadian state stepped in and began providing welfare and other social services previously regarded as the domain of the private sector.

But how could a society that had preached self-reliance now justify allowing government to accept responsibility for private concerns? The theoretical underpinning for this new view was provided by the British economist John Meynard Keynes, who argued that in bad economic times, the government could step in and prime the pump of economic growth by investing and spending. Spending on infrastructure as well as on social programs was thus justified.

The Keynesian welfare state resulted. In Canada, it included a commitment to full employment as well as the construction of the social safety net (welfare, unemployment insurance, pensions, family allowance, medicare, etc.) which began in the 1940s. The acceptance of Keynesianism implied that the government would be providing more and more services, which in turn spurred growth in the public sector. A large, sophisticated, well-trained civil service emerged first at the federal level, and later at the provincial level. Indeed, because the provinces in Canada have constitutional responsibility for most social policy issues, overall provincial government growth actually outstripped that of the federal government.

The Neoconservative State

More recently, we have entered a new era that in many ways reflects the attitudes and ideologies that rationalized the original minimalist state. Globalization has prompted questions about the apparent inability of the Keynesian welfare state to perform as theory predicted. Growing deficits, both real and exaggerated, informed the ideological framework within which the expanded interventionist role of the state was brought under question. A concerted attack on the state, by business and right-wing think tanks and the corporate-controlled media, successfully conveyed the image of Canada on the edge of a precipice, and convinced many citizens that we could only pull back from sure disaster if we curtailed the state. From the 1970s onward, provincial governments in Manitoba under Conservative Sterling Lyon, in British Columbia under Social Crediters Bill Bennett and Bill Vander Zalm and Liberal Gordon Campbell, in Alberta under Conservative Ralph Klein, and Ontario under Conservative Mike Harris, as well as federal governments under Conservative Brian Mulroney and Liberal Jean Chrétien, preached fiscal responsibility above all else. This emphasis on efficiency, economy and effectiveness usually translated into massive cutbacks in the public sector, coupled with drastically reduced government spending on social policies.

A period of retrenchment of the public sector has resulted. Privatization, contracting out of services, deregulation, firing of civil servants, reengineering, restructuring, devolution and other buzzwords have become commonplace. Transferring services to the private sector and to the newly emergent "third sector"— i.e., non-profit, voluntary and similar organizations—has become a significant development. Moreover, the role of the family, church and private charities has reemerged, as in earlier times, to fill the void left by the retreating state.

We can measure and compare the three eras by looking at how the expenditures and revenues of Canadian governments have changed over time. One common method for doing so is to note the percentage of Canada's Gross Domestic Product (GDP) accounted for by government. GDP represents the total value of all goods and services produced in the country. In 1950, for instance, federal government revenues accounted for 15.8 percent of GDP, while its expenditures accounted

FIGURE 1.1   **Public Finance in Canada: Revenue and Expenditure as Percentages of GDP for Each Level of Government, 1950 and 1994**

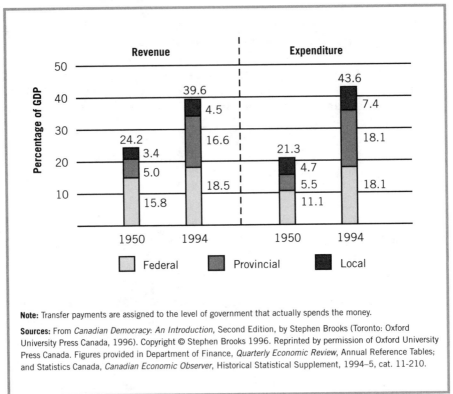

Note: Transfer payments are assigned to the level of government that actually spends the money.

Sources: From *Canadian Democracy: An Introduction*, Second Edition, by Stephen Brooks (Toronto: Oxford University Press Canada, 1996). Copyright © Stephen Brooks 1996. Reprinted by permission of Oxford University Press Canada. Figures provided in Department of Finance, *Quarterly Economic Review*, Annual Reference Tables; and Statistics Canada, *Canadian Economic Observer*, Historical Statistical Supplement, 1994–5, cat. 11-210.

for 18.5 percent of GDP. Provincial government revenues accounted for 5 percent of GDP, while local government revenues accounted for 3.4 percent. Thus, the total of all federal, provincial and local government revenues accounted for 24.2 percent of GDP in 1950. By 1994, federal government revenues accounted for 18.5 percent of GDP, while provincial government revenues accounted for 16.6 percent, and local government revenues accounted for 4.5 percent. Thus, total government revenues accounted for 39.6 percent of GDP by 1994 (Figure 1.1).

Consider the other side of the government ledger: expenditures as a percentage of GDP. In 1950, federal government spending accounted for 11.1 percent of GDP, provincial government spending accounted for 5.5 percent, and local government spending accounted for 4.7 percent. By 1994, federal government spending accounted for 18.1 percent of GDP, provincial government spending also accounted for 18.1 percent of GDP, and local government spending accounted for 7.4 percent of GDP. You will notice that these numbers went up across all three levels of government, but the greatest increase occurred at the provincial level. Why is this? The period under consideration, 1950–1994, covers the era of the expansion of the social welfare state when a variety of social security programs was enacted by governments in Canada. Since the constitution stipulates that the provinces are primarily responsible for social policy fields such as health, education and welfare, we should not be surprised that most government growth occurred at this level. Between 1994 and 2001, federal government spending as a percentage of GDP actually declined due to efforts by the government to eliminate its deficit. By 2001, program spending as a percentage of GDP was down to 11.3%, its lowest level since 1948–1949, and down more than 5 percentage points from 1993–1994. Federal revenues accounted for 16.9% of GDP in 2001, an increase of 1% over 1993–1994.[31]

As we proceed from here, ask yourself why the state was originally small in scope, and what factors contributed to its growth. Today, can you think of an area of your own life in which the state does *not* have a role? These kinds of questions are central to public administration because they touch on the issue of what size, shape and form the government ought to take. We will examine these questions in more detail in Chapter 3, when we look at factors affecting the organization of government.

WHAT YOU HAVE LEARNED

Now that you have read through this chapter, you should be comfortable with some of the basic concepts employed in the study and practice of public administration. More specifically, you should now be able to answer the questions posed at the outset of this chapter.

At this stage, you should ask yourself the following: Can I adequately define public administration? Can I define and explain the function of bureaucracy? Are the differences between public administration and private administration clear to me? And do I know enough about the role of the state to be able to explain how and why the public sector has been undergoing a period of restructuring?

There are several more issues surrounding public administration than the ones we have taken up so far. They are addressed in the next chapters in this book. For now, the best way to summarize what we have studied so far, as well as to signal what is to come, is to consider political scientist David Johnson's top-ten list for public administration (with apologies to David Letterman).[32] See Box 1-3.

The list highlights some of the seminal issues surrounding the practice and theory of public administration. As you can see, the concerns of public administration are many and varied. We will begin to examine them in more depth in the next chapter, which looks at theories of organization.

BOX 1-3

David Johnson's "Top Ten List for Public Administration"

1. Public Administration and Political Power
2. Public Administration and Public Policy
3. Public Administration and Institutions
4. Public Administration and the Public Service
5. Public Administration and Democracy
6. Public Administration and Law
7. Public Administration and Management
8. Public Administration and Evaluation
9. Public Administration and Ethics
10. Public Administration and Accountability

Sources: David Johnson, "Public Administration's Top Ten List," in John James Guy, ed. *Expanding Our Political Horizons: Readings in Canadian Politics and Government*, (Toronto: Harcourt Brace, 1997): 124–132.

ENDNOTES

1. Howard E. McCurdy, *Public Administration: A Bibliographic Guide to the Literature*, (New York: Marcel Dekker Inc., 1986): iii.

2. See E.N. Gladden, *A History of Public Administration*, (London: Frank Cass and Company, 1972).

3. On various definitions of public administration, see David H. Rosenbloom, *Public Administration: Understanding Management, Politics and Law in the Public Sector, Fourth Edition*, (New York: McGraw-Hill, 1998): 4–5. For one of the earliest definitions of the field, see Leonard D. White, *Introduction to the Study of Public Administration*, (New York: Macmillan, 1926). See also Grover Starling, *Managing the Public Sector*, (Homewood, Illinois: The Dorsey Press, 1977): 1; and Frederick C. Mosher, "Public Administration," in Frederick S. Lane, ed. *Current Issues in Public Administration*, (New York: St. Martin's Press, 1978): 4.

4. See Dwight Waldo, "Education for Public Administration in the Seventies," in Frederick C. Mosher, ed. *American Public Administration*, (University, Alabama: University of Alabama Press, 1975).

5. See Woodrow Wilson, "The Study of Administration," in Jay M. Shafritz and Albert C. Hyde, eds. *Classics of Public Administration, Third Edition*, (Pacific Grove, California: Brooks Cole Publishing, 1992): 11–24.

6. A. Paul Pross and V. Seymour Wilson, "Graduate Education in Canadian Public Administration: Antecedents, Present Trends and Portents," *Canadian Public Administration*, 19, (Winter, 1976): 515–541.

7. Robert MacGregor Dawson, *The Principle of Official Independence With Particular Reference to the Political History of Canada*, (London: P.S. King, 1922); *The Civil Service of Canada*, (London: Humphrey Milford, 1929); *The Government of Canada*, (Toronto: University of Toronto Press, 1947).

8. See J.E. Hodgetts, "The Intellectual Odyssey of Public Administration in English Canada," *Canadian Public Administration*, 40, 2 (Summer, 1997): 171–185.

9. See Donald J. Savoie, "Studying Public Administration," *Canadian Public Administration*, 33, 3 (Fall, 1990): 389–413; and Sanford F. Borins, "The Role of Universities in Public Administration Education," *Canadian Public Administration*, 33, 3 (Fall, 1990): 348–365.

10. David A. Good, "2002 CAPPA/CCMD Survey of Schools and Programs of Public Administration and Public Policy: Report of the Findings," Presentation to the University Seminar of the Canadian Centre for Management Development, (Ottawa: April, 2002).

11. See Leslie A. Pal, *Beyond Policy Analysis: Public Issue Management in Turbulent Times*, (Scarborough: Nelson, 2001): chapter 4; and Nicolas Baxter-Moore, "Policy Implementation and the Role of the State: A Revised Approach to the Study of Policy Instruments," in Robert J. Jackson *et al.*, eds. *Contemporary Canadian Politics: Readings and Notes*, (Scarborough: Prentice Hall, 1987): 336–355; and M.J. Trebilcock *et al.*, *The Choice of Governing Instrument: A Study Prepared for the Economic Council of Canada*, (Ottawa: Minister of Supply and Services, 1982).

12. James L. Perry and Kenneth L. Kraemer, *Public Management: Public and Private Perspectives*, (Palo Alto, California: Mayfield, 1983): x. Cited in Shafritz and Hyde, eds. *Classics of Public Administration*, (1992): 443.

13. See, for example, J.L. Granatstein, *The Ottawa Men: The Civil Service Mandarins 1935–1957*, (Toronto: Oxford University Press, 1982).

14. See Anthony A. Cupaiuolo and Michael J. Dowling, "Are Corporate Managers Really Better?" *Public Welfare*, (Summer, 1983): 13–17.

15. See Graham T. Allison, "Public and Private Management: Are They Fundamentally Alike in All Unimportant Respects?" in Jay M. Shafritz and Albert C. Hyde, eds. *Classics of Public Administration: Third Edition*, (Pacific Grove, California: Brooks Cole Publishing, 1992): 457–475.

16. See Graham T. Allison, "Public and Private Management: Are They Fundamentally Alike in All Unimportant Respects?" cited in Jay M. Shafritz and Albert C. Hyde, *Classics of Public Administration: Third Edition*, (Pacific Grove, California: Brooks/Cole, 1992): 462.

17. See Evert Lindquist, "Government Restructuring and Career Public Service in Canada: Introduction and Overview," in Evert Lindquist, ed. *Government Restructuring and Career Public Services*, (Toronto: Institute of Public Administration of Canada, 2000): chapter 1; and Kenneth Kernaghan, "Career Public Service 2000: Road to Renewal or Impractical Vision?" *Canadian Public Administration, 34,* 4 (Winter, 1991).

18. For a discussion of the merit principle, see Fred Ruemper, "Beyond Merit: The Representative Principle," in Randy Hoffman *et al.*, *Public Administration: Canadian Materials, Third Edition*, (Toronto: Captus Press, 1998): 252–271; and Herbert A. Simon, Victor A. Thompson and Donald W. Smithburg, *Public Administration*, (New Brunswick, New Jersey: Transaction Publishers, 1991): 315–321.

19. Paul Appleby, *Big Democracy*, (New York: Alfred A. Knopff, 1945): 7, cited in Howard E. McCurdy, *Public Administration: A Synthesis*, (Menlo Park, California: Cummings Publishing Company, 1977): 107.

20. See Canada, Office of the Auditor General of Canada, *Auditing for Parliament*, (Ottawa: Minister of Public Works and Government Services Canada, 1997): 1.

21. See Janice Gross Stein, *The Cult of Efficiency*, (Toronto: Anansi, 2001).

22. James John Guy, *How We Are Governed: The Basics of Canadian Politics and Government*, (Toronto: Harcourt Brace, 1995): 189.

23. See Ralph Heintzman, "Introduction: Canada and Public Administration," in Jacques Bourgault, Maurice Demers and Cynthia Williams, eds. *Public Administration and Public Management: Experiences in Canada*, (Quebec: Les Publications du Quebec, 1997): 1-12.

24. Reginald Whitaker, "Politicians and Bureaucrats in the Policy Process," in M.S. Whittington and G. Williams, eds. *Canadian Politics in the 1990s, Fourth Edition*, (Toronto: Nelson, 1995): 426.

25. See Gene Swimmer, Michael Hicks and Terry Milne, "Public Service 2000: Dead or Alive?" in Susan D. Phillips, ed. *How Ottawa Spends 1994–1995: Making Change*, (Ottawa: Carleton University Press, 1994): 165–204.

26. Marcel Masse, "Getting Government 'Right': The Challenges of Governing Canada," in James John Guy, ed. *Expanding Our Political Horizons: Readings in Canadian Politics and Government,* (Toronto: Harcourt Brace, 1997): 13.

27. See Canada, Privy Council Office, *Fifth Annual Report to the Prime Minister on the Public Service of Canada*, (Ottawa: March 31, 1998).

28. See Gilles Paquet and Robert Shepard, "The Program Review Process: A Deconstruction," in Gene Swimmer, ed. *How Ottawa Spends, 1996–1997: Life Under the Knife*, (Ottawa: Carleton University Press, 1996): 39–72.

29. Kenneth Kernaghan and John W. Langford, *The Responsible Public Servant*, (Halifax: The Institute for Research on Public Policy: 1990): 3.

30. Elaine Todres, "The Ethical Dimension in Public Service," *Canadian Public Administration*, 34, 1 (Spring, 1991): 14.

31. Canada, Department of Finance, *Budget 2001: Canada's Fiscal Progress Through 2000-2001*, (Ottawa: Department of Finance, 2001): 9-10.

32. See David Johnson, "Public Administration's 'Top Ten List,'" in James John Guy, ed. *Expanding Our Political Horizons: Readings in Canadian Politics and Government*, (Toronto: Harcourt Brace, 1997): 124–132.

KEY WORDS AND CONCEPTS

public administration (2)

democratic society (6)

elected representatives (6)

politics-administration dichotomy (6)

merit principle (6)

bureaucracy (7)

accountability (8)

private sector/public sector (9)

patronage (14)

minimalist state (18) *laissez faire*

Keynesian welfare state (18)

neoconservative state (19) - *period of retrenchment*

REVIEW QUESTIONS

This chapter was divided into five substantive sections, each reflecting a key issue for public administration. You should be familiar with these issues, and be able to address the questions associated with each.

1. What Is Public Administration?

This introductory section addressed the following questions: How do we define public administration, and what key terms and concepts are used in its study and practice?

2. Public Administration and Democratic Government

The second section concerned the tensions between democratic representation and bureaucracy, and asked the following: If elected officials as representatives of the people are responsible for government policy, how do unelected bureaucrats influence the policy agenda, policy decisions and way in which policies are implemented? What is meant by the "politics-administration dichotomy"? Is it a realistic description of public bureaucracy? Why or why not?

3. Bureaucracy

The nature of bureaucracy was briefly examined in this section. The issues of personnel, formal rules, policy instruments, conventions of behaviour, and institutions were reviewed. It asked you to consider this question: What happens when the values of democracy and efficiency clash within the organizational structure of bureaucracy? Is it more important to increase the efficiency of the modern public service, or its democratic accountability? Can the two values be reconciled?

4. Comparing Public and Private Sectors

The fourth issue compared the public and private sectors, and noted important differences between the two. It asked the following: How do the mandates and goals of the public sector differ from those of the private sector? How do the issues of efficiency and service differ in each? What roles do professionalism and ethics play in the one compared to the other?

5. Restructuring the Public Sector and the Role of the State

The fifth section addressed the extent, significance and consequences of government restructuring. It asked, Why is organizational change taking place? What forms does it take? How has organizational change redefined the nature and scope of public administration? What are the main differences between private and public administration? Is it true that the two are "fundamentally alike in all unimportant respects"? List as many public services as you can. Select one and argue why it should, or should not, be turned over to the private sector.

FURTHER READING

1. What Is Public Administration?

White, Leonard D. "Introduction to the Study of Public Administration," in Jay M. Shafritz and Albert C. Hyde, eds. *Classics of Public Administration. Third Edition.* Pacific Grove, California: Brooks Cole Publishing, 1992: 57–65.

Wilson, Woodrow. "The Study of Administration," in Jay M. Shafritz and Albert C. Hyde, eds. *Classics of Public Administration. Third Edition.* Pacific Grove, California: Brooks Cole Publishing, 1992: 11–24.

2. Public Administration and Democratic Government

MacDonald, Flora. "Who is on Top? The Minister or the Mandarins?" and Mitchell Sharp, "A Reply From a Former Minister and Mandarin," in Paul W. Fox and Graham White, eds. *Politics Canada. Eighth Edition.* Toronto: McGraw-Hill, 1995: 448–456.

Thomas, Paul. "The Administrative Machine in Canada," in Paul Fox and Graham White, eds. *Politics: Canada. Eight Edition.* Toronto: McGraw-Hill, 1995: 527–534.

Whitaker, Reginald. "Politicians and Bureaucrats in the Policy Process," in M.S. Whittington and G. Williams, eds. *Canadian Politics in the 1990s. Fourth Edition.* Scarborough: Nelson, 1995: chapter 21.

3. Bureaucracy

Brooks, Stephen. "Bureaucracy," in James P. Bickerton and Alain-G. Gagnon, eds. *Canadian Politics. Second Edition.* Peterborough: Broadview Press, 1994: 307–327.

Kernaghan, Kenneth, Brian Marson and Sandford Borins. *The New Public Organization.* Toronto: Institute of Public Administration of Canada, 2000.

4. Comparing Public and Private Sectors

Allison, Graham T. "Public and Private Management: Are They Fundamentally Alike in All Unimportant Respects?" in Jay M. Shafritz and Albert C. Hyde, eds. *Classics of Public Administration. Third Edition.* Pacific Grove, California: Brooks Cole Publishing, 1992: 457–475.

5. Restructuring the Public Sector and the Role of the State

Doern, G. Bruce, "Efficiency-Democracy Bargains in the Reinvention of Federal Government Organization," in Susan D. Phillips, ed. *How Ottawa Spends: A More Democratic Canada? 1993–1994.* Ottawa: Carleton University Press, 1993: 203–229.

Johnson, David. "Public Administration's 'Top Ten List,'" in James John Guy, ed. *Expanding Our Political Horizons: Readings in Canadian Politics and Government.* Toronto: Harcourt Brace, 1997: 124–132.

Masse, Marcel. "Getting Government 'Right': The Challenges of Governing Canada," in James John Guy, ed. *Expanding Our Political Horizons: Readings in Canadian Politics and Government.* Toronto: Harcourt Brace, 1997: 8–14.

Roberts, Alasdair. "A Fragile State: Federal Public Administration in the Twentieth Century," in Christopher Dunn, ed. *The Handbook of Canadian Public Administration.* Toronto: Oxford University Press, 2002: 18–36.

WEBLINKS

Institute of Public Administration of Canada (IPAC)
www.ipaciapc.ca

Canadian Association of Programs in Public Administration (CAPPA)
uregina.ca/~ramussk

Public Service Commission of Canada
www.psc-cfp.gc.ca

Canadian Political Science Association
www.cpsa-acsp.ca

Chapter ②

Theories *of* Organization

WHAT YOU WILL LEARN

In this chapter, we will focus on theoretical approaches to public administration by examining several schools of thought on bureaucratic organization. The discussion is organized around three central issues.

1. — *Perspectives on Bureaucratic Organization*

This section provides a brief overview of how we can approach organizations from a theoretical perspective, and why we should do so to enhance our understanding of the development of bureaucracy and public administration over time. It notes the contribution of business management thinking and its uneasy marriage with public sector values and concerns. This section asks the following questions: What are the main concerns of organization theory? What are the origins of organization theory? What contesting values underlay the development of theories of public administration?

2. — *The Classic Theorists*

This section focuses mainly on the vital contributions of Karl Marx and Max Weber to our understanding of bureaucratic organizations. It outlines the seminal contributions of these two great thinkers, as well as the influence they have had on subsequent theorizing. It asks, What are the major classical theories and theorists of organization?

3. — *Structuralist and Humanist Theories*

This section looks at the two main schools of thought that have, historically, dominated the theories of organization literature. It introduces you to the scientific management approach pioneered by F.W. Taylor, as well as the backlash it spawned in the form of *organizational humanism*. A variety of theorists are canvassed in this section. It poses the following questions: What types of debates have ensued over the nature and form of organization in both the private and the public sectors? What exactly are theoretical innovations meant to accomplish when translated into practice? After reading this chapter, you should have a firm grasp of the major contending theories of public administration, and be familiar with the thinkers associated with each.

Perspectives on Bureaucratic Organization

The literature on bureaucratic organization is rich and well developed. Indeed, there are a multiplicity of approaches to understanding the role and impacts of bureaucracies (both private and public sector).[1] You will recall from the first chapter that public bureaucracy is the organizing principle of government. Despite its pejorative connotations, it is nonetheless central to the study and practice of public administration.

Bureaucratic organizations are ubiquitous; that is, they exist everywhere in all parts of our lives. When you registered in your program at university and signed up for your courses, you dealt with a bureaucratic organization. If you ran into difficulties, you might have cursed the "red tape" and bureaucratic mindset that held up the smooth processing of your registration. But chances are that you have spent little time thinking through the reasons for that red tape, or the complexities of processing your application. What factors lay behind it? Why is it done the way it is done? How can it be made more efficient? More fair? Cheaper? Quicker? More convenient? If you have ever pondered any of these questions (and who hasn't, while standing in a line or waiting on hold on the phone?), then you have confronted questions about the role of bureaucracy in organizational life.

While bureaucratic organizations are ubiquitous, opinion over their role and function is quite divided. Most organization theory originated from studies about how to improve the management of private sector organizations, particularly large corporations. Hence, academically, organization theory is often associated with schools of business management. But issues that affect how businesses organize themselves are also of great concern to both practitioners and scholars in public administration. In some cases, theories derived from business practices have been adapted to the public sector in an attempt to understand how government organizes itself. In other cases, the social sciences, and especially sociology, have developed their own unique explanations and analyses of government organization. In either case, when we talk about "organization theory," we are talking about our need to understand what people do, how things get done, and why we have organizations.

In the 19th and 20th centuries, organizations became increasingly administered according to values of rationality and impersonality aimed at maximizing efficiency. If you designed an organization based on these values, what might that organization look like? In the public sector, other values come into play, such as democracy and fairness. Compare the design of an organization premised on rationality, impersonality and efficiency to one based on democracy and fairness. Chances are, you would come up with two quite different animals. The problem has been how to marry these sets of values in organizations whose primary task is to serve the public interest through the formulation, implementation and evaluation of government policies. So in a sense, the history of the development of the theory and practice of public administration has been the story of struggling to adapt and extend aspects of private sector management into the public sector over time, and blend those aspects with theory and practice unique to the problems and opportunities of governing.

The following section provides you with an overview of some of the main thinkers and theories on organization as it applies to public administration. It is thematically divided into sections. The first presents the ideas of *classic* public administration thinkers. The next addresses what are termed *structuralist* and *humanist* theories. In the next chapter, we will consider the impact of these theories on the actual practice of public administration in Canada, including the most recent development: incorporating more businesslike management techniques into the public sector.

The Classic Theorists

We begin with an overview of what might be called the "classic theorists" of bureaucracy and organizations—Karl Marx and Max Weber—as well as some other important contributors to the foundations of our thinking about organizations. The classic theorists dealt with the question of the effect of the development of large-scale organizations on the power structure of society. How does "big" government or "big" business influence the political life of a society? Is bureaucracy simply an administrative apparatus designed to meet societal goals? Or does it actually come to shape those goals? Again, we find ourselves confronting the nature of the relationship between bureaucracy and democracy first raised in Chapter 1.

Karl Marx

The first major figure in the classic school of thought is **Karl Marx (1818–1883)**, for whom the concepts of **class conflict** and **alienation** were central to understanding bureaucracy. Marx was influenced in his ideas about bureaucracy by the German philosopher Hegel. For Hegel, the bureaucracy represented a bridge between the state and civil society. Civil society was made up of the various interests in society outside the government itself. The state, on the other hand, represented the overall general or common interest. The state bureaucracy, in Hegel's view, was the medium through which the transformation of the particular interest into the general interest could take place. For Hegel, the bureaucracy was in fact the "universal class" par excellence because it represented the generalized communal interest of all.

Marx rejected Hegel's characterization of the state bureaucracy. For Marx, bureaucracy was not some kind of ideal representation of the general will of society. It was more concrete than that: it was real people involved in a particular set of social relationships involving the exercise of power. Marx particularly disagreed with Hegel's conception of the bureaucracy as the "universal" element in society.

Such a notion was illusory, according to Marx, since the bureaucracy's interests were anything but universal. The bureaucracy was nothing more than a special interest in itself. It might hide behind the more dignified picture of a faithful servant of the general will, and therefore appear somehow to be above personal interests, but reality was quite different. Marx pointed to where bureaucratic interests lay. Whereas in society various interests struggled for possession of private property (the basis of wealth in capitalist societies), he said, within the bureaucracy the struggle was over positions. The desire to claw one's way up the bureaucratic career ladder in the quest for increased power, status and prestige is what motivates bureaucrats.

Hegel had raised the question of how the people were to be safeguarded against abuse from bureaucratic authority. He answered by referring to **hierarchy**. The hierarchical structure of government meant that abuse by lower officials could be redressed by their superiors. Marx refuted this contention. He argued that hierarchy only leads to the punishment of officials who commit offenses against the hierarchy itself. However, it protects the official whenever the hierarchy commits an offense against the people through the official. Hierarchy, then, was far more likely to abuse citizens than were the petty actions of lower officials.

Marx's theory is distinctive because in it bureaucracy is not seen as merely an unfortunate tumour on the otherwise healthy body of the state, but rather as inherent and inseparable from that body itself. In a capitalist society, Marx said, the role of the bureaucracy was to maintain the class distinctions and domination that sustained the rule of the business class. But at the same time, the bureaucracy must mask this domination by presenting itself as representing the general interest. To maintain this facade, it must retain a certain degree of **autonomy** (freedom of action) from the ruling business class. Because of this autonomy, the bureaucracy occasionally acts in a way that may appear to be counter to the interests of the business class. But overall, it will always act in the long-term interests of the capitalist class, since its main purpose is to sustain the power of the dominant class in society. Moreover, it is an organization that serves as an instrument of rule from above, institutionally detached from the mass of the people it is ostensibly designed to serve.

The concept of alienation is a major aspect of Marx's views about bureaucracy, and he sees bureaucracy as one of the primary institutions responsible for the creation of alienation in society. Bureaucracy is seen and felt by most citizens as a distant, impersonal and oppressive force—a perception promoted by bureaucrats themselves through the invention of special myths and symbols that serve to make the bureaucracy a bewildering institution that compels compliance. Moreover, alienation occurs not just in the relationship between citizens and the bureaucracy, but also within the bureaucracy itself. The true nature of the bureaucracy is hidden from itself so that those occupying its posts view their jobs as essential rather than as oppressive or parasitic, as Marx would contend. This image is sustained within the bureaucracy by the institutions of hierarchy, discipline and authority, all of which promote alienation among bureaucrats themselves. For Marx, bureaucracy stifled its workers' initiative and imagination, while reinforcing the fear of taking any responsibility and risk. See Box 2-1.

When he first set out to critique Hegel, Marx did not initially consider that bureaucracy might in fact be a class unto itself. He was only concerned with disabusing Hegel's notion of the "universal class." But as he began to examine the historical role of bureaucracies, he concluded that during the transition from feudalism to capitalism (the transition from rule by the aristocracy to rule by the bourgeoisie), there was a contest for political power in which the state took a "rel-

> ### BOX 2-1
>
> ## Karl Marx on Bureaucracy
>
> In his *Critique of Hegel's Philosophy of Right* (1844), Marx outlines the true character of bureaucracy and presents some ideas that would be expanded upon later by the other great classic theorist, Max Weber. Marx wrote,
>
> *Authority is... the principle of its knowledge,... authority is its mentality. But inside the bureaucracy itself spiritualism becomes a crass materialism, faith in authority, mechanization of a fixed and formal behaviour, fixed principles, views, and traditions. As far as the individual bureaucrat is concerned, the state's ends become his private ends, namely, chasing after higher posts and carving out a career.... The state continues to exist only as various bureau mentalities connected by relations of subordination and passive obedience.*
>
> *The universal spirit of bureaucracy is secrecy, the mystery, which it secures internally by hierarchy, and against external groups by its character as a closed corporation.*[2]

atively autonomous" position. He felt that the bureaucracy was able to stay above the fray, more or less, and gain an "abnormal" level of independence and political influence. The bureaucracy helped pave the way for capitalism, according to Marx, but once capitalism was established, the bureaucracy reverted to its previous role of supporting the ruling interests of society. As a result, Marx saw bureaucracy as a "parasitic" body that did not contribute to the productive forces of society, but rather fed off the rest of society, its real task being to maintain the status quo.

Marx's hope for society was for the triumph of communism over capitalism. Under communism, exploitation of one class by another would end, and therefore there would no longer be any need for institutions that sustained that exploitation. As a result, the state would wither away along with the bureaucracy and we would have a classless society. Beyond this, Marx said little about this new world.

To summarize briefly, Marx argued the following:

- Capitalist society is marked by class conflict in which the capitalist (business class) oppresses and exploits the working class in the pursuit of profitability.
- The state (of which the bureaucracy is a key part) is "relatively autonomous" from the capitalist class, but ultimately serves its long-term interests.
- The bureaucracy also has interests of its own, focused on its own survival and the career-building activities of its employees.
- Both the society at large and bureaucrats suffer from alienation derived from the hierarchical nature of bureaucracy.
- Class struggle will result in revolution, leading to a classless society in which the state (and bureaucracy) will gradually wither away.

The Neo-Marxists

Marx inspired a number of subsequent thinkers who have modified his original ideas, such that we can talk about a school of thought known as neo-Marxism. In general, these theorists consider the modern capitalist state to have two primary functions. One is to foster capital **accumulation**, meaning that the state passes policies that make it possible for capitalist enterprises to make profits. These might include low corporate tax rates, subsidies, grants or other similar measures. The second is to ensure that the working class does not rise up and revolt against the dominant class. Thus, the state passes policies of **legitimation** that are designed to appease the working class without interfering with the accumulation of profits by capitalists. These may include social welfare policies, but if they do not keep the workers more or less quiescent, the state may also use coercion or even force to ensure that the working class complies with the needs of the capitalist class.

Neo-Marxists are divided, though, over the precise nature of the state and its role in supporting capitalism. Some, like political economist Ralph Miliband, point to the close personal and professional relationships and networks between senior state officials and the corporate elite as evidence of the commonality of interests between the state and the bureaucracy. In a groundbreaking study, Canadian sociologist John Porter (although not a Marxist himself) documented the common social origins and ties between these groups as evidence that public policy naturally tends to favour the dominant classes in society.[3] Other neo-Marxists, such as Nicos Poulantzas, contend that bureaucracy serves the capitalist class not because of common social origins, but because the state operates in a capitalist system and is thereby constrained by the structures of that system. Because of these "structural constraints," the interests of the state and the capitalist class coincide.

Neo-Marxists do agree, however, on the notion that the modern bureaucratic state is a threat to democracy. They contend that it has grown so powerful that it is no longer as responsible to elected legislatures as it should be, and that in any case, the bureaucracy is politicized in many countries, which enables the ruling party to appoint its own supporters to influential positions within the bureaucracy.

Criticisms of Marxist Theory

One of the basic problems with Marx's analysis is that he himself did not elaborate on his ideas in this area to any great extent. Thus, his ideas have been subject to a variety of interpretations (and misinterpretations). More concretely, the neo-Marxists have been criticized for trying to have their cake and eating it too. They claim that any state policy that assists capital is evidence of the state serving the capitalist class. But any policy that assists the working class is also interpreted as ultimately serving the interests of capital by legitimating the capitalist system. They are also criticized for arguing that the bureaucracy is merely a tool of the capitalist class, while arguing that the bureaucracy has become too powerful in its own right. In any event, there is no doubt that Marx and his followers have exerted a tremendous influence over the way we think about the role and nature of bureaucracy.

Max Weber

Perhaps the greatest influence on our thinking about organizations is derived from the literature on the sociology of organization, and the dominant writer in this area remains **Max Weber**.

Contemporary thinking... [about bureaucracy] begins with the work of the brilliant German sociologist Max Weber (1864–1920). His analysis of bureaucracy, first published in 1922 after his death, is still the most influential statement—the point of departure for all further analyses—on the subject. Drawing on studies of ancient bureaucracies in Egypt, Rome, China and the Byzantine Empire, as well as on the more modern ones emerging in Europe during the 18th and 19th centuries, Weber used an "ideal-type" approach to extrapolate from the real world the central core of features characteristic of the most fully developed bureaucratic form of organization.[4]

Weber argued that bureaucracy was essentially a system of administration carried out on a continuous basis by trained professionals according to prescribed rules. He identified four main features common to modern systems of organization:

1. **hierarchy**, in which everyone has a clearly defined role within a division of labour and answers to a superior
2. **continuity**, in the sense of full-time salaried occupations and career structures
3. **impersonality**, in which work is based on prescribed rules and a written record
4. **expertise**, whereby personnel, selected on the basis of what they know rather than who they know (that is, on the basis of merit), are trained, and control access to knowledge stored in files.[5]

Weber felt that the closer an organization could be to this model, the more efficient it would be (see Box 2-2). Moreover, the more efficient the organization, the larger it would grow. Weber identified bureaucracy with efficiency since its central feature is rationality. Rationality is reflected in bureaucracy's complex division of labour, coupled with its impersonality and uniformity in the treatment of all citizens—all of which enhanced its potential for efficiency. Weber felt that bureaucratic organization was becoming more prevalent in all political systems and in all organizations where complex and large-scale administrative tasks were undertaken, including businesses, trade unions, political parties, etc. Weber saw bureaucracy as central to modernization. Its source of power was the monopolization of knowledge and organization, and the concentration of this power was within the political domain.

Weber regarded the growth of the modern organization and the bureaucratic form it took as the single most important phenomenon of the modern world. That growth was the result of the superiority of bureaucratic forms of organization based on rationality and efficiency. Because individuals working within the structures of such an organization develop skills through training and experience, they develop into a body of professionals and experts. Because their positions are determined by their skills, and not by inheritance or purchase, as was common in

BOX 2-2

Weber's Views on Organization

Weber's views on organization are summarized by Adie and Thomas in the following way:

In bureaucracy there is a clearly defined layering of authority, a hierarchy, with each person under the control and supervision of a superior. Each person in the organization fills an office, or position, on the basis of free, contractual agreement, and following from a division of labour based on specialization of function, each person is appointed to a position on the basis of competence demonstrated to superiors. Each office has a specified sphere of competence, in that duties are specifically attached to it along with the necessary authority to carry them out. Each person obeys authority because that authority is attached to the position above his or her own. Each person obeys another only because the other has the "legal" right to give orders. At the same time, no person is entitled to give orders to others unless his or her office clearly allows it, and the orders must pertain to the functions of that office. At all times, however, the individual is subject to strict and systematic supervision and discipline based on the principle of hierarchy. To avoid arbitrary, personalistic use of authority, it is clearly stated that the individual is always free to resign but that the employing authority can end a subordinate's appointment only under certain circumstances, e.g. dereliction of duty.[6]

earlier times, there is an ineluctable logic in the expansion, development and evolution of bureaucracy as the dominant organizational form in modern society.

Weber saw bureaucratization as a rational, systematic, logical and scientific approach to organization. Weber argued that historically, people and societies were guided in their actions and behaviours by tradition, habit, instincts and passions. But in the 16th and 17th centuries, the ideas of the Enlightenment period elevated reason and rationality, and largely replaced those earlier guides to action. Consider the concept of *authority*, for instance, and the decisions in society about who has the right to wield it. Weber argued that in the past, authority could be attributed to tradition (e.g., you are the king because your father was the king, as was his father, etc.) or to the charisma of an individual leader (e.g., you are able to secure compliance to your authority by the force of your personality). But the increasing rationalization of modern life undermined the grounds upon which these justifications stood. An ideally rational organization in the Weberian sense was an organization performing its tasks with maximum efficiency. But bestowing authority on an individual for reasons of tradition or charisma was not logical in that it did not guarantee that the best person for the job would exercise authority. As a result, efficiency could actually be impeded. An ideal type of organization would be perfectly rational, since rationality enhanced efficiency, whereas tradition and charisma did not, according to Weber.

But Weber also noted that the pervasiveness and thoroughgoing nature of bureaucratic organizations had a profound effect on people as individuals. The tendency toward impersonality of bureaucracy, which is realized through the application of impersonal rules (i.e., rules that apply to all, regardless of station in life), means that bureaucracy depersonalizes individuals. Also, the idea that bureaucrats advance through the strict application of rules contributes to that spirit of impersonality that pervades bureaucracy, since it promotes the pursuit of personal career goals through rigid application of formulistic rules. In some cases, following these rules supersedes other considerations due to the bureaucrat's desire for advancement and security within the organization. We will examine these kinds of pathologies in more detail later on.

Criticisms of the Weberian Model

We know that organizations do not always work the way Weber prescribed. There is a discrepancy between his model and the real world, and herein lies a problem with organization theory in general. It seeks to describe and explain *what is,* but often falls short of achieving this elusive goal. For example, we know that many organizations that display Weber's characteristics of an ideal bureaucracy (i.e., are hierarchical, have continuity, are impersonal, and are staffed by experts) are in fact inefficient! Moreover, some are downright dysfunctional. For instance, hierarchy can generate a lack of initiative and individual responsibility; continuity can lead to ennui and apathy in the delivery of services; impersonality can foster indifference and insensitivity; expertise can result in inflexibility, hidebound tradition and arrogance.

Moreover, while the impersonality of bureaucratic rules and authority is consistent with the democratic ideal of the equality of everyone before the law, in some cases it actually impedes values such as democracy and equality. For instance, the education level required for one to hold a position of authority in a government bureaucracy prevents many individuals from disadvantaged circumstances from becoming rule-makers themselves. Or, while impersonal rules may protect individuals from arbitrary treatment at the hands of officials, they may also be used to frustrate popular demands for social justice. For instance, the hiring criteria of your local fire department might require individuals who are a certain height and weight. Ostensibly, these are objective criteria that are deemed necessary due to the physical requirements of fighting fires. But what if they inadvertently discriminate against a whole group of people who do not meet those qualifications? For instance, women and some visible minorities tend to be shorter and of slighter stature than the white male average against which the standards were set. As a result, demands for equality of opportunity in employment run up against allegedly impersonal and objective rules and regulations. The result, systemic discrimination, is neither foreseen nor desired by the rule-makers, but is nonetheless a reality in this situation.

Some argue that bureaucracy has significantly contributed to the destruction of privileges based on heredity (due to the merit principle) and made the organization of large-scale industry and commerce possible. But right-wing critics of the Weberian view argue that increasing government bureaucracy, marked by greater regulation and intervention in the economy, has hindered capitalist development and the risk-taking initiative and entrepreneurial spirit of capitalism.

Critics on the left focus on a different problem with the Weberian model. They suggest that Weber's model assumes a view about human nature that is contestable, to say the least. Weber sees humans as constantly striving for power and self-gain and in need of discipline and control. Workers in the bureaucratic machine are subsumed under the organization, rather than possessing some sense of individuality. Thus, "the impact of bureaucracy on the individual is the extreme limitation of our personal freedom and spontaneity, and an increasing incapacity to understand our own activities in relation to the whole organization. We become cogs in a machine."[7]

From this perspective, bureaucracy has profoundly negative implications for democracy. Democracy requires participation by citizens who have a strong sense of self and belonging and who feel able to participate in decision-making, but bureaucratic forms of organization stress obedience to authority, and the sublimation of the self to the greater interests of the organization. These points are important to keep in mind when we look at some later theorists who argue that managers in bureaucracies would be more successful in attaining their goals if they permitted more democratic forms of decision-making and participation to take place within organizations.

Weber's work on bureaucracy was premised on the notion of an *ideal-type*; that is, a model of the perfect bureaucratic machine. In his view, the closer you come to approximating the ideal-type, the closer you come to creating the most perfectly efficient type of organization. But the work of subsequent social scientists, who observed how bureaucratic organizations actually functioned in the real world, gave rise to some trenchant critiques of Weber's views. Such observations led to the conclusion that there was more to bureaucracy than the rules and structures of Weber's ideal model. There were informal patterns of behaviour co-existing with the formal rules which, when they functioned in harmony, could produce greater efficiency and effectiveness. But when they were in conflict, efficiency and effectiveness were impeded.

The work of several theorists who followed Weber modified his views about bureaucracy. For instance, they took Weber's notion that politicians were at the top of the hierarchical ladder, giving orders to faithful public servants, and examined real-life cases where it appeared that the bureaucrats were actually following their own agendas. These new theorists noted that the politician was often at a distinct disadvantage in that he was a generalist with a lack of specific technical knowledge of how government departments functioned or how policy was made and implemented. The bureaucrats, on the other hand, were often technical experts with many long years of experience. Picture yourself in the following situation:

You are the newly elected member of Parliament for your riding, and the prime minister calls to tell you that she wants you to be the minister of the Environment in her Cabinet. Chances are, you may not be an expert in environmental issues. But even if you are, the first day you walk into your office, you are met by the deputy minister and other senior bureaucratic officials who have spent years developing policy in this area. Moreover, they have all developed an intimate knowledge of how government works. You, as the rookie, will have to be an awfully quick study to get up to speed, but in the meantime you may find yourself at the mercy of the "experts" who are supposedly also your "servants."

While Weber acknowledged that tensions could develop between politicians and their bureaucrats, it took the work of other theorists to document how this could affect the running of governmental bureaucracies. For instance, S.M. Lipset, in his book *Agrarian Socialism,* used a case study that showed that the political values and ideologies of bureaucrats could directly influence and even override the express wishes of their political masters.[8] Lipset studied the 1944 Co-operative Commonwealth Government (CCF), the forerunner of the New Democratic Party (NDP), in Saskatchewan and the difficulties it had in initiating its socialist platform. Many of the top civil servants in the province were opposed to socialism and were successful in having the CCF's reforms modified or even thwarted altogether, often by arguing that the reforms were "administratively unfeasible," although this was not necessarily the case. Although they did not have it all their own way, some senior bureaucrats boasted of "running my department completely" and of "stopping the harebrained radical schemes" of the CCF.

Lipset's study clearly outlined how the values and ideological predispositions of top civil servants could have an important impact on the formal orders passed down from their political superiors. This also revealed that the bureaucracy was not simply a passive tool, but could itself develop informal values and even policy goals.

Another feature of bureaucracy not accounted for by Weber is its pathological or distorted character. An example from popular culture is presented in the novel *One Flew Over the Cuckoo's Nest* by Ken Kesey, which was made into a movie starring Jack Nicholson.[9] In the story, a nurse in a mental hospital runs a ward in an authoritarian manner, following the rules and regulations of the organization with no flexibility or allowance for individual circumstance or personality. The inmates passively accept the nurse's orders, but are never "cured." When a new patient arrives (played by Nicholson in the movie), he challenges the nurse's authority and her insistence that "therapy" consists of routine schedules and rigid rules of behaviour. He organizes poker and basketball games, and tries to have the nurse rearrange the patients' schedule so they can watch the World Series. The nurse refuses, but with every refusal to indulge the patients in new activities outside the rigidly defined rules of the institution, the new patient introduces ever more radical and risky activities, culminating in a daylong fishing trip outside the institution, and a wild party with alcohol and prostitutes. This is too much for the nurse to bear, even though the patients display a marked improvement in their conditions. She orders the disruptive new patient to the surgical wing of the hospital, where he is lobotomized—the thinking part of his brain removed.

This is a highly dramatic and fictional account of how a bureaucracy with the best of intentions can display pathological behaviour that actually impedes the goals it sets for itself. The rules of the organization came to take precedence over the very objectives the rules were intended to realize. When the new patient defied the established routine and rules, the nurse used those same rules to beat him down, even though his unorthodox solutions to the patients' mental disorders were having positive effects.

The sociologist Robert K. Merton studied such dysfunctions in bureaucracies. In an important article entitled "Bureaucratic Structure and Personality," he argued that certain aspects of bureaucratic procedure may in fact be dysfunctional to the organization and actually discourage behaviour that might otherwise be beneficial to the organization's goals.[10] He suggested that when an official is trained to comply with a set of rules and regulations, any situation that arises that is not covered by those rules may lead to inflexibility and timidity. The bureaucrat is not taught to be innovative or creative, but simply to follow the rules. He may actually be afraid to deviate from the rules, even in the face of absurd outcomes, because of fear of jeopardizing chances for promotion. This is sometimes referred to as *trained incapacity*, referring to the state of affairs in which one's learned abilities function as inadequacies or blind spots. The analogy is sometimes used of chickens trained to interpret the sound of a bell as a signal for food. That same bell may also be used to summon the trained chickens to the slaughterhouse!

Merton also notes that the devotion to rules often becomes an end in itself for officials (see Box 2-3). The bureaucrat loses sight of the goals of the organization, and instead becomes bound up in red tape, trying to ensure that the rules are followed without deviation. Merton characterizes this kind of behaviour as *goal displacement*, an example of which is clearly present in *One Flew Over the Cuckoo's Nest*. But it is worth remembering that Weber's model bureaucracy stressed the importance of impersonally applying prescribed rules and regulations to maximize efficiency. In many cases, bureaucrats are trained to be skeptical of complaints, since they are led to believe that universal impersonal application of rules is for the good of the organization. In time, bureaucrats come to identify the disciplined application of rules with their own self-interest and desire for promotion and status.

This notion of the substitution of self-interest for organizational interest is crucial. It means that bureaucrats will come to interpret any challenge to the existing rules as a threat to their own security. To protect themselves, they will apply the rules even more rigidly, since this is the only procedure they know that will bring the praise of their superiors. In time, they will cease to question whether the rules are relevant to the objectives of the organization. For example, in 1803, the British government created a post that required a civil servant to stand on the cliffs of Dover with a spyglass, and ring a bell if he saw Napoleon coming. The position was not abolished until 1945!

Merton also focused on the impersonality of bureaucratic procedures and the problems this raised. He noted, in particular, the cold impersonal treatment jobless individuals met when applying for benefits from employment offices. The bureaucrats interpreted their own behaviour as "businesslike." They had little time for pleasantries since they were so rushed and overworked, so they went about applying the rigid rules of the application process with little regard to the feelings of their clients, who were often emotionally distressed due to their unemployment. But the clients interpreted the clerks' behaviour as arrogance, and felt that they were being looked down upon. Many complaints from the public resulted, but no action was taken in response by the bureaucrats, who had been trained to impersonally apply a set of predetermined rules in a prescribed manner.

BOX 2-3

The Dark Side

Merton's observations on the cold, impersonal characteristic of welfare officers were first made in 1940. The following article, though, shows the persistence of these attitudes over time:

There is a dark side to living in Newfoundland which the average employed person knows nothing about. The welfare recipient, or the applicant, is the one who knows about it; he knows less than civil treatment from civil servants, gets the feeling that he is a criminal-minded scrounger and is not sure whether he should walk in like a man and demand his rights or should crawl in on his hands and knees and beg for mercy.

Most welfare recipients live in fear and dread of the welfare officer. They look on him as the all-powerful lord who can give or take away. A frown from the welfare officer is almost the same as a death sentence, and few people are brave enough to risk the wrath of these lords of welfare.

At most welfare offices the recipient is treated with less respect than the mat on the floor... in most areas the welfare officer is lord and master of all he surveys and those who seek his time and attention must put up with his whims, his quirks of personality and any mean or vicious streak that may be included in his character. Most of the people who deal with him treat him with fear rather than respect. They have learned from experience that to make an enemy of the welfare officer is unhealthy and unwise....[11]

Two other post-Weberians, Victor Thompson (*Modern Organizations*) and Alvin Gouldner (*Patterns of Industrial Behaviour*), approached these issues from another angle.[12] They focused on the behaviour of clients, that is, those on the receiving end of the bureaucracy. They argued that clients are notoriously insensitive to the needs of bureaucrats, and that clients tend to act like children when they encounter big organizations. They seem to want instant gratification and fulfillment of their needs, irrespective of how difficult or complicated it is for the bureaucrat to fulfill those needs. They argued that clients tended to view bureaucratic organizations in personal terms, as either a friend or an enemy. All attempts by bureaucrats to evaluate clients are perceived as intrusions upon their personal lives. While the clients are willing to accept the services provided by bureaucracies, they resent having to give anything in return. Moreover, while clients realize that they depend on large institutions for a variety of services, they feel powerless in their presence, which fosters feelings of alienation and anger. Such responses, Thompson insisted, were nothing more than the dysfunctional persistence of childish patterns of behaviour.

Thompson and Gouldner had come across the role of *passion* in human affairs as it related to large organizations. Bureaucracies require that people be patient, accept impersonal treatment, submit to evaluation, and place obligation above rights—in short, that they substitute self-discipline for passion. In the era of large bureaucracies, passion is a human attribute that is out of place, since bureaucracy draws its morality from the old Protestant work ethic, with its commitment to self-discipline.

Weber's ideas were reassessed from another perspective as well. His work was the basis of what other theorists called the politics-administration dichotomy; that is, the notion that politics and administration are separate things, as Frank J. Goodnow explained in his book *Politics and Administration*, published in 1900.[13] Goodnow took the view that public administration, as practised under the party "boss system" in the United States, was in many ways corrupt and thereby inefficient. An ardent reformer, he argued for the separation of politics and administration. But while this "principle" of public administration prevailed for many years, it also increasingly came under attack. Indeed, few would admit the theory has much utility today. It is factually inaccurate in that politics and administration are inextricably linked in countless large and small ways, even if we do not want them to be. Nonetheless, as a "principle" it remains desirable in guiding public administration in areas such as appointments to the public service (where merit has replaced patronage).

But Herbert Simon, the only non-economist to ever win the Nobel Prize in economics, postulated that the "principles of public administration" were really nothing more than "proverbs of administration."[14] As a result, they were often contradictory, inconsistent, inapplicable and confusing. In short, it was anything but scientific, notwithstanding the claims of a couple of generations of theorists. For example, he noted that proverbs often come in mutually contradictory pairs ("look before you leap" is countered by "he who hesitates is lost"). Similarly, in administration, apparently contradictory principles seem to be at work. The Peter Principle states that every individual reaches her level of competence in an organization; yet the Great Shelf Principle suggests that individuals are generally shelved somewhere in the organization long before they have realized their potential. More directly, Simon cited the example of the span of control in organizations. **Span of control** refers to the structure of the hierarchy within an organization. Traditional literature had argued that efficiency was maximized with a narrow span of control; that is, each manager "controls" only a limited number of subordinates. The theory was that too many subordinates resulted in poor communications within the organization and a progressively looser and less effective control. But Simon pointed out that the literature also argued that, for an organization to maximize effective communications, there should be as few hierarchical levels as possible. These are two mutually contradictory principles, making it impossible for managers to "do the right thing" as far as the structure of their organization is concerned. The two span of control systems are represented in Figure 2.1.

As you have seen, Weber's basic model contained vitally important insights, but it has not gone unchallenged. The fact that he really only considered the formal

FIGURE 2.1   SPAN OF CONTROL

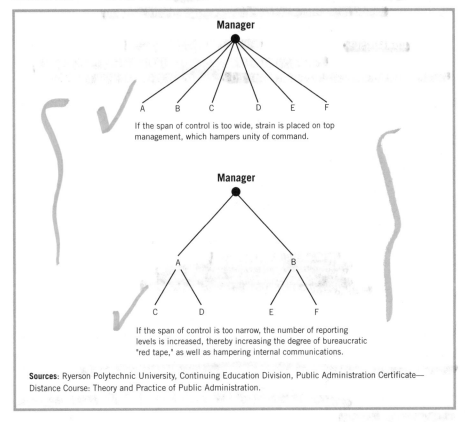

If the span of control is too wide, strain is placed on top management, which hampers unity of command.

If the span of control is too narrow, the number of reporting levels is increased, thereby increasing the degree of bureaucratic "red tape," as well as hampering internal communications.

Sources: Ryerson Polytechnic University, Continuing Education Division, Public Administration Certificate— Distance Course: Theory and Practice of Public Administration.

structure of bureaucracy, with its official rules and procedures and authorized structure of hierarchy, meant that he ignored the unofficial practices that also contribute to the functioning of organizations. But various **bureaucratic pathologies** also exist that impede the achievement of maximum efficiency and rationality as espoused in the Weberian model. Many of these new insights found expression through the theorists we will now turn to in the structuralist and humanist schools of thought.

Structuralist and Humanist Theories

Generally speaking, the **structuralist** theories tend to view workers in administrative organizations as little more than interchangeable parts—cogs in a machine lubricated by money. In this view, the goal of organization theory is to devise structures within which the work of individuals could be maximized so as to maximize the efficiency of the organization. Little regard is paid to the needs or desires of the individual workers, who are expected to subsume their interests to those of the administrative machine. These theories rely on a particular view of human nature that suggests individuals are motivated by material gain (wages, career advancement, etc.) and that workers require a strict regime of rules and regulations, determined and clearly spelled out by management, in order to function at maximum efficiency.

The **humanist** school arose as a critique of the structuralist approach. Humanist theorists argued that to maximize efficiency required paying attention to the workers as individuals with identifiable needs beyond mere material rewards or advantages. It was the job of managers, according to this school of thought, to be sensitive to those needs in order to maximize efficiency, since a happy and contented worker who feels a part of the decision-making process is more likely to produce efficiently than one who is disgruntled and must be coerced by restrictive institutional structures and rules.

Scientific Management

A profoundly important development in the evolution of thinking about public administration came about as a result of new demands from business managers arising at the turn of the 20th century, as a consequence of the growth of industrial capitalism. The term **scientific management** came to characterize this school of thought. Increasing industrialization and technological change in the workplace in the late 1800s created a great deal of disorganization in industry. Major adjustment problems were encountered in the transition from small-scale, craft-based production to large-scale, industrial factory-based production where the work of employees was increasingly deskilled (for example, on the newly invented assembly line). As a result, a growing class of capitalist owners and workers had to adapt to new forms of workplace organization to remain competitive, if large-scale efficiency was going to be achieved.

Moreover, the growth of business operations increasingly separated owners from the daily routine of workers. Thus, a more rationalized form of organization and control was needed to maximize productivity and profit. But who was best positioned in the newly emerging organizations of 20th-century capitalism to determine how improvements could be realized? The pioneers in this reorganizational challenge became those in industry who were strategically located in the production process—namely the mechanical engineers—because of their central position in facing the problem of organizing factory production on a daily basis. The cost accountants also became key players, due to their role of measuring and controlling costs. These people and the theorists who supported their work tackled the question of organizations and administration from the point of view of what can be called the managerial tradition. Thus, scientific management's origins and ideas were clearly directed at and for management, in contrast to the humanist theories of bureaucracy.

The person generally considered to be the father of scientific management is Frederick Winslow Taylor (1856–1915) (see Box 2-4). He was not so much interested in the organizational problems of society's power structure as in the practical problem of efficiency. In other words, Taylor's main unit of analysis was not society as a whole or bureaucracy as such, but the individual worker in the bureaucratic/organizational setting (i.e., the workplace). Taylor began to develop his

BOX 2-4

Frederick Winslow Taylor: The Father of Scientific Management

Although he is regarded as the father of scientific management, the term originated elsewhere.

Strangely enough, while Taylor's 1911 book Principles of Scientific Management *is the work for which he is best known, the credit for coining the term scientific management belongs not to Taylor but to an associate of his, Louis D. Brandeis (1856–1941). Brandeis, who would later be a Supreme Court justice, needed a catchy phrase to describe the new style management techniques of Taylor and his disciples when he was to present arguments before the Interstate Commerce Commission that railroad rate increases should be denied. Brandeis dramatically argued that the railroads could save 'a million dollars a day' by applying scientific management methods. The highly publicized hearings beginning in 1910 caused a considerable sensation and vastly expanded Taylor's reputation. Ironically, Taylor was initially opposed to the phrase, thinking that it sounded too academic. But he quickly learned to embrace it. So did the rest of the country. In the first half of the century, scientific management was gospel and Frederick W. Taylor was its prophet.*[15]

system in the 1880s while employed as a pattern maker and machinist at the Midvale Steel Works in Philadelphia. At the time, work in factories was still not particularly "routinized" or "rationalized." The idea of the craft worker still predominated, which meant that to a large measure, workers were left on their own to perform their duties; the pace of the work was not yet set by the machines; and the individual worker placed his own "stamp" on the product, i.e., work was individualized. Foremen were also generally left to set their own standards and to regulate work breaks, etc. The tyranny of the clock had not yet been imposed.

Taylor came to regard such practices as haphazard and inefficient. The Midvale plant where he worked was run on a piecework basis: machines ran around the clock, and labourers were paid on the basis of how many pieces they produced. Taylor observed this process and determined that workers could triple their productivity (and their wages) simply by reorganizing the flow of work. So Taylor attempted to regulate the work routine and speed up its pace. Rather than allow individual workers to set the pace and to carry out their tasks in their own individual ways, Taylor set a time for how long any particular job should take, and outlined in a strict way the manner in which the job should be done. The workers reacted unfavourably to Taylor's attempted reorganization. They called him a "piecework hog" for working so hard; he was the kind of guy you love to hate in the workplace—the keener who volunteered to work on Sundays, and who rose every day at 5:00 a.m. to walk the two miles to work, never leaving before 5:00 p.m., etc. He was born into an upper-class Philadelphia family, and studied law at

Harvard for a while, but quit, complaining that he was going blind from all the reading. It was after this that he signed up with the Midvale plant and engaged his fascination with time management and scientific solutions to workplace problems. (Incidentally, this was a type of thinking that he applied to his personal life too. Plagued by nightmares, he noticed that he always woke up on his back. He therefore concluded that if he did not sleep on his back, he would not have nightmares. So he rigged up an elaborate harness of leather straps and wooden prods that he wore while sleeping. If he rolled onto his back, he would be prodded awake. Thus he applied a scientific-type solution to his problem.)

In the workplace, Taylor sought to scientifically discover the shortest time possible for performing any particular task, and his tool was the stopwatch. Standing behind each worker, Taylor would record the time it took to perform even the most elementary motions: finding a steel rod, setting it on a lathe, picking up a tool, and so on. By studying a large number of workers, he felt he could identify the shortest possible time for performing each individual motion. By combining the best times, discarding useless motions, and adding gaps for unavoidable delays or rest breaks, Taylor could establish a pattern of work that was invariably shorter than the workers' informal pace. These experiments became known as the infamous **time and motion studies**.

When Taylor asked for help from management to implement his system, the workers responded by running their machines so fast and hard that pieces fell off! Taylor responded by fining them; and ultimately, he convinced management to use the penultimate weapon against the workers: cut the piecework rate in half so that the workers would have no choice but to speed up their production in order to financially survive. Taylor's battles with the Midvale workers were to last three years (see Box 2-5). Before leaving Midvale, Taylor astonished the plant engineers by revealing that he had conducted upwards of 50 000 experiments on these problems, which he published in the book *On the Art of Cutting Metal.*

He then began to look beyond time and motion studies to determine that workers were also using improper tools and defective equipment. He contended that there was "one best way" of performing any task, and his work resulted in a complete reorganization of the firm—planning, engineering, purchasing and inventory control were all centralized, as was maintenance, and cost accounting; assembly line techniques were introduced as well. Management's job, Taylor argued, was to "discover" this "one best way" by applying scientific principles to the design of work procedures. The workers should not be left to solve the problems of production themselves; this was management's role. The worker should simply be told how to carry out the "one best way." What this implied was a radical separation of planning and performing, of thinking and doing.

While Taylor's theories were initially developed for and applied to the private sector, Taylor also attempted to introduce his system into public administration, beginning in 1906 in government-run arsenals and navy yards. The most famous incident involving the application of Taylor's approach took place at Watertown Arsenal near Boston. The arsenal was run by rule of thumb; the workers would receive an order for a set number of gun carriages and fill it by milling assorted

---

BOX 2-5

Taylor's View of Workers

Taylor based part of his view of the division of labour in the workplace on a view of workers that can only be considered repulsive by today's standards. Consider the following quote from his book *The Principles of Scientific Management*:

Now one of the very first requirements for a man who is fit to handle pig iron as a regular occupation is that he shall be so stupid and so phlegmatic that he more nearly resembles in his mental make-up the ox than any other type....Therefore the workman who is best suited to handling pig iron is unable to understand the real science of doing this class of work. He is so stupid that the word "percentage" has no meaning to him, and he must consequently be trained by a man more intelligent than himself into the habit of working in accordance with the laws of this science before he can be successful.[16]

---

parts found in the yard according to designs someone sketched in chalk on the factory floor. Taylor contended this was not the "one best way" of doing the job. Furthermore, he argued that the selection of workers must be based upon scientific criteria too; i.e., some workers were better suited for some jobs than others, and the best person for each job must be determined and chosen. When the workers at Watertown heard that Taylor was coming, they went on strike, and the army was sent in to guard the arsenal with fixed bayonets. Later, a special congressional committee was formed that summoned Taylor to explain his system. So contentious was Taylor's time and motion system that the U.S. Congress passed a law banning stopwatches in government-run factories—a law that remained in place for 40 years. Congress had been prompted to act because of the unpopularity of Taylor and his ideas among working class voters.

These developments distressed Taylor, who knew that the workers had to "buy into" his system in order for it to work. He felt that he was genuinely aiding the workers too, since his system would lead to greater productivity and higher wages. He attempted to win workers over with an incentive system—a carrot-and-stick arrangement in which workers were encouraged to keep up with the standards imposed by the production engineer with the slogan "A big day's work for a big day's pay."

Two more theorists in the scientific management tradition argued that there are universal principles of administration that should govern arrangements for human organizations. Luther Gulick and Lyndall Urwick produced an important collection of papers on the state of the art of organization theory entitled "Papers on the Science of Administration."[17] Gulick regarded these principles as relevant, no matter what the organization's purpose, personnel or goal. He encapsulated these principles in a famous acronym, **POSDCORB**, which he claimed summarized all the functions of management executives in organizations. It stands for Planning, Organizing, Staffing, Directing, Coordinating, Reporting and Budgeting. By subdividing all the tasks of an organization along these lines, all of administrative life could be understood, and efficiency maximized. This was Gulick's attempt to define the "one best way" for organization management. Gulick's approach was to focus on the top of the hierarchical pyramid in organizations. He was concerned with developing scientific principles and practices that management should systematically employ.

But it is the underlying philosophy behind Taylorism and scientific management, which begins with the assumption of worker-management cooperation, that was problematic. In the absence of this, all other principles of his approach were useless. Taylor saw scientific management as a solution both to productivity problems and to class conflicts, which he viewed as wasteful. He wrote, "Once the natural laws governing work and production are discovered, the determination of the proper time for doing a job and the proper amount of pay can be determined in an objective, scientific way." Once these things were scientifically established, there would be no need or room for bargaining or conflict between labour and management, because one could not bargain with scientific fact. Thus, Taylor was hostile to trade unions, feeling that they served to generate conflict and were against the real best interests of the workers. He preferred to deal with workers as individuals rather than in groups (unions) because he felt that workers in groups exerted social pressure on individuals to conform to unscientific, more comfortable production norms (i.e., to "slack off"). Taylor wished to prevent such groups from developing, by making it in the workers' economic interest to cooperate with scientific management techniques.

It is interesting to note that the underlying premise of scientific management in terms of the relationship of workers to the industrial environment was explained by Taylor in analogies between people and machines. First, in terms of production, people were considered to be like machines (the mechanomorphic world image) whose specifications and performance could be scientifically measured and rated, and whose efficiency could be improved through mechanical adjustments such as reducing superfluous motions. Second, it was argued that the factory structure should be considered as a complex productive mechanism—a combination of machines and workers involved in the process of transforming raw material in the cheapest possible manner. Rationalization was the key, defined as producing a product in the most efficient manner. Goals were to be set and achieved by using workers and machines as standardized, interchangeable parts to be manipulated with the aim of maximizing productivity at minimum cost.

Mechanization of industry in the late 1800s and early 1900s had resulted in unprecedented productivity growth, particularly in America, it is true. But it also resulted in human organizational problems, the solution to which, according to scientific management, was to treat humans as machines. In terms of efficiency, this was a solution that resulted in amazing gains in productivity. Thus, scientific management represents not just a theory of organization, but one of motivation and human behaviour. It characterizes the individual as driven by fear of hunger and deprivation, and a desire for profit. These characteristics were easily manipulable, according to scientific management, in a manner compatible with efficiency, so long as it was possible to view humans as mere appendages to machines.

Taylor saw the **division of labour** as a basic principle controlled by a hierarchical pyramid of authority driven by efficiency. The emphasis on managerial control attracted American capitalists engaged in a bitter struggle with labour over control of the modern industrial workplace. But even once Taylorist measures were implemented in workplaces, they did not have all the desired effects of transferring decision-making authority to management and producing the most efficient and profitable form of operation. The adoption of scientific management by Henry Ford in his assembly line, for instance, did not result in the workers quietly acquiescing to the highly regulated and automated routine of the production line. Instead, they unionized and adapted their own defensive techniques to counter management's attempts to gain total control over the labour process. Their responses culminated in the sit-down strikes of the 1930s, the wild-cat strikes of the 1940s, as well as labour militancy in the 1960s and 1970s. These struggles showed the alienating power for workers of Taylor's approach, and demonstrated that scientific management rationality did not necessarily result in the most efficient, effective production process. Instead, it often resulted in worker resistance or even sabotage of the production process. The often inhumane working conditions fostered by Taylor's techniques functioned to impede efficiency, which ironically destroyed the very "rationality" of the system. Thus, the observation is appropriate that the quickest way of doing a job may not be the most efficient way.

Nonetheless, Taylorism attracted a diverse range of supporters. Besides American capitalists and industrialists, Italian Fascists in the 1930s made scientific management an important plank in their ideology; but it was also picked up by the left too. Lenin, the father of the Communist revolution in Russia, was an enthusiastic admirer of Taylor, as were several socialist parties in the U.S., strangely enough. The attraction can be explained by remembering that there was widespread admiration in societies of the day for "scientific" advancement, which often overcame more ideologically based concerns about the welfare of workers.

Criticisms of Scientific Management

Scientific management techniques caught on across the United States and the industrialized world. But critiques of scientific management also emerged, and sometimes found expression in popular culture. Charlie Chaplin's *Modern Times* and Fritz Lang's *Metropolis,* for instance, were trenchant and biting commentaries on the dehumanizing tendencies of this approach to workplace organization. By now, some of the weaknesses of the scientific management school should be apparent to you. For instance, by focusing on the individual worker as the main unit of analysis, it fails to see the worker as a member of a broader social group—with all that entails. There is no recognition that the worker is socially influenced in his behaviour and attitudes by colleagues and by the social structure and culture of the group.

Moreover, Taylorism represents a theory of organization based upon a particular model of human behaviour: a machine model. This was an engineer's perspective, which saw human relations in mechanistic terms. The organization member was seen as an instrument of production like any other tool, to be manipulated and used. Taylor assumed that the individual feelings of workers were more or less irrelevant to the problems of productivity. In this sense, Taylor's conception of the worker is very similar to Weber's view of the ideal bureaucrat: both are devoid of personal feelings, ambitions and independent actions that might jeopardize the systems Taylor and Weber constructed. Thus, there is no consideration of the feelings, attitudes and private goals of the individual. In short, Taylor (like Weber) neglected the psychological and sociological variables of organizational behaviour.

Thus, the same types of criticisms levelled against Weber by the post-Weberians apply in some instances to Taylor. Taylor, for instance, looks at the problem of morale and productivity exclusively in terms of economic reward and punishment; the primary motivation of workers is assumed to be economic. But this is obviously an oversimplified view of human nature; clearly other, non-economic motivations also guide worker behaviour (e.g., alienation). Furthermore, Taylor's pro-management perspective led him to mistakenly believe that the interests of management and labour were reconcilable and could exist in harmony through scientific management. But this is naive; as long as there are bosses and workers and a prevailing capitalist economy wherein a dollar that goes to profit cannot also go to wages, tensions and hostilities will persist.

Over the years, a growing chorus of criticisms of Taylorism lead to a contrary school of thought, which we can classify as the humanist or human relations approach to organization theory.

The Human Relations Approach

As we saw above, the main concern of Taylorism was with scientifically selecting workers for particular jobs on the basis of their aptitude for the position. Given such an orientation toward work, it was only a matter of time before the move to rationalize work would take a further turn; that is, the industrial psychologist would join the engineer to discover the most efficient conditions for work. The turn toward the industrial psychologist was largely prompted by the fact that workers had such hostile reactions to scientific management's attempts to implement its mechanistic principles in the working environment. Industrial psychologists went beyond scientific management in that they sought to take into account more than the mere physical elements of the human in relation to work suitability. They attempted to modify scientific management's "machine model" of organizational behaviour, and were concerned with the following: how to devise tests to select the best person for a job; how to discover whether that person was working at full efficiency or not; how work conditions such as lighting, humidity and temperature affect productivity; how the effects of boredom, brought on by doing repetitive tasks, impeded productivity, etc. This approach, then, began to emphasize the human element in the work enterprise, hence the name *human relations approach*.

Serious labour disruption brought about by the introduction of scientific management to the worksite prompted certain more enlightened managers to begin to take into account how workers themselves felt about the organization of work.

They began to employ techniques such as questionnaires to gain insight into the feelings and opinions of the workers in their organizations. They wished to tap into the influence of the "human factor" in their operations. This new view was reflected in a slogan adopted by much of the American business community beginning in the 1930s: "The human element is the most important element in business." This gave recognition to problems inherent in scientific management.

The receptiveness of some business people to such studies provided industrial psychologists with a real working environment in which to apply academic theories. The worksite became their "laboratory" for studying human behaviour in an organizational (primarily industrial) setting. Among the most famous of these experiments were the **Hawthorne experiments**. In 1924, the American National Academy of Sciences sent a team of researchers to the Western Electric Company's Hawthorne Works near Chicago to study the effects of illumination on worker efficiency. Taylor had pointed to the need for well-placed work breaks that would give workers relief from the strains of their job and thereby improve efficiency. The researchers in the Hawthorne study were keenly aware of the studies of fatigue and monotony that had attempted to reduce these phenomena and consequently cut down on the problems of absenteeism and turnover and increase overall worker productivity. Researchers believed that an improved physical work environment would result in increased worker productivity.

The Hawthorne Works employed about 29 000 men and women. It was a massive industrial complex geared toward the production of telephones and telephone equipment. The researchers initially conducted their lighting tests on various broad groups of workers throughout the plant, but the results were inconclusive, so they decided to focus on a narrower, more controlled group of workers who wound small induction coils onto wooden spools. The researchers improved the lighting in the room, and found that for every increase in lighting, worker productivity went up. But some researchers were not convinced of the certainty of the results; they argued that if productivity was tied to illumination, then a *decrease* in lighting would result in a *decrease* in productivity. So the scientists then tested this proposition; they replaced the higher intensity light bulbs with lower ones, and what happened surprised them: productivity slowly but steadily increased! The scientists kept lowering the light level, and productivity continued to slowly rise. Finally the experimenters replaced the electric lights with three-foot candles; at this point the workers complained—noting that they were hardly able to see what they were doing—and the production rate decreased.

The researchers attempted to check their unusual findings by establishing a control group in another area of the plant. Here the level of lighting was never altered in the work room, yet the productivity of the workers in this control group continued to increase! This baffled the scientists. So they began a second series of experiments in 1927, in which they recruited five women who built telephone relays and segregated them from the other employees. They worked in a special room where the scientists could control temperature and humidity; even their hours of work were manipulated. The objective of the experiment was to test the role of fatigue and monotony on productivity. The scientists experimented with longer rests and shorter workdays. In their conversations with the women, they discovered that the women frequently had no time to have breakfast, so the scientists provided them with sandwiches, coffee and soup. Productivity went up. Moreover, productivity steadily went up until the rumour spread through the plant that the Hawthorne executives were about to dismiss the research team because of the effects of the experiments on other workers in the plant. At this point the workers in the experiment began producing an extraordinarily large number of telephone relays. At about the same time, scientists decided to observe the effects of increasing the women's fatigue by restoring the old 48-hour workweek. Productivity continued to climb! They eliminated the lunch break. Absenteeism went down! They cut down the rest breaks. There were still no signs of fatigue! No matter how the researchers tinkered with the rest periods or the workweek, they could not get the women to slow down.

What they finally figured out after about five years of study was that the workers were actually responding to the researchers, not to the conditions imposed on them or to the manipulation of their work environment. In the beginning, the women had responded to the novelty of having the researchers there; they felt it meant that management was worried about productivity. Then the women began to respond to the style of supervision. Given greater freedom, said the researchers, less strict supervision, and the opportunity to vary from a fixed pace without reprimand by a gang boss, worker morale increased, as did productivity.

The researchers felt they needed to know more about the effects of supervision, so they interviewed 20 000 workers, but got so many different responses that they decided to conduct another experiment. This time the researchers would not supervise the workers directly, but watch them from a distance. The most important of these experiments began in 1931 in the bank wiring room where workers produced telephone switchboards. At the time, management was trying to improve worker productivity through a combination of wage incentives and low-key supervision. By industrial standards of the time, Hawthorne was a good place to work (given the Great Depression of the 1930s, *anywhere* was a good place to work). But the employees were naturally concerned about losing their jobs. As a result, they artificially depressed their own productivity so that each worker wired no more than two banks a day. Any worker, of his own initiative, could have made more money by working harder. But the employees attacked those who did, and berated those who worked too slowly. Thus, two banks a day was considered by all to be a fair day's work.

This phenomenon finally revealed the source of the researchers' confusion over their findings: the **informal group**. The researchers concluded that the dominant factor in employee productivity was the informal group and its attitudes. The most powerful motivators on the job were the social norms and values of the group, and the ability of supervisors to act as leaders in modifying those norms and values. Workers might acquire their sentiments on the basis of individual experience, but on the job they acted as members of groups.

Elton Mayo, who was one of the key researchers from the Harvard Business School at Hawthorne, is considered to be the father of the human relations approach in the same way that Taylor was the father of scientific management.[18] Mayo made the following observation: Human collaboration in work has always depended upon the evolution of a nonlogical social code that regulates the relations between persons and their attitudes to one another. Insistence upon a merely economic logic of production interferes with the development of such a code and consequently gives rise in the group to a sense of human defeat. The human relations school came to the conclusion that economic incentives, rest breaks, free breakfasts, improved physical working conditions, etc., could never be as powerful as the "social controls" exercised by the group in the workplace. In other words, the key finding of the decade-long study was one that we might assume is rather obvious today: workers are more responsive to peer pressure than to management controls. Thus, the Hawthorne experiments are thought to be the genesis of the human relations school.

Still, the scientific management movement remained largely predominant. The human relations approach did not really begin to catch on until the late 1930s, with the publication of a book in 1938 called *The Functions of the Executive* by Chester Barnard, a career executive and president of the New Jersey Telephone Company.[19] Barnard was closely associated with the experimenters from the Harvard Business School who conducted the Hawthorne experiments. Barnard argued that organizations by their very nature were cooperative, rather than mechanical, in nature. They were held together by good communications and the continuing desire of individuals within an organization to see it thrive. Members of an organization make contributions to it, but only when they receive adequate inducements to do so. There must therefore be a balance between the two, and it was the task of the executive to maintain the dynamic equilibrium between the needs of the organization and the needs of the employees. Inducements include not only money, but loyalty, good working conditions and pride. Barnard gave credence to such ideas as upward communications, and authority from below, rather than hierarchical structuring. He recognized the existence of natural informal groupings in the work setting—giving support to the growing human relations school by pointing out that one cannot understand how an organization works simply by studying its organization chart, its charter or its rules and regulations. You cannot really understand how the government of Canada works, for instance, by simply reading the Constitution. "'Learning the organization ropes' in most organizations," he claimed, "is chiefly learning who's who, what's what, why's why, of its informal society."[20]

Two other Hawthorne experimenters from 1927–1932, F.J. Roethlisberger and William Dickson, published *Management and the Worker*—the first empirical study to test for the relationship between productivity and social relations.[21] This book, containing the definitive account of the Hawthorne studies, investigated the importance of informal groups, and looked into the effects of psychological manipulation of workers and resulting productivity. They tended to confirm empirically some of Barnard's earlier intuitive assertions concerning the efficient functioning of organization and the existence of informal groups.

This work, and Elton Mayo's contributions, are key to understanding the significant findings of this school of thought. Mayo developed a general philosophy concerning problems brought about by industrial civilization. He said these problems stem largely from the social disorganization generated by industrialization (i.e., the weakening of the family and other traditional groups that the individual had been associated with, such as the church and community). He said this resulted in the atomization (isolation) of the individual, leading to loneliness and anxiety and a sense of defeat called *anomie* (a term coined by the French sociologist Emile Durkheim). This created a social vacuum whereby a person might be in a crowd (in the workplace or community) but still feel alone, and feel no real sense of identity with her social surroundings. Mayo contrasted this with the past social cohesion rooted in the neighbourhood centred around small towns and villages. He hoped, through the human relations approach, to recreate the communal village of rural times within the work group of a modern factory. For Mayo, this required a new society within the workplace to replace the decaying family and social institutions of the past. It is in this workplace that individuals will find emotional security and social satisfaction as a result of the harmony of both the formal and informal organizations. Such individual worker satisfaction, Mayo argued, rested upon open communications between the ranks, participation in decision-making by workers, job security, and a spirit of democracy wherein the administrator became concerned not just with the work, but with the workers.

It was felt that the application of human relations to the work setting would bring an end to industrial strife, and establish a new industrial order based on co-operation and harmony. This was the philosophy that guided Mayo's work and the early stages of the human relations approach. The key question in this approach became: How do you marry harmony and efficiency?

Mayo's philosophy, plus the research findings from Hawthorne, outlined the basic principles of human relations, which can be summarized in the following five points:

1. **Social Norms** The level of organizational effectiveness is determined by social norms. The early experiments on illumination and fatigue demonstrated that the physiological capability of the worker was not the crucial factor in productivity; neither were the principles of administration, such as the division of work. Neither was as important as the social norms. To put it another way, the amount of work carried out by a worker is not determined by his physical capacity, but rather by his social capacity.

2. **The Group** Group standards strongly influence the behaviour of individuals in organizations. The bank wiring room experiment showed how the group could enforce a standard level of productivity upon all members. The group also provided a shield against executive reprisals. In both ways the group acted as a restraint on management power.

3. **Rewards and Sanctions** Social rewards and sanctions are the strongest motivators on the job. The Hawthorne workers responded to the respect, affection and appeals to group loyalty provided by their fellow workers. Management's system of economic incentives was, by contrast, less powerful.

4. **Supervision** The most effective system of supervision is created when the managers consult the group and its informal leaders in order to win acceptance of organizational objectives. Human relations specialists would advise managers to a) be human, b) be good listeners, c) not be "bosses," and d) give the impression that the workers are making the decision. They believe that effective communication, supplemented by a willingness to allow workers to participate in decision-making, is the key to effective supervision.

5. **Democratic Administration** Workers will achieve their highest level of effectiveness when they are allowed to manage their own affairs with no gang boss looking over their shoulder. Re-analysis of the Hawthorne experiments revealed that improvements in productivity in the relay assembly room followed the decision of the researchers to allow the women to become a collegial, self-managing group. This point also relates to the issue of specialization: democratic administration also implies that specialization is by no means the most efficient form of division of labour.

Another theorist, psychologist Abraham Maslow, took the Hawthorne findings a step further. The experiments had challenged the scientific management view that workers were essentially economic animals who could be motivated to produce simply by offering financial incentives. Maslow argued that the notion of monetary incentives for workers was too simplistic and failed to recognize motivation from other sources. He argued that people were motivated by a **hierarchy of human needs**, of which there were five categories, ranging from physiological to self-actualization. People are motivated to satisfy the first categories, the most basic physiological ones, and only once those have been satisfied do they move up to the next level (see Box 2-6). Moreover, once they have satisfied the lower needs, these cease to be motivators of human behaviour. But higher needs cannot be satisfied until lower ones are met.[22] Contrary to the scientific management literature, Maslow contended that there was no "one best way" to motivate employees. Instead, management had to be sensitive to the idea that workers have a variety of needs and motivations.

BOX 2-6

Maslow's Hierarchy of Human Needs

1. **Physiological** Food, shelter, clothing, sex, sleep
2. **Safety** Security, stability, freedom from fear
3. **Belongingness and Love** Friendship, love, membership in some community
4. **Esteem** Achievement, competence, independence, prestige, status
5. **Self-Actualization** Self-fulfillment, attaining ultimate goals in life

Sources: Maslow, A.H. *Motivation and Personality, Second Edition*. (New York: Harper and Row, 1970).

Thus, the human relations school no longer saw the worker as an isolated physical being, but considered her as a group member whose behaviour is greatly controlled by group norms and values, and motivated by a complex hierarchy of needs and desires. The lesson, then, was that management must *not* try to destroy the informal organization on the worksite, but rather take into consideration this informal structure and use supervisors trained in human relations to harmonize the informal norms and values with the goals of the formal organization. Ultimately, then, the human relations skills of the people in the leadership positions of the organization by and large set the tone of human relations. The good leader was one who was considerate of the workers' positions and problems.

From an historical perspective, the Hawthorne study began a new direction—a recognition that human beings are a complex and influential factor in organizational performance. Humans are not machines, and scientific management's "one best way" approach had to be tempered to recognize the effect of group behaviour. Many have taken the human relations movement as a great counterbalance to the more orthodox principles of administration as advanced by Taylor and scientific management, and it is true that human relations certainly filled a blind spot in the earlier school of thought. However, in reality, the distinction between the two is more academic than practical. What managers in the real world tended to do was graft the principles of human relations onto the more formal principles of scientific management, seeking to maximize production as efficiently as possible behind the facade of a humane face. After all, it should be remembered that the Hawthorne experiments were no less interested in improving efficiency than was Taylor; they shared the common desire to find principles that would aid managers in running a better, more efficient shop. This leads us to consider some criticisms of the human relations approach.

Criticisms of the Human Relations School

Criticisms of human relations theory are often centred on its neglect of organizational conflict in favour of a one-sided emphasis on harmony, and on the fact that, notwithstanding their apparent concern with the needs and motivations of workers, human relations theorists ultimately display pro-management values. For instance, one of the Hawthorne experiments involved 300 workers who were given the job of wandering around the factory floor, listening to the complaints of other employees. But management never intended to do anything about the complaints; it simply wanted to create the impression that it actually cared about the workers. In any event, these theorists' preaching about the virtues of internal democracy and worker-participation in decision-making were, when viewed against reality, certainly utopian. Advising that workers be given active participation in the workings of the firm immediately gives rise to a dilemma—either they construct a pseudo-democracy where employees are given the opportunity to participate only in decisions that do not hurt management, or they propose real meaningful participation, which in the end means that management must voluntarily cede part of its power and prerogatives over their employees. Given this situation, it becomes clear that managers would be unwilling to sacrifice their own power interest for such an altruistic purpose. Real participation on a large scale would imply sacrificing the predominant position of management—an unlikely development in a capitalist enterprise. To put it another way, human relations theorists wanted to revolutionize the organization without a revolution, without touching its societal foundations.

Some critics, such as the sociologists Clark Kerr and Abraham Siegel, challenged the notion that industrial cooperation rested primarily on the skills and understanding of industrial leaders.[23] They pointed to areas of work activity where industrial conflict was persistent (in Canada, the Post Office, or resource extraction industries such as logging; in Britain, coal mining) and they pointed to other areas where conflict was rare (in Canada, the federal civil service and the textile industry). Kerr and Siegel asked if they could really be expected to believe that differences in workplace harmony could be accounted for in terms of the leadership skills (the human relation skills) of management. Was it that some industries adopted a human relations approach and others did not? Or were the roots of these differences in workplace conflict to be found elsewhere? Kerr and Siegel pointed to the powerful influence of job structure upon human relations on the job. For instance, the resource industries are notoriously strike-ridden because of structural factors—the jobs are dangerous, it is a boom-and-bust industry, employment is often centred in small, highly class-polarized towns, etc. All of these factors contribute to the conflict-prone nature of the industry, notwithstanding the best efforts and theories of the human relations model. In Canada, for postal workers, the issue of technological change is vital. For the textile industry, the lack of conflict can be explained by the large numbers of unorganized marginal workers—mainly women and immigrants—who are less likely to strike. The reason for differing job structures in various working environments also has much to do with the nature of the work, and in most cases little to do with the orientation of management, whether trained in human relations or not.

Furthermore, human relations theorists have given little consideration to the effect on work behaviour of the worker's experience beyond the confines of the organization. It makes little sense, in this view, to talk about basic needs of all workers. If such needs exist, they are conditioned by the individual's place in the social structure or class structure outside work (e.g., white-collar versus blue-collar individuals). Thus, the human relations school is limited by its failure to look beyond the factory gates for explanations of the behaviour of humans in organizations.

Another criticism is that human relations is management-centred and therefore biased. Human relations theorists were accused of being as preoccupied with efficiency as were scientific management theorists. The human relations specialists simply emphasized different principles; they were concerned with informal groups and improved communications, and thought that executives should be benevolent toward employees because this would raise productivity and make workers happy. But critics found this view superficial and irrelevant to the real needs of workers. For instance, the position of Mayo and other human relations theorists on collective bargaining was that unions were divisive. Collective bargaining emphasized the divisions between workers and management, preventing effective communication and increasing the kind of conflict that bred anomie. The assumption that there was a natural community of interests between worker and management was not substantiated by the human relations specialists, according to the critics. In addition, the point that financial incentives were not all that important in motivating workers was challenged; after all, wages and benefits are usually at the heart of collective bargaining disputes. These criticisms undermined the human relations approach to a certain extent, though it continues to play an influential role in the corporate world.

Other Theoretical Approaches

Our survey of organization theory, while covering a lot of ground, cannot of course be comprehensive. To round out this overview, though, we will finish by briefly noting the importance of a sampling of other modern theoretical approaches.

Among the post–Second World War developments in organization theory, systems theory came to the fore and established itself as the predominant approach to understanding organizations. Systems theory sought to explain organizations as open systems through the application of computers, statistical analysis, information systems and quantitative measurement. These techniques attracted the attention of theorists who expressed a confidence in the same kind of rationality espoused generations earlier by structuralist theorists. The seminal work in this area was by Robert Katz and Daniel Khan, who wrote *The Social Psychology of Organizations* in 1966.[24] This was followed in 1967 by the publication of *Organizations in Action* by James D. Thompson.[25] Katz and Khan's notions of organizations as open systems suggested that organizations must constantly change in response to environmental factors, but that the working environment is also influenced by the decisions of managers. This stands in contrast to classical theory, which saw organizations as closed and static creatures in pursuit of economic efficiency. Thompson's insight was to acknowledge that, although parts of organizations may be closed at the technical level of operations, they contain other elements which are designed to adjust to the uncertainties inherent in the outside environment.

Systems theory sees organizations as made up of complex and dynamic interconnected elements. They consist of inputs, processes, outputs and a feedback loop whereby outputs reenter the system as new inputs. There are elements in this process that are knowable and understandable, but there are also others whose presence and impact is hard to discern. Thus, when a manager makes a decision, she sets in motion unanticipated consequences due to the dynamic, multidimensional and interconnected nature of the organization as a whole. Systems theorists sought to study this by focusing on decision-making processes, the flow of information through the system, and the measure and degree of controls present in it. They noted the ability of an organization to adapt in order to keep functioning.

The adaptability of an organization was given attention through the work of theorists in the field of cybernetics. This is a term derived from the Greek word for "steersman"; as applied to organizations it means "the multidisciplinary study of the structures and functions of control and information processing systems in animals and machines. The basic concept behind cybernetics is self-regulation— through biological, social, or technological systems that can identify problems, do something about them, and then receive feedback to adjust themselves automatically."[26] But another stream of thought within systems theory, known as *contingency theory*, suggested that there are no absolutes or universal rules that apply to all organizations in all circumstances. "... the effectiveness of an organizational action (for example, a decision) is viewed as dependent upon the relationship between the element in question and all other aspects of the system—at the particular moment."[27] Everything depends on (is contingent upon) the situation at hand. This view places a large emphasis on the ability of an organization to develop rapid and accurate information systems to successfully adapt.

Systems theory ran into criticisms by the 1970s, however. In particular, human relations theorists argued that the systems theory model paid inadequate attention to issues like the negative role of computers and information technology in dominating human organizations; the impact of centralized decision-making; and the freedom of individuals within organizations to escape the tyranny of technological imperatives. Methodological problems arose as well. Faith in computer analysis, econometric modeling and statistical analysis often proved misplaced when analyses of organizations revealed outcomes different from those predicted by the model. In Canada, cybernetics and systems theory received the imprimatur of Prime Minister Trudeau and his government, which attempted to initiate reforms built on the inherent rationalism of the approach.[28] But repeated frustrations led to its virtual abandonment by the 1980s. The standard diagrammatic depiction of systems theory as applied to the Canadian government is captured in Figure 2.2, which shows a model of the political system that contains the essential elements of inputs, process and outputs feeding back into the inputs.

FIGURE 2.2   A Model of the Political System

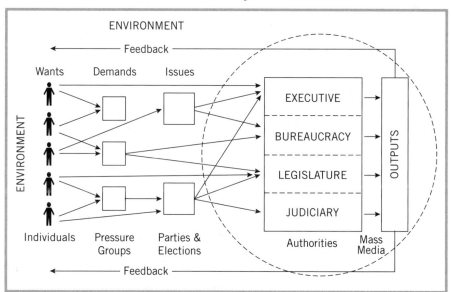

One of the offsprings of systems and contingency theory is *population ecology theory*. Theorists working in this area view organizations as organisms with a life cycle of birth, growth and death. They also note the diversity of organizational types that exist. In these regards they owe an intellectual debt of gratitude to Darwinism, since much of their approach can be likened to evolution theory. Competition for scarce resources among populations, the need to reproduce, and survival of the fittest are all concepts borrowed from the natural sciences and ap-plied to organizations. Population ecology theory also pays attention to the different environments within which organizations exist and attempts to understand the impact of environment on organizational form and durability. It also argues that a process of natural selection is at work among organizations. Those which adapt, thrive; those which remain static, die. At a more subtle level, this theory suggests that decision-making by managers does not in itself lead to adaptation. Instead, pop-ulation ecology theory argues that the environment itself selects organizational forms (consistent with the process of natural selection in the animal world).[29]

As with the other theoretical models outlined above, population ecology had its share of critics. They begin with the question of the applicability of models from the natural sciences to organization theory, and proceed to the methodolog-ical difficulties inherent in tracing causal factors for the success and failure of or-ganizations which do not lend themselves to easy identification or measurement. Still, the approach added to the diversity of organization theory and offers yet an-other way of thinking about how organizations function.

Given the diversity of approaches outlined (and again, this is not a compre-hensive overview), students of public administration may be forgiven for feeling a little overwhelmed. One way of sorting through the morass of approaches is pro-vided by management professor Gareth Morgan. He developed a typology of dif-ferent "images" of organizations—a classification system of several different metaphors which can be used to describe the attributes of organizations. He sug-gests we can classify organizations as, among other things: machines; organisms; brains; cultures; and instruments of domination.[30] If you give some considera-tion to the theories and theorists studied here, you should be able to make some sense of them in terms of this template. For instance, it is clear that some theorists, like Weber and Taylor, undertake their study of organizations while regarding them as machines, as we noted. The work of the human relations school can be seen to privilege the view of organizations as organisms, as can systems, contingency and population ecology theories. Proponents of TQM, cybernetics and similar models see organizations as brains. Marx, and to some extent Weber, view organizations as instruments of domination. In short, a rich and varied set of perspectives has been brought to bear on our understanding of organizations.

But what about Canadian public administration more specifically? How have these varied approaches affected the organization of the public sector in Canada? This is the concern of the next chapter.

WHAT YOU HAVE LEARNED

This chapter has focused on the theory side of the study of public administration. As such, it has sought to elucidate the ideas behind that ubiquitous presence of contemporary life—the modern organization. It is important, in studying public administration, to understand the theoretical premises upon which organizations are constructed. It is also important to appreciate that organization theory crosses from the private to the public sector and back again. This makes for some difficulty in drawing conclusions and in constructing organizations, since, as you saw in Chapter 1, the public and private sectors are two quite different beasts. Nonetheless, theoreticians tell us that the study of one aids us in the understanding of the other. Hence, this examination of the theoretical literature reveals the interrelationship between the dominant ideas that animate our understanding of both sectors.

But another point about organization theory needs to be emphasized. It should be obvious to you by now that no one theory explains all there is to know about organizations. You should therefore be considering the utility of particular theories by subjecting them to a series of questions:

➤ What aspects of organizational reality does a given theory purport to explain? Is it concerned with the methods managers use to maximize efficiency, or with the well-being of workers and their role in decision-making?

➤ What level of analysis is the theory aimed at? Individuals within organizations? Parts of organizations? The whole organization? The society within which the organization is located? Or some combination of all of these?

➤ What conception of human nature underlies the theory? We saw that Taylor assumed people were lazy and indolent unless motivated by personal monetary gain. But Maslow felt that humans were motivated by a much more complex set of factors. What does this tell us about the way each theorist viewed human nature?

➤ Does the theory appear to make sense of what actually goes on in the real world of organizations? Does it explain only the workings of private sector organizations, or is it applicable to the public sector as well?

➤ Does the theory make sense in light of your own knowledge and experience?

This is not a comprehensive list of questions, but should nonetheless give you some idea of the nature and utility of the theoretical aspects of public administration as it has been affected by organization theory.

ENDNOTES

1. See Jay M. Shafritz and J. Steven Ott, eds. *Classics of Organization Theory: Fourth Edition*, (Fort Worth: Harcourt Brace College Publishers, 1996).

2. Karl Marx, "Contribution to the Critique of Hegel's *Philosophy of Right*," in Robert C. Tucker, ed. *The Marx-Engels Reader, Second Edition,* (New York: Norton, 1978): 25.

3. John Porter, *The Vertical Mosaic: An Analysis of Social Class and Power in Canada,* (Toronto: University of Toronto Press, 1965).

4. Jay M. Shafritz and Albert C. Hyde, eds. *Classics of Public Administration, Third Edition,* (Pacific Grove, California: Brooks/Cole Publishing, 1992): 40.

5. See H.H. Gerth and C. Wright Mills, eds. *From Max Weber: Essays in Sociology*, (New York: Oxford University Press, 1946): 196–244.

6. Robert F. Adie and Paul G. Thomas, *Canadian Public Administration: Problematical Perspectives, Second Edition,* (Scarborough: Prentice-Hall, 1987): 17–18.

7. Adie and Thomas, *Canadian Public Administration,* (1987): 18.

8. S.M. Lipset, *Agrarian Socialism,* (Berkeley: University of California Press, 1950).

9. This example is cited in Howard E. McCurdy, *Public Administration: A Synthesis,* (Menlo Park, California: Cummings Publishers, 1977).

10. See Robert K. Merton, *Social Theory and Social Structure,* (New York: The Free Press, 1957).

11. "The Dark Side," *St. John's Evening Telegram,* 1973. Cited in Albert J. Mills and Tony Simmons, *Reading Organization Theory: A Critical Approach,* (Toronto: Garamond, 1999): 41–42.

12. See Alvin Gouldner, *Patterns of Industrial Bureaucracy,* (New York: The Free Press, 1954), and Victor A. Thompson, *Modern Organization,* (New York: Alfred A. Knopf, 1961).

13. Frank J. Goodnow, *Politics and Administration: A Study in Government,* (New York: Russell and Russell, 1900).

14. See Herbert A. Simon, "The Proverbs of Administration," in Jay M. Shafritz and Albert C. Hyde, eds. *Classics of Public Administration, Third Edition,* (Pacific Grove, California: Brooks/Cole Publishing, 1992): 150–65; and Herbert A. Simon, *Administrative Behaviour,* (New York: The Free Press, 1954).

15. Jay M. Shafritz and Albert C. Hyde, *Classics of Public Administration, Third Edition,* (Pacific Grove, California: Brooks/Cole Publishing, 1992): 3.

16. F.W. Taylor, *The Principles of Scientific Management,* (New York: Harper and Brothers, 1911): 59.

17. See Luther Gulick and L. Urwick, eds. *Papers on the Science of Administration,* (New York: Augustus M. Kelly Publishers, 1937).

18. See Elton Mayo, *The Human Problems of an Industrial Civilization,* (New York: The Viking Press, 1960). The first five chapters of this book provide short summaries of some of the Hawthorne experiments.

19. Chester Barnard, *The Functions of the Executive,* (Cambridge, Massachusetts: Harvard University Press, 1938).

20. Chester Barnard, "Informal Organizations and Their Relation to Formal Organization," cited in Jay M. Shafritz and Albert C. Hyde, eds. *Classics of Public Administration, Third Edition,* (Pacific Grove, California: Brooks/Cole Publishing, 1992): 99.

21. F.J. Roethlisberger and William J. Dickson, *Management and the Worker,* (Cambridge, Massachusetts: Harvard University Press, 1939).

22. A.H. Maslow, "A Theory of Human Motivation," in Jay M. Shafritz and Albert C. Hyde, eds. *Classics of Public Administration, Third Edition,* (Pacific Grove, California: Brooks/Cole Publishing, 1992): 129–137.

23. See Clark Kerr *et al. Industrialism and Industrial Man: The Problems of Labour and Management in Economic Growth, Second Edition,* (Harmondsworth, England: Penguin Books, 1973).

24. Robert Katz and Daniel Khan, *The Social Psychology of Organizations,* (New York: Wiley, 1966).

25. James D. Thompson, *Organization in Action,* (New York: McGraw-Hill, 1967).

26. Jay M. Shafritz and J. Steven Ott, eds. *Classics of Organization Theory: Fourth Edition,* (Fort Worth: Harcourt Brace College Publishers, 1996): 255.

27. Jay M. Shafritz and J. Steven Ott, eds. *Classics of Organization Theory: Fourth Edition,* (Fort Worth: Harcourt Brace College Publishers, 1996): 258.

28. See Peter Aucoin, "Organizational Change in the Machinery of Canadian Government: From Rational Management to Brokerage Politics," *Canadian Journal of Political Science*, 29, 1 (March, 1986): 3–27.

29. See Michael Hannan and John Freeman, "The Population Ecology of Organizations," *American Journal of Sociology*, 82 (1977): 929–64.

30. Gareth Morgan, *Images of Organization: Second Edition*, (Thousand Oaks, California: Sage Publications, 1997). Morgan also uses the metaphors of organizations as political systems, psychic prisons, and unfolding logics of change.

KEY WORDS AND CONCEPTS

Karl Marx (29)
class conflict (29)
alienation (29)
hierarchy (30)
autonomy (30)
accumulation (32)
legitimation (32)
Max Weber (33)
span of control (40)

bureaucratic pathologies (41)
structuralist and humanist theories (41)
scientific management (42)
time and motion studies (44)
POSDCORB (45)
division of labour (47)
Hawthorne experiments (49)
informal group (50)
hierarchy of human needs (53)

REVIEW QUESTIONS

This chapter was divided into three sections, each of which addressed key issues regarding theoretical approaches to understanding organizations within public administration. You should now be able to answer the questions associated with each.

1. Perspectives on Bureaucratic Organization
The development of bureaucratic organizations is central to public administration. This section noted the contribution of business management thinking and its uneasy marriage with public sector values and concerns, asking the following questions: What are the main concerns of organization theory? What are the origins of organization theory? What contesting values underlay the development of theories of public administration?

2. The Classic Theorists
Karl Marx and Max Weber are two thinkers whose contributions to understanding organizations and bureaucracy, though widely divergent, are the basis for much subsequent theorizing. The section examined the strengths and weaknesses of their ideas, and asked, What impact have the classic theories and theorists had on public administration? What are the strengths and weaknesses of their respective theories?

3. Structuralist and Humanist Theories
Two main schools of thought have dominated historically in the theories of organization literature. The scientific management approach, pioneered by F.W. Taylor, and human relations theories arose in response to the need to improve the efficiency of large-scale modern organizations, as well as the conditions of those who worked in these structures. This led us to ask the following: What types of debates have ensued over the nature and form of organization in both the private and the

public sectors? What exactly were these theoretical innovations meant to accomplish when translated into practice?

FURTHER READING

1. Perspectives on Bureaucratic Organization

Denhardt, Robert B. *Theories of Public Organization: Third Edition.* Fort Worth: Harcourt Brace, 2000.

Mills, Albert J. and Tony Simmons. *Reading Organization Theory: A Critical Approach.* Toronto: Garamond, 1999: chapter 2.

2. The Classic Theorists

Marx, Karl. "Contribution to the Critique of Hegel's *Philosophy of Right*," in Robert C. Tucker, ed. *The Marx-Engels Reader. Second Edition.* New York: Norton, 1978.

Merton, Robert K. "Bureaucratic Structure and Personality," in Jay M. Shafritz and J. Steven Ott, eds. *Classics of Organization Theory. Fifth Edition.* Belmont, California: Wadsworth Publishing, 1999: 103–11.

Weber, Max. "Bureaucracy," in Jay M. Shafritz and J. Steven Ott, eds. *Classics of Organization Theory. Fifth Edition.* Belmont, California: Wadsworth Publishing, 1999: 73–78.

3. Structuralist and Humanist Theories

Barnard, Chester. "Informal Organizations and Their Relation to Formal Organization," in Jay M. Shafritz and Albert C. Hyde, eds. *Classics of Public Administration. Third Edition.* Pacific Grove, California: Brooks/Cole Publishing, 1992: 96–100.

Gulick, Luther. "Notes on the Theory of Organization," in Jay M. Shafritz and J. Steven Ott, eds. *Classics of Organization Theory. Fifth Edition.* Belmont, California: Wadsworth Publishing, 1999: 79–87.

Kernaghan, Kenneth. "Empowerment and Public Administration: Revolutionary Advance or Passing Fancy." *Canadian Public Administration*, 35, 2 (Summer, 1992).

Maslow, A.H. "A Theory of Human Motivation," in Jay M. Shafritz and J. Steven Ott, eds. *Classics of Organization Theory. Fifth Edition.* Belmont, California: Wadsworth Publishing, 1999: 167–78.

Simon, Herbert. "The Proverbs of Administration," in Jay M. Shafritz and Albert C. Hyde, eds. *Classics of Public Administration. Third Edition.* Pacific Grove, California: Brooks/Cole Publishing, 1992: 150–165.

Taylor, Frederick W. "Scientific Management," in Jay M. Shafritz and J. Steven Ott, eds. *Classics of Organization Theory. Fifth Edition.* Belmont, California: Wadsworth Publishing, 1999: 61–72.

 ## WEBLINKS

Marx/Engels Archive
www.marxists.org

Max Weber
www.faculty.rsu.edu/~felwell/Theorists/Weber/Whome.htm

Dead Sociologists Index
www2.pfeiffer.edu/~lridener/dds/index.html

F.W. Taylor
attila.stevens-tech.edu/~rdowns

Chapter ③

Organization Theory *and* Canadian Public Administration

WHAT YOU WILL LEARN

One notable characteristic of the theorists surveyed thus far is that few are Canadian. Indeed, the United States and Europe (especially Britain and Germany) have proven most influential in the spread of ideas about public administration. We will now assess in turn the impact of each of the major schools of thought on Canadian public administration. To begin with, it is worth asking how inspirational the classic thinkers have been. The answer is not easy, for their influence has sometimes been subtle. But there are also some obvious ways in which the work of particular individuals and schools of thought have come to shape both the practice and theory of Canadian public administration. This chapter looks at this issue in two sections.

1. The Impact of Organization Theory

How powerful have Marx, Weber and the other theorists been in the Canadian context? In what ways have Canadian thinkers adopted their ideas, or developed their own counterpoints to those ideas? Are there concrete instances of the impact of their thinking on the form and structure of the public sector?

2. Contemporary Developments

This section considers the most recent developments in the theory and practice of public administration in Canada in light of the perspectives sketched out in Chapter 2. It raises questions such as the following: How effective have applications of participatory management theory been in Canada? What is the New Public Management, and how has it influenced thinking about recent reforms in Canadian public administration?

The Impact of Organization Theory

Among the classic thinkers, Marx's critique of bureaucracy has shed light on how the power structures in society affect democracy and the governing of the nation. For instance, his assertion that the most important division in society is the class division has important implications for the question of who occupies the most important decision-making posts in the political and bureaucratic realm. Some research in Canada points to the existence of a dominant **elite** representing, directly or indirectly, the capitalist class in Canada. It suggests, moreover, that a network of social, economic and political ties reinforces the dominance of this elite. Thus, it is not uncommon to find that this relatively small proportion of the population is connected through family, social and business ties. They hang out at the same exclusive clubs; send their children to the same private schools; sit on the same boards of directors of major corporations; are wealthy and well educated; and are generally an ethnically and religiously homogeneous group in that they have historically tended to be white, Anglo-Saxon male Protestants (if they are English) or Catholic (if they are French).[1]

In organizational terms, this elite dominates the top positions in government. Thus, many of the senior bureaucrats as well as the politicians belong to this exclusive agglomeration of individuals, who generally act in the best interests of their own class. For instance, many former prime ministers and Cabinet ministers were first corporate lawyers and business persons. Many have been directors of important corporations. There is a good deal of mobility in this group among corporate, political and bureaucratic careers.

Marxist theory suggests that therefore we should not be surprised to discover that the organizations of the state are designed in a way that perpetuates the power and influence of this class. On one level, the bureaucracy is a cold, uninviting and alienating place that is difficult to penetrate and understand. This tends to thwart ordinary citizens, most of the time, in questioning the actions of government. On the other hand, it permits those in control of its complicated mechanisms to use them for their own ends. This is not to suggest that the state is solely organized for the purpose of the elite. This is too simplistic an assertion. Rather, it is to suggest that the bureaucratic state is set up in such a way that most of the time it acts in the long-term interests of the capitalist class. There are many debates among Marxist scholars in Canada about exactly how this process works, as well as criticisms of the theory by non-Marxists.

As for Weber, there is no doubt that his theories have been profoundly influential in Canadian public administration. For instance, the 1918 reforms to the civil service, which we alluded to in Chapter 1, reflect very strongly a Weberian sensibility. You will recall that those reforms were intended generally to introduce the concept of merit into the public service and entrench hierarchy, a job classification system, professionalism, competitive exams, etc. The intent—true to Weber's ideas—was to put the Canadian public service on a more rational basis and have it operate according to prescribed rules and regulations.

It is also evident that Taylor's scientific management approach has been tremendously influential in Canadian public administration. Taylor's major contribution was in the development of two main principles adapted by public administration theorists and practitioners. First, there was the division of work, or the principle that work ought to be divided up so as to take maximum advantage of the skills of the employees. The assembly line is the most obvious application of this principle in the private sector. In the public sector, elaborate job classification schemes have existed at least since the 1918 *Civil Service Act*. Second, there was the principle of **homogeneity**, also called **unity of direction**, which asserts that similar activities ought to be grouped together in the same unit under a single supervisor and a single plan. In public administration, then, work ought to be grouped according to purpose, e.g., those things related to health under one department, to education under another, etc. Moreover, within departments, there is a further division of labour, with scientists grouped in one unit, policy analysts in another, clerical staff in yet another, and so on, for purposes of job function, promotion and wages.

Furthermore, as applied to the civil service, scientific management attempted to eradicate imprecise job criteria based on the personal characteristics of workers (i.e., patronage) by setting out the very careful specification of job duties and requirements (i.e., merit). Civil service recruits were expected to display only those "scientific qualities" that made them fit for the job. This was reflected in the *Civil Service Reform Act* of 1918 in Canada, which was bent on eliminating all irrelevant considerations in the hiring of government workers. Thus, in Canadian public administration, the impact of scientific management was felt fairly early, and was reflected in the concerns about efficiency and economy within the civil service that eventually gave rise to the reforms of 1918.

The reforms called for the creation of a Civil Service Commission that would be responsible, in part, for choosing government personnel based on scientific principles, and would develop an elaborate classification scheme for government workers. What was being called for, in short, was a system of scientific management that could satisfy the rising demand for the elimination of patronage in government, coupled with the demand for more efficient administration. It was felt this would only be possible if all civil service positions were classified by function. Thus, an attempt to analyze the component elements of jobs was inspired by the example of scientific management in studying the component elements of work; once these were analyzed, examinations could be devised to determine which candidates were best qualified to fill specific positions (the central concern of a merit system of selection). At the same time, development of new methods of uniform cost accounting necessitated a uniform job terminology, which would allow the legislature to more efficiently control the finances of the bureaucracy.

Having said all this, it is also important to note that the many units of organization within the complex machinery of government are structured in a variety of ways. Some are close to the models set out by Weber or Taylor. Think about the organization of the Canadian army, for example, or the fire and police services. These all come closest to Weber's model. But other departments and agencies approximate the Weberian model too. Still others reflect scientific management techniques.

For instance, in the Canada Customs and Revenue Agency (formerly Revenue Canada), large numbers of employees work in data processing centres that are much like large factories, and there is strong pressure on employees to conform to the rules and regulations of the organization to maximize the efficient processing of tax returns and other financial information. The organization is highly structured, with rules emanating from the top downward, and little attempt is made to seek employee input into management decisions. But not all government departments are best run in this way. For example, in some departments the workplaces are scattered throughout the country in small, regional offices, with a good deal of local control and initiative being allowed. Control is decentralized, and reporting systems are less hierarchical. Input from below is encouraged, since frontline employees often have a better idea of what works than their seniors in distant Ottawa.

The point here is to ask yourself, Does any one model explain all there is to know and understand, given the complexity of modern government in Canada? Is there homogeneity in organizational types across government departments? Within departments? Are there some government organizations that display two or more of the models under consideration simultaneously?

Overall, we might conclude that the human relations school has been less successful in seeing its perspective adopted in Canadian public administrative structures and practices. You will recall that human relations theorists argued that organizations would produce the best work environments when they implemented nonroutinized tasks, recognized the goals of their employees, decentralized decision-making, and worked against a hierarchical decision-making structure. But in Canada, there seems to be little overt evidence that public administration was profoundly influenced by human relations; government in this country has persistently been characterized by rigid hierarchies, inflexible job classification structures, and other elements more reminiscent of Weber and of scientific management than of human relations theories.

One exception in Canada is that decentralization became a major theme that reached into government organizational thinking. In 1965, the Glassco Commission pushed it, under the catchphrase "Let the managers manage." Decentralization was aimed at securing the participation and commitment of subordinates and was seen as a tool for reducing delays and red tape in decision-making. Of course, politicians saw decentralization as aiding certain political objectives, and this was probably a greater motivation to its implementation than was human relations theory *per se*. But it can be said that the human relations school did sensitize the Canadian government and public to its uses in curbing excess bureaucracy. It also aided in introducing freedom of information legislation and creating specialized government offices that were motivated by the drive to improve democracy within bureaucracies. Human relations theories helped give greater credence to these types of ideas. Yet, 30 years after Glassco, another review of public administration practices entitled part of its report "Let the Managers Manage." Have we really gotten anywhere?

Contemporary Developments

Most recently, organization theory has evolved further into a set of concepts that can loosely be referred to as participatory management. The general goal of this school of thought was to go beyond the platitudes of human relations theorists and implement genuine worker participation in the decision-making functions of the workplace. It was premised on the view that there is an innate tension in the work organization, and that this is natural and unavoidable; but it can be controlled and directed. Many different approaches exist under the broad heading of participatory management, including Management by Objectives (MBO), Organization Development (OD), and Total Quality Management (TQM). But alongside participatory management, another set of developments has occurred, uneasily coexisting with the first. This is the New Public Management approach, which seeks to incorporate management techniques and strategies from the business sector in a much more deliberate and systematic manner than has been the case in the past. We will look briefly at some major trends in participatory management before turning our attention finally to the New Public Management.

Participatory Management

Management by Objectives (MBO) is derived from a theory by Peter Drucker, founder of MBO, that stood Weber's basic argument on its head.[2] It is centred on the notion that specialization and hierarchy can be overemphasized at the expense of the overall efficiency of the organization. If you subdivide an organization into numerous specialized agencies each with their own functions, the actions of one agency may conflict with the goals of another. For instance, the human resources department may require savings to be realized by eliminating employees to reduce payroll costs. But other departments may already be stretched to the limit in terms of personnel. Thus, if human resources does its job well, other parts of the organization may suffer. The problem, then, according to Drucker, is the inability of the specialized parts of the organization to focus on the overall goals of the whole. The solution is MBO. While there is little agreement over the precise means of implementing MBO, several steps can be identified:

1. Consultation between top managers and their immediate subordinates to determine the broad goals of the organization.

2. Preparation of a statement by top management of the overall results expected in the upcoming year.

3. Meeting between top managers and their subordinates to parcel out the responsibility for these results to individual organizational units. This task is subdivided by focusing on a) routine objectives; b) problem-solving objectives; and c) innovative objectives.

4. Repetition of the process of parceling out the responsibilities (outlined in step 3) throughout the organization.

5. Management review of this plan for consistency and to ensure that the desired goals are met.

6. Year-end comprehensive review.[3]

Some critics claim that MBO is a system that only pretends to offer greater participation in decision-making, but that ultimately leaves control in the hands of senior management. Any participation in decision-making that does take place is not really meaningful. Another problem is that establishing clear and measurable objectives is often difficult to do, especially in public administration (as was suggested earlier in Chapter 1). Still, MBO did catch on in many organizations and was used with varying degrees of success.

Organization Development (OD) begins with the premise that organizations become rigid and inflexible over time. They develop means and methods of doing things that make responding to changed conditions difficult, if not impossible. The purpose of OD is to identify rigidities and prepare the organization to be flexible enough to adjust to changes in the broader environment before crisis or collapse occurs. OD requires the recognition of a culture or history within every organization that is often an impediment to positive reform, and the development of strategies to overcome that culture or history. Dysfunctional organizational behaviour is identified, and the organization is encouraged to "unlearn" that behaviour. For instance, objections to new innovations are often framed this way: "We tried something like that before, and it didn't work." This reflects the historical memory of the organization, but ignores that circumstances may have changed, making the suggested reforms more applicable. Then the reforms needed are identified and implemented. Finally, new behaviours are instituted to prevent the organization from slipping back into its old dysfunctional ways.

Total Quality Management (TQM) is an approach to participatory management that began to emerge in the 1980s. It was partly a response to Japanese management techniques and is associated with the work of W. Edwards Deming, who taught Japanese business leaders his techniques after the Second World War.[4] In particular, the auto industry in Japan embraced TQM. In the American model, production fo-

FIGURE 3.1

cused on maximizing output and then employing a separate quality control group to detect and repair problems after the fact. The Japanese approach was to make each employee responsible for the quality of his segment of the work. Thus while it might take longer to build a car, the overall quality was better, resulting in cost savings for the organization in the longer term, since repair and recalls were fewer. The guiding principle of TQM is "Get it right the first time." Thus quality control is no longer considered a discrete function of part of the organization, but rather an integral part of what the entire organization does.

In Canadian public administration, these ideas were instituted by the federal government and some provinces in the mid-1970s with varying degrees of success. For instance, the federal Department of Energy, Mines and Resources, the Office of the Auditor General, and Industry, Science and Technology all adopted TQM. Committee structures were put in place, composed of both management and elected worker representatives. But most of these experiments failed, due primarily to the imbalance of power between management and workers, which was reinforced by the public service's rigid job classification system, which simply could not be overcome.

These examples reveal that attempts to institute participatory management theories in the Canadian public service have run into some serious roadblocks. The entrenched hierarchical system reflective of Weberian and Taylorist models has proven remarkably resistant to change. Even with the best of intentions, efforts to increase the participation of workers in decision-making structures have frequently floundered on the rocks of rigid job classification systems, rules and regulations, and hierarchy, which predominate in the organization of the Canadian public service.

The New Public Management

Much contemporary organization theory centres on the **New Public Management (NPM)**, which is the last development that we will consider in this chapter. NPM is a term loosely used to describe a set of administrative doctrines and practices that have dominated not only in Canada, but in several other countries as well. Indeed, NPM found its origin in the approach to governing pioneered by the administration of Britain's former prime minister Margaret Thatcher. It has been motivated by three things: the increased debt and deficit problems of contemporary governments that have resulted in a search for ever more economical ways of governing; a growing alienation from politics and politicians among ordinary citizens, a rise in apathy, distrust of governments, and a decline in public confidence in public policies and services provided by governments; and globalization and the emergence of a new economic order in which the traditional nation-state has declined in significance in comparison to transnational corporations and other global actors.

Thatcher's basic response to these developments was to argue for a rolling back of the state and its withdrawal from a number of areas. The problems and their proposed solutions have spread to other countries, including Canada. Recent changes in public administration have focused on **privatization**, **deregulation**, **contracting out** of public services, decentralization, **downsizing** and expenditure reduction initiatives (including layoffs of public servants, and wage freezes and rollbacks), the introduction of **user fees**, commercialization of public enterprises, and other similar measures. Responses have varied from province to province and from the provincial to federal levels of government, but the general trend seems clear. The new job of politicians and public sector managers has been to cope with these changes. The new paradigms for the administration of public affairs has led to a variety of reforms.

According to political scientist Peter Aucoin, the NPM requires state administrators to accommodate themselves to certain assumptions: bureaucrats have gained too much power over politicians in recent years; the organizational mechanisms of government have become too complex and now actually impede the ability of political leadership to exercise authority and manage government; management in government has become too concerned with rigid adherence to rules and procedures and too prone to bureaucratic pathologies.[5] Thus, criticisms of government bureaucracy have emerged that focus on *reengineering* the whole apparatus and role of government. More precisely, this criticism has prompted a search for management techniques that put the operation of government on a more businesslike footing.

Among the most influential proponents of the NPM are David Osborne and Ted Gaebler. Their 1992 book *Reinventing Government* outlined 10 principles of reinventing government, based on the assumption that government is necessary but that it does not necessarily have to act like government. They argued the following:

Most entrepreneurial governments promote competition *between service providers. They empower citizens by pushing control out of the bureaucracy, into the community. They measure the performance of their agencies, focusing not on inputs but on outcomes. They are driven by their goals—their missions—not by their rules and regulations. They redefine their clients as customers and offer them choices—between schools, between training programs, between housing options. They prevent problems before they emerge, rather than simply offering services afterward. They put their energies into earning money, not simply spending it. They decentralize authority, embracing participatory management. They prefer market mechanisms to bureaucratic mechanisms. And they focus not simply on providing public services, but on catalyzing all sectors—public, private, and voluntary—into action to solve their community's problems.*[6] [Emphasis in original.]

You will recall from Chapter 1 that the idea that government should be run like a business is not a new idea. You will also recall that the idea has traditionally been regarded by theorists of public administration as reflecting a lack of understanding of the differences between the public and private sectors. Nonetheless, a veritable revolution has been going on in public administration in Canada for the last 10 to 20 years, in which the practices of the private sector have been incorporated much more overtly into the public sector than previously in Canada's past.

The NPM in the public sector is thus now being driven by the same values that underlie those of the private sector: the bottom line is the **three Es**: *efficiency, effectiveness* and *economy*. These are placed within the framework of "quality service" to citizens, who are now referred to as "customers" or "clients." A much greater level of attention is being paid to the relationship between expenditures and revenues, even at the cost of sacrificing long-established and cherished government policies and programs. Confronted with clients demanding improved services at less cost, government's response has been to look to new business management practices. As Aucoin notes, "Concerns for economy and efficiency have thus been given a new priority in public management. Enhancing cost-consciousness, doing more with less and achieving value for money became the objectives of this finance-centred perspective on public management reform."[7] This entails creating management structures and practices that effectively "debureaucratize" organizations. Donald Savoie suggests that "the philosophy [of NPM] is rooted in the conviction that private sector management is superior to public administration. The solution, therefore, is to transfer government activities to the private sector through privatization and contracting out." But, as he goes on to suggest, it is hardly practical to transfer *all* government activities to the private sector, so "the next best solution is to transfer business management practices to government operations."[8] Box 3-1 shows how government attempted to incorporate new public management principles through a government-wide program review undertaken in 1994.

BOX 3-1

The Six Tests of Program Review

The federal government in Canada instituted NPM through the Program Review in 1994. This review was guided by six tests:

Public Interest Test

Does the program area or activity continue to serve a public interest?

Role of Government Test

Is there a legitimate and necessary role for government in this program or activity?

Federalism Test

Is the current role of the federal government appropriate, or is the program a candidate for realignment with the provinces?

Partnership Test

What activities or programs should or could be transferred in whole or in part to the private or voluntary sector?

Efficiency Test

If the program or activity continues, how could its efficiency be improved?

Affordability Test

Is the resultant package of programs and activities affordable within the fiscal restraint? If not, what programs or activities should be abandoned?

Sources: Canada, Privy Council Office, "Program Review and Getting Government Right." 1994. Reproduced with the permission of the Minister of Public Works and Government Services, 1998.

Some of the purported changes to Canadian public administration in recent years are shown in Table 3.1. It contrasts traditional bureaucratic structures with the main features of newer models. The reality, of course, is that change has come about much more slowly and has encountered considerable resistance. Still, the table at least outlines the attempts that have been made to reconfigure the public sector in Canada.

TABLE 3.1 Traditional Bureaucratic Organizations[9]

Traditional Bureaucratic Organizations	The New Public Sector Organization
A. Hierarchy and Central Command	Flattened and Decentralized Organization and Decision-Making
B. Rule-Governed and Upward Accountability	Results-Centred • achievement of goals rather than process is what counts
C. Static/Status Quo • all change is initiated and driven from above • emphasis given to continuity over continuous change	Change-Driven High Performance Organizations • risk-taking, continuous improvement and innovation are encouraged from all levels of the organization
D. Standardized Citizen's Right to Public Services • emphasis on universal legal rights to services	Client-Focused • emphasis upon individual customer satisfaction and service to selective client groups • clients as taxpayers
E. Tayloristic-Style Operating Structure	Empowering Employees • use of new human resource strategies such as Total Quality Management
F. Process-Driven Organization • static tasks, hierarchical institution, rigidly specified job categories	The Learning Organization • workforce is multiskilled • a learning and adapting environment
G. Fordist Production System • workforce based upon economies of scale, i.e., large workforce involved in all aspects of production and service delivery	The Flexible Workplace • "just-in-time" lean production • extensive use of part-time and contract workers • contracting out of tasks • alternative service delivery

In any event, a literature on public administration has already emerged that suggests NPM was never very thoroughly applied in the Canadian context, or more precisely, that a Canadian variant of NPM evolved that was softer than the model imposed on Britain, New Zealand and other places. Some theorists argue that in any event we are already moving beyond NPM.[10] In Chapters 9 and 10 we will more thoroughly consider the argument that Canadian public administration is moving toward a "post-bureaucratic state" model. For now, it is suffice to note that the impact of NPM is apparent in a series of reforms instituted by the federal government in the 1990s, like PS 2000 (discussed in Chapter 10), which called for improved service to the public, support for innovation, better human resource management practices, and new forms of accountability focused on results and performance.

But a variety of impediments frustrated the wholesale application of the NPM model, not the least of which was lack of political will, with the result that Canadian reforms paled in comparison to those in other countries.[11] Nonetheless, the introduction of reforms like the 1995 Quality Service Initiative, which sought to improve client satisfaction with government services, and an array of new innovations deemed "alternative service delivery" mechanisms proliferated. What emerged was "an increasing number of instruments, ranging from traditional ones such as departments, Crown corporations and mixed enterprises to newer ones such as special operating agencies, privatized public organizations, single-window service-delivery units, and partnerships," which, according to some theorists of public administration, are derived from NPM but move beyond it to the post-bureaucratic model.[12]

Critics of NPM point out that in many cases wholesale reform has been taking place without any effort at public consultation or popular approval. Others suggest that the changes in public sector management techniques represent yet another fad in a long line of changing tastes. Moreover, the critics contend, it would appear that proponents of the NPM have forgotten Wallace Sayre's law that public and private administration are fundamentally alike in all unimportant respects.

Peter Aucoin argues that

it is increasingly acknowledged that public service reform cannot be based on a paradigm that assumes that public administration is essentially the same as private administration. The public policy dimension is unique to public management as governance. Citizen-centred service requires attention to critical issues of law, rights, and due process not present in the marketplace of private service delivery. And managing the public service entails managing in a context of constraints and motivations that are distinct to the public sector. To the degree that privatization and contracting out cannot be extended to all functions of government, public administration, even in a highly devolved management regime, remains subject to political and administrative dynamics that require their own distinctive modes of reform and renewal.[13]

In a sense, this brief overview of the NPM and other recent developments brings us full circle. Many of the ideas of NPM are a reformulation of traditional models of organization management. There are shades of both structuralist and humanist approaches, for instance. Elements of scientific management and Weberian notions of hierarchy and control are present in the NPM. As you can see, the development of organization theory has proceeded through several different stages, each having had an impact on the public administration of Canada. To put these developments into more focus, we turn in the next chapter to the "real world" of organizations, looking at the actual machinery of government to see more concretely what impact theory has had on practice.

WHAT YOU HAVE LEARNED

This chapter has illuminated some of the ways in which various theoretical approaches to the concept of organization have influenced Canadian public administration. It observed that Canadian ideas have been heavily influenced by foreign ones in this area, particularly American, British and German. An assessment of the impact of each of the major schools of thought on Canadian public administration in turn reveals that the classic thinkers have been influential, though sometimes in subtle ways. The basic Weberian-type model has largely prevailed in the structure and organization of Canadian public administration. Structuralist and humanist theories have waxed and waned over time.

ENDNOTES

1. The groundbreaking study in this regard was John Porter's *The Vertical Mosaic: An Analysis of Social Class and Power in Canada*, (Toronto: University of Toronto Press, 1965). See also Dennis Olsen, *The State Elite*, (Toronto: McClelland and Stewart, 1980); Wallace Clement, *The Canadian Corporate Elite: An Analysis of Economic Power*, (Toronto: McClelland and Stewart, 1975); and Wallace Clement, *Class, Power and Property: Essays on Canadian Society*, (Toronto: Methuen, 1983).

2. Peter F. Drucker, *The Practice of Management*, (New York: Harper and Row, 1954).

3. See Drucker, *The Practice of Management*, (1954). Adapted from *Public Administration in Canada*, by Kenneth Kernaghan and David Siegel (ITP Nelson: 1995): 71. Reprinted by permission of ITP Nelson.

4. See W. Edwards Deming, *Quality, Productivity and Competitive Position*, (Cambridge, Massachusetts: M.I.T. Centre for Advanced Engineering Study, 1982).

5. Peter Aucoin, *The New Public Management in Canada in Comparative Perspective*, (Montreal: The Institute for Research on Public Policy, 1995): 3–4.

6. David Osborne and Ted Gaebler, *Reinventing Government: How the Entrepreneurial Spirit is Transforming the Public Sector*, (New York: Penguin, 1993): 19–20. Cited in Leslie A. Pal, *Beyond Policy Analysis: Public Issue Management in Turbulent Times*, (Scarborough: Nelson, 1997): 56–57.

7. Aucoin, *The New Public Management*, (1995): 9.

8. Donald Savoie, "What is Wrong With the New Public Management?" *Canadian Public Administration*, 38, 1 (1995): 113.

9. Aucoin, "Beyond the 'New' in Public Management Reform in Canada," (2002): 50.

10. Source: John Shields and B. Mitchell Evans, *Shrinking the State: Globalization and Public Administration "Reform,"* (Halifax: Fernwood, 1998): 44.

11. See Peter Aucoin, "Beyond the 'New' in Public Management Reform in Canada: Catching the Next Wave?" in Christopher Dunn, ed. *The Handbook of Canadian Public Administration*, (Toronto: Oxford University Press, 2002): 36–52; and Kenneth Kernaghan, Brian Marson and Sandford Borins, *The New Public Organization*, (Toronto: The Institute of Public Administration of Canada, 2000).

12. See Donald J. Savoie, *Thatcher, Reagan and Mulroney: In Search of a New Bureaucracy*, (Toronto: University of Toronto Press, 1994); and Peter Aucoin, *The New Public Management in Comparative Perspective*, (Montreal: Institute for Research on Public Policy, 1995).
13. Kernaghan, Marson and Borins, *The New Public Organization*, (2000): 26.

KEY WORDS AND CONCEPTS

elite (64)
homogeneity (65)
unity of direction (65)
New Public Management (69)
privatization (69)

deregulation (69)
contracting out (69)
downsizing (69)
user fees (70)
three Es (efficiency, effectiveness and economy) (70)

REVIEW QUESTIONS

This chapter was divided into two sections addressing the impact of organization theory on Canadian public administration. You should now be able to answer the questions associated with each.

1. The Impact of Organization Theory

Sometimes it is hard to see the relevance of theoretical arguments to the real world. To overcome this liability, this section explored the ways in which theory has been concretely applied in the Canadian experience. This was done to discern which approaches have been most influential in shaping the organization of the Canadian government. We asked the following questions: What theories have had the most influence on the development of Canadian public administration? How have contending schools of thought affected the actual organization and functioning of the Canadian public sector?

2. Contemporary Developments

Finally, the most recent developments in the theory of organizations were briefly examined. Again, in trying to wed the theoretical with the concrete, we asked, How have recent theoretical developments affected organizations in the public sector in practice?

After reading this chapter, you should have a firm grasp of the major contending theories of public administration, the thinkers associated with each, and the impact of organizational life on the Canadian government and on us as individuals.

FURTHER READING

1. The Impact of Organization Theory

Albo, Gregory. "Democratic Citizenship and the Future of Public Management," in Gregory Albo, David Langille and Leo Panitch, eds. *A Different Kind of State? Popular Power and Democratic Administration*. Toronto: Oxford University Press, 1993: 17–33.

Kramer, Fred A. "Organization Theories of Public Bureaucracies," in Kenneth Kernaghan, ed. *Public Administration in Canada: Selected Readings, Fifth Edition*. Toronto: Methuen, 1985: 1–22.

Lindquist, Evert A. and Graham White. "Streams, Springs, and Stones: Ontario Public Service Reform in the 1980s and the 1990s," *Canadian Public Administration*, 37, 2, (Summer 1994).

2. *Contemporary Developments*

Borins, Sandford. "The New Public Management Is Here to Stay," *Canadian Public Administration*, 38, 1 (1995).

Hood, Christopher. "A Public Management for All Seasons," *Public Administration*, 69, (Spring, 1991): 3–19.

Johnson, David. *Thinking Government: Public Sector Management in Canada.* Peterborough: Broadview Press, 2002: Chapter 5.

Savoie, Donald. "What is Wrong With the New Public Management?" *Canadian Public Administration*, 38, 1, (1995): 113.

WEBLINKS

La Relève
leadership.gc.ca/categories.asp?lang=e&sub_id=582

Canada Site/Site du Canada
canada.gc.ca/

Canada Gazette
canadagazette.gc.ca/

Canadian Government Publishing
cgp-egc.gc.ca/

Chapter ④

Public Administration
and Democracy

WHAT YOU WILL LEARN

This chapter considers how the concepts of democracy and power relate to the theory and practice of public administration in Canada. In order to examine Canadian public administration in any serious way, we must address the basics. So we must ask ourselves, What do we understand by the terms *democracy* and *power*? This is not as straightforward as it might seem. We will then proceed to examine some questions related to this basic starting point. What is politics? What is the state? What is government? Are they the same things? If not, how are they different, and how are they related? Why might we draw a distinction among them?

What we want to try to do is demystify Canadian public administration and its democratic context, to show that it has a very real and practical impact on our everyday lives. So we will draw connections among what happens, how it happens, to whom it happens and why it happens. By the end you will hopefully find yourself empowered toward the political system and prepared as a citizen to participate in and engage yourself with public administration in a proactive manner, beyond simply casting a ballot once every five years, or passively submitting to the bureaucratic machine as it steamrolls along.

Once we feel we have a working understanding of these concepts, we can go on to ask other fundamental questions. How, for example, is power exercised in Canada? Who has it and who lacks it? What is the basis of power relations within society? Is it notions of equity? Equality? Freedom? Or is it simply that the person with the most toys gets to determine the rules of the game? In other words, what role do economic factors play in Canadian public administration?

Accountability is a prominent issue in any consideration of democracy and public administration. But since it is given fuller treatment in Chapter 12, it is raised here only in passing, as a subset of the broader philosophical approach to democracy.

This chapter is divided into five sections, each dealing with a particular but related aspect of democracy, political power and public administration. It is prefaced with a brief section defining power and politics, followed by a consideration of the concept of democracy. This is followed by a brief analysis of the concepts of state and government. Some observations on political culture are made, and its interplay with the democratic context of public administration is then assessed by examining the issues of the constitution and the key parliamentary and extra-parliamentary actors who play a role in public administration in Canada. The chapter is divided in the following way:

1. — *Power, Politics and Public Administration*

Call for referenda from / Citizen's Assembly on Electorial Reform.

This brief section sets the table for our discussions of democracy by asking simply, What is power? What is influence? Who has these things in Canadian society, and why? What is politics? What is the relationship between power and politics? This section also presents the debate about the public sector versus the private sector in a slightly different manner than in Chapter 1, where it was first raised. Here, the issues are recast in light of democratic theory. We ask, How is it determined what is rightly in the public domain? What kind of struggle must be engaged to move issues from the private world to the public, or vice versa?

2. — *What Is Democracy?*

This section asks us to pause and consider what exactly we mean by the term *democracy*. In defining this term, we ask, What is democratic theory? What does democracy mean to the theory and practice of public administration? What is the relationship of democracy to political power? This section assesses the concepts of direct democracy and representative democracy, both of which are central to the underpinnings of the institutions and structures of public administration, which we will discuss in the next chapter. We ask, What is direct democracy, and what is representative government? How does the application of these terms affect the way government is structured, organized and run in Canada?

3. — *State and Government*

These two terms are often used interchangeably. But they actually refer to two different things. We ask the following: What is the difference between state and government? Why is it important to have a conceptual difference between the two in the study and practice of public administration?

4. — *Political Culture*

This section looks at several definitions of this concept, as well as several theories that seek to explain the nature of democracy and governance in Canada. It poses the following questions: What are the major theoretical explanations for the quality and type of democratic life in Canada? Is there a single theory that explains how democratic Canada is (or is not)? What impact does this have on public administration in Canada?

5. — *The Interplay of Democracy, Political Culture, and the Institutions of Public Administration*

Finally, this section resurrects the theme of democratic theory to introduce both parliamentary and extra-parliamentary actors who influence and exercise power in the state and government in Canada. We ask: What is a constitution, and what impact does the Canadian constitution have on the relations of power within Canadian public administration? We further ask: What are those relations? Who are the actors? What are the key institutions, both parliamentary and extra-parliamentary, that have an impact on the unfolding of public administration?

Power, Politics and Public Administration

Politics is and always has been fundamentally about the issue of **power**. The element of power always lurks beneath the surface of public administration, and in many cases is overt and plain to see (see Box 4-1). If you could imagine the origins of society, you might begin to see where the exercise of power comes from. You might see the interactions of individuals devolving into conflict or evolving into co-operation over the division of goods among them. There will virtually always be conflict or cooperation simply because there will never be enough goods for all those who want them, all the time. Therefore, some means must be devised to divide those goods, and to prevent conflict from degenerating into violence. This is where the exercise of power comes into play. Someone must be designated (or designate themselves) the arbiter over the division of the goods desired by the members of the society. In other words, someone must have **authority** to exercise power and make decisions on behalf of the members of the society. This scenario is the core of politics. Public administration, in turn, is the mechanism by which these political decision-making processes take place.

Power is typically defined in the literature on public administration and politics as the ability to authorize, influence or coerce behaviour. In other words, someone has power over you because they can direct or instruct you to do something (or refrain from doing something) by virtue of their legal position of authority; they can persuade you to do something (or refrain from doing something) by virtue of their status or position; or they can force you to do something (or refrain from doing something) by virtue of their use of force if you fail to consent.

Why people consent to alter their behaviour is a fascinating sociological question. Max Weber suggested that those in positions of power derived their authority from one of three sources of legitimacy. The first is **traditional legitimacy**, wherein rule is justified on the basis of long-established custom or habit. The fact that things have always been ordered in a certain way means that the exercise of power is justified. The second is **charismatic legitimacy**. Under these circumstances, a leader is believed to be vested with exceptional and extraordinary personal qualities that make her uniquely suited to the role of leader. In many cases, these leaders will claim to have been divinely chosen. Third, Weber refers

Box 4-1

Power in the Nation's Capital

This description of power in the nation's capital was written by Christina McCall-Newman more than 20 years ago. While the roles of women have changed, it still has resonance today:

Ottawa is a city that talks incessantly about power: who has it, who wants it, who's misusing it, who's losing it. The talk starts first thing in the morning as soon as the busses begin to lumber around Confederation Square and the sun glances off the windows of the West Block. As the day wears on, the buzz becomes nearly visible, blowing in the wind like the sulphur fumes that used to waft over the area from the paper company on the Ottawa River's farther shore.

Everybody talks about power. Secretaries talk in the corridors of the commons at a quarter to ten on their way to the cafeteria for coffee; commissionaires gossip at the main door and the sound reverberates from the vaulted ceilings, rivalling the chatter of school children lining up for official tours. MPs harangue each other while sprawling on leather sofas in each other's offices or hovering over the cold buffet in the parliamentary restaurant at noon. Deputies arrange to lunch late at Le Cercle Universitaire so they can sound out each other's weaknesses while glancing over their shoulders to see who else is talking there and to whom. Lobbyists reserve tables in the alcoves of the Chateau Grill and over underdone beef and overpriced Bordeaux float deals in voices that sound like chain saws. Ministers greet each other behind the gold curtains of the Commons chamber after Question Period, exchanging innuendos and anxieties. Diplomats display their volubility in Rockcliffe houses between six and eight, eating anchovies and uttering banalities with effortless sophistication in two languages and fifty-four accents. Hostesses call their best friends for advice while writing out place-cards for little dinners at eight, hopefully placing the assistant deputy minister's wife, who is famous for intelligently listening, between the privy councillor who is famous for continuously yapping and the ambassador who is famous for unstintingly imbibing. Late at night back room boys and executive assistants of varying shapes and political hues meet in dark downtown bars to complain confidentially about the press, the Leader, the cabinet, and the drawbacks of their lives and wives. Everybody talks, talks, talks about power all day long, spreading rumours, flying kites, seeking leaks, formulating strategies, and telling lies.

Source: Christina McCall-Newman, *Grits: An Intimate Portrait of the Liberal Party*, (Toronto: Macmillan, 1982): 177–78.

to **legal-rational legitimacy**, in which a set of rationally created rules and legal statutes serve as the basis of power and sanctioned authority.[1]

Increasingly, modern states have moved to systems of legal-rational legitimacy, although there are still plenty of examples of the other two systems as well. Still, tradition-based and charisma-based systems of authority and power tended to predominate in nondemocratic societies in the past. The reasons for the rise of the legal-rational model are many. They include the fact that modern societies, unlike their predecessors, tend to have a high degree of literacy and education with which to question the basis of power and authority. At one time it may have served the purposes of a king to suggest to his subject that some holy book decreed that he should rule. As long as the majority of the population lacked the skills to read and interpret such a source of authority, the king could maintain his power. But the rise of mass literacy was accompanied by the rise of "public opinion," which increasingly could intelligently ask (and answer) the question "Who ought to rule?" This example also illustrates the diminishing role in many societies of religion, which often served as the rationale for charismatic and some traditional systems of legitimacy.

Moreover, a rational-legal system makes clear the answer to the question "How will they rule?" It sets out the parameters of rule much more obviously and clearly than do the other two systems. For instance, leaders could justify their actions in traditional and charismatic systems simply by stating that this was what they had ordained. Under a legal-rational system, however, this kind of arbitrariness is reduced by features such as the rule of law and rules of accountability. In a democratic society, decisions about who holds power—and can therefore legitimately authorize, influence or coerce you into behaving in a certain way—are made through both the elected and the nonelected institutions of public administration. These range from the prime minister, Cabinet, bureaucracy and Parliament to the judiciary, police and army—all of whom are given clearly prescribed roles.

Where does politics come into play in all of this? Politics is as old as human history. As political scientist Larry Johnston suggests, "The world we inhabit is political. We may choose to study politics or not, or having studied politics, decide that we will do so no more, but we *cannot choose to opt out of the political world*."[2] [Emphasis in original.] But it is not always perfectly obvious what we mean by "politics," though we may have a commonsense feeling about it. For some, it is simply the goings-on on Parliament Hill, far removed from real life, which intrude on our everyday life only when a scandal or particularly flashy issue emerges. Relatively few Canadians are passionately involved in this sphere. The majority remain at a distance from political life. If you are typical of most Canadians, you probably are not a member of a political party, and follow politics only casually, if at all.

Still, politics is all around us, and failure to come to grips with this too often makes us citizen-victims, as other interests in society play the political game to their advantage. For the most basic fact about politics is that it arises out of scarcity. There are not enough resources available in the world for all people to satisfy all of their basic wants and needs all of the time. Limits on what is available, especially on what is desirable, such as wealth, mean that conflicting claims will be made as to who gets what. So competition over scarce resources is at the heart of understanding what politics is all about. But if it were just a situation of perpetual conflict, then presumably we would be in a state of perpetual war with our neighbours, with other countries, and so on. So politics is about more than just conflict; it is also about how rival claims are settled. It is about the resolution of conflict.

Moreover, it is obvious that conflict and competition are not the only forces driving humans. Cooperation is also important, indeed inevitable, whenever individuals come together to settle disputes over scarce resources. If you think back to our discussion of organization theory in Chapter 2, it should be obvious that cooperation, as much as conflict, has led us to create many complex systems of cooperation, which we call organizations. Since humans are naturally sociable animals, it did not take us long to deduce that cooperation with one another over a variety of matters could further the interests of all. Hence we developed the organization, with its division of labour and hierarchy, to realize societal goals through a process of cooperation. Thus, in our understanding of power and politics, we might just as easily speak of the use of cooperation as the resolution of conflict.

We must be aware that this is not the only definition of politics. Indeed, there are almost as many definitions as there are writers on the subject. But at the core of every definition is the notion that politics is about the exercise of power. One commonly cited definition is by American David Easton, who developed what is known as the systems approach to the study of politics. His definition is somewhat general and abstract: politics is the authoritative allocation of values.[3] What this mouthful of abstract terms means is really quite simple when you break it down. *Authoritative* refers to the idea we discussed above, namely, that there must be a legitimate authority who can make decisions on behalf of the society as a whole. Decisions about what? About what values will prevail. For instance, you may value freedom, but someone else may value security. So how do we decide whether society should invest in bureaucratic structures such as human rights commissions to safeguard our freedoms, or in the armed forces to safeguard our security? We give the job to authorities, who then allocate values.

Another definition, perhaps more straightforward in its terminology, was offered by Harold Laswell, who said that politics always concerns "who gets what, when and how."[4] This is essentially another way of expressing what Easton said. But its virtue—besides brevity—is clarity and simplicity. Lenin, the leader of the Bolshevik revolution in Russia and founder of the Soviet Union, said politics was "who does what to whom."[5] China's great Communist leader Mao Tse Tung called politics "bloodless war."[6] Bismark, the Chancellor of Germany, called politics "the doctrine of the possible: the attainable."[7] Karl Marx argued that "political power, properly so called, is merely the organized power of one class for oppressing another."[8] Virtually all definitions of politics have this common underlying theme of power.

Now, we engage in conflict resolution and cooperative activities in all aspects of our lives: in familial disputes, in the workplace, over grades in school, etc. But there are two things about politics that distinguish it from other forms of conflict resolution and cooperation: first, the nature of the issues are public, not private; second, we use public authority to settle them.

The issue of which relations within society count as political ones is a contentious one. And so part of the process of politics is establishing which relationships in society are political, i.e., public, and which are private. It was not until the 20th century, for example, that relations between men and women were deemed political. But the explosion of the women's movement, especially in the past 30 years, has raised people's consciousness about the political factors underlying the subjugation of women. Where public administration is concerned,[9] it has been argued that the very structures of bureaucracy have themselves contributed to the oppression of women by men. According to Camilla Stivers,

the images of expertise, leadership, and virtue that mark defenses of administrative power contain dilemmas of gender. They not only have masculine features but help to keep in place or bestow political and economic privilege on the bearers of culturally masculine qualities at the expense of those who display culturally feminine ones. Far from being superficial window-dressing or a side effect, the characteristic masculinity of public administration is systemic: It contributes to and is sustained by power relations in society at large that distribute resources on the basis of gender (although not solely on this basis) and affect people's life chances and their sense of themselves and their place in the world.[10]

Similarly, at one time relations between bosses and workers were considered to be a private affair in which public authorities had no business. That has changed with the advent of a strong labour movement that politicized workplace relations and appealed to public authorities—the government—to do something about wage levels, unsafe working conditions, child labour, and so on.[11] In these views about women's role in society and politics, and the conflict between capitalists and the working class, the idea of power is related directly to the concept of oppression; the manifestations of oppression are the key to understanding the concept of power.

The boundary between what can be considered political (or public) and what can be considered private may not be very distinct, but it is crucial for understanding the politics of any society. For much of political conflict occurs over where exactly this line should be drawn: what should be considered a matter for public life and decisions by the state, and what should remain private.

This is important to us for a fundamental reason, for it is only by clarifying the line between public and private that our democratic rights and responsibilities can be discerned. The reason for this is that only those power relations that take place in the public realm can legitimately be associated with the use of coercion or force. Only public authorities—the state—have the legitimate right to back up decisions with the full power of society at their disposal, because the state is the only entity in society that can claim to speak and act on behalf of the entire community. It alone is responsible for some measure of social order, which is a necessary condition for all other social activities. Without it, there is no peaceful basis for reconciling conflicts in society.

What Is Democracy?

The term *democracy* is one of those words that everyone uses, but no one defines. We all have an intuitive sense of what democracy is. If you were asked what it is, what would you reply? Elections? Parliamentary government? Freedom? The reality is that democracy is what political scientists call a "contested concept," meaning there is not always agreement on what the term means. If you sat down with a group of people—say, the other students in this course—and canvassed their views, you might find broad agreement on the outlines of democracy, but differences on the details. It may be quite hard, in fact, for your group to reach unanimity.

We are interested here in noting where democracy intersects with public administration, and so will not digress too far into the definitional quagmire. But it is important to keep in mind the extent to which democracy is a value-based term; the values an individual or a society holds will help determine what they mean by democracy. In turn, these values are translated into political institutions and structures, roles and actors that assume responsibility for enacting the public will; in other words, for governing.

Given the variety of nations with different governmental forms, politics and policies, all of which call themselves "democratic," how can we be sure what the concept really entails? The word *democracy* comes from two Greek roots: *demos*, meaning the people, and *kratos*, meaning authority. In ancient Greek culture, democracy meant government by the many. In some Greek city-states, all citizens participated in making and implementing laws (all, that is, except women and slaves, but then they were not considered citizens). Save for a few rare examples, such as some Swiss Cantons and the New England "town halls" of the 17th and 18th centuries, such systems, known as **direct democracy,** no longer exist. In direct democracy, citizens exercise authority and power personally. Instead, most democracies, including Canada, now consist of a system of elected representatives who make laws for the land. This is **representative democracy,** in which citizens delegate others to exercise authority and power on their behalf. Let us briefly consider each model.

Direct Democracy

The model of democracy that approaches most people's conception of "pure" democracy is one in which popular assemblies are constituted by the people to directly govern themselves. Strictly speaking, this ideal did not even prevail in the Athenian example, since elections were often carried out by lotteries rather than voting. The Athenians believed that elections could be manipulated by wealthy individuals who could afford to put themselves forward as candidates, but other citizens would be effectively shut out of the process (much like the impression that prevails today). Currently, few people expect democracy to be rule by the people as a whole, since societies have become so large and complex. Ironically, though, for the first time, we may have the technological capability to effect direct democracy with the Internet and interactive telecommunications developments, although few concrete steps have yet been taken in this direction.[12]

There are, however, some mechanisms that approximate the direct democracy model in Canada. These include, for instance, *referenda*, in which citizens directly express their approval of or objection to a particular issue via a simple vote. Two referenda, in 1980 and 1995, asked Quebecers whether they would authorize their provincial government to negotiate sovereignty with the rest of Canada. Referenda results are generally binding on the government. Another form of direct vote is a *plebiscite*, which is a vote, the results of which are not binding on the government. Shades of direct democracy can also be seen in extending the election of governmental officials to include not just politicians, but also judges and other administrative officials. Other direct democracy mechanisms include recall, wherein voters can effectively "fire" their representative before an election by getting a certain number of voters to sign a petition to that effect (see Box 4-2). However, it is noteworthy that in jurisdictions that employ these techniques of direct democracy, there is often a low participation rate by citizens. And, as the example in Box 4-2 shows, wealthy and powerful interests are often the only ones who can afford to spend money on campaigns that will influence citizens' choices.

Box 4-2

Direct Democracy in Canada

There are few examples of direct democracy in the Canadian experience, although there have been some instances that approximated it. For example, two attempts were made in 1998 to fire sitting New Democratic Party cabinet ministers in British Columbia. The drive was organized by a powerful right-wing corporate-sponsored and -financed organization. It claimed that the government had lied about the level of the provincial deficit prior to the last election, and therefore had surrendered its moral right to govern. The petitions it launched were unsuccessful when organizers failed to get the sufficient number of signatures in each of the ministers' constituencies to effect a recall.

A third attempt at recall was more grassroots in that ordinary citizens were behind it. On April Fools' Day, 1998, the *Qualicum Beach Morning News* ran a front-page article stating that "MLA Reitsma is a liar, and we can prove it." The newspaper reported that Liberal Bob Reitsma had written fake letters to the editor under an assumed name in support of his work as a member of the Provincial Legislative Assembly. In this case, the MLA resigned after organizers produced more than 25 000 signatures on a recall petition and appeared well on the way to getting the requisite number to force his recall.

Representative Democracy

Democracy in Canada is not equivalent to rule by the people as a whole. The Canadian form of government is, properly speaking, a representative democracy in which those elected to public office derive legitimacy to act authoritatively for others in society. They are thus vested with power to make decisions having the force of law. Less involved than a system of direct democracy, in which we all participate actively in exercising power, this system allows a method of choosing representatives and monitoring their activities on an ongoing basis. It also permits regular opportunities for changing those responsible for governing through the institution of elections.

In a representative democracy, then, citizens are one step removed, as it were, from the actual exercise of decision-making. Almost all modern democracies are representative democracies. Government is carried out by an elected legislature that represents the people. Citizens delegate law-making authority to their representatives, holding them responsible for their actions through various institutions of government (Parliament, for instance) and through periodic elections. Representative democracy can be summed up as a system in which "public policies are made, on a majority basis, by representatives subject to effective popular control at periodic elections which are conducted on the principle of political equality and under conditions of political freedom."[13]

Political Democracy

It is useful to take these basic conceptions about representative democracy in Canada and further subdivide them by focusing on what might be called "political democracy" and "economic democracy." Both direct and representative democracy have at their core some notion of equality. This implies, for example, that all citizens have equal rights. But in the real world, equality is an elusive quantity. Certain features of the Canadian system are associated with the idea of political democracy, including majority rule; one person, one vote; competitive elections; and cabinet-parliamentary government. Theoretically, we might expect that with all these principles and mechanisms in place, some measure of equality could be realized. And in fact, a formal political type of equality does apply in that we all have rights to and access to these political mechanisms. Thus, oppressive government in which equality is undermined or denied should be virtually impossible.

But consider the following possibility: What if the majority of Canadians voted for a party that supported the suppression of French-language rights? Would that be democratic? The point is that the appearance of equality as vested in the mechanisms of democracy can be deceiving. What this hypothetical example points to is the imperfection of a democracy in which the simple principles, such as majority rule, can actually be used to achieve ends that seem antidemocratic, since there is nothing "democratic" about depriving citizens of their rights.

To avoid these consequences, we build protection against what may be called the "tyranny of the majority" into our institutions and processes. These might take the form of constitutional limits on the power of the state. For example, while a majority might vote to suppress French-language rights, no law calling for such action could stand up against the rights and freedoms enshrined and protected in the constitution. In other words, formal guarantees are entrenched in the constitution and other institutions of government.

As well, particular protection for groups and individuals in society may be entrenched in the formal and informal rules and procedures of politics. For example, the Canadian electoral system reinforces the power of the country's French Canadian minority, most of whom live in Quebec and can therefore vote as a block to protect their own interests. Moreover, federalism and the division of powers in the constitution mean that citizens aggrieved by one level of government can seek redress from the other.

But beyond formal and informal constitutional rules and procedures, the social and cultural values of a society also come into play. This is a point made by political scientists Gabriel Almond and Sidney Verba in their book *The Civic Culture*.[14] A political culture that acknowledges and recognizes a multiplicity of group identities is likely to give rise to values such as tolerance. These group identities become important in protecting minority rights when individuals perceive, and society recognizes, that some members of society belong to discrete groups, whether religious, ethnic, linguistic, regional, occupational, etc., in addition to sharing a common citizenship with everyone else. Under these circumstances, the likelihood of a democratic state being turned to oppressive ends is reduced, since everyone ultimately has a stake in the tolerance of society.

Can we say that political democracy ensures freedom and equality—two values of primary importance in contemporary Canadian society? If all the rules and procedures are followed, and if there are guarantees for minority rights against the tyranny of the majority derived from political culture, have we achieved some near-ideal form of representative democracy? To answer this question, we must look at democracy from yet another angle, and consider what may be called *economic democracy*.

Economic Democracy

In Canada, we claim to have a democratic system because there is a fairly equal chance that all citizens can participate in one way or another in the political system, and because we as citizens have an opportunity to "throw the rascals out" if we disagree with the government of the day. But in the absence of economic and social equality, can we really claim to have a democratic society?

Look at it this way. Political democracy guarantees that there are institutions in place through which the will of the people can be realized. These include Parliament, and theoretically everyone has a chance to run for election, become a member of Parliament, and exercise authority on behalf of the people. However, it is prohibitively expensive to run for Parliament. Increasingly, it seems this key symbol of Canadian democracy is becoming the preserve of the wealthy. Certainly lower-income Canadians, welfare recipients and those on social assistance, among other less well-off Canadians, are grossly underrepresented in the halls of power. The same holds true for the upper reaches of the bureaucracy. The senior civil servants tend to be well educated and from middle- and upper-income families. They can afford the university education that prepares them for a position in the upper echelons of the bureaucracy. The question that arises is whether they, along with their parliamentary masters, can adequately and fairly represent and understand the views and needs of those who are systematically excluded from positions of power. There is no easy answer to this question. Though we explore it in more detail in Chapter 9, it is flagged here as a disputed element in any discussion of the quality of democracy in a society.

Socialists critique democracy as it currently exists by suggesting that it is unrealistic to expect ordinary citizens, who are overburdened with the concerns of making ends meet, to have the time, energy and resources to engage the political system in a meaningful way. They argue that political equality without economic equality is a sham. Politics becomes the preserve of the idle rich, while the majority toil endlessly with little time or opportunity to substantively affect the political system. Marxists go a step further and argue that any system, democratic or not, that exists within the framework of capitalism, is by its nature unequal. This is because capitalism divides society into classes, with the upper (capitalist) class exploiting the lower (working) class through their disproportionate ownership of property and the means of production. The minority, then, exploits the majority, and this makes a mockery of notions of political democracy. In this view, only when some form of economic democracy is realized through the overthrow of capitalism can there be true equality.

In short, political democracy lacks any sense of a commitment to economic or social equality. There are examples of societies that devote a considerable amount of effort to ensuring the economic and social equality of their citizens, but which lack many of the institutional features that we assume characterize democracy, such as free, fair open elections. So, does attaching greater importance to the social and economic equality of individuals than to rules and procedures make those societies any less democratic than our own?[15]

There is one more aspect to democracy that needs to be considered—one still related to the question of equality. That is respect for rights and freedoms. But which rights and freedoms warrant protection in a democratic society, and which may be legitimately limited by government? These questions form the basis of a perhaps unsolvable debate about democracy, ongoing since ancient Greek times. For example, some would argue that any level of taxation is a restriction on the personal freedom of individuals to dispose of their income as they see fit. Others argue that taxation promotes freedom by paying for policies that provide opportunities that the disadvantaged in society might not otherwise enjoy. Even a value such as freedom of speech becomes controversial. Are limits on spending to advertise a political point of view during an election a legitimate limit on freedom of speech, since only the wealthy and powerful in society can afford to try to influence public opinion in this way?

Rights and freedoms are important, but almost everyone recognizes that no right is absolute, and that certain kinds of limits on rights actually promote democracy. The struggle between expanding and limiting rights is sometimes seen as the struggle between the competing pulls of individual rights and group rights, or between the private and public realms. Society must constantly find the balance between these conflicting impulses if it is to be considered democratic. And it expresses its findings through the mechanisms of public administration.

In summary, then, the formal political institutions of society, including the constitution, Parliament, elections and so on, are only part of what constitutes democracy. We must also consider social and cultural values, particularly regarding issues of equality; the protection of rights and freedoms; socioeconomic and ideological factors of society; and other formal and informal features of the political system. Ultimately, several complex elements come into play, so that even defining the term is perilous.

State and Government

We will now move to a more specific consideration of the role of the state. We are, most of us, familiar to a certain extent with the debate over issues such as how much the state should be involved in the economy, for example: in public broadcasting through the CBC; in the airline business, as with Air Canada; or in the business of selling gas and oil, as with Petro-Canada. There is a long history of state involvement in the economy in Canada, stretching back to the pre-Confederation era, when the state took on the responsibility for canals, railroads and other similar types of infrastructure development. Canadian society has evolved over the past 130 years from one in which there was little need or desire for state involvement in the lives of its citizens, to one in which the state is intimately and intricately involved in our lives in countless ways—to the point that this larger role is now under attack.

This has given rise to a great clamorous debate about the appropriate role of the state in society, largely organized around ideological world views. We are naive if we think that the level and extent of state involvement in the economy and in society is somehow "natural"—that it is the result of forces beyond our control. For what it clearly reflects is the nature of power relations in society. It reflects in whose interests the power of the state has been exercised. Why did the welfare state develop in Canada over the past 50 years? Was it simply because politicians in power felt generous? Why has that same welfare state been under a savage attack for the past 20 years? Who benefits and who loses when you have a strong state, as opposed to a laissez-faire system in which the state disengages itself from involvement with the economy and social life? How do these interests affect public administration?

To sort out these issues we must ask the following: What exactly do we mean when we use the term "the state"? Some use it interchangeably with "government," but, in fact, it means something somewhat different. For example, to argue that a government is corrupt or wasteful and that it should be turfed out, is not the same as arguing for the overthrow of the state. It simply challenges the authority of the particular people who at a particular moment in time have their hands on the levers of power of the state. Most political activity is aimed at influencing and changing the government, rather than at reforming the state.

Weber suggested that it is most useful to view the state, not in terms of its ends, but of its means. He quoted the Communist revolutionary Leon Trotsky, who said that "every state is founded on force," and went on to suggest that the elemental characteristic of any state is this feature of the legitimate use of violence and coercion. Weber wrote,

A state is a human community that (successfully) claims the monopoly of the legitimate use of physical force within a given territory. Note that "territory" is one of the characteristics of the state. Specifically, at the present time, the right to use physical force is ascribed to other institutions or to individuals only to the extent to which the state permits it. The state is considered the sole source of the "right" to use violence. Hence, "politics" for us means striving to share power or striving to influence the distribution of power, whether among states or among groups within a state.[16]

Marx claimed that society as a whole was more and more splitting up into two great classes directly facing each other: bourgeoisie (the capitalist class) and proletariat (the working class). In a famous and often-quoted line from the *Communist Manifesto,* he claimed that "the executive of the modern State is but a committee for managing the common affairs of the whole bourgeoisie."[17] But if class differences were obliterated by a revolution in which private property was abolished, there would be no need for the state to continue to exist, since the bourgeoisie in whose interests it acted would no longer exist. Hence, Marx argued, the state would "wither away."

Political economist Ralph Miliband explained the importance of the state in this way:

> More than ever before men [sic] now live in the shadow of the state. What they want to achieve, individually or in groups, now mainly depends on the state's sanction and support. But since that sanction and support are not bestowed indiscriminately, they must, ever more directly, seek to influence and shape the state's power and purpose, or try and appropriate it altogether. It is for the state's attention, or for its control, that men compete; and it is against the state that beat the waves of social conflict. It is to an ever greater degree the state which men encounter as they confront other men. This is why, as social beings, they are also political beings, whether they know it or not. It is possible not to be interested in what the state does; but it is not possible to be unaffected by it.[18]

According to Brooks, the state has three main characteristics:[19]

1. territorial boundaries, beyond which the state has no legitimate authority;

2. a complex set of institutions that wield public authority;

3. power.

It enjoys a "monopoly of the legitimate use of physical force in the enforcement of its order."

Asserting, as Weber has, that the state has a legitimate monopoly on the use of force to maintain order says nothing about in whose interests this power is exercised. Some have tried to incorporate this question into their understanding of the state. Marxists, for example, see the state as an instrument used by the ruling class to oppress and exploit the working class. Feminists view the state as a patriarchal institution designed and maintained to ensure the dominance of men over women in society.

Later on, we will consider whose interests the state serves. But for now, we want to make sure that we understand the difference between, and the relationship between, the state and government. The latter is a term usually reserved for those who have been elected to power. This is a more personal conception than the state, usually being associated with a particular group of people, often through the instrument of a political party. We speak of the "Chrétien government," but not of the "Chrétien state," even though the prime minister and the political party and the elections that he may contest are all part of the larger state structure. Governments come and go; but the rules, procedures and institutions of the state are more enduring than is the government and its policies. You might think of the state as the forum within which government exists.

A state is also characterized by the feelings its citizens have about it. In developed democracies such as Canada, the state elicits widespread public identification with its institutions and values. Normally, the people strongly identify with their state. When citizens accept that a government ought, or has the right, to make decisions for them, political scientists refer to the system as having *legitimacy*.

Legitimacy in this sense is closely linked to the concept of authority: the legitimate right to exercise power. Underlying the distinction between state and government is an important practical difference in the basis on which each compels the obedience of citizens within its jurisdiction. The willingness of citizens to obey the decisions of the government, even though they may strongly disagree with them (for example, the Goods and Services Tax), is fundamentally based on the view that the state's authority is legitimate; that is, the rules and institutions of the state that determine how governments are chosen are accepted by most people as reasonable. The legitimacy of the state is therefore based on the consent of those who are governed.

Government may be upheld by consent of the governed. Or it may be upheld by the use of force. Usually both come into play to a varying extent. The state's authority may be questioned from time to time, as when citizens stage a tax revolt, or when unionists protest in the streets over wage controls, or when the police themselves, who are charged with upholding the authority of the state through the use of force, protest on the lawns of the legislature over policing regulations they do not like, as was the case in 1991 in Ontario. Thus the state's authority is sometimes questioned, and sometimes when this happens the state may have to resort to the use of force, crushing civil disobedience to maintain its ability to govern. Of course, governments that rely on threats or violence to stay in power are usually unstable. As well, they actually serve to undermine the legitimacy of the state, because one of the cornerstones—consent by the governed—is missing. How consent is manufactured is the topic of some debate. In some societies such as Canada, it arises out of the combined ideological forces of the education system, the media, family, government, the workplace and various other political, social and economic institutions that influence the ideological outlook of citizens. In other societies, more overt and sometimes quite crude attempts are made to manufacture the consent of the people through propaganda, or the stifling of opposition parties or media censorship, and so on. This is frequently resorted to in totalitarian systems.

The ability of a state and its political institutions to govern a given population and territory rests on its legitimacy to exercise power. In the resolution of conflict, a government requires the consent necessary to authoritatively allocate values and resources. All states attempt to maintain political order and viability, to resolve societal conflicts without tearing the country apart, to defend the territory against external enemies, and to maintain essential services for its citizens. The manner in which these and other policy-making activities are performed, while a balance is maintained between power on the one hand and legitimacy on the other, is at the core of the study of politics and government.

Political Culture

To fully understand the nature of political power and democracy, we must also understand the context and environment within which it takes place. We therefore must look at the question of **political culture** in Canada. Political culture is an important concept to public administration, though it is not without some controversy as to its precise meaning and application. For example, understanding political culture can help us understand why western Canada feels alienated from the rest of Canada, and what this means for public administration. It can assist in understanding the impact of language; the relationship between Quebec and the rest of the country; the growing participation of women in politics, in the workplace and in public life; how multiculturalism has affected the governance of the country; and a legion of other issues.

There is a vast literature dealing with political culture, and definitions of it abound. Most refer to the values, attitudes and beliefs citizens possess in relation to political life in the society. It was first introduced as a concept by Gabriel Almond in his essay "Comparative Political Systems," where he claimed it was "the particular distribution of patterns of orientation toward political objects among the members of the nation."[20]

By looking at the questions students of political culture wrestle with, we can get a more concrete sense of the central ideas of the concept itself. First, some students of political culture look at attitudes toward political symbols and institutions. They ask, How strongly do you, as a citizen, feel about political symbols such as the flag? Do you feel sheepish about singing the national anthem at sporting events, or do you belt it out with gusto? Are there historical heroes from Canada's past that you look back on with pride? Or villains? Do you believe political institutions such as Parliament, the courts and the bureaucracy are effective? Can government, the prime minister, and elected and appointed officials be trusted to do the right things? What kinds of duties and obligations are implied by the idea of "citizenship"? How do citizens view their own constitution?

Second, students of political culture look at attitudes towards others in the political system. Do citizens have strong loyalties to particular groups or regions of the country? Are you a "Canadian" first and foremost, or are you an "Albertan" or a "Newfoundlander"? How tolerant should majorities be toward minorities? Should you be tolerant of those expressing alternative political viewpoints, or who are critical of the status quo? What types of protest are acceptable behaviour? How important is freedom of speech?

The third thing students of political culture look at is political knowledge, values and evaluations. They ask how much do you, as a citizen, know about politics, about the workings of institutions, policy-making and political leaders? What kinds of beliefs, values and sentiments do citizens have? How widely are they shared? What, do they feel, is the proper role of government in society and the economy? How should resources be distributed? How much support should be given to the poor or disadvantaged groups in society?

(margin note: acquisition ; transmission of pol. belief)

Finally, the fourth thing students of political culture look at is the acquisition and transmission of political beliefs. They ask, Where do your beliefs and expectations about political life come from? How are they learned? How effectively are they transmitted from one generation to the next? Are citizens' beliefs becoming more coherent, more ideological? Or are citizens becoming more "issue driven"?

This long list of questions suggests that political culture, as a concept, covers an awful lot of ground. This is partly because political cultures are so dynamic; that is, they are constantly changing and evolving. Indeed, the broad configuration of political culture today may well be the result of events from the distant past. Conditions change over time, populations grow or change, and remote historical episodes that were at one time terribly important, fade from our collective memories. But just because we don't consciously remember the events of our collective past does not mean that they don't continue to influence the way we view political life today and affect public administration.

Much of political culture is oriented toward our subjective perspectives on political life (that is, how we feel things are, as opposed to how they actually are). But political culture nonetheless relates very directly to our political behaviour, *(margin note: voting)* that is, how we vote, the way parties work, the effectiveness of political institutions, the formation of policy, interest group behaviour, the workings of the constitution and so on. Public administration must respond to these subjective perspectives, which give rise to actions that can ripple through the entire sociopolitical and economic system, affecting it in large and small ways (see Box 4-3).

Box 4-3

Charlie Brown and Seniors' Pensions

In the late 1980s, the government of Brian Mulroney attempted to create some cost savings by de-indexing seniors' old age pensions. There was an outcry from "grey power" groups across the country. Many seniors developed the subjective perception that their income was under threat. Whether this was the case was a matter of some dispute, but ultimately incidental. Once they felt threatened, they mobilized. A demonstration on Parliament Hill encapsulated the feelings and power behind this threat. Prime Minister Mulroney waded into the crowd, affecting his most statesman-like demeanour for the cameras, no doubt sensing a photo opportunity in the making. But he was confronted by a tiny octogenarian who loudly berated him for his government's stand. The sight of this ordinary Canadian standing up to the power of the prime minister created a striking image. She admonished him for messing around with seniors' pensions, loudly proclaiming, "You lied to us, Charlie Brown." The prime minister's blustering reply was lost in the face of this forthright challenge, which was repeated on the airwaves for days afterward. The government backed down from its plan to de-index pensions.

Isolating and analyzing the precise way that Canadians feel about political life is a difficult task. It is not hard to see that Canada shares with many other industrialized democracies certain political values rooted in the Western tradition. This value system contains a set of essentially liberal elements modified by democratic practices that have evolved since the 18th century. Thus, Canadian political culture embraces such values as equality before the law, the right to hold private property, the right of free speech and assembly, the right to vote and run for office, and so on. But these values do not set us apart from numerous other political communities that also share the same general type of political culture. So to understand the uniqueness of the Canadian political culture, we need to consider how geography, economics, culture and politics historically combined to shape this country.

Geography

First, the sheer geographic size of Canada has had an immense impact on its political development and the structure of political life. Canada is the second largest country in the world, after Russia; it occupies some 9.2-million square kilometres; it spans six time zones; and it sprawls across half an entire continent. Distance, climate, and natural geographic barriers such as the Canadian Shield, the St. Lawrence Seaway, the Prairies, the Rockies, and the tundra have all had an impact on attempts to carve a political community out of this land mass.

Demography

Relative to its land size, Canada's population is small. As well, the population is unevenly distributed. About 80 percent of all Canadians live within three hours of the U.S. border, and 60 percent reside in two provinces: Ontario and Quebec. The cultural distribution of the population is also uneven. Eighty percent of all francophones live in Quebec, and Canada's native peoples form majorities in the largely uninhabited Nunavut, Yukon and Northwest Territories.

So the physical size and expanse of the country, and the size, makeup and distribution of the population, posed unique problems of communication, transportation and governance in the early years of the nation's history, and indeed continue to do so. The decision to adopt a federal political framework—that is, a division of powers among regional and central governments—can be seen as an institutional response to those kinds of problems; one of federalism's aims was to make government less remote to a far-flung and diverse population.

Three Founding Cultures

The presence of a significant linguistic minority—francophones—concentrated in one part of the country is a significant factor that sets Canadian political culture apart from other similar countries. The differences and ongoing debate between French and English have had a profound impact on Canadian political life from the start, and continue to influence Canadian culture, politics and economics in profound ways. This condition is sometimes summed up by the term *dualism*, and was captured in Lord Durham's famous 1839 pronouncement that Canada was "two nations warring in the bosom of a single state." Add to this the presence of a civilization that predates European settlement by several thousand years—Native Canadians—and which has always played a significant but largely ignored role in political, economic and cultural affairs, and you have a unique mixture that defines Canadian political culture.

Continentalism

The relationship between Canada and the United States as co-tenants on one continent, who share "the longest undefended border in the world," is difficult to analyze because it is so basic to the essence of both countries. But it is perhaps more significant to Canada because of the immense imbalance in power between the two countries, which has resulted in an ongoing challenge to Canadians to find and define their "national identity." Canadians may not be good at articulating what they *are,* but at least most can agree that what they are *not* is American. But the ongoing struggle by Canada to maintain itself as a distinct political culture north of the 49th parallel has been seriously compromised by the penetration of U.S. economic and cultural influences. The continuous fight against absorption into the U.S. empire is a particularly important theme in the study of Canadian political culture, as was the struggle to emerge from the shadows of Great Britain in an earlier age. Indeed, this process has been called "the evolution of Canada from colony to nation to colony."

Interpretations of Canadian Political Culture

There is widespread agreement that factors such as geography, demography, the presence of three founding cultures—English, French and Native—and proximity to the U.S. all contributed to the early formation of Canadian political culture. But how? When presented together, it is easy to see that these different elements must have created immense barriers to the creation of a single, united and focused political culture. This has given rise to several different interpretations of how these factors combined to give Canadian political culture its unique colouration. We will look at the contributions of four important theorists: Louis Hartz, Seymour Martin Lipset, John Porter and Harold Adams Innis.[21]

One very influential interpretation has been that offered by the U.S. sociologist Louis Hartz in his book *The Founding of New Societies.*[22] There are three main points in Hartz's thesis: the nature of the founding "fragment"; the point of departure of the emigrants; and the point of congealment in the new society. Hartz argued that "new" societies, such as Canada, Australia and the United States, were profoundly shaped by the values carried to those societies by early settlers and immigrants (he tended to ignore the presence of Natives in his study). So you had to look at the specific segment of the culture that the settlers came from in order to understand the political culture they established in the new land. Second, he called these early immigrants "fragments," for they brought with them segments or parts of the ideological worlds from which they came. So you had to look at these fragments' point of departure from the Old World to see the dominant political culture and ideology there. By looking at the specific segment of European ideologies from which the new settlers came—that is, by looking at the moment in the ideological evolution of the originating culture of which the fragment was an off-shoot—you could explain the dominant ideologies of the new societies. Third, you had to ask, what was the "point of congealment" in the new society? When did the values of the new society take on a distinctive and self-sustaining character?

The Hartzian approach could be used to explain, for example, the radical working-class ideology of Australia by looking at the predominantly English working-class emigrants who settled Australia after they had already been exposed to the ideas of radical socialism in England. By contrast, Canada and the U.S. were settled earlier than Australia by English middle-class settlers who brought with them liberal and conservative ideological world views. Similarly, settlers in New France came from a prerevolutionary France, which was heavily Catholic and conservative, and these attributes were reflected in the new society they constructed.

Hartz's thesis has been widely accepted, though it is not without its critics. Gad Horowitz, for example, shows that Hartz underemphasizes the differences between Canadian and U.S. political cultures.[23] Horowitz argues that while the U.S. adopted an overwhelmingly liberal ideological political culture, which does not permit for the adoption of dissentient views such as socialism or communism, Canada developed a much more heterogeneous and tolerant political culture that contains a healthy and vibrant socialist element, as well as a more distinct conservative one, to counter the dominant liberalism here. Both this socialism and conservatism find their origins in British political culture, and this helps to explain not only the historic attachment to the British Crown and a deference to elites that are traits of Canadian society, but also the greater role played by our government in society and the economy than by the U.S. government in its own.

A second, complementary explanation of Canadian political culture is offered by the American sociologist Seymour Martin Lipset in his book *Continental Divide*.[24] He emphasizes the importance of what he calls "formative events," historical episodes such as the British conquest of Quebec, which has forever since shaped Quebecers' views about their position in Canadian society. Evidence of the impact of this can even be found in the vitality of the sovereignist movement in Quebec, as well as in something as prosaic as Quebec licence plates, whose motto, *Je me souviens* (I remember), is a reference to the conquest. Other formative events include the American revolution, which resulted in the displacement of tens of thousands of Americans loyal to Britain. These United Empire Loyalists fled to Canada, carrying with them conservative, elitist, loyalist world views. In addition, the rebellions of 1837 and 1838 in Upper and Lower Canada, and the Riel rebellions of 1870 and 1885, are all examples of the kind of nation-shaping events to which Lipset is referring. Canadians, he argues, are more accepting of authority because of these formative events, and thus give government a greater role in society and the economy. Lipset further concludes that Canada is a less open society than the U.S.; there are fewer opportunities for upward social mobility; the Canadian welfare state is more developed, and so on.

A third interpretation focuses upon the central role elites play in Canadian society. John Porter's important book *The Vertical Mosaic* is a study of how power is organized and exercised in Canadian society.[25] It provides a provocative analysis of the ways in which Canadian elites exercise far more influence over the state and Canadian society than is typical in other advanced industrial states. These elites, he contends, are crucial "gatekeepers," who exercise control over the economy, the bureaucracy, elected officials, the media, and intellectual and religious life. All societies have elites, but Porter argues that Canadian elites are particularly powerful because they are a small, closed group with overlapping membership in different sectors of Canadian society. Moreover, because such small groups exercise influence over all these domains, they have been able to deflect attention away from class division in Canadian society, and towards ethnic, religious and regional divisions.

Porter's groundbreaking work has been emulated by others, who have focused on the corporate elite, the political elite, the bureaucratic elite, the intellectual elite, the religious elite, the social elite, and so on.[26] But most have concluded, as did Porter, that the ability of these elites to act as power brokers, with few constraints on their actions, has been greatly facilitated by the widely held political culture value that has already been described, namely, the deference to authority figures common in Canadian society.[27]

Harold Adams Innis has been one of the most influential interpreters of Canadian society, spawning a whole subdiscipline called the *staples approach* within the academic discipline of Canadian political economy.[28] He contended that an understanding of the broad economic forces, and particularly the importance of such primary resources as fish, fur, lumber, minerals and wheat, is germane to understanding Canadian political culture. These primary resources, or "staples," formed the core of the Canadian export economy from the outset, and that economy in turn has shaped the political and cultural outlines of Canadian society. A country such as Canada, which is overly dependent on the whims of the international marketplace into which it seeks to export its goods, has little control over its economy. Demand is dictated by economic forces beyond its boundaries. Thus, Innis maintained, Canadians have developed conservative, cautious and even pessimistic or fatalistic attitudes, largely because they are not able to control their own economic destinies. This cautiousness is not just limited to economic matters, though; it filters through to the way Canadians think about their society and about political life, and helps to explain why Canadians hold such cautious views about social and political change.

These four interpretations of Canadian political culture do not necessarily contradict one another. In fact, in many ways they are complementary, though each scholar emphasizes different areas. Hartz focuses on founding peoples; Lipset emphasizes founding events. Porter's analysis of elites is narrower in scope, but his findings might well be interpreted as a result of cultural, social and economic forces that Hartz, Lipset and Innis see in a more sweeping historical context.

However you want to explain the making of Canadian political culture, a long-range, historical perspective on Canadian society is useful—indeed necessary. When we turn to more recent developments, however, it would seem that we are as far as ever from a single, harmonious, unified national culture. We are bedeviled by ongoing debates about constitutional change, Senate reform, Native rights, language rights, multiculturalism, and so on. This suggests that in fact there are deep fractures or divisions in Canadian society. And one way to look at these fractures is in terms of different political cultures within society, in conflict with one another.

Why has Canada become so politically fragmented? At least part of the answer can be found when we look more closely at three key dynamics of Canadian society: Quebec nationalism, and relations between the English and French in this country; the ongoing vitality of regionalism; and the pull of continentalism.

When the English General Wolfe defeated his French counterpart Montcalm on the Plains of Abraham at Quebec City in 1760, the immediate problem facing the French was how to sustain a viable francophone culture under British rule. The solution presented itself in the form of the *Quebec Act* of 1774, whereby the French were permitted to retain their religion and legal traditions—their culture— in return for not supporting the Americans in their revolution against the English. Loyalty to the British Crown was exchanged for guaranteed legal and religious rights.[29] These rights remain intact, and are at the root of Canada's linguistic duality. They have also worked as the chief instruments of the survival of Canada's francophone community. Those rights, along with the expanding shield of the provincial government, have formed the historical basis of Quebec's political self-definition as a "nation" and, by extension, the moral claim to national self-determination.

Describing Canada as "two nations within a single state" focuses attention on the historic role that anglophone-francophone relations and conflicts have played in the evolution of Canadian political culture. Language, however, is but one aspect of political culture, and it is clear that other relevant regional divisions also shape the collective lives of Canadians in significant ways. In fact, some observers have gone so far as to suggest that Canadian politics is the politics of regions.

Evidence of the political importance of regions is all around us. Imagine, for instance, that you are the prime minister and you want to form a Cabinet composed of the best and the brightest of your members of parliament. But there is a long-standing tradition of taking regional representatives into the federal Cabinet, for example by making sure the minister of Fisheries is from the Atlantic region or British Columbia, that the minister of Agriculture is from the Prairies, that the minister of Finance is from Toronto or Montreal, and so on. Think about the regular spectacle of the First Ministers' Conference, at which the premiers get to unload their regional concerns into the lap of the prime minister. Think about the way debates about the distribution of economic resources take place: Why did Ontario want lower oil prices in the 1970s and 1980s, while the western provinces wanted higher ones? Think of the regional orientation of the party system. We have two major parties, the Canadian Alliance and the Bloc Québécois, that are regional in nature, the latter of which does not even try to run candidates in all parts of the country. In these and a thousand other ways, regionalism intrudes on Canadian political life, and must be accommodated within the workings of public administration.

Regionalism is partly a function of patterns of immigration and settlement. Different groups of people have settled in different parts of the country at various times in our history, reinforcing the regional nature of the political culture. But immigration and settlement are also a function of economics. In economic terms, regional differences in economic activity have contributed to the development of regional political cultures. Innis was among the earliest proponents of this view. In the industrialized heartland of Quebec and Ontario, the occupational mix of working populations is quite different from that found in the prairies, the Atlantic provinces, or British Columbia, all of which rely heavily on resource-based economic activities, or staples. Economies that overrely on staples are subject to the fluctuations of world demand for their products, a factor over which they have no control. So the regional economies fluctuate in terms of prosperity at different rates and times depending upon the particular economic base of the region. Thus, while some regions enjoy prosperity, others falter, and the uneven performance of different segments of the Canadian economy aggravates regional political differences.

What is the importance of the regional dynamic of political culture for the political community as a whole? Well, one thing it does is frustrate the development of a strong national political community. First, there is the bare fact of electoral arithmetic; that is, about 60 percent of Canada's population live in two provinces, which means that the votes in that region carry enormous electoral weight; they can make or break nationally elected governments. Indeed, it is often said that elections are over before voters in western Canada have even had a chance to cast their ballots. This can only contribute to a feeling of alienation and powerlessness among Canadians in regions other than Quebec and Ontario, who have few reasons to believe that their influence will be felt nationally, that their influence can be exercised effectively, or that their interests will ever occupy a place of importance on the national agenda.

Second, it has been argued that Canada's particular style of federal parliamentary institution tends to aggravate rather than moderate regional divisions. The fact that Canada's Senate is an appointed body, in the first place, decreases the legitimacy of the institution for many people. And the fact that the appointment process is highly politicized—that is, often based on political patronage rather than on merit—is another blow to the Senate's legitimacy. The Senate's seeming ineffectuality in the main task for which it was created, representing regional interests, also decreases respect for the institution, and creates the feeling among regional populations that they are without an effective champion in Ottawa's halls of power.

Party discipline is a third institutional practice that frustrates balanced regional representation, and hence the development of a national political community. In the British parliamentary tradition that Canada follows, party discipline is central to the workings of **responsible government**, which is government in which the prime minister and Cabinet are accountable to, and can be removed by a majority of, the legislature. While MPs from various regions may be able to try to influence their colleagues on the merits of a certain course of action for their region, they have few real opportunities to place the interests of their region over those of the party, due to party discipline.

The electoral system, the weakness of institutions such as the Senate that were supposed to be regionally sensitive, and the workings of party discipline all combine to frustrate the national representation of regional concerns. One consequence of these factors has been the emergence of provincial premiers as strong regional advocates on the national stage—a development we will explore in more detail later on.

Linguistic duality and regionalism are both dynamics that appear to be undermining the development of a clear, single political culture in Canada. However, there is another contextual dynamic at work, namely, Canada's continental location, which also obscures the evolution of a strong and easily identifiable political culture. There is a multiplicity of ways in which the United States dominates the North American continent: its population size, the power of its economy, the vitality of its cultural institutions, and so on. Most recently, questions related to the security of the continent in the wake of September 11, 2001 have brought to the fore issues of identity and sovereignty.

The extent of Canada's economic ties to the United States is astonishing. Canada and the United States have the largest single trading relationship in the entire world. Since the Second World War, U.S. direct and indirect investment in Canada has grown to account for more than 75 percent of all foreign investment in the country. Furthermore, U.S. control over a variety of key industrial sectors, such as fuels, rubber, chemicals, transportation and others, is remarkably high. U.S. enterprises account for more than 60 percent of the Canadian manufacturing sector, for example. Virtually no other free and sovereign country in the world has permitted this kind of foreign economic domination of its domestic economy. But our ambivalence as a nation about these issues is apparent through the lens of public administration. Free trade with the United States was a central issue in the 1911 election, in the late 1940s, and in the 1980s and 1990s. In the past 25 years, we have seen the Canadian government create an agency to *monitor and limit* foreign direct investment in Canada (the Foreign Investment Review Agency), then replace it with an agency that *facilitates and welcomes* it (Investment Canada).[30]

This U.S. penetration of Canada is, of course, a mixed blessing. Undoubtedly Canada enjoys a high standard of living partly because of high levels of American investment. But at the same time, the levels and types of U.S. investment in Canada have limited the abilities of the Canadian government to exercise complete control over domestic economic policy-making. Indeed, it has been suggested that with the progressive integration of Canada into the U.S. economy, Canada has become little more than a branch plant of the United States.[31] The **Free Trade Agreement (FTA)** and its successor, the **North American Free Trade Agreement (NAFTA)**, according to this view, simply provide the institutional mechanism or framework to continue this process. It is also argued that the continentalization of the economy both undermines Canadian political sovereignty and erodes the distinctiveness of Canada's social and cultural fabric. Consequently, some have called NAFTA Canada's "real constitution."[32]

Economics has had a major effect on the continentalization of Canada, but it is difficult to precisely measure the extent to which it has consequences for political and cultural life in Canada. The supporters of the FTA and NAFTA argue that these are merely economic agreements with no impact on politics or culture. They are simply tools to enhance the economic well-being and strength of the nation. Nor is it possible to measure the extent to which Canadians have absorbed American

values. But certainly economic ties, proximity, population distribution, and the
fact that a majority of Canadians share a language with Americans means that U.S.
cultural values are easily transmitted to Canadians.

What else shows the distinctiveness of Canadian political culture?[33]
Researchers have noted the apparent absence of a strong or consistent relationship
between class and vote in Canada. In other words, Canadians do not tend to
support political parties that appeal to them on the basis of which class they belong to. A second significant finding that sets Canadian political belief systems apart
from those in other countries is the apparent weakness of left-right orientations
within the population. In other words, Canadians do not generally think of themselves in class or ideological terms in relation to the political system—although this
may be changing.

Until recently, it was commonly observed that one thing Canada shares with
other nations is a citizenry that demonstrates a high level of political trust, which is
reflected in a fairly high regard for those who govern. But this too seems to be changing. It has been noted that Canadians were more likely to defer to authority figures
than are citizens of the U.S. and publics in other industrial countries., but that recently
there has been a "decline in deference" amongst Canadians.[34] Canadians and
Americans are also quite different in their attitude toward the role of government
in society and the economy. Canadians have a much more positive view of the state.

What you should begin to see by now is that despite the linguistic and regional differences that raise substantial obstacles to the development of an easily
identifiable national political identity, and despite the powerful pull of continental forces, a distinctive combination of political values are discernible that together
delineate Canadian political culture. But what is the relationship of political culture to the other topics raised in this chapter, such as democracy and power? This
is the concern of the next section.

The Interplay of Democracy, Political Culture, and the Institutions of Public Administration

While the next chapter looks at some of the key actors and institutions of public administration, a brief introduction to this topic is included here in the context of
our discussion of democracy. Specifically, we are interested in briefly sketching out
how the interplay of democracy and political culture produces certain types of institutions, and in turn how those institutions contribute to democracy and political culture. Rather than viewing the relationship as one-way and linear, then, we will
look at the interplay between these things as circular and mutually reinforcing.

The Canadian Constitution

The starting point for our exploration of the context of policy-making in Canada
is the Canadian Constitution. The Constitution, as both the written document
and the unwritten set of conventions that accompany it, is the guidepost of society. It is the supreme law of the land, embodying the fundamental beliefs and

3 functions of Constitution

values of a society, such as democracy and freedom. Any constitution typically does three things: it orders the relationship between the state and its citizens; it orders the relationship between citizens; and, in a federal system such as Canada, it orders the relationship between the different levels of government. It is within the parameters set by the Constitution that public administration takes place.

The Canadian Constitution has evolved to reflect changing conditions in Canadian society. For example, the *British North America Act, 1867*, reflected the nature of Canadian society at Confederation. It set out a division of powers between the federal government and the provinces that reflected the roles of the state in the latter half of the 19th century. And it sketched out the responsibilities of some of the major institutions of government. It is perhaps a testament to the flexibility of the original constitutional agreement that it has been formally amended only 18 times. Strikingly, most constitutional change has occurred outside the written Constitution, through alterations to the informal traditions and customs known as *constitutional conventions,* as well as to the common law. For example, the prime minister is clearly the most powerful figure in government, yet nowhere are the duties and responsibilities of this post spelled out in the *BNA Act*. They have evolved largely through habit and tradition, rather than in formal written constitutional rules.

The most significant amendment to the Constitution came in 1982, when it was patriated (that is, brought home from Great Britain where it had resided as an ordinary statute of the British Parliament) and a *Charter of Rights and Freedoms* was added to it. The addition of the *Charter* most obviously signalled changing attitudes in the Canadian political culture about democracy, the role of the state, and the relationship of citizens to the institutions of government.[35] It has spawned a whole new set of issues for public administration, including, for example, the question of whether the judges who interpret the legality of legislation through the prism of the *Charter* are in fact usurping Parliament's traditional role.[36] Citizens have embraced the *Charter* to protect their basic freedoms (of conscience and religion, association, and peaceful assembly), as well as basic legal rights (such as the right to be secure against unreasonable search and seizure, and the right to life, liberty and the security of the person). In addition, the *Charter* guarantees equal protection and equal benefit of the law without discrimination based on race, national or ethnic origin, colour, religion, sex, age or mental or physical disability. All these and other rights specified in the *Charter* are only subject to such reasonable limits by law as can be demonstrably justified in a free and democratic society. The catalogue of rights and freedoms strongly reflects the prevailing political culture, and their protection has had a profound effect on the practice of public administration, in that government institutions and bureaucrats have had to conform in policy and behaviour to the *Charter.*

The veritable orgy of constitutional politics in Canada over the past 30 years is another important indicator of the political culture. Why was our political elite so focused on the Constitution? What explains the Meech Lake and Charlottetown accords? Was this simply a temporary bout of national constitutional insanity, or are we a cursed people, forever destined to wallow in the morass of arcane constitutional discussions and debates? These are difficult questions, but on one level they can be seen as part of the nature of a political culture that includes a healthy respect for democratic processes. After all, it has been said that while the U.S. constitutional order was the result of revolution, we Canadians preferred the route of evolution—which is, of course, a much slower process.

The North American Free Trade Agreement

The great debate that raged in Canada around the 1988 election concerning free trade is deeply resonant of the political culture of the country, and touches on all aspects of public administration. Essentially, the nationalists who opposed the signing of a free trade agreement with the United States argued that Canada's national identity was at risk if it submitted to the lure of the U.S. empire. They argued that as Canada integrated itself economically with the United States, it would only be a matter of time before Canada was culturally and politically integrated as well. The continentalists scoffed at these charges, arguing that the Free Trade Agreement was nothing more than an economic arrangement that would bring enhanced economic wealth and opportunity to Canada. It had nothing to do with sovereignty, or political or national identity.[37]

The continentalists prevailed, and the FTA was signed into law in 1989. It was extended to Mexico in 1990 and rechristened NAFTA. Its provisions created a tariff-free border among Canada, the United States and Mexico, and improved market access in areas such as services, agriculture and resources. But it does much more than this. It entrenches a supranational dispute resolution process that requires the Canadian government to sacrifice decision-making powers over the economy to a commission. In addition, Canada cannot act unilaterally in certain policy initiatives. Instead, it must give advance notice of its intentions to its partners. Moreover, it cannot apply traditional trade remedies in the event of a dispute with the United States or Mexico. Thus, some have argued that NAFTA is a new pillar in the constitution of the country that constrains the state from taking certain policy actions. Moreover, in political culture terms, the free trade debate has become a flash point for those who argue for the supremacy of the free market versus those who argue for a positive, interventionist state—all of which has a direct impact on public administration.

Federalism

Fundamentally, the Constitution reflects the power relationships within society and helps us understand the basic values of a society. The Canadian Constitution divides jurisdiction between a federal government and provincial governments (municipal governments fall under the jurisdiction of the provinces). Why don't we have a unitary system with just one government? The Fathers of Confederation struck a bargain in 1867, in which the rights of linguistic and religious minorities would be protected. The only practical way they could see to do that was to create two levels of government and divide jurisdiction between the two. The federal government was given the majority of powers to construct and maintain the national economy, while the provinces were given powers to safeguard social and cultural issues.

Clearly, the decision to divide powers in this way reflects the political culture of the country at the time, and has also had a lasting effect on public administration. One inescapable issue which continuously resurfaces is the French presence in Canada. At the basis of Canada's constitutional regime is a concern for the survival of French Canada, as evidenced by various elements of the Constitution and by federalism itself. At the same time, though, we must consider the other regions of Canada that are acknowledged through the Constitution and federal system. Ultimately, federalism is based on the desire to balance regional interests with a sense of national unity. Concretely, it tries to do this through sections 91, 92 and 95 of the *Constitution Act, 1867*. Section 91 lists powers that are the exclusive preserve of the federal government. Section 92 lists provincial powers. And section 95 indicates that agriculture and immigration are areas of shared jurisdiction, but that in the event of a dispute, federal law prevails.

Conflict between the two levels over this division of powers is endemic in Canadian federalism. The resolution of disputes can occur in one of two main ways. The two levels of government can sit down at the bargaining table and talk through their problems, a process that necessarily gives a prominent role to provincial premiers as the spokespersons for regional interests. A whole machinery of intergovernmental relations has arisen around this development, including ministries in each government responsible for relations with the other level of government, and permanent intergovernmental secretariats to coordinate relations between Ottawa and the provinces.[38] This process has come to be known as *executive federalism*, since it is the executive of each level of government (the prime minister, premiers and Cabinet ministers and their senior bureaucratic advisors) who take the lead role.[39]

The second major form of dispute resolution is the courts. The role of the judiciary in federalism has been vital. In a long series of judgments since Confederation, the judges have interpreted the division of powers between the two levels of government whenever governments could not settle their differences at the bargaining table. In some instances, the judges have tended to rule in favour of the provinces, shifting the pendulum of power toward a decentralized form of federalism. In other instances, they have upheld Ottawa's position, contributing toward a centralized federal system. In any event, the role of the judiciary has been key to shaping the federal system.[40]

The Parliamentary Actors

One of the elemental questions of public administration is "Who decides?" Who decides, for example, that tuition is going to be increased? Did you? Who decides that we should purchase sophisticated helicopters for the Canadian navy at a cost of some $5 billion? Did you? Who decided that we should forgo a national, universally accessible day-care system? Did you? Who decided that we should enter into a free trade agreement with the U.S., and extend it to Mexico? Did you? Who decided that the community-based policing model is the preferable approach to dealing with modern crime problems? Did you?

Perhaps the facile answer to these questions is that our elected politicians decide these things. But a sophisticated analysis reveals that the waters of public administration run much deeper than this. There is a whole legion of players, some known to us, but most not known to us, that makes the decisions about our everyday lives. Who are these people? How public is the process of public administration? Do we as ordinary citizens have access to the decision-making process in any meaningful way? Do we even understand the stages of the decision-making process? Hopefully we can cast a little light on this aspect of Canadian public administration, if only to bring some understanding to the sometimes seemingly incomprehensible decisions our political representatives take. As well, it may help us to understand where, within the complex process, effective input is possible, and help to reveal who the main players are in the system of decision-making.

We will begin with the *parliamentary actors*. These are the important individuals, groups and organizations within government that influence public administration. They include the executive, legislative and judicial branches of government. We will then look at the *extra-parliamentary actors*; that is, the individuals, groups and organizations that influence public administration from outside government. These include political parties, interest groups and the media.

The Executive What is the **executive** branch of government? It is first the Crown, represented in Canada by the governor-general, whose role has evolved into a purely symbolic one. But it is the prime minister and the Cabinet that compose the politically significant parts of the executive branch. Together, they direct and control the bureaucracy, which is also part of the executive. (These relationships are presented in more detail in the next chapter). The prime minister and the Cabinet are the key decision-makers. Together they initiate policy and legislation, and have their hands on the purse strings of government. Cabinet is organized into committees, and its overall work is coordinated by powerful central agencies.

Of course, the prime minister and Cabinet do not act alone or in isolation. Instead they are supported and assisted by a veritable army of civil servants, whose job it is to proffer advice and carry out the decisions of their political masters. This largely faceless, nameless cast of thousands is headed by senior bureaucrats who not only administer on behalf of their political masters, but also influence the policy process with their advice and actions. Among the important issues this raises is this: To whom are they accountable? We need to understand how an appointed authority such as the civil service, which wields so much influence and power, can be held accountable and is reconcilable to a system of responsible government. This raises all sorts of thorny questions. For example, if there is a major screwup or scandal in the government, who would you hold responsible? Is it the minister who heads the department? Or is it the civil servant who gave bad advice? Furthermore, how responsive is this massive bureaucratic machine to individual citizens and interest groups? Is it just the wealthy and powerful who have the wherewithal to gain access to the corridors of power? What about ordinary citizens who may lack the financial resources, organizational skills or sophisticated knowledge and understanding of how government works? These questions have important implications for public administration and democracy.

The Legislature We also must consider the role of the **legislature** in the Canadian political system. After all, is this not what democracy is all about? We elect representatives to take our concerns to Parliament, where free and open debate about the merits of different positions takes place, and decisions are taken and passed into law on the basis of what is good for Canadians. This is typical of what many Canadians think the legislature is and what it does.

The Canadian Parliament is based on the British model. It consists of two parts: the elected House of Commons, and the appointed Senate. Given that the Senate is appointed, it generally lacks legitimacy in the eyes of most Canadians. Its members are appointed by the prime minister, usually as a reward for faithful service; it is thus a major vestige of patronage. The Senate was originally meant to fulfill two roles: a forum for regional interests, and a voice to protect minority rights. As to the second function, the property requirements for membership in the Senate ensured that it became a preserve of the well-off, but as Sir John A. Macdonald noted, the Senate should protect minorities—and the rich are always a minority. Macdonald also saw the Senate as a forum for "sober second thought." This attitude reflects the elitist political culture that is cautious and conservative and wary of the democratizing influences of the House of Commons. As for defending regional interests, the Senate has failed miserably in this regard. Since, proportionately, Ontario and Quebec have the most seats in the Senate, central Canadian interests have tended to prevail there. Hence calls, emanating particularly from western Canada, to reform the Senate on the lines of a triple-E model: elected, equal and effective.

The House of Commons is really where most of the action is. Democratically elected in one of 301 geographically defined constituencies, each member of Parliament (MP) is charged with holding the government to account. He or she does this by supporting or opposing the party that has the majority of seats. This is the essence of responsible government. The party with the most seats, whose leader is the prime minister, is primarily responsible for the initiation of policy, especially through the powers of taxing and spending. But it only retains power so long as it retains the support of the majority in the House. This would appear to give ordinary MPs a tremendous amount of leverage and power. But the practice of party discipline constrains them. This is the convention whereby MPs vote in the House according to the wishes of their leaders. In this way, some stability is achieved in government, and the business of passing laws is facilitated. But this also means that in many circumstances, ordinary MPs are caught between a rock and a hard place: that is, they are forced to support their leader even when their constituents demand they act otherwise. Failure to subscribe to the rules of party discipline can mean a short and inglorious parliamentary career: rogue MPs are denied promotion to Cabinet minister or any of the other perks and privileges that the prime minister dishes out to ensure the loyalty of the troops. This means, effectively, that the dominance of the executive branch over the legislative branch is firmly entrenched.[41]

This is not to suggest that Parliament is completely toothless and ineffectual. Legislators do play an important role in holding the executive accountable through mechanisms such as Question Period in the House of Commons, through various legislative committees that investigate government policies, and through the actions of the opposition parties in mobilizing public opinion. But overall, it is best to regard Parliament as a *law-passing* body rather than as a *law-making* body, whose role is secondary to that of the executive.

Can Parliament control the prime minister and Cabinet, or keep the bureaucracy accountable for its actions? Should the Senate be reformed, or should we just abolish it and put it out of our misery? Does Parliament respond to the needs of ordinary citizens? Where party discipline is concerned, should MPs be allowed to vote according to their conscience—assuming they have one? Should they be allowed more free votes in the House of Commons? Or does this pose a threat to the underpinnings of responsible government? All these questions animate public administration where these parliamentary actors are concerned.

The Judiciary. The courts and the judges constitute the third branch of government in Canada: the **judiciary**. Judges are appointed rather than elected. The top court is the Supreme Court of Canada, which became so only in 1949. Prior to this, the Judicial Committee of the Privy Council, a British body of law lords, was the final court of appeal for Canadian judicial cases.

The judicial branch of government is important to public administration in two ways. First, it is responsible for interpreting constitutional law.[42] Within the purview of this responsibility, the judges are asked to make judgments on two broad types of issues. The first involves the division of powers in the Constitution. They are asked to determine whether a law passed by one level of government is within its jurisdiction as spelled out in the Constitution. If it infringes on the jurisdiction of the other level of government, the courts rule that it is *ultra vires*, and therefore illegal. If it does not infringe on the other level of government, the courts rule that it is *intra vires*, or legal. As well, since the introduction of the *Charter of Rights and Freedoms* in 1982, the courts have been asked to rule on the constitutionality of laws related to human rights.

Second, the judicial branch is responsible for the area of administrative law.[43] This essentially means that the judges are required to ensure that government bureaucrats do not overstep the law in fulfilling their duties and obligations, that regulations are followed according to the rules and procedures set out in legislation, that citizen rights are not abridged or denied in the process of carrying out the instructions of government, and that penalties are levied for violations of administrative procedure and process.

Besides the judicial, legislative and executive branches of government, there are a range of other actors that influence and impinge upon the practice of public administration, and that also reflect the dominant values, attitudes and beliefs of the political culture of the country. We turn our attention now to these extra-parliamentary actors.

The Extra-Parliamentary Actors

Political Parties The traditional view of political parties in Canada is that they play an important role in recruiting political leaders, and that they aggregate and artic-ulate disparate interests, which are then mobilized for electoral purposes.[44] In Canada, the political party system has evolved from two dominant parties (the Liberals and the Conservatives) to three (add the New Democratic Party) to a mul-tiparty system with as many as five parties holding seats in Parliament at any one time. Parties are a particularly important reflection of the political culture. For ex-ample, the Liberals and Conservatives—the only two parties to form the government at the federal level—have usually been viewed as "brokerage parties" engaged in the task of downplaying divisions within Canadian society and forging the broad-est possible coalition of voters to win power. This typically means pitching their ap-peal to the region with the most votes: central Canada. They are often regarded as subsuming principles to the pursuit of power, which has resulted in a range of "protest parties" popping up on the horizon. These include the NDP and its pre-decessor, the Cooperative Commonwealth Federation, as well as the Social Credit Party, the Progressives, and several others. Regionalism is mirrored in the party system, as we can see from the contemporary rise of the Canadian Alliance (for-merly the Reform Party) and Bloc Québécois, two parties firmly rooted in the West and Quebec respectively.

Elections and political parties are of course central to our general under-standing of democracy in Canada. But think about parties in political culture terms. They reflect a political culture in which class issues are subordinated to is-sues of language and region (and earlier in our history, religion). Moreover, low par-ticipation by Canadians in the party system reflects our tendency to defer to elites. We lack the kind of mass populism that characterizes party systems in some other countries. Parties generate policy ideas, but these are rarely acted on unless they have the support of the leadership of the parties. In other words, they do not tend to reflect "grassroots" democracy. Still, they are the key organizational variable in the House of Commons, as we saw earlier in the section on party discipline.

Interest Groups **Interest groups** are organizations of like-minded individuals that attempt to further their common interests by affecting public policy. Increasingly they seem to dominate the policy-making process in Canada.[45] They arise as a result of citizens banding together to promote their own interests, but they often end up in conflict with other groups doing the same thing. All these competing groups try to get the attention of bureaucratic and political decision-makers. Almost every imag-inable interest in Canadian society is represented by organized groups; you yourself are probably a member of several such groups at any one time. Besides the major busi-ness and labour groups, there are hundreds of organizations representing women, students, environmentalists, seniors, Aboriginals, farmers, musicians and artists, religions and so on.

Clearly, though, not all interest groups are equal in their influence. As a result, it is perhaps overstating the case to say that the system of interest groups repre-sents the pinnacle of democracy in large, complex modern societies, since everyone can be represented. Some groups are well-funded, institutionalized, and have the resources to pursue their interests effectively. Others, though, are just the opposite. They lack financial resources, knowledge of who the key decision-makers are, and how to get to them. This is not to say that they are totally ineffective, but clearly the odds of success are improved if you have the wherewithal to play the game well. Typically, business groups have the resources at their disposal to target decision-makers and public opinion at the same time; thus the ideological dominance of business values is reinforced through the interest group system. While business interests do not "win" on every issue they try to influence, clearly their position is predominant in the constellation of interest groups trying to influence public administration.

It is perhaps axiomatic that a society that values free association should feature interest-group politics. Interest groups provide important services to their members, but are also oriented toward influencing policy-making by advocating change or mobilizing to prevent change unfavourable to their interests. They also provide expert knowledge and information to policy-makers, and often support governments sympathetic to their aims. They target Cabinet ministers and senior bureaucrats as well as ordinary MPs. They use techniques such as personal lobbying, public information campaigns, the media, protests and other tactics to get their messages across.

The Media. Finally, we need to consider the role of the **media** and its influence on public administration.[46] Again, political culture reveals that Canada is a society that values freedom of speech and a free press as a cornerstone of democracy. Hence the media plays an important role as a purveyor of information as well as of political attitudes and values. The media is constantly engaged in a process of defining what is political, and of setting political discourse—that is, the way we talk about politics.

The media plays an extremely important role in matters such as the selection and evaluation of political leaders. As well, it plays a key role in the communication functions of government. But in so doing, it should be noted that the media carries its own set of biases, contrary to the widely held view that the media is objective. This means that what the media chooses *not to report* can be every bit as important as what it chooses *to* report. In this way it helps set the agenda for public discussion and debate, legitimizing certain actors and institutions, and conferring or withholding status.

In the context of a nation that sits next door to the most powerful media empire on earth, a whole other set of issues becomes important, such as the Americanization of Canada and the national identity question. The decision to have a public broadcasting network, the CBC, was in part a reaction to this reality. Moreover, the regulatory regime that has been developed in Canada concerning the media is complex and contains many contentious issues. Should the CBC be privatized? Do we need Canadian content regulations as stipulated by the Canadian Radio-television and Telecommunications Commission (CRTC)? Should Canadian magazines be protected from U.S. competition? Should the reporting of poll results be restricted during elections? All these questions, and many others, imply that the role, function and place of the media are issues of ongoing concern for public administration.

WHAT YOU HAVE LEARNED

We began this chapter with some basic concepts: power, politics, democracy, state and government. Each term, while susceptible to a variety of interpretations, plays an important part in the world of Canadian public administration. We then examined some related questions to demystify Canadian public administration and its democratic context. It is important to draw connections between *what* happens, *how* it happens, *to whom* it happens and *why* it happens. This helps us understand how power is exercised in Canada, who has it, and who lacks it. Furthermore, by introducing the topic of political culture and its interplay with democracy and public administration, we can begin to see the basis of power relations within society and the importance of values such as equality and freedom.

This chapter considered how the concept of democracy relates to the theory and practice of public administration in Canada. Finally, the context of public administration was assessed by examining the issues of the constitution, NAFTA, federalism and the key parliamentary and extra-parliamentary actors who play a role in public administration in Canada.

ENDNOTES

1. Max Weber, "Politics as a Vocation," in H.W. Gerth and C. Wright Mills, eds. From *Max Weber: Essays in Sociology*, (New York: Oxford University Press, 1958): 79.
2. Larry Johnston, *Politics: An Introduction to the Modern Democratic State*, (Peterborough: Broadview, 1997): 15.
3. David Easton, *Systems Analysis of Political Life*, (New York: John Wiley and Sons, 1965): 21.
4. Harold D. Laswell, *Politics: Who Gets What, When and How*, (New York: McGraw-Hill, 1936).
5. V.I. Lenin, "Left Wing Communism: An Infantile Disorder," in *Selected Works*, (New York: International Publishers, 1943).
6. See Stuart Schram, ed. *The Political Thought of Mao Tse Tung*, (New York: Frederick A. Praeger, 1969): 287.
7. Cited in James John Guy, *People, Politics and Government: A Canadian Perspective, Fourth Edition*, (Scarborough: Prentice Hall, 1998): 2.
8. Karl Marx and Frederick Engels, "The Communist Manifesto," in Arthur P. Mendel, ed. *The Essential Works of Marxism*, (New York: Bantam Books, 1961).
9. For an overview of the role of women in the public service, see Caroline Andrew, "Women and the Public Sector," in Christopher Dunn, ed. *The Handbook of Canadian Public Administration*, (Toronto: Oxford University Press, 2002): 159–68.
10. Camilla Stivers, *Gender Images in Public Administration*, (Newbury Park, California: Sage Publications, 1993): 4. See also Susan D. Phillips, "Discourse, Identity and Voice: Feminist Contributions to Policy Studies," in Laurent Dobuzinskis, Michael Howlett and David Laycock, eds. *Policy Studies in Canada: The State of the Art*, (Toronto: University of Toronto Press, 1996): 242–265.
11. See Leo Panitch and Donald Swartz, *The Assault on Trade Union Freedoms: From Wage Controls to Social Contract*, (Toronto: Garamond, 1993).

12. See Cynthia J. Alexander and Leslie A. Pal, eds. *Digital Democracy: Policy and Politics in the Wired World*, (Toronto: Oxford University Press, 1998); Mark Kingwell, "Geek With an Argument," *Saturday Night*, (February, 1996): 75–77; and Arthur Kroker and Marilouise Kroker, *Hacking the Future: Stories for the Flesh-Eating 90s*, (New York: St. Martin's Press, 1996).

13. Henry B. Mayo, *An Introduction to Democratic Theory*, (New York: Oxford University Press, 1960): 70.

14. Gabriel A. Almond and Sidney Verba, *The Civic Culture*, (Princeton, New Jersey: Princeton University Press, 1963).

15. See C.B. Macpherson, *The Real World of Democracy*, (Toronto: CBC Enterprises, 1965).

16. H.H. Gerth and C. Wright Mills, *From Max Weber: Essays in Sociology*, (New York: Oxford University Press, 1946): 78.

17. Karl Marx and Frederick Engels, "The Communist Manifesto," in Arthur P. Mendel, ed. *Essential Works of Marxism*, (New York: Bantam Books, 1961): 15.

18. Ralph Miliband, *The State in Capitalist Society: The Analysis of the Western System of Power*, (London: Quartet Books, 1969): 3.

19. Stephen Brooks, *Canadian Democracy: An Introduction, Second Edition*, (Toronto: Oxford University Press, 1996): 7.

20. Gabriel Almond, "Comparative Political Systems," *World Politics*, 18 (1956): 396.

21. For an overview, see David J. Bell, *The Roots of Disunity: A Study of Canadian Political Culture*, (Toronto: Oxford University Press, 1992).

22. Louis Hartz, *The Founding of New Societies: Studies in the History of the United States, Latin America, South Africa, Canada and Australia*, (New York: Harcourt, Brace and World, 1964). See also H.D. Forbes, "Hartz-Horowitz at Twenty: Nationalism, Toryism and Socialism in Canada and the United States," *Canadian Journal of Political Science*, 20, 2 (June, 1987): 287–316.

23. Gad Horowitz, "Conservatism, Liberalism and Socialism in Canada: An Interpretation," *Canadian Journal of Economics and Political Science*, 32, 2 (May, 1966): 143–177.

24. Seymour Martin Lipset, *Continental Divide*, (New York: Routledge, 1990).

25. John Porter, *The Vertical Mosaic: An Analysis of Social Class and Power in Canada*, (Toronto: University of Toronto Press, 1965).

26. See, for example, Wallace Clement, *The Canadian Corporate Elite: An Analysis of Economic Power*, (Toronto: McClelland and Stewart, 1975).

27. A recent interpretation argues that deference is less of a factor in the makeup of the Canadian political culture than it once was. See Neil Nevitte, *The Decline of Deference: Canadian Value Change in a Cross-National Perspective*, (Peterborough: Broadview Press, 1996). See also Michael Adams, *Sex in the Snow: Canadian Social Values at the End of the Millennium*, (Toronto: Penguin Books, 1998).

28. Harold Adams Innis, *The Fur Trade in Canada: An Introduction to Canadian Economic History*, (Toronto: University of Toronto Press, 1956).

29. See Bayard Reesor, *The Canadian Constitution in Historical Perspective*, (Scarborough: Prentice Hall, 1992): 9.

30. See Stephen Clarkson, *Canada and the Reagan Challenge: Crisis and Adjustment 1981–1985*, (Toronto: James Lorimer, 1985); and David Thomas, ed. *Canada and the United States: Differences That Count*, (Peterborough: Broadview, 1993).

31. Among the first statements of this position was Kari Levitt, *Silent Surrender: The Multinational Corporation in Canada*, (Toronto: Macmillan, 1970).

32. See Stephen Clarkson, *Uncle Sam and Us: Globalization, Neoconservatism and the Canadian State*, (Toronto: University of Toronto Press, 2002).

33. See Adams, *Sex in the Snow*, (1998). For an earlier look at this question, see Richard Simeon and David Elkins, *Small Worlds: Provinces and Parties in Canadian Political Life*, (Toronto: Methuen, 1980).

34. See Neil Nevitte, *The Decline of Deference*, (Peterborough: Broadview Press, 1996).

35. See Alan Cairns and Cynthia Williams, eds. *Constitutionalism, Citizenship and Society in Canada*, (Toronto: University of Toronto Press, 1985).

36. See Michael Mandel, *The Charter of Rights and the Legalization of Politics in Canada*, (Toronto: Thompson Educational Publishing, 1994).

37. See Gregory J. Inwood, *Continentalizing Canada: The Politics and Legacy of the Macdonald Royal Commission*, (Toronto: University of Toronto Press, forthcoming). See also Jeffrey M. Ayres, *Defying Conventional Wisdom: Political Movements and Popular Contention Against North American Free Trade*, (Toronto: University of Toronto Press, 1998). For arguments against free trade, see Duncan Cameron, ed. *The Free Trade Deal*, (Toronto: Lorimer, 1988). For arguments in favour of free trade, see John Crispo, ed. *Free Trade: The Real Story*, (Toronto: Gage, 1988). A collection of papers on both sides of the debate can be found in Marc Gold and David Leyton-Brown, eds. *Trade-Offs on Free Trade*, (Toronto: Carswell, 1988).

38. See Gregory J. Inwood, Carolyn M. Johns and Patricia L. O'Reilly, "The Impact of Administrative Reform on Intergovernmental Officials," in Harvey Lazar and Peter Meekison, eds. *The State of the Federation 2002-2003: Managing Tensions: Evaluating the Institutions of the Federation*, (Montreal: McGill-Queen's University Press, forthcoming 2003). See also Richard Simeon, *Federal-Provincial Diplomacy*, (Toronto: University of Toronto Press, 1972).

39. See D.V. Smiley, *The Federal Condition in Canada*, (Toronto: McGraw-Hill Ryerson, 1987).

40. See Peter H. Russell. *Constitutional Odyssey: Can Canadians Become a Sovereign People? Second Edition*, (Toronto: University of Toronto Press, 1993).

41. See Donald J. Savoie, *Governing From the Centre: The Concentration of Power in Canadian Politics*, (Toronto: University of Toronto Press, 1999).

42. See Peter H. Russell, *Leading Constitutional Decisions, Fourth Edition*, (Ottawa: Carleton University Press, 1987).

43. See David Phillip Jones and Anne S. de Villars, *Principles of Administrative Law, Second Edition*, (Scarborough: Carswell, 1994).

44. See Hugh G. Thorburn, ed. *Party Politics in Canada, Seventh Edition*, (Scarborough: Prentice Hall, 1996); and M.J. Brodie and Jane Jenson, *Crisis, Challenge and Change: Party and Class in Canada*, (Toronto: Methuen, 1980).

45. See Susan D. Phillips, "Competing, Connecting, and Complementing: Parties, Interest Groups and New Social Movements," in A. Brian Tanguay and Alain-G. Gagnon, eds. *Canadian Politics: Second Edition*, (Peterborough: Broadview Press, 1996). See also Paul A. Pross, *Group Politics and Public Policy*, (Toronto: Oxford University Press, 1986).

46. See Rand Dyck, *Canadian Politics: Critical Approaches, Third Edition*, (Scarborough: Nelson, 2000): chapter 11; and Edwin R. Black, *Politics and the News*, (Toronto: Butterworths, 1982).

KEY WORDS AND CONCEPTS

power (79)

authority (79)

traditional legitimacy (79)

charismatic legitimacy (79)

legal-rational legitimacy (80)

direct democracy (84)

representative democracy (84)

political culture (92)

responsible government (99)

FTA (100)

NAFTA (100)

Charter of Rights and Freedoms (102)

executive (105)

legislature (106)

judiciary (107)

interest groups (108)

media (109)

REVIEW QUESTIONS

The chapter was divided into five sections. You should now be able to address the following set of questions:

1. *Power, Politics and Public Administration*

This brief section set the table for our discussions of democracy by asking simply, What is power? What is influence? Who has these things in Canadian society, and why? What is politics? What is the relationship between power and politics? This section also addressed the debate about the public sector versus the private sector in a slightly different manner than in Chapter 1, where it was first raised. Here, the issues are recast in light of democratic theory. We asked the following: How is it determined what is rightly in the public domain? What kind of struggle must be engaged to move issues from the private world to the public, or vice versa?

2. *What Is Democracy?*

This section asked us to pause and consider what exactly we mean by the term democracy. In defining this term, it asked the following: What is democratic theory? What does democracy mean to the theory and practice of public administration? What is the relationship of democracy to political power? This section assessed the concepts of direct democracy and representative democracy, both of which are central to the underpinnings of the institutions and structures of public administration, which we will discuss in the next chapter. It asked the following: What is direct democracy, what is representative government, and what is the difference between political and economic democracy? How does the application of these terms affect the way government is structured, organized and run in Canada?

3. *State and Government*

These two terms are often used interchangeably. But they actually refer to two different things. We asked the following: What is the difference between state and government? Why is it important to have a conceptual difference between the two in the study and practice of public administration?

4. *Political Culture*

This section looked at several definitions of this concept, as well as several theories that seek to explain the nature of democracy and governance in Canada. We posed the following questions: What are the major theoretical explanations for the quality and type of democratic life in Canada? Is there a single theory that explains the elusiveness of the "Canadian identity," and what impact does this have on public administration in Canada?

5. *The Interplay of Democracy, Political Culture, and the Institutions of Public Administration*

Finally, we resurrected the theme of democratic theory to introduce both parliamentary and extra-parliamentary actors who influence and exercise power in the state and government in Canada. We asked, What is a constitution, and what impact does the Canadian Constitution have on the relations of power within Canadian public administration? It further asked, What are those relations? Who are the actors? What are the key institutions, both parliamentary and extra-parliamentary, that have an impact on the unfolding of public administration?

FURTHER READING

1. Power, Politics and Public Administration

Almond, Gabriel. *Comparative Politics: A Theoretical Framework*. New York: HarperCollins, 1993.

Blair, R.S. and J.T. McLeod. *The Canadian Political Tradition. Basic Readings. Second Edition.* Scarborough: Nelson, 1993.

Easton, David. *A Framework for Political Analysis*. Englewood Cliffs, New Jersey: Prentice Hall, Inc., 1965.

2. What Is Democracy?

Dahl, Robert. *Democracy and Its Critics*. New Haven: Yale University Press, 1989.

Esberey, Joy and Larry Johnston. *Democracy and the State: An Introduction to Politics*. Peterborough: Broadview, 1994.

Pocklington, T.C., ed. *Representative Democracy: An Introduction to Politics and Government*. Toronto: Harcourt Brace, 1994.

3. State and Government

Clement, Wallace, ed. *Understanding Canada: Building on the New Canadian Political Economy*. Kingston: McGill–Queen's University Press, 1997.

Miliband, Ralph. *The State in Capitalist Society: The Analysis of the Western System of Power.* London: Quartet Books, 1973.

Panitch, Leo, ed. *The Canadian State: Political Economy and Political Power.* Toronto: University of Toronto Press, 1977.

4. Political Culture

Bell, David V.J. "Political Culture in Canada," in Michael S. Whittington and Glen Williams, eds. *Canadian Politics in the 1990s. Third Edition.* Scarborough: Nelson, 1990: 137–157.

Christian, William and Colin Campbell. *Political Parties and Ideologies in Canada. Second Edition.* Toronto: McGraw-Hill Ryerson, 1983.

Pye, Lucian W. and Sidney Verba, eds. *Political Culture and Political Development*. Princeton: Princeton University Press, 1965.

5. The Interplay of Democracy, Political Culture, and the Institutions of Public Administration

Bradford, Neil. *Commissioning Ideas: Canadian National Policy Innovation in Comparative Perspective*. Toronto: Oxford University Press, 1998.

Nevitte, Neil. *The Decline of Deference*. Peterborough: Broadview Press, 1996.

Simeon, Richard and David Elkins. "Regional Political Cultures in Canada," *Canadian Journal of Political Science*, 7, 3 (September, 1974).

 ## WEBLINKS

Canadian Political Science Association
www.cpsa-acsp.ca

Political Science Links
www.umich.edu/~mjps/links.html

Political Science Resources
sun3.lib.uci.edu/~dtsang/pol.htm

Chapter 5

Public Administration *and* Institutions: The Real World *of* Organizations *and the* Machinery *of* Government

WHAT YOU WILL LEARN

In this chapter we will consider the place at which theory and practice intersect. We will be looking at the actual practice of public administration in Canada in light of the theories examined earlier. Chapter 5 is divided into the following sections:

1. — *Factors Influencing Organizational Structure*

   Here we look at the basic framework of the Canadian political system and ask the following: How have capitalist democracy, federalism and cabinet-parliamentary government influenced the organizational structure of the Canadian government? How have the very outlines of the state influenced the nature of public administration?

2. — *Political-Administrative Relationships*

   Chapter 1 introduced you to some issues surrounding the nature of the relationship between public administration and democratic government. This section elaborates on and examines the nature of this relationship by focusing on the roles of politicians and bureaucrats in more detail, and addresses a very fundamental question: Who is in control of the machinery and actions of the state?

3. — *Departmental Organizations*

Why do governments grow and shrink over time? Why do some prime ministers prefer large Cabinets with many departments, while others opt for more stripped-down models? We will consider these types of questions in this section to introduce you to the actual organizational units of the Canadian government, including the new mechanisms which fall under the heading of alternative service delivery (ASD). In so doing, we will explain why, organizationally speaking, the government looks the way it does.

4. — *Regulatory Agencies*

What role do these bodies play in public administration? In an era of deregulation and downsizing government, we have been rethinking the areas of life that government should be regulating. Why is this?

5. — *Crown Corporations*

The role of Crown corporations in the development of Canada has been important. But recently, we have been questioning the wisdom of public ownership (i.e., the use of Crown corporations) to achieve policy goals. What explains their use over time in Canada, and why are we reevaluating Crown corporations as policy instruments?

After reading this chapter, students should be able to explain the relationship between politicians and bureaucrats, and the main factors influencing the organizational structures of the Canadian public sector, including departments, regulatory agencies and Crown corporations, while keeping in mind the organizational theories studied earlier.

Factors Influencing Organizational Structure

Before we dive right into the nature of political and administrative relationships, it is important that we be clear about some fundamentals of the organization of the Canadian government. The first point to consider is that public policy-making takes place within the parameters of a capitalist democracy. Second, Canada has a federal system. And third, within that federal system, we have a cabinet-parliamentary government. What exactly do these terms mean? It is worth spending a moment clarifying them, since these systems are the framework for the structures and organizations of Canadian public administration. Then, we will look more closely at the organization of government within these structures, including, particularly, the political and administrative relationship, departments, regulatory bodies and Crown corporations.

Capitalist Democracy

The first thing to note about the factors shaping the organization of government— which shapes organizations in the public sector, according to political scientist Neil Bradford—is that governing in Canada takes place within the context of capitalist democracy.[1] This is a political-economic system whose broad rules impose themselves on the scope of action of governments in obvious and subtle ways. At the most basic level, it is the combination of capitalist relations of production with democratic electoral institutions that shape public policy-making and to which organizational life must ultimately conform.

You might look at it this way. At the root of capitalist economic systems is the right to private property. To defend that right, state structures are created that act in the interests of those who hold property. If we define property here to mean the "means of production" (i.e., capital, machines, factories, natural resources, information systems, etc.), then in a capitalist system, this means the capitalists. In other words, business interests (capital) must be defended through the structures of the state. But at the same time, in a democratic society, the will of the majority must prevail. And since the majority of Canadians are not capitalists (ownership of the means of production in Canada is concentrated in few hands), this means that the state must also respond to the democratically expressed will of ordinary citizens. As Bradford asserts,

This combination of capitalism and democracy must reasonably be seen to set broad and general parameters on policy-making. Elected officials clearly rely heavily on private investors to sustain growth, employment, revenue, and so forth. Given the value voters placed on these outputs, this dependence on "business confidence" reduces the political incentive for certain kinds of policy innovation, for example, those that directly challenge the existing property system.[2]

So the organization of government in Canada must meet the needs of the property-holding capitalists by creating the conditions for profitability, to ensure that business confidence is maintained. But this must be balanced against the interests of others in the system, whose interests may be in direct contrast to the capitalists.

For instance, it may enhance profitability for a corporation to simply dump its waste in a nearby river. But that action certainly is not in the interests of the communities situated along the river. The citizens may mobilize and demand that the government do something about industrial pollution, and hence a ministry of the environment is created. But the corporation may resist attempts by the new ministry to impose restrictions on polluting by threatening to move its plant to some other jurisdiction that has less severe environmental laws. Less drastically, it may look to other parts of the state structure for assistance. There may be, for instance, a ministry of industry that provides subsidies for the purchase of pollution-control equipment for corporations. Or the ministry of finance may provide tax breaks to corporations that promise to meet certain environmental goals. Whatever the case, the structure and organization of the state flows in a very direct way from the interaction and tension between capitalism and democracy.

Federalism

A federal system of government is one in which the constitutional authority to make laws is divided between a national government and some number of regional governments. Neither the national government acting alone, nor the regional governments acting together, have the authority to alter the power of the other level of government. They are coordinate and equal in their own constitutional spheres. Where there is a dispute between the levels of government, the courts are called upon to adjudicate. According to K.C. Wheare, the great British authority on federalism, "federal government exists... when the powers of government for a community are divided substantially according to the principle that there is a single independent authority for the whole area in respect of some matters and that there are independent regional authorities for other matters, each set of authorities being co-ordinate with and not subordinate to the others within its own prescribed sphere."[3]

What does this mean in the Canadian context? Simply that we have a national government as well as 10 provincial governments. Beyond this obvious point, though, lies a range of complex issues, problems and opportunities that affect the public administration in Canada in a myriad of ways.

In the Canadian federal system, power is divided between the two levels of government through the Constitution. Section 91 lists most of the federal government's powers, and section 92 lists most of the provincial governments' powers. Therefore, the structures and organization of both levels of government are shaped by their respective responsibilities and the nature of the relationship between the two levels of government. For example, in section 91.15, the Constitution confers the power to enact laws in the area of "Banking, Incorporation of Banks, and the Issue of Paper Money" exclusively to the federal government. Therefore it would make little sense, and indeed would be in violation of the Constitution, for the provinces to create a department to pass laws or create programs in this area.

Complicating this issue, though, is the fact that the language of much of the Constitution is ambiguous. This, coupled with the overlapping nature of many issues confronting modern governments, means that often both levels of government set up administrative organizations (e.g., departments, regulatory bodies, Crown corporations, etc.) in the same area of jurisdiction. For instance, even though the Constitution stipulates that health care is a provincial responsibility, there is a federal Ministry of Health as well as provincial ministries of health. While this may at first appear to contradict the constitutional division of powers, it in fact reflects the reality that the federal system is flexible. In this case, the federal government lacks jurisdictional authority over health care. But it alone has the fiscal resources to support such an expensive policy area. And in federalism, it is said that the golden rule always prevails: He who has the gold makes the rules. In constitutional terms, this is derived from the fact that the national government has what is called the "spending power" in its arsenal. Although not listed anywhere in the formal written Constitution, the spending power is nonetheless the convention that if the federal government offers to spend money in an area of provincial jurisdiction to set up a program or enact a policy, the provinces generally acquiesce.

An important irony shapes the nature of the Canadian federal system. In 1867, the Fathers of Confederation gave most powers over issues such as education, health and social policy to the provincial level of government. In the context of the times, these were relatively unimportant areas in which governments were only minimally involved. Furthermore, the Fathers of Confederation gave most of the powers to raise and spend money to the federal level of government, in the interests of creating a national economic and social union. The result is that today, the provinces are constitutionally responsible for the most expensive policy areas, but lack the fiscal capacity to pay for them. The federal government, on the other hand, has tremendous fiscal resources at its disposal, but lacks the constitutional jurisdiction to enact policies in the most expensive policy areas.

The ongoing search for ways around this basic dilemma is at the root of structural and organizational reform for both levels of government where relations with each other are concerned. As a result, an elaborate network of intergovernmental institutions has emerged.[4] Bureaucrats and ministers from both levels of government regularly meet to discuss and shape policy across the whole range of issues confronting governments today. So entrenched is the network of intergovernmental committees and other bodies that, argues political scientist Richard Simeon, a system of federal-provincial diplomacy has emerged.[5] By the 1960s, meetings of federal and provincial ministers and their expert advisers became so numerous that they were supplanting legislatures as the primary area of Canadian policy-making, according to political scientist Peter Russell.[6] For instance, the federal government has long had a permanent secretariat to deal with federal-provincial issues. And one by one the provinces have established their own ministries of intergovernmental affairs as well.

As you can see from this brief review, federalism is an important factor in shaping the type and number of organizational units and structures in Canadian public administration. The constitutional division of powers, constitutional conventions, and other factors play an important role in determining the responsibilities of each level of government. Increased interaction over time has seen a complex and elaborate machinery of institutions develop to facilitate policy-making in areas where both the federal and provincial governments have a stake. This, in turn, helps determine the structures and organization of government within each level.

Cabinet-Parliamentary Government

The third major part of the framework of Canadian public administration is cabinet-parliamentary government. To place this in context, look at Figure 5.1, which outlines the major branches of the Canadian government.

The Canadian governmental system is divided into three branches. The **executive branch** consists of the monarch, the governor general and the Cabinet (which includes the prime minister). The bureaucracy is considered a part of the executive as well, in that it administers the programs devised by the executive and tenders advice on the formulation of those programs. The **legislative branch** consists of Parliament, which in turn is divided into a lower elected chamber called the House of Commons and an appointed upper chamber called the Senate. Finally, the **judicial branch** consists of the Supreme Court and all the courts and judges below it in the federal and provincial court systems.

FIGURE 5.1   Basic Institutions of Canadian Government

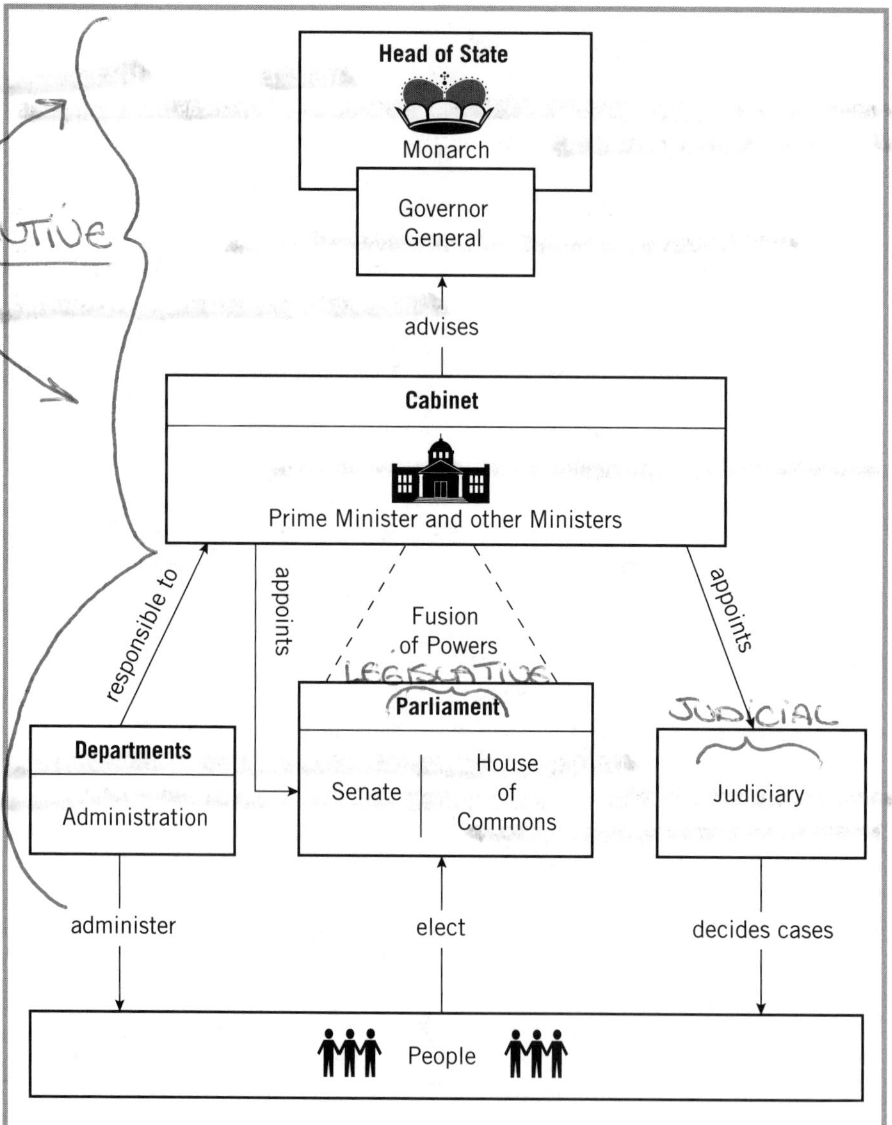

EXECUTIVE

Head of State

Monarch

Governor
General

advises

Cabinet

Prime Minister and other Ministers

responsible to

appoints

Fusion
of Powers

LEGISLATIVE

Parliament

Departments

Administration

Senate | House
of
Commons

appoints

JUDICIAL

Judiciary

administer

elect

decides cases

People

Source: James John Guy, *People Politics and Government: A Canadian Perspective*, Fourth Edition. (Scarborough: Prentice Hall, 1998): 142.

There are two main features of cabinet-parliamentary government with which you need to familiarize yourself. The first is the nature of the relationship between the various branches of the government. The second, related feature is that the Constitution tells us that certain offices are conferred with tremendous powers, but practice reveals that those offices do not actually exercise those powers. In effect, to understand the nature of the relationship between the branches of government, you need to understand the "myth and reality" of cabinet-parliamentary government. Another way to conceive of this is to consider the "formal" powers of each branch of government and compare those to the "political" powers each wields.

To begin with, the "myth" asserts that tremendous powers are accorded by the Constitution to the monarch as the formal head of state. In Canada, the monarch is represented by the governor general, who has the power on behalf of the monarch to decide which political party will be asked to form the government, when Parliament will be dissolved and when a new election will be called, and the right to confer royal assent upon all federal and provincial legislation. In reality, all of these powers are almost completely symbolic. Because of the historical evolution of democratic government, the role and position of the nonelected monarch and governor general have become essentially ceremonial.

So, in reality, who gets to exercise the formidable powers cited in the Constitution as the prerogative of the monarch? The answer: another part of the executive branch of government, the **Privy Council**, which is an advisory body. This is a term with which you might not be familiar, since it is hardly ever used anymore. Strictly speaking, it consists of all current and former ministers of the Crown; more commonly it is known nowadays as the **Cabinet**. Only current members of the Cabinet exercise the powers spelled out in the Constitution, and they are usually members of the House of Commons selected by the prime minister, who heads the Cabinet. Indeed, so much power has come to be vested in the prime minister and the Cabinet that it is common to refer to the Canadian system as executive-dominated.[7]

Why does the Constitution tell us that power is held in one place, while in reality it is exercised somewhere else? Partly because of **constitutional convention**. This is the idea of habit or tradition; that is, when things have been done a certain way for a long period of time, it becomes a convention, which can be every bit as important as the actual written Constitution. The other reason is the doctrine of **responsible government**. This is the principle that states that the government of the day (as represented by the Cabinet) must explain itself and be accountable to the elected representative of the people. For this to take place, there must be some mechanism by which power can be removed from the hands of the government by the people's representatives. This point reflects the doctrine that in order to govern, the prime minister and Cabinet must have the confidence of the elected House of Commons. If a government loses that confidence (i.e., loses the support of the majority of members of the House), it loses the right to govern, and can therefore be removed from power. Thus the doctrine of responsible government has evolved to ensure that those who actually hold and exercise power (in the Cabinet) can be held accountable in the exercise of that power (by Parliament).

The other important thing to note here in the relationship between the executive and legislative branch is the question of where the Cabinet comes from. Since its members are also members of the House of Commons, we talk about a fusion of powers in the Canadian system. This differs from the American system, for instance, where there is a separation of powers. In the United States, the president (the executive branch) is not a member of Congress (the legislative branch). He does not sit there, nor does he require the support of a majority of its members to retain power. This is a crucial difference, and needs to be fully understood to comprehend the fusion of powers in the Canadian system that facilitates accountability, in that the prime minister and Cabinet must participate every day in Question Period and other activities of the House of Commons. They must explain their policies and actions (or inaction) on a daily basis to their opponents and to the country as a whole. This is the heart of cabinet-parliamentary government.

You should be able to infer from these comments that the second branch of government—the legislative branch—plays a significant role in the theory of responsible government. It is here in Parliament, and particularly in the House of Commons within Parliament, that the executive is held to account. Some people mistake this power for the power to make laws. The truth about the legislative branch is that it is a law-*passing*, rather than a law-*making*, body. The main decisions about what laws the government seeks to introduce are made in Cabinet, and indeed in almost all cases it is Cabinet ministers who introduce legislation into Parliament for debate and approval. Ordinary members of Parliament in the governing party who are not in the Cabinet (called *backbenchers*) and opposition party members of Parliament have a circumscribed role in law-making. This is because of the doctrine of party discipline, which suggests party members always vote according to the instructions of their leaders. This is necessary to ensure that Cabinet can have its legislative desires realized, since the government, to pass laws, must have the support of the majority in the House of Commons.

The third branch of Canadian government is the judicial branch which, unlike in some other countries, is composed of appointed rather than elected officials. The judges and courts that make up this part of government are called upon to act as arbiters in the event of disputes between the other branches of government, between the two levels of government, and between citizens and government. Where constitutional law is concerned, the judicial branch mediates two types of disputes. The first are disputes related to the division of powers in the Constitution, which sets out the powers and responsibilities of the federal and provincial governments. If one or the other level of government passes a law that infringes on the jurisdiction of the other, a court action can be initiated to see if the law is *intra vires* (constitutional) or *ultra vires* (unconstitutional). The other type of constitutional law the judicial branch deals with relates to the relationship of government and citizens. When citizens feel their rights have been infringed or denied, they may appeal to the courts to rule whether a government's actions or law has violated the *Charter of Rights and Freedoms*. The *Charter*, added to the Constitution in 1982, provides a list of rights that governments may not infringe when they pass laws.

In addition to constitutional law, the judicial branch is also concerned with administrative law. This entails making sure that the administrative processes, rules, and regulations of policy are followed. This essentially means ensuring that the administrators conform to the law, that they do not transgress the law in carrying out their duties, and that there are penalties assigned if they do. The courts are the principle agency through which controls over the administrative process are exercised.[8] The courts may examine three aspects of the administrative process.

First, they may consider the validity of the way in which power was delegated to an administrative unit by the legislature. Here the courts are looking to make sure that the delegation of power does not violate the principles of law, including the Constitution, and that there has not been an inappropriate or excessive delegation of power. Second, the courts may look into the rule-making process to ensure that the administrative body has not exceeded the powers granted to it in the making of rules and procedures. Finally, the courts may investigate whether the administrative body has applied the rules with which it is empowered in a fair and consistent manner to individual citizens.

The hallmark of the relationship between the judicial branch and the other two branches is that the judicial branch is regarded as independent of the control of the other two branches. It is meant to be far removed from the taint of political interference or partisanship. The principle of noninterference in judicial affairs is reflected in the fact that individual judges have complete liberty to hear and decide any cases that come before them. How do we know how important this principle is? Consider the number of times Cabinet ministers have been forced to resign their positions because of the reality, or even the perception, that they have interfered with a member of the judiciary. This was the downfall of Cabinet ministers Francis Fox in the Trudeau government, Jean Charest in the Mulroney administration, and several others over the course of Canadian history.

In summary, you should now have a basic understanding of the importance of capitalist-democracy, federalism, and cabinet-parliamentary government for public administration in Canada. All three are important as the framework within which administering the public's affairs takes place. To illustrate their importance, try to conceive of a Canada in which business interests and property rights are not preeminent in influencing public policy. For instance, what would the organization of public administration look like if the state, rather than private interests, owned everything? Or consider what Canada would look like with a unitary system of government. What would be different if there were no provincial governments? What if there were no division of powers between two levels of government in the constitution to worry about? Now think about a government without a cabinet-parliamentary form. Imagine, for instance, that power had not devolved through historical practice and convention into the hands of the Cabinet held accountable by the elected representatives of the people, but had instead been retained in the hands of the monarch. How different would the provision of services and the formulation, implementation and evaluation of public policy be?

Now imagine that it is July 1, 1867. Prime Minister Sir John A. Macdonald invites you into his office to tell you that he has an important task for you. You are to organize the government of the new Dominion of Canada by providing him with a plan for the structure and responsibilities of his new government. What would that government look like? How many and which ministries and departments would be needed to serve the needs of Canadians in the mid- to late-1800s? What would the composition of Macdonald's new government be?

Flash ahead to the year 2005. The new prime minister has invited you into her office with the same assignment Macdonald gave you. Would the government you now design look the same as the earlier one? What would be different? Why? What factors did you take into account as you thought about how government would be designed in each of the two eras?

Let's suppose that the first principle you settled on was that the organization of government should allow for the most efficient provision of services possible. Presumably you would opt for a streamlined model of government, with as few departments as possible. This requires you to think very precisely about what exactly government should do, i.e., what activities it should engage in and what services it should provide. You might start, for instance, by noting the obvious ones: you need structures that serve the interests of the main actors in a capitalist democracy, that respond to the opportunities and constraints of a federal system, and that respond to the rules and processes of cabinet-parliamentary government.

Within these parameters, you must ask what government is to be responsible for. The safety and defence of the nation might be a starting point. Therefore, you would want to create an army, and a department of defence to run it. Governments are also responsible for dealing with foreign countries, so you would need a department of foreign affairs. Beyond these two, what else does government need to do? Communications and transportation are important services, and therefore you might consider creating a post office and a department of transportation. There ought to be a department responsible for coordinating the government's spending and revenues, so a finance ministry seems like a logical choice.

We could continue adding to this list in a number of other areas too. But keep in mind that each time you add a department, agency, board commission or other government body, you increase the complexity of governing and thereby potentially decrease its efficiency.

But where do you draw the line? What interests in society need to be served? When considering a country like Canada, there are certain obvious features that need to be taken into consideration when designing a government: regionalism, class, language, gender, ethnicity, economic factors (business, labour, popular sector), geography, climate, and so on. At some point, you will also need to think about how to coordinate the various organizations that you have created within the government to ensure that there is no overlap of duties, and that money is being raised and spent in the most propitious manner. So you need to construct some "watchdog" organizations, adding another layer of complexity to the scheme you have designed.

While speculating in this manner is an interesting intellectual exercise, the fact is that capitalist democracy, federalism and cabinet-parliamentary government prevail in the real world of Canadian public administration. In some ways, the basic conundrum of making a society run smoothly can be expressed this way: the pursuit of common goals requires organization. Within the bounds of capitalist democracy, federalism and cabinet-parliamentary government, we have a variety of structures and organizations designed to facilitate the public's business.

To illustrate, let us now focus on the actual organizational features of the federal government. The federal government in Canada employs more than 500 000 people working in about 400 different organizations. In addition, the provincial governments in Canada employ about 650 000, while local governments employ another 330 000. This should give you some sense of the complexity and size of the public sector. For now, we will focus only on the organization of the federal government. The structure of the federal government is divided into three broad components: departments, regulatory agencies, and Crown corporations. Before considering each specifically, we will provide a brief overview of political-administrative relationships in general.

Political-Administrative Relationships

Let us return here to a concept we introduced in Chapter 1: the politics-administration dichotomy. You will recall that this is the principle that insists that in the organization of government, there is a division between the elected officials and the appointed ones. The elected officials (the politicians) are the key decision-makers because, as the theory of representative government tells us, they represent the people. They are elected to govern on behalf of the citizenry. The appointed officials—the bureaucrats or civil servants—are there to take orders and assist the politicians in the formulation, implementation and evaluation of the government's policies.

But, as we also noted in Chapter 1, this relationship does not always work the way the theory suggests. Politicians run for public office as members of political parties. But ask yourself this: Does it really matter which party wins office in an election? Doesn't the ongoing, professional bureaucracy march to the beat of its own drummer, regardless of which party wins elections? Sometimes it seems like this is the case. For instance, the Chrétien Liberals campaigned in the 1993 federal election against the dreaded Goods and Services Tax and the North American Free Trade Agreement, promising to repeal both pieces of legislation passed by the earlier Conservative government. Yet once in power, the Liberals kept both. Is it possible that the bureaucrats within government convinced the new ruling party to keep both policies? If so, what does this suggest about the politics-administration dichotomy?

At various times in history, the alarm has been raised that the public interest, as represented by the elected officials, has been sacrificed to the self-interest of bureaucrats and their organizations. The fear of "rule by officials" is often cited in connection with bureaucracies that appear to be too powerful. This raises questions about the goals and values that bureaucrats may have. After all, the traditional view is that bureaucrats are supposed to be concerned with the means by which government accomplishes its goals—not the ends that society aims for. In recent years, though, there has been a growing recognition that the values bureaucrats have as individuals should be expressly acknowledged, and that they should use those values to guide them in their actions. But this brings us back to the age-old problem of accountability. How can bureaucrats, who are not elected, be held accountable for their actions? What if bureaucrats, guided by their own personal value systems, take actions that contradict official rules or procedures?

Imagine yourself in this position: You are a frontline worker in a government employment office. The rules say that each and every applicant for a job must be treated in exactly the same manner. Over time, you have gotten to know the case of one hard-luck individual who has just about used up his employment insurance benefits, who has a young family to care for, and is about to lose his apartment. His search for a job has been futile. One day, you are contacted by an employer who needs someone immediately. Your hard-luck case meets all the qualifications. But the rules say that you must post the job so that everyone has a fair chance to apply, and that you can only send the employer a maximum of three applicants. Your hard-luck case has just been in to see you before you learned of this new job. What do you do if your value system says that this person should be given first crack at the job, but the rules say that the job must be processed in the usual manner, even if it means the individual concerned will have virtually no opportunity to apply?

If you follow your own value system, you contribute to the concern that powerful bureaucracies acting in their own interests can actually undermine democracy, since you are accountable to no one in this example but your own conscience. You will recall that some of the theorists of public administration, such as Marx (and others), raised just this issue. But if you follow the prescribed rules, an individual may suffer dire consequences.

Think about it this way. Governments are involved in making countless choices about what policies to enact. This necessarily involves making compromises between competing groups and individuals in societies, since not everyone is going to get all of what they want all of the time. It is the people's representatives who theoretically make the choices about whose interests are to be satisfied, since they have the legitimacy to exert authority in democratic societies. And if the people do not like the decisions made by their representatives, they can replace those representatives in the next election with a more agreeable group. Elections are the mechanisms by which governments are held to account for their actions (or inactions) by the citizens. But what if the function of compromising is tainted by the fact that those responsible for enacting the compromises bring their own narrow self-interest to the process? What if, instead of faithfully serving the government of the day in a nonpartisan manner regardless of which party is in power, the bureaucracy really only serves its own interests? Clearly the democratic process would be undermined.

What this reflects is the underlying tension between bureaucracy and democracy that is a recurrent theme in public administration. It is one that has been wrestled with by theorists and practitioners since the first bureaucracy appeared. Clearly there are no easy answers to the dilemmas raised by these tensions. Perhaps at best all we can hope is that the structures and organizations of government are constructed to minimize the inherent limitations, and to facilitate the efficient and democratic functioning of government.

Departmental Organizations

About half the employees who work in the federal public service work directly or indirectly in **departments** (also referred to as **ministries**). These are **statutory bodies**; that is, they are created by law passed by Parliament. The head of each department is the **minister**, who is appointed by the prime minister. The prime minister and the other ministers together constitute the Cabinet and are responsible individually for their departments and collectively for the actions of the government as a whole.

The convention exists that the prime minister will always select Cabinet ministers from individuals who sit in Parliament. This means that both senators and members of Parliament are eligible to become ministers; in reality, the prime minister virtually always limits his or her selection of ministers to those who are elected to the House of Commons rather than to the Senate. This is because senators are appointed to the Senate (by the prime minister), and therefore have less legitimacy as representatives of the people.

This means, of course, that the talent that the prime minister can draw on ultimately depends on the composition of the House of Commons, which is determined by voters in elections. There is usually a strong correlation between the distribution of Cabinet seats and provincial population. Moreover, certain regional, linguistic and other constraints limit the prime minister's choices. For instance, a French-Canadian prime minister will usually select an English-Canadian to be deputy prime minister. A western Canadian is usually made minister of Agriculture, while a Maritimer or British Columbian is usually made minister of Fisheries.

There has been a gradual growth in the number of departments (and hence of Cabinet ministers) over time until recently in Canada (see Table 5.1). Sir John A. Macdonald got by in 1867 with 13 ministers, but since the 1970s the wholesale growth in government responsibilities has necessitated ever larger Cabinets. Brian Mulroney felt compelled to appoint 40 in 1984! Pierre Trudeau's largest Cabinet had 37 members, which was nine more than that of his predecessor, Lester Pearson. Joe Clark, who followed Trudeau, reduced the Cabinet to 29 members, the same number used by John Turner. Mulroney's successor, Kim Campbell, began the trend toward a reduced Cabinet with just 24 ministers, which has been followed by Jean Chrétien, who currently has 23 ministries (although he also maintains a large number of "Secretaries of State," which are like junior ministers).

The number of departments (and hence Cabinet ministers) is entirely at the discretion of the prime minister. She or he may decide, as well, which ministries are needed; that is to say, the prime minister decides if there should be a ministry of "this" or of "that," or indeed of both.

The federal government, under the *Financial Administration Act* and the *Public Service Employment Act,* defines departments and the other parts of government in terms of statutory lines of control and accountability according to financial and personnel criteria. More broadly, political scientist J.E. Hodgetts defines a department as an administrative unit consisting of one or more organizational components under the direct management and control of a minister of the Crown.[9] Departments provide services and administer programs either for the public or for other parts of the government. Personnel are mainly drawn from the Public Service Commission, which establishes merit-based hiring criteria and administers the hiring and firing process. Funding for each department comes from an annual appropriation act passed by Parliament as part of the government's overall budget.

One typology of departments divides them into three broad types of organizations (see Table 5.2).[10] First, and most commonly, there are the *vertical constituency*

TABLE 5.1   Government Departments, 1867 and 2002

Government Departments in 1867	Government Departments in 2002
Agriculture	**Government Departments**
Customs	Department of Agriculture and Agri-Food
Finance	Department of Canadian Heritage
Inland Revenue	Department of Citizenship and Immigration
Justice	Department of Environment Canada
Marine and Fisheries	Department of Fisheries and Oceans
Militia and Defence	Department of Foreign Affairs and International Trade
Post Office	Department of Health
Privy Council Office	Department of Human Resources Development
Public Works	Department of Indian Affairs and Northern Development
Receiver General	Department of Industry Canada
Secretary of State	Department of Justice Canada
Secretary of State for Provinces	Department of Labour
	Department of National Defence
	Department of Natural Resources
	Department of Public Works and Government Services Canada
	Department of Transport
	Department of Veterans Affairs
	Solicitor General of Canada

Central Agencies
Department of Finance
Prime Minister's Office
Privy Council Office
Treasury Board Secretariat

Special Agencies and Other Bodies
Atlantic Canada Opportunities Agency
Canada Customs and Revenue Agency (Formerly Revenue Canada)
Canadian International Development Agency
Economic Development Agency of Canada for the Regions of Quebec
Western Economic Diversification

Source: Updated for 2002 from Government of Canada's Privy Council Office Information Resources section online at http://www.pco-bcp.gc.ca/default.asp?Language=E&Page=home

TABLE 5.2   A Typology of Departments

Horizontal Policy Coordinative	Horizontal Administrative Coordinative	Vertical Constituency
Finance	Public Works and Government Services	Agriculture and Agri-Food
Foreign Affairs and International Trade		Canadian Heritage
Justice		Citizenship and Immigration
Privy Council Office		Environment
Treasury Board Secretariat		Fisheries and Oceans
		Health
		Human Resources Development
		Indian Affairs and Northern Development
		Industry
		Labour
		National Defence
		Natural Resources
		Solicitor General
		Transport
		Veterans' Affairs

[Handwritten margin notes: "central agencies"; "Provide services to other departments"; "① coordinate Policies & programs"; "② dev. P policy framework w/in which other gov't functions are carried out"; "Provide services directly to the public (link b/w gov't & citizens)"; "Vertical Constituency"]

departments. Their primary function is to provide services directly to the public (e.g., Health or Industry), or some particular segment or group thereof (e.g., Indian Affairs and Northern Development). They are described as *vertical* departments, since they represent direct links between citizens and the government.

These are typically the most visible and high-profile parts of the government, in terms of citizen awareness of how government affects their lives. They also tend to have the most personnel and largest budgets. But that does not imply that within government they are necessarily the most influential players. The Department of Health and the Department of Agriculture and Agri-Food fall into this category, for instance.

The second type of department is the *horizontal administrative coordinative* type. These are departments whose main role is to provide services to other departments rather than directly to the public. For instance the Department of Public Works and Government Services provides and coordinates a range of services, such as printing and purchasing, real estate and office space, for other departments.

The third type of department is the *horizontal policy coordinative* one, whose responsibilities include developing the broad policy framework within which other government functions are carried out. These departments also coordinate policies and programs across government. The Department of Finance is among the most important in this regard, along with other "central agencies" (described below). This group also includes the Department of Foreign Affairs as well as Justice. Each provides coordination and policy advice to other departments regarding external relations and legal issues respectively. Although usually small in size and budget, these are generally the key actors in terms of the overall coordination of government policy. They can intervene in the affairs of the other departments, for instance, in the interest of providing government policy that is coordinated across the entire structure of governing.

Not all departments are alike in organization or function. (See Table 5.3.) But we can generalize about the structure of departments to some extent. They are hierarchical bodies with the minister, as the political head, at the apex. Below the minister is the administrative head of the department, the deputy minister (who is discussed in more detail below). Below that are a number of deputy ministers, directors, managers and so on down the line. The problem with this type of structuring is that it is very difficult to know just how many subdivisions or units optimize both efficiency in decision-making and democracy in terms of accountability. While increased bureaucratization of government functions has been the response to the increased complexity of governing modern society, at some point bureaucracy becomes dysfunctional, as we saw in Chapter 2.

Just as too many departments overall can make the process of Cabinet decision-making too unwieldy (and as we have seen, there have been recent attempts by prime ministers to get by with smaller Cabinets), similarly too many internal subdivisions within departments can hamper their effective operation. The question of how many subdivisions to have is part of the span of control problem that confronts any bureaucratic structure. *Span of control* refers to the number of subordinates that report to one supervisor. Ideally, a balance must be reached between too narrow and too broad a span of control. In a narrow span of control, there are too many supervisors and the number of reporting levels is increased, thereby increasing the degree of red tape and impeding internal communications. In a broad span of control there are too few supervisors, and thus strain is placed on top management. As noted in Chapter 2, Luther Gulick was among the first to think systematically about this problem. "Just as the hand of man [sic] can span only a limited number of notes on the piano," he wrote, "so the mind and will of man can span but a limited number of immediate managerial contacts.... The limit of control is partly a matter of the limits of time and of energy. As a result the executive of any enterprise can personally direct only a few persons. He must depend upon these to direct others, and upon them in turn to direct still others, until the last man in the organization is reached."[11] (See Figure 5.2.)

There is no sure way of knowing what constitutes an acceptable span of control, since any of a number of factors can come into play in the functioning of an organization. For instance, the number and type of tasks to be performed, the compe-

FIGURE 5.2   Department of Foreign Affairs and International Trade

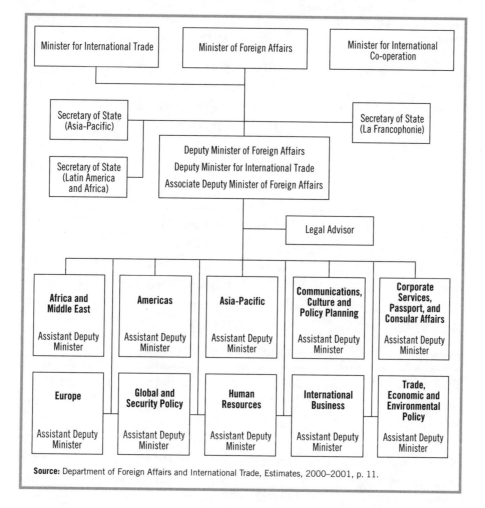

Source: Department of Foreign Affairs and International Trade, Estimates, 2000–2001, p. 11.

tence of individuals within the organization, the quality and amount of assistance available to the manager, and the geographical and physical setting (whether, for example, a department must have a number of regional offices, or can be centralized in Ottawa) can all be factors influencing the organizational design of departments.

These points can be illustrated by looking at the organizational chart of a typical federal government department. Figure 5.2 shows the organizational structure of the Department of Foreign Affairs and International Trade. Notice the hierarchical arrangement of offices, beginning with the ministers for each of International Trade, Foreign Affairs, and International Co-operation, where ultimate authority rests. Below the ministers are the deputy ministers and other top management, including an associate deputy minister. There are six functional branches, and four geographic branches. What type of span of control is evident here?

TABLE 5.3   Largest Departments in the Federal Public Service, 1912–1999

1912		1935	
Total employment	20,016	Total employment	40,709
Post Office	5,082	Post Office	10,780
Transport	4,235	National Revenue	5,374
Customs	3,214	Transport	4,678
Public Works	1,400	Public Works	3,620
Interior	1,270	Agriculture	2,280
1945		**1970**	
Total employment	115,908	Total employment	244,197
National Defence	28,137	Post Office	45,482
Post Office	13,770	National Defence	39,027
Finance	12,772	National Revenue	18,967
National Revenue	10,706	Transport	17,556
Veterans Affairs	7,364	RCMP	12,253
1985		**1999**	
Total person-years	260,049	Total employment	186,314
National Defence	37,018	Revenue Canada	43,216
Solicitor General (RCMP)	32,462	Human Resources Development	21,848
National Revenue	29,594	National Defence	18,644
Employment and Immigration	24,823	Correctional Service	12,232
Transport	22,976	Public Works and Government Services	11,418

Sources: Data for 1912 to 1970: (Leacy, 1983). Data for 1985 from Estimates. Data for 1999: (Treasury Board Secretariat, 1999). The Post Office became a Crown corporation in 1981 and was excluded from the public service count after that date. Before 1970 and after 1985, only RCMP administrative staff were included in the public service count.

Cited in Alasdair Roberts, "A Fragile State: Federal Public Administration in the Twentieth Century," in Christopher Dunn, ed. *The Handbook of Canadian Public Administration*, Toronto: Oxford University Press, 2002: 20.

A generic model of the general categories of offices in federal government departments would look like this: The deputy minister (DM) sits at the apex of a pyramidal hierarchy, with two or more assistant deputy ministers (ADMs) heading branches or bureaus of the department and reporting directly to the DM. Below the

ADMs are directorates or branches, each headed by a director-general or director. These directorates are in turn subdivided into divisions headed by directors or divisional chiefs, which are also subdivided into sections, regions, districts and areas. In general, this structure is used at both the federal and provincial levels, although different titles are sometimes used for roughly the same position in the hierarchy.

Central Agencies ~appoint of my acts in Cabinet.

Another way of thinking about government departments is to divide them into two categories in terms of their main functions. In this typology, some departments are simply referred to as *line departments,* which means they have direct responsibility for the delivery of goods and services to the people of Canada. These departments tend to consist of a large number of subunits and employ a large staff to deal with the public. The Department of Agriculture and Agri-Food, for instance, is a line department employing thousands of civil servants in a wide range of jobs.

Other departments are referred to as *central agencies,* which means that they are responsible for coordinating the policy actions and expenditures of the line departments. Their main purpose is to support the decision-making activities of Cabinet, which they do in a variety of ways.[12] For instance, they supply Cabinet with information and advice, and they communicate Cabinet decisions to other parts of the bureaucracy, to the public and to other governments. Central agencies ensure there is some consistency and harmony across various departments—in other words, that there is *horizontal coordination*—and that the overall spending habits of the departments fit with the revenue-raising capacity of the government as a whole. Until 1993, there were five central agencies in the federal government: the Finance Department; the Privy Council Office (PCO); the Prime Minister's Office (PMO); the Treasury Board Secretariat (TBS); and the Federal-Provincial Relations Office (FPRO). The latter central agency, however, has been folded into the PCO. Let us consider briefly the role of each central agency.

Department of Finance In many respects, this is the most powerful actor in the federal government. It plays a leading role in making economic policy, which contributes to its informal reputation as the centre of key economic decision-making in the government. Preparation and delivery of the government's revenue and expenditure budgets rest with this department, as does jurisdiction over taxation and trade and tariff policy. Moreover, the Finance Department manages federal borrowing on financial markets, and administers major federal transfers to provinces and territories. It also develops regulatory policy for the financial sector (for example, determining whether the big banks can merge), and represents Canada within international financial institutions. It provides the government with analysis and advice on the broad economic and financial affairs of the country.

To fulfill its mandate, the Finance Department monitors and researches the performance of the Canadian economy in all important aspects, from output and growth to employment and income to price stability and monetary policy to the impact of globalization, and so on. In addition, the Finance Department is in constant communication with the other departments of government to coordinate and harmonize all federal initiatives that have an impact on the economy. Created in 1867 to replace the old office of Inspector General, Finance officials numbered 38. The department grew as large as 6000, but currently employs about 600 civil servants. It is generally conceded that the best and the brightest in the public service aspire to work in this powerful central agency.

Concerns expressed by the Finance Department about the economic health of the country usually become the concerns of other departments as well. In other words, Finance often sets the tone for the rest of government in terms of whether new policies and programs can be launched, or whether there will be cutbacks and restraint. Initiatives from other departments in government generally require the support of Finance if they are to go ahead, since Finance controls the purse strings.

Treasury Board Secretariat The Treasury Board Secretariat (TBS) is the administrative arm of the Treasury Board, which is a Cabinet committee. The TBS has a mandate to support the Treasury Board as a committee of ministers, and to fulfill certain statutory (i.e., legal) responsibilities. Indeed, among the Cabinet committees, only the Treasury Board has a statutory basis. TBS supports the Treasury Board by providing advice on policies, directives, regulations and program expenditure proposals regarding the management of the government's financial, human and material resources (e.g., lands and buildings). TBS also supports the Treasury Board in its role as the general manager and employer of the public service. It is "management" where employee relations are concerned within government. In other words, it is the agency that assumes the interest of employer in collective bargaining and personnel issues within government. But not only is TBS the lead agency in making personnel policy; it is also the key actor in administrative policy within the government. To this end, it oversees departmental audits, and ensures that accounting practices and standards are uniformly adhered to across the government.

TBS is also responsible to a large degree for the evaluation of policy and particular programs. TBS assists the Cabinet by providing information about departmental expenditures and the financial and personnel resources required by each department. And TBS also prepares the main estimates for the government, which are the detailed spending plans that the government introduces each year in the House of Commons.

The Privy Council Office As an organizational body, the Cabinet requires support to function on an ongoing, day-to-day basis. This support primarily comes from the Privy Council Office (PCO), which acts essentially as the Cabinet's secretariat (see Figure 5.3). The PCO reports directly to the Prime Minister, and is headed by the Clerk of the Privy Council and Secretary to the Cabinet, which is the highest position in the bureaucracy (see Box 5-1). The Clerk and the PCO are intimately involved in the sensitive process of Cabinet decision-making, and particularly in strategic planning and the formulation of policy. The PCO is both the Cabinet secretariat and the prime minister's source of public service advice across the entire spectrum of policy questions and operational issues that confront the government. This includes matters relating to the management of federal-provincial relations and constitutional issues.

Box 5-1

Clerk of the Privy Council and Secretary to the Cabinet

This is the most senior public servant in the government. In his or her role supporting the prime minister, the clerk has three primary responsibilities:

➤ as the prime minister's deputy minister, provides advice and support to the prime minister on a full range of responsibilities as head of government, including management of the federation;

➤ as the secretary to the Cabinet, provides support and advice to the ministry as a whole, and oversees the provision of policy and secretariat support to Cabinet and Cabinet committees;

➤ as the head of the Public Service, is responsible for the quality of expert, professional and nonpartisan advice provided by the Public Service to the prime minister, the ministry and to all Canadians.

The PCO also provides support to the deputy prime minister, government leaders in the House of Commons and the Senate, the president of the Privy Council and minister of Intergovernmental Affairs, as well as the minister designated as the federal interlocutor for Métis and nonstatus Indians.

The Prime Minister's Office The Prime Minister's Office (PMO) stands apart from the other central agencies in at least one key regard. It is staffed by partisan supporters of the government in power, rather than by nonpartisan public servants. This is the prime minister's personal staff (see Figure 5.4). As such, the PMO performs functions such as dealing with the prime minister's voluminous correspondence; speech writing; scheduling the prime minister's time and appearances; dealing with media relations; liaising with other ministers, the government caucus and party; and providing advice on appointments and policy. The PMO is headed by a chief of staff, who has ongoing daily contact with the prime minister. The PMO drafts the annual Speech from the Throne, which is the statement of the government's legislative and policy intentions for the coming year.

To a large extent, the success or failure of any given prime minister rides on the quality of advice he or she gets from the PMO. Not surprisingly, the style of the prime minister is reflected in the role and functioning of the PMO. Pierre Trudeau was the first prime minister to really expand the size and role of the PMO, which previously had been a relatively small organization in government. Today it is an extremely influential body, having grown in size and influence ever since.

Taken together, these four central agencies play a vital series of coordinating and supportive roles for the government. They are powerful and important actors in the overall structure. An understanding of their place in the organization of the Canadian government is vital to understanding public administration.

FIGURE 5.3   Basic Privy Council Office Structure Under Jean Chrétien

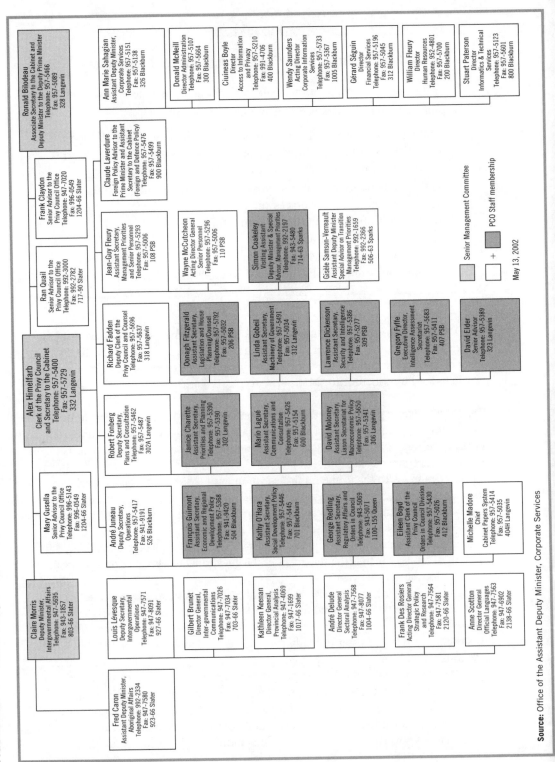

Source: Office of the Assistant Deputy Minister, Corporate Services

FIGURE 5.4   The Prime Minister's Office (Basic Form)

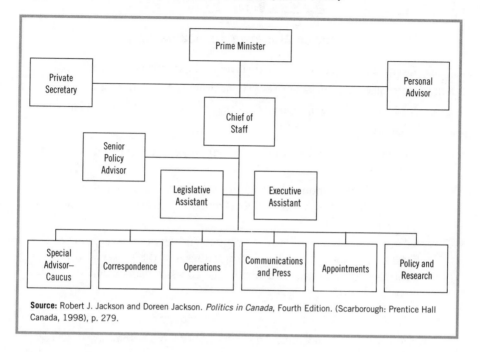

Source: Robert J. Jackson and Doreen Jackson. *Politics in Canada*, Fourth Edition. (Scarborough: Prentice Hall Canada, 1998), p. 279.

Alternative Service Delivery

Apart from the traditional structures reviewed above, governments have been re-sorting to a variety of new innovations to provide services to Canadians (see Box 5-2). These so-called **"alternative service delivery"** (ASD) arrangements come in a number of packages. They include: bodies that have been created by restruc-turing existing departments and institutions within government; partnering with actors in other departments within government, with other governments or out-side government altogether; and structures outside government entirely. According to the Treasury Board Secretariat, "While departments continue to play an im-portant role in service delivery, a growing need for flexibility, interdependence and innovation has produced an increasing diversity of organizational forms and service delivery arrangements to provide more responsive service to Canadians."[13]

The motivations behind ASD are varied. They include the desire to offer a more "citizen-centred" approach to service provision, in response to the growing disillusionment with government evident in the broader society. They also are a re-sult of the drive toward "less government" which has been predominant in recent years. In addition, they are seen as potential cost-saving innovations in many cases. Moreover, the rigidities in existing institutions have increasingly come to be seen as impediments to service delivery, and it is thought that more flexible alternatives to departments might address this problem. In particular, there is the desire to break down the "silo mentality" in which different government departments exist in isolation from each other, resulting in unnecessary duplication of activities

Box 5-2

Policy on Alterative Service Delivery

The Government of Canada constantly reviews its programs and services to identify opportunities to improve services to Canadians. In this context the Government supports innovative organizational arrangements, which are driven and guided by its commitment to:

➤ achieve measurable results in improving citizen-centred service to Canadians;

➤ ensure value for money by creating efficiencies and establishing partnerships that can enhance the government's delivery of responsive programs and services;

➤ balance the drive for innovative program and service delivery, on the one hand, and respect for public sector values and the preservation of the public service of Canada as a vibrant and cohesive national institution, on the other hand.

Alternative Service Delivery entails the pursuit of new and appropriate organizational forms and arrangements, including partnerships with other levels of government and other sectors, in order to improve the delivery of programs and services. Innovative organizational arrangements for delivering government programs and services can result in:

➤ more cost-effective, responsive delivery to Canadian citizens;

➤ changes in organizational culture and management practices so that the organization performs more effectively; and

➤ the granting of greater authority to managers, thus moving decision-making closer to the point of delivery, to the communities served and to Canadian citizens.

A federal public sector that is committed to championing innovation through a wide range of promising avenues is key to the continuing success of the Canadian experience with alternative service delivery. These avenues include:

➤ innovative organizational arrangements and transformations within the Government of Canada;

➤ horizontal integration of service delivery between federal departments and agencies;

➤ vertical integration of service between governments, as they share the responsibility of serving citizens; and

➤ strategic alliances and partnerships with the private sector and with volunteer and not-for-profit organizations.

Source: Canada, Treasury Board Secretariat, "Policy on Alternative Service Delivery," (April 1, 2002): 1–2.

FIGURE 5.5   **Opportunities for Program Delivery Alternatives**

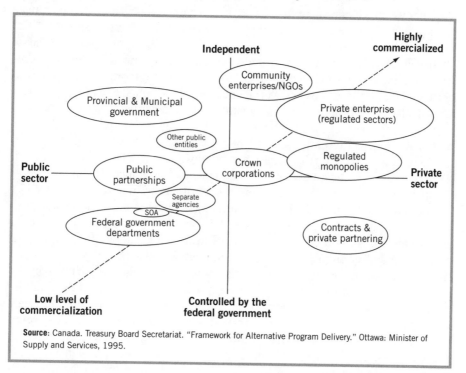

Source: Canada. Treasury Board Secretariat. "Framework for Alternative Program Delivery." Ottawa: Minister of Supply and Services, 1995.

and frustration for citizens trying to find information across departments which never speak to or interact with one another. This is directly related to the trend toward "horizontality" in management, wherein attempts are made to cut across traditional boundaries (be they departmental, programmatic, issue-based, etc.) to more fully integrate and rationalize service delivery. ASD promotes horizontality by requiring different institutional actors to learn to work together in new ways. Finally, ASD mechanisms are often designed to accommodate the growing desire for greater citizen participation in governance. They provide interested actors with the "hands-on" opportunity to shape, create and implement programs in ways traditional structures cannot or will not.

The scope of ASD is impressive[14] (see Figure 5.5). It can include special operating agencies (SOAs), service agencies, and Crown corporations within its purview. But it also includes a variety of partnership arrangements and the devolution of programs and services to other governments. It sometimes involves the commercialization of services, such that they are run in a more "business-like" fashion than government is typically able to achieve. This might take the form of innovations such as employee takeovers, contracting out, and the application of user fees. In addition, outright privatization of government services is an option. In short, the last decades of the 20th century have seen a plethora of new institutions arise alongside the traditional line department and central agency model.[15]

Ministerial Responsibility

Whether we are talking about line department, central agency or ASD, the ultimate responsibility for what government does or does not do rests with the political head of the institution, namely the minister. As a member of Cabinet, she is responsible for all the official acts of the bureaucrats under her supervision. This is known as the doctrine of ministerial responsibility, which is an extremely important concept in understanding how the actions of government are held accountable to the people. This is particularly significant when you remember that a department can employ thousands of people and be responsible for spending millions of dollars of taxpayers' money. Reinforcing this principle is another: collective ministerial responsibility. This is the convention that says that ministers must always show solidarity with their colleagues in Cabinet. Once a decision has been taken in a Cabinet meeting, the whole Cabinet supports it publicly. These concepts are discussed in detail in Chapter 12.

But how can an individual minister heading up a department employing thousands of people, and spending millions of dollars, really be held responsible for everything that goes on in that department? Realistically and logistically, it is impossible for a given minister to know the intimate details of the thousands of decisions that are taken every year within his department, let alone those taken by the government as a whole. Still, there is the expectation that the principle of ministerial responsibility will be observed. Thus, for example, during the Mulroney years, John Fraser, then minister of Fisheries, resigned when it was discovered that officials in his department had allowed tainted tuna to be sold to the public in supermarkets. Obviously Fraser would have had no personal knowledge that this was being done. But as the minister responsible for the department, he was compelled to accept responsibility. In this way, a link was established that saw the bureaucracy connected to the political realm through the minister. Political scientists Jackson and Jackson put it this way:

The Prime Minister appoints members of the Cabinet to assume responsibility for particular ministries or portfolios, and their associated departments, commissions, boards and corporations. Ministers are constitutionally responsible for all of the operations of their departments. Thus, legally, it is ministers who are assigned the powers and duties to be exercised by their departments. Departmental officials, on the other hand, are given scant attention in the law and are responsible exclusively to their ministers, not to Parliament. They are supposed to be non-partisan, objective and anonymous—shielded from the glare of public attention and from the partisan political arena of Parliament by their minister—in order to safeguard their neutrality and ensure their ability to serve faithfully whichever government is in power. In the event of a serious error in the formulation or administration of policy within a department, convention dictates that the minister, rather than officials, be held responsible to Parliament; and if the minister cannot account for the failures to the satisfaction of Parliament, then convention dictates that the minister should resign.[16]

The Deputy Minister

While the minister is the political head of a department, the administrative head is the **deputy minister** (DM). This is the senior-most public servant, an extremely powerful and influential post in the workings of government. DMs receive their positions "at the pleasure of the Prime Minister," which is to say that it is the prime minister who hires and fires them. (Most other personnel in departments are recruited through the Public Service Commission, which is like a giant human relations department for the government.)

What exactly is the nature of the relationship between a minister and his top bureaucratic advisor—the deputy minister? This is an important question. The popular British sitcom *Yes, Prime Minister* portrays a series of often hilarious episodes in which the senior advisor to the prime minister is engaged in a constant game of trying to control and shape the prime minister's decisions. The series portrays the clash between the "political will and the administrative won't." Interestingly, the writers for the series were former bureaucrats, and claim their inspiration came from real-life examples within the British government.

In the real world of governing, there are several factors that may make it difficult for a minister to resist the influence of her DM or other senior advisors. The experience of Flora MacDonald, former secretary of state for External Affairs in the Joe Clark government, points to this. A minister is typically pulled in several different directions at once. There are Cabinet responsibilities, party duties, attendance in the House of Commons, press conferences, constituency work, foreign travel, political brushfires, and countless other distractions. As to administration, invariably most ministers have little time to effectively concentrate on the day-to-day administrative needs of their departments. This must be left to the deputy minister and other senior bureaucratic staff. But MacDonald claimed that her senior staff went beyond simply tendering advice on the administration of the department she headed. MacDonald claimed that her senior advisors engaged in a concerted effort to impose their own agendas on both the running of the department and the development of policy. She felt that as a rookie Cabinet minister, she was at the mercy of the more experienced bureaucrats.[17]

Another view is provided by Mitchell Sharp, who was a bureaucrat in his early career, and later a Cabinet minister. He argued that top civil servants are powerful individuals in the machinery of government. After all, they hold their positions because they have demonstrated a high level of skill and ability in administrative matters. And while Sharp suggests that weak ministers may be susceptible to manipulation by crafty civil servants, he also argues that most of the time this is not the case. A government, he argues, cannot be run by amateurs, and so a trained and professional civil service is vital. But ministers must be able to determine what constitutes good advice from their bureaucratic advisors, and must be able to weed out sycophants who echo their superiors' views. Moreover, Sharp felt that a first-class nonpartisan civil service dedicated to the public interest was one of the hallmarks of parliamentary government that enabled elected "amateurs" to make the political decisions needed to govern effectively.[18]

There is also the issue of the longevity of ministers. Most serve for relatively short periods of time before being shuffled to another position in the Cabinet (or removed from Cabinet altogether). To ensure that there is some continuity in departments, DMs are not appointed by the ministers they serve. Rather, the prime minister is responsible for selecting and appointing them. The DM thereby has some measure of security, knowing that he will not lose his job if the minister changes. This is reinforced by the nonpartisanship of the DM. He is not a member or supporter of any political party, but rather serves the government of the day no matter who is in power. This is meant to ensure that the minister gets the best possible advice at all times, rather than advice tainted by political considerations. Thus, when the government changes hands, the senior bureaucrats retain their jobs, allowing for a measure of stability and continuity in the administration of government. Admittedly, though, this places the DM in a somewhat awkward position, sandwiched between the nonpolitical bureaucracy and the political minister.

Apart from the appointment question, there are other questions surrounding the DM. What exactly are her role and duties? And what is the relationship of the DM to other actors in the political-administrative structure?[19] At a general level, it is the primary duty of the DM to create the conditions under which the minister and prime minister can provide the best possible government. To this end, the DM plays a vital role in both the formulation and the implementation of policy. There are several important conventions that guide the DM in her role: neutrality, anonymity, the politics-administration dichotomy, and loyalty. Let us consider each in turn.

The convention of *neutrality* suggests that the DM is nonpartisan, as we noted above. He should be politically neutral in serving the minister, but this convention is often difficult to maintain. Political pressures swirl around the DM constantly. Political interaction occurs in almost all facets of his job, from dealing with Parliament and Cabinet, to meeting with interest groups and citizens, all of whom have some vested stake in policy matters. Moreover, while remaining officially nonpartisan, the DM must be sensitive to political developments, trends and issues. This is an extraordinarily difficult balancing act.

The second convention is that of *anonymity*. Can you name a Cabinet minister? Most people can. Can you name a deputy minister? Most of us would be hard-pressed to identify a single one at either level of government. Since it is the minister who is formally responsible for the actions of the government, it is the minister who must accept praise or blame for those polices. The DM toils anonymously in the shadows for two reasons. First, the DM is not elected by anyone, and therefore is not directly accountable to anyone other than the minister and the prime minister. Second, the DM must be free to provide frank and impartial advice in a private and confidential manner. In return, the DM is shielded from public attack by the minister, who rightly accepts public responsibility for the actions of the department.

This is part of the doctrine of ministerial responsibility. Having said this, it should be noted that this doctrine of anonymity has been eroding in recent years. Senior bureaucrats have been singled out and asked to explain their actions in public in a number of high-profile scandals. But overall, to retain anonymity the DM must renounce any desire for public recognition of his efforts, or personal identification with the government's policies.

The third convention relates to the *politics-administration dichotomy*. It is the duty of the minister to direct the bureaucracy, and of the DM to see to it that directions are executed faithfully. In reality, as we discussed earlier in Chapter 1, this is an artificial division of duties. The senior civil service is very much involved in both administration and policy formulation. Interestingly enough, though, the same cannot be said of the minister, who is so consumed by other duties that she is mainly concerned with formulation, but rarely concerned with the administration of the department.

Ironically, while the precepts of the politics-administration dichotomy are supposed to be followed, it is also expected that the DM will regularly provide policy advice to the minister. What does this policy advisory role cover? It entails initiating policy suggestions without seeking to usurp the decision-making role of the minister. In other words, the DM should be able to say, "The government ought to adopt policy X for all these reasons." But the minister ultimately says "yes" or "no" to this suggestion. Some have criticized this as providing the DM with "power without responsibility." Others have said that it is quite the opposite: "responsibility without power." Whichever view is correct, there is a fine line that DMs ought not to cross, between simply providing advice and making decisions.

Finally, there is the convention of *loyalty*. The DM must in all circumstances remain loyal to the minister in the interest of helping the minister to provide the best possible government. But the DM's loyalties conflict, making this a complicated problem. DMs have a loyalty to Parliament as well as to the policies their departments implement. And the DM has a loyalty to the profession of public servant. These various pressures may compel the DM to speak out against certain policies as a matter of conscience. But his position compels him to remain silent. For instance, when the Mike Harris government in Ontario began systematically dismantling many government programs and changing long-established policies, many senior bureaucrats were deeply troubled, and had to decide whether they could continue to serve the government of the day as neutral, faithful public servants. Many determined they could not, and in the first three years of the Harris government, more than half of the DMs left or were replaced.

The relationship of the DM to her staff is also an important consideration. As the head of the administration of the public service, the DM must set the example for the other bureaucrats. She must instill a sense of public service, an understanding of the power of bureaucracy, and a respect for what is most important in every department, program and policy: the rights of the citizen. The DM also has a responsibility to keep abreast of public reaction to government policies, and to have a staff that can evaluate when policies are working properly or not. Thus the DM must keep in close touch with her subordinates and be sensitive to their views.

In relation to the public, the DM typically must develop a good working relationship with the interest groups and citizens most directly affected by the policies of the government in a given area. The DM actively seeks out public opinion on these issues so as to be able to represent the most current views of the public to the minister in the development of policy. At the same time, the DM must be careful not to become captive to any one group or interest. To avoid this pitfall, good DMs constantly seek countervailing sources of information and advice. They talk not only to the proponents of a particular policy, but also to those affected by the policy. Independent advice is sought on various issues, often from disinterested parties such as academics. To effectively do their jobs, DMs canvass a range of views to get the best possible advice to tender to the minister.

A major job of the DM is to implant in the ministry an understanding and perspective of the broader social and economic trends in the land, and to effectively evaluate those trends in relation to the responsibilities and programs of the department. This means that besides administering the day-to-day minutiae, the DM must also be able to see the big picture of governing. She is responsible for understanding the long-term impacts of social and economic change, and anticipating when and where those changes will affect her department. This contrasts with the short-term view typical of the minister, whose main concern is the next election just over the horizon. The juxtaposition of these two views often creates tensions and difficulties within the relationship of the DM and minister that a skillful and sensitive DM must nonetheless work around.

The DM has some particular administrative responsibilities in the area of personnel and finance. He must deal with matters of personnel, such as changes in the collective agreement, employment equity, bilingualism in the public service, and so on. As well, the DM is responsible for the overall preparation of departmental expenditure budgets. In these duties, the DM must be responsible to other actors in government besides his minister. Where personnel decisions are concerned, the DM must answer to the Public Service Commission and the Treasury Board. Regarding financial matters, the Ministry of Finance as well as the Treasury Board must be accommodated.

Clearly, the role of the DM is a demanding and complex one that requires an incredible amount of administrative management ability combined with a remarkable degree of political sophistication. The DM must constantly satisfy, at the same time, the demands of both his bureaucratic constituency and his political master. It is a remarkably sensitive balancing act, but one which must be maintained for a department to be successful in fulfilling its mandate.

Regulatory Agencies

Besides *making* policy, government is also in the business of *enforcing* policy. Enforcement can take many forms, the most common of which is regulation. According to the Economic Council of Canada, regulation is "the imposition of constraints, backed by government authority, that are intended to modify economic behaviour of individuals in the private sector significantly."[20] In other words, regulation is intended to ensure that the behaviour of private sector actors is in conformity with the desires of government. It involves modifying the behaviour of private sector actors through a number of possible mechanisms. For instance, the government may decide that the promotion of Canadian culture is a worthwhile goal, and craft a series of regulations to ensure that private sector broadcasters include a certain percentage of Canadian content on the airwaves. The Canadian Radio-television and Telecommunications Commission (CRTC) does exactly this.

Among their varied functions, **regulatory bodies** can influence private sector behaviour with respect to a range of things: prices, conditions and quality of service, contents of goods for sale, methods of production, and so on. Many regulatory agencies also have investigative powers and can undertake research and launch inquiries within their fields of competence. Some regulatory bodies are imbued with quasijudicial power. This means they can "judge specific cases involving the granting, denial, or removal of licences, the approval of rates or fares and the censuring of failure to comply with terms of licences."[21] The senior levels of regulatory bodies are staffed by individuals appointed by government, usually for five- or ten-year terms, often as patronage appointments. In general, they enjoy an arm's-length relationship with the department that oversees their activities, thus creating a climate of independence from direct political interference by the government of the day. With some exceptions, their members are not appointed by the Public Service Commission, nor are they employees of the Treasury Board. But accountability is maintained, in that regulatory bodies must submit their budgets to the Treasury Board for review, and present annual reports through the responsible minister to the House of Commons.

Regulation takes place in a range of areas. Besides radio, television and telecommunications cited above, the government also regulates matters as varied as atomic energy (Atomic Energy Control Board), labour relations (Canadian Labour Relations Board), old age pensions (Canadian Pension Commission), and many others. Regulatory agencies receive their powers—which are often considerable—and their mandates through legislation. While some regulations are actually laws that require enforcement by the police and judicial system, most are simply administrative directives managed on an ongoing basis by a specialized government body.

Political scientists Howlett and Ramesh point out that the nature of regulations varies depending on whether they are economic or social in nature:

Economic regulations control prices and the volume of production, or return on investment, or the entry into or exit of firms from an industry. Their objective is to correct perceived imbalances that may emerge as a result of the operation of market forces. Economic regulations have been the traditional form of regulation; their social counterparts are of more recent origin.

Social regulations refer to matters of health, safety and social practices such as discrimination of various sorts in employment. They have more to do with our physical and moral well-being than with our pocketbooks. Examples of social regulation include rules regarding consumer product safety, occupational hazards, water-related hazards, air pollution, noise pollution, discrimination on the basis of gender or ethnicity, and pornography. Environmental protection is a hybrid between economic and social regulation, because the problems usually have economic origins but their adverse effects are mostly social. Social regulations do not focus on any particular industry (for example banks or telecommunications), as do economic regulations, but on broader problems or functions such as pollution, safety or morality. Thus a social regulation might cut across several industries and come under the jurisdiction of several government agencies.[22]

Regulation can take many different forms. In some cases, regulation is directed at placing directed constraints on behaviour, leaving little or no discretion to the body concerned in the implementation of the regulations. In other cases, the government steps back from the regulatory processes somewhat and allows the private actors to self-regulate, sometimes through the adoption of voluntary codes of conduct.[23] This is the case, for instance, with the medical and legal professions, which are given substantial power to regulate their members and their activities. These powers are only limited where they contradict the broad guidelines provided in the government regulations. The government will choose this option in certain cases because it is often the least expensive form of regulation. It reduces administration costs for the government by passing them on to the profession concerned. In addition, it allows those with the most intimate knowledge of the activity being regulated to administer the rules. Governments have neither the time nor the inclination to enter the labyrinthine worlds of doctors and lawyers, and so are content to allow these (and other) groups to regulate themselves.

Why do governments use regulation rather than other administrative or organizational forms? First, it has frequently been argued that regulation was justified on the grounds of "public interest." This means that government intervention in the market is sometimes needed to correct market failures; that is, situations in which private sector actors cannot or will not act as effective regulatory instruments themselves. The most obvious case of market failure is monopoly. Regulation is justified in this case on the grounds that monopoly firms may earn excessive profits by exploiting consumers by charging excessive rates for their services, or engaging in discriminatory behaviour toward certain customers. This argument has been under fire for some time, though, on the basis that the public interest is not always served by regulation in these circumstances. Instead, the regulator becomes "captured" by the interests that it was supposed to be regulating. As a result, the very public purposes of the regulatory agency are undermined and the private corporate interest is promoted at public expense.

Another motivation for regulation is to create conditions within which individual firms can be protected from competition. Such was the case, for instance, when Air Canada was created. Another reason still is to create a policy tool that can engage in some planning for a specific sector of the economy. This may be most obvious in the telecommunications sector, where ongoing planning under the auspices of the CRTC has been used to moderate the impact of new television technologies, from antennae to cable to satellites, for instance.

The most important recent development concerning the issue of regulation is the contemporary trend toward deregulation.[24] According to political economists Shields and Evans, "deregulation may entail the complete or partial withdrawal of the state from a specific activity, such as enforcement of labour standards or occupational health and safety, through privatizing the enforcement function, shifting towards a compliance framework based on workplace or sectoral self-regulation, or both."[25] Deregulation is an important component of the New Public Management, discussed in Chapter 2.

In 1978 Prime Minister Trudeau and the premiers of the provinces jointly called for a reduction in the burden of government regulation on the private sector and the elimination of the burden of overlapping federal and provincial jurisdictions. Thus began the current mania for downsizing the government's role in the economy through deregulation (although it should be noted that Lester Pearson introduced the *National Transportation Act* in 1967, which reduced the regulation of the Canadian railways). While the Trudeau government embraced deregulation in only a lukewarm manner, the Mulroney and Chrétien governments made it central to administrative reform for their governments. At the provincial level, Ralph Klein in Alberta, Mike Harris in Ontario and Gordon Campbell in British Columbia also adopted deregulation as a key element in the restructuring of government in those provinces.

Federally, the government has deregulated the oil and gas industry, foreign investment, financial services, transportation, and other areas. Indeed, in terms of organizational structures, the Mulroney government signalled its desire to proceed with deregulation in a pronounced manner. It created an Office of Regulatory Affairs, attached to the Treasury Board, with its own minister, who was also a member of the most powerful Cabinet committee.[26]

Sociologist Gary Teeple argues that there are three main reasons for the accelerating pace of deregulation.[27] First, he suggests that there is usually a strong relationship between the development and application of new technology and the use of regulation or some other form of government intervention in the economy. When new technology comes on line, a number of consequences are discernable: increased competition between producers with the same technology; competition between producers with different technology; monopolies in which only one or a small number of firms have access to the new technology for a period of time; damage to humans or the natural environment. In all of these situations, regulation can be justified, according to Teeple. Thus, he argues, the growth of government regulation corresponds more or less to the rate of technological growth in society. Since the Second World War, technological growth has proceeded at a pace unprecedented in human history, and, not surprisingly, so too has the growth in regulatory bodies and agencies established to respond to the varied impacts of technology. But "with the present stage of permanent technological revolution beginning in the 1970s, the imposition of government regulations can no longer keep up with industrial innovation and its implications for society and nature."[28] Thus regulation has come under attack as a hindrance to innovation and development.

Second, Teeple argues that the original rationale for much regulation was to prevent or control monopolies and other market failures. But increasingly, the global economy is made up of global monopolies, oligopolies and cartels. So the rationale for seeking to control competition among national corporations is being swept aside. In any event, global corporations can move their operations to countries with minimal regulations as a means of lowering the costs of doing business. The mere threat of this action by a major employer in Canada is often enough to send government officials scurrying to find ways to repeal or tone down the regulatory framework. Moreover, the construction of global trade regimes and international free trade areas often means that one country has to modify its regulations to match those of its partners. In Canada's case, there is pressure to lessen regulations to the lowest common denominator of its NAFTA partners. Since both the United States and (especially) Mexico have much less government intervention than Canada, this implies reducing the regulatory role of the Canadian state to match that of the other two parties.

Teeple goes on to argue, though, that the impact of deregulation is frequently negative. For instance, deregulation actually reduces competition in some cases. It sometimes even opens the doors to illicit financial activities, since the watchdog role of regulatory bodies is relaxed. Nonetheless, deregulation has recently been embraced by governments of many different ideological stripes struggling to reduce deficits and debt and get their spending under control.

Recently, governments have moved toward a program of regulatory reform, according to economist John Strick, in which they:

'regulate smarter' through greater efficiency, greater accountability, and increased senstitivity to those affected by regulation. Regulatory procedures were streamlined to reduce bureaucratic red tape and delays. Regulations were relaxed and modified in areas where it was deemed they impeded efficiency in the marketplace. A form of regulating the regulators was introduced through the application of cost-benefit analysis to new regulatory proposals in recognition of the potential high costs to the economy of regulation.[29]

A moment's reflection about your own personal daily routine will reveal that, notwithstanding the recent deregulation craze, government is still intimately involved in almost every aspect of your life. And regulations are a prominent part of that involvement. Bleary-eyed, you wake up to the sound of your alarm clock-radio, the electronic parts of which are regulated by safety standards set by the government. The D.J. screams at you to rise and shine, as he plays the latest Canadian hit song, as required by government regulations covering Canadian content on the airways. You stumble into the bathroom, flip on the light and turn on the water, both of which are supplied by public utilities heavily regulated with regard to delivery, service and maintenance. You fumble for the toothpaste, whose ingredients are carefully monitored and regulated to ensure that they do not include anything harmful. As you head out for your morning walk with the dog, you put its leash on, mindful of municipal regulations (which also require that you suffer the indignity of having to "stoop and scoop"). If you drive to school, you are travelling in an invention that is among the most regulated technologies ever developed, from the additives in the fuel that propels it, to its safety systems, to the speed at which it can travel, and so on. If you take public transit, another legion of regulations governs everything from smoking to numbers of passengers to hours of operation. As you stare blankly at the advertisements plastered throughout your bus or subway car, you are vaguely conscious of the fact that there are no alcohol or cigarette ads—a result of regulations concerning commercial advertising. Glancing down at your magazine, you see a story on the contentious issue of Canadian content in print and on the airwaves. You realize that even the popular culture you consume is regulated. And on and on the list goes. In short, the world of regulation has truly penetrated every aspect of our lives. Former Prime Minister Pierre Trudeau once said that the state had no place in the bedrooms of the nation. He might have reconsidered that observation in light of the pervasive growth of the state's regulatory powers.

Crown Corporations

Another important organizational unit of government is the **Crown corporation**. Even if you are not sure what these are, you are influenced by them on a daily basis (as with the other structures of government). Crown corporations include a variety of nondepartmental organizations involved in regulation of the private sector through public ownership. There are about 400 such federal corporations in Canada, usually headed by boards of directors, members of which are usually appointed by the prime minister. These are typically patronage appointments. The legal definition of Crown corporations revolves around the issue of government ownership. Government doesn't have to own 100 percent of an enterprise for that enterprise to be publicly owned; a minority holding of less than 50 percent of the shares of a corporation qualifies as public ownership. But the legislation covering Crown corporations only refers to enterprises which are 100-percent government owned.

A general definition supplied by Adie and Thomas suggests that "a Crown corporation could be described as an institution with a corporate form brought into existence by government action to serve a public function."[30] Crown corporations are a sort of blend between the private and public sectors. They function in most cases like private corporations, but under conditions of greater accountability to government than private corporations. They enjoy a higher level of autonomy from Parliament than do departments, although they are ultimately responsible to Parliament through a designated minister. For instance, one of the most prominent Crown corporations is the Canadian Broadcast Corporation (CBC), which reports to Parliament through the Canadian Heritage minister. But Crown corporations are not subject to direct ministerial control. As a result, they have more autonomy with regard to personnel, finance and service provision than do regular departments.

Why would governments create Crown corporations in the first place? Why not simply rely on the traditional structures of government—that is, on departments? These questions are central to any explanation of the role of government ownership in Canada. We will consider several related explanations: nation-building, resistance to the pull of continentalism, regional economic development, other economic rationales, ideology and efficiency.

Crown corporations have historically been used in Canada as nation-building tools in the promotion of transportation, communication and resource development, and to make Canada competitive with its neighbour to the south. For instance, pre-Confederation governments were heavily involved in developing infrastructure, such as canals and roads, a practice that continued after 1867 in other areas, such as airports. The Canadian National Railway and Air Canada were created to unite the country through transportation links from sea to sea. More recently, Petro-Canada was created to give the Canadian government a "window" into the oil and gas industry, which was mainly foreign (i.e., U.S.) owned and controlled. The CBC was created to protect and promote Canadian culture and cultural industries. At the provincial level, countless Crown corporations have been created over the years to pursue the goals of economic development and diversification. Ontario Hydro was created in 1906 by taking over the many private utility companies in the province so as to provide cheap and reliable sources of electric power to the manufacturers in the province. By the 1970s and 1980s, every province in the country had established some sort of provincial development corporation to attract investment and jobs. So nation- and province-building have been important factors in explaining the proliferation of Crown corporations at both levels of government in Canada.

Sir John A. Macdonald once said in defence of government involvement in the economy that without it Canada would become "a bundle of sticks... without binding cord, [which would] fall, helpless, powerless, and aimless, into the hands of the neighbouring republic."[31] Later in the 1930s, an early advocate for a national public broadcasting system, Graham Spry, argued that the choice for Canadians was either "the state or the United States." These arguments reflect what economist Hugh G.J. Aitken termed the practice of "defensive expansionism." This is the notion that Canadian governments adopt an active role in the economy in order to resist or prevent continentalism—the economic, cultural and ultimately political domination of Canada by the United States. In this view, Crown corporations are viewed as policy tools that permit Canadian governments to resist the overwhelming influence of the world's most powerful nation.

The third common explanation for the use of Crown corporations also has economic roots. This is the view that says that these policy tools are needed to promote regional economic development. Canada is regionally divided in a number of ways. Uneven economic development means that some regions are poorer and less economically diversified than other regions. At various times in Canadian history, governments have attempted to overcome this problem by targeting economic development at particular areas to stimulate the economies of these regions. For example, the Cape Breton Development Corporation was established by the federal government in 1967 to take over some failing coal mines that the private sector was about to abandon. The Maritime provinces have been particular targets of federal intervention in the form of Crown corporations, but such corporations have also been used in other depressed regions from time to time. In many of these situations, the government steps in to an area where the private sector has failed or refuses to go. The bottom line of the private sector is profits, but governments must also take into consideration the health and welfare of communities, the costs of unemployment insurance and welfare, the possibility of mass migrations of people out of depressed regions into other parts of Canada and so on. These are considerations that corporate officials do not need to worry about.

Regional economic development is also fostered when governments create Crown corporations in industries that tend to have wide fluctuations in prices and incomes from year to year. For instance, the Canadian Wheat Board was established to add some stability to the price of wheat by regulating supply and demand, and ensuring that farmers would get a fair price year in and year out, notwithstanding fluctuations in the world price for their products. Finally, some Crown corporations are used in order to provide low-interest loans and risk capital to private sector corporations to promote economic activity in particular regions. All these measures are intended to ensure that some healthy level of economic activity exists in all the regions of Canada.

Another economic argument for Crown corporations says that in some circumstances, particular industries may lend themselves to a natural monopoly. For instance, until recent technological change altered the landscape, it was often argued that the provision of services such as transit, sewage, telephone, hydro or natural gas were most efficiently and effectively provided by one big company in each field. Whether the one company was to be public or private was a matter of some debate, but in many instances it appeared that there was a proper and defensible role for the state, as the monopoly provider of a given service, to ensure that customers were not gouged by high prices, poor service or discriminatory practices.

Besides the economic arguments, there are also ideological ones. Some commentators have focused on the differences between Canadian political culture and U.S. political culture, arguing that Canada has a stronger sense of the collective or community, and is more willing to use the state to defend that sense of community than are the Americans, where a more "rugged individualism" prevails. This manifests itself in a more pluralistic set of political ideologies than is found in the United States. The political scientist Gad Horowitz ascribes a specific content to the ideologies of conservatism, liberalism and socialism in Canada. Each has important consequences for the choice and implementation of economic development strategies by the Canadian state,[32] and will be considered in turn:

➤ Socialism is associated with the idea that society should be organized on the basis of cooperation rather than competition, and that the collective is of paramount importance in securing the liberty of the individual, whose self-worth is recognized in the idea that all in society are equal. In this view, the state is seen as an active agent of intervention in the marketplace, up to and including nationalization of industry.

➤ Liberalism asserts that the individual is the single most important element in a society, a notion derived from political philosophers, such as Thomas Hobbes and John Locke, who essentially saw the community as an atomistic collection of individuals who best further societal living by pursuing their self-interests in healthy competition with others. The liberal, like the socialist, believes in equality. But unlike the socialist, the liberal asserts that equality of opportunity is sufficient for the pursuit of personal fulfillment, while the socialist asserts that equality of condition is necessary. Freedom of the individual from state interference is of primary importance for liberals, and shapes their view of economic development, which is that the market should operate unencumbered by state intervention.

➤ In conservatism, the organic community is most important, and notions of social equality give way to a deference to authority and tradition that guide societal relations. This view asserts that society is naturally hierarchically organized, and is evidenced in the Canadian tradition by such well-known features of Canadian history and development as the absence of a lawless, egalitarian, American-style frontier, by a preference for Britain rather than the United States as a social model, and generally by a weaker emphasis on social equality than is found in either socialism or liberalism. A particular trait of Canadian conservatism is the willingness of the political and business elites to use the power of the state for developing and controlling the economy, especially where staples (i.e., natural resource) development is concerned. This partly explains why it was Conservative governments in Canada that created Crown corporations such as the CBC, Air Canada, Ontario Hydro and others.

The presence of conservatism and socialism alongside liberalism permits a greater diversity of views about the role of the state to exist in Canada than does the more monolithic ideology of liberalism that dominates in the United States. Hence the more common use of public ownership in Canada than in the United States.[33]

Indeed, almost all aspects of social and economic life in Canada are represented in the proliferation of Crown corporations that has occurred at both the federal and the provincial levels. Their use as policy tools has some advantages over the use of regular departments in providing services for citizens. For instance, as alluded to above, Crown corporations are one step removed from direct political control. As a result, they enjoy a measure of independence. This immunizes Crown corporations from compromising positions, for example where the provision of a good or service may appear as a political favour from a minister to a supporter or friend (e.g., in the awarding of a contract).

In addition, there is often an advantage of efficiency in Crown corporations that is absent in departments. Departments can be weighed down with processes, procedures, rules and regulations that impede the speedy and efficient achievement of a particular goal. Departments may also be less efficient due to contradictory, competing or multiple goals. Budgeting and personnel policy may be more streamlined in Crown corporations than in government departments. For instance, labour relations in many Crown corporations come under the *Labour Code* instead of the more onerous *Public Service Staff Relations Act,* which governs personnel in departments. This allows for greater flexibility in a number of areas, such as setting wages and salaries. Finally, Crown corporations may be preferable to departments under certain circumstances for the simple reason that departments have enough on their plates already, making it preferable to "farm out" tasks and work to another government body.

In general, Crown corporations have been created to serve a public policy purpose that cannot be served by traditional departments. That purpose may involve nation-building, resistance to the pull of continentalism, regional economic development, other economic rationales, ideology, efficiency, or a combination of all or some of these factors. In addition, they are often created in areas that the private sector will not or cannot enter. But recently, Crown corporations have been under sustained attack by the right wing in Canada as costly, bloated, unresponsive and unaccountable creatures, which compete unfairly in the marketplace against private sector corporations. What began in the 1970s and 1980s as a call for increased accountability and control over Crown corporations has evolved into a call for their dismantling. Thus neoconservatives in Canada have argued fairly success-fully that many such corporations have outlived their usefulness, and that, more im-portantly, they are inappropriate as a policy instrument, draining away taxpayer money and doing a job poorly that could be better done by the private sector. Thus there has been a trend lately toward privatization of Crown corporations—that is, selling them to the private sector.

Advocates of privatization argue that the original public policy purposes of Crown corporations no longer apply, or that the public policy goals involved could be pursued more efficiently through private sector ownership. This has been the fate of Air Canada and Petro-Canada at the federal level (see Table 5.4). At the provincial level in Alberta, the Liquor Control Board has been privatized. In Ontario, the Liquor Control Board, TVO, Ontario Hydro and other Crown cor-porations are subject to ongoing speculation that they may be privatized. Most governments in Canada have established departments or units within departments to look at which Crown corporations can be turned over to the private sector.

Those who oppose privatization argue that it is premised on pretty shaky eco-nomic and ideological grounds. There is a good deal of skepticism that the free mar-ket can perform as well as its proponents claim. Certainly there are underlying questions about whether nation-building or resistance to continentalism can be re-alized without public ownership. And there is the lingering issue of whether the public interest is best served under conditions of free markets or under some mix of private and public ownership. Moreover, if privatization proceeds, who exactly will be able to afford to buy the assets put on sale by the government? Generally, it will be those corporate actors who are already powerful to begin with. Therefore, it is argued that privatization simply contributes to an undesirable concentration of wealth and power in fewer and fewer hands. In any event, the ongoing discus-sion in Canadian society about the usefulness of these policy instruments is part of the larger ideological debate about the proper role of government in general.

WHAT YOU HAVE LEARNED

The three categories of departments, regulatory bodies and Crown corporations do not encompass all organizational units within the federal bureaucracy. As we noted, several new mechanisms for alternative service delivery have emerged. And certain other offices and institutions exist, for example the Office of the Auditor General and the Commissioner of Official Languages. These are independent of Cabinet and report directly to Parliament. But the majority of organizational units do fall within the ambit of departments, regulatory bodies and Crown corporations. Let us sum-marize this part by returning to some general observations about bureaucracy and how these units fit in the overall bureaucratic scheme of things.[34]

TABLE 5.4   Privatization of Federally Owned Enterprises, 1985–1999

Enterprise	Activity	Year
Northern Transportation	trucking	1985
de Havilland Aircraft of Canada	aircraft manufacture	1986
Canadair	aircraft manufacture	1986
Canadian Arsenals	munitions	1986
Nanisivik Mines	mining	1986
Pêcheries Canada	fish processing	1986
Route Canada	trucking	1986
Teleglobe Canada	telecommunications	1987
Canada Development Corporation	venture capital	1987
Fishery Products International	fish processing	1987
CN Hotels	hotels	1988
CNCP Telecommunications	telecommunications	1988
Northern Canada Power Commission	electricity generation and distribution	1988
Terra Nova Telecommunications	telecommunications	1988
Air Canada	air transportation	1989
Eldorado Nuclear	uranium mining and processing	1991
Co-Enerco Resources	oil and gas production	1992
Nordion International	nuclear-based industrial and medical products	1992
Telesat Canada	satellite telecommunications	1992
Canadian National Railways	rail transportation	1995
Petro-Canada	petroleum production and retailing	1991–5
Nav Canada	air navigation systems	1996
Canada Communications Group	printing and publishing	1996–7
National Sea Products	fish processing	1997
Theratronics International	radiation therapy equipment	1998

Source: Alasdair Roberts, "A Fragile State: Federal Public Administration in the Twentieth Century," in Christopher Dunn, ed. *The Handbook of Canadian Public Administration*, Toronto: Oxford University Press, 2002: 29.

FIGURE 5.6

Sources: Josh Beutel, St. John, N.B.

You will recall that the term *bureaucracy* refers to a kind of organization with particular structural characteristics. As Weber pointed out, bureaucracies are characterized by a well-developed division of labour within which officials perform certain clearly defined roles by following prescribed rules and regulations. Moreover, those roles are defined by the office held, not by the individual occupying the role. This ensures that there is some continuity in the functions and structures of government. Detailed written records of all the actions taken by bureaucrats are also a feature of this system, which allows for a body of precedents to build up to guide future actions. The fact that office-holding is a full-time occupation also contributes to continuity. Finally, the organizational structure is characterized by hierarchy. Decision-making flows downward from above in a rigidly defined structure in which each level of the bureaucracy is responsible to the level above.

Adopting this type of bureaucratic organization has its benefits. It allows for a kind of equality of treatment of all citizens. It does this by "routinizing" the decision-making process, which in turn allows for maximum impartiality in dealing with citizens. It also allows for predictability, and thus fairness, in that the application of the law by bureaucratic officials must be the same for everyone. But clearly, these strengths are also weaknesses. Citizens with special circumstances may not fit into the routinized bureaucratic process. For example, certain university students applying for financial assistance may find they are unfairly disadvantaged by a bureaucratic interpretation of what constitutes an asset, which is appropriate in most cases, but not their own. You have no doubt encountered a situation in which you pleaded for treatment appropriate to your own circumstances, only to be told by some bureaucratic official, "If we change the rules for you, we'll have to change them for everyone."

Notwithstanding these limitations, bureaucracy is the worst system we have—except for all the others (to paraphrase Winston Churchill on democracy). The organization of the Canadian bureaucratic system into departments, regulatory bodies and Crown corporations both reflects the major characteristics of bureaucracy and represents our best attempts to construct a complex organizational structure that responds to the needs of citizens and can balance the tensions between democracy and efficiency within the framework of bureaucracy. The fact that alternative service delivery mechanisms have evolved, but not supplanted traditional mechanisms, speaks to both the strengths and weaknesses of the latter.

This chapter began by examining some of the factors influencing organizational structure. Presented was the basic framework of the Canadian political system, particularly capitalist democracy, federalism and cabinet-parliamentary government. You should now be able to indicate how each of these factors influences the nature of public administration in terms of organization and structure of the state. Political-administrative relationships were overviewed. The nature of the relationship between public administration and democratic government underlay this section, which examined the nature of the relationship between politicians and bureaucrats, while addressing a fundamental question: Who is in control of the machinery and actions of the state? You should now be able to answer this question, and particularly be able to say something about the relationship of the branches of government to each other, as well as the roles of ministers and deputy ministers.

We next asked why governments grow and shrink over time. Why do some prime ministers prefer large Cabinets with many departments, while others opt for more stripped-down models? Some answers to these questions were provided by considering the actual organizational units of the Canadian government. In so doing, we explained why the government looks the way it does, organizationally speaking, in terms of departments, regulatory agencies, Crown corporations, and alternative service delivery agencies. You should now be able to explain what role these bodies play in public administration. In addition, we briefly considered the issues of deregulation and privatization, and the general rethinking of the areas of life that government should be involved in. This led us to think about the choice of governing instrument used in achieving policy goals and the general reevaluation of traditional tools employed by Canadian governments to date.

ENDNOTES

1. Neil Bradford, *Commissioning Ideas: Canadian National Policy Innovation in Comparative Perspective*, (Toronto: Oxford University Press, 1998): 15.
2. Bradford, *Commissioning Ideas*, (1998): 15–16.
3. For a discussion of Wheare's views and other definitions of federalism, see Garth Stevenson, *Unfulfilled Union: Canadian Federalism and National Unity*, Third Edition, (Toronto: Gage, 1989): chapter 1. For an overview of the evolution of federalism, see Gregory J. Inwood, "Federalism, Democracy and the (Anti-) Social Union," in Mike Burke, Colin Mooers and John Shields, eds. *Restructuring and Resistance: Canadian Public Policy in an Age of Global Capitalism*, (Halifax: Fernwood Press, 2000).
4. See Gregory J. Inwood, Carolyn M. Johns and Patricia L. O'Reilly, "The Impact of Administrative Reform on Intergovernmental Officials," in Harvey Lazar and Peter Meekison, eds. *The State of the Federation 2002–2003: Managing Tensions: Evaluating the Institutions of the Federation*, (Montreal: McGill-Queen's University Press, forthcoming 2003).
5. See Richard Simeon, *Federal-Provincial Diplomacy: The Making of Recent Policy in Canada*, (Toronto: University of Toronto Press, 1972).
6. Peter H. Russell, *Constitutional Odyssey: Can Canadians Become a Sovereign People? Second Edition*, (Toronto: University of Toronto Press, 1993): 81. See also Herman Bakvis and Grace Skogstad, "Canadian Federalism: Performance, Effectiveness, and Legitimacy," in Herman Bakvis and Grace Skogstad, eds. *Canadian Federalism: Performance, Effectiveness, and Legitimacy*, (Toronto: Oxford University Press, 2002): 3–23.6.
7. See Donald Savoie, *Governing From the Centre: The Concentration of Power in Canadian Politics*, (Toronto: Univeristy of Toronto Press, 1999).
8. Victor S. MacKinon, "Introduction to the Legal Environment: Theories and Principles," in Randy Hoffman *et al.*, *Public Administration: Canadian Materials*, Third Edition, (Toronto: Captus Press, 1998): 199.
9. J.E. Hodgetts, *The Canadian Public Service: A Physiology of Government 1867–70*, (Toronto: University of Toronto Press, 1973): 89.
10. Robert J. Jackson and Doreen Jackson, *Politics in Canada: Culture, Institutions, Behaviour and Public Policy*, Third Edition, (Scarborough: Prentice Hall, 1994): 376–377.
11. Luther Gulick, "Notes on the Theory of Organization," in Jay M. Shafritz and Albert C. Hyde, eds. *Classics of Public Administration*, Third Edition, (Pacific Grove, California: Brooks/Cole Publishing, 1992): 83–84.
12. See Canada, Privy Council Office, "Decision-Making Processes and Central Agencies in Canada: Federal, Provincial and Territorial Practices," (Ottawa: Privy Council Office, 1998).
13. Canada, Treasury Board Secretariat, "Policy on Alternative Service Delivery," (April 1, 2002): 2.
14. See David Zussman, "Alternative Service Delivery," in Christopher Dunn, ed. *The Handbook of Canadian Public Administration*, (Toronto: Oxford University Press, 2002): 55.
15. See John C. Strick, *The Public Sector in Canada: Programs, Finance and Policy*, (Toronto: Thompson, 1999): Chapter 6.
16. See Jackson and Jackson, *Politics in Canada, Third Edition*, (1994): 384–385.
17. Flora MacDonald, "Who is on Top? The Minister or the Mandarins?" in Paul Fox and Graham White, eds. *Politics: Canada, Eighth Edition*, (Toronto: McGraw-Hill, 1995): 488–552.

18. Mitchell Sharp, "A Reply from a Former Minister and Mandarin," in Paul Fox and Graham White, eds. *Politics: Canada, Eighth Edition*, (Toronto: McGraw-Hill, 1995): 453–456.

19. See Gordon F. Osbaldeston, *Keeping Deputy Ministers Accountable*, (Toronto: McGraw-Hill Ryerson, 1989).

20. Economic Council of Canada, Interim Report: Responsible Regulations. Cited in Jackson and Jackson, *Politics in Canada, Fourth Edition*, (1998): 346.

21. Richard Schultz, "Regulatory Agencies," in M.S. Whittington and G. Williams, eds. *Canadian Politics in the 1980s, Second Edition*, (Toronto: Methuen, 1984): 438.

22. Michael Howlett and M. Ramesh, *Studying Public Policy: Policy Cycles and Policy Subsystems*, (Toronto: Oxford University Press, 1995): 87–88.

23. See John C. Strick, "Regulation and Deregulation," in Christopher Dunn, ed. *The Handbook of Canadian Public Administration*, (Toronto: Oxford University Press, 2002): 262–78.

24. See Strick, "Regulation and Deregualtion," (2002): 276.

25. John Shields and B. Mitchell Evans, *Shrinking the State: Globalization and Public Administration "Reform,"* (Halifax: Fernwood Press, 1998): 69–70.

26. Richard J. Schultz, "Regulating Conservatively: The Mulroney Record, 1984–1988," in Andrew B. Gollner and Daniel Salèe, eds. *Canada Under Mulroney: An End of Term Report*, (Montreal: Véhicule Press, 1988): 198.

27. Gary Teeple, *Globalization and the Decline of Social Reform*, (Toronto: Garamond Press, 1995): 85–89.

28. Teeple, *Globalization and the Decline of Social Reform*, (1995): 87.

29. Strick, "Regulation and Deregulation," (2002): 277.

30. Robert F. Adie and Paul G. Thomas, *Canadian Public Administration: Problematical Perspectives, Second Edition*, (Scarborough: Prentice Hall, 1987): 377.

31. Cited in Adie and Thomas, *Canadian Public Administration*, (1987): 387.

32. See Nelson Wiseman and David Whorley, "Lessons on the Centrality of Politics from Canadian Crown Enterprise," in Christopher Dunn, ed. *The Handbook of Canadian Public Administration*, (Toronto: Oxford University Press, 2002): 383–4.

33. See W. Christian and C. Campbell, *Political Parties and Ideologies in Canada, Second Edition*, (Toronto: McGraw-Hill Ryerson, 1983): 25–26.

34. See Richard J. Van Loon and Michael S. Whittington, *The Canadian Political System: Environment, Structure and Process, Fourth Edition*, (Toronto: McGraw-Hill Ryerson, 1987): 541–542.

KEY WORDS AND CONCEPTS

spending power (118)
executive branch (119)
legislative branch (119)
judicial branch (119)
Privy Council (121)
Cabinet (121)
constitutional convention (121)
responsible government (121)

departments (126)
ministries (126)
statutory bodies (126)
minister (126)
alternative service delivery (137)
deputy minister (140)
regulatory bodies (145)
Crown corporation (149)

REVIEW QUESTIONS

This chapter was divided into five sections, each reflecting a key issue for public administration. You should be familiar now with these issues, and be able to answer questions associated with each.

1. *Factors Influencing Organizational Structure*

Among the many factors influencing Canadian public administration, we isolated three for particular attention. We asked the following: How have capitalist democracy, federalism and cabinet-parliamentary government influenced the organizational structure of the Canadian government? How have the very outlines of the state itself influenced the nature of public administration?

2. *Political-Administrative Relationships*

We returned here to some issues surrounding the relationship between public administration and democratic government. This section elaborated and examined the nature of the relationship between politicians and bureaucrats, and addressed a fundamental question: Who is in control of the machinery and actions of the state?

3. *Departmental Organizations*

This introduction to the main organizational units of the Canadian government asked: Why do governments grow and shrink over time? Why do some prime ministers prefer large Cabinets with many departments, while others opt for more stripped-down models? We also asked what alternative service delivery agencies are, and why they have emerged.

4. *Regulatory Agencies*

This section concerned another of the most common organizational forms of government, but one which is increasingly under attack. It asked: What role do regulatory bodies play in public administration? In an era of deregulation and downsizing government, why have we been rethinking the areas of life that government should be regulating?

5. *Crown Corporations*

An understanding of the historical place of public ownership was conveyed in this section. But we also pointed out that the role of Crown corporations as a policy tool has recently been questioned. We asked the following: What explains the use of Crown corporations over time in Canada, and why are we reevaluating them now as policy instruments?

FURTHER READING

1. *Factors Influencing Organizational Structure*

Johnson, David, *Thinking Government: Public Sector Management in Canada*. Peterborough: Broadview Press, 2002.

Lindquist, Evert A. "Recent Administrative Reform in Canada as Decentralization: Who is Spreading What Around to Whom and Why?" *Canadian Public Administration,* 37, 3 (Fall, 1994).

Peters, B. Guy and Donald J. Savoie, eds. *Governance in the Twenty-First Century: Revitalizing the Public Service*. Montreal: McGill-Queen's University Press, 2000.

2. *Political-Administrative Relationships*

Bourgault, Jacques, "The Role of Deputy Ministers in Canadian Government," in Christopher Dunn, ed. *The Handbook of Canadian Public Administration*. Toronto: Oxford University Press, 2002: Chapter 23.

Brooks, Stephen. "Bureaucracy," in James P. Bickerton and Alain-G. Gagnon, eds. *Canadian Politics. Second Edition*. Peterborough: Broadview Press, 1994: 307–327.

Dwivedi, O.P. and James Iain Gow, *From Bureaucracy to Public Management: The Administrative Culture of the Government of Canada*. Peterborough: Broadview Press, 1999.

MacDonald, Flora. "Who is on Top? The Minister or the Mandarins?" in Paul Fox and Graham White, eds. *Politics: Canada. Eighth Edition*. Toronto: McGraw-Hill, 1995: 488–552.

Sharp, Mitchell. "A Reply From a Former Minister and Mandarin," in Paul Fox and Graham White, eds. *Politics: Canada. Eighth Edition*. Toronto: McGraw-Hill, 1995: 453–456.

3. Departmental Organizations

Lindquist, Evert A. "Has Federal Cabinet Decision-Making Come Full Circle?" in Paul Fox and Graham White, eds. *Politics: Canada. Eighth Edition*. Toronto: McGraw-Hill Ryerson, 1995: 544–552.

Tardi, Gregory, "Departments and Other Institutions of Government," in Christopher Dunn, ed. *The Handbook of Canadain Public Administration*. Toronto: Oxford University Press, 2002: Chapter 16.

Thomas, Paul B. "Central Agencies: Making a Mesh of Things," in James B. Bickerton and Alain-G. Gagnon, eds. *Canadian Politics. Second Edition*. Peterborough: Broadview, 1994: 288–306.

4. Regulatory Agencies

Johnson, David. "Regulatory Agencies and Accountability: An Ontario Perspective." *Canadian Public Administration*, 34, 3 (Fall, 1991): 417–434.

MacDonald, Donald C. "Ontario's Agencies, Boards & Commissions Come of Age." *Canadian Public Administration*, 36, 3 (Fall, 1993): 349–363.

Schultz, Richard. "Regulatory Agencies," in M.S. Whittington and G. Williams, eds. *Canadian Politics in the 1990s. Third Edition*. Scarborough: Nelson, 1990: 468–480.

5. Crown Corporations

Langford, John W. "Crown Corporations as Instruments of Policy," in G. Bruce Doern and Peter Aucoin, eds. *Public Policy in Canada: Organization, Process and Management*. Toronto: Gage, 1979: 239–274.

Laux, Jeanne Kirk. "Shaping or Serving Markets? Public Ownership After Privatization," in Daniel Drache and Meric S. Gertler, eds. *The New Era of Global Competition: State Power and Market Power*. Montreal and Kingston: McGill-Queen's University Press, 1991: 288–315.

 WEBLINKS

The Prime Minister of Canada
pm.gc.ca

The Privy Council Office
www.pco-bcp.gc.ca/

Treasury Board
www.tbs-sct.gc.ca/

Cabinet Ministers and Their Portfolios
canada.gc.ca/howgoc/glance_e.html

Parliament of Canada
www.parl.gc.ca/

Federal Government Departments Canada.
canada.gc.ca/depts/major/depind_e.html

Canadian Public Service Commission
www.psc-cfp.gc.ca/

Auditor General of Canada
www.oag-bvg.gc.ca/oag-bvg/html/menue.html

La Relève
leadership.gc.ca/categories.asp?lang=e&sub_id=582

Supreme Court of Canada
www.scc-csc.gc.ca

Chapter 6

Public Administration *and* Law

Clearly, public administration is intimately connected to the law, particularly constitutional law and administrative law. Constitutional law deals with the rules, practices and institutions that constitute the state. Constitutional law issues occur when the courts are asked by an individual, group, corporation, or other government to declare a particular law unconstitutional. If they succeed, the law becomes null and void. There are two primary grounds upon which the constitutionality of a law can be tested. One ground is that it violates the division of powers as set out in the *Constitution Act, 1867* (formerly the *British North America Act, 1867*). This is the section of the Canadian Constitution that lays out the jurisdiction of the federal and provincial governments. The other ground is that it violates fundamental rights and freedoms as set out in the *Charter of Rights and Freedoms*.

Administrative law is closely related to constitutional law. It regulates the relationships between the individual and the state. If constitutional law looks at the *macro-legal* picture, administrative law looks at the *micro-legal* level. It is more concerned with the day-to-day legalities of how administration takes place.

In this chapter, we will frame our discussion of public administration and the law by first looking at the more general question of what a constitution is, and what it does. We will also explore the question of the relationship between the Constitution and the institutions of the state. As well, we will bring elements of political culture into this analysis by asking how the *British North America Act, 1867(BNA Act)* reflected the nature of Canadian society at Confederation, compared to how the *Constitution Act* of 1982 reflects the changed nature of Canadian society. We will also, of course, look at the extent to which a constitution deals with the question of rights and freedoms in a society, and to that end we will examine the *Canadian Charter of Rights and Freedoms*. Finally, we will seek to understand how the Canadian Constitution has evolved and changed, or, alternatively, why it has changed so little in over 135 years, by looking at constitutional politics. We will then turn our attention to administrative law. This chapter is divided into the following sections:

1. The Law and the Courts

   This section asks you to consider the political-culture origins and application of the rule of law in Canada. It asks, What is the rule of law? What are common law and civil law? What is the structure of the court system in Canada?

2. What Is a Constitution?

   This section asserts that while constitutions are fundamental to every society, they vary widely in their utility and application. It asks the following: What is a constitution? What three main functions do constitutions serve? What are the component parts of the Canadian Constitution? What is constitutional law? How did the Canadian constitutional order come about?

3. Constitutional Law

   This section addresses constitutional law in terms of conflict over the division of powers in the Constitution. It asks the following: How are disputes resolved before the courts when federal and provincial governments cannot agree on the jurisdiction of a law? What powers in the division of powers have proven the most contentious, and how have disputes over them been resolved? What role have the courts played in the resolution of conflict? What has been the legacy of judicial review of constitutional law?

4. Administrative Law

   Finally, the last section in this chapter examines administrative law. It asks, What is administrative law? What is the power of discretion held by civil servants? What happens when a dispute arises over the exercise of legal powers by an administrative agency? What is the relationship between constitutional and administrative law? What is the role of judicial review in administrative law?

The Law and the Courts

Canadians have a reputation as a peace-loving, orderly, cautious people. Our Constitution, it is said, reflects this in that its most memorable phrase is "peace, order and good government." Compare this to the U.S. Constitution's declaration of "life, liberty and the pursuit of happiness," or the French constitution's affirmation to "liberty, equality, fraternity." These phrases speak volumes about the political cultures of the three countries. Canada is said to be a nation that sent its police force into the wilderness to precede settlement and establish loyalty to the Crown, and hence the patterns of deference to authority were sown early on.

The early establishment of this firm belief in the law became fundamental to the evolution of the Canadian society. Moreover, we embraced the **rule of law**, which is the principle that both the rulers and ruled are answerable to the law. In other words, both are prohibited from interfering with the independence of the courts, which uphold the rule of law through their positions as independent arbiters of societal disputes. This cornerstone of the Canadian constitutional order is evidenced daily by our obvious respect as a society for duly constituted authority and reason.

The function of law is essentially to regulate human behaviour.[1] But to be effective, the law must be knowable—that is, people must be made aware of the standards of behaviour they are expected to uphold. And it must be predictable—that is, it cannot be arbitrary in its application. The law in Canada is based largely on statutes passed by the legislatures of the federal and provincial governments, and on the English common law tradition. This is a system of law wherein judges dispense justice on the basis of past custom and the precedents built up over the years in prior legal findings. The cumulative body of law dating from the 13th century in England serves as the basis of common law.

Canada also has a system of civil law, most particularly in Quebec. This is based on Roman law. Napoleon ordered the codification of French law on the model of Roman law, and the Napoleonic Code came to represent an attempt to produce an authoritative written record of the laws of the land. When French settlers came to North America, they brought this system with them. Judges in a civil law system are more constrained in making judgments than in common law. The continued use of the civil code in Quebec, a legacy of the early relationship between French and English after the Conquest in 1759, is a key aspect of the distinctive political culture of the province.

Because Canada is a federal country, the courts are federal. There are separate federal and provincial courts in Canada, although in some circumstances cases from provincial courts can be appealed to the Supreme Court of Canada, illustrating that a degree of horizontal integration exists between the two levels of court. The Supreme Court stands at the apex of the court system.[2] It was established in 1875, but did not become the final court of appeal until 1949. All types of law cases (common, civil, criminal, statutory, administrative, constitutional, federal, provincial) can be appealed to and be heard in the Supreme Court. It consists of nine learned and senior justices appointed by the prime minister. Three judges from Quebec hear civil law cases.

This brief sketch needs to include another important court that relates particularly to administrative law. In 1970 the Federal Court of Canada was created to replace the Exchequer Court, which had been responsible for hearing cases concerning federal taxes, patents and copyrights. The Federal Court of Canada consists of a Trial Division and an Appeals Division, and its tasks were expanded to include federal administrative law cases concerning agencies, boards, commissions and tribunals.

The law and the courts only exist within the framework of the Constitution. The Constitution encapsulates the rule of law, even though it is nowhere explicitly mentioned in the written documents of the Constitution. And it orders the positions and the roles of the courts—not always explicitly, but certainly implicitly. We now turn to a consideration of the Constitution, before returning in more detail to constitutional and administrative law.

What Is a Constitution?

Constitutions are fundamental to the existence of virtually every organized society on earth.[3] They come in every size, description, length and style. Some contain rules of behaviour and guidelines that are religiously adhered to even though they are nowhere written down. Others are not worth the paper they are written on. The simple fact that a nation has a constitution is no guarantee that it is necessarily a "democratic" society, that its constitution is observed, or even that the rights of citizens enshrined in the constitution will be protected. The constitutions of the former Soviet Union contained ringing declarations of the rights of its citizens, but at the same time a form of state terrorism was conducted against those citizens, often depriving them of liberty and even life. The constitution of South Africa in the apartheid era denied the fundamental equality of all its citizens. A constitution, then, is no guarantee in and of itself that rights will be protected or that states will stay within the rules of the game.

But without a constitution, the concept of rights, as well as the delineation of the appropriate limits to be placed on the actions of the state, would not even exist. A constitution is the fundamental law of a political system. All other laws are supposed to follow from, and be subordinate to, the laws of the constitution. A constitution provides us with a set of rules or guidelines that permits the peaceful and civilized resolution of most conflicts within society. Without it, there is no way of predicting either the powers of government, or the rights of citizens. As political scientist J.R. Mallory put it, "the essence of a constitutional order is that it provides effective means of preventing abuses of power, and ensures that those in authority cannot take away the ultimate right of the governed to remove them or reject their policies."[4] Imagine a hockey game without a rule book. You can still play, but the game becomes largely meaningless unless there is some order imposed on the conduct of the participants. Otherwise, the law of the jungle may prevail, and only the strongest, biggest, meanest hockey players would be able to impose their version of the game on the rest of us.

So constitutions exist, in part, to establish order, and to allow for the peaceful resolution of conflict over scarce resources in society. Imagine a society in which there is no constitution; a society in a "state of nature," in which chaos and anarchy prevail; a society in which no individual could feel secure in the possession of her property or life; a society in which life was, as 17th-century political philosopher Thomas Hobbes put it, "solitary, poor, nasty, brutish, and short." The insecurity fostered by this state of nature can only be remedied when people agree to establish a set of binding and authoritative rules; hence the development and evolution of constitutions.

All constitutions are meant to do three things. First, constitutions define the relationship between citizens and the state. They empower the state to regulate the behaviour of citizens by passing laws on behalf of the community; and generally they delineate the boundaries of the state's powers. They do this by identifying both individual rights and collective rights that the state is not allowed to violate. For example, the constitution prohibits the state from censoring the free expression of ideas, and therefore protects the individual right to freedom of speech. However, it also allows the state to place limits on those individual rights in the interests of the greater community through anti-hate laws, libel and slander laws, and so on.

Second, constitutions define the responsibilities and relationships of the different parts of the state and the ways in which those parts relate to one another. In particular, there are three main parts of the state whose relationships are spelled out in a constitution. These are: a) the executive, which makes and implements the law; b) the legislature, which passes the law; and c) the judiciary, which interprets the law. Since each of these elements is complex, we need to have an understanding of their roles, and of how they relate to one another in their functioning. A constitution provides us with this information. Two political scientists put it this way:

In modern times, political power is understood to consist of three distinct types: Legislative power is the power to make law or policy. For instance, a political community might use its legislative power to pass a law stipulating that no one may drive an automobile when their blood has an alcohol content above .08%. Executive power is the power to "execute" or administer that law or policy. This would include the power to establish and maintain a police force to catch drunk drivers. Judicial power is the power to settle questions about specific violations of law (is there appropriate evidence to prove the driver's blood-alcohol level exceeded .08%?) and to choose a suitable punishment, from among those permitted in the relevant legislation, for those found guilty.[5]

So the rules that govern the various parts of the state are an important part of any constitution.

Because Canada is a federal state, our constitution is given a third function. Constitutions in federal systems also lay out the rules governing the relations between the levels of government. This aspect of the Canadian Constitution has captured the attention of politicians and constitutional experts throughout our history, during which federal-provincial disputes have played a prominent role.

If you were asked what the Canadian Constitution was composed of, what would you say? In essence, there are three basic elements:

1. written documents, such as the *BNA Act, 1867,* the *Constitution Act, 1982,* and the *Charter of Rights and Freedoms;*
2. the common law; and
3. constitutional conventions—that is, practices that emerge over time and that are generally accepted as binding rules of the political system.

Note that constitutional conventions are not written anywhere into the constitutional documents; they are simply traditional habits and practices. But they can be just as significant as the other parts of the Constitution. Conventions are rules of the Constitution that are not enforced by the law courts. They can be regarded as nonlegal rules. An example would be the convention that the leader of the party that captures the most seats in the House of Commons is called on to form the government. Another example concerns the exercise of the powers of the governor general. Convention stipulates that the governor general will only use his or her considerable powers in accordance with the advice of the Cabinet or prime minister. For instance, the Queen, through the governor general, enjoys the power of withholding royal assent from a bill that has been enacted by Parliament, but convention stipulates that royal assent will never be withheld.

In Canada, the first two components of the Constitution—written documents and the common law—together make up the **constitutional law**. Conventions, while part of the Constitution, do not have the status of constitutional law. But this should not be interpreted to mean that constitutional law is more important. The major difference is that constitutional law is enforceable through the courts, whereas constitutional conventions are not.

In most countries, the bulk of the constitutional law is contained in a single constitutional document that can and usually is described as "the constitution." In most cases this document came into being after independence, or after a revolution, or war, and was intended to symbolize and legitimize a new regime of law.[6] As we will see, the Canadian case is somewhat different. Before we turn our attention to the actual constitutional documents, let us look briefly at the reasons and effects of Confederation, which resulted in the constitutional order we now have.

A History of Canada's Constitution

You are probably familiar with the less-than-stirring history of Canada's march from "colony to nation"[7] (and back to colony again, some would add). The outlines of the picture are clear: conservative, loyal Canada, turning its back on and rejecting the U.S. revolutionary experience, decides to take the slow, evolutionary path to nationhood. If nothing else, this picture seems to accurately reflect Canadian political culture, rooted as it is in the formative experiences of accommodation with French Canada rather than assimilation, and the loyalist influence on English Canada. The Confederation experience seemed to reflect Canada's cautiousness and moderation in action, its preference for evolution over revolution, and its reluctance to break the imperial/colonial ties that bound it to Britain.

Thus, it is to British constitutional practices we must turn to discover the essential foundations of Canada's constitutional order. Long before Confederation, for example, the colonists had adopted many of the practices of British constitutionalism: the Crown, Parliament, Cabinet, responsible government, an independent judiciary, and the rudiments of party politics. Much of this heritage took the form of constitutional conventions; that is, rules, habits and practices that had evolved over a much earlier period of political experimentation in Britain. And, as well, it is to Britain we must turn to find the legislation that created and expanded upon so much of Canada's constitutional life, both pre- and post-Confederation.

The *BNA Act, 1867*, gave effect to Confederation following conferences in Charlottetown in 1864, Quebec City in 1864, and London, England, in 1867. It united the provinces of Canada, Nova Scotia and New Brunswick into a single "Dominion" under the name of Canada. It established a bicameral national Parliament with representation by population in the elected, lower House of Commons, and representation by region in the appointed, upper house, the Senate. It established a common market, and allocated important economic powers to the new federal Parliament for maintaining peace, order and good government, and authority over trade and commerce, transportation and communication, banking, currency, customs and excise, and other forms of taxation. Criminal law also became a federal responsibility, as did marriage and divorce. The provincial legislatures were given other powers, notably over property and civil rights, municipal institutions, education and the administration of justice, the power of direct taxation, and matters of a purely local or private nature within the province. Nova Scotia and New Brunswick retained their existing legislatures and other institutions of government. The province of Canada was divided into two new provinces: Ontario (the old Canada West, formerly Upper Canada) and Quebec (the old Canada East, formerly Lower Canada). The Act also established a legislature and other institutions of government for each of Ontario and Quebec. Thus, the *BNA Act* established the rules of federalism, allocating governmental power between the central and provincial institutions of government.

The *BNA Act* did not follow the U.S. model of codifying all the new nation's constitutional rules, since, as the preamble to the Act stated, the new nation was to have "a constitution similar in principle to that of the United Kingdom," which is not a written constitution. Apart from the changes needed to establish the new federation, the British North Americans wanted the old rules to continue in both form and substance exactly as before. After 1867, therefore, much of Canada's constitutional law continued to be found in a variety of sources outside the *BNA Act*, such as in conventions and in the common law, as mentioned earlier.

The result is that the *BNA Act* is silent on a number of issues you might suppose would be basic to the constitutional order. For instance, there is no general amending clause in the *BNA Act*, since the framers of the Constitution were content to let the amending power rest in the hands of the British Parliament. Later generations of political leaders in Canada could not agree on how the Constitution could be changed. Because of the absence of an amending clause in the *BNA Act*, the British parliament enacted amendments to it right up until 1982, when the *Constitution Act, 1982* finally supplied amending procedures that could be operated entirely within Canada.

The field of foreign relations is another notable gap in the *BNA Act*. It contains no express provision, for example, for a treaty-making power for the Canadian Parliament, except as it may relate to the responsibilities that it might assume as part of the British empire. Yet another gap in the *BNA Act* concerns the Office of the Governor General. The Act vests executive authority for Canada in the Queen, and confers several specific powers on a governor general. But the Office of Governor General is nowhere created by the *BNA Act*, and no rules are provided for the appointment or tenure of that officer. The reason for this gap was the assumption that the office would be created and filled in the same way colonial governorships had always been created and filled: by the Queen acting on the advice of the British colonial secretary. The Office of the Governor General has never been formalized in an amendment to the *BNA Act*. The office is still constituted by royal prerogative, and appointments are still made by the Queen, although, needless to say, she now acts on the advice of her Canadian ministers.

Not even the system of responsible government receives explicit mention in the *BNA Act*. It never seemed to occur to anyone to write the rules of this system into the *BNA Act*, and so there is no mention of the prime minister, or of the Cabinet, or of the dependence of the Cabinet on the support of a majority in the House of Commons. All these rather significant details were left in the form of unwritten conventions, as in the United Kingdom. Nor did the Canadians write into their *BNA Act* a new supreme court. Section 101 of the Act gave authority for such a court to be established, but it did not actually establish it, since we were accustomed to appealing our legal cases to the British Judicial Committee of the Privy Council (JCPC). Indeed, even the JCPC is not mentioned in the *BNA Act*. The Supreme Court of Canada was finally established in 1875, but through an ordinary federal law or statute, and the right of appeal to the JCPC was retained until 1949, when our Supreme Court at last became "supreme." Meanwhile, the existence, composition and jurisdiction of the Supreme Court of Canada still depend upon that 1875 statute. As we will see, the JCPC played a significant role in determining the balance of powers between the federal and provincial governments, by ruling in a long series of court cases over the years in favour of the expansion of provincial powers.

Finally, the *BNA Act* did not even include a bill of rights. The civil liberties of Canadians were instead left in the hands of our legislative bodies and the rules of common law, as in Great Britain. In 1960, the Canadian government of John Diefenbaker enacted a Bill of Rights—not as an amendment to the Constitution, but as a simple statute that applied only to the federal government. The *Constitution Act, 1982* finally added to the Constitution the Canadian Charter of Rights and Freedoms, which is now entrenched (that is, alterable only by the process of constitutional amendment) and applies to provincial as well as federal laws. We will expand on the importance of the *Charter* below.

The *BNA Act* served as Canada's central written constitutional document for 115 years. Changes were made to it occasionally prior to 1982, but most were relatively minor. With the passage of time, however, it became apparent that the original document was deficient for modern Canada, and so attempts were made at different times to overhaul and reform it. These attempts did not succeed until 1982, when, under then Prime Minister Pierre Trudeau, the *BNA Act* was patriated and reformed.

Repeated efforts had been made, dating from the 1930s, to correct the anomaly of British control over the amending of the Canadian Constitution. But in every case, Canadian provincial premiers and prime ministers failed to agree on any domestic **amending formula** until, in 1980, Trudeau forced the issue by deciding to attempt to do it unilaterally. That decision, after a long battle with the provinces for public support and in the courts, eventually led to renewed federal-provincial negotiations in the fall of 1981. A settlement was finally reached on November 5, 1981, despite the vigorous opposition of René Lévesque, then premier of Quebec.[8] In the past, when Quebec had alone dissented from proposed amendment procedures—as with the 1964 Fulton-Favreau formula and the 1971 Victoria Charter—the deals fell apart, implying that Quebec enjoyed a veto over constitutional change.[9] This time, in 1981, a Supreme Court judgment ruled that Trudeau simply needed the "substantial agreement" of the provinces—and not their unanimous consent—for his patriation plan. After obtaining the consent of all provinces but Quebec, a constitutional resolution was passed by the Canadian Parliament on December 8, 1981, and transmitted to Westminster for its approval on March 29, 1982. Proclamation of the *Canada Act, 1982,* and the *Constitution Act, 1982* by Queen Elizabeth followed in Ottawa on April 17, 1982.[10]

The constitutional deal of 1982 essentially did three things:

1. it added a domestic amending formula requiring the consent of seven of 10 provinces representing 50 percent of the population for most constitutional amendments;

2. it terminated the authority of the United Kingdom parliament over Canada; and,

3. it created and adopted the *Charter of Rights and Freedoms.*

But the struggle was a long and arduous one, and it left some Québécois with a sense of betrayal. Indeed, November 5, 1982, the date the deal was struck between the federal government and the nine English-speaking provinces, is still referred to by some in Quebec as "the night of the long knives." The legitimacy of the 1982 deal, then, is diminished: Quebec still has not signed the *Constitution Act, 1982.*

Subsequent attempts to bring Quebec back into the constitutional fold have been stunning failures, and have fed the momentum of separatist forces in the province. First, in 1985, then Prime Minister Brian Mulroney initiated discussions between Ottawa and the 10 provinces, aimed at producing a constitutional amendment that would satisfy Quebec's concerns (see Box 6-1). The result—the Meech Lake Accord—would have, among other things, declared Quebec a "distinct society," and would have given all the provinces a veto over constitutional amendments affecting certain national political institutions such as Parliament and the Supreme Court. This entailed changing the amending formula arrived at in 1982, and so required unanimous consent of all the provinces, plus Ottawa. But some of the premiers who signed the Meech Lake Accord were replaced in subsequent elections by others less sympathetic to it, before they could get the Accord ratified in their legislatures. Moreover, the three-year ratification period allowed opponents of the Accord to launch a long and loud denunciation of both the secretive closed-door manner in which the deal was made, as well as the substance of the deal. In the end, both Manitoba and Newfoundland failed to ratify the Accord—and it died.[11]

Two years later, Mulroney tried again. Only this time, the issue was immensely complicated by the broadened focus of the negotiations to include not just Quebec's concerns, but those of all the provinces and Aboriginals too. The result was an unwieldy shopping list of demands known as the Charlottetown Accord. Whereas

BOX 6-1

The Meech Lake Accord

The Meech Lake Accord was the first attempt to amend the Constitution using the new amending formula added to the Constitution in 1982. Meech Lake was the 1987 agreement between then Prime Minister Brian Mulroney and the 10 provincial premiers. It was developed in response to a series of five demands that Quebec government of Robert Bourassa made as conditions before Quebec would sign the Constitution. The main demands were as follows:

1. **Immigration policy** Some federal powers over immigration would be transferred to Quebec. This would have constitutionalized an agreement that Ottawa and Quebec had already worked out in 1978 anyway. Other provinces would also be able to assume these expanded powers if they wanted to.
2. **Distinct society** Quebec would be recognized as a "distinct society," and the government and legislature of the province would have a responsibility to "preserve and promote the distinct identity of Quebec." The distinct identity referred to in this section was explicitly linked to the French language. As well, this section of the Accord declared that the Constitution of Canada would be interpreted in a manner consistent with the recognition of Quebec as a distinct society.
3. **Supreme Court** Provincial governments would have been given the right to nominate candidates for the Supreme Court of Canada. When filling a vacancy on the nine-member court, Ottawa would be obliged to select from the provinces' list of nominees and to select three from Quebec (already a conventional practice).
4. **Shared-cost programs** Any provincial government would have the right to receive reasonable compensation from Ottawa in the event that it decided not to participate in a new national shared-cost program. The only stipulation was that the provincial program would have to be "compatible with the national objectives."
5. **Amending procedures** Two important changes were proposed to the amending formula. The first would have changed the provision that allows a province to opt out of constitutional amendments, so that a dissenting province would receive reasonable financial compensation

to finance its own programs in the case of any transfer of legislative power from the provinces to Ottawa. The second change involved the list of subjects requiring the unanimous consent of the provinces. The Accord would have doubled the length of this list, adding to it the following: Senate reform, the principle of proportionate representation of the provinces in the House of Commons, any change to the Supreme Court, and the establishment of new provinces.

the Meech Lake Accord contained only the five basic demands of the Quebec government, the Charlottetown Accord contained 60 substantive sections. While Meech was known as the "Quebec round" of constitutional negotiations, Charlottetown was clearly the "Canada round" (see Box 6-2). But this attempt to accommodate the many interests that felt they were left out of the Meech Lake Accord only resulted in an overly complex document. Moreover, the massive level of public consultation surrounding the development of the Charlottetown Accord failed to dispel the perception that this was still, ultimately, a deal among elites. A national referendum was held on the Charlottetown Accord on October 26, 1992. A majority of Canadians—54.4 percent—rejected the proposed reforms, including provincial majorities in British Columbia, Alberta, Saskatchewan, Manitoba, Quebec and Nova Scotia, as well as the Yukon. In Ontario, it was virtually a tie. Ironically, it became clear during the referendum debate that while many English Canadians said "no" to Charlottetown because they thought that it gave too much to Quebec, many Québécois said "no" because it did not give them enough![12]

The Meech Lake and Charlottetown episodes fanned the flames of Quebec nationalism, and led to the second referendum in Quebec on sovereignty association in 1995. The result—the narrowest of victories by the federal government—prompted Prime Minister Chrétien to introduce the "Clarity Bill" (discussed below) to test the constitutional validity of Quebec independence. In August 1998, Chrétien asked the Supreme Court of Canada to clarify whether Quebec enjoyed the legal right to unilaterally cecede from Canada. The courts ruled that Quebec could not *unilaterally* cecede, but that the rest of Canada would be obliged to negotiate terms of secession if a *clear* majority of Qubecers voted to do so on the basis of a *clear* referendum question.[13]

An integral part of the 1982 *Constitution Act* was the inclusion of the **Charter of Rights and Freedoms**, which entrenched our rights in a way that they never were before. The *Charter* makes formal distinctions among different kinds of rights that we enjoy: 1) fundamental political freedoms; 2) democratic rights; 3) mobility rights; 4) legal rights; 5) equality rights; and 6) language rights. Most of these rights were part of Canada's Constitution before 1982; some can be found in the *BNA Act,* 1867; some are considered part of the common law. But by specifically delineating these rights and including them in the Constitution, an important shift has occurred in the distribution of power in the Canadian constitutional system. Now, Canadian citizens are far more conscious of their common rights and the

BOX 6-2

The Main Features of the Charlottetown Accord

If Meech Lake can be considered the "Quebec round" of constitutional negotiations, the Charlottetown Accord can be considered the "Canada round." The main features of the Charlottetown Accord were as follows:

➤ a Canada clause listing the fundamental characteristics of Canadian society

➤ recognition of Quebec as a distinct society

➤ entrenchment of the rights of Aboriginal self-government

➤ an elected Senate with equal representation from the provinces and, eventually, special seats for Aboriginal representatives

➤ a francophone veto in the Senate regarding bills affecting the French language or culture

➤ guarantee of three Quebec judges on the Supreme Court and provincial input in the selection of judges

➤ a guarantee that Quebec would always have at least 25 percent of the seats in the House of Commons

➤ entrenchment of Ottawa's right to spend money on matters within provincial jurisdiction, but with the provision that any province could opt out of any shared-cost program and be entitled to reasonable compensation to run its own program

➤ confirmation of the province's exclusive jurisdiction in several policy areas, and some decentralization of powers to the provinces in the area of immigration and labour policy.

ways in which they can defend them. This has given rise to an increase in individual citizens becoming more "judicially conscious," i.e. more willing to use the courts to defend their rights. It has also meant that interest groups have become more aware of this avenue of challenging governmental power. Court challenges to established authority have been on the rise, as Canadians get used to employing this new tool in the constitutional arsenal. Finally, it also means that the judges and the judicial branch of government have come to play an enhanced role in the Canadian political system, and that old notions of parliamentary supremacy have had to be reassessed in light of a more activist judiciary.[14]

Federalism and the Constitution

At this stage, it is useful for us to return to the issue of federalism first raised in Chapter 5, and focus on the way in which the Constitution defines the nature of the relationship between the different levels of government and judicial interpretation of the division of powers. You will recall that a federal system of government is one in which the constitutional authority to make laws is divided between a national government and some number of regional governments. Neither the national government acting alone, nor the regional governments acting together, have the authority to alter the power of the other level of government. They are coordinate and equal in their own constitutional spheres.

The very existence of federalism depends upon its articulation within the Constitution; that is to say, federalism is a legal term based in the Constitution. It is a system that vests power in at least two levels of government by virtue of a country's basic constitutional law. Within that constitutional law, certain areas of authority are assigned to a central government, and others to regional governments; theoretically, neither can interfere with the jurisdiction of the other. So each level of government has independent power, free from the dominance and control of the other.

In this theoretical model of perfect federalism, or classic federalism, there are "watertight compartments" of power.[15] The delineation of jurisdictional authority is clearly laid out, and neither level of government ever crosses the line. In Canada, we have never really had "classic federalism." When we look at the original Constitution, it is apparent that the Fathers of Confederation consciously developed a system whereby the federal level of government would have certain powers that would permit it to intrude in provincial jurisdiction; thus, we have never had the "watertight compartments" of classic federalism. We were handed a federal system in which the federal government was clearly intended to be the more powerful of the two levels of government, and was even to be permitted to intrude into provincial areas of jurisdiction. Indeed, Sir John A. Macdonald prophesied a role of little significance for provincial governments; he saw them as glorified municipal councils.[16] Macdonald turned out to be a better prime minister than he was a prophet.

The key sections of the Canadian Constitution that deal with federalism are those laying out the division of powers, primarily sections 91 and 92, but also sections 93, 94, 95, 101, 117 and 132. Sections 91 and 92 are the most significant. As we will see, each section listed a number of powers to be held exclusively by the national and provincial governments. But only a few subsections within sections 91 and 92 have provided the basis for most of the power of the national and provincial governments, and these have formed the basis of most of the legal and political debate over jurisdiction.

Federalism divides political authority along territorial or regional lines. The extent to which this occurs depends on a variety of factors particular to the society in question. Thus, power may be centralized—that is, held mostly by the national government, or decentralized—that is, held mostly by the regional governments. This is determined by such things as the particular geographic, social and political conditions within a country.

Not surprisingly, the different players in the Confederation struggle had differing conceptions of the new system. We have already noted that Macdonald wanted to create a strong central government and weak, insignificant provincial governments. Others, though, felt differently. Oliver Mowat, for example, who would go on to become the longest serving premier in Ontario history and a champion of provincial rights, resisted the establishment of too strong a central government.[17] In any event, the agreement reached gave the central government what were then considered to be the most important legislative powers and sources of public revenue. Ottawa was thus given authority over trade and commerce, shipping, fisheries, interprovincial transportation, currency and banking, the postal service, and several other subjects largely related to the managing of the economy. Responsibility for immigration and agriculture was divided between the federal and provincial governments, but in the event of a conflict, Ottawa's legislation would prevail. The federal government was also assigned the job of building an intercolonial railway from Halifax to Montreal. Together, these powers seemed to establish Ottawa's clear superiority over the provinces in economic matters. When we consider that the two main functions of the state in the 19th century were military defence and economic growth, Ottawa certainly was assigned the major legislative powers of that era.

Ottawa was also given the most important taxation powers. Customs and excise taxes were the most important sources of government revenue prior to Confederation, and these became the exclusive preserve of the federal government, which could raise money "by any Mode or System of Taxation," according to s. 91(3) of the *BNA Act*. The provinces were limited to the less lucrative field of "direct taxation" through s. 92(2), as well as royalties on provincially owned natural resources through s. 109. So the provincial revenue sources were meagre compared to those available to the federal government. Recognizing this, the Confederation agreement also established the practice of transferring federal funds to the provinces. Thus, the economic dependence of the weaker provinces on federal funding began in 1867, and continues to this day.

In addition, there were several parts of the Confederation agreement that took Canada farther away from the model of classic federalism and watertight compartments. In fact, there are sections of the *BNA Act* that appear to establish an almost colonial relationship between Ottawa and the provinces, by permitting the federal government to disallow laws passed by the provincial legislatures. In addition, the *BNA Act* gives provincial lieutenant-governors—appointees of Ottawa—the power to reserve approval of any act passed by a provincial legislature for up to one year after its passage. These powers of **reservation** (s. 57) and **disallowance** (s. 56) were widely used in the early years of Confederation, and periodically in the first 40 years of the 20th century, and clearly established the primacy of the federal government over the provincial governments. In most cases, the federal government used these powers when a province challenged Ottawa's supremacy over economic matters. And s. 92(10c) gives the federal government the authority to intervene in a provincial economy by declaring that the construction of a "public work" (which could mean a road or bridge, or similar type of structure) was in the national interest. This power was used more than 470 times since Confederation, although not since 1961. Finally, ss. 93(3) and (4) give Ottawa the power to pass laws respecting education, an area of provincial jurisdiction. It may do so when education rights, held by denominational minorities when a province entered Confederation, are abrogated by provincial law. This power has never been used.

It is clear that the Fathers of Confederation did not establish a system true to the principles of classic federalism. Instead, they developed what we might call a quasi-federal system. Instead of watertight compartments, there are several examples of spillover and outright intrusion by the federal government in provincial areas. So we can conclude from this that the Fathers of Confederation intended to create a federal system with a strong central government and subordinate provincial governments. The irony is that today Canada is considered to have one of the most decentralized federal systems in the world; that is, the central government is easily challenged by the regional governments for supremacy in a variety of areas. Why is this the case, given the intentions of the Fathers of Confederation? The answer lies in a number of areas that we will consider. But first, let us look at the way the federal bargain came to be interpreted by the federal and provincial governments of Canada.

Federal versus Provincial Rights

Soon after Confederation, Ontario and Quebec began to agitate for more power and more control over their own destinies within Confederation. Then Premier Mowat of Ontario and then Premier Honoré Mercier of Quebec launched what came to be known as the Provincial Rights movement,[18] based on a theory developed about the original Confederation agreement that was used to argue that the provinces were the equals of the federal government, and not subordinate to it. Quebec judge T.J.J. Loranger first articulated the theory in the early 1880s, when he declared, "The confederation of the British Provinces was the result of a compact entered into by the Provinces and the Imperial [British] Parliament which, in enacting the *British North America Act,* simply ratified it." As political scientist Kenneth McRoberts points out, "[F]rom this it followed that there could be no enhancement of federal powers without the consent of all the provincial governments."[19] The provinces agreed to give up certain powers to a new national government that they (the provinces) had created, but they maintain that the federal "bargain" could not be changed without the mutual consent of those who agreed to it. In the case of the compact theory, this means that Quebec should enjoy a veto over constitutional change affecting the division of powers and Quebec's position within national institutions such as Parliament and the Supreme Court, because Quebec has a majority of one of the original signatories to the compact—French-Canadians. As we noted above, this view was rejected in the 1981 Patriation Reference by the Supreme Court, and in practice when the Constitution was patriated against the express will of the Quebec government in 1982. The view of federalism as a contract among the provinces claims that each province has a veto over constitutional changes that affect provincial powers or their representation in national institutions.[20]

In terms of constitutional law, it is striking that neither the compact theory nor the contract theory has any legal, constitutional basis. But their importance lies in their political and symbolic strength. This is clear because for years Canadian politicians were unable to agree on a basic amending formula for the Canadian Constitution. This anomaly persisted because the federal government and the provinces could not agree as to which theory best applied to the Canadian condition. As of 1982, of course, we have an amending formula, but both compact and contract theory continue to have political importance. Quebec's refusal to sign the Constitution in 1982, and the subsequent attempts to reform the Constitution in the Meech Lake and Charlottetown rounds of constitutional negotiations, were recent examples of the provinces and the federal government arguing over what theory of federalism best applies to Canada. Is Canada a binational compact between English and French? Or is it a contract among 10 equal partners? We have still not solved that basic question.[21]

Whatever theory best explains the federal-provincial relationship, both levels of government exercise a range of powers assigned to each by the Constitution. So if you want to know what level of government is responsible for your particular misery, look at sections 91 and 92 of the *Constitution Act, 1982*. However, any reading of these sections must be undertaken cautiously, since conditions have changed considerably since they were first drafted. Moreover, a raft of new issues has arisen that could not even have been imagined by the Fathers of Confederation. In 1867, the framers of Confederation did not have to wrestle with problems such as old age pensions, air transportation, broadcasting and telecommunications technology, nuclear energy, environmental protection, and so on. So none of these are explicitly assigned to either Ottawa or the provinces. In addition, issues that were of minor significance in 1867 took on tremendous importance in the 20th century, as the role of the state has evolved over the past 135 years in ways unfathomable to the generation of the 1860s.

In addition, it is important to note that some powers are held even though they are nowhere listed in the Constitution. The most important of these is federal **spending power**. There is no mention of such a thing in the Constitution, so it is an implied power rather than a stated one. Ottawa spends billions of dollars every year on social and education policies and programs that fall, strictly speaking, under provincial authority. As political scientist Keith Banting explains, "[A]ccording to the federal view, the spending power allows the federal government to make payments to individuals, institutions, or governments for purposes on which Parliament does not necessarily have the power to regulate. That is, it claims the power to give money away, and attach conditions if it wishes, even if the purposes involved clearly fall within provincial jurisdiction, as specified by the *BNA Act*."[22] Ottawa's "right" to spend money in any way it sees fit has never been definitely established by the courts, and provokes a good deal of controversy.[23] But nonetheless, the spending power has provided the constitutional basis for many major federal expenditures. Needless to say, this can cause friction between the two levels of government, as Ottawa wades into a field with its massive spending power and consequently distorts or usurps related provincial initiatives. Recently, for the first time, Ottawa agreed to certain limitations on the use of the spending power in an agreement signed with the provinces (except Quebec) and territories known as the Social Union Framework Agreement (SUFA) (discussed below).[24] But the impact and extent of the limitiations are yet to be tested.

Contention over the federal use of spending power is but one area of federal-provincial conflict, though. And how are disputes resolved over the division of powers within federalism? In several ways, including going to court—an issue we will now look at.

Constitutional Law

One of the advantages of listing the **division of powers** in the Constitution is that it theoretically delineates what jurisdictional authority each level of government enjoys, or so we might think. In fact, the list of federal and provincial powers in sections 91 and 92 has actually fuelled more conflict between the two levels of government than perhaps any other institution of government, because items on the list are subject to a variety of interpretations. Powers such as "trade and commerce," "property and civil rights," and "direct taxation" may seem straightforward enough. But when important material interests are at stake for the constitutional experts, lawyers, judges and citizens who launch constitutional challenges against federal or provincial law, words and phrases take on whole new meanings unintended by the Fathers of Confederation. Thus, the supposedly clear-cut list of powers becomes a source of endless haggling and interpretation, and, in fact, we find that court interpretations over the division of powers have produced some unexpected results, which have effectively recast the face of Canadian federalism, for better or worse.

Let us begin by looking at the ways in which the courts interpreted what was perhaps meant to be the most sweeping power handed to the federal government. The preamble to section 91 authorizes the Parliament of Canada "to make Laws for the Peace, Order and Good Government of Canada, in relation to all Matters not coming within the Classes of Subjects by this Act assigned exclusively to the Legislatures of the Provinces...," while section 91(2) authorizes the federal government to make laws for "The Regulation of Trade and Commerce."[25]

Peace, Order and Good Government

At first blush, "Peace, Order and Good Government" (P.O.G.G.) may appear to be a wide power, under which a variety of laws could be justified. But over time, this power has been reduced to one available to the federal government only in times of emergency. The restrictions on the use of P.O.G.G. began with a ruling by the JCPC in a case called *Local Prohibition,* in 1896. The issue revolved around regulation of the lucrative sale of liquor. In an earlier case, *Russell v. The Queen* (1882), the JCPC held that the *Canada Temperance Act,* a federal law that established a local-option temperance scheme, was constitutional, since temperance did not fall under provincial jurisdiction. But later, in the *Local Prohibition* case, the provinces tried to introduce their own local-option temperance schemes, and the JCPC ruled in their favour. However, to do so, it had to argue that the *Local Prohibition* case was upheld on the basis of the P.O.G.G. power, even though this had not been articulated at the time of the case. In rationalizing this decision, the judges argued that the federal government could only use P.O.G.G. if the issue at hand was one of "national dimensions"; that is, if it was important nationally. Since, in the view of the judges, temperance was not an issue of national concern, the federal government was not justified in using P.O.G.G. to launch its own temperance scheme. But meanwhile, they left open the question of how to determine what constitutes "national dimensions."[26] Nonetheless, these cases represent the beginning of the winnowing-away of the federal power of P.O.G.G.

The question of what exactly qualifies as "national dimensions" became moot in a sense, since later cases determined that a new standard had to be met for the federal government to justify a law under P.O.G.G.: national emergency. This view developed in three subsequent court cases. In the *Board of Commerce Act and Combines and Fair Prices Act*, 1919, a case heard in 1922, the JCPC struck down two federal laws intended to prevent the development of monopolies and hoarding of essential goods (food, clothing and fuel), and which required fair prices for those goods after the First World War.[27] The courts struck down the laws, but said that they might have been justifiable laws under the conditions of a national emergency. In so saying, the courts specified that P.O.G.G. should only be applied during times of war, or famine or some similar condition. So in the *Board of Commerce* case, the courts actually made it harder for the federal government to employ this power than if they had simply argued that an issue had acquired "national dimensions," as they suggested in the earlier *Local Prohibition* case. The fact that an issue had acquired "national dimensions" would no longer be sufficient to justify such exceptional legislation.

Subsequent rulings on P.O.G.G. also suggested that it was essentially a power to be employed only in wartime or other similar, exceptional circumstances. In the *Fort Frances Pulp and Power Company v. the Manitoba Free Press*, 1923, for instance, the JCPC declared that war-related circumstances were sufficient to warrant legislating under P.O.G.G., and indicated that the courts would be out of line in questioning Parliament's authority to do so under the conditions of a war or war-related emergency.[28] In this case, the courts argued that controlling the price and supply of newsprint would normally be a matter of provincial jurisdiction under the province's power in section 92(13), "Property and Civil Rights in the Province." But it was willing to concede that under wartime conditions, P.O.G.G. could be used to "trump" provincial jurisdiction. Subsequent court rulings backed up this view.

In fact, in cases where the courts rejected the federal government's use of P.O.G.G. as a valid basis for federal legislation, the legislation dealt with peacetime circumstances. The first of these was the decision in *Toronto Electric Commissioners v. Snider*, 1925, in which the JCPC struck down Canada's major industrial relations legislation. It argued that relations between employers and employees were a matter of civil rights in the province, and therefore within provincial jurisdiction. The JCPC also struck down the peacetime use of P.O.G.G. in three decisions in 1937 concerning the federal government's right to make laws regarding unemployment and social insurance, agricultural marketing boards and labour relations.[29] The government of R.B. Bennett passed the laws as part of its New Deal legislation to mitigate the ravages of the Great Depression. But Bennett lost the 1935 election, and his successor, William Lyon Mackenzie King, referred the legislation to the courts to test their constitutionality. The Bennett government had attempted to justify the law on the basis that the Depression of the 1930s was a national concern, and that it threatened the well-being of the country. In all three cases, the JCPC considered this argument inadequate.

In the 1970s, the courts were once again confronted with a federal government that wanted to use the P.O.G.G. to justify legislation intended to deal with economic problems outside wartime. In a ruling on the constitutionality of Ottawa's *Anti-Inflation Act,* 1975, the federal government argued that growing inflation constituted an emergency justifying legislation that infringed on provincial jurisdiction. The judges agreed. This ruling made it easier for the federal government to use the P.O.G.G. power by detaching it from the emergency doctrine. The court also declared that it was really up to Parliament, and not the courts, to determine when an emergency existed.[30]

The "Regulation of Trade and Commerce" power in section 91(2) of the Constitution also appears to be a broad source of authority for Ottawa, but it too has been interpreted narrowly by the courts. It has come to be limited largely to interprovincial and international trade. In contrast, the provincial power over "Property and Civil Rights in the Province" in section 92(13) has been interpreted more the way you might expect the trade and commerce power to have been interpreted. *Citizen's Insurance v. Parsons,* 1881, was the first major case to limit trade and commerce power.[31] The JCPC ruled that a broad, literal interpretation of "trade and commerce" would unnecessarily restrict provincial rights under property and civil rights, and would bring all aspects of economic life under the authority of Ottawa. Never mind that this was the intention of the framers of Confederation! The JCPC nonetheless limited Ottawa's powers over trade and commerce in this case by suggesting that what the phrase "trade and commerce" meant was the regulation of trade in matters of interprovincial concern, and the general regulation of trade affecting the whole country.

The legacy of the *Parsons* case has been problematic. For example, it is possible that some federal laws that regulate trade between provinces may also affect trade that occurs strictly within a province. Is such a law constitutional? Until the 1950s, the courts said "no." But over the years, a series of court decisions gradually loosened the restrictions placed on the trade and commerce power in the *Parsons* case.[32] Nonetheless, the overall effect of the *Parsons* case, and others like it, was to severely restrict the powers of the federal government.

Federal-Provincial Bargaining

This brief overview of select examples of constitutional law judgments shows the impact of judicial review on federalism, and ultimately on public administration in Canada. But the courts are only one avenue for settling conflicts between Ottawa and the provinces, and their decisions do not always put an end to that conflict. Besides determining the constitutionality of law, another power the courts have is to force the two levels of government back to the bargaining table.[33] For example in *Employment and Social Service Act Reference,* 1937, the JCPC decision to strike down a federal law establishing a program to deal with national unemployment precipitated federal-provincial negotiations that led to a constitutional amendment giving the federal government power over unemployment insurance in 1940. In *Public Service Board v. Dionne,* 1978, the Supreme Court confirmed Ottawa's exclusive jurisdiction to regulate television broadcasting. But right after the decision by the courts, Ottawa indicated its willingness to negotiate with the provinces to share authority over this area. In *CIGOL v. Government of Saskatchewan,*

1978, a provincial tax on natural gas was found to be a direct tax, and therefore outside provincial jurisdiction. Later, during the constitutional negotiations of 1981–1982, control over natural resources was negotiated that appeared to broaden the powers of the provinces in this area and permit some form of resource taxation in section 92A of the *Constitution Act, 1982,* which was ruled ultra vires in an earlier decision. In the *Patriation Reference,* 1981, the Supreme Court ruled that Ottawa's proposal to patriate the *BNA Act* and to change it in ways that affected provincial power was legal, but that it was not constitutional in the conventional sense. This gave the federal government a legal victory, but at the same time suggested that the political consequences for proceeding were too high. The provinces and the federal government were forced back to the negotiating table.

More recently, the 1998 decision of the Supreme Court on the right of a province to unilaterally secede from Confederation is illustrative of the role of the courts in encouraging discussion and negotiations between the two levels of government. In this decision, the federal government asked the Supreme Court of Canada to rule on three questions:

1. Under the Constitution of Canada, can the National Assembly, legislature or government of Quebec effect the secession of Quebec from Canada unilaterally?

2. Does international law give the National Assembly, legislature or government of Quebec the right to effect the secession of Quebec from Canada unilaterally? In this regard, is there a right to self-determination under international law that would give the National Assembly, legislature or government of Quebec the right to effect the secession of Quebec from Canada unilaterally?

3. In the event of a conflict between domestic and international law on the right of the National Assembly, legislature or government of Quebec to effect the secession of Quebec from Canada unilaterally, which would take precedence in Canada?[34]

The court response to this potentially explosive set of questions gave a little bit to both sides (the federal government and the separatist government of Quebec) in that it suggested that unilateral secession was illegal and unconstitutional, but that if the citizens of Quebec voted to separate, the federal government would be bound to negotiate the terms of the secession with the Quebec government. As with the 1981 *Patriation Reference,* the ball was thrown squarely back into the laps of the politicians.

Constitutional law, though, is not the only way to resolve conflicts between the federal and provincial governments. In fact, in many instances, it is not even the best way to do so. Over the years, a system of intergovernmental bargaining and negotiation has developed, whereby the two levels of government get together to discuss their differences in much the same way that countries carry out international negotiation; that is to say, at the highest political and bureaucratic levels.[35] At these meetings, each province puts its own particular regional concerns on the table, while the federal government attempts to bring national concerns to the discussion. Since each province comprises many different economic, social and cultural interests, intergovernmental conflict is to some extent the clash of conflicting regional demands in Canada.[36] As well, the state, whether federal or provincial, has its own set of interests, whether it is to constantly expand in size and influence and power, or to seek jurisdictional control of a particular area.[37] Thus, intergovernmental relations are driven by both the demands of regional societies within Canada, and the demands of the states that represent those regions.

Intergovernmental negotiations frequently focus on issues of jurisdiction: Who has the authority to tax and spend in which areas? The arcane discussions and disputes that arise from these negotiations between the federal and provincial governments often seem remote and detached from the lives and concerns of ordinary Canadians. But from the state's point of view, how revenue sources and legislative jurisdiction are divided affects the ability of politicians to pursue their interest in reelection, career advancement and personal prestige. The same is true of bureaucrats.

The provincial governments in Canada have a long history of trying to wrestle power and jurisdiction away from the federal government. And frequently, provincial governments are backed up, from within, by powerful economic interests. We refer to this process as **province-building**, when the political needs of governments are reinforced by the demands of provincially oriented economic interests. This is, in effect, the provincial counterpart to the nation-building initiated by Sir John A. Macdonald. The term "province-building" was originally applied to the efforts of then Ontario Premier Oliver Mowat and then Quebec Premier Honoré Mercier, who aggressively tried to expand the powers and rights of their provincial governments vis-à-vis the federal government. More recently, it refers to the aggressive British Columbia, Alberta and Quebec governments, since lately these have been the most vocal in their demands.

We have already seen how the Constitution does not provide a neat division of powers between the two levels of government. Clearly, both levels of government have come to have a share in a variety of tax and legislative areas, and this fact causes conflict between the two. The basic fact of divided jurisdiction has given rise to a sprawling and complicated network of relations linking the two levels of government. There are two basic elements to this network of relations: the part we see, and the part we don't. The part we see involves meetings between the prime minister and provincial premiers (First Ministers' Conferences). These meetings always generate a great deal of media interest, and at least part of their proceedings usually takes place before the cameras. Less publicized, but far more frequent, are the hundreds of meetings between federal and provincial Cabinet ministers and their bureaucratic advisors. Some of these are established as regular annual (or more often than annual) meetings; others are called as a new issue or demand arises. In any event, a complex web of intergovernmental meetings and conferences is now a regular feature of Canadian federalism, which, as we noted earlier, in some ways reflects the way sovereign countries carry on international negotiations.[38]

The meetings and relations between the prime minister and premiers, and between Cabinet ministers from both levels of government, have evolved into a formalized and regularized feature of Canadian federalism.[39] It has its own name, executive federalism, because it involves meetings between the executives of both levels of government.[40] Executive federalism, by its nature, excludes the public, and it excludes the elected members of the federal and provincial legislatures. Instead, negotiations and agreements are usually undertaken with little input from anyone but the federal and provincial executives and their closest bureaucratic advisors. This, plus the fact that these negotiations are secret and private, often raise the charge that executive federalism is undemocratic. It is considered undemocratic because it undermines the elected legislatures, whose role, if they are given any role at all in this process, is simply to approve what the executives have come up with. As well, there is usually no opportunity within this structure and process of executive federalism for public input or debate. Thus decisions about important public issues, such as health care, education, taxation, and other matters of real concern to ordinary citizens, are removed from the public realm and discussed behind closed doors. Citizens, political parties, interest groups, and others are generally excluded from a process of decision-making dominated by the prime minister, premiers, and Cabinet ministers and their bureaucratic advisors.[41]

In addition to these criticisms, executive federalism has been blamed for distorting the political agenda by reinforcing regional differences and obscuring the national interest. At the same time, it undervalues the importance of nonregional interests. As well, it fuels government expansion, because competitive relations between the two levels of government produce duplication of services. And it perpetuates intergovernmental conflict by, in effect, giving provincial premiers a stage from which to publicize and air their grievances. Still, in the absence of an alternative, executive federalism appears as an enduring institution of contemporary Canadian politics. Perhaps the most prominent recent example of the process of intergovernmental relations through executive federalism was the failed Meech Lake Accord. The five demands were all agreed to by the prime minister and the 10 premiers in the kind of secret, closed-door negotiations that are the hallmark of executive federalism.

What did we learn from this experience? First, it seemed to show that nothing much had changed as a result of our newfangled amending formula. The proposal in Meech Lake represented a deal struck by 11 heads of government—a deal that was reached with no public input or legislative debate. In fact, Mulroney and some of the premiers betrayed a stunning arrogance in insisting that no changes could be made to "their" deal, that it could not be altered in any respect, even after it became apparent that there were many problems with it. It was submitted to the legislatures for ratification—not modification. In effect, Meech Lake came to represent elitist deal-making at its worst.

The death of Meech Lake did not end the constitutional wrangling. However, it did teach the politicians—or at least some of them—a lesson. So when they reopened constitutional negotiations, they broadened them to include the public, to a certain extent. The next two years saw dozens of government-sponsored public hearings on the Constitution, and hundreds of conferences and forums organized by academics, political parties and interest groups. Ottawa and the provinces were determined to avoid charges of elitist deal-making that had been levelled against the Meech Lake process. But in this they failed. Despite ample opportunities for citizens and groups to express their views on constitutional reform, the proposals presented to Canadians in the October 26, 1992, referendum were widely viewed as yet another instance of the elites cutting a deal and trying to foist it on the public.

Is executive federalism more problematic than helpful? It would seem that overlapping powers are unavoidable, given the nature of our federal Constitution. But can we realistically expect that the complex negotiations and discussions needed to sort out this reality can be undertaken in public forums? The answer to this question remains to be seen, although political scientists Malcolmson and Myers seem to believe that the Charlottetown referendum has created the expectation in the minds of the public that it will be consulted on future constitutional change. Malcolmson and Myers go so far as to suggest that a new constitutional convention may be emerging before our eyes.[42] Indeed, another round of negotiations (sans Quebec, which refused to participate) involved a meeting of provincial premiers in Calgary in 1997. They produced the Calgary Accord in September 1997, which contains a seven-point framework for bringing Quebec back into the Constitution by declaring it a "unique society," but not before each government has conducted extensive public consultations with its citizens[43] (see Box 6-3). Moreover, Alberta and British Columbia have legislated that provincial referenda must be held before constitutional change can be ratified by their legislatures. Clearly, there is a trend toward more democratic and accountable forums through which to involve the public and debate major issues.

The need to address the charge that executive federalism is elitist and undemocratic has been acknowledged in the latest attempt by the federal and provincial and territorial governments to define their relationship. SUFA, agreed to by all the governments except Quebec in February 1999, contains provisions for enhanced public accountability and public participation. But, strikingly, SUFA was also the product of closed-door negations between the governments involved. In any event, its impact remains to be determined.[44] But to their credit, our political leaders have at least signalled with SUFA that the seemingly interminable round of constitutional haggling that obsessed our first ministers from the 1960s to the 1990s has drawn mercifully to a close. SUFA represents, in part, a move toward a new focus on non-constitutional bargaining[45] and an acknowledgement of the constitutional fatigue that citizens expressed in their rejection of Meech Lake and the Charlottetown Accord.

As this overview suggests, constitutional law is multifaceted and complex. It ranges across a number of issues having to do with the relations between the state and citizens (the *Charter of Rights and Freedoms,* for instance), and the relations between the two levels of government (the division of powers in the Constitution). Administrative law is related to constitutional law, but is focused more exclusively on the relations between citizens and the administrative arm of government. We now turn our attention to administrative law.

BOX 6-3

The Calgary Accord

Reached in Calgary after 10 hours of closed-door meetings between the provincial premiers (excluding the premier of Quebec, who boycotted the meeting), the Calgary Accord contains seven points in a framework for discussion:

➤ All Canadians are equal and have rights protected before the law

➤ All provinces, while diverse in their characteristics, have equality of status

➤ Canada is graced by a diversity, tolerance, compassion and an equality of opportunity that is without rival in the world

➤ Canada's gift of diversity includes Aboriginal peoples and cultures, the vitality of the English and French languages, and a multicultural citizenry drawn from all parts of the world

➤ In Canada's federal system, where respect for diversity underlies unity, the unique character of Quebec society, including its French-speaking majority, its culture and its tradition of civil law, is fundamental to the well-being of Canada. Consequently, the legislature and government of Quebec have a role to protect and develop the unique character of Quebec society within Canada

➤ If any future constitutional amendment confers powers on one province, these powers must be available to all provinces

➤ Canada is a federal system in which federal, provincial and territorial governments work in partnership while respecting each other's jurisdictions. Canadians want their governments to work cooperatively and with flexibility to ensure the efficiency and effectiveness of the federation. Canadians want their governments to work together, particularly in the delivery of their social programs. Provinces and territories renew their commitment to work in partnership with the government of Canada to best serve the needs of Canadians.

Administrative Law

The most visible government institution of which most citizens are conscious is the department or ministry, but below this is a huge array of other bodies with lesser powers and narrower functions. These bodies are termed "agency," "board," "commission," "tribunal," "bureau," or any of a number of other names. Indeed, the variety of names for administrative bodies, and the fact that the same name may imply different functions in two bodies, is one thing that makes administrative law complicated and confusing to the outsider. For instance, the National Energy Board makes licensing decisions; sets rates and conditions regarding energy matters; revokes, suspends or imposes conditions on licence holders; conducts research; and advises government on energy matters. By comparison, the Pension Review Board has a much more constrained and limited role, primarily involving the review of decisions by the Canadian Pension Commission.[46] This lack of uniformity in terms makes administrative law a challenging field. So too does the legalistic language typical of administrative law. Moreover, procedures are not uniform across different agencies, and are a source of many problems in the administrative process. Personnel selection is uneven, and often complicated by patronage appointments. And the process by which citizens launch grievances against administrative bodies is not coordinated. As administrative law expert Alan Leadbeater has noted,

Independent administrative agencies at the federal level in Canada are not easily described or understood. They have a variety of powers and duties; their procedures differ and are not always formalized; their members are appointed in a closed and informal selection process; there is no uniform right of appeal from their decisions and no single appeal body to deal with those appeals; finally, their success in performing delegated functions efficiently and effectively is not regularly or adequately evaluated.[47]

It is to both departments and to these less visible fora that much of administrative law relates.

Lawyer Sara Blake draws our attention to the ubiquity of officials, whose decision-making powers affect our lives: immigration officers, securities commissioners, building inspectors, parole boards, labour relations boards, professional colleges (for example of physicians and surgeons) and so on. She reminds us that:

Much of our lives is governed by decisions made by administrative tribunals and government officials. Parliament and the provincial legislatures enact statutes that set out the framework of rules for a field of activity and then delegate the day-to-day decision-making power to tribunals and officials. These tribunals and officials then decide whether to admit an immigrant, whether to permit a person to trade in the stock market, whether to order an industry to clean up pollution, whether a person is eligible for Employment Insurance, whether to issue a building permit, whether to release a person from prison before the end of the sentence, the rights of employees, the licensing conditions imposed on a television broadcaster, professional discipline, and so on.... In Canada there are thousands of tribunals and officials who have statutory power to make decisions affecting our lives.[48]

An enormous amount of what government does takes place at the discretion of civil servants. This is because virtually no piece of legislation can be drafted in such a way as to foresee every circumstance that might arise in the day-to-day application of its provisions. As a result, a great deal of power is left in the hands of bureaucratic officials to determine how legislation is actually operationalized. But what happens when these officials stray from the spirit, intent or letter of the law that they are implementing? What recourse do citizens have when they feel wronged by the actions or inactions of bureaucratic officials? This is where administrative law comes into play.

The growth of public administration has been accompanied by the concern that arbitrariness and inconsistency might arise in the treatment of citizens by the growing legions of administrators. Personal liberty and control over your own destiny seem increasingly under siege as a result of administrative mechanisms and measures that, while effective in achieving their own internal goals, may fail to take into consideration the rights and freedoms of individuals. Moreover, the growth in administrative bodies has not always been well coordinated, either within the federal government, or across federal-provincial boundaries. Finally, a key problem for the administrative machine has been to develop norms and standards of behaviour that will guarantee effectiveness while simultaneously retaining a measure of discretion and flexibility in the role performed by civil servants.[49] This is a circle not easily squared.

Administrative law is concerned with the manner in which government departments and regulatory agencies actually exercise the legal powers that they have been granted. When a dispute arises (for instance, if a citizen feels that a board is failing in its duties as prescribed by legislation), departments and regulatory agencies are obligated to abide by certain fundamental rules of administrative law that are enforced by the courts. Two theorists of administrative law put it this way:

Administrative Law deals with the legal limitations on the actions of governmental officials, and on the remedies which are available to anyone affected by a transgression of these limits. The subject invariably involves the question of the lawful authority of an official to do a particular act which, in the absence of such authority, might well be illegal.... In our legal system, the mere fact that the government is the government does not give it any particular rights or powers. On the contrary, all governmental actions must be specially authorized by either legislation or the Royal Prerogative. This need for governmental officials to be able to point to the lawful authority permitting their actions makes Administrative Law a close cousin to Constitutional Law.[50]

The modern state is characterized by a substantial delegation of authority and responsibility to various administrative bodies. One observer puts it this way:

The fact of the matter is that while the legislators may give legal effect and governmental force to certain directions in policy or priorities in terms of programmes and activities, it is in the process of implementation, by way of delegated powers and authority, that policies become meaningful and make their impact on particular groups or the society as a whole. It is no secret that much of the legislation which is enacted by Parliament or the legislative authority (as much as 80–90%) originates within the Civil Service, and certainly the regulations made to give practical effect to enabling legislation are almost always subject to the decisive influence of civil servants.[51]

Delegation is limited not just by the Constitution but by administrative law, which embodies principles of fairness and justice developed by the courts. What techniques are used to control delegated power and influence the conduct of administrative bodies? What mechanisms exist, both internally and externally, to watch over administrative bodies and examine the role and practice of administrative tribunals and courts in reviewing administrative decisions and actions? These will be the concerns of this section.

Administrative law is, of course, intimately related to constitutional law, although it is a very young branch of the law overall. But constitutional law may be distinguished from administrative law "mainly by the fact that the former provides a skeleton of broad principles which the latter fleshes out."[52] Frank Scott, the great Canadian constitutional lawyer, once described constitutional law as "a law for the making of laws." Administrative law, then, is concerned with the administrative actions of officials whose powers are derived from laws enacted under the Constitution. A law found to be unconstitutional therefore deprives the administrator of any right to exercise those powers, and further, may give rise to citizens who are adversely affected by the administrator's actions seeking remedies, in the event that the administrator's (illegal) actions caused damages. Administrative law has been defined as the branch of law that "is concerned with the legal limits on the actions of government or its agencies and with the remedies that are available to persons who feel aggrieved by an improper, illegal, or unauthorized act by the government or one of its agencies."[53]

Typically, a statute passed by the government contains only the bare bones of a law. It must then be fleshed out during the implementation stage by the bureaucrats who actually operationalize the law. But in so doing, many of their actions are left to discretion, and herein lies the need for administrative law. In effect, there must be a check against the arbitrary and discretionary interpretation of the law by unelected officials whose job it is to implement the wishes of the elected politicians, and through them, the people. These checks are provided in administrative law by administrative tribunals and, ultimately, the courts. The courts are the principal means by which controls over the administrative process are exercised through the power of judicial review.[54]

The courts play a role at several points in the review of administrative practice. Initially they might examine the validity of power delegated to an administrative body. They may look at the granting of power to the agency to ensure that it is authorized by the principles of law, including the Constitution, or that there has not been an excessive or inappropriate delegation of power. As well, the courts may look into the rule-making process; that is, they may check to see if the regulatory body that has been given power is exercising that power in its own rule-making, or whether it has exceeded the grant of power in constructing its own rules. Finally, the courts may investigate the propriety of the way in which the administrative body has exercised its adjudicative power, which is the power to make decisions involving individual citizens.[55]

A whole series of legal principles, some of them centuries old, has infused the development of administrative law. For instance, there is the principle of *audi alteram partem,* which means that the individual must be given an opportunity to represent her side of an issue in a formal hearing or by some other process.

Moreover, citizens generally have the following rights: to be represented by legal counsel, to be given advance notice of any proceedings and disclosure of evidence that the state may bring, to be given the opportunity to cross-examine witnesses, and to be heard by an impartial adjudicator. Not every one of these principles is necessarily in effect in every single case of administrative law. But over the years the courts have reinforced the importance of these principles of natural justice to an ever-widening range of administrative individuals and organizations. This ensures that civil servants who are challenged by citizens cannot run roughshod over the rights of those citizens in their zeal in interpreting Parliament's will.

These principles contribute to the elaborate decision-making process judges engage in, in deciding to overturn or support a particular administrative action. Judges must decide within the context of these principles whether an administrative action is based upon an error of law, an error of fact, or inadequate evidence or information. They must also determine when not to intervene in an issue, allowing administrators to exercise their **discretion** in acting. But in the event that the judges do decide a wrong is committed, they must next determine what the remedy is for the aggrieved citizen. The courts have a number of options where remedies are concerned, ranging from simply quashing the administrative action or decision of the agency concerned, to ordering the agency to take some action that it had failed to take, to ordering the agency to compensate the citizen.

Complicating our study of administrative law is the fact that there are four main actors involved, each with his own perspective. These are citizens, politicians, bureaucrats and judges. Each has a unique take on whether a law is working or has been administered properly. Somehow, at the intersection of these four groups of disparate perspectives, public policy must be made to work. It can be an imposing challenge.

Assuming that a given law is constitutionally valid, the next task is to determine the exact nature and scope of the powers delegated to officials. It is striking that most of the business of government is actually contained in delegated powers instead of in the actual laws passed by Parliament. Power can be delegated to a number of places (see Box 6-4). The legislation can say, for instance, that power is delegated to Cabinet, to a particular Cabinet minister, a particular bureaucrat, a judge, or even to a private citizen. In theory, there is no limit to the powers that Parliament can delegate to others, because of the doctrine of parliamentary supremacy, which means that Parliament has the right to make or unmake any law whatsoever, and no other body has the right to "override or set aside the legislation of Parliament."[56] Therefore, an important aspect of administrative law involves how Parliament devises ways to supervise and control the delegation of powers to administrators.

What happens when the delegated authority oversteps the bounds of the instructions imparted to it by Parliament? The judges are asked to step in and ask the delegate to reveal what statutory authority permitted her to take action. If the delegate cannot demonstrate that her actions are justified under the relevant statute, then her actions are declared *ultra vires* by the court, and thereby beyond the delegate's jurisdiction to act. This can be a daunting process, since legislation is often vague and unclear. Therefore the judges are asked, essentially, to determine precisely what the legislation was intended to do or allow. Upon a court finding an admin-

BOX 6-4

Delegating Power

According to Jones and de Villars, there are several reasons why Parliament delegates authority, including the following:

a) The sheer magnitude of the business of government means that not everything can be dealt with by Parliament or a legislature.

b) Much governmental activity is technical in nature, and only broad principles should be contained in legislation.

c) Delegating power to an administrator allows greater flexibility in applying broad statutory provisions to changing circumstances.

d) It may not be possible to devise a general role to deal with all cases, which may be more conveniently determined in the discretion of a delegate.

e) The need for rapid governmental action may require faster administrative response than can be accommodated by the necessity of legislative amendment.

f) Innovation and experimentation in solving social problems may not be possible if legislation is required.

g) Someone actually has to apply legislation, and that person has to have authority to do so.

h) Emergencies may require broad delegation of powers with respect to a wide range of matters which would normally be dealt with by legislation.

Source: David P. Jones and Anne S. de Villars, *Principles of Administrative Law*, Third Edition, (Toronto: Carswell, 1999): 4–5.

istrator's actions *ultra vires*, the next step is to find a legal remedy. This process of **judicial review** is generally limited to determining whether an administrator has acted strictly within the statutorily delegated powers. In other words, it looks at whether the administrator has legal jurisdiction to act.

One of the important court cases that illustrates the working of judicial review in relation to the question of jurisdiction involved the premier of Quebec in the 1950s. Then Premier Maurice Duplessis had ordered the revocation of a liquor licence belonging to a bar owner who had posted bail for some Jehovah's Witnesses.[57] They had been arrested for distributing religious literature that attacked the Catholic Church. In predominantly Catholic Quebec, this was seen by the premier as a provocation. However, in a court case entitled *Roncarelli v. Duplessis*, the courts ruled that there were jurisdictional errors in the administrative action of revoking Roncarelli's liquor licence. First, the legislature had not delegated power to revoke liquor licences to the premier, but rather to a liquor licensing board. As well, revoking a licence because of posting bond for a group being prosecuted for their religious activity was an irrelevant and improper motive for the exercise of the power granted to the board. As a result, the board's actions (acting at the behest of the premier) were declared *ultra vires;* Roncarelli got to keep his licence and he was awarded damages.

Judicial review can occur for a number of reasons. If an action appears to be *ultra vires,* as the case above illustrates, it can be reviewed. Moreover, exercising discretion for an improper purpose, with malice, in bad faith, by reference to irrelevant considerations, or by not considering relevant matters, through procedural errors or through making an error in law, can all lead to judicial review. There are three central features of administrative law: the Rule of Law, which is the requirement that all government action must be expressly permitted by validly enacted laws; the denial of any special status to the government merely because it is the government; and the right of ordinary courts to determine such questions of legality.[58]

If judicial review concludes that a delegated authority has overstepped the bounds of her authority, administrative law allows for the application of one of several types of remedies (see Box 6-5). But there are also nonjudicial remedies that can be sought. Parliamentarians are often alert to perceived abuses by administrative officials and, especially if they are from the opposition, eager to point them out. The resulting embarrassment for the government may cause a review of administrative practices. In addition, the office of the ombuds is an increasingly common institution. It is responsible for reviewing the propriety and fairness of government actions. Reporting directly to Parliament, the ombuds draws attention to administrative action in such a way that few bureaucrats want to be highlighted in its reports. Finally, administrative practice is itself sometimes self-correcting; that is, administrators learn through trial and error or public criticism which practices are permissible, and alter their behaviour and actions accordingly.

In any event, judicial review can be entirely avoided if the legislation contains what are called *privative clauses.* These deprive the courts of any jurisdiction to review the actions of delegates. Thus, the legislation can expressly state that the administrator's actions shall not be reviewed in any court. The courts, naturally, do not appreciate being frozen out in this manner, and have devised a number of imaginative rulings to allow them to review administrator's actions even when privative clauses have been in effect.

In summary, administrative law, closely related to constitutional law, deals with the legal remedies available to citizens aggrieved by administrative actions. Determining what Parliament means when it delegates powers and authority is a large measure of what administrative law is all about. Thus, administrative law deals with three broad areas of public administration: the ways in which power is transferred from Parliament to administrative agencies; how those agencies use that power; and how the actions taken by administrative agencies are reviewed by the courts.[59] Administrative power has grown tremendously in Canada in terms of powers delegated to administrative bodies, raising questions about control in democratic society. As arcane as it may seem to the uninitiated, administrative law is thus fundamentally important. Those concerned with administrative law must wrestle with many important questions: How much power should be delegated to administrative agencies? How much administrative discretion is too much? What constitutes a fair hearing for those aggrieved by administrative behaviour? Is it reasonable to allow administrative agencies to make law, implement law and determine the fairness of that same law? How can administrative abuses be effectively checked? What internal and external safeguards are needed to prevent abuse by administrators? When should the courts become involved in the review of agency decisions? How can Parliament control the many and diverse administrative agencies for which it is ultimately responsible? Fundamentally, administrative law is about the making of fair procedures in administrative agencies, but this is a complex and daunting task.

Box 6-5

Remedies

When a citizen feels aggrieved by the actions of an administrative official, he can apply for a *prerogative remedy:* a declaration, an injunction, damages or a statutory appeal to a court or another administrative body. Each is explained briefly below:

➤ **Certiorari** an order from the superior court compelling an inferior tribunal or other statutory delegate to render up all records of its proceedings to permit the superior court to determine its lawfulness

➤ **Prohibition** similar to *certiorari*, except that this order occurs before the conclusion of the proceedings by the inferior body, and prohibits it from proceeding in a manner that would take it outside its jurisdiction

➤ **Mandamus** a command by the superior court compelling an inferior body to fulfill a delegated statutory duty

➤ **Habeas corpus** a command that compels the respondent to bring the person of the application before the superior court in order to determine the lawfulness of the respondent's detention of the applicant

➤ **Quo warranto** an order that requires the respondent to demonstrate by what authority she exercises the powers of a particular statutory office

A declaration can be used to determine the lawfulness of an administrator's actions, or the validity of the parent legislation. Claims for damages may be successful if the court finds that an illegal administrative action causes harm. Statutory appeal is sometimes expressly granted by the legislation setting up the administrative machinery in question.

Source: David P. Jones and Anne S. de Villars, *Principles of Administrative Law, Second Edition*, (Toronto: Carswell, 1994): 10–11.

WHAT YOU HAVE LEARNED

This chapter has shown that public administration is intimately connected to the law. While constitutional law deals with the rules, practices and institutions that constitute the state and can be considered the macro-legal environment, administrative law is the micro-legal level, and deals with the discretionary actions of bureaucrats in operationalizing the instructions of Parliament on a day-to-day basis.

Constitutional and administrative law issues are reflective of the broader political culture of the society. In Canada, our proclivity for constitutional wrangling is almost unprecedented anywhere else in the world. And the development of a complex web of administrative bodies and the judicial regime to ensure the laws of the land are being observed by administrators is impressive, if somewhat arcane.

In this chapter, we discussed public administration and the law by examining the following: what a constitution is and what it does; the relationship between the constitution and the institutions of the state; political culture and the legal order; the question of rights and freedoms; the evolution of constitutional politics; the role of the courts in interpreting the division of powers; and finally, administrative law.

ENDNOTES

1. For a discussion of the legal system in Canada see F.L. Morton, *Law, Politics and the Judicial Process in Canada,* (Calgary: University of Calgary, 1984).

2. For a history of the Supreme Court of Canada, see Peter H. Russell, *The Judiciary in Canada: The Third Branch of Government,* (Toronto: McGraw-Hill Ryerson, 1987).

3. The following discussion draws from Stephen Brooks, *Canadian Democracy: An Introduction, Second Edition,* (Toronto: Oxford University Press, 1996): chapter 4.

4. J.R. Mallory, *The Structure of Canadian Government,* (Toronto: Gage, 1971): 1.

5. Patrick Malcolmson and Richard Myers, *The Canadian Regime,* (Peterborough: Broadview Press, 1996): 31.

6. Peter Hogg, *Constitutional Law of Canada, Student Edition 2002,* (Toronto: Carswell, 2002): 2.

7. See A.R.M. Lower, *From Colony to Nation,* (Toronto: University of Toronto Press, 1946).

8. See Robert Sheppard and Michael Valpy, *The National Deal: The Fight for a Canadian Constitution,* (Toronto: Fleet Books, 1982).

9. On the Fulton-Favreau formula, the Victoria Charter, and the ongoing search for an amending formula for the Canadian Constitution, see Garth Stevenson, *Unfulfilled Union: Canadian Federalism and National Unity, Third Edition,* (Toronto: Gage, 1989): chapter 10.

10. See Keith Banting and Richard Simeon, *And No One Cheered: Federalism, Democracy and the Constitution Act,* (Toronto: Methuen, 1983).

11. See Andrew Cohen, *A Deal Undone: The Making and Breaking of the Meech Lake Accord,* (Vancouver: Douglas and McIntyre, 1990); and Patrick Monahan, *Meech Lake: The Inside Story,* (Toronto: University of Toronto Press, 1991).

12. See Martin Westmacott, "The Charlottetown Accord: A Retrospective Overview," in Martin Westmacott and Hugh Mellon, eds. *Challenges to Canadian Federalism,* (Scarborough: Prentice Hall, 1998): 100–111; and Robert M. Campbell and Leslie A. Pal, *The Real Worlds of Canadian Politics: Cases in Process and Policy, Third Edition,* (Peterborough: Broadview Press, 1994): chapter 3.

13. See Jose Woehrling, "The Supreme Court's Ruling on Quebec's Secession: Legality and Legitimacy Reconciled by a Return to Constitutional First Principles," in Hugh Mellon and Martin Westmacott, eds. *Political Dispute and Judicial Review: Assessing the Work of the Supreme Court of Canada,* (Scarborough: Nelson, 2000): 83–101.

14. See Michael Mandel, *The Charter of Rights and the Legalization of Politics in Canada,* (Toronto: Thomson Educational Publishing, 1994); and David P. Shugarman and Reg Whitaker, eds. *Federalism and Political Community: Essays in Honour of Donald Smiley,* (Peterborough: Broadview Press, 1989).

15. See Nathalie Des Rosiers, "Federalism and Judicial Review," in Martin Westmacott and Hugh Mellon, *Challenges to Canadian Federalism,* (Scarborough: Prentice Hall, 1998): 66.

16. Macdonald's view of Confederation is discussed in J.R. Mallory, *The Structure of Canadian Government,* (Toronto: Gage, 1971): 331–334. See also P.B. Waite, ed. *The Confederation Debates in the Province of Canada, 1865,* (Toronto: McClelland and Stewart, 1963).

17. See John Ibbitson, *Loyal No More: Ontario's Struggle for a Separate Destiny*, (Toronto: HarperCollins, 2001); and Donald Swainson, ed. *Oliver Mowat's Ontario,* (Toronto: Macmillan, 1972).

18. See François Rocher and Miriam Smith, "Four Dimensions of the Canadian Constitutional Debate," in François Rocher and Miriam Smith, eds. *New Trends in Canadian Federalism,* (Peterborough: Broadview Press, 1995): 45–66.

19. Kenneth McRoberts, *Misconceiving Canada: The Struggle for National Unity,* (Toronto: Oxford University Press, 1997): 16–17.

20. Brooks, *Canadian Democracy: An Introduction,* (1993). See also Robert C. Vipond, *Liberty and Community: Canadian Federalism and the Failure of the Constitution,* (Albany, New York: State University of New York Press, 1991).

21. See Peter H. Russell, *Constitutional Odyssey: Can Canadians Become a Sovereign People? Second Edition,* (Toronto: University of Toronto Press, 1993).

22. Keith Banting, *The Welfare State and Canadian Federalism, Second Edition,* (Kingston: McGill-Queen's University Press, 1987): 52.

23. See, for instance, David Kwavnick, *The Tremblay Report,* (Toronto: McClelland and Stewart, 1973).

24. See Gregory J. Inwood, "Federalism, Globalization and the (Anti-)Social Union," in Mike Burke, Colin Mooers and John Shields, eds. *Restructuring and Resistance: Canadian Public Policy in an Age of Global Capitlaism,* (Halifax: Fernwood Press, 2000).

25. Canada, Department of Justice, *A Consolidation of the Constitution Acts 1867 to 1982,* (Ottawa: Minister of Supply and Services, 1989): 26–27.

26. See Peter H. Russell, *Leading Constitutional Decisions, Fourth Edition,* (Ottawa: Carleton University Press, 1987): 54–63.

27. Russell, *Leading Constitutional Decisions,* (1987): 69–75.

28. Russell, *Leading Constitutional Decisions,* (1987): 77–81.

29. Russell, *Leading Constitutional Decisions,* (1987): 113–130.

30. See Peter H. Russell, "The Anti-Inflation Case: The Anatomy of a Constitutional Decision," *Canadian Public Administration,* 10, 4 (Winter, 1977): 632–665.

31. Russell, *Leading Constitutional Decisions,* (1987): 33–40.

32. See Brooks, *Canadian Democracy,* (1993): 150.

33. See Brooks, *Canadian Democracy,* (1993): 150–151.

34. Canada, Supreme Court of Canada, "Reference Re Secession of Quebec," (August 20, 1998), [online] http:www.scc-csg.gc/reference/hn.htm

35. On intergovernmental bargaining and negotiation concerning health care, for instance, see Patricia L. O'Reilly, "The Federal/Provincial/Territorial Health Conference System," in Duane Adams, ed, *Federalism, Democracy and Canadian Health Policy,* (Montreal: McGill-Queens Press, 2001).

36. See Stevenson, *Unfulfilled Union,* (1989): chapter 4.

37. See Alan Cairns, "The Past and Future of the Canadian Administrative State," in Douglas E. Williams, ed. *Reconfigurations: Canadian Citizenship and Constitutional Change,* (Toronto: McClelland and Stewart, 1995): 62–96.

38. The classic analysis of this phenomenon remains Richard Simeon, *Federal-Provincial Diplomacy: The Making of Recent Policy in Canada,* (Toronto: University of Toronto Press, 1971). See also Gordon Robertson, "The Role of Interministerial Conferences in the Decision-Making Process," in

Richard Simeon, ed. *Confrontation and Collaboration: Intergovernmental Relations in Canada Today,* (Toronto: The Institute of Public Administration of Canada, 1979): 78–88; and Kathy Brock, "The End of Executive Federalism?" in François Rocher and Miriam Smith, eds. *New Trends in Canadian Federalism,* (Peterborough: Broadview Press, 1995): 91–108.

39. See O'Reilly, "The Federal/Provincial/Territorial Health Conference System." On the roles and responsibilities of intergovernmental officials, see Gregory J. Inwood, Carolyn M. Johns and Patricia L. O'Reilly, "The Impact of Administrative Reform on Intergovernmental Officials," in Harvey Lazar and Peter Meekison, eds. *The State of the Federation 2002–2003: Managing Tensions: Evaluating the Institutions of the Federation,* (Montreal: McGill-Queen's University Press, forthcoming 2003).

40. On executive federalism, see J. Stefan Dupre, "Reflections on the Workability of Executive Federalism," in Richard Simeon, ed. *Intergovernmental Relations,* (Toronto: University of Toronto Press, 1985): 1–32; Donald V. Smiley, "An Outsider's Observations of Federal-Provincial Relations Among Consenting Adults," in R.D. Olling and M.W. Westmacott, eds. *Perspectives on Canadian Federalism,* (Scarborough: Prentice-Hall, 1988): 279–284; and Albert Breton, "Competition and Cooperation in the Canadian Federal System," in *Report of the Royal Commission on the Economic Union and Development Prospects for Canada, Volume III,* (Ottawa: Minister of Supply and Services, 1985): 486–526.

41. See Inwood, "Federalism, Globalization and the (Anti-)Social Union," (2000).

42. Malcolmson and Myers, *The Canadian Regime,* (1996): 53.

43. "Premiers Develop Unity Plan," *Globe and Mail,* (Monday, September 15, 1997): A1.

44. See Inwood, "Federalism, Globalization and the (Anti-)Social Union," (2000). On SUFA see Kathy O'Hara, with the assistance of Sarah Cox, *Securing the Social Union,* (Ottawa: Canadian Policy Research Networks, 1998); and Alain-G. Gagnon and Hugh Segal, eds. *The Canadian Social Union Without Quebec: Eight Critical Analyses,* (Montreal: Institute for Research on Public Policy, 2000). To view SUFA see http://www.unionsociale.gc.ca/menu_e.html

45. See Harvey Lazar, ed. *Non-Constitutional Renewal: Canada: The State of the Federation 1997,* (Kingston: Institute of Intergovernmental Relations, 1998).

46. See Alan Leadbeater, *Council on Administration: Administrative Law Series Prepared for the Law Reform Commission of Canada,* (Ottawa: Minister of Supply and Services, 1980): 3.

47. Leadbeater, *Council on Administration,* (1980): 1.

48. Sara Blake, "An Introduction to Administrative Law in Canada," in Christopher Dunn, ed. *The Handbook of Canadian Public Administration,* (Toronto: Oxford University Press, 2002): 466.

49. See René Dussault and Louis Borgeat, *Administrative Law: A Treatise, Second Edition, Volume 1,* (Toronto: Carswell, 1985): 4.

50. David P. Jones and Anne S. de Villars, *Principles of Administrative Law, Second Edition,* (Toronto: Carswell, 1994): 3–4. The following discussion of administrative law is derived from their overview.

51. George E. Eaton, "Understanding Canadian Parliamentary Government," in Randy Hoffman *et al. Public Administration: Canadian Materials, Third Edition,* (North York: Captus Press, 1988): 63.

52. Dussault and Borgeat, *Administrative Law,* (1985): 13. See also Margot Priest, "Structure and Accountability of Administrative Agencies," in *Administrative Law: Principles, Practice and Pluralism: Special Lectures of the Law Society of Upper Canada,* (Toronto: Carswell, 1992): 63–78.

53. Donald J. Bourgeois, *Public Law in Canada,* (Scarborough: Nelson, 1990): 195.

54. See Des Rosiers, "Federalism and Judicial Review," (1998): 63–75.

55. Victor S. MacKinnon, "Introduction to the Legal Environment: Theories and Principles," in Randy Hoffman, *et al. Public Administration: Canadian Materials, Third Edition,* (North York: Captus Press, 1998): 199–200.

56. A.V. Dicey, *Introduction to the Study of the Law of the Constitution,* (London: Macmillan, 1920): 40.

57. See Hogg, *Constitutional Law of Canada,* (2002): 668–9.

58. Jones and de Villars, *Principles of Administrative Law,* (1994): 9.

59. See Kenneth F. Warren, *Administrative Law in the Political System, Abridged Third Edition,* (Upper Saddle River, New Jersey: Prentice Hall, 1997): 23.

KEY WORDS AND CONCEPTS

rule of law (165)
constitutional law (168)
amending formula (170)
Charter of Rights and Freedoms (173)
reservation (176)
disallowance (176)
spending power (178)

division of powers (179)
province-building (183)
administrative law (188)
discretion (190)
ultra vires (190)
judicial review (191)

REVIEW QUESTIONS

The four sections of this chapter each dealt with a specific set of issues related to public administration and the law. You should now be able to address the following questions:

1. The Law and the Courts
This section asked you to consider the political-culture origins and application of the rule of law in Canada. It asked the following: What is the rule of law? What are common law and civil law? What is the structure of the court system in Canada?

2. What Is a Constitution?
This section asserted that while constitutions are fundamental to every society, they vary widely in their utility and application. It asked, What is a constitution? What three main functions do constitutions serve? What are the component parts of the Canadian Constitution? What is constitutional law? How did the Canadian constitutional order come about?

3. Constitutional Law
This section addressed constitutional law in terms of conflict over the division of powers in the Constitution. It asked the following: How are disputes resolved before the courts when federal and provincial governments cannot agree on the jurisdiction of a law? What aspects of the division of powers have proven the most contentious, and how have disputes over them been resolved? What role have the courts played in the resolution of conflict? What has been the legacy of judicial review of constitutional law?

4. Administrative Law
Finally, the last section examined administrative law. It asked, What is administrative law? What is the power of discretion held by civil servants? What happens when a dispute arises over the exercise of legal powers by an administrative agency? What is the relationship between constitutional and administrative law? What is the role of judicial review in administrative law?

FURTHER READING

1. The Law and the Courts
Canada, Law Reform Commission. *Judicial Review and the Federal Court*. Ottawa: Minister of Supply and Services, 1980.

Gall, Gerald. *The Canadian Legal System. Third Edition.* Toronto: Carswell, 1990.

Hogg, Peter. "Judicial Review: How Much Do We Need?" *McGill Law Journal*, 20 (1974): 157–66.

McCormick, P. and I. Greene. *Judges and Judging: Inside the Canadian Judicial System.* Toronto: Lorimer, 1990.

2.   What Is a Constitution?

Cheffins, R.I. and P.A. Johnson. *The Revised Canadian Constitution: Politics as Law.* Toronto: McGraw-Hill Ryerson, 1986.

Milne, David. *The New Canadian Constitution.* Toronto: Lorimer, 1982.

Morton, F.L. *Law, Politics and the Judicial System in Canada. Second Edition.* Calgary: University of Calgary Press, 1992.

3.   Constitutional Law

Finkelstein, Neil R. and Brian MacLeod Rogers, eds. *Administrative Tribunals and the Charter.* Toronto: Carswell, 1990.

Heard, Andrew D. "The Charter in the Supreme Court of Canada: The Importance of Which Judges Hear an Appeal," *Canadian Journal of Political Science,* 24 (June, 1991): 289–308.

Hogg, Peter W. *Constitutional Law of Canada: Student Edition 2002.* Toronto: Carswell, 2002.

Mellon, Hugh and Martin Westmacott, eds. *Political Dispute and Judicial Review: Assessing the Work of the Supreme Court of Canada.* Scarborough: Nelson, 2000.

Millar, Perry S. and Carl Barr. *Judicial Administration in Canada.* Montreal: McGill-Queen's University Press, 1981.

4.   Administrative Law

Blake, Sara. *Administrative Law in Canada.* Toronto: Butterworths, 1992.

Brown, Donald J.M. and John M. Evans. *Judicial Review of Administrative Action in Canada.* Toronto: Canvasback Publishing, 1998.

Canada, Law Reform Commission. *Toward a Modern Federal Administrative Law.* Ottawa: Law Reform Commission of Canada, 1987.

Finkelstein, Neil R. *Recent Developments in Administrative Law.* Toronto: Carswell, 1987.

Macaulay, Robert W. and James L.H. Sprague. *Practice and Procedure before Administrative Tribunals.* Toronto: Carswell, 2001.

Steele, G. "Private Lawyers, Public Law. Administrative Law in the Making." *Canadian Public Administration*, 35, 1 (Spring, 1992).

 WEBLINKS

Canadian Constitutional Documents
insight.mcmaster.ca/org/efc/pages/law/cons/Constitutions/Canada/English.html

Law Commission of Canada
www.lcc.gc.ca/

Canada's Court System
canada.justice.gc.ca/en/dept/pub/trib/index.html

The Supreme Court of Canada
www.scc-csc.gc.ca

Supreme Court Decisions on the *Charter of Rights and Freedoms*
canada.justice.gc.ca/en/dept/pub

Chapter 7

Public Administration *and* Public Policy

WHAT YOU WILL LEARN

Public policy is a vitally important aspect of public administration, and this chapter will provide an overview. You will recall that we talked earlier about the practice of public administration as the formulation, implementation and evaluation of public policies.

This chapter is divided into four sections, each dealing with the issue of policy-making in public administration. By the end of this chapter, you should be able to answer the following questions: What is public policy? What theories of public policy decision-making explain the way public officials (both bureaucratic and political) make decisions on behalf of citizens? What is the policy cycle of formulation, implementation and evaluation? These central issues are highlighted:

1. — *Defining Public Policy*

   This brief introductory section will ask you to consider what public policy is. You will discover that a number of definitions exist.

2. — *Formulating Public Policy*

   There are several different theoretical explanations that seek to illuminate the question of how and why policy is made. This section asks the following: Does any one theoretical model comprehensively explain *how* policy is made as well as *why* policy is made (or not made)?

3. — *Implementing Public Policy*

   The issue of how policy is acted upon once it is identified is the main concern of this section. It asks, What policy instruments are available for governments to use in realizing their goals? How do they choose among these instruments?

4. — *Evaluating Public Policy*

A relatively new concern of governments has been how to test whether their policy actions have been effective. While this issue is dealt with in detail in Chapter 8, it is introduced here as part of the policy framework of formulation, implementation and evaluation. How do public officials and others assess the quality, utility and success of public policies?

Defining Public Policy

Public policies in general cover a wide range of fields, and you can tell something about the interests of particular governments by the policies they tend to emphasize or focus on, according to Stephen Brooks.[1] One government may stress economic policy; another, social policy. Yet another might see foreign and defence policy as important, while others do not. Justice policy, language policy, multicultural policy, education policy, and environment policy are just some of the countless areas with which public administration deals.

The range of policy fields and their importance for the government of the day can be influenced by a number of factors. A particular prime minister may have a strong personal interest in an issue, as did former Prime Minister Trudeau on constitutional and national unity policy. Or interest groups may be particularly effective in persuading the government to focus its energies on one area, as did the big business lobbies with the free trade issue in the late 1980s and 1990s. In other cases, public opinion may dictate that a government proceed with a certain policy only at its peril. Sometimes a crisis such as September 11, 2001, will catapult an issue to the forefront. The mix of factors that determines which issues will be addressed as public policy is complex and changes over time. But whatever the public policy, it is the job of public administration to formulate, implement and evaluate it.

There is a large and well-developed literature in Canada on public policy.[2] Public policy has been defined as "a set of interrelated decisions taken by a political actor or group of actors concerning the selection of goals and the means of achieving them...."[3] One of the most often cited definitions of public policy is by American political scientist Thomas Dye, who said that public policy is "whatever governments choose to do or not to do."[4] The utility of this definition is that it points out that "policy" can be a case of either action or inaction. Thus, passing a law is an obvious, deliberate and conscious policy act on the part of a government. But not passing a law may be as well.

Consider, for instance, a situation in which a government passes a law, but the courts find that the law violates the Constitution. Therefore the law is of no force or effect. The government is then faced with a number of options. First, it can decide to redraft the law to bring it into conformity with the Constitution. It can override the court's decision by employing the *Charter of Rights and Freedoms* (in certain select areas). Or it can do nothing. All these responses are "public policy." A case in point occurred in January 1988, when the Supreme Court of Canada struck down the government's abortion law on the basis that it violated certain sections of the Constitution. The government of the day took stock of the judgment and decided to do nothing! That is, it declined to either overrule the court, or redraft and reintroduce the law. Thus, there is currently no abortion law in Canada. Why did the government take this "inaction"? It simply weighed the political costs of taking sides in the incredibly controversial abortion debate in Canada, and wisely decided not to do so.

In many ways, public policy involves conscious choices by governments that lead to action or inaction. These take many forms, such as passing a law or regulation, creating a Crown corporation, spending or raising money (i.e., taxing), holding a royal commission or inquiry, and so on. But there are other less obvious examples of public policy too. For instance, consider when a politician or government official gives a speech to an interest group. Suppose the Minister of Education came to your campus to speak on the future of post-secondary education. This may be considered part of the ongoing process of public policy-making, in that the minister may use the speech to signal a new direction in government thinking, test the reaction of educators and students to existing government policy, defend the status quo, or float trial balloons by laying out various options the government is examining. All this activity represents the nebulous world of public policy. Therefore, it is necessary to look at both official claims and concrete policy action and inaction to determine what actually constitutes public policy.

A useful way to think about public policy is to look at it in terms of scope, means and resources.[5] Simply put, this means considering public policy from the point of view of how much government involvement in our lives is appropriate (scope), what form that involvement ought to take (means), and how it is to be provided (resources). Let us consider each in a little more detail.

Scope

Canadian governments at all levels (federal, provincial and municipal) do more now than they have ever done in the past. They pass more laws, create more regulations, spend and raise more money, employ more people, etc. The tangible representation of this phenomenon and symbol of the growth of government has been the *welfare state*. This phrase refers to the growing interventionist role of government in the economy and in social life through policies such as state ownership (Crown corporations) and regulation of the private sector, and especially the growing role in social policy fields such as welfare, education and health. As the scope of government activity has increased, the size of the machinery of government, and of the decision-making process, has increased and become more complex.

But recently, this growth of the welfare state has been under ideological attack on the basis that it costs too much, that it interferes with the operations of the "free" market, that deficits have become uncontrollable, and so on. Regardless of the accuracy of these claims (and many are wildly exaggerated for ideological reasons), the welfare state has developed a tarnished image. This is sometimes explained with reference to the *overload thesis*, which is expressed in two ways:[6] First, it is argued that the state has taken on more functions than it can perform or afford; second, the policy-making process has become too cumbersome and complicated. The overall result is that citizens have lost faith in the capacity of their governments to deliver on promises. And there has been a backlash against "big government"—a backlash felt strongly in the realm of public policy.

The question "How much government is too much?" is central to the issue of public policy-making. Once we figure out the proper scope of government, then we can know what areas government ought to be acting in. But how do we answer that question? Fundamentally, we must confront our own political values; we must make value judgments as individuals and as a society to determine what areas of life we believe it is appropriate for the government to be involved in. These value judgments are shaped and constrained by our socialization, which includes our family life, education, workplace experience, exposure to popular culture, and so on. Once we identify our core values as a society, we construct constitutional rules that influence the actions of government. Beyond these broad constitutional boundaries are the laws, regulations, Crown corporations, and so on, through which public policy is realized (see Box 7-1).

An alternative perspective on the question of the scope of government activity asks not whether the state needs to be made bigger or smaller, but whether it can be made more democratic, regardless of its size. This view argues that the debate over the scope of the state is misplaced. It suggests that no matter what government does, empowering citizens and popular movements should be the real focus, along with training public administrators to increase the democratic capacity of citizens.[7]

Thus, much of public policy-making comes down to value judgments about how to achieve societal and private goals within the confines of a broad set of "rules of the game." For example, as a society we may generally agree that care of children is a predominant value. But we disagree over whether that care can best take place within the structure of a government-funded national day-care system. By contrast, we long ago agreed as a society to permit the state to take on the major responsibility for the education of children. But we have not yet reached the point where we have collectively agreed to place the care of preschool children in the hands of the state. Put another way, we have not yet determined that the "private" issue of child care should become a "public" issue of state concern. Thus the scope of government activity in this, as in other public policy areas, is set by the value judgments that predominate at any given time in society.

Means

Once we sort out the thorny problem of whether the government ought to be involved in a particular issue, we are still only partway to understanding public policy. We must also ask what form that involvement ought to take. Put another way, we need to consider how the government can achieve its goals, once those goals are articulated. Governments have a variety of tools at their disposal, and we refer to the ongoing selection of these tools as the "choice of **governing instruments**" (discussed in more detail below). Which tools should government use under what circumstances?

Box 7-1

The Scope of Governments in Canada

The scope of government is truly amazing when you think about it. Think about the following:

Consider the effects of three levels of government active in virtually every sphere of life, from the social to the economic and cultural. In 1993–94, for example, the federal government (through Public Works and Government Services) issued over 100 million payments to Canadians, including 37 million Child Tax Benefit payments, 41 million Old Age Security payments, and 35 million Canada Pension payments. Another random example: the 1931 Canadian Government Publications Catalogue was a 96-page document listing everything available from the federal government—some 3000 entries. In 1989–90, Ottawa published 3000 new entries every six months. A 1993 guide to federal government programs and services listed 145 organizations working in 1256 program areas.

The sheer scope and minutiae of government regulation and activity is often breathtaking. Among the regulations published in the Canada Gazette *of September 21, 1994, were the following: (1) an amendment to National Parks Cottages Regulations, affecting the building codes of cottages within national parks, including a definition of the term "One-half storey"; (2) United Nations Rwanda Regulations passed by the United Nations Security Council, including the prohibition against exporting, selling, supplying or shipping arms to Rwanda; (3) an Aircraft Seats and Safety Belt Order, requiring the use and specifying the type of safety belts used by adults and infant passengers and by the crew on Canadian aircraft; (4) an amendment to the* Canadian Environmental Protection Act *affecting the disposal of industrial and radioactive waste at sea; and (5) the designation of October 9–15, 1994, as Fire Prevention Week. All in a day's work for Ottawa."* [8]

Unfortunately, the process of selecting appropriate instruments is rarely straightforward. It can be influenced by any of a number of factors, such as by the way things have been done in the past, by dominant ideas and ideologies, by the personal preferences of particular politicians or bureaucrats, by the availability of resources, by the relative strengths of interest groups trying to influence the government, by the media, by public opinion, etc. For example, taxation on personal and corporate income has become one of the chief policy instruments by which modern governments have achieved their goals. Yet now, most governments feel severely constrained by the notion that any more personal taxation may invoke a taxpayers' revolt in Canada, while any more corporate taxation might provoke a "capital strike" by business. Similarly, while regulations and Crown corporations have traditionally been important policy instruments in Canada, they are currently out of vogue.

But even knowing what policy instrument is needed leaves unanswered the question of whether the government has the *policy capacity* to achieve its goals. There is a growing literature on the concept of policy capacity,[9] which has been defined as "the institutional ability to conduct policy analysis and implement its results effectively and efficiently."[10] In general, it is being increasingly acknowledged that during the past 10 years, governments have experienced a reduced capacity to develop policy.[11] This is generally attributed to factors such as cutbacks and re-structuring exercises in which policy analysts and policy shops in government were the first things reduced or eliminated. At the same time, there has been in-creased focus on management as opposed to policy. However, as political scien-tist Leslie Pal reports, "policy is popular again."[12] Governments are realizing that to achieve their objectives, a greater emphasis must be placed on developing strong policy capacity.

As political scientist Stephen Brooks suggests, part of the issue of determining the means by which policy is to be achieved is tied up with the notion of what goal is to be served—Justice? Efficiency? Equality? Security? What do we do when these goals clash? What standard do we use to measure the success or failure of a particular policy?[13] These are difficult questions. Consider, for instance, the great free trade debate in the late 1980s. As the Canadian government sought the right economic policy to ensure growth and prosperity, it was confronted by two value-based arguments. On the one hand were the pro-free-traders, arguing that the economic gains from free trade were unassailable and that the goal of economic ef-ficiency should be the guide in determining which policy instrument (free trade) ought to be adopted. On the other hand were the anti-free-traders, who argued that intangible values such as national identity and culture would be threatened by free trade, and who therefore preferred the policy option of tariffs.

Related to these kinds of value problems are those associated with cost. Policies, more often than not, have some kind of price tag attached. It is up to government to determine whether a particular price is worth paying for a given policy. These costs are both financial and political. There is the "dollars and cents" aspect to policy. The fiscal means must be present in order to embark on policy projects. But there is also the political question of whether a particular action (or inaction) by the government will cost votes. The policy of regional economic development grants may be popular in depressed regions of the country that require economic assistance to spur employment and growth, for instance. But they may be un-popular in the regions of the country that have to help pay for them via transfer pay-ments from the rich provinces to the poorer ones. All these types of issues influence the question of the "means" of public policy.

Resources

Politics is said to be about who gets what, when and how. The making of public policy partly answers that question. But when you get something in the form of policy by the government, someone else may be deprived of something, since there are finite resources to spread around. For instance, you may desire a policy calling for lower personal taxes. This may mean that the quality of health care must diminish, because there is now less money to spend on it. Or tuition must go up, since governments have less tax revenue to put into the post-secondary education system. Thus, the issue of who benefits and who pays is central to policy decisions. Given that resources are scarce and there is not enough of everything to go around for everyone at all times, governments must constantly make difficult decisions about how to apportion the resources of society through the policies they enact.

How governments deal with this through public policy is related again to values. In Canada, one dominant idea is that those least able to help themselves should be assisted by those who can. But this has lead to controversy over the role of government in redistributing wealth through taxation policy, social programs, regional economic development programs, etc. Major government expenditures to the less well-off regions of Canada through policy tools such as equalization programs, income transfers to individuals (Employment Insurance, etc.), and industrial assistance programs that subsidize businesses, are controversial, even if most Canadians subscribe to the principle that the better-off should help the less well-off. Thus, governments are constantly trying to strike a balance in devising policy that will help redistribute wealth, but not infringe too much on the right to private property or the workings of the free market.

Where public policy is concerned, one answer to the question of how resources are spent or apportioned by government comes from the observation that policy choices reflect the **mobilization of bias**. This means that any individual or group with a particular interest or concern (a "bias") can organize and mobilize itself to influence government to act in its favour. At first blush, this argument would tend to support the view that Canadian society is democratic, in that anyone can have his fondest policy wishes realized. But closer inspection reveals that, naturally, those with the fiscal and organizational means will tend to be more successful at getting the attention of government, and therefore are more likely to have their interests served by public policy than are the unorganized, the marginalized and the less well-off. Thus, it is best to remember that the decision-making process where public policy is concerned is weighted in favour of certain actors in Canadian society, and that the question of how the scarce resources of society are divided up is never the result of an equal competition.

Finally, besides looking just at the material or financial costs of resources, we must also consider the symbolic resources that can be spent and saved in various ways by governments. Perception is vitally important in politics and public administration—and perception is often shaped by symbols. The flag is a symbol of national unity that costs relatively little to disseminate, but that can reap large rewards or cause deep division. The *Charter of Rights and Freedoms*, language law, multiculturalism, etc., are all powerful symbols that can be invoked virtually without having to spend a cent. Thus, it is wise not to overlook the importance of symbols in calculating the resources available to governments in the making of public policy.

The concepts of scope, means and resources, then, all play a large role in public policy, and help us to organize our thinking about this important aspect of public administration. We can also think about policy-making as a cyclical exercise involving three distinct but related steps. These steps are formulation, implementation and evaluation. Figure 7.1 depicts the relationship of the three parts of the **policy cycle**. It shows that we can conceptualize each of the three as distinct stages in an ongoing process of policy-making. In addition, each stage of the process is the responsibility of certain individuals and institutions. For instance, the **formulation** stage is the responsibility of the Cabinet and Legislature. Public servants play an advisory role at this point. **Implementation** is the responsibility primarily of the public service: the Cabinet and Legislature oversee this stage to ensure that their orders are being followed faithfully. Finally, the **evaluation** stage is the responsibility of the public service and of citizens. Bureaucrats are constantly engaged in checking their own work, while citizens (often acting as interest groups or through the media) keep an eye on the government and its officials to ensure that their tax dollars are being spent wisely, and that they are getting the level and quality of service that they asked for.

But in reality, the policy-making cycle is less clear-cut than Figure 7.1 depicts. In fact, the boundaries among the three stages are rather indistinct, as are the roles assigned to key actors and institutions. The boundaries are blurred and the steps, rather than unfolding sequentially, may occur simultaneously or in some other order. In any event, the three steps constantly influence one another. Figure 7.2 depicts more realistically the overlapping nature of the three parts of the policy-making process. The next three sections of this chapter deal with the formulation, implementation and evaluation of policy.

FIGURE 7.1   The Policy Cycle

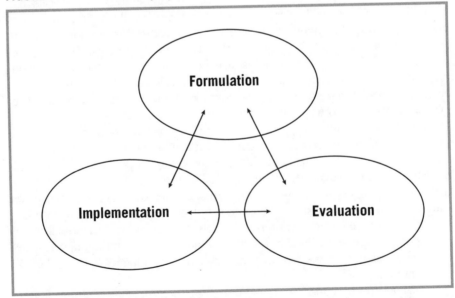

FIGURE 7.2   The Policy Cycle Revisited

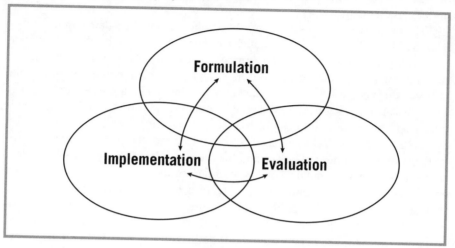

Formulating Public Policy

The key decision-makers, where public policy is concerned, are the politicians and the bureaucrats. More specifically, the prime minister and Cabinet are the central actors who enjoy the ultimate decision-making authority. They are assisted by senior bureaucrats in this process, but retain the final "yes" or "no" in determining the policy goals of the government, whether a proposal will be translated into policy, and which policy instrument will be employed. Parliament plays the role of scrutinizing government and passing legislation, and the courts play the role of judging whether policy is "legal" or not. This oversimplifies the complex functions and activities of the executive, legislative and judicial branches of government, but nonetheless summarizes the main features of the relationship among them as regards policy-making.

But let us consider the question of how public policy is made in a little more detail by placing it in theoretical perspective. Several models of decision-making have been developed to explain exactly how the process of making public policy unfolds. These models can help us to understand how the mobilization of bias takes place in the real world of policy-making. Imagine yourself, for example, as a key decision-maker in the government. How exactly do you arrive at decisions about what policies ought to be pursued by government? Do you try to anticipate the demands of the society you serve and initiate action accordingly? Or do you wait until various societal interests and actors have demanded action? Once you acknowledge that there are demands for government to respond to an issue, how do you then determine what the best response is—Inaction? A new law? A regulation? An inquiry? A treaty with a foreign country? Education? The huge array of policy choices with which you are confronted demands some sort of decision-making process. This is where *models* can help us. Models sketch out the parameters of the decision-making process and explain why certain policy choices are made under certain circumstances.

The most basic model says that public policy-making is a democratic process in which the will of the people is translated into policy through the work of competitive political parties and elected representatives, who play the crucial role in determining which issues advance. But however appealing it is to think that public policy is a reflection of the "will of the people," this view is simplistic, for it ignores a number of realities. These include the idea that there is no unified, single "will" out there. There is a multiplicity of voices all clamouring for attention. Moreover, this view ignores the fact that sometimes governments act in the absence of public demand. Sometimes politicians and bureaucrats take initiatives for which there seems to be little or no public demand. In other words, the decision-makers are not simply passive receptors of instructions from the people. They are active players themselves in the development of policy initiatives. Thus, we need a more sophisticated theory than traditional democratic theory to explain public policy.

First, though, let us consider the broad framework within which policy-making takes place. Political scientist Richard Simeon has suggested that there are five key variables that help us understand why we get the policy that we do. Simeon begins with the assumption that

the political machinery and the policy-makers at any point in time work within a framework which greatly restricts the alternatives they consider and the range of innovations they make. This framework, or set of constraints and opportunities, defines a set of problems considered to be important, a set of acceptable solutions or policy responses, [and] a set of procedures and rules by which they will be considered.[14]

He suggests that we approach public policy by first examining these five complementary characteristics of a society. He cites environmental factors, the distribution of power, social attitudes and ideas, institutional structures, and procedural factors as all being important contributing factors in the design and makeup of public policy. Let us consider each in turn.

Environmental Factors

At the root of all policy are certain basic socioeconomic realities. For instance, the geography, demography, level of industrialization, rate of urbanization, relative affluence, level of education, and similar elementary features of a society are going to shape the type of policy a government embarks upon. It is obvious, for instance, that one of the first concerns of the new Dominion of Canada in the late 19th century was to facilitate communications and transportation links across the great stretches of territory that formed the new country. Hence, many public policy initiatives focused on issues such as the construction of a transcontinental railway, and immigration to settle the vast expanses of the western prairies. Thus these basic *environmental factors* play a significant part in shaping public policy. In addition, in the Canadian case, proximity to the United States means that the environment of our public policy is inevitably shaped by *continentalism,* which simply refers to the powerful influence of our southern neighbours. Hence, issues such as tariff policy and free trade, cultural protectionism and nationalism have loomed large in policy-making in Canada.

Distribution of Power

This is a more nebulous concept. While we can agree that public policy reflects the exercise of power and influence, it is difficult to measure and quantify the concept of power itself. What is it? Who has it? How is it measured? In seeking answers to these questions, a variety of positions have evolved. Some suggest that power is widely diffused in a democratic society such as Canada, and that a plurality of interests have a more or less equal chance of influencing policy-makers to create policy. This is the ***pluralist view*** that there is a healthy competition among groups that expresses itself through the competitive political party system. The ***elitist view***, by contrast, argues that power is tightly held and concentrated in few hands; and that there is a network of corporate, political and bureaucratic elite that, for the most part, dominate the development of public policy in their own interests. Various interpretations of these views are elaborated below.

Social Attitudes and Ideas

Within any given society there is a set of broadly held attitudes, values and beliefs. These core ideas shape the contours of public policy by helping to determine what ideas are and are not acceptable. Simeon suggests there are two sets of social attitudes and ideas that are especially relevant to public policy-making. The first is the set of *procedural* attitudes that a society holds. These are the accepted rules of the game. For instance, nearly everyone agrees in Canada that the political system ought to be democratic, and that certain features of democracy must be adhered to in the process of making public policy, including free, fair and open elections, free speech, parliamentary procedures, and so on. The second are *substantive* values, which reflect beliefs about the scope and purpose of government. For example, historically, Canadians have been more willing than have Americans to use the state in the pursuit of societal goals, with the result that public policy in the two countries is qualitatively different in a number of ways. Overall, social attitudes and beliefs are broad and general in nature, but help to define the problems and the range of policy alternatives open to government. Indeed, the great British economist John Meynard Keynes attributed a great deal of importance to the role of ideas. He wrote,

The ideas of economists and political philosophers, both when they are right and when they are wrong, are more powerful than is commonly understood. Indeed the world is ruled by little else. Practical men, who believe themselves to be exempt from any intellectual influences, are usually the slaves of some defunct economist. Madmen in authority, who hear voices in the air, are distilling their frenzy from some academic scribbler of a few years back.[15]

Keynes, of course, provided the intellectual underpinnings for the modern welfare state with his own theoretical writings, and so could speak with some authority on the influence of ideas.

Institutional Structure

The nuts and bolts of government help determine the types of public policy. The way power and authority are distributed across the various structures of government has an important impact on the translation of will into action. As we noted in Chapter 4, institutions such as federalism and cabinet-parliamentary government, departments, regulatory bodies and Crown corporations, as well as the Constitution and other institutional features, all influence the exercise of power and the type of public policy produced.

Procedural Factors

This concept is closely related to the foregoing one. It refers to the way that those closest to the development of public policy (primarily politicians, bureaucrats and interest groups) interact in developing policy. They follow rules and processes based on certain norms, with the result that policy is formulated, implemented and later evaluated in a certain manner. There is considerable dispute, though, over exactly how the process unfolds, which we will explore in more detail below.

Overall, then, many variables affect the development of public policy. To fully understand it, we need to take into consideration what these factors are and how they interact to influence policy. Still, while these factors are useful for understanding the broad parameters of public policy-making, they do not really address the issue of how individual policy-makers make policy. Another set of models addresses this question more closely.

Political scientists Robert and Doreen Jackson have usefully categorized the major models as *micro-level* and *macro-level* approaches—a distinction we will use here.[16] Micro-level models focus primarily on the role of individual decision-makers, while macro-level models tend to be concerned with broader societal and state factors. The micro-level models we will briefly look at are called the *rational-comprehensive theory*, the *incremental theory*, and the *mixed-scanning theory*, as outlined by political scientist James Anderson.[17]

To understand how these theories help us comprehend public policy-making, imagine the following scenario. You are a key decision-maker in the government, charged with the development of a policy on some important matter. You take as a given the following influences on your decision-making: the environment that constrains you (i.e., the demographic, geographic, urban-industrial, bilingual, multicultural, and other characteristics of Canada); the current distribution of power (both within the country as a whole and within the government); the predominant ideas and attitudes that Canadians hold; the institutional constraints; and the procedural rules of the game you are required to follow. Beyond these factors, though, how do you actually make a policy decision? Consider the following options.

The Rational-Comprehensive Theory

You wake up in the morning confident that for every policy problem confronting the government and Canadians, there is a rational solution. You arrive at work and are met by a problem that is clearly separate from other problems you deal with. You carefully draw up a list of goals, values or objectives related to the problem, and rank them according to their importance. You next carefully consider various alternatives for dealing with the problem, and examine them thoroughly. In so doing, you weigh the consequences of each alternative by considering the costs and benefits of each, and the advantages and disadvantages of each. Next you compare the alternatives to one another. Finally, you choose the alternative that maximizes the attainment of your goals, values and objectives. Voila! You have created public policy through a rational decision-making process that most effectively achieves the ends you seek. At the end of the day you head home, confident that your rational application of problem-solving skills has saved the day for Canada.

This, in a nutshell, is the **rational-comprehensive model**. This is a widely accepted approach rooted in a Weberian perspective that suggests policy-making is a rational, logical process of decision-making involving a number of discrete steps or stages. All the decision-maker has to do is follow the steps, and the result will be effective public policy. This approach has a good deal of appeal in that it suggests a clean, surgical approach to the problems of making public policy. But it is not without significant criticisms.

First, it is somewhat unrealistic, in that problems confronting decision-makers are not always clear-cut and concrete, or even well defined. For instance, when car drivers in major urban centres begin to complain about "squeegee kids," what exactly is the problem that needs to be addressed? Is it a matter of enforcing existing traffic safety laws, or drafting new ones to keep the kids off the streets? Or is it an issue of poverty, homelessness, lack of meaningful employment opportunities, etc.? In other words, is it a matter of treating the symptom (squeegee kids), or the cause (youth alienation)? Clearly, your definition of the problem will condition the policy response you devise.

A second criticism focuses on the unrealistic scenario built into the model of unlimited time and resources for the decision-maker. There is the assumption that the decision-maker can relatively easily collect whatever data is needed to make an informed decision, and take the time to reflect on it carefully and thoughtfully. This is clearly not possible in the pressure-cooker of the real world. Moreover, many of the "alternatives" proposed will be derived from value judgments on the part of those affected by the issue, and of the decision-makers themselves. In other words, personal biases and interests impinge on the cold rational calculations that the model calls for. And those interests can become particularly entrenched if past policy decisions have tended to favour them. For instance, there may be broad agreement in society that health-care costs are escalating too rapidly. But the health-care professions may be reluctant to accept any fiscal solution to the problem that erodes their own privileged financial solution, such as reducing doctors' pay, de-institutionalizing health care, etc.

In addition, the rational model has been criticized for excluding other, non-rational ways of knowing, based as it is on a narrow Western tradition rooted in ancient Greek and European civilizations. Non-Western cultures may use decision-making processes that rely less on the rationalistic traditions of the Western world, but which are nonetheless every bit as valid.[18]

Notwithstanding these criticisms, the rational-comprehensive model has a good deal of appeal. In a perfect world, it would indeed be useful to follow the steps it outlines (see Box 7-2). In an imperfect world, though, perhaps the best we can hope for is to adhere to the main precepts of the model, while recognizing its shortcomings.

Box 7-2

The Rational-Comprehensive Theory

Perhaps the most widely accepted and best-known theory of decision-making is the rational-comprehensive theory, which can be summed up in the following points:

1. The decision-maker is confronted with a given problem that can be separated from other problems, or at least considered meaningfully in comparison with them.
2. The goals, values or objectives that guide the decision-maker are clarified and ranked according to their importance.
3. The various alternatives for dealing with the problem are examined.
4. The consequences (costs and benefits, advantages and disadvantages) that would follow from the selection of each alternative are investigated.
5. Each alternative, and its attendant consequences, can be compared with the other alternatives.
6. The decision-maker will choose the alternative (and its consequences) that maximizes the attainment of his goals, values or objectives.[19]

Source: Anderson, *Public Policy-Making, Third Edition,* (New York: Holt Rinehart and Winston, 1984): 9–10.

The Incremental Theory

Returning to your role as decision-maker, let us assume that you are unable to live up to the rigorous process implied by the rational-comprehensive model. So, when you arrive at work, you embark on a slightly different path toward developing policy. To begin with, you implicitly recognize that your goals and objectives are closely connected to the empirical data you need in order to attain them. As well, you recognize that realistically, you can only consider some of the alternatives and a limited number of the most important consequences. You do not cast your net broadly in the search for solutions; instead, you begin by looking for solutions that require only minimal change from the status quo. In other words, you look for *incremental* change, rather than wholesale change. You engage in a process of give-and-take and mutual consent among interested parties to the issue. This approach allows you to avoid proposing radical change that might involve an all-or-nothing policy solution. Instead, you can offer pragmatic, moderate change to the status quo that does not upset entrenched interests. This, in brief, is the **incremental model** (see Box 7-3).

Box 7-3

The Incremental Theory

This approach avoids many of the problems associated with the rational-comprehensive approach, and may describe the actual decision-making process of policy-makers more accurately.

1. The selection of goals or objectives and the empirical analysis of the action needed to attain them are closely intertwined with, rather than distinct from, one another.
2. The decision-maker considers only some of the alternatives for dealing with a problem, and these will differ only incrementally (i.e., marginally) from existing policies.
3. For each alternative, only a limited number of "important" consequences are evaluated.
4. The problem confronting the decision-maker is continuously redefined. Incrementalism allows for countless ends/means and means/ends adjustments that have the effect of making the problem more manageable.
5. There is no single decision or "right" solution for a problem. The test of a good decision is that various analysts find themselves directly agreeing on it, without necessarily agreeing that the decision is the most appropriate means to an agreed objective.
6. Incremental decision-making is essentially remedial and is geared more to the amelioration of current, concrete social imperfections than to the promotion of future social goals.[20]

But incrementalism has been criticized too. It has been suggested that it is really a conservative approach to policy development, which, by its nature, favours the status quo and entrenched interests. Moreover, in crisis situations, incrementalism may actually be detrimental to finding solutions to problems. Nonetheless, incrementalism is also an approach with strong explanatory value in terms of trying to understand the decision-making process undertaken by policy-makers, and, particularly, why government appears to be such a slow lumbering beast. Economist Charles Lindblom suggested that policy-making is best described as "muddling through."[21]

The Mixed-Scanning Theory

Mixed scanning is a model developed by sociologist Amitai Etzioni, who tried to synthesize the most useful aspects of the rational-comprehensive theory with those of the incremental model.[22] In this way, the difficulty of attending to every detail inherent in the rational-comprehensive model is overcome, and more profound change is possible than the incremental model allows. In this model, as the decision-maker, you explore the main alternatives to the existing policy (rather than all possible alternatives), and thereby avoid getting hung up on paralyzing details and minutiae. An overview of possible change is developed that avoids the conservatism of incrementalism and the unrealistic characteristics of rational-comprehensive approaches.

Some applications of the mixed-scanning theory have suggested that the type of decision-making process you employ may depend on your position within the hierarchy of the organization. It may be that the lower-level functionaries lean toward incremental means of decision-making, lacking the authority and information for large-scale alterations to policy. The higher officials probably engage in a more comprehensive scanning of the alternatives, given that they have the "big picture" before them.

In any event, it should be clear that no one theory explains everything in relation to the decision-making process. Instead, it is probably accurate to say that each theory surveyed explains some aspects of the process. Thus far, this examination of decision-making models has focused on how decision-makers go about their business in the realm of public policy. We now turn our attention to why they make the decisions they do, and thus to the macro-level models of decision-making, which provide a broader perspective on the role of the state and its relationship with society. To this end, we will now consider as explanatory models the theories of pluralism, public choice and neo-Marxism.

Pluralism

Thus far we have examined some theoretical approaches to the way individual decision-makers might go through the process of making public-policy decisions. But some theorists argue that these approaches are incomplete without a broader perspective on the forces that shape decision-making. They point out that decision-making does not occur in a vacuum; it is part of a larger process of influences derived from the society within which policy-makers work.

One view asserts that individuals in society join together to pursue common goals. In so doing, they form groups or organizations to influence policy-makers. These groups are many in number, and indeed you probably belong to several at one time. For instance, as a student, you belong to organized interests—such as your student council, or the Canadian Federation of Students—which attempt to influence government. But at the same time, you may also be working full or part time, in which case you may belong to a union that puts its views regarding policy to decision-makers. Your employer may belong to a business association as well. There are countless groups and associations which, when they turn their attention toward influencing government, are generally referred to as *interest groups*.[23]

The theory that focuses on the role and nature of these interest groups, as well as political parties, is called **pluralism**. Pluralism suggests that there is an ongoing competition among shifting groups in society who all attempt to influence you, the policy-maker, to create public policy that favours their interests.[24] Individuals may band together with others on the basis of common religion, ethnicity, language, class, gender, region, ideology or other factors. Sometimes alliances between groups with common interests will be constructed, occasionally under the banner of a political party. In this view, government is seen as a neutral arbiter among the groups—a sort of referee overseeing the group struggle and responding to the wishes of the majority on each issue by producing appropriate public policy.

An essential component of this theory is that power is widely diffused in society. A concentration of power is avoided, and no one individual or group can monopolize public policy. Therefore, all have a more-or-less equal opportunity to influence the government to pass policies favourable to their own interests through organization and mobilization. As long as groups play by the rules of the game—that is, the broadly accepted societal political values and procedures—they all have a potentially equal influence on public policy-making.

More sophisticated versions of the theory point out that in fact in contemporary society, the main competition between groups tends to occur at the elite level. The leadership of each interest or coalition of interests engages in bargaining and negotiation with the government. The reward for the interest group elite is to obtain policies that promote and protect their interests, and the interests of their supporters. For the political elite, the competition is for votes and the reward is reelection.[25]

As a description of politics, pluralism provides a powerful explanation for how state policy is made. But the early proponents of this view ignored the fact that, while there did seem to be some basis to the organizational focus of pluralism in that people did band together into groups around common interests, these groups were patently unequal in resources. Some were wealthy, sophisticated and powerful. Others were lacking fiscal and other resources, knowledge of the political system, and influence. It is obviously easier, for instance, for the big banks to organize and mobilize their resources to influence government decision-makers than it is for the poor to do so. In a famous formulation of this critique of pluralism, political theorist E.E. Schattschneider wrote, "[T]he flaw in the pluralist heaven is that the heavenly chorus sings with a strong upper-class accent."[26] Moreover, it is argued that some issues that might otherwise be placed on the public policy agenda are actually "organized out" of politics. You will recall that our definition of public policy indicated that it is both *decisions* and *non-decisions* by governments. Thus, powerful groups influence government not only *to do* things on their behalf, but also *not to do* things, effectively preventing some issues from ever seeing the light of day.

Marxist Analysis

You will recall from Chapter 4 that capitalist democracy is part of the framework within which public administration takes place in Canada. The interrelationship between capitalism and democracy is explained by **Marxist analysis** in terms of class theory, and this in turn explains how public policy gets made. The first thing that you, the policy-maker, are influenced by is the fact that modern capitalist society is divided into classes. Moreover, the basis of the relationship between the two main classes is antagonism. The working class and the capitalist class (the owners of the means of production) are locked in a conflictual relationship in which gains for one mean losses for the other. The second point is that class is the single most important concept in terms of the divisions within society, superseding religious, linguistic, regional, gender, age, ethnic, or any other divisions. Marxists argue that class is the preeminent determining factor in shaping political, social and economic relations within society. The third point is that there is always inequality between the classes, which gives rise to conflict. The capitalist class enriches itself at the expense of the working class in a relationship of dominance and subordination. Finally, the fourth point is that the capitalist class does this by enlisting the aid of the state, which then passes policies that tend to favour the capitalist class and ensure its continued dominance.

One of the main reasons that the state supports capital through the policies it passes is the threat of a *capital strike* if it failed to do so. This is the threat by business to pull up stakes and move to jurisdictions more accommodating of capitalist interests. Capital thus has a powerful weapon in reserve to ensure that the state acquiesces to its demands. If you, the policy-maker, propose to bring in legislation favouring the working class through new trade union laws, business might threaten to move to the United States or elsewhere where legislation makes it difficult or even impossible for workers to organize. The threat is a serious one; if businesses follow through, the result can be decreased tax revenues, investment and jobs. This may translate into working-class anger with the government of the day, and, as a result, the loss of votes. Thus, the imperative of maintaining "business confidence" overshadows public policy-making and must always be taken into consideration by the policy-maker.

An example of this phenomenon occurred with the Bob Rae NDP government in Ontario. When it looked as though the NDP was about to live up to campaign promises to reform rent control, liberalize labour laws, and nationalize automobile insurance (as Quebec, Saskatchewan and British Columbia had previously done), the "suits" fought back in a massive display of opposition that included threatening widespread job losses, disinvestment and a loss of business confidence.[27]

But only the crudest form of Marxist theory would suggest that the state is simply the tool of the capitalist class. The relationship is far more nuanced than this simplistic view suggests.[28] Indeed, you can probably think of lots of examples of public policy that seem to run counter to the interests of capital. How do Marxists explain them? You will recall that in Chapter 2 we noted that Marxists allude to two types of policies: *accumulation* and *legitimation* policies. Accumulation policies are intended to be supportive of the profit-making activities of capital. They include things such as tax breaks, grants, expenditures on public works and infrastructure (roads, airports, harbours, canals, bridges, etc.), and so on. Legitimation policies are intended to mitigate interclass conflict and promote social harmony, and include policies such as employment insurance (formerly called *unemployment* insurance), welfare and other social policies whose effect is to legitimize capitalism for those least able to benefit from it. The public policy that results reflects a pattern in which the state does not do everything capital wants all the time. But it acts in the general interest of capital, since policy-makers believe that to do so reflects the broader public interest.

Public Choice Theory

The next theory to consider, known as **public choice**, is heavily influenced by economic theory, which derives its premises and arguments from the view that individuals are rational, self-interested, utility-maximizing creatures. This is precisely the view held by classic liberal economics, which argues that our pursuit of individual fulfillment is constrained only by a world in which scarcity is the prevailing condition. As noted earlier, there is not enough of everything for everybody at all times. Therefore, we make rational calculations based on self-interest as to how to get the things we want, need and desire. But we are in a constant competition with other individuals engaged in the same basic process of fulfilling their desires.

Decision-making about how to fulfill those desires in the political realm is no different from the process in the economic marketplace, according to the theory. Thus, you make decisions about spending and saving in the economic marketplace on the basis of a rational calculation of your self-interest (e.g., I am hungry; how much money do I have in my pocket? How much is that pizza compared to that submarine sandwich?). So, too, will you support political parties that promote policies most likely to maximize your individual well-being. Moreover, when you, the policy-maker, set about your job, you do so on the basis of a rational calculation of self-interest. This might mean enacting policies that will bring you the greatest chances for reelection if you are a politician, or that will expand your bureaucratic empire or secure your own position and promotion if you are a bureaucrat. From this perspective, it is folly to talk about some vague "public interest" or "will of the people," since all are engaged in a competition to see their own particular and narrow self-interest prevail.

As you can see, whereas the pluralist sees the group as the most important actor in the policy process, and Marxists see class as most significant, for public choice theorists, it is the individual that is the primary unit of analysis. Another important feature of public choice theory is that it departs from the pluralist view that the state is somehow a neutral arbiter among the competing interests in society. Instead, bureaucrats and politicians engage in a complex process of negotiating and bargaining to maximize their own individual self-interests.

The problems with the public choice approach are twofold. First, its assumptions about rationality are largely unsupported. It is not clear that we are rational utility-maximizing creatures at all times and in all circumstances. However appealing it may seem to base our actions on science, facts and reason, we clearly do not do this in all things. Second, and related, is that the theory assumes a view of human nature that is by no means universally accepted. It assumes that people are inward-looking and self-interested competitors, while making no allowance for other values such as altruism and cooperation. Still, it does seem to present some intriguing explanations as to how policy is produced.

All these theories go some way toward helping us understand how and why public policy is made. But it should be obvious by now that each contains limitations, and no single theory explains all there is to the issue. Some focus on the factors that influence policy-making from outside the government; others make observations from the perspective of those within government. Still, these are the dominant conceptual models in the current literature on public policy. But we still need to know something about how policy is actually implemented, and what tools policy-makers have at their disposal to achieve their goals. These are the concerns of the next section.

Implementing Public Policy

What exactly happens once a policy decision has been taken? Two things. First, it must be implemented. It is of little use for the government to decide on a course of action if there is no effective way of carrying out its intentions. Following this, the policy must be evaluated to see that it is successfully attaining the objectives set out by the government.

In theory, the implementation stage of the policy process is dominated by the bureaucrats. They are the ones mainly responsible for carrying out the will of the elected representatives who made the key decision to proceed with a particular policy. In an ideal policy-making world, the politicians impart directions to the bureaucrats, who then faithfully carry them out. While the Cabinet and Legislature retain a role in this stage of the policy cycle by overseeing the actions of their underlings—the bureaucrats—the primary responsibility for implementation rests in the hands of the public servants. And part of the implementation process involves deciding exactly what policy instrument will be used to realize the government's goals. A variety of options is available. The choice of governing instrument is discussed below. First, though, the next section provides some insights into problems associated with implementation.

The Process of Implementation: How Does Anything Get Done?

When scholars first turned their attention to the implementation process, they noticed that there was often a disturbing gap between the expectations of political actors who formulated policy, and the actions of bureaucratic actors charged with implementing policy. For instance, if legislators passed a law to eliminate poverty among children by the year 2000, why is it that poverty among children has actually been increasing over the past few years? If tough new environmental standards have been enacted to limit the discharge of toxins into the atmosphere, why has pollution been getting worse? In these and countless other examples, there seems to be a void between intention and action. This realization has led to the conclusion that the implementation aspect of policy-making deserves more thorough attention.

Among the important first studies of implementation as a distinct part of the policy cycle is a study by Public Management theorists Jeffrey Pressman and Aaron Wildavsky.[29] They examined a $23-million initiative by the U.S. government to revitalize an Oakland, California neighbourhood. They discovered the initiative suffered from contradictory legislative mandates, antagonisms between federal agencies, and the skepticism of the local business community. In short, implementation of a laudable project got bogged down by the impracticability of having so many actors working at cross-purposes.

In fact, the implementation of public policy is hardly a straightforward process. It is complicated by numerous factors.[30] Let us review just a few. To begin with, governments are increasingly forced to draft legislation in broad and general terms. Indeed, the objectives of policy are often unclear, and may be expressed in fuzzy, multiple or contradictory terms. It is then left up to the bureaucrats to interpret the meaning of those terms, and ultimately to provide the actual content of the policy in the sense of day-to-day implementation. What this implies is that public servants enjoy a generous amount of discretion in translating into action the legislative expectations of their political masters. In turn, it is conceivable that narrow bureaucratic goals may displace those of the legislators. For instance, if legislation is passed that calls for reform of the delivery of certain social services, and this reform threatens the positions of bureaucrats in the department responsible for enacting the reforms, those reforms may be sabotaged in the implementation stage. Or conversely, the reforms may be exaggerated if their impact is to expand a bureaucratic empire. But this may then lead to conflict with other administrative agencies over the appropriate areas of involvement of the first agency, with the result that implementation is thwarted by bureaucratic in-fighting. A further layer of bureaucratic interference may occur when the coordinating agencies (i.e., Finance Department, Treasury Board, the Privy Council Office or the Prime Minister's Office) stick their noses into the process. Thus, it is worth noting that in the implementation stage, the content of policy can be modified, elaborated or even reversed.

Within the bureaucracy itself, then, there may be resistance to implementing policy. Old habits, ideas and programs die hard. Individuals or institutional offices that are accustomed to doing things a certain way are often reluctant to change procedures and processes. Thus, when a section of a department is given instructions to draft the regulatory framework that will assist in enacting a new law, it may draft those regulations so as to minimize change to customary procedures. Or there may be costs associated with change that are difficult to overcome. Prevailing values may be challenged. In any case, policy objectives may not always be clear. This problem is often compounded by the differing perspective of the participants in implementation relative to the perspective of the policy formulators. While a program may set out with laudable objectives, the individuals actually enacting the program may decide, for whatever reason, that they will focus on the one or two aspects of the program with which they are most comfortable—leaving the other objectives to fall by the wayside.

The question of political feasibility also often gets in the way of implementation. Consider the following case. Scientists with the Ministry of Fisheries conduct research and gather data that suggest that the east-coast fishing stocks are in dire circumstances. Using the latest computer modelling and fish survey techniques, they determine that there simply are not enough fish to sustain the traditional level of fishing. So they recommend that quotas be imposed on the amount of fish taken from the ocean, and that the fishery be open only during strictly monitored times of the year. The scientific basis of their policy is unassailable. And most everyone agrees that saving the long-term viability of the fishing industry is a worthwhile goal. But is implementing this policy politically feasible? Will those most affected by the new policy—namely, the fishers and their families—support such drastic actions, when it could mean the end of their way of life? Probably not, and they will express their displeasure with this policy by withholding their support from the political party that tries to implement it. Thus, local politicians will quickly calculate that whatever the merits of the policy, it is too politically costly, and, besides arguing against it at the formulation stage, they may also resist its implementation.

Another actor to consider in the implementation process is the frontline worker who actually meets with the public and is responsible for delivering a policy, program or service. These people could be the ones who issue your driver's licence, give you a parking ticket, pick up your garbage, collect your bus fare, etc. Consider your teachers as frontline workers, for instance. Each is instructed to follow policy that is sent down from "on high" from the Ministry of Education. But despite the best intentions of legislators and bureaucrats who dictate through policy that children are entitled to a "good education," they are not the ones responsible for delivering that policy to its ultimate users: children in the schools. It is the teacher—the frontline worker—who holds that responsibility. Thus the frontline worker has a great deal of influence over the quality of the delivery of services, and often has a direct influence on the success or failure of a given policy.

It is important to note as well that since Canada is a federal state, initiatives at one level of government can be affected by the other level. For instance, the federal government and the provinces are engaged in numerous shared-cost and joint federal-provincial programs. But disputes constantly arise as to the implementation of these programs. For instance, under the *Canada Health Act,* the federal government articulated a set of five principles that guide the delivery of health services by the provinces. Health care is a provincial responsibility, but since the federal government kicks in the lion's share of funding, it feels entitled to set some of the rules regarding implementation. This has caused a series of disputes between the two levels of government over issues such as extra billing.[31]

In addition, it is important to look at forces outside government that influence the implementation stage of policy-making. Policy decisions are often the result of compromise and negotiation between interests with conflicting views. This means that a decision will spawn both proponents and opponents, winners and losers. In many cases, the losers will not simply give up and go away once a policy is announced. Rather, they will move from trying to influence the formulation stage to influencing the implementation stage. They may, for instance, carefully monitor the implementation of a certain policy to ensure that whatever regulations and guidelines have been enacted adhere to the letter of the law. Or they may even take the extreme step of trying to impede the policy's implementation. For example, in 1997 when the Ontario government passed Bill 160, governing education reform, the teachers in the province staged a two-week strike and promised to

FIGURE 7.3

POLITICAL PLOY # 3726

DO IT DURING THE PLAYOFFS!...

Source: Reproduced with permission, Dennis Pritchard.

fight the policy until it was reversed. In addition, they launched a court challenge claiming the policy was unconstitutional.

Alternatively, opponents of a given policy may carefully monitor it for weaknesses in implementation. They may vigilantly stand guard to uncover any perceived injustices that might result from the policy, or any errors in its implementation— ready to pounce on the government and expose its malfeasance.

Ever since the enactment of the *Charter of Rights and Freedoms,* the implementation of public policy has been subjected to heightened scrutiny. The courts have always been an avenue that could be used to check the constitutional legality of legislation, but primarily with regard to whether a law was within the jurisdiction of the level of government that passed it. With the advent of the *Charter,* however, the constitutional validity of laws can be challenged on the basis of whether they violate human rights. The range of policies subjected to *Charter* challenges has been incredibly broad, including abortion, fetal rights, mandatory retirement, strikes and secondary picketing, Sunday shopping, children's advertising, minority language education rights, French-only signs, official bilingualism, extradition, drunk driving, cruise missile testing, narcotics, breathalyser testing,

Box 7-4

Conditions for Effective Implementation

Daniel Mazmanian and Paul Sabatier have studied the issue of implementation and concluded that it is most easily accomplished if the following conditions prevail:

1. The objectives of legislation should be clear and consistent.
2. The legislation that establishes a policy should be based on sound theory.
3. The agencies that are chosen to implement a policy should be sympathetic to it.
4. Agencies responsible for implementation of a policy must have good managers.
5. Strong supporters of a policy must be engaged in the policy during its formative period. Otherwise it will probably fade away.
6. Socioeconomic change must be anticipated.[32]

refugees, assisted suicide, pornography, hate literature, political rights of public servants, constituency boundaries, dangerous offenders, sexual assault, battered women, prisoners' rights, prostitution, and other issues. Analysis of *Charter* cases in the first 10 years of its life reveals that legal rights, mainly dealing with the enforcement of criminal law, were the most common basis of *Charter* cases. The result, according to some analysts, is that the *Charter* has effectively created a "new constitutional code of conduct for Canadian police officers in dealing with suspects and accused persons, and in the process has pushed the Canadian criminal process away from the 'crime control' side of the ledger toward the 'due process' side of the ledger."[33] In other words, the legality of the implementation of policies has served as the most common form of *Charter* violation complaint. More particularly, the implementation of policies regarding police actions concerning procedural fairness has dominated the dockets of the courts.

It may appear from this brief survey of some of the factors affecting implementation that policy as articulated by formulators does not stand a chance of being enacted as planned. Yet a tremendous amount of progress is made, year after year, by governments in enacting a panoply of policy (see Box 7-4).

In the meantime, the question of how policy is implemented needs to be addressed. We now turn to the issue of the choice of governing instrument.

Choice of Governing Instrument

One of the key steps in implementing any policy involves deciding on the means by which the policy will be enacted. And one way of exploring this question is to look at governing instruments, which political scientists Doern and Phidd define as "the major ways in which governments seek to ensure compliance, support and implementation of public policy."[34] In other words, is it better to use the carrot, the stick or the sermon?[35] Most studies of instrument choice trace their intellectual origins to the work of Theodore Lowi, who was among the first to try to categorize the types of instruments available to governments, as well as to differentiate them according to how coercive they were.[36] We will look at various governing instruments in terms of their level of intrusiveness in the economy and lives of citizens. This expands upon the issues raised earlier regarding scope of government, while also bringing to mind the related issues of means and resources.

Fundamentally, when government creates public policy, it is trying to get us to adjust our behaviour in some way. When it passes a law calling for a stop sign at the corner of Maple and Elm streets, this requires us to adjust our driving habits. When it provides tax breaks for purchasing Registered Retirement Savings Plans, this encourages us to adjust our savings and investment habits. And when we fail to comply with the state in these matters, various penalties can be applied. Failure to stop at a stop sign might result in a ticket. Failure to purchase RRSPs might mean higher real tax rates and a diminished quality of life when we retire. In short, the state has at its disposal a range of policy instruments to influence our behaviour, backed up by a range of sanctions and coercive measures to ensure our compliance.

But what motivates policy-makers to select certain policy instruments and not others? For one answer, consider the role of the state in terms of the level of intrusiveness of policy instruments, an approach outlined by political scientist Nicolas Baxter-Moore. Intrusiveness means "the extent to which various instruments as means of government intervention intrude directly and publicly on private decision-making."[37] Baxter-Moore developed a scale of government intrusiveness in which he categorized the various instruments available for government use (see Figure 7.4). The scale has the advantage of accounting for both *decisions* and *non-decisions* of government, and thus accords with our definition of public policy. It ranges from minimum to maximum degrees of intrusiveness.

The scale is divided first into non-decisions and decisions. Each of these categories is then subdivided into degrees of state intrusiveness, ranging from minimum to maximum. At the extreme end of the minimum end of the scale is the idea that conflict between citizens is privatized. Indeed, government may concretely signal that it refuses to get involved, as in instances where certain professions are given the power to regulate themselves rather than have the government regulate them. Medicine and law, for instance, are self-governing professions. There is no government public policy at this point, but moving across the scale we encounter our first example of government intrusiveness. This takes the form of a *symbolic gesture or response* wherein, for instance, the prime minister makes a speech, or establishes a royal commission or task force to inquire into an issue without actually committing the government to take a course of action. It also includes conferences, information, studies and research, the reorganization of government departments and other similar devices.

Privatization of conflict and symbolic responses both fall under the heading of non-decisions. Other policy instruments fall under the heading of decisions, which in turn is subdivided into incentives and directives. Incentives begin with exhortation,

FIGURE 7.4   A Reconstruction of the Policy Instruments Continuum

Non-Decisions		Decisions				
		Incentives (Indirect Public Intervention)		Directives (Direct Public Intervention)		
Privatization of Conflict	Symbolic Responses	Exhortation	Tax Expenditures	Public Spending	Regulation	Taxation	Public Ownership	State of Emergency

Minimum -------- Degree of State Intrusiveness -------- Maximum

Source: Nicolas Baxter-Moore, "Policy Implementation and the Role of the State: A Revised Approach to the Study of Policy Instruments," in Robert J. Jackson et al., *Contemporary Canadian Politics*, (Scarborough: Prentice-Hall, 1987).

which means political and bureaucratic leaders attempt to secure the compliance of citizens without threats or inducements. Examples include the government using persuasion to get us to buy into what it is trying to accomplish. Moving along the scale of intrusiveness, we next find tax expenditures, which permit individuals and corporations to retain money that would otherwise normally go to taxes. This policy instrument essentially entails the failure to do something (e.g., collect taxes) that might otherwise have been done. It is estimated that the Canadian federal government currently has $30 billion worth of tax expenditures on the books. Among the more well-known are those that encourage investment in the Canadian film industry. But there are many more obscure examples that are the domain of tax accountants and lawyers, and otherwise remain largely hidden from view.

Public spending is the next most intrusive category of public policy. It includes items such as subsidies, grants and transfer payments, loans and loan guarantees, and some cases of joint public-private ownership where the government is a minority shareholder. Exhortation, tax expenditures and public spending are examples of incentives involving indirect public intervention. Directives are the final category, within which the government takes an increasingly intrusive role. Regulation (see Box 7-5). is the first example of a directive, but is somewhat less intrusive than taxation. Public ownership is more intrusive that either regulation or taxation. The most intrusive public policy in the government's arsenal, however, is to declare a state of emergency. In this case, all normal civil liberties and government institutions are suspended, control is exercised autocratically, and state security forces (the army and police) are used to support the government's directives, using force if necessary.

Given this scale of intrusiveness and the range of policy choices available, how do decision-makers decide which policy to employ? The answer to this question takes us back to the issues of scope, means and resources. Policy-makers are constrained in their choice of governing instruments by societal views regarding what the appropriate level of state involvement should be in the society. They are constrained by the appropriateness of various means at their disposal. (It would make little sense, for instance, to try to secure the compliance of citizens to obey traffic laws by imposing a state of emergency.) And finally, the resources need to be available to ensure that a policy goal is realistically achievable. The creation of a national universally accessible federally funded day-care system seemed improbable in an age of spiralling debt and deficits. But now that we have entered the post-deficit era, and resources may be available, we may see this issue resurface on the public policy agenda.

Returning to the scale of intrusiveness, as a policy-maker, you might go through the following process: Upon being confronted with an issue or problem, you first decide whether to make a non-decision or decision. If you select non-decision, you then decide whether to leave the issue in private hands, or employ symbolic responses. If you opt to make a decision, then you need to determine whether to employ incentives or directives. The decision-making process is, of course, less straightforward in the real world of policy-making. But by breaking down the options available to policy-makers in this way, we impose some structure on a process

Box 7-5

When to Select "Regulation"

In October 1992, the Canadian government issued a directive to all departments outlining the conditions each must meet when deciding whether to employ the policy instrument of regulation. To create new regulatory programs or for substantive new or amended regulations, the directive said, departments and agencies must demonstrate the following:

1. A problem or risk exists, government intervention is justified, and regulation is the best alternative.
2. Canadians have been consulted and have had an opportunity to participate in developing or modifying regulations and regulatory programs.
3. The benefits of regulation outweigh the costs, and the regulatory program is "structured" to maximize the gains to beneficiaries in relation to the costs to Canadian
    ➤ government,
    ➤ business, and
    ➤ individuals
4. Steps have been taken to ensure that the regulatory activity impedes Canada's competitiveness as little as possible.
5. The regulatory burden on Canadians has been minimized through such methods as cooperation with other governments.
6. Systems are in place to manage regulatory resources effectively. In particular,
    ➤ compliance and enforcement policies are articulated, as appropriate; and,
    ➤ resources have been approved and are adequate to discharge enforcement responsibilities effectively, and to ensure compliance where the regulation binds the government.[38]

that is inherently disordered, messy and sometimes seemingly incomprehensible. Doern and Wilson suggest that "politicians have a strong tendency to respond to policy issues (any issue) by moving successively from the least coercive governing instruments to the most coercive."[39] Trebilcock *et al.* argue that the choice of governing instrument is explainable in public choice terms. They suggest that most political behaviour is guided by the calculus of *vote maximization*. The instrument choice will be determined by whichever policy and means of achieving it is likely to garner the most electoral support. This consideration, they argue, even outweighs considerations about the cost of programs and policies.[40]

Recent Developments in Policy Implementation

What is important to note in the current political climate is that implementation of policy is undergoing some drastic changes. As with other aspects of public administration, the trends toward decentralization, downsizing and devolution of responsibilities to the private sector means that in many instances the traditional governmental role of policy implementation is being taken over by nongovernmental actors. The current thinking among the New Public Management (NPM) advocates is that government should "steer" rather than "row."[41] A major premise of this approach is that government should arrange for the provision of services, but not deliver (or implement) those services itself.

To put it another way, many policy decisions fall on the least intrusive end of the scale discussed above, namely, *privatization of conflict*. These changes are reflected in the adoption of the NPM discussed in Chapter 3. Implementation has been influenced by the rigorous demands of NPM for reorganization and restructuring. But it has also been affected by the recent increases in demands for greater privatization and deregulation, coupled with citizen participation and control, democracy and responsiveness of government institutions.[42] The impact of NPM on policy implementation is summarized in Box 7-6.

BOX 7-6

The Impact of the NPM on Policy Implementation

1. NPM assumes traditional government structures are rule-bound, inflexible and incapable of adapting quickly.
2. NPM questions government involvement in a variety of traditional policy fields.
3. Policy-makers increasingly look to nongovernmental actors to deliver policies (private sector corporations, community groups, nonprofit organizations, citizens, the family, etc.)
4. There is a new emphasis on outcomes of policy in terms of quality of service.
5. NPM looks to hybrid forms of policy delivery that have greater flexibility than traditional governmental forms, including contracting out, partnerships and other forms of nongovernmental implementation of policy.[43]

Recent government reviews of bureaucratic performance, from PS2000 to La Relève to the Program Review, have either implicitly or explicitly included concerns about the implementation of policy. Consider, for instance, the entreaty contained in PS2000 that the public service of Canada undergo a fundamental culture change. Why? To enable it to become a public service that recognizes the primacy of service to clients. It suggested more than 300 ways in which central controls and the number of job classifications could be reduced, and staffing could be made easier.[44] All this reflects the underlying concern that policy implementation (as well as formulation, of course) needed to be improved.

Similarly in 1996, the Treasury Board document "Getting Government Right: A Progress Report" identified four objectives for improving government services. These were as follows: a) clarification of government federal roles and responsibilities; b) better targeting of resources on high-priority social and economic issues; c) better and more accessible government "involving clients more in decision-making and using modern and practical service delivery tools"; and d) more affordable government. The report presented new thinking on the way government implements policy.

A central thrust of the renewal agenda has been to determine where the federal government is best placed to deliver programs or services and where these programs and services are more appropriately delivered by others. The net result is significant changes both in the services the federal government provides and in how it delivers them. The federal government is increasing its use of partnerships with other levels of government, the private sector and citizens to better manage collective and particular interests within Canada's economic and social union. In addition, by paying greater attention to how well it delivers services, the federal government is finding better ways to manage its operations efficiently and provide quality service to Canadians.[45]

NPM, then, has insinuated itself into the formulation and implementation stages of public policy.

Yet the outcomes of NPM policy innovations are sometimes not clear (as with other systems of management). For instance, massive restructuring of the health-care sector brought new efficiencies and cost savings in Ontario. But it also unexpectedly brought a 4000-percent increase in the incidence of certain bacterial infections in hospitals. This was because fewer staff, dealing with greater caseloads, had less time to wash their hands between treating patients, with the result that bacterial infections soared. This is an example of the unforeseen consequences of policy implementation under the NPM. But unforeseen consequences frequently seem to bedevil implementation, whatever form it takes.

All in all, the concept of implementation is a difficult one to analyze, much less execute. It involves so many factors and actors: Cabinet and Legislature, courts, bureaucrats, interest groups, citizens, etc. And it involves an evolving process of bargaining, negotiation, incentives, decisions, log-rolling, discretion, and so on. It is also hard to say with authority where the formulation process ends and implementation begins, since the two are continuous and interrelated. Still, it is crucial to understanding the public policy aspects of public administration. In any event, once formulated and implemented, some mechanism must exist to ensure that the policy has achieved its objectives. The evaluation of policy is the third step in the policy cycle and, although discussed in detail in Chapter 8, is introduced below.

Evaluating Public Policy

Evaluation is one of the areas that distinguishes the public and private sector. It is relatively straightforward to determine whether or not a widget company is making a profit. On the basis of this "bottom-line" standard, an evaluation can be made. But in the public sector, as we noted in Chapter 1, this clear-cut bottom-line standard does not exist. Thus, evaluation can be more of a challenge in the public sector than in the private sector. We will explore the conundrums of evaluation in some detail in Chapter 8. But for now, we will simply make a few general observations about how evaluation fits in with the other two aspects of the policy cycle: formulation and implementation.

As noted above, evaluation is that part of the policy cycle that is mainly conducted by the public service and the attentive public. It is an ongoing process that can be conducted either formally and systematically, or informally and haphazardly. The former case might involve, for instance, a team of forensic accountants being contracted by a municipal government to determine if county finances are in order. The latter case might involve the casual observation by a citizen that a parking meter is not functioning properly. In both cases, some form of evaluative exercise is going on that forces government officials to account for their action (or inaction). In short, public policy is being scrutinized and assessed.

It might seem surprising that the systematic evaluation of public policy is a young art. It is only in the past 20 or 30 years that theorists of public administration acknowledged how little was being done academically in this area. Furthermore, while it could be argued that practitioners of public administration had always carried on some form of evaluation of public policy—however informal it might have been—the Canadian federal government only initiated ongoing, professional and rigorous self-evaluation in the last few decades. According to political scientist Ray Rist,

Policy evaluation began and rapidly expanded at a time in many western democratic societies when there were strong pressures to address the social problems of these same societies. The 20 years from 1960–1980 witnessed a dramatic increase in the use of the public sector to address social issues as far-ranging as drug abuse, education of poor children, crime, availability of affordable housing, environmental pollution and health care for the elderly, to name but a few....

But while large sums of funds were to be spent, there was also the need to ensure that the funds were spent effectively. Stated differently, there was a need to ensure that the policies and programs delivered on what they had promised. Assessing the impacts and performances of the new initiatives fell to the emergent field of policy and program evaluation.[46]

Initial attempts to employ the burgeoning field of evaluation theory, though, faltered on the faulty premise of rationalism. Theorists and practitioners alike assumed it was possible to make a factual, objective assessment of a policy based largely on quantitative methods derived from scientific inquiry. But as Rist suggests, over time it was realized that there was no simple linear relationship between evaluation and its use by policy-makers to produce sound policy. The emergent problems of applying evaluation theory to practice will be analyzed in Chapter 8.

As with formulation and implementation, it is possible to identify the key actors who should be involved in evaluation. These are the bureaucrats and the public. But it is also important to acknowledge that the boundaries are blurred between the three stages and between who performs each stage. Thus, the Legislature has an important evaluative role through the mechanisms of the opposition parties and Question Period in the House of Commons. As well, the courts are frequently asked to judge whether public officials are implementing what the formulators have asked, in accordance with the Constitution and the rules and regulations set out in legislation.

But once evaluation has taken place, then what? Usually evaluation will reveal one of three things. First, the policy is working just fine, and so needs no further refinement or change. Second, the policy is deficient in certain regards, but on the whole is redeemable. Perhaps it only requires some tinkering. Third, the policy is an abject failure and should be entirely scrapped, and a new approach developed. Notice that in all three cases, information is being fed back into the policy cycle that will affect the future formulation and implementation of policy. If the first scenario prevails and the policy does not need any change, then formulators can go on to another issue, and implementers can continue to do their job, secure in the knowledge that they are doing the right thing. But if either of scenarios two or three prevail, then both formulators and implementors are confronted with a new set of challenges. Thus the process cranks (or creaks) back into gear, with either minor reform or wholesale change by the formulators and implementors. Such is the never-ending, dynamic and evolving world of the policy cycle.

WHAT YOU HAVE LEARNED

Public policy is a vitally important aspect of public administration, difficult though it is to define. It is convenient for us to think of the public policy process as a cycle involving the continuous interplay of formulation, implementation and evaluation of various public policies. While the three steps of the process can be conceptualized as discrete, in fact in the real world there is considerable overlap between them, and each influences the other. You should now be able to answer the following questions: What is public policy? What theories of public policy decision-making explain the way that public officials (both bureaucratic and political) make decisions on behalf of citizens?

ENDNOTES

1. See Stephen Brooks, *Public Policy in Canada: An Introduction, Third Edition,* (Toronto: Oxford, 1998): chapters 1–2.

2. See, for example, Laurent Dobuzinskis, Michael Howlett and David Laycock, eds. *Policy Studies in Canada: The State of the Art,* (Toronto: University of Toronto Press, 1996); Brooks, *Public Policy in Canada,* (1998); G. Bruce Doern and Richard W. Phidd, *Canadian Public Policy: Ideas, Structure, Process,* (Toronto: Methuen, 1983); Michael Howlett and M. Ramesh, *Studying Public Policy: Policy Cycles and Policy Subsystems,* (Toronto: Oxford University Press, 1995); Leslie A. Pal, *Beyond Policy Analysis: Public Issue Management in Turbulent Times, Second Edition,* (Scarborough: Nelson, 2001); Andrew F. Johnson and Andrew Stritch, eds. *Canadian Public Policy: Globalization and Political Parties,* (Toronto: Copp Clark, 1997); and Ronald Manzer, *Public Policies and Political Development in Canada,* (Toronto: University of Toronto Press, 1985).

3. W.I. Jenkins, *Policy Analysis,* (London: Martin Robertson, 1978): 15. Cited in Doern and Phidd, *Canadian Public Policy,* (1983): 33–34.

4. Thomas R. Dye, *Understanding Public Policy, Fifth Edition,* (Englewood Cliffs, New Jersey: Prentice-Hall, 1992): 1.

5. See Richard Simeon, "Studying Public Policy," *Canadian Journal of Political Science,* 9, 4 (December, 1976): 559–562. Stephen Brooks refers to "scope," "choice of policy instrument," and "who benefits and who pays?" See Brooks, *Public Policy in Canada,* (1998): 8–17

6. Robert J. Jackson and Doreen Jackson, *Politics in Canada: Culture, Institutions, Behaviour and Public Policy, Fifth Edition,* (Scarborough: Prentice Hall, 2001): 22.

7. Gregory Albo, David Langille and Leo Panitch, eds. *A Different Kind of State? Popular Power and Democratic Administration,* (Toronto: Oxford University Press, 1993): 5.

8. Cited in Keith Archer *et al., Parameters of Power: Canada's Political Institutions,* (Scarborough: Nelson, 1995): 271. Reprinted with permission of ITP Nelson.

9. Canada. *Strengthening Our Policy Capacity,* Report of the Task Force on Strengthening the Policy Capacity of the Federal Government, (Ottawa: Canadian Centre for Management Development, April, 1995); B. Guy Peters, *The Policy Capacity of Government,* (Ottawa: Canadian Centre for Management Development, 1996); George Anderson, "The New Focus on Policy Capacity in the Federal Government," *Canadian Public Administration,* 39, 4, (1996): 470–71; Canada. Policy Research Secretariat, *Policy Research in Canada: A Capacity for the Future: A Discussion Document,* (March, 1999); Herman Bakvis, "Rebuilding Policy Capacity in the Era of the Fiscal Dividend: A Report from Canada," *Governance,* 13, 1, (2000): 71–103.

10. Pal, *Beyond Policy Analysis,* (2001): 35.

11. For a consideration of policy capacity in an intergovernmental context, see Patricia L. O'Reilly, Gregory J. Inwood and Carolyn M. Johns, "Intergovernmental Policy Capacity in Canada," Paper presented to the Annual Meeting of the Canadian Political Science Association, University of Toronto, May 31, 2002; and Gregory J. Inwood, Patricia L. O'Reilly and Carolyn M. Johns, "A Comparative Analysis of Intergovernmental Policy Capacity in Trade, Environment and Health," Paper Presented to the Annual Meeting of the Canadian Political Science Association, Laval University, May 29, 2001.

12. Pal, *Beyond Policy Analysis,* (2001): 23.

13. Brooks, *Public Policy in Canada,* (1998): 11.

14. See Richard Simeon, "Studying Public Policy," *Canadian Journal of Political Science,* 9, 4 (December, 1976): 548–580. Simeon's views, in turn, were influenced by the work of Anthony King. See "Ideas, Institutions and the Policies of Governments: A Comparative Analysis," Parts I–III, *British Journal of Political Science,* 2 (July and October, 1973): 291–313 and 409–423.

15. John Meynard Keynes, *The General Theory of Employment, Interest and Money,* (London: Macmillan, 1936): 383.

16. Jackson and Jackson, *Politics in Canada,* (2001): 500 ff.

17. See James E. Anderson, *Public Policy-Making, Third Edition,* (New York: Holt, Rinehart and Winston, 1984): 8–10.

18. Leslie A. Pal, *Beyond Policy Analysis: Public Issue Management in Turbulent Times, Second Edition*, (Scarborough: Nelson, 2001): 17–18.

19. Anderson, *Public Policy-Making*, (1984): 8.

20. Charles E. Lindblom, "The Science of 'Muddling Through,'" *Public Administration Review*, 19, 2 (Spring, 1959): 79–88.

21. See Amitai Etzioni, "Mixed Scanning: A 'Third' Approach to Decision-Making," *Public Administration Review*, 27, 5 (December, 1967); and *Modern Organizations*, (Englewood Cliffs, New Jersey: Prentice-Hall, 1964).

22. Anderson, *Public Policy-Making*, (1984): 9–10.

23. See Hugh G. Thorburn, "Interest Groups in the Canadian Federal System," in R.S. Blair and J.T. McLeod, eds. *The Canadian Political Tradition, Second Edition*, (Scarborough: Nelson, 1993): 316–329; and Paul Pross, *Group Politics and Public Policy*, (Toronto: Oxford University Press, 1986).

24. The classic statement of pluralist theory is Robert A. Dahl, *Who Governs?*, (New Haven: Yale University Press, 1961).

25. See Joseph Schumpeter, *Capitalism, Socialism, and Democracy*, (New York: Harper, 1943).

26. E.E. Schattschneider, *The Semisovereign People: A Realist's View of Democracy in America*, (Hinsdale: Dryden Press, 1975): 34.

27. See Chuck Rachlis and David Wolfe, "An Insider's View of the NDP Government of Ontario: The Politics of Permanent Opposition Meets the Economics of Permanent Recession," in Graham White, ed. *The Government and Politics of Ontario, Fifth Edition*, (Toronto: University of Toronto Press, 1997): 331–364.

28. See Leo Panitch, "The Role and Nature of the Canadian State," in Leo Panitch, ed. *The Canadian State: Political Economy and Political Power*, (Toronto: University of Toronto Press, 1977): 3–27.

29. See Jeffrey L. Pressman and Aaron Wildavsky, *Implementation, Second Edition*, (Berkeley: University of California Press, 1979).

30. Cases adapted from Jeffrey D. Straussman, *Public Administration, Second Edition*, (New York: Longman, 1990): 244–245.

31. See Carolyn Tuohy, *Policy and Politics in Canada: Institutionalized Ambivalence*, (Philadelphia: Temple University Press, 1992): chapter 3.

32. F.L. Morton, Peter H. Russell and Troy Riddell, "The Supreme Court's First Decade of *Charter* Decisions: Judging the Judges, 1982–1992," in Paul Fox and Graham White, eds. *Politics: Canada. Eighth Edition*, (Toronto: McGraw-Hill, 1995): 80.

33. G. Bruce Doern and Richard W. Phidd, *Canadian Public Policy: Ideas, Structure, Process*, (Toronto: Methuen, 1983): 110.

34. Adapted from Daniel Mazmanian and Paul Sabatier, *Implementation and Public Policy*, (Glenview, Illinois: Scott, Foresman, 1983). See also Paul A. Sabatier and Daniel Mazmanian, "The Implementation of Public Policy: A Framework for Analysis," in Daniel A. Mazmanian and Paul A. Sabatier, eds. *Effective Policy Implementation*, (Lexington, Massachusetts: D.C. Heath and Company, 1981): 3–35; and Brian W. Hogwood and Lewis A. Gunn, *Policy Analysis for the Real World*, (Oxford: Oxford University Press, 1984): chapter 11.

35. See Marie-Louise Bemelmans-Videc, Ray C. Rist and Evert Vedung, *Carrots, Sticks and Sermons: Policy Instruments and Their Evaluation*, (New Brunswick, New Jersey: Transaction Publishers, 1998).

36. Theodore Lowi, "Distribution, Regulation, Redistribution: The Functions of Government," in R.B. Ripley, ed. *Public Policies and Their Politics: Techniques of Government Control*, (New York: W.W. Norton, 1966): 27–40.

37. See Nicolas Baxter-Moore, "Policy Implementation and the Role of the State: A Revised Approach to the Study of Policy Instruments," in Robert J. Jackson *et al. Contemporary Canadian Politics: Reading and Notes*, (Scarborough: Prentice Hall, 1987): 336–355. See also Rand Dyck, *Canadian Politics: Critical Approaches. Third Edition*, (Scarborough: Nelson, 2000): 467–70.

38. Source: Reprinted by permission of Transaction Publishers. "The Stick: Regulation as a Tool of Government," by Donald Lemaire, in Marie-Louise Bemelmans-Vedec, Ray C. Rist and Evert Verding, eds. *Carrots, Sticks, and Sermons: Policy Instruments and Their Evaluation*, (New Jersey:

Transaction Publishers, 1998): 66–67. Copyright © 1998 by Transaction Publishers. All rights reserved.

39. G. Bruce Doern and V. Seymour Wilson, *Issues in Canadian Public Policy*, Toronto: Macmillan, 1974): 339.

40. M.J. Trebilcock *et al*, *The Choice of Governing Instrument*, (Ottawa: Economc Council of Canada, 1982): 27.

41. David Osborne and Ted Gaebler, *Reinventing Government*, (Reading, Massachusetts: Addison-Wesley, 1992): chapter 1.

42. See Pal, *Beyond Policy Analysis*, (2001): 192 ff.

43. Source: Leslie A. Pal, *Beyond Policy Analysis: Public Issue Management in Turbulent Times*, (Scarborough: Nelson, 1997): 158–159.

44. Donald J. Savoie, *Thatcher, Reagan and Mulroney: In Search of a New Bureaucracy*, (Pittsburgh: University of Pittsburgh Press, 1994): 228–229.

45. Canada, Treasury Board of Canada, *Getting Government Right: A Progress Report*, (Ottawa: Minister of Supply and Service, 1996).

46. Ray C. Rist, "Introduction," in Ray C. Rist, ed. *Policy Evaluation: Linking Theory to Practice*, (Aldershot, England: Edward Elgar Publishing: 1995): xv.

KEY WORDS AND CONCEPTS

public policy (199)	rational-comprehensive model (211)
governing instruments (202)	incremental model (212)
mobilization of bias (205)	mixed scanning (214)
policy cycle (206)	pluralism (215)
formulation (206)	Marxist analysis (215)
implementation (206)	public choice theory (217)
evaluation (206)	

REVIEW QUESTIONS

This chapter was divided into four sections, each dealing with the issue of policy-making in public administration. These central issues were highlighted:

1. *Defining Public Policy*

This brief introductory section considered what "public policy" is and explained that, while a number of definitions exist, we would focus on the idea that public policy is "a set of interrelated decisions taken by a political actor or group of actors concerning the selection of goals and the means of achieving them..." More simply, we quoted Thomas Dye's maxim that public policy is "whatever governments choose to do or not to do."

2. *Formulating Public Policy*

There are several different theoretical explanations which seek to illuminate the question of how policy is made. Does one theoretical model comprehensively explain how policy is made as well as why policy is made (or not made)?

3. *Implementing Public Policy*

This section dealt with the tools and means by which will is translated into action. It showed that policy is not self-executing, but must be enacted to be effective.

Decisions about the level of intrusiveness are among the first that policy-makers must consider when deciding on a policy. But the process of carrying out a decision and of transforming ideas into action is fraught with peril. This section asked, What policy instruments are available for policy-makers, and in what circumstances are they likely to be employed? What factors influence the choice of policy instruments?

4. Evaluating Public Policy

This brief section introduced the relatively new issue of testing the utility and success of various public policies, an issue returned to in detail in Chapter 8. It asked, What is evaluation? Who are the key actors involved in the evaluation process? Finally, you need to ask yourself the following: What is the relationship between formulation, implementation and evaluation? Who is responsible for each? Do these three terms adequately sum up the policy process? Or is there more to it than this apparently simple illustration would imply? In an era of downsizing and cutbacks, what is the capacity of the state to manage policy-making? How much is being left of the private sector and the voluntary sector? What is the impact of the NPM on public policy formulation, implementation and evaluation?

FURTHER READING

1. Defining Public Policy

Anderson, James E. *Public Policy-Making. Third Edition.* New York: Holt, Rinehart & Winston, 1984.

Brooks, Stephen. "Policy Analysis in Canada," in Christopher Dunn, ed. *The Handbook of Canadian Public Administration.* Toronto: Oxford University Press, 2002: 192–203.

Howlett, Michael and M. Ramesh. *Studying Public Policy: Policy Cycles and Policy Subsystems.* Toronto: Oxford University Press, 1995.

Pal, Leslie A. *Beyond Policy Analysis: Public Issue Management in Turbulent Times.* Scarborough: Nelson, 2001.

2. Formulating Public Policy

Burke, Mike, Colin Mooers and John Shields, eds. *Restructuring and Resistance: Canadian Public Policy in an Age of Global Capitalism.* Halifax: Fernwood Press, 2000.

Simeon, Richard. "Studying Public Policy," *Canadian Journal of Political Science,* 9, 4 (December 1976): 548–580.

3. Implementing Public Policy

Howlett, Michael. "Policy Instruments, Policy Styles, and Policy Implementation: National Approaches to Theories of Instrument Choice," *Policy Studies Journal,* 19, 2 (Spring, 1991): 1–21.

Prince, Michael. "The Return of Directed Incrementalism: Innovating Social Policy the Canadian Way," in G. Bruce Doern, ed. *How Ottawa Spends 2002–2003: The Security Aftermath and National Priorities.* Toronto: Oxford University Press, 2002: 176–95.

4. Evaluating Public Policy

Posavac, Emil J. and Raymond G. Carey. *Program Evaluation: Methods and Case Studies. Fifth Edition.* Upper Saddle River, New Jersey: Prentice Hall, 1997.

Van Loon, Richard and Michael Whittington. "Kaleidoscope in Grey: The Policy Process in Ottawa," in Michael Whittington and Glen Williams, eds. *Canadian Politics in the 1990s. Third Edition.* Toronto: Methuen, 1989: 448–467.

 **WEBLINKS**

Canadian Public Policy Resources
www.cpac.ca/links/policies_e.asp

Canadian Public Policy (newsmagazine)
OttawaBureau.com/CanadianPublicPolicy/

Institute for Policy Analysis
www.epas.utoronto.ca/ipa/

Association for Public Policy Analysis and Management (APPAM)
www.appam.org

Canadian Centre for Policy Alternatives
www.policyalternatives.ca/

Government of Canada Policy Research Initiative
policyresearch.gc.ca

Chapter (8)

Public Administration *and* Evaluation

WHAT YOU WILL LEARN

Canadians need to know whether or not the policies and programs instituted by government are working properly. But how is this to be determined? As noted in earlier chapters, the public sector, unlike the private sector, does not have the standard of the bottom line against which to measure success. Nonetheless, the evaluation of the decision-making and actions of government must be accomplished with efficiency and economy. There are further difficulties associated with evaluation of government policies and programs. Governments often have vague and ambiguous goals, and thus policies are expressed in broad terms. And in other cases, different departments may be faced with contradictory goals. Evaluating whether each department has done its job well, let alone whether the government as a whole has met the expectations of citizens, is extremely hard in many circumstances.[1] Chapter 8 examines the difficulties around effective evaluation in the public service in Canada, noting that evaluation is the third component of the policy cycle (along with formulation and implementation) introduced in Chapter 7. This chapter is divided into the following sections:

1. — *The Development of Evaluation*

This section provides a brief overview of the development of evaluation processes and approaches. It asks the following: What is evaluation? How is it conducted, both formally and informally? What early developments contributed to the emerging role of evaluation in the policy cycle? What do early examples of evaluation suggest about the practice?

2. — *Problems of Evaluation*

The exercise of evaluation studies is fraught with difficulty. This section asks, What are the major impediments to effective evaluation? How can they be overcome? What methodological and other problems confront evaluators? Can evaluation practices be made effective such that the public can be assured that it is getting the most bang for its buck?

3. — *Evaluation in Action*

This section considers the actual practice of evaluation. It explores the following questions: Who is primarily responsible for evaluation? How is it undertaken? What factors contribute to successful evaluation?

4. — *Contemporary Evaluation Practices*

This section asks, How has the New Public Management had an impact on evaluation? What changes in perspective have been brought to the process of evaluation by the new emphasis on running government like a business? What results have been produced in the area of evaluation by the Program Review exercise launched in 1994?

The Development of Evaluation

There is no consensus in the literature as to what exactly **evaluation** should entail. It is a multidisciplinary creature, drawing on political science, accounting, economics, education, industrial engineering, management sciences, medicine, psychology, sociology, statistics, mathematics, urban studies, and a handful of other areas. Evaluation should not to be confused with policy analysis, which is embarked upon before a policy is implemented. Rather, program evaluation is a retrospective consideration of how a policy has worked.

As the third element in the policy cycle after policy formulation and implementation, evaluation is an important but ambiguous concept. A number of problems associated with trying to undertake evaluation are reviewed below. For now, though, to illustrate the nature of the evaluation process, think about your own experience, for instance, as a student. First, it is natural that people are reluctant to have their work assessed, for fear of being criticized. So we approach evaluation with some reluctance. Still, you hand in an essay that you regard as first-rate, and patiently wait for that A+ that you are sure it deserves. But your paper is now in the hands of someone who had little or no part in its creation, has a different perspective on what an essay ought to look like, and has extremely high expectations about its content. After receiving your C, you wonder what planet your professor is from. In particular, you wonder what standards of evaluation were applied to your work. If you pursue the question, you will probably find that a set of "objective" criteria exist against which every student's essay was graded, including proper spelling, punctuation and grammar, a coherent thesis and argument, a clear structure and organization, and evidence of research and familiarity with the literature in your field of study. But how objective are these criteria, in reality? Your professor invariably has a strong background in certain aspects of your topic, but may not be an expert in everything about it. And what if she was not feeling well when she graded your paper, or was distracted by other work or family responsibilities? How do you know that she does not hold the opposite ideological position from the one adopted in your essay, and is therefore inclined to disagree with your stance, no matter how eloquently put?

All these issues colour the evaluation of your work. Similarly, a host of problems interfere with the easy and objective evaluation of the work of the public service. The purpose of program evaluation is, in part, to ensure that government can be held accountable for the public monies for which it is responsible. In addition, it is expected to assist managers in making informed decisions about how to provide financial and human resources for their programs. In short, evaluation helps in determining a program's worth. And it helps in the provision of useful advice to Cabinet. Moreover, it permits the government to anticipate future problems and plan ahead to avoid them. It is also suggested that self-analysis of programs by managers and their employees will promote experimentation and innovation. Finally, evaluation helps to legitimize government programs, since evidence is presented to citizens of the effectiveness and efficiency of programs and policies. Still, notwithstanding all these laudable goals and effects of evaluation, the practice is regarded with suspicion and disdain by those being evaluated.

Evaluation has always been a part of government activity, both formally and informally. It is shaped in the first instance by constitutional arrangements and the way in which government operations are managed. Evaluation can be usefully categorized into three types: administrative evaluation, judicial evaluation, and political evaluation.[2] **Administrative evaluation** generally involves the examination of the efficient delivery of government services, and attempts to ascertain whether the best value for money is being realized within the framework of democracy and justice. **Audits** of budgetary systems, personnel reviews, managerial performance reviews, and the like are typical of this type of evaluation, which is usually conducted within government by specialized agencies. Methodologically, administrative evaluation tends to be technical in nature, involving the compilation and analysis of data on program costs and benefits.

Judicial evaluation is related to the practice of judicial review (discussed in Chapter 6). It is concerned with the legal issues arising out of administrative actions when government programs are implemented. Judicial evaluation is a facet of constitutional and administrative law involving the judges and the courts passing judgment on the behaviour and practices of the public service. They can do so either on their own or at the behest of a government, corporation or citizen filing a case against a government agency.

Political evaluation is a more vague concept, since it is an ongoing process that can occur formally or informally, and one that lacks technical and methodological sophistication. This type of evaluation is less interested in objectively establishing the utility and value of a particular policy, and more interested in subjectively establishing a case for its demise and replacement with a policy more favourable to the interests of the evaluator. Perhaps the most visible manifestation of this type of evaluation occurs at election time when citizens are asked, in a sense, to evaluate the overall performance of their government. This is evaluation as it is most broadly understood. Political evaluation also occurs, though, in other places such as royal commissions and task forces, parliamentary committees, central agencies, line departments, Cabinet, through the actions of interest groups, via protests, lobbying, the media, and so on. When you write a letter to the editor of your local newspaper or member of Parliament to protest against the impact of some government program on your life, you are engaging in an informal and uncoordinated form of government policy evaluation. In short, evaluation occurs anywhere that "politics" takes place. We will be concerned in this chapter with *administrative evaluation*.

We are interested in the more formalized methods and processes that have become part of the public administration landscape in the past 30 years or so. This means that we are more interested in evaluation as a management function of the public service, generally involving a focus on the resources used by government institutions (that is, the dollars spent and the numbers of people employed), how the resources are utilized, and the purposes and impacts of programs on society. As we will see, there has been an evolution in the emphasis of evaluation. At first, it was thought sufficient to simply count the dollars and the employees, and make some kind of rough calculation as to whether citizens were getting a good return for their taxes. But government activities have become increasingly varied, complex and immune to a simplistic bean-counting approach. Many government programs and policies are sophisticated, multilevel, cross-jurisdictional, wide-ranging attempts to deal with complicated issues. They involve a plurality of interests and actors, both governmental and nongovernmental. Moreover, much government activity has come under increased public scrutiny. Hence the need for more refined forms of evaluation.

According to the Program Evaluation Branch of the **Office of the Comptroller General** of Canada, program evaluation "is the formal assessment of the continued relevance and of the effectiveness of existing [government] programs. That is, it involves the systematic gathering of verifiable information on a programme and demonstrable evidence of its results." Moreover, program evaluation is the periodic, independent and objective review and assessment of a program to determine, in light of current circumstances, the adequacy of its objectives, its design and its results—both intended and unintended. Evaluations will call into question the very existence of the program. Reviewed are such matters as the rationale of the program, its impact on the public, and its cost-effectiveness as compared with alternative means of program delivery.[3]

The Office of the Comptroller General was created in 1978 and was given broad authority and responsibility for administrative practices and controls in the areas of financial management and procedures for program evaluation. The office is responsible for ensuring that departments and agencies have established program evaluation processes consistent with policy as articulated by the Treasury Board (discussed in Chapter 3).

The 1960 Royal Commission on Government Organization (the Glassco Commission, mentioned earlier in connection with other administrative reforms), is the starting point for the evolution of evaluation concerns, from those focused on the *amounts* of government expenditures to those focused on the *results* of government expenditures. This is an important qualitative difference in approach to evaluation. Prior to the Glassco Commission, evaluation tended to rely mainly on the annual audits of government expenditures conducted for Parliament. The **Auditor General** conducted a post-audit of government department activity and spending. And a pre-audit was conducted by the comptroller of the Treasury. Each audit ensured the probity of expenditures; that is, checked that due process was followed and that the honesty and integrity of the expenditure process was upheld. In other words, these audits looked at the inputs into programs—the finances.

But gradually the realization dawned that despite money being raised and spent religiously following every rule in the book, the results expected of program and policies might not be obtained. So eventually a mind-set took hold that suggested the purposes and results of programs ought to be evaluated alongside their probity. The outcome of the Glassco recommendations was a more decentralized management and financial system, and more modern management techniques. The Glassco Commission reported as follows:

Just as the scope and character of federal activity must respond to the changing character and needs of the Canadian community, so the government's structure and methods must take account of new resources and techniques... budgetary and accounting systems which permit better control over the allocation of financial resources and the assessment of performance; operational research and other techniques for evaluating alternative courses of action and for designing and appraising methods and systems.[4]

Thus, a new concern developed that broadened the traditional function of financial audits and created a concern for evaluating programs in terms of their legislated intent and outcomes. By the 1960s, program evaluation had developed into a more sophisticated art, drawing on the new tools of social science that were emerging in this period.

There are three basic questions evaluation is intended to answer: Is a policy relevant? Is it successful? Is it cost effective? To answer these questions, various attempts were made from the 1960s onward to reorganize the roles of departmental managers by allowing them to assume more responsibility for managing their affairs. For instance, a new financial management approach was introduced in 1968 called the **Planning, Programming, Budgeting System (PPBS)**, designed to define program objectives and show the full cost of each government program (as opposed to simply showing the cost of departments, each of which housed many discrete programs). Moreover, it was intended to produce multi-year plans so there would be some predicability in the financial management work that the Treasury Board carried on. The Trudeau government briefly embraced this system, consistent as it was with the prime minister's own stated preference to bring rationality and reason to politics, and it was adopted by several provincial governments as well. (Ironically, the U.S. government abandoned this system as unworkable just as Canadian governments were embracing it.) The Treasury Board oversaw the introduction of PPBS, encouraging all departments to state their goals and objectives, list specific costs associated with each program designed to meet those goals, and detail the resources required for each program.[5] Once these steps had been initiated, it was thought, comparisons between departments and programs for evaluation purposes could be made relatively easily. The rationalism underlying the approach made it attractive to the technocrats who dominated the senior reaches of the civil service. As political scientist Donald Savoie suggested,

PPB[S] was seen as the instrument that would enable departments to define objectives and assess the full cost of programs. It was also seen as the means by which the cost-benefits of alternative programs could be evaluated, as well as providing a capacity to ascertain the costs of future programs and spending proposals. This would leave ministers free to consider larger issues and broader questions.... The extent to which it was regarded in Ottawa as a dramatic and effective new approach to budgeting is best exemplified by the minister of finance's statement at the time the approach was introduced. "PPB," he boldly declared, "is a major budget breakthrough."[6]

But "the articulation of rational budgeting philosophies is not to be equated with their actual practice. Practice could not help but part company with theory to some significant extent, since politics (viewed as both power and ideas) imposes a rationality of its own."[7] In other words, PPBS failed to live up to its advance billing, since the underlying rationalism of the system seemed to ignore the fact that it was being grafted onto a political rationality quite different from the one called for in PPBS. As a result, the system never quite fulfilled its promise.[8]

It did contribute to the new emphasis on approaching evaluation in a results-oriented manner, however. One impact was to introduce a trend toward more systematic and professional evaluation, rather than relying on the rough-and-ready, seat-of-the-pants judgments that had often passed for evaluation in the past. An increase in computer modelling and highly sophisticated, quantitative research assisted the evolution of evaluation into more of a science and less of an art. This is reflected in the growing business of evaluation consultants, and the formation of professional standards for evaluators. Beginning with PPBS, both quantitative and qualitative assessments began to be done on programs and policies. In 1977, formal, systematic evaluations of programs were initiated by the Treasury Board; henceforth, departments and agencies were expected to periodically review their programs to evaluate their effectiveness in meeting objectives. As well, they were expected to analyze the efficiency with which they were being administered. But as political scientist Sharon Sutherland reported, there were important differences between the original PPBS initiative and subsequent Treasury Board guidelines that followed in 1977 and 1981. To begin with, the PPBS framework implicitly called for automatic evaluations of programs. Moreover, they would consist primarily of cost-benefit analyses, and generate comparisons across government departments. But the updated policy was looser than this in its expectations. It left in the hands of administrators much of the decision-making about when and what kinds of evaluations to undertake—and left out any serious requirements for comparisons.[9] Political scientist Leslie Pal concluded about these developments that "with a kind of logic that would delight Lewis Carroll, program evaluation became both universally mandated for all federal government programs over time, and yet was left up to the discretion of departmental managers as to targets and techniques of evaluation."[10] As a result, evaluation as a tool of accountability declined.

Subsequent developments, though, breathed new life into the moribund practices of evaluation that resulted from the shortcomings of PPBS. In the mid-1970s, a professional accountant named J.J. Macdonnell was appointed Auditor General. He wanted to see the federal government adopt private sector accounting practices, and began to push for the creation of an Office of the Comptroller General to be responsible for overseeing the government's evaluation systems. The government was reluctant to embrace the idea, but it was galvanized into action when Macdonnell imperiously announced in his 1976 annual report to Parliament: "I am deeply concerned that Parliament—and indeed the Government—has lost, or is close to losing, effective control of the public purse."[11] The ensuing storm resulted in a royal commission on financial management and accountability, and, ultimately, Macdonnell's desire to establish the Office of the Comptroller General (OCG) was realized. Although part of the motivation for establishing the OCG was to head off political criticism, it nonetheless came to play an important role in the design, development, implementation and monitoring of evaluation systems. As a result, according to Savoie, "[P]rogram evaluation did indeed develop into a growth industry, and it grew around the Office of the Comptroller General."[12]

Lest there is some confusion in your mind now about who does what concerning evaluation, look at it this way. A three-cornered relationship has developed around evaluation, involving departments, the OCG and the Auditor General. Departments conduct their own evaluations based on guidelines provided by the OCG. The Auditor General cannot independently conduct evaluations, but reports on the success or failure of evaluation across government.[13]

This was roughly the evaluation regime that persisted until the early 1990s. Before picking up the story to date, though, a slight digression is in order to report on the difficulties encountered by this new emphasis on evaluation. We will return to more recent developments below. But first, here is an overview of the problems associated with conducting evaluation.

Problems of Evaluation

Program evaluation is fraught with difficulties, not the least of which is that it can be expensive. In 1992–1993 the federal government spent $28.5 million on program evaluation. Moreover, program objectives are not always straightforward or clearly defined, and therefore defy easy assessment. In particular, politicians and bureaucrats are often reluctant to expressly state the goals of a particular program, lest it offend those not served by it. In addition, they may want to avoid blame, should something go wrong, so legislation objectives are often vaguely worded. Politicians often derive their support from broad coalitions of interests in society; they frame legislation in terms that appeal to disparate groups so that each can interpret the intent of the legislation as serving their own goals.[14]

The root of the problem is not that programs lack objectives; rather it is that program objectives are not easily measurable. If the government provides increased funding for scholarships for post-secondary students, and there is a decrease in student indebtedness, how can we be sure the one caused the other? Perhaps more students found summer or part-time work; perhaps more well-off students entered the system; perhaps Kraft Dinner was on sale more often in the year under review! Or consider the program objectives of the Department of External Affairs. How does one determine whether improved relations with foreign countries has been attained? Or that trade has been increased due to the efforts of our ambassadors schmoozing with foreign dignitaries? Measuring whether program objectives have been met is difficult.

Even in situations where goals are clear and measurable, things that are easily measured will attract the eye of those charged with conducting evaluations. This phenomenon twists and contorts the rationale of evaluation, and may result in influencing the program such that it seeks to conform with that which is measurable. A related consideration is raised by political scientist Alan Maslove. He asks what indicators can be used to measure success, and then poses the dilemma of bureaucrats developing indicators that result in sympathetic reports of their work.

Indicators may emerge from the political-bureaucratic process which minimize problems or make them more amenable to solutions and which suit the emotional commitments and interests of the decision-makers and those who influence them. Indicators may be selected to promote the adoption of desired policies, to make these policies appear as successful as possible, and to direct public discussion in the desired directions.[15]

There are methodological problems too. For instance, measuring outputs when many are intangible is difficult. Establishing control groups to test whether a policy applied to one group but not to another is effective is next to impossible. Even establishing causality—that is, showing that program X caused a certain result—can be challenging, because of the difficulty of isolating the impact of a particular program. Outside factors may intrude on the success or failure of a program. For instance, is a decline in drunk driving the result of increased educational campaigns, increased police spot-checks, or an aging population less inclined to consume alcohol? Another problem is related to the fact that some programs themselves constitute several subprograms. Does the measurement of the success of the subprograms add up to the measurement of the success of the overall program? Methodologically, it is hard to establish such a straightforward and linear connection. Or consider that the world of public policy is constantly changing. Programs may have a short shelf life, and there may simply not be enough data about a program to make a reasonable assessment of its utility or benefit.

Moreover, governments often have unclear or multiple goals and objectives, making measurement a mug's game. In some cases goals—for example, those regarding national security or sensitive financial information—cannot be stated publicly or explicitly. In other cases, new and innovative programs may defy easy assessment simply because they are in uncharted waters. Programs devised to promote racial tolerance or gender equality may fall into this category. More specifically, objectives for these types of programs may be deliberately left vague to permit flexibility in their implementation. And then, there are some things governments do not want to know. For instance, if a government is committed ideologically or politically to a course of action, it may not want to know that it will not work. The opponents of the Free Trade Agreement (FTA) and the North American Free Trade Agreement (NAFTA), for example, argued that trade deals were to blame when tens of thousands of workers were thrown out of work in the early 1990s. But the government insisted that since it had conducted no evaluations of the impact of free trade, it could not confirm that free trade was responsible for the recession that gripped the country.

The lack of sufficient resources to conduct meaningful evaluation is another potential hazard. Evaluation proposals must first scale the wall of skepticism that surrounds policy-makers concerning evaluation, convincing them to commit sufficient resources to projects that might in the end criticize their work. They must then traverse the minefield of policy reversals, changes in funding and personnel, and changing priorities that characterize the realm of public policy. In addition, mustering capable troops to conduct evaluations has been a problem in the past, given the lack of expertise in government (and elsewhere) in this relatively new field. In any event, given the wide range of disciplines that evaluation practices draw on, findings of particular assessments may be contested by "experts" from disparate fields. In addition, the assumption that only the "experts" know best sometimes flies in the face of the real, lived experiences of people affected by government programs. For instance, marine biologists and other scientists working for the Ministry of Fisheries may scientifically assess an east-coast cod fishery and determine that it should be closed to preserve the dwindling stock of fish. But for the fishers who make their livelihood there, that recommendation is disastrous. Moreover, the fishers' evaluation of previous attempts by scientists to monitor the cod stock may have pointed out gross errors in their calculations. But because the fishers are not "experts," their concerns may be ignored.[16]

In addition, some programs serve several masters. Public service managers are accountable to more than one agency. This may result in the manager being pulled in several different directions at once, which may in turn detract from the overall quality of the program. Finally, public servants are often reluctant to subject their work to critical examination. It is often said in this context that a dog will not bring the stick with which it will be beaten. Public servants resist evaluation as costly and time-consuming, and, more importantly, they may fear results that might turn out to be disparaging of their work. Political scientist Timothy Plumptre rather pithily expresses some of the problems associated with evaluation when he compares it to chastity. "People support it in principle," he suggests, "but in practice they prefer if it is mandatory for others and optional for them...."[17]

Evaluation in Action

Notwithstanding these difficulties, a culture of evaluation has gradually infused the public service. The Treasury Board is primarily responsible for ensuring that individual departments conduct ongoing evaluation. It also sets the standards for these evaluations. Evaluation is seen as an important aspect of accountability and responsibility, in that almost all evaluations conducted by the public service are available for public scrutiny.

A range of evaluations has been employed by the government over the years, using a variety of techniques. Methods as complex as econometric modelling and computer simulations exist alongside the more traditional interviewing of program beneficiaries and experts in a field. This means that great care must be taken by public servants even in determining what type of evaluation is suitable for the particular program. And evaluation can be costly in terms of human and financial resources. Indeed, many evaluation exercises have floundered on the rocks of inadequate consideration over "appropriate" evaluation. Hence, evaluation assessment studies are a part of the broader evaluation landscape.

An appropriate evaluation study of a program requires consideration of six factors.[18] First, the nature of the program to be evaluated must be considered. A definition or description of what is to be evaluated is needed, since it is not always obvious what constitutes a "program" for evaluation purposes. In addition, the length of time that a program has been running is an important consideration, since a program should be "field-tested" before attempts are made to evaluate. Another consideration is the type of state intervention employed in the program; that is, whether it involves regulation, expenditure, taxation, or any other policy instruments (discussed in Chapter 7).

Second, the questions to be addressed by the evaluation must be carefully thought through. Without this step, program evaluation can lack focus, and wander far and wide in search of answers that may in the end prove to be irrelevant to the task at hand. To this end, evaluators need to consider whether their evaluation is dealing with the rationale of the program, its impacts and effects, its objective achievements, or alternatives to the program. Each of these categories will prompt a different set of questions.

Third, the client of the evaluation study must be clearly identified. It was noted above that sometimes programs serve more than one master. Potential clients include Cabinet, the media, Parliament, program planners and managers, the public, researchers and senior civil servants. This list represents a diversity of interests. Consider again a program designed to ease student debt load. The questions that concern Cabinet about the impact of the program might be different from those that concern the public (i.e., students). The former might ask if the program is having a demonstrable effect on fiscal resources dedicated to student loans, and the political impact of garnering the electoral support of students. The students themselves might ask whether enough is being done to ease their debt load, and why the government is not doing more. The program manager might ask whether the program is being delivered effectively and efficiently (regardless of outcomes), or whether a new computer system or other technology or redeployment of staff would help in the program's delivery.

The fourth component of an evaluation study relates to the actual technique used to conduct the evaluation. A range of methodologies is available to program evaluators, but the selection of a technique should not be haphazard. Great care must be taken to ensure the right type of evaluation is conducted. A written survey administered to illiterates in an adult education program is not likely to produce useful results. Decisions must be made about whether to employ quantitative or qualitative methods, analysis, description, surveys, research, etc. Questions must be asked about how rigorous and systematic the evaluation needs to be, or how casual and informal, and so on.

Fifth, every program evaluation study must carefully consider the resources and time available. These can be very important constraints on what reasonably can be done. Almost invariably, trade-offs must be made to meet time and money resource constraints, with the result that findings may sometimes be compromised. The short-term perspective of the governmental budget cycle means that long, languorous time-consuming studies are a luxury that few program managers can afford to engage in. Moreover, clients often want results "yesterday." Evaluations that must be reported to Parliament must subscribe to the parliamentary cycle and timelines. As to the costs involved, these must be justified. This in itself can entail a considerable amount of effort that detracts from the evaluation. In any event, the amounts budgeted for evaluation can be prohibitive. But in an era of cutbacks and reduced departmental spending, high quality evaluation is often among the early casualties.

Sixth, and finally, evaluation studies must be credible. They must have legitimacy—in the eyes of clients as well as other observers of the process—derived from factors such as impartiality, accuracy and honesty. Without these qualities, evaluation studies will not be taken seriously either by the client directly, or by the broader public. Ideally, credibility is enhanced if the evaluator has an arm's-length relationship from the subject being evaluated, as well as from the client being served. This is where institutions such as the OCG, the Office of the Auditor General, and the Treasury Board are useful. They establish criteria and guidelines for evaluation that help ensure the evaluation is impartial, accurate and honest. Ultimately, though, the test of credibility is in the hands of the public. If a program is perceived by citizens to be a boondoggle, all the evaluation studies in the world are unlikely to change their minds. In this regard, recent Access to Information legislation has given citizens (as well as bureaucrats) improved tools with which to conduct their own evaluations of government programs.

Assuming evaluators pay heed to these six conditions for evaluation studies, they can achieve some success in assessing the worth of programs. In short, the terms of reference must be carefully thought through before embarking on the perilous exercise of evaluation. But a little foresight can temper expectations and bring about realistic appraisals of what evaluation can and cannot, and should and should not do.

Contemporary Evaluation Practices

You will recall that earlier in this chapter we traced the evolution of evaluation up to the early 1980s. We pick up the story here by noting that the Treasury Board evaluation guidelines of 1981 were updated in 1991 in response to **PS2000**, which called for a new emphasis on "quality of service" to the public. The OCG published a document entitled "Into the 90s: Government Program Evaluation Perspectives," in which it laid out the relationship of PS2000 to evaluation.[19] A link was drawn between successful and careful evaluations, and better quality service to the public. It also emphasized broadening the evaluative process beyond simply consulting with direct stakeholders about how a program affects them, to a more participatory model of assessing the quality of service to the public as part of a broader change-based environment.

Still, by the early 1990s, the original zeal for evaluation was diminished. The Auditor General was critical of a trend that saw a quantitative decline in evaluations, as well, apparently, as a qualitative one. Moreover, the time and resources dedicated to evaluation were in decline in this period. This is not to suggest that evaluation was inconsequential. Indeed, in this period many useful reforms arose as a result of a variety of evaluation studies. But as Savoie pointed out in 1990, the question of "who was evaluating the evaluators" was left unanswered. In other words, internal assessment was lacking regarding how effective evaluation was in practice. The OCG and program evaluation "seem to be concerned only with methodologies and how many programs have been evaluated," according to Savoie. "Put more bluntly, evaluators seem to be kept busy turning cranks not connected to anything. The result is that one would be hard-pressed to point to even a handful of programs that have been reduced or eliminated as a result of an evaluation study."[20]

However, the advent of contemporary management practices, including those inspired by the New Public Management (NPM) (discussed in Chapter 3), has reinvigorated evaluation.[21] In 1994, the Treasury Board issued an updated framework for evaluation that, in concert with **Program Review**, superseded the earlier efforts under PS2000. As a result, a distinction can be drawn between the evaluation concerns of traditional management practices in the public service and contemporary practices arising in the early 1990s. The traditional approach focused on effectiveness, efficiency and economy. It initially was concerned with government processes rather than outcomes. It placed much less emphasis on issues such as customer satisfaction, public participation and procedural due process, all of which have come to the forefront in recent efforts to reconfigure evaluation. As well, a clear and unambiguous link has been established between the purposes of evaluation and deficit control. The Treasury Board argued that "the fiscal burden carried by Canadian taxpayers, pressures to control and reduce the cost of government programs and operations, and management reform within the Public Service are all factors that make it essential to have information on results."[22] In addition, according to Pal, the 1994 statement on evaluation "highlights performance, service, clients, and decentralization—all shibboleths of the new thinking on management."[23]

In the Annual Report to Parliament in 1996, the president of the Treasury Board said, "[W]e must equip ourselves with better systems for evaluating the actions of government so that we can genuinely answer for our actions, first and foremost to our fellow citizens who are both clients and taxpayers. This is the only way our government can evaluate and debate the merits of the decisions we make every day on the public's behalf."[24] Government performance, then, is measured in terms both of the benefits citizens derive from programs, and the broader government objectives, such as reducing total government expenditures, cooperating with other levels of government and establishing a more results-oriented management culture in the public service.

This raises the issue of how government-wide evaluation can take place, given these wider parameters of evaluation. The Treasury Board addressed this question in 1996 when it recommended that, while different approaches could be used to identify and report on broad economic and social goals, establishing a few "core indicators" of government performance, and regularly measuring and reporting on them, was a useful tactic. Their characteristics include the following:

➤ a single comprehensive perspective on the most important information that shapes the government's priorities and decisions;

➤ a stable and more strategic vision of the government's objectives;

➤ a persuasive context to show the links between programs, which encourages greater cooperation within and among departments and agencies; and

➤ a more open and disciplined approach to showing the values of policies and programs, which also provides for public involvement beyond consultation on specific issues.[25]

The use of core indicators has been adopted by several federal government departments to measure economic performance based on data supplied by Statistics Canada. It is an ongoing process that involves asking the following: Which indicators are most useful? How should they be selected, measured and reported? How can the public be assured that the measurement is reliable? How can the core indicators be linked back to specific programs and initiatives while involving the public in the process?

In 1995 the federal government outlined an action plan for improving results measurement and accountability. In "Strengthening Government Review," it identified initiatives in three areas: identifying expected results for programs and services, improving results measurement and improving results reporting.[26] Where departmental results were concerned, the government focused on essential services, and identified expected results in three ways. First, it restated the government's commitment to Program Review, policy reviews, the Business Planning process and the Service Standards Initiative. Second, it focused on the development of broadly based accountability frameworks. Third, it required each department to report its key results commitments. Across the whole government, efforts have been made to categorize government-wide performance indicators, which can take several forms. For instance, they might be policy issues such as a secure social safety net, or activities connected to changes in related legislation.

It was noted above that a variety of techniques and methodologies is available to enact evaluation. According to the Treasury Board, "[T]o make continuous improvements to programs, services and meet decision-making needs, the information produced must be timely, relevant and credible in the eyes of managers, other users and the public. So that performance information can focus more on the impact of programs on the public, program managers and departments must expand their measurement tools and skills, and they must involve the public more directly in the performance assessment process."[27] To this end, the federal government has been seeking ways to improve communication of its review findings. As well, departments are looking for ways to enhance the involvement of the public in the process of performance measurement. For instance, the Treasury Board reported these findings:

➤ Statistics Canada relies on a network of professional advisory committees in major subject areas to ensure the continuous review of statistical outputs, help determine priorities and foster program relevance.

➤ The Veteran's Independence Program helps veterans remain healthy and independent in their own homes and communities. An expert panel and a working group composed of Canadian home care experts, representatives from Health Canada, provincial home care programs and Veterans Affairs Canada staff helped to review the program. The review confirmed that the program helped minimize the need for more costly institutional care and made it easy to improve the delivery of services to veterans.

➤ Natural Resources Canada's Model Forest Program is a network of large-scale living laboratories established to test sustainable forest management principles and practices. A national advisory committee composed of representatives from academia, industry, First Nations, other levels of government, and nongovernmental organizations oversaw the program's evaluation. The evaluation concluded that the program had made important progress in furthering sustainable forest management. Most notable was the progress in establishing partnerships among diverse groups, and in developing tools for sustainable forest management. As a result, the committee recommended the program be modified and extended for five years.[28]

Another important aspect of results measurement and analysis concerns educating managers, since not all of them are well versed in the new techniques of evaluation. For instance, several departments are sharing information on best practices in decision-making and accountability.

Finally, results reporting and access is another important issue. This revolves around the notion that the public deserves timely information and the results of performance measurements so that it can make informed judgments about the quality of government performance. This information is disseminated through a variety of sources, including parliamentary reports, press releases and media reports on government policies and programs, government databases, ministerial announcements, and so on. The three integrated steps of identifying expected results, taking action to improve results measurement and analysis, and taking action to improve results reporting and access are summarized in Box 8-1.

Box 8-1

A Strategy for Improving Results Measurement and Accountability

The federal government, as part of its exercise "Getting Government Right," reported specific actions as a core part of improving evaluation.

Actions related to identifying expected results

➤ continuing to improve the Business Planning process, implementing service standards, and including results commitments in spring planning information as part of the Improved Reporting to Parliament initiative;

➤ identifying government-wide, citizen-centred and sectoral (e.g., science and technology as one area of federal activity) results, developing performance indicators and examining review plans against government priorities; and

➤ encouraging departments and new agencies to develop results-based accountability frameworks.

Actions to improve results measurement and analysis

➤ updating the 1995 Treasury Board Secretariat's analysis of departmental capacity to measure and report results, based on the Secretariat's evaluation of the 16 departmental pilot reports, and continuing to strengthen evaluation and internal audit functions;

➤ implementing the Financial Information Strategy;

➤ testing information by improving communication of findings, and sharing lessons learned and best practices with federal departments and other levels of government and think tanks;

➤ increasing external participation in reviews; and

➤ promoting the cost-effective use of review tools and educating managers to obtain, understand and use performance information.

Actions to improve results reporting and access

➤ ensuring the practical implementation of improved performance reporting to Parliament at the government-wide and departmental levels;

➤ strengthening the Review and Performance Database in terms of information it can provide, links to other databases, and Internet access; and

➤ encouraging benchmarking and synthesis work to provide broader-based reports.

Program Review can be considered the largest macro-exercise ever undertaken in evaluation of government programs. Consistent with increasing concern that government had grown out of control, Program Review sought to provide the rationale and means by which government could be "shrunk" to a more manageable size. This involved evaluation of existing practices and programs. The results to date have included ending inappropriate programs, changing how some programs are delivered, and improving the efficiency of ongoing initiatives. Moreover, it is estimated that Program Review has helped effect savings of some $11 billion in direct program spending over the period 1994–1995 to 1998–1999. Alongside Program Review, several other management initiatives have been undertaken to improve evaluation (see Box 8-2).

With the advent of the NPM, evaluation exercises are increasingly concluding that many services traditionally provided by government can be provided by others outside government. Part of restructuring, then, has meant undertaking new arrangements, such as devolving authority to provincial or municipal governments, creating alternative service delivery vehicles, and developing new mechanisms and partnerships. While these initiatives may indeed increase the flexibility of program delivery, they raise important questions about evaluation and accountability. As a result, actors outside government are more and more engaged in new forms of evaluation. As the government relies increasingly on third parties, and empowers employees to achieve public purposes, new methods are being developed to evaluate the effectiveness of policy. For instance, where the government contracts out a service, the contract will usually require specific observable and measurable performance requirements that can be assessed. Scheduled and surprise inspections by government personnel, client surveys, "hot lines," and other strategies are more often being built into the evaluation process of the changing public service. Clearly, though, a balance needs to be struck between these new activities and the age-old requirement of accountability. This point will be explored more thoroughly in Chapter 12.

Related to these developments is the introduction of the **Business Planning** process, first initiated by the government of Alberta and then adapted by other governments in Canada. This is a means by which departmental planning is put on a more businesslike footing, involving the identification of core results and programs as well as statements of performance expectations and performance reviews. Performance is measured in terms of what is being delivered by a given department (for instance, new policies, or improvements in the delivery of existing ones), or in terms of the impact of programs (for instance, new job creation or economic growth). Under this approach, evaluation results are fed back into the system, to be used in determining the future course of action. Decisions are generated about how to better manage programs and make continuous improvements in the provision of services. Sound administrative and financial controls, and information systems, are fine-tuned. Business Plans and reports to Parliament incorporate the evaluation information as feedback in their development. And citizens (now referred to as "clients" in the Business Plans) are sounded out for further feedback and results monitoring.

Box 8-2

Evaluation: Case Studies

➤ The Atlantic Groundfish Strategy is a five-year, $1.9-billion program that started in 1994 to provide income support and adjustment services, including training, for about 40 000 Canadians affected by the collapse of the east-coast groundfishery. Reviewing early implementation of Human Resources Development Canada's portion of the program helped management to deal with higher-than-expected enrolments and to adjust the program priorities to keep within the budget.

➤ An audit of the Military Pay Service for the Regular Force in National Defence used international benchmarking and focus group techniques. This audit concluded that reducing annual service delivery costs by more than $26 million was possible in the long term. This would be a saving of more than 40 percent. Notwithstanding that existing delivery costs are comparable to other militaries, management is now reengineering the military pay services, taking into account the audit recommendations. Alternative service delivery mechanisms are being studied actively.

➤ Natural Resources Canada conducted a review of the use of credit cards and electronic data interchange for electronic receipt and payment of credit card purchases. The review concluded that the initiative has generated significant benefits in terms of streamlined processes, and has resulted in savings of $1 million to date, with potential annual savings of $4 to $5 million over the longer term. As a result, the department has extended electronic receipt and payment to other types of purchases.

➤ An evaluation led to the total reorganization of a billion-dollar program. The objective of the National Defence Ammunition Program is to ensure an appropriate level of Canadian Forces readiness, and the effective, efficient and safe management of ammunition. Reviewing the program has led to the complete reorganization of the management process, including developing a disposal strategy to eliminate stocks and surplus ammunition, establishing an Ammunition Information System to monitor use more accurately, and reviewing ammunition requirements for training.[29]

Where financial management is concerned, evaluation efforts have concluded that improved financial information can assist in meeting the government's overall goals. To this end, the Treasury Board Secretariat, the Office of the Auditor General, and other departments have been working toward improved financial accounting methods through a Financial Information Strategy, which has been implemented to improve the quality and timeliness of financial information. The goal is to give departments more flexibility in meeting their financial management needs, while also allowing for full accountability of how tax dollars are being spent. In addition, government regulations have undergone an evaluation under a program entitled Regulatory Review, launched in May 1996 and aimed at regulatory reform.

It has been recently pointed out that "many governments are now engaged in what is commonly described as results-based management, involving the development of performance indicators and measures related to an organization's business objectives, measuring the outputs and outcomes of programs and services, and using these data to evaluate the performance of the organization and its employees."[30] In 2001, Treasury Board updated its policy on evaluation, reemphasizing the importance with which evaluation should be regarded by public service managers and focusing sharply on the practice of "managing for results." The new policy is based on three fundamental principles:

➤ first, that achieving and accurately reporting on results is a primary responsibility of public service managers;

➤ second, that rigorous and objective evaluation is an important tool in helping managers to manage for results; and

➤ third, that departments, with the support of the Treasury Board Secretariat, are responsible to ensure that the rigour and discipline of evaluation are sufficiently deployed within their jurisdictions.[31]

Managing for results has become the mantra for public service managers, who are now expected as a matter of routine to define the anticipated results of their work, continuously focus attention on results achievements, and measure performance regularly, all with an eye on improving efficiency and effectiveness. In this regard, it has been said that "evaluation—like internal audit, risk management capacity and other management tools—helps managers to operate effectively in this environment. Evaluation can support managers' efforts to track and report on actual performance and help decision-makers objectively assess program or policy results."[32] In addition, as a contemporary management tool, evaluation increasingly is entangled with new forms of service delivery, such as partnerships within government bodies, across departments and with outside actors.

According to Treasury Board, managers are expected to "embed the discipline of evaluation into the lifecycle management of policies, programs and initiatives."[33] Furthermore, it argues:

The success of evaluation depends on a number of important factors. It requires clarity of roles, application of sound standards, ongoing support for rigorous, professional practice, and developing a conducive environment where managers embed the discipline of evaluation into their work. The organizational positioning of evaluation should reflect the unique needs of the department. Evaluation discipline should be used in synergy with other management tools to improve decision-making. Heads of evaluation should work to ensure that evaluation in their organization is healthy in respect of all these factors.

The Treasury Board Secretariat, in its role as the government's management board, should support the practice of evaluation in departments by providing advice on best practices, setting standards, monitoring the evaluation capacity in departments and using the products of evaluation to inform decision-making at the centre.[34]

This overview of recent developments in the world of the evaluation of public policy shows that interest in the process has waxed and waned over time. After an initial outburst of interest in the 1960s and 1970s, the place of evaluation in the realm of government activities declined in stature and status. Many of the difficulties associated with the practice asserted themselves, and no sustained effort was made to ensure that evaluation became a regular feature of government accountability. This has changed somewhat in the 1990s. The advent of new management philosophies and techniques has resulted in a renewed interest in evaluation. It is now linked to the overarching goals of deficit reduction, quality of service, program review, management for results, and other related issues that have arisen in contemporary governance. So the next time you feel aggrieved by a government action (or inaction), rest assured that it has probably undergone a process of evaluation that has concluded that—like cod liver oil—it is good for you.

WHAT YOU HAVE LEARNED

Evaluation, as the third element in the policy cycle, can be an elusive concept. Ironically, nearly everyone recognizes, at least intuitively, that some measure of the worth of public policies needs to be taken. Citizens want to know, and have a right to know, whether they are getting value for their tax dollars. They also need to know and have a right to know that the rules of the game are being followed—that fairness, objectivity and honesty are applied to all cases. Evaluation should go some way toward telling citizens whether this is the case. But because of the difficulties associated with evaluation, it is not always clear-cut. The recent emphasis on evaluation is motivated less by traditional concerns of probity and honesty than by the values of the three Es. This generalization does not apply in all cases, of course, but sufficiently illustrates the differing emphases of the art and science of evaluation, past and present.

ENDNOTES

1. Stephen Brooks, "Bureaucracy," in James B. Bickerton and Alain-G. Gagnon, eds. *Canadian Politics, Second Edition*, (Peterborough: Broadview Press, 1994) : chapter 16.

2. See Michael Howlett and M. Ramesh, *Studying Public Policy: Policy Cycles and Policy Subsystems*, (Toronto: Oxford University Press, 1995): 170–175.

3. Canada, Office of the Comptroller General, *Program Evaluation: An Introduction*, (Ottawa: February, 1981): 2.

4. Canada, The Royal Commission on Government Organization (the Glassco Commission), *Management of the Public Service, Volume I*, (Ottawa: The Queen's Printer, 1962): 45–46.

5. See Government of Canada, *Planning, Programming and Budgeting Guide*, (Ottawa: Information Canada, 1969).

6. Donald J. Savoie, *The Politics of Public Spending in Canada,* (Toronto: University of Toronto Press, 1990): 57.

7. Allan M. Maslove, Richard Schultz and G. Bruce Doern, *Federal and Provincial Budgeting,* (Toronto: University of Toronto Press, 1985): 18.

8. See Sharon L. Sutherland, "The Evolution of Program Budget Ideas in Canada: Does Parliament Benefit From Estimates Reform?" *Canadian Public Administration,* 33 (Summer, 1990): 133–164.

9. Sutherland, "The Evolution of Program Budget Ideas in Canada," (1990): 144–145.

10. Leslie A. Pal, *Beyond Policy Analysis: Public Issue Management in Turbulent Times, Second Edition,* (Scarborough: Nelson, 2001): 297–298.

11. Canada, Auditor General of Canada, *Annual Report 1976,* (Ottawa: Information Canada, 1976): 9.

12. Savoie, *The Politics of Public Spending in Canada,* (1990): 114.

13. Pal, *Beyond Policy Analysis,* (2001): 298.

14. See, for example, James E. Anderson, *Public Policy-Making,* (New York: Holt, Rinehart and Winston, 1984): 139–143.

15. Alan M. Maslove, "Indicators and Policy Formation," *Canadian Public Administration,* 18, 3 (Fall, 1975): 483.

16. See Susan McCorquodale, "Federal Spending on the Atlantic Fisheries," in Susan Phillips, ed. *How Ottawa Spends 1995–1996: Mid-Life Crisis,* (Ottawa: Carleton University Press, 1995): 364.

17. Timothy Plumptre, *Beyond the Bottom Line: Management in Government,* (Halifax: The Institute for Research on Public Policy, 1988): 267.

18. Recently, the Treasury Board developed guidelines for evaluation in the context of a results-based management and accountability framework. See Canada, Treasury Board of Canada, "Guide for the Development of Results-Based Management and Accountability Frameworks," (August 2001) http://www.tbs-sct.gc.ca/eval/pubs/rmafcgrr-PR_e.asp.

19. See Canada, Treasury Board of Canada, *Into the 90s: Government Program Evaluation Perspectives,* (Ottawa: Office of the Comptroller General, 1991).

20. Savoie, *The Politics of Public Spending in Canada,* (1990): 115.

21. See Christopher Pollitt, "Management Techniques for the Public Sector: Pulpit and Practice," in B. Guy Peters and Donald J. Savoie, eds. *Governance in a Changing Environment,* (Kingston: McGill–Queen's University Press, 1995): 226–231.

22. See Canada, Treasury Board of Canada, *Treasury Board Manual— Review, Internal Audit and Evaluation,* Amendment RIE/94-1, (Ottawa: Treasury Board of Canada, July 1994): 2.

23. Pal, *Beyond Policy Analysis,* (2001): 302.

24. Canada, Treasury Board, "Getting Government Right: Improving Results Measurement and Accountability," (Ottawa: Minister of Public Works and Government Services Canada, 1996): preface. Online www.tbs-sct.gc/rma/communic/prr96/PRR96.e.htm

25. Canada, Treasury Board, "Getting Government Right: Improving Results Measurement and Accountability," (1996): 2.

26. See Canada, Treasury Board, "Getting Government Right: Improving Results Measurement and Accountability," (1996): 8–9.

27. Canada, Treasury Board, "Getting Government Right: Improving Results Measurement and Accountability," (1996): 8.

28. Canada, Treasury Board, "Getting Government Right: Improving Results Measurement and Accountability," (1996): 4.

29. Source: Canada, Treasury Board, "Getting Government Right: Improving Results Measurement and Accountability," (1996): 4.

30. Ken Kernaghan, Brian Marson and Sandford Borins, *The New Public Organization*, (Toronto: Institute of Public Administration of Canada, 2000): 273.

31. Canada, Treasury Board Secretariat, *Evaluation Policy*, (April 1, 2001): 1.

32. Canada, Treasury Board Secretariat, *Evaluation Policy*, (April 1, 2001): 1.
33. Canada, Treasury Board Secretariat, *Evaluation Policy*, (April 1, 2001): 2.
34. Canada, Treasury Board Secretariat, *Evaluation Policy*, (April 1, 2001): 2.

KEY WORDS AND CONCEPTS

evaluation (238)
administrative evaluation (239)
audits (239)
judicial evaluation (239)
political evaluation (239)
Office of the Comptroller General (240)

Auditor General (241)
Planning, Programming, Budgeting
 System (241)
PS2000 (248)
Program Review (248)
Business Planning (252)

REVIEW QUESTIONS

This chapter reviewed the important role of policy evaluation as a key part of the policy cycle. It was divided into four sections:

1. *The Development of Evaluation*

This section provided a brief overview of the development of evaluation processes and approaches. It asked, What is evaluation? How is it conducted, both formally and informally? What early developments contributed to the emerging role of evaluation in the policy cycle? What do early examples of evaluation suggest about the practice?

2. *Problems of Evaluation*

The exercise of evaluation studies is fraught with difficulty. This section asked the following: What are the major impediments to effective evaluation? How can they be overcome? What methodological and other problems confront evaluators? Can evaluation practices be made effective enough to assure the public that it is getting the most bang for its buck?

3. *Evaluation in Action*

This section considered the actual practice of evaluation. It explored the following questions: Who is primarily responsible for evaluation? How is it undertaken? What factors contribute to successful evaluation?

4. *Contemporary Evaluation Practices*

In looking at recent developments, this section asked, How has the New Public Management had an impact on evaluation? What changes in perspective have been brought to the process of evaluation by the new emphasis on running government like a business? What results have been produced in the area of evaluation by the Program Review exercise launched in 1995?

FURTHER READING

1. The Development of Evaluation

Braybrooke, David and Charles E. Lindblom. *A Strategy of Decision.* New York: Free Press of Glencoe, 1963.

Rist, Ray C., ed. *Policy Evaluation: Linking Theory to Practice.* Aldershot, England: Edward Elgar Publishing Limited, 1995.

Weiss, Carol H. *Evaluation. Second Edition.* Upper Saddle River, New Jersey: Prentice Hall, 1998.

2. Problems of Evaluation

Pal, Leslie A. *Beyond Policy Analysis: Public Issue Management in Turbulent Times. Second Edition.* Scarborough: Nelson, 2001: chapter 7.

Seidle, F. Leslie. *Rethinking the Delivery of Public Services to Citizens.* Montreal: Institute for Research on Public Policy, 1995.

3. Evaluation in Action

Doern, G. Bruce. *Progress and Constraints in Five Canadian Federal Agencies: The Road to Better Public Services.* Montreal: Institute for Research on Public Policy, 1994.

Howlett, Michael and M. Ramesh, *Studying Public Policy: Policy Cycles and Policy Subsystems.* Toronto: Oxford University Press, 1995: chapter 9.

4. Contemporary Evaluation Practices

Leclerc, G. "Institutionalizing Evaluation in Canada," in J. Mayne, J. Hudson, M.L. Bemelmans-Videc and R. Conner, eds. *Advancing Public Policy Evaluation: Learning From International Experiences.* Amsterdam: North Holland, 1992: 49–58.

WEBLINKS

Treasury Board, "Getting Government Right: Improving Results Measurement and Accountability"
www.tbs-sct.gc.ca/rma/communic/prr96/PRR96.e.htm

Expenditure Management System
www.tbs-sct.gc.ca/pubs_pol/opepubs/TB_H/EXMA_e.asp

Chapter (9)

Public Administration *and the* Management *of* Human Resources

WHAT YOU WILL LEARN

In Chapter 1, we identified personnel as a key issue in the study and practice of public administration. Under the guidance of their political masters, public servants—the people who work in the central agencies, departments, regulatory bodies, Crown corporations and other government institutions—are responsible for formulating, implementing and evaluating public policies. To coordinate the vast range of services government offers, and manage the issues it deals with, a large, sophisticated merit-based public service has emerged, made up of professionals from many occupations who offer an astonishing array of skills.[1]

The federal government is one of the largest employers in the country. Because it is a public sector organization rather than a private sector one, the issues relating to the organization and structure of the federal workforce are of particular importance. We consider these issues here in Chapter 9, in the following sections:

1. *A Brief History of the Public Service: Who Works There, Anyway?*
This section provides an overview of the development of the public sector workforce and introduces some of the basic issues that have confronted the public service over time. It asks the following: What is the public service? What has been the historical development of the institution? What issues have animated the evolution of the public service over the past 130 years? How is the public service workforce organized, and who works for the public service? Merit and patronage have been raised as important issues several times already in this book, but we take another look at them here. Their enduring importance centres around the constant tension between them. On the one hand, there is the need to reward faithful supporters and friends of the governing party. On the other hand, there is the need to maintain a professional, objective

and neutral civil service. So this section also asks, What steps have been taken to find a balance between patronage and merit?

2. — *The Public Service Today: An Overview*

This section looks at several key issues related to the contemporary nature and role of the public service. In many respects, the public sector has pioneered progressive change in the workplace, but not without a struggle. This section asks the following: How large is the public service? What factors affect its current composition? Why are region, language, equity and unionization important? What have the most important issues been with regard to equality in the workplace? How has the public service changed to reflect the face of Canada? What is the importance of representativeness? The unionization of the public service in the past 30 years has introduced a whole range of issues, not the least of which is the political rights of workers in the public service. This section also asks the following: How was the right to collective bargaining achieved in the public service? What collective rights do workers in the public service enjoy? How has the presence of unions changed the relationship of the public service to the government? The special relationship of public servants to the political system has important implications for understanding public administration. Beginning with the notion that the political rights of ordinary citizens are different from those of public servants, this section asks several questions: What political rights do public servants enjoy? What is the doctrine of political neutrality, and how does it affect the work that public servants do? What trends currently dominate in the relationship between public servants and the political system?

3. — *Human Resources Management*

The issue of how the tens of thousands of public servants in the federal government are organized and managed requires consideration. To this end, this section asks these questions: How are systems of accountability established and maintained in the public service? What opportunities and constraints do managers have in the hiring and firing of personnel, and in setting pay levels and conditions of employment? How do merit and representativeness mesh or conflict with one another? Recent demographic shifts have left the pubic service in a precarious position. So this section also asks: What is being done around issues of recruitment, retention and succession planning?

A Brief History of the Public Service: Who Works There, Anyway?

In this chapter, we first look at the public service in historical context. Thus, a general overview of the development of the public sector is followed by a brief sociological profile that documents who works there. The impact that region, language, equity, unionization and the political rights of public servants have had on the nature and composition of the Canadian public service is explored.

A famous National Film Board documentary on bureaucracy by the late, great Canadian filmmaker Donald Brittain captured the disparaging attitude many people have towards the bureaucrat, whom he characterized in this way:

He is that most despised of human creatures. His activities have brought down upon his shoulders the scorn and outrage of history's multitude. He is homo bureaucratus; *the bureaucrat. He is the paper-pusher of the world.... He has been compared to the cockroach. Like the cockroach, he appears to have no useful function. Like the cockroach, he has many enemies. Like the cockroach, he has survived all attempts at extinction.*[2]

Some studies reveal that compared to private sector organizations, the public service has made a very poor impression in the minds of many Canadians when it comes to service provision. (See Figure 9.1.) Government, and indeed society, could scarcely function without the legions of public servants who every day process our forms, regulate our behaviour and punish our crimes and misdemeanors. Despite this, pervasive, if facile, negative attitudes about public servants abound.

This reality helps to explain, perhaps, the fact that reform of the public service reaches back to the earliest days of Confederation. And Canada is not alone in this regard. In many other countries, wholesale reform of the public service is the

FIGURE 9.1 **Impression of Service Provided by Public- and Private-Sector Organizations in Canada**

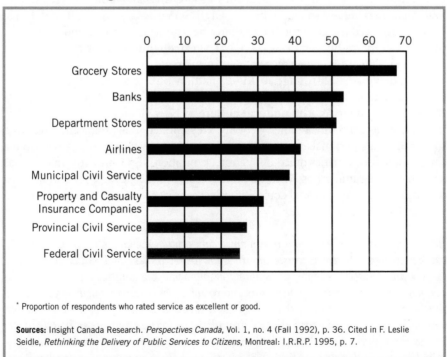

* Proportion of respondents who rated service as excellent or good.

Sources: Insight Canada Research. *Perspectives Canada*, Vol. 1, no. 4 (Fall 1992), p. 36. Cited in F. Leslie Seidle, *Rethinking the Delivery of Public Services to Citizens*, Montreal: I.R.R.P. 1995, p. 7.

order of the day. The United States, Britain, Finland, New Zealand, Australia, Sweden, Singapore, Malaysia, and countless other jurisdictions are trying to respond to globalization, fiscal crises, and citizens' growing disillusionment with government by changing the way their public services do their jobs. But the history of public service reform is a series of pitfalls. When Pierre Trudeau became prime minister in 1968, he promised to reduce the number of government employees by 25 000. Ten years later, their numbers had grown by 40 000. Brian Mulroney assumed office in 1984 with the promise that he would issue "pink slips and running shoes" to the public service. By the time he left in 1993, the public service had increased by over 13 000. The Chrétien government reversed this between 1993 and 1999, when there was a 23 percent reduction in the federal public service. By the end of 1999, public service employment had reached an historic low of 186 314.[3] But these reductions created serious workload issues, as we will see below. In 1999 the first employment increase in seven years took place, and the public service grew by 2.6 percent or 3800 employees.

To place this in some context, let us consider the history of the public service through the lens of the issues of merit and patronage. You will recall that in Chapter 2 you were introduced to some of the main theories of organization, including the Weberian notion of hierarchically ordered structures marked by a definitive chain of command, with each employee responsible to a superior. The Weberian model emphasized rationality in the name of efficiency, but frequently sacrificed some degree of both, due to bureaucratic pathology. It was also noted in Chapter 1 that the professionalization of the Canadian public service (along Weberian lines) really started with the **Civil Service Acts of 1908 and 1918**, which introduced the concept of merit into the recruitment, hiring and promotion practices of the public service. The **Civil Service Commission** was created in 1918 to implement and oversee the merit principle.

The origins of patronage in the Canadian public service reach back to pre-Confederation times, and find their roots in the colonies of New France and British North America. The political culture of New France was shaped by the fact that it was primarily a military colony. This implied a hierarchically organized society in which personal ambition was rewarded (or denied) through service to the King, whose functionaries doled out patronage positions. British North America was shaped by the same ethos, with its citizens serving the needs of the monarchy, who held centralized political control. But by the mid-1800s, the importance of patronage had changed.

[P]atronage played an important role in nineteenth-century Canadian political culture because of its role as a vehicle for social promotion for the professional middle classes. In a largely pre-industrial economy, the many employment possibilities offered by an expanding state—from customs inspectors and postal clerks to appointments to the judicial bench—were irresistibly attractive to the middle classes in search of security and prestige. The pursuit of such social rewards provided the foundation for political life in nineteenth-century Canada and gave rise to an intensely partisan political culture.... [Sir] John A. Macdonald used the patronage potential of an expanding state with mastery to build up his federal Conservative Party across the new federation and to dissolve, as *far as possible, the forces of regionalism which threatened the stability of the new federal state. However, his success and example stimulated emulation and competition at the level of provincial governments, especially in Ontario, where long-serving Liberal Premier Oliver Mowat built up a smoothly functioning patronage machine based on an expanding and centralizing provincial state, that eclipsed even Macdonald's federal Conservative machine for impartial and impersonal efficiency.*[4]

Political scientist Laurent Dobuzinskis suggests that the move toward a meritocratic system of administration along Weberian lines began in Western Europe, but had spread to North America by the 1880s.[5] The need for professional administrators in both government and industry had become increasingly obvious by then.

Geography heavily influenced the structure of Canada's early federal bureaucracy. The dominant departments were those associated with the settlement of the West, and the vast territory to be serviced there required a decentralized bureaucracy with widely dispersed public servants. But the complexity of this system increased over time, bringing new issues and a larger bureaucracy. The creation of the Civil Service Commission in 1908 and the extension of its authority in the 1918 reforms marked the drive toward professionalization of the Canadian public service. Moreover, it reinforced the independence of the public service from political interference—a factor that remains a cornerstone of the **Public Service Commission** today. It was thought that unlike the government, fixated as it inevitably is on short-term political advantage, the permanent public service would be able to take a longer view of professionalism and integrity. Moreover, the drive to a merit-based professional civil service, which traced its origins to British practice, was wedded to the influence of scientific management wafting up from the United States. The result was a sort of hybrid of British and American traditions.

As time went by, the growth of the state severely tested the politics-administration dichotomy. While Woodrow Wilson's distinction between politics and administration stood as the standard against which the quality of administration was measured for many decades, by the middle of the 20th century it had become evident that public servants were, in fact, playing an active role in policy formulation. The emergence of the welfare state was indeed partly attributable to the increasingly activist role of public servants. They provided the technical, managerial and professional capability to mobilize the resources of the Canadian government towards a massive shift in the traditional relationship between the state and society. In the area of federal-provincial relations, for instance, an era of "administrative" or "cooperative" federalism emerged. Political scientist Garth Stevenson suggests,

As bureaucracies became larger, more powerful, more functionally specialized, and more removed from partisan influence and pressure, they assumed increasingly autonomous roles in seeking accommodation with their counterparts at the other level of government. As specialists of various kinds came to predominate in certain sectors of the public service, they tended to discover that they held interests, goals and assumptions in common with similar specialists at the other level of government, and that these took precedence over considerations of intergovernmental competition, party rivalry, or even constitutional propriety. Thus administrative methods of problem-solving were preferred.[6]

These developments characterized not just federal-provincial relations, but a range of other areas of public policy development and public administration. Thus, an overlap developed between politics and administration.

By the 1950s, the state was assuming an ever-larger role in the management of the economy and the day-to-day lives of Canadians. The earlier metaphors derived from Weber's and Taylor's views of a mechanistic, rigid, rule-bound hierarchical organization were reinforced by increasingly rigid structures, rules and processes, and, simultaneously, challenged by new thinking about the roles of public servants. Two post-war developments, in particular, changed the nature and role of the public service in profound ways. The first was a rudimentary affirmative action plan put in place in the late 1940s to provide employment for the large number of Canadian soldiers returning from the Second World War (a similar, more modest effort had been initiated after the First World War, as well). Over about 12 years from 1940, the public service tripled in size, absorbing surplus labour, and helping to prevent a return to the conditions of the Great Depression of the 1930s. However, this development, while impressive quantitatively, had relatively little qualitative effect. As Nicole Morgan, an authority on public service management, put it,

[T]he first period of growth was unparalleled but had no effect on the traditional structure of the public service. In this instance, growth was carefully managed; it was concentrated in a few departments, distributed fairly evenly across the country, and made up of older men whose outlook had been shaped by the Hungry Thirties and the war. In a period of intensive growth, the civil service, as it was then called, was modeled on our military.[7]

The second development occurred when the first cohort of baby boomers began to graduate from the expanded university system in the 1960s and 1970s. From 1965 to 1975, the public service doubled in size as a result. Many of these new, young employees began to see themselves not just as loyal servants, but as agents of change. Morgan suggests that "although the second period of growth was less important in terms of numbers, it revolutionized both the structure and role of the public service."[8] These highly skilled and well-trained graduates, mainly from business schools, the social sciences and economics, increasingly challenged the traditional views of civil servants, pursuing organizational objectives and career goals that greatly transformed the public service. A new climate developed that encouraged policy experimentation and initiative. The technocratic expert who could provide sophisticated policy advice based on the new sciences of cybernetics, computer modelling, systems theory and other innovations came to be valued. The number of government departments, regulatory bodies and Crown corporations mushroomed. New planning techniques were introduced, including financial management systems such as Planning, Programming, Budgeting Systems (PPBS) (discussed in Chapter 8) and its successors. But this explosion of new systems left a troubling legacy. As Dobuzinskis reports,

[T]raditional administrative tasks (e.g. personnel management) received relatively less attention; thus a gap was created between the macro-policy concerns of the upper echelons of the public service and the more strictly managerial concerns of middle-ranking officials. This gap was to become more and more pronounced, until it was finally acknowledged in the late 1980s. The same preoccupation with policy issues, as distinguished from the study of public administration, also gripped the academic community in the same period. (For instance, most graduate programs offering a Master's degree in public administration placed a greater emphasis on policy analysis than on organizational and managerial problems).[9]

Moreover, even the merit system began to reveal itself as a barrier to sound management practices. By the 1980s, it was apparent that the elaborate system of exams and the rules and regulations governing recruitment and promotion had set up systemic barriers to certain socioeconomic groups, and that, consequently, the public service had largely become the preserve of white Anglophone males (especially at the upper levels).This failure of the public service to be **representative** of the society it served developed into an important issue, as did the proposed solutions.

Organizationally, the public service experienced growing pains in the post-war years. For instance, the ***Civil Service Act* of 1961** was passed after it became apparent that the Civil Service Commission and the Treasury Board were stepping on each other's toes in terms of authority over government personnel. The Act gave the Treasury Board sole responsibility for determining pay levels and administrative organization. This was followed in 1967 by the *Public Service Staff Relations Act,* which allowed the Civil Service Commission to enter into collective agreements in the name of the government. Classification of jobs, pay levels and most conditions of employment remained under the purview of the Treasury Board. Also in 1967, the *Public Service Employment Act* gave authority for staffing and training to the Civil Service Commission, which was renamed the Public Service Commission. The independence of the Public Service Commission from interference by government was maintained by having it report to Parliament rather than to Cabinet, although the three commissioners who head the Public Service Commission are appointed by the Cabinet for a set term of 10 years.

A variety of societal changes affected the growth and the development of the public service in the post-war years. To begin with, technological change drove the state to broaden its role and functions. In part, the expansion of the public service was a response to the necessity of keeping the regulatory regime up to speed with the rapid technological changes of the 20th century.[10] Second, the rise of new social movements around a variety of issues, such as women's rights and gender equality, environmentalism, gay and lesbian rights, animal rights, seniors' rights, and the rising militancy of youth, demanded a response from the state. The public service has had to scramble to respond to the demands of these activists "engaged in the politics of identity and... interested in the democratization of both everyday life and governance."[11] Finally, a fiscal crisis gripped the state from the 1970s onward, reshaping thinking about what the public service should be doing and what it should look like. Public sector managers, as a result, have been forced to shift their attention from designing grand systems for policy planning to the more prosaic details of managerial and administrative concerns.

Throughout the 1980s and 1990s, the combination of these factors seemed to overwhelm the public service, and a malaise settled over it. The rise of neoconservatism, first in Great Britain under Margaret Thatcher, then in the United States under Ronald Reagan, and finally in Canada under Brian Mulroney and Jean Chrétien, brought increased disparagement of the public service. For instance, former finance minister Michael Wilson said this in his May 1985 budget speech:

[G]overnment is not only too big, it also reaches too far into almost every corner of the economy. It over-regulates some industries and over-protects others. In trying to facilitate investment, government too often distorts it. Instead of encouraging strength, many actions perpetuate inefficiency. Too often, government frustrates entrepreneurship and discourages initiative.[12]

These arguments reflect the concerted attack that was launched against the public service by those who believed the state had become too large, complex and unwieldy. They focused much of their attack on the public service as a primary instrument of obstruction to the free operation of markets. The rise of globalization reinforced these perspectives by raising the idea that states (that is, the public sector) interfere with the flow of goods and services in the global marketplace. The growing chorus of demands to reduce the size of government and to put the art of governing on a more businesslike footing profoundly affected the public service's identity, role, composition and morale.

The neoconservative arguments were challenged by those who saw a legitimate role for government intervention in the economy, particularly in times of recession and unemployment. As political economist Isabella Bakker suggests, the supporters of this "Keynesian" viewpoint "argued for active government fiscal and monetary policies, as well as regulations aimed at curbing the excesses of corporate concentration and abuses of consumers. In addition, some Keynesians embraced the proposition that redistributive measures such as social security, and income supplements such as unemployment insurance, were effective safeguards, because they gave workers money to buy the goods the economy produced even during economic downturns."[13] Even Jocelyne Bourgon, then Clerk of the Privy Council and Secretary to the Cabinet (the top civil servant in the public service) reminded Canadians that those reinventing government, while perhaps doing the inevitable, must not make government more businesslike, since the public and private sectors are inherently different. She also argued that the challenges of reinventing government were tremendously more complex than those faced in the private sector. "The management of change in the private sector may be a question of financial survival," she argued, "but for those of us in the public sector, it is about the future of the country, the national interest and the public good. We must guard against the simplistic notion that the public sector should be run like a private enterprise."[14] But these arguments largely succumbed to the powerful juggernaut of professional economists, business lobbies and think tanks propounding the neoconservative doctrine.

As a result of the spread of neoconservative ideas in Canada, the public service has had to undergo a major self-examination over the past 15 years. In her *Report to the Prime Minister on the Public Service of Canada*, Jocelyne Bourgon described a "quiet crisis" in the Canadian public service. The years of downsizing and pay freezes, criticism and insufficient recruitment efforts have made it difficult to retain, motivate and attract the people essential to the work of the public service. Moreover, the premature departure of experienced public servants who took early retirement buyouts or simply left in frustration, coupled with insufficient hiring of new young blood, meant that the public service was bulging with middle-aged managers and workers.[15] The historical memory and institutional experience and knowledge of the "old-timers" was being drained away. As well, there was an absence of the invigorating new ideas and perspectives that new recruits would normally bring to an organization. It was as though someone had cut off the head and feet of the organization and left the bloated body (see Figure 9.2). Bourgon maintained that the crisis was a quiet one simply because no one was willing to talk about or confront these emerging problems.

Thus, exercises such as PS2000 and La Relève were launched (discussed in greater detail below) and some concrete changes to the public service have resulted. For instance, in 1992, as a result of PS2000, the *Public Service Reform Act*

FIGURE 9.2 **Age Distribution of Public Service Management vs. Canadian Labour Force Senior Management (1996 Census)**

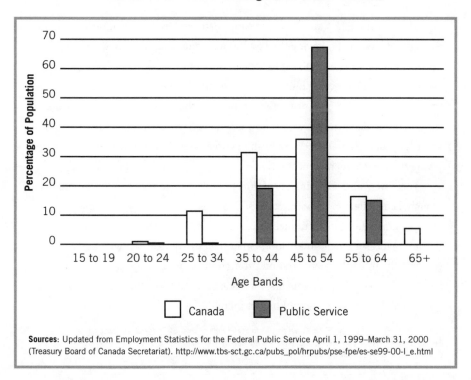

Sources: Updated from Employment Statistics for the Federal Public Service April 1, 1999–March 31, 2000 (Treasury Board of Canada Secretariat). http://www.tbs-sct.gc.ca/pubs_pol/hrpubs/pse-fpe/es-se99-00-l_e.html

was passed.[16] This helped lessen the bureaucratic red tape around hiring and firing decisions. Perhaps more significantly, it also mandated employment equity programs. These reforms did, however, lead to some contention over the extent to which the merit principle has been compromised for the goal of increased efficiency, as Box 9-1 shows.

Moreover, a general rethinking of the place of the public service ensued, as represented by the "mission statement" of the Public Service Commission (PSC) (see Box 9-2). The key issues identified by the PSC included merit, the ability to perform duties without political interference, representativeness, and access by all Canadians to employment opportunities within the public service.[17]

Box 9-1

Public Service Reform Act (PSRA, 1992)

As a consequence of the PS2000 recommendations, and a recognition that flexible staffing arrangements were required to allow managers to provide the best possible service to the public, the *Public Service Reform Act (PSRA)* was passed in November. 1992. The Act made amendments to two pieces of legislation, the PSSRA and PSEA. These changes represented the first major set of amendments to staffing legislation since 1967.

Many of the *PSRA* amendments simplified the job classification system and the staffing process. Following the PS2000 recommendations, a new system of deployments was initiated, subject to Treasury Board direction, which enabled managers to move employees more easily to a position of the same level, either to meet operational requirements or to give employees the opportunity to acquire new skills. As well, departments would now be allowed to respond quickly to urgent or short term operational needs by hiring people on a short term basis without applying the normal merit process.

There were also amendments of direct significance to the PSC. For example, although the requirement to select people on the basis of merit was retained as the basis of appointment, a new amendment enabled the PSC to prescribe standards of competence to measure merit in isolation rather than by comparison, with other persons (not simply on deployments but on promotions as well). Although these changes largely promoted efficiency benefits, the trade off would seem to be an erosion of the traditional definition and upholding of merit.

Source: Trevor Bhupsingh and Peter Edwards. *Tracking the Role of the PSC in the Governance System of the Federal Public Service.* (Ottawa: Public Service Commission of Canada, April, 1997). http://www.psc-cfp.gc.ca/research/merit/role_psc_e.htm

---

Box 9-2

Mandate, Roles and Responsibilities, and Mission Statement of the Public Service Commission of Canada

Our Mandate

The Public Service Commission of Canada is an independent agency responsible for safeguarding the values of a professional Public Service: competence, nonpartisanship and representativeness. It does this in the public interest as part of Canada's governance system. It does this by administering the *Public Service Employment Act (PSEA)* and a merit-based system and, *inter alia*, being responsible for the appointment of qualified persons to and within the Public Service; by providing recourse and review in matters under the *PSEA*; by delivering training and development programs; and by carrying out other responsibilities as provided for in the *PSEA* and the *Employment Equity Act (EEA)*.

Our Mission

The mission of the PSC is, through its statutory authorities, to:

➤ maintain and preserve a highly competent and qualified Public Service in which appointments are based on merit: and

➤ ensure that the Public Service is non-partisan and its members are representative of Canadian society.

The PSC a an active partner in developing the broad framework for human resource management and ensuring the health of the federal human resource system, within the scope of its mandate.

Source: Canada. Public Service Commission of Canada Mandate, Roles and Responsibilities.
http://www.psc-cfp.gc.ca/centres/mission_e.htm

Over time, the Public Service Commission has been forced to effectively redefine itself and state in a nutshell what its responsibilities are, and how it will fulfill them.

In 2001, Mel Cappe, the Clerk of Privy Council, reported to the prime minister that "a more modern public service is emerging to respond to the challenges of today's rapidly changing, interdependent world focused on knowledge." He went on to argue that:

We are moving away from a traditional model of public service based on hierarchical, directive management. We are leaving behind a public service where jobs were based primarily on repetitive, well-defined tasks and predicable activities and where vertical, top-down communications approaches were the norm.

We have begun the transformation to a modern, people-centred Public Service of Canada, one which is more flexible and responsive, adaptive and innovative.[18]

Some important institutional changes have been made to realize these goals. For instance, in 1999–2000, two new federal agencies were created which significantly reduced the number of employees traditionally under the purview of Treasury Board. First, Parks Canada was created in April 1999. This resulted in the transfer of 3900 employees from the Ministry of Canadian Heritage. But a more significant change occurred in November 1999 when Revenue Canada became a separate agency known as the Canada Customs and Revenue Agency, resulting in the transfer of about 40 000 employees. These innovations represent new ways to contain the growth of the public service and to reconfigure the universe of government human resources management. The new agencies fall outside of the *Public Service Staff Relations Act* (the legislation that gives the Treasury Board the authority to act as the manager and employer of the federal public service) and are therefore subject to different rules.

But, as Mel Cappe also points out, "the transformation is taking place too slowly. Current laws, rules and structures for managing people in the Public Service are neither flexible nor responsive enough to allow us to compete for talent in a knowledge economy. As well, the industrial era mindset and culture is still alive in many parts of today's Public Service."[19] Still, the process of reform, however incremental, is ongoing. Currently the challenges of recruitment and retention are uppermost in the minds of human resources managers in the public service. (See Box 9-3.) We return to these two issues in more detail below.

Clearly, many changes have occurred in the public service in Canada since 1867. Originally a relatively small, patronage-based haven for friends of the governing party, it has evolved into a huge, complex, merit-based professional institution composed of legions of highly skilled and technically gifted people. It has changed in other important ways too. For instance, it has become more representative in nature. Once the preserve of white Anglophone middle- and upper-class males, it has recently taken proactive and progressive steps to become a more inclusive equal opportunity employer. To ensure the public service reflects the regional, ethnocultural, linguistic and gender makeup of Canada, procedures such as affirmative action, employment equity and pay equity programs have been introduced to encourage and promote the employment of women, visible minorities, the disabled, and Aboriginals. Moreover, since the Second World War, the public sector has been the fastest-unionizing sector of the Canadian economy. This development—the culmination of a long struggle—has given workers in the public service collective agreements and expanded their political rights, which were once severely circumscribed.

Jocelyne Bourgon summarized the post-war efforts of the public service in a 1994 speech to the Association of Professional Executives of the Public Service of Canada.

Throughout the history of Canada, successive generations of public sector managers have been asked to assist the government in meeting the challenges of their times. This generation is no different: In the 1950s, the public sector embarked on the massive task of postwar

Box 9-3

Employment Trends in the Federal Public Service

The following [summary] reviews the major changes that have occurred in the composition of the federal public service workforce in recent years. For purposes of comparison, however, Revenue Canada (now the CCRA) has been excluded from the historical data. Here is an overview of the main trends:

1. The size of the federal Public Service shrank by about 40,000 employees when Revenue Canada became a separate agency at the end of November 1999. For ease of comparison, if we exclude Revenue Canada from the workforce represented by the Treasury Board, the workforce would have increased by 3,738 employees (2.6 per cent).

2. The proportion of employees in the federal Public Service who hold positions in the Executive, Scientific and Professional, or Administrative and Foreign Service categories is still on the rise. Eight of the 10 occupational groups whose numbers have grown the most over the past five years belong to one of these three categories.

3. The proportion of federal public service jobs held by women has been rising for more than 15 years and has surpassed the proportion of men about two years ago.

4. The percentage of employees holding indeterminate positions who fall in the age band 45 to 54 has continued to increase and represented about 42 per cent of the total federal public service workforce as at March 31, 2000. The high concentration of employees in this age group will have repercussions on the number of separations from the federal Public Service five to 10 years from now. Over the next 10 years, the proportion of employees age 55 and over is also expected to increase by at least 75 per cent.

5. Although the proportion of term and casual employees has fluctuated over the past 15 years, in March 2000 it reached its highest level in at least 10 years.

6. The proportion of federal employees who hold positions in the Executive, Scientific and Professional, or Administrative and Foreign Service categories is appreciably higher in the National Capital Region than elsewhere in the country.

Source: Canada. Treasury Board of Canada Secretariat. *Employment Statistics for the Federal Public Service April 1, 1999–March 31, 2000.* (Ottawa: Treasury Board of Canada Secretariat, 2000): 3. http://www.tbs-sct.gc.ca/pubs_pol/hrpubs/pse-fpe/es-se99-00-1_e.html

rebuilding, in order to lay the foundation of the modern society Canadians now enjoy. In the '60s, the public sector was called upon to invent and implement most of the social security programs that have since become a hallmark of our society. The public sector was up to the challenge.

In the '70s, the public sector extended its reach to virtually every aspect of life in Canadian society. Trade, energy, the environment, consumer protection—all these sectors benefitted from the contributions of public servants.

In the '80s, the public sector was asked to focus on macro-economic policies to help Canada adapt to a more open economy. We were also asked to streamline the operations of government. The public service responded to the challenge.[20]

Each of these developments has contributed significantly to the fact that Canadians enjoy a very high standard of living in a country with a highly developed and sophisticated provision of public services. Indeed, in 1996, the United Nations rated Canada first in terms of its Human Development Index, a scale devised to measure purchasing power, life expectancy, literacy and educational attainment.[21] But at the same time, each of the developments cited above has also been marked by controversy reflecting disputes over what the public service (that is, the state) should or should not do.

At this stage, you may feel you understand something about the historical development of the public service, but remain a little unsure about what it looks like today. Thus, it will be useful to examine the nature of the public service as it is currently constituted.

The Public Service Today: An Overview

Attitudes about the public service in Canada are currently changing. Recognizing some of the damage that has been done to a once-great institution, efforts are being made to restore a sense of pride and worth to a public service career. In its Speech From the Throne in 2001, the government of Jean Chrétien pronounced:

To assist the government in fulfilling its responsibilities, Canada must have a public service distinguished by excellence and equipped with the skills for a knowledge economy and society. The government will seek bright, motivated young women and men to accept the challenge of serving their country in the federal public service. The Government is committed to the reforms needed for the Public Service of Canada to continue evolving and adapting. These reforms will ensure that the Public Service is innovative, dynamic and reflective of the diversity of the country—able to attract and develop the talent needed to serve Canadians in the 21st century.[22]

How thoroughly this attitude has permeated the political leadership in government across the country is hard to say. Certainly a contrasting view is apparent in Box 9-4, wherein one of the unions in the Ontario public service (the Association

Box 9-4

Five Questions That Drive Ontario Public Service Recruiters Nuts

1. Why should I work for 12% to 21% less than I could make any-where else?
2. What future will I have in an organization that has cut thousands of jobs in the last decade?
3. Why won't my salary even keep up with the cost of living?
4. How can you expect me to work unlimited overtime without compensation?
5. Why do current Ontario Public Servants feel forced to put out ads like this?

Think twice before joining Ontario's Public Service.

www.amapcco.on.ca

Source: *Metro Today* (Toronto. January 28, 2002): 10.

of Management, Administrative and Professional Crown Employees of Ontario) rather bluntly articulated their displeasure with the status of public employees in that province. And certainly the British Columbia government's announcement in early 2002 that it was committed to cutting one-third of its workforce as a cost-saving measure indicates that some old attitudes die hard. Nonetheless, a decade or more of retrenchment may be receding.

Even if you have never worked in the public sector, chances are that you know someone who has or does. With over half a million employees, the federal government is a significant employer in Canada. Indeed, when you account for federal, provincial and local governments, the public sector in Canada employs about one in four Canadians. By comparison, prior to Confederation, the public service employed about 2700 people, and by 1896 it had grown to about 10 000.[23] In 1993, 196 674 people were employed under the authority of the federal Public Service Commission alone. By 1999 this number had been reduced to 142 906 (see Figure 9.3).[24] But if the transitions involving Parks Canada and the Canada Customs and Revenue Agency are taken out of the equation, the public service actually began to grow again in 2000. The rest of the federal workforce is under the jurisdiction of the armed forces, RCMP, Crown corporations, agencies and other bodies that together make up the broader public service.

The question of how to organize all those people is vital to the smooth functioning of government. Currently, the public service is divided into six occupational categories: management, scientific and professional, administrative and foreign service, technical, administrative support, and operational. These categories are used to help determine pay levels and occupation. According to the Treasury Board's guidelines, the policy objective of the classification system is "to ensure that the

FIGURE 9.3   Total Number of Employees in the Federal Public Service

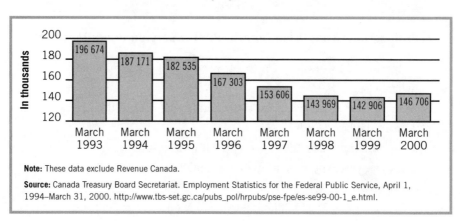

Note: These data exclude Revenue Canada.

Source: Canada Treasury Board Secretariat. Employment Statistics for the Federal Public Service, April 1, 1994–March 31, 2000. http://www.tbs-set.gc.ca/pubs_pol/hrpubs/pse-fpe/es-se99-00-1_e.html.

relative value of all jobs in the Public Service is established in an equitable, consistent and effective manner and provides a basis for the compensation of public servants."[25] Within these six categories, virtually every profession and trade known to modern society is found, organized in a uniform manner that permits rational staffing and appointments consistent with the merit principle. No matter which department an employee works in, he receives the same remuneration as any other employee in that level and category. The categorization of jobs in this manner reflects a clear chain of command and responsibility, and within each department a descending order of command is organized such that each employee is responsible to a superior. In many cases, the complexity of this system, given the size of the public service, means that communication within and across departments is bogged down by red tape and the requirements of triplicate copies of memos, directives and forms. Hence, efficiency is sacrificed, but accountability is maintained.

Currently, the major issues confronting human resource managers in the public service include: the adoption of performance management measures; an increased focus on human resources planning, particularly retention and recruitment problems; exploring new forms of partnerships, including employee takeovers; pension reform; the development of a new employment classification system; and interest-based bargaining.[26] The agenda is large and daunting. Demographic trends, government downsizing, hiring freezes and shifts in the occupational makeup of the public service are particularly troubling. One of the most significant results of these developments is a growing concentration of the 45–54 age group in the federal workforce. This group constitutes over 40 percent of all federal employees. Furthermore, the number of employees aged 55 or over is expected to almost double over the next 10 years, imposing a greater strain on the public service in terms of sick leave and higher health-care costs, as well as the prospect of large numbers of early retirements. The rate at which employees leave the public service is expected to dramatically increase, especially at the senior levels of the public service. According to Treasury Board estimates:

In March 2000, of the total number of indeterminate employees in the federal Public Service, the proportion aged 45 to 54 was over 42 per cent. Since 1989, their proportion in the workforce has doubled.

According to our forecasting models, the proportion of employees age 55 and over will increase by at least 75 per cent over the coming 10 years. For this reason, separation rates are expected to increase gradually over the years, then reach a plateau at levels comparable to those recorded in the last two years of Program Review (1997–98 and 1998–99).

Much of the growth in the proportion of indeterminate employees age 45 to 54 has been at the expense of indeterminate employees below age 35. The proportion of federal public servants in this latter age group has dwindled considerably over the years—from 23 per cent as at March 31, 1992 to only 12.8 per cent of the total workforce as at March 31, 2000.[27]

Not surprisingly, the move to a knowledge-based economy has affected the composition of the public service. According to a survey of the federal workforce conducted by the Treasury Board, "the occupational mix of the federal Public Service is undergoing major changes, with a growing percentage of employees holding scientific, technical, and professional jobs that require high levels of skill and education. Factors that have contributed to this change in the employment mix include increased automation of office work, changes in federal areas of activity, and devolutions and privatizations of federal departments and agencies."[28] About 52 percent of federal public servants hold positions in the Executive, Scientific and Professional, or Administrative and Foreign Service categories, which represents an increase of over 10 percent in about 10 years. The fastest growing occupational groups include: computer systems administration; law; economics, sociology and statistics; welfare programs; physical sciences; correctional services; and information services. Together, these seven groups account for approximately 17 percent of the total federal public service workforce, compared with 9 percent in 1993. Another interesting recent development is the trend toward increased numbers of term and casual employees. This human resources strategy gives managers more flexibility in their operations, it is argued, besides saving money. Nearly 20 percent of the total federal public service is now composed of these types of employees (see Figure 9.4). But as noted below, this creates a recruitment problem for the public service, since it makes the prospect of a public service career less tenable.

If you decide on a career in the public service, you will first have to write an entrance exam to determine whether you are a qualified candidate. The Public Service Commission sponsors various recruitment programs. Once you secure a position, there are competitions for promotions, as well as an appeal process to ensure that every employee has a fair chance to advance through the ranks. In some cases, new job openings will be deemed "open," meaning that individuals from outside the public service can apply. In other circumstances, the candidate search will be "closed," meaning that it is limited to those who already work within the bureaucracy.[29]

FIGURE 9.4   **Use of Term and Casual Employees on the Rise**

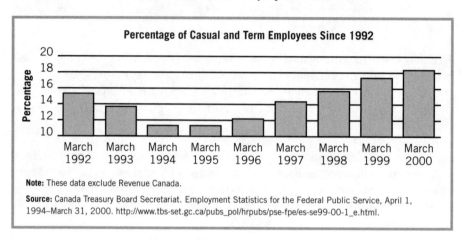

Percentage of Casual and Term Employees Since 1992

Note: These data exclude Revenue Canada.

Source: Canada Treasury Board Secretariat. Employment Statistics for the Federal Public Service, April 1, 1994–March 31, 2000. http://www.tbs-set.gc.ca/pubs_pol/hrpubs/pse-fpe/es-se99-00-1_e.html.

Analyzing employment in the public service is not simply a matter of "How many?" Looking at a variety of factors will give us a more nuanced picture. We will consider the following issues here: region, language, equity, and unionization. But first we will consider the extent to which the public service is, or ought to be, representative of the society it serves.

The Theory of Representativeness

The *Public Service Employment Act* forbids discrimination in hiring or promotion on the basis of race, national or ethnic origin, colour, religion, age, sex, marital status, disability, or conviction for an offence for which a pardon has been granted. The use of an entrance exam ostensibly reinforces the merit principle. Since the 1992 reforms, the Public Service Commission's staffing decisions are still guided by the merit principle, but it has also been instructed to initiate employment equity plans for historically underrepresented groups: women, Aboriginal peoples, persons with disabilities and visible minorities. The broad goal has been to make the public service more representative of the society it serves. Social changes have seen more women enter the paid workforce, and immigration has brought about demographic change. The difficult question is how to adapt the public service to these changes so that it reflects the broader Canadian society.[30]

Essentially, the theory behind representativeness is that if the public service reflects the population it serves, it will make decisions in the best interests of those it serves. The demographic composition of the public service should resemble that of society to ensure that the values of both are commensurate. Of course, there is no guarantee that the values of an individual public servant will be the same as those of the group she comes from, since socialization is a complex thing. Thus, critics of the theory of representativeness suggest that you cannot guarantee a sensitive and responsive public service simply by creating one that is composed of individuals whose numbers are in proportion to the size of their group in the broader society. In any event, it is often suggested that the public service itself has its own institutional values and interests that often supersede those of individuals, no matter how those individuals were previously socialized. The other side of this coin, though, is that there is no guarantee that a responsive public service need be representative. There are countless examples in Canadian history of the elite, exclusive upper echelons of the public service enacting policy that benefits minorities and other groups different from those who hold offices of power.

In any event, the theoretical arguments about representativeness seem moot in light of real-life experience. A regime of representativeness is under construction in Canada, and has been for more than 30 years. Proactive steps have been taken in a number of areas to promote regional and linguistic representativeness. Moreover, various equity initiatives concerning women, visible minorities, Aboriginals and the disabled have been enacted. We will now consider each in turn, bearing in mind that despite these recent efforts, the Canadian public service is still not a "microcosm" of the society it serves, and that the further up the bureaucratic hierarchy you go, the truer this statement is.

Region

It may not seem obvious at first, but where public servants work is an important consideration. The assumption that the "government" is in Ottawa is a mistaken one. It is true that about one-third of Canada's public servants work in the Ottawa-Hull region. But another one-third work in Ontario and Quebec outside Ottawa-Hull. About 17 percent of public servants are found in the Atlantic provinces, and another 24 percent work in the West, Yukon and Northwest Territories. A small percentage work outside Canada, for instance in our embassies and trade missions.

The proportion of public servants found in each region of the country has both symbolic and pragmatic importance. First, there has been a deliberate effort to decentralize the functions of government away from Ottawa. This has been done to help combat alienation from the nation's capital, by putting the face of the government in the very communities that it affects. In other words, establishing field offices across the country lets Canadians see their tax dollars at work, and in a sense personalizes the distant and aloof structures of power found in Ottawa. Second, and more pragmatically, locating government offices outside Ottawa creates jobs in regions that might lack other employment opportunities. Nothing puts a smile on the face of a Cabinet minister like the prospect of opening a federal facility in his riding! As a result of the decentralization of federal government functions, the Atlantic provinces have slightly more than their fair share of federal public servants compared to their proportion of the overall population, and the West has slightly less. Ontario and Quebec's shares of federal public servants roughly match their proportions of the overall population.

Language

Linguistic considerations have always played a prominent role in the development of the public service. In the era of patronage, a certain number of French-Canadians could always count on receiving appointments to the public service from the handful of French-Canadian Cabinet ministers. But when patronage was eliminated as the basis of hiring, there was no mechanism put in place to ensure that the proportion of French-speaking civil servants matched the proportion of the French-speaking population in Canada. As a result, the use and importance of French within the halls of power diminished over time. Political scientist J.E. Hodgetts reported that between 1918 and 1945, for instance, the number of French-speaking civil servants dropped by more than 10 percent.[31] At the senior levels of the public service, the numbers were particularly dismal. Former prime minister Pierre Trudeau recalled arriving in Ottawa in the late 1950s to work as a public servant in the Privy Council Office, and being astonished to discover that if he—a French-Canadian—wanted to write a memo to another French-Canadian civil servant, he had to do so in English!

Political scientists Robert and Doreen Jackson explain the lack of French-Canadian representation in the civil service this way:

Many factors combined during these years to reduce levels of francophone recruitment in the federal bureaucracy. The public service became less attractive for French-Canadians because no provisions were made to ensure service to French-Canadians. Nor were francophones' bilingual skills included in an assessment of their qualifications. Francophones were also hindered by the merit system's examinations and interviews, which reflected the patterns of thought and cultural styles of English-speaking Canada. The competitions also emphasized the technical and commercial skills taught in the English educational system, placing French-Canadians, with their classical education, at a disadvantage.[32]

Incidents like the one experienced by Trudeau in an ostensibly bilingual country and federal public service prompted Trudeau to pass the *Official Languages Act* in 1969 to rectify this type of discrimination. Trudeau embarked upon an ambitious exercise to make "French power" a reality in Ottawa, and to make the federal government truly bilingual.

Much of the groundwork for this process was laid by the Royal Commission on Bilingualism and Biculturalism, which reported between 1967 and 1970.[33] The Royal Commission handed the Public Service Commission the responsibility for language training, instructing it to walk a tightrope between, on the one hand, promoting the use of French in the federal bureaucracy and recruiting more bilingual workers, and on the other hand, ensuring that the merit principle was respected. Progress has been slow, especially at the upper reaches of the bureaucracy, where French-Canadians continue to be underrepresented relative to their numbers in of the population. Still, they now represent about 28 percent of all public servants, which approximates the percentage of French-Canadians overall. Table 9.1 shows the number and percentage of appointments by language group and type of appointment for 2000–2001.

Equity

Employment equity is a term that came into widespread use in the 1980s and is similar in meaning to **affirmative action**. It was coined by Judge Rosalie Abella in her groundbreaking Royal Commission Report on Equality in Employment.[34] The

TABLE 9.1   Appointment Type and Language Group

Number and percentage of appointments by appointment type and language group, April 1, 2000 to March 31, 2001

| Language Group | Appointments to the Public Service | | Appointments *within* the Public Service: Type of Appointment | | | | | | | |
| | | | Promotions | | Lateral movements | | Action appointments (a) | | Total | |
	No.	%	No.	%	No.	%	No.	%	No.	%
Anglophones	13,613	68.9	14,287	66.4	9,744	66.6	7,383	61.9	45,007	66.2
Francophones	6,131	31.1	7,235	33.6	5,118	34.4	4,543	38.1	23,027	33.8
Total	20,124	100.0	21,534	100.0	14,922	100.0	11,952	100.0	68,532	100.0

(a) Excludes acting appointments of four months or less.

Source: Canada. Public Service Commission of Canada. *Annual Report 2000–2001*. (Ottawa: Public Service Commission of Canada, 2001).
http://www.psc-ofp-gc:ca/centres/annual-annuel/2001/ann2001-e.pdf

Public Service Commission defines it as "employment practices designed to ensure that the regular staffing process is free of attitudinal and systemic barriers in order that the Public Service reflects all groups present in the Canadian labour force, and designed to ensure that corrective measures are applied to erase any historical disadvantage experienced by certain designated groups."[35] Judge Abella intended it to help eliminate discrimination in the workplace, which, she noted, had affected various groups in Canadian society. "One hundred years ago, the role for women was almost exclusively domestic," she wrote. "Fifty years ago some visible minorities were disenfranchised; 25 years ago, native people lacked a policy voice; and 10 years ago, disabled persons were routinely kept dependent. Today, none of these exclusionary assumptions is acceptable."[36]

In 1967, women made up only 27.3 percent of the employees in the public service, compared to 51.7 percent today (about 75 836 women; see Figure 9.5). According to Treasury Board statistics, "at the end of fiscal 1999–2000, there were 4,984 fewer men than women in the federal Public Service. Compare this with five years ago (March 1995), when there were 15,000 more men than women, excluding Revenue Canada."[37] However, women have historically been heavily "ghettoized" in "pink-collar" occupations. For instance, 83 percent worked in "office and administrative support" positions in 1967, compared to about 46.5 percent today. While fewer than 3 percent of those working in financial administration in 1967 were women, today some 40.5 percent are women. Whereas only 11.5 percent of those working in program administration 30 years ago were women, today 52.5 percent are women. These gains are impressive, but there are several occupational groups where women have made virtually no progress. Consider, for instance, that women only constitute 8.5 percent of engineers and land surveyors, 2.5 percent of electronics experts, 1.5 percent of firefighters and 3.3 percent of general labour and trades, and it is evident that progress is uneven across the public service. At the executive level of the public service, fewer than 1 percent of senior officers were women in 1967, whereas today 23 percent are women. The first woman

FIGURE 9.5   Percentage of Women in the Federal Public Service

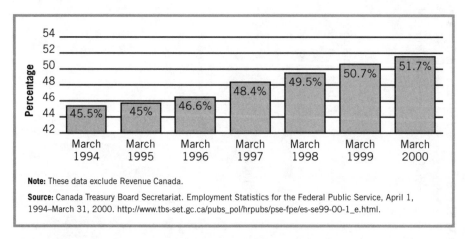

Note: These data exclude Revenue Canada.

Source: Canada Treasury Board Secretariat. Employment Statistics for the Federal Public Service, April 1, 1994–March 31, 2000. http://www.tbs-set.gc.ca/pubs_pol/hrpubs/pse-fpe/es-se99-00-1_e.html.

FIGURE 9.6   **Percentage of Women Working in the Executive, Scientific and Professional, or Administrative and Foreign Service Categories**

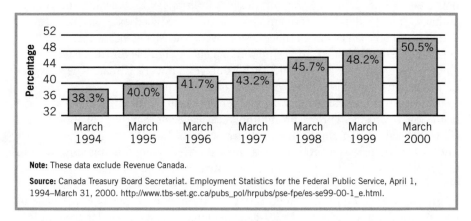

Note: These data exclude Revenue Canada.

Source: Canada Treasury Board Secretariat. Employment Statistics for the Federal Public Service, April 1, 1994–March 31, 2000. http://www.tbs-set.gc.ca/pubs_pol/hrpubs/pse-fpe/es-se99-00-1_e.html.

to be appointed to the position of the top public servant—the Clerk of the Privy Council—was Jocelyn Bourgon, who served in that role from 1994 to 1999, and recently as many as 11 of 31 deputy ministers were women.[38] Overall, "the percentage of female public servants who work in the Executive, Scientific and Professional, or Administrative and Foreign Service categories has been rising since the 1980s. Today these categories account for more than half of the women working in the federal Public Service." (See Figure 9.6) Moreover, "Women hold a proportionally smaller number of administrative support jobs than they used to, partly because each year an average of about 2.5 per cent of the women in such positions are appointed to positions in the Scientific and Professional or Administrative and Foreign Service categories."[39]

However, one recent study concluded that a more focused assessment of these developments reveals some lingering problems.[40] For instance, there is a significant difference between the genders in the percentages of employees in term and casual positions, with male employees constituting less than 15 percent of this group, compared with close to 22 percent of female employees. While the overall number of women in the executive category has increased, most are concentrated in the lower reaches of that category. At the lowest executive level, women constitute 27 percent of the total, whereas at the highest executive level, they constitute only 11.7 percent. However, a spate of retirements means that up to 70 percent of the executive category could retire by 2005. Since most (about 87 percent) are men, this potentially opens the doors for women in senior management positions. Furthermore, more men than women overall are leaving the public service. Indeed, the number of men who left the federal Public Service was 63 percent higher than the number of women between 1995 and 2000, a trend that is expected to grow in the short term. As the Treasury Board points out, "as at March 31, 2000, 5.6 per cent of male public servants were eligible for immediate retirement with no actuarial penalty, compared with 2.0 per cent of female public servants. At the same time, more women than men are being recruited into indeterminate positions in the federal Public Service. Over the past five years, 18 per cent more women than men have been hired into indeterminate positions, and over the past fiscal year the figure was 35 per cent."[41] However, under conditions of downsizing and budget cutbacks, most federal departments have actually reduced external recruitment and demand for management trainees. Moreover, downsizing means more work for fewer people. Since women are disproportionately responsible for "home work" and child-rearing, they are at a distinct disadvantage in a work climate where expectations are that ever more time will be spent at the office.[42]

In any event, attitudes toward women working in the public service have been slow to change. Hiring, promotion, sick leave and handling of absenteeism have all been implemented differently for women than for men. Consider that until 1955, there was a prohibition against married women being employed in the public service! This reflected the view that men were the natural breadwinners and that women belonged in the home. Prior to 1969 it was permissible for hiring requests going to the Public Service Commission to specify either male or female, and, even more recently, it was considered normal to ask female employees about their plans to marry and have children, as part of any assessment of their qualifications! Camilla Stivers, a professor of public administration, argues that both the study and the practice of pubic administration are structurally male. She claims that the "images of expertise, leadership, and virtue that mark defences of administrative power contain dilemmas of gender. They not only have masculine features, but help to keep in place or bestow political and economic privilege on the bearers of culturally masculine qualities at the expense of those who display culturally feminine ones."[43]

But it is further argued that differences between the way men and women relate to their work environment mean that traditional "male" approaches are still overused in the public service. In particular, fostering a "competitive" management style reflects a male way of thinking. As Martha Hynna, a management consultant and former senior public service mandarin, explains, "[T]he contrasting 'integrative' style of management, which values team-building, participation, responsiveness, and the ability to integrate various points of view, more closely reflects the way in which many women have been socialized and behave in a work environment..." She further suggests that "there are important differences in the way men and women communicate. These differences can lead to misinterpretation and misunderstanding, and, in a culture where 'toughness' is valued, this can sometimes result in men underestimating the competence and effectiveness of women."[44]

But while the Public Service Commission lauds the goal of developing a truly representative workforce, it admits to falling short of that goal in relation not only to women, but also to Aboriginals, persons with disabilities and members of visible minorities. Table 9.2 shows the number, percentage and type of appointments by employment equity designated groups for 2000–2001. Aboriginals (including status and non-status Indians, Metis and Inuit) suffer from an appalling number of barriers to representation in the public service. Isolated culturally, they lack role models in the upper reaches of the bureaucracy. Poor educational opportunities make entry to and advancement in the public service prohibitively difficult.

TABLE 9.2   Appointment Type and Employment Equity Designated Groups

Number and percentage of appointments by appointment type and employment equity designated group April 1, 2000 to March 31, 2001

Employment equity designated groups	Appointments to the Public Service			Appointments within the Public Service: Type of Appointment									Total	
				Promotions			Lateral movements			Action appointments (a)				
	No.	%	External availability (b) %	No.	%	Internal availability %	No.	%	Internal availability %	No.	%	Internal availability %	No.	%
Women	9,056	58.1	50.8	12,321	59.0	58.2	8,949	62.0	59.0	7,223	61.7	60.2	37,549	60.0
Members of visible minorities	1,290	8.3	7.0	1,356	6.5	6.5	1,059	7.3	6.2	664	5.7	5.9	4,369	7.0
Persons with disabilities	485	3.1	5.4	983	4.7	5.6	642	4.5	5.3	518	4.4	5.8	2,628	4.2
Aboriginal peoples	722	4.6	2.2	786	3.8	3.8	646	4.5	3.9	438	3.7	3.8	2,592	4.1
Total (c)	15,589	100.0		20,883	100.0		14,423	100.0		11,701	100.0		62,596	100.0

(a) Excludes acting appointments of four months or less.

(b) Availability estimates are based on Statistics Canada Labour Market Availability data adjusted to reflect the positions staffed during the fiscal year *within* the Public Service. As a consequence, these numbers will not match those published elsewhere by Treasury Board Secretariat (TBS) which are adjusted to reflect the total population in the Public Service as of the end of the fiscal year.

(c) The counts for employment equity designated groups exclude specified period appointments of less than three months and appointments *to* and *within* separate employers as TBS does not collect self-identification information on these populations. The sum of employment equity designated groups does not equal the total as a person may be in more than one group and men are included in the total. Consequently, the totals do not match other tables.

Source: Canada. Public Service Commission of Canada. *Annual Report 2000–2* (Ottawa: Public Service Commission of Canada, 2001).

Moreover, the traditional emphasis in the public service on formal educational qualifications over life experience has discriminated against Aboriginals. Some Aboriginals do not recognize Ottawa as their legitimate government, which dissuades them from entering the federal public service. To overcome these barriers, the federal government has instituted programs and strategies used earlier in its history to promote French-Canadians and women, including aggressive recruitment campaigns and training assistance. But there is still a long way to go. The same is true of the representativeness of visible minorities and the disabled. They experience several of the same types of barriers, both inside the public service and in the broader society.

The initiation of the 1995 *Employment Equity Act* and other progressive changes to the public service have brought a variety of challenges, including that of "managing diversity."[45] For example, there is the difficulty of promoting changes in organizational values and ensuring that managers are sensitive to cultural and other differences. In addition, there is the view that many equity initiatives constitute reverse discrimination, and therefore ought to be scrapped. Such was the position of the Harris government in Ontario, for instance, which campaigned in the 1995 Ontario election on a promise to get rid of so-called "quota laws" that promoted disadvantaged groups within the Ontario bureaucracy.[46]

Moreover, in times of fiscal conservatism, the view is put forward that equity is not "affordable." For instance, consider the issue of **pay equity**, which involves determining equal pay for work of equal value. In the spring of 1998, the federal government was ordered by the Canadian Human Rights Commission Tribunal to pay public servants "equal pay for work of equal value." The ruling required the government to provide back pay to some 200 000 (mostly female) public servants who were determined to have been underpaid in comparison to those in male-dominated jobs. The controversial ruling is expected to cost the federal government about $4 billion, and is under appeal. But it signals the complexity of issues that surround remuneration and fairness in the public service (see Box 9-5). As various such court cases wind their way through the judicial system, greater clarity will be added to the murky question of representativeness and equity.

Constitutional and administrative law heavily influence the equity regime in Canada. For instance, the provinces and federal government have enacted human rights codes, the first of which was created by the CCF government of Saskatchewan more than 40 years ago. These codes generally prohibit discrimination in employment against women, visible minorities and other designated groups. Moreover, section 15 of the 1982 *Charter of Rights and Freedoms* guarantees "equal protection and equal benefit of the law without discrimination," but importantly, it goes on to suggest that this guarantee "does not preclude any law, program or activity that has as its object the amelioration of conditions of disadvantaged individuals or groups, including those that are disadvantaged because of race, national or ethnic origin, colour, religion, sex, age or mental or physical disability." In addition, the *Canadian Human Rights Act,* passed in 1977, established the Canadian Human Rights Commission to investigate complaints about discrimination by federal departments, Crown corporations, and business under federal jurisdiction. A variety of other federal and provincial legislation reinforces the equity regime.

Box 9-5

Representativeness and Fairness in the Public Service

The issue of pay equity is an important aspect of contemporary public administration, involving value judgments, administrative law, the application of scientific reason and rationality to policy-making, politics, gender issues, fairness, administration of the public's money, labour-management relations and a cornucopia of other disputatious concerns. The *Globe and Mail* summarized the key issue of pay equity this way:

The pay-equity debate breaks down into a squabble over how the wage gap gets calculated. It is a complex statistical question, made more so because two judicial bodies—the Canadian Human Rights Tribunal and the Federal Court—have recently produced opposite interpretations of equal pay for work of equal value....

What everyone agrees on: In the 1980s, 3200 public servants working in jobs defined as being dominated by either men or women were asked to complete a 27-page questionnaire. The questionnaire asked them to describe their work broken into four parts: the skills they needed, their responsibility, their working conditions and how much effort their jobs required.

The questionnaires were scrutinized by their supervisors, a special team in the Treasury Board, and, finally, by a job-evaluation committee of union and Treasury Board officials. Based on the questionnaires, the job committee ranked the four components of each job on a scale of 1 to 10, assigned a specific number of points to each ranking and then added the points. This standardized system is not limited to pay-equity cases; employers have been using points for decades to create fair wages scales.

For example: A typist in the public service ended up with just about the same ranking as a deckhand, although for different reasons. The deckhand scored high for working conditions, but needs fewer skills to complete the job. The typist enjoys a better working environment but earned more points in the skills category. Despite similar scores, the typist and the deckhand do not earn the same wage. In 1989, according to figures supplied by the Human Rights Commission, the deckhand received an annual salary of $23 843—close to $5000 more than the typist.

Source: "The Fight Over Formulas," *Globe and Mail*, (Friday, August 28, 1998): A4.

In the meantime, the Public Service Commission, the Treasury Board, the Human Rights Commission and Statistics Canada have been conducting analyses of the public service and broader Canadian workforce to assist the public service in becoming more representative. The Public Service Commission and the Treasury Board have developed an Employment Systems Review Guide to help departments and agencies of the public service identify systemic barriers to employment for

TABLE 9.3   Representation of Visible Minorities in the Federal Public Service (1991–99)

	Non-visible minorities	Visible minorities	Visible minority representation
1991	230719	9815	4.1%
1992	232158	10332	4.3%
1993	229729	10630	4.4%
1994	225023	10613	4.5%
1995	216615	10507	4.6%
1996	197956	9979	4.8%
1997	183545	9525	4.9%
1998	176104	10809	5.8%
1999	168292	10586	5.9%

Source: Population files of the PSC, as of March 31, 1999, and TBS employment equity data base.

Douglas Booker, Natalie Dole, Stan Lee, Kathy Malizia, Daniel O'Connor and Rhonda Nause, *Demographic Study of the Visible Minority Community in the Federal Public Service.* (Ottawa: Public Service Commission of Canada, February 2000): 6. http://www.pse-cfp.gc.ca/research/merit/merit practices e.htm

the four designated employment equity groups, and determine what measures are needed to remove those barriers.

Recent studies reveal that external recruitment of visible minorities has not been sufficient to overcome the lack of representativeness of the public service (Table 9.3). Furthermore, at the current rates of recruitment, this situation will still prevail by 2023. "Achieving a more representative public service (using the 1996 census as the benchmark) by 2005 would require that 1 in every 5 new recruits to the public service be a visible minority," according to the Public Service Commission. "The magnitude of this task speaks to the need for increased corporate efforts and policy initiatives to build a more representative public service."[47]

Unionization of the Public Service

The struggle by Canadian public servants to unionize was a long and arduous one. Prior to 1872, trade unions were illegal in Canada. After that, public service unionization was put off by the convenient fiction that the rights of government workers could be restricted because of the principle of the supremacy of Parliament. Even when federal civil servants finally won the right to collective bargaining in 1967, the government imposed restrictions on their rights well beyond those imposed on private sector workers. "Vital issues, including pensions, job classifications, technological change, staffing, and use of part-time or casual labour, were wholly or partly excluded from the scope of bargaining," according to political economists Leo Panitch and Donald Swartz. "Serious consideration was given to denying federal workers the right to strike as well, but in the end, the right to strike was granted, largely because the postal employees, particularly in British Columbia and Quebec, waged a number of what, in effect, were recognition strikes in the mid-1960s."[48]

As noted above, about one in four members of the labour force in Canada works in the public sector. But public sector employees make up slightly more than half of all union members, and the three largest unions in Canada are public sector unions. They represent a new political dynamic that has emerged in the labour movement in Canada over the past 30 years, for a couple of reasons. First, because of their relative "youth," public sector unions are not steeped in the history of labour militancy that characterizes many private sector unions. Public sector workers tend to be "white collar" rather than "blue collar," and therefore do not necessarily feel an affinity or solidarity with their brothers and sisters in the private sector. In addition, the massive growth of public sector unions in the 1960s and 1970s added a new "nationalist" dimension to the union movement in Canada. Prior to the rise of public sector unions, the majority of union members belonged to so-called "international unions"—a euphemism for U.S. unions. Today, that situation has reversed itself, with prominent private sector unions—such as the former United Auto Workers, now the Canadian Auto Workers—breaking away from their U.S. cousins. As a result, there is a more nationalist flavour to the union movement in this country, which is traceable in large measure to the growth of national public sector unions.[49]

The unique nature of public sector bargaining gives rise to a number of issues absent in the private sector. As one observer states, in the public service

collective bargaining, which is generally an exercise in economic power, becomes an exercise in political power. Public opinion and the prospects of re-election substitute for profit maximization in the employer's calculus. A related issue is whether government policy should be decided at the bargaining table, instead of the appropriate legislature. Is bilingual air-traffic control a legitimate employee relations issue, or does Parliament reign supreme?[50]

These and other issues make the issue of **collective bargaining** controversial from a number of perspectives.

Prior to the era of collective bargaining, the federal government established a National Joint Council of the Public Service made up of representatives of staff associations and managers representing the government.[51] This was intended as a mechanism through which employees could be consulted regarding matters such as conditions of employment. It proved unsatisfactory, however, and by the late 1950s and 1960s, public servants were increasingly agitating for full unionization. In 1961, a new *Civil Service Act* gave employees the right to be consulted on pay determination, a major point of contention that was not covered under the National Joint Council. But even this advance proved difficult to realize, due to the complex way in which consultations were structured. Still, the 1961 reforms meant that henceforth public servants would be paid as a matter of right rather than as a matter of privilege of the Crown, as was previously the case.

The three main political parties campaigned in the 1963 election with a promise, if elected, to introduce collective bargaining in the public service. After the election, the Liberal minority government of Lester Pearson established a Preparatory Committee on Collective Bargaining in the Public Service, which reported in 1965. Legislation followed in 1967, when the *Public Service Staff Relations Act* was passed, giving employee organizations the right to negotiate directly with the government as trade unions, with the right to compulsory arbitration conciliation, and the right to strike. The Act is administered by the Public Service Staff Relations Board, which is an arm's-length body.

In fact, the legal framework for unionization of the public service is found in three statutes. First, the *Financial Administration Act* was amended to make the Treasury Board the "employer" for purposes of collective bargaining. As well, it assumed responsibilities for staff requirements, pay, job classification and training policy from the Civil Service Commission. Second, the *Public Service Employment Act* was passed, replacing the Civil Service Commission with the Public Service Commission. It became the central staffing agency of the government. Finally, the *Public Service Staff Relations Act* was passed to provide the "machinery" of collective bargaining. For example, the authority to certify bargaining units and administer dispute resolution was handed to the Public Service Staff Relations Board.

Despite these advances for public sector workers, certain public servants are denied the right to strike, since they are considered to provide "essential services" for public safety or security. Moreover, there are restrictions on what the government deems "negotiable." Job security, classification and other issues have been excluded in the past from the set of issues that public servants can bargain over with their employer. As well, several classes of employees are specifically excluded from the legislation governing collective bargaining. Still, the introduction of collective bargaining in the federal public service in 1967 completely altered relations between the government, as employer, and its employees.[52]

Public Servants and Politics

The political rights of public servants are also protected by the Public Service Commission, as is the responsibility to see to it that public servants can speak the truth to those in power without fear of reprisal. The fact that Cabinet ministers cannot recruit, assign, transfer, promote or make any other decision regarding the career of a public servant serves to maintain the integrity and nonpartisanship of the public service and keep it free from undue political interference, by freeing public servants from feeling beholden to the politicians.

Ultimately, politicians must be able to trust that their public servants will not engage in partisan politics, but will serve them loyally. PS2000 expressed the point this way:

[T]here is nothing more important to the effectiveness of the Public Service than that Ministers of successive Governments have confidence in the loyalty of Public Servants. Those who advise them... must be without partisan associations.... These conditions form

the basis of careers in the Public Service, enabling Public Servants to carry out their essential duty of serving successive Governments of different political parties without any legitimate questioning of their loyalty and commitment.[53]

This reality stands in marked contrast to the early history of public service appointments, most of which were actually patronage rewards for political service. And indeed, when reforms to the Civil Service were enacted in 1918, serious penalties were imposed on any public servant engaging in political activities. The zeal with which reformers sought to eradicate patronage meant that, though they could still vote, public servants suffered the curtailment of virtually all other political rights that we, as citizens, take for granted.

This continued until 1967, when the *Public Service Employment Act* loosened the constraints on the political rights of public servants. It allowed public servants below the rank of deputy minister to run for election themselves under certain circumstances, and to attend political meetings and donate funds to candidates or parties. They still could not work for or against a candidate or political party. In 1991, the Supreme Court struck down the sections of the *Public Service Employment Act* containing these remaining prohibitions, on the grounds that they violated the political rights of public servants. As lawyer Michael Mandel reports, "[T]he Supreme Court held that the limits on federal civil servants' partisan political activity were too broad in that they included every employee without any distinctions for type of job and type of political activity."[54] As a result, today's federal public servants, with the exception of deputy ministers, are free to participate fully in the political system. Current *Public Service Employment Act* regulations state that public servants who seek to be nominated as candidates and to stand for election in the House of Commons, or any other legislature in Canada, must apply to the Commission for a leave of absence without pay. In the 1997 federal election, the Public Service Commission granted 11 such requests, and in the 2000 election, four such requests were granted.[55]

There are some particular principles that set the parameters of the relationship between the public service and the political system.[56] Prominent among them is the doctrine of **political neutrality**.[57] In short, this convention states that public servants must consistently act in ways that assure their political impartiality. They are not members of the governing party, nor are they party activists who happen to be working within the government. Instead, they occupy a special position of trust through which they are expected to serve the government of the day faithfully, no matter which party is in power.

The various issues surrounding the relationship between the public service and politics can be summed up by the doctrine of political neutrality, which is made up of several elements. First is the politics-administration dichotomy, which, you will recall, states that policy and administration are separate activities. Politicians make policy; public servants administer it. Second is the merit principle. In the context of the relationship between the public service and politics, this implies that positions are awarded not on the basis of political affiliation or membership in a political party, but on the skills and qualifications of the applicant for a position. Third, and related, is the notion that public servants do not engage in partisan political activities. To do so would compromise their positions as neutral advisors to the government. Fourth, although public servants have their own personal views of the quality of the government's policy and administration, it is not their place to express those views publicly. Fifth, in return for honest and straightforward advice to their political masters, the anonymity of public servants is guaranteed. Thus, politicians accept public responsibility for the government's action or inaction; they take the blame when things go wrong, and the praise when things go right. The public servant toils anonymously in the background. Finally, public servants enjoy tenure in their positions as long as they perform their jobs satisfactorily. In return, they are expected to offer loyal service and to execute the decisions of the government irrespective of their personal opinions.

Overall, striking a balance between the need for political neutrality and the political rights of public servants is a challenging task. But recent developments, both federally and provincially, suggest a trend toward broadening the political rights of public servants. The extent to which this trend may compromise the quality of advice and service provided to politicians is yet to be seen. But early indications are that erring on the side of democratic freedom has not diminished the professionalism or effectiveness of the public service.

Human Resources Management

Here we examine the issue of public service personnel from the perspective of management. Like financial management (discussed in Chapter 10), human resources management is consumed with debates. For instance, at times, public service managers may find that the merit principle clashes with other values important to Canadians, such as representativeness.[58] If society decides that it is important to have a public service that is representative of the society that it serves, then remedial action may have to be taken that conflicts directly with the merit principle. For instance, as we noted, it has been deemed desirable that the federal public service in Canada reflect the bilingual nature of the nation. Thus, attempts have been made to increase the proportion of French-Canadians in the bureaucracy, such that they represent about 28 percent of the personnel in the federal civil service. This number approximately reflects their proportion of the total population of the country. And efforts have been made to address the question of whether others in Canadian society should be targeted for affirmative action and employment equity programs, so that the public service will accurately reflect those groups as well. Such policies cause disputes, both inside government and out in the broader society, with which public service managers must wrestle. One side argues that these measures are needed to make the public service truly representative; the other claims that the measures are reverse discrimination and violate the merit principle.

 The debate also revolves around the extent to which the values of efficiency conflict with those of representativeness. Public sector managers are constantly under pressure to produce results in the most efficient and economical manner possible. But when staffing decisions routinely take up to 90 days because of the sensitivity of issues such as representativeness, and owing to regulations requiring detailed candidate searches with reporting to numerous departmental and central agency superiors, these values are impeded. From a purely administrative point of view, then, balancing merit, representativeness and fairness is a challenging objective. Furthermore there is the question of whether "members of a bureaucracy chosen from various relevant groups will be likely to act as agents or spokesmen [sic] for their groups and group interests."[59] The public sector manager must be conscious of all these potential value conflicts.

Another issue that infuses human resources management in the public sector is collective bargaining, as noted above. The fact that the public sector has become the largest and fastest-growing sector of the economy to unionize has raised a host of issues for managers, not the least of which is the addition of another level of bureaucracy to the process of hiring and firing. More recently, restructuring, cutbacks, wage freezes, layoffs, mass firings, contracting out and privatization have cast large shadows over the issue of human resources management in the unionized setting of the public sector. And the issues of retention and recruitment have come to the fore as well. To sort out the role of the public sector manager in human resources management, it is useful for us to present an overview of some of the major developments in this area. Necessarily, this will take us through a reconsideration of merit and patronage, representativeness, and several of the other issues raised in connection with human resource management in other chapters. The place to begin this overview, though, is with a brief look at the origins of human resource management policy.

The patterns of public service human resources management were established in colonial times, when public servants received their posts for life. This generated stability for the governance of the colony, and laid the basis for a "professional" career-based civil service, despite the presence of patronage politics. For instance,

[I]mmediately prior to Confederation, out of nine deputy departmental heads in the Province of Canada, six had risen through the ranks by promotion, four had over twenty years' experience, and the most senior among them, the clerk of the Executive Council, could claim well over forty years' public service employment! The pattern was continued after 1867. At the time of the First World War, for example, the two dozen deputies at the federal level had an average of twenty years' experience.[60]

Thus, while we generally assume that the major "human resources policy" of the early days of this country was essentially the widespread use of patronage to reward friends of the government, in fact a "meritocracy" of sorts was evident quite early on at the upper reaches of the civil service.

However, citizen outrage over the pettiness of patronage lower down in the bureaucracy, coupled with the example of merit systems introduced in Great Britain and the United States, prompted the 1918 civil service reforms (described earlier). Indeed, between 1867 and 1918, five federal royal commissions devoted at least part of their investigations to the evils of patronage. The reforms of 1918 were directly predicated, strangely enough, on a U.S. model, not particularly suited to Canadian conditions. Political pressures surrounding the government of Sir Robert Borden during the First World War forced the prime minister to reform the civil service to end the squabbling between Conservatives and Liberals over patronage appointments. A U.S. consulting firm was called in to make recommendations for reform. It devised a blueprint for a complex, rigid, inflexible, and highly centralized human resources system designed for the conditions of corrupt machine politics in U.S. cities. This was Taylor's scientific management with a vengeance.

The reforms of 1918 influenced human resources management and the shape of the public service for the next 50 years. According to one observer, the 1918 reforms contained

a mechanistic view of the world of work, of clear-cut and precise specialization of labour, one that assumed considerable organizational stability—so much stability that each step in the process of classifying and filling jobs should be done thoroughly even if it took many months, because each appointment was expected to last for years and years. This resulted in heavy, time-consuming processes and not a great deal of concern for human resource management. Employees were, in essence, seen as cogs in a large machine.[61]

The reforms of 1918 were taken to heart by a generation of public service managers. They desired a professional, technically skilled and competent career public service, and actually constructed one. But it was one firmly rooted in the Tayloristic model. Thus, the pattern of human resource management was set and reinforced by these developments.

Several senior civil servants subsequently played a vital role in shaping the managerial class and human resources policy and outlook of the Canadian public service. A new intellectual community, rooted mainly in the universities (especially Queen's University in Kingston), began to emerge; it turned its attention to how the state could be used to better manage the new issues of rapid industrialization and urbanization that were becoming prominent government concerns. Specifically, a cadre of individuals trained in the social sciences developed the conceit that they could play a role in making Canada a better country through improved human resource management and, ultimately—with a professional, skilled public service in place—in public policy-making.[62] Individuals such as O.D. Skelton and Clifford Clark left Queen's University in the 1920s and 1930s to become deputy ministers (of External Affairs and Finance, respectively), attracting a new generation of like-minded university graduates, many of them economists, to form what historian J.L. Granatstein termed a new "mandarin" class of influential senior public managers.[63] Through the 1940s and 1950s, this small group played an influential role in professionalizing the public service.

Recruitment to the ranks of the upper reaches of the public service is noteworthy because of the way it reinforced the position and power of the mandarins. For instance, over the past 50 years, nearly 95 percent of the deputy ministers (DMs) have come up from the ranks of assistant or associate deputy ministers. And even though the authority to appoint DMs is widely regarded as one of the more potent aspects of prime ministerial power, in fact, DMs are rarely recruited directly by the prime minister. Instead, most are recommended and approved on the advice of the secretary to the Cabinet (who, you will recall, is the senior-most civil servant). This has led one observer to conclude that "the senior public service in Canada, then, has developed a pattern of internal recruitment, professionalism and political neutrality, although some deputy ministers in later life have become Cabinet ministers or senators."[64] But it also meant that the senior levels of the public service were remarkably homogeneous, a fact remarked upon in a ground-breaking study by sociologist John Porter. He noted in his 1965 book *The Vertical Mosaic* that the senior bureaucrats in the public service were part of an intercon-nected political, economic, social and intellectual elite, which shared certain char-acteristics: they tended to be white, Anglo-Saxon, Christian males who were well educated, moved in the same social circles, and acted as "gatekeepers" to keep out others who were not like themselves.[65] But perhaps more to the point, this group of managers seemed to regard human resources management as almost in-cidental to their work. They were greatly concerned with the broad picture of policy-making, and with macro-economic management of the country and related issues. But they paid little concrete attention to the day-to-day issues of employee satisfaction, morale, working conditions, or even the performance and compe-tence of their underlings. Indeed, it is not an exaggeration to suggest that despite its huge significance, human resources management has been a central concern of government for only the past 20 years.

However, the rapid changes brought about by immigration, as well as the changing role of women in Canadian society, made anachronistic this "clubby" public service elite. Gradually, new attitudes crept into the thinking of public ser-vice managers, not the least of which was the notion that the entire public ser-vice, and most particularly its senior levels, should bear some resemblance to the society it serves. Hence, the more recent era of wholesale reform of human re-source policies, such as affirmative action, employment equity, pay equity, and so on. Ironically, when some attention was finally paid to this area, it occurred in an era of financial constraint—such that the much-needed reforms were severely im-peded by fiscal realities.

The post-war years saw a massive expansion of government at all levels in re-sponse to the growth of society and technological change, but a lag in renewing human resources policy. Departmental expansion meant that more employees were brought into the public service, but more important, qualitative changes to human resources policy were needed. Moreover, a variety of new professional, technical and managerial careers were made a part of the public service. For example, the wide-spread introduction of computerized systems meant that positions for technically skilled computer technicians had to be created and categorized, and their pay lev-els and job descriptions had to be formalized. Given the rigid and bureaucratic na-ture of human resources management in this era, this was no easy task. It also had to be done for the countless other new positions created to keep pace with the broader changes in Canadian society. The depths of the difficulties in this era of rapid expansion were encapsulated in the Glassco Commission of 1961, and were expressed in the need to make the management of human resources (and indeed of government generally) more efficient, economical and effective.[66]

Moreover, as the 1960s and 1970s unfolded, the issues of language training and bilingualism, unionization, affirmative action and departmental reorganization converged. By this time, the literature of business management was replete with theories derived from the human relations school of organizational theory (see chapters 2 and 3). New management techniques were washing over the public service, and a new public service ethos was emerging that saw the public servant as an agent of change in the community, and not just a passive servant of the people, awaiting policy directives and instructions from Parliament. Participatory democracy became the watchword of the day (although in practice it meant "you participate, we'll decide"), and the rapidly changing public sector scrambled to keep up.

Renewal of the public service became a pressing concern, and the strong expectation developed that new recruits to the upper levels of the bureaucracy would produce a more representative public service. Contemporary demographic patterns, and the fact that so many senior managers have left the public service in recent years (as noted below), means that recruitment from outside the ranks of the public service is becoming more commonplace. And since the broader society from which those recruits will come is changing, it is axiomatic that the public service will continue to evolve into an institution far removed from the days of the old boys' network.

Two political scientists have produced a profile of the career patterns of deputy ministers. Bourgault and Carroll note that close to 90 percent of federal government DMs have spent their entire careers in the federal public service, serving first as associate or assistant deputy ministers; over a 23-year career, they will have served, on average, in five departments. As well, about 60 percent of DMs will have spent at least some of their career in central agencies, which, it is argued, allows them to absorb the "culture of the mandarinate." Furthermore,

The age and years of experience that deputy ministers had at appointment steadily decreased over the period since 1977 but seems to have stabilized at age 47 and 18 years of experience around 1988. In the eight years that they will serve as deputy ministers, on average, they will usually have about three appointments. Increasingly, they are retiring at an earlier age, leaving at 55 years (33 percent) and going into another career in business or public interest consulting. The ranks are also well educated, with all holding undergraduate degrees, and most having some postgraduate training. The field of education has increasingly been law, economics or business rather than science or engineering....

The first female deputy minister was appointed in 1975. But by 1988 12 percent were female, and by 1996 31 percent were women, including the head of the public service. Over the same period the number of Francophones has hovered around 30 percent, exceeding the percentage of Francophones within the overall population. All deputy ministers are fluent in both official languages (English and French).[67]

The "culture of the mandarinate" referred to above is an interesting phenomenon. Presumably, a DM might be focused on seeing that his ministry gets every advantage in terms of human and financial resources, as well as favourable policy decisions by Cabinet, even at the expense of other ministries. However, the shared culture among the senior managers of the civil service fosters a good deal of cooperation aimed at achieving better overall government. This is partly the result of recruitment patterns, the selection of individuals who share values, and crisscrossing career paths. In addition, DMs work closely with each other in strategy sessions, seminars, committees and so on, all of which also helps to encourage camaraderie.[68]

Still, there are severe stresses and strains produced by various issues intersecting with one another. As a result, reevaluation of human resources management has been a constant feature of the public service. Merit is under review, and representativeness is an ongoing concern. Organizational confusion between the Treasury Board and the Public Service Commission as to who should be doing what continuously challenges the regime of accountability. One response to these challenges was the call for the creation of an institution "to inculcate corporate values and prepare senior managers to work in rapidly changing internal and external environments. The idea of a 'university' for senior managers had been in circulation for over 20 years and, in 1988, the Canadian Centre for Management Development (CCMD) was established.... its mandate included commissioning research from public servants and from academics on public management issues, and providing a forum for the exchange of ideas."[69]

Given the organization and structure of management where human resources is concerned, it is no wonder that specialized training, such as that being developed by the CCMD, is needed. Consider, for instance, the complexity of the organizational duties and roles of the main bodies responsible for human resources management. As currently constituted, the Treasury Board, as the "manager" in employer-employee relations, has the following powers: generally, a) it develops and interprets policies, programs and procedures related to the organization of the public service; b) it is responsible for setting positions, compensation, training and development, official languages, discipline, working conditions, classification of employees, employee benefits, and terms and conditions of employment; and c) it represents the government in collective bargaining.

The Public Service Commission is authorized within the guidelines established by the Treasury Board to recruit, select, promote, transfer, demote and fire public servants; it is also responsible for staff development and training, and language training. It hears appeals related to appointments or dismissals and investigates allegations of discrimination in public service employment practices. It also administers regulations for political activities by public servants. A good deal of the responsibilities held by the Public Service Commission are actually delegated to departments, which remain accountable to the Public Service Commission for the undertaking of these responsibilities. Besides the Treasury Board and the Public Service Commission, there is another administrative body involved in coordinating human resources management. This is the Public Service Staff Relations Board. This body certifies bargaining units, handles complaints of unfair practices, deals with procedural aspects of collective bargaining, and administers the *Public Service Staff Relations Act*.

At this point, it may be worth reflecting on the administrative complexity of the picture so far. Consider all the bodies to which you are accountable if you are a senior administrator in a department about to make a hiring decision.. You must ensure that you comply with the Treasury Board's guidelines and the Public Service Commission's regulations. You must answer to the Public Service Staff Relations Board. You must also act in accordance with the directives of your own superiors within the department, and with whatever rules they impose on the selection of the person for the job. You must be versed in the merit principle, but also be sensitive to the value of representativeness, and be aware of the latest government policies with regard to employment equity. But the list of bureaucratic and administrative responsibilities does not end here, since several other sectors of government have a stake in your hiring decision. These include the Human Rights Commission, whose provisions you must not violate, and the Privy Council Office, especially if the hiring is for a senior position. And even this is not a comprehensive list of the government bodies that could potentially be involved, at some level, in your decision. Moreover, you must determine what job classification to use, how your hire fits into the broad human resource planning goals of your department, what your staffing needs will be for the new position, whether the candidates have all had an equal chance to meet the selection criteria for the job (including language requirements), and so on. To say that the process is complex is an understatement.

Now imagine that you must make a firing decision. There is a widespread assumption that once a person has been hired in the public service, she is essentially "set" for life. This is inaccurate, as recent mass layoffs and firings at all levels of government amply demonstrate. Nonetheless, there is a complex procedure that must be followed before any public servant can be let go. Every employee is subject to a rigorous performance assessment on an annual basis that has an important bearing on pay, opportunities for training and upgrading, and promotion. A government-wide system of staff assessment is administered by management. The Performance Review and Appraisal Report, developed by the Treasury Board and the Public Service Commission, is used to rank an employee's performance on a five-point scale, from Outstanding to Unsatisfactory. It also assesses an employee's abilities, also on a five-point scale, for purposes of determining promotion, probation, transfer and other actions. As political scientist James Simeon reports, this process "provides a structured method for assessing their employees and assisting them in realizing their full potential. In fact, managers are assessed on how well they do staff performance reviews and appraisals."[70]

Simeon goes on to point out that disciplinary measures are another important aspect of human resources management. There are five measures used in the federal public service in relation to discipline. In ascending order of severity, these are as follows: oral reprimand, written reprimand, suspension, financial penalty, and discharge. Immediate supervisors may dispense the first two, but more serious offences and penalties are dealt with by senior managers. The deputy minister ultimately has the discretion to determine which penalty should be applied for various sorts of misconduct. These penalties are partly determined, though, by guidelines set through established precedents within the public service. In setting penalties, managers must not violate collective agreements. And employees have the right to appeal disciplinary measures and be represented in a hearing by legal counsel (see Chapter 6 on administrative law). Furthermore, there are prescribed steps that must be followed prior to taking disciplinary action, including giving the employee an opportunity to explain the circumstances surrounding their actions. "Determining an appropriate penalty for misconduct always requires good judgement," according to Simeon. "With respect to the federal government, its explicit policy is that the primary object of discipline is not punishment but to rehabilitate the employee, to make them a better and more productive worker. This is referred to as 'corrective discipline.'"[71] At the very least, all of this suggests that where human resources is concerned, management is far more difficult in the public sector than in the private.

Finally, managers in today's public service are increasingly consumed with the issues of retention and recruitment as part of a broader process of human resources modernization.[72] Recruitment is a concern due to the steady erosion in the public's faith in the public service, coupled with the denigration of public service careers from within. The institutions of government have been suffering for a long time now from a serious image problem in the public mind, and have been overseen by political masters whose own view is that the public service is an inefficient, slow, ponderous, expensive and ineffective machine. As a result, the idea of the "career public servant" has eroded. Where once it was commonplace to work toward a lifetime of service to the public, today there is a much higher rate of outward migration to the private sector, the not-for-profit sector, the voluntary sector and so on. Morale is low and downsizing is endemic.

As a result, public sector managers are faced with the task of reinvigorating the public service and making it into an "employer of choice" for prospective job-seekers. The challenge, according to professor of public administration Evert Lindquist, is to offer opportunities for a career that: is challenging; allows for knowledge-building; provides opportunities to work with people from diverse backgrounds; allows for learning from experienced staff; enables people to move from position to position to work in a variety of areas; permits creativity; makes a difference and has an impact on the community and public policy; is well compensated in a manner which is competitive with other sectors; and provides people with recognition for a job well done.[73]

The recruitment challenge is partly derived from the demographic reality noted above, namely that the public service is aging and is not being renewed.[74] Public service employers now face a "seller's market" when looking to hire, and must aggressively compete with other employers for a limited pool of talent. The trend toward short-term and temporary staffing in the 1990s exacerbated the problem of recruitment, too. As the Public Service Commission reports, "the number one reason for joining the Public Service was also the number one reason for wanting to leave. Employees drawn to the promise of work in their area of specialization would be difficult to retain without a long-term commitment to deliver on that promise."[75] Moreover, many of those who would traditionally seek a career in the public service—such as new graduates in public administration, political science and other disciplines—are choosing other career paths. Some of the new strategies used by public service recruiters to win these people back have included: aggressive on-campus recruiting at universities and colleges; emphasizing public sector strengths and learning opportunities to prospective employees; expanding beyond their usual recruitment sources (to, for example, electronic recruitment strategies); and developing selling points to make the idea of a career in the public service more appealing.[76]

Of course, once recruitment efforts are successful, retention becomes an issue. Skilled employees will continue to be in demand, there will be a high level of job mobility, and competitors (in both public and private sectors) will be recruiting aggressively. Knowledge workers are especially valued, as governments embrace technological innovations in the delivery of programs and services. Thus, governments will have to continue to innovate and flexibly respond to changing labour market conditions in order to fulfill the ongoing demand for the provision of public goods and services.

WHAT YOU HAVE LEARNED

Can the public service move forward in the area of human resources management under the current stresses and strains that it faces? Issues such as patronage versus merit, the growth of government, the return of war veterans and arrival of new university graduates, and bilingualism challenged the public service in the early years. Later, issues such as shrinking government, affirmative action, employment equity and pay equity, as well as the need to do more with less in an era hostile to the very institution of the public service, lowered morale and brought other new problems. Currently, retention, recruitment and succession planning are among the most significant challenges. In sum, the public service has had to change constantly. What, then, are the expectations that Canadians currently hold of their public service? According to the Public Service Commission,

Canadians want some things to change, but they wish that basic Public Service values be protected. The Public Service Commission plays a key role in addressing this requirement. Its role is to meet the dual challenge of preserving the values of merit-based, non-partisan and representative staffing that are the cornerstone of our staffing process, while helping create for managers and public servants the conditions for creativity and innovation that will need to be the hallmarks of the Public Service of the future.[77]

The extent to which the challenges of the current era have been met is a matter of some dispute. Certainly the Auditor-General is critical of the human resources reforms of the 1990s, calling human resource management "a major weakness" of government.[78] The next chapter focuses on the management of the public service, including fiscal management, to place the issues raised in Chapter 9 in a broader context.

ENDNOTES

1. See Reginald Whitaker, "Politicians and Bureaucrats in the Policy Process," in M.S. Whittington and G. Williams, eds. *Canadian Politics in the 1990s, Fourth Edition,* (Scarborough: Nelson, 1995): chapter 21.

2. Donald Brittain, *Paperland: The Bureaucrat Observed,* (Ottawa: National Film Board of Canada, 1979).

3. This number refers to all federal public service employees working in departments and agencies listed under Schedule 1, Part 1 of the Public Service Staff Relations Act. See Canada. Treasury Board of Canada Secretariat. *Employment Statistics for the Federal Public Service April 1, 1999–March 31, 2000.* Ottawa: Treasury Board Secretariat, 2000:2. http://www.tbs-sct.gc.ca/pubs_pol/hrpubs/pse-fpe/es-se99-00-1_e.html

4. Ralph Heintzman, "Introduction: Canada and Public Administration," in Jacques Bourgault, Maurice Demers and Cynthia Williams, eds. *Public Administration and Public Management: Experiences in Canada,* (Sainte-Foy, Quebec: Les Publications du Quebec, 1997).

5. Laurent Dobuzinskis, "Public Administration," in Michael Howlett and David Laycock, eds. *Puzzles of Power: An Introduction to Political Science, Second Edition,* (Toronto: Oxford University Press, 1998): 156. The following paragraphs are derived from Dobuzinskis's overview of the development of the public service.

6. See Garth Stevenson, *Unfulfilled Union: Canadian Federalism and National Unity, Third Edition,* (Toronto: Gage, 1989): 221–223.

7. See Nicole Morgan, *Implosion: An Analysis of the Growth of the Federal Public Service in Canada 1945–1985,* (Montreal: Institute for Research on Public Policy, 1986): xvi–xvii.

8. Morgan, *Implosion,* (1986): xvii.

9. Dobuzinskis, "Public Administration," (1998): 157.

10. See Gary Teeple, *Globalization and the Decline of Social Reform,* (Toronto: Garamond Press, 1995).

11. See Susan D. Phillips, "A More Democratic Canada...?" in Susan D. Phillips, ed. *How Canada Spends: A More Democratic Canada...? 1993–1994,* (Ottawa: Carleton University Press, 1993): 6–7.

12. Canada, Ministry of Finance, *Budget Speech by the Honourable Michael Wilson,* (Ottawa: Ministry of Finance, May 23, 1985).

13. Isabella Bakker, "The Size and Scope of Government: Robin Hood Sent Packing?" in Michael S. Whittington and Glen Williams, eds. *Canadian Politics in the 1990s, Third Edition,* (Scarborough: Nelson, 1990): 423–424.

14. Canada, Public Service Commission, "Change and Management in the Public Service. Talking Points for Mme. Jocelyne Bourgon, Clerk of the Privy Council and Secretary to the Cabinet to the Association of Professional Executives of the Public Service of Canada," (Ottawa: Public Service Commission of Canada, May 11, 1994): 3. Online www.pco-bcp.gc.ca/ClerkSP/Manageme.htm

15. See Trevor Bhupsingh and Peter Edwards, *Tracking the Role of the PSC in the Governance System of the Federal Public Service,* (Ottawa: Public Service Commission of Canada, April, 1997). http://www.psc-cfp.gc.ca/research/merit/role_psc_e.htm. See also Darryl Hirsch, *Merit Systems in Western Democracies: Current Problems and Selected Best Practices,* (Ottawa: Public Service Commission of Canada, (December, 1999): 16. http://www.psc-cfp.gc.ca/research/merit/merit_practices_e.htm

16. See David Zussman, "Managing the Federal Public Service as the Knot Tightens," in Katherine A. Graham, ed. *How Ottawa Spends 1990–1991: Tracking the Second Agenda,* (Ottawa: Carleton University Press, 1990): 247–275.

17. Canada, *The Public Service Commission,* (Ottawa, The Public Service Commission, 1998). Online www.psc-cfp.gc.ca/mission/pscrre2.htm

18. Canada, Privy Council Office, *Eighth Annual Report to the Prime Minister on the Public Service of Canada,* (Ottawa: Privy Council Office, 2001): 3.

19. Canada, Privy Council Office, *Eighth Annual Report to the Prime Minister on the Public Service of Canada,* (Ottawa: Privy Council Office, 2001): 3.

20. Canada, Public Service Commission, "Change and Management in the Public Service. Talking Points for Mme. Jocelyne Bourgon, Clerk of the Privy Council and Secretary to the Cabinet to the Association of Professional Executives of the Public Service of Canada," (Ottawa: Public Service Commission of Canada, May 11, 1994): 2. Online www.pco-bcp.gc.ca/ClerkSP/Manageme.htm

21. United Nations, *Human Development Report 1996,* (New York: Oxford University Press, 1996): 135.

22. Canada. *Speech From the Throne to Open the First Session of the 37th Parliament of Canada.* Ottawa: January 30, 2001. http://www.sft-ddt.gc.ca/sftddt_e.htm

23. Heintzman, "Introduction," (1997): 5.

24. Canada. Treasury Board of Canada Secretariat. *Employment Statistics for the Federal Public Service April 1, 1999–March 31, 2000.* Ottawa: Treasury Board Secretariat, 2000: 2. http://www.tbs-sct.gc.ca/pubs_pol/hrpubs/pse-fpe/es-se99-00-1_e.htmlX Canada. Treasury Board Secretariat. *Classification System.* http://www.tbs-sct.gc.ca/Pubs_pol/hrpubs/TBM_111/CHAPT1_e.html

25. Canada. Treasury Board of Canada Secretariat. *Employment Statistics for the Federal Public Service April 1, 1999–March 31, 2000.* Ottawa: Treasury Board Secretariat, 2000: 1. http://www.tbs-sct.gc.ca/pubs_pol/hrpubs/pse-fpe/es-se99-00-1_e.html

26. Canada. Treasury Board of Canada Secretariat. *Employment Statistics for the Federal Public Service April 1, 1999–March 31, 2000.* Ottawa: Treasury Board Secretariat, 2000: 1. http://www.tbs-sct.gc.ca/pubs_pol/hrpubs/pse-fpe/es-se99-00-1_e.html

27. Canada. Treasury Board of Canada Secretariat. *Employment Statistics for the Federal Public Service April 1, 1999–March 31, 2000.* Ottawa: Treasury Board Secretariat, 2000: 5. http://www.tbs-sct.gc.ca/pubs_pol/hrpubs/pse-fpe/es-se99-00-1_e.html

28. Canada. Treasury Board of Canada Secretariat. *Employment Statistics for the Federal Public Service April 1, 1999–March 31, 2000.* Ottawa: Treasury Board Secretariat, 2000: 5. http://www.tbs-sct.gc.ca/pubs_pol/hrpubs/pse-fpe/es-se99-00-1_e.html

29. For a current listing of career opportunities in the public service see the Public Service of Canada website, www.psc-cfp.gc.ca/centres/empl_e.htm

30. For an early consideration of these issues, see V. Seymour Wilson and Willard A. Mullins, "Representative Bureaucracy: Linguistic/Ethnic Aspects in Canadian Public Policy," *Canadian Public Administration,* 21 (Winter, 1978): 513–538.

31. J.E. Hodgetts, *et al. The Biography of an Institution: The Civil Service Commission of Canada 1908–1967,* (Montreal: McGill–Queen's University Press, 1972): 473.

32. Robert J. Jackson and Doreen Jackson, *Politics in Canada: Culture, Institutions, Behaviour and Public Policy, Fourth Edition,* (Scarborough: Prentice Hall, 1998): 354–355.

33. Canada, Royal Commission on Bilingualism and Biculturalism, *Report,* Five Volumes, (Ottawa: Queen's Printer, 1967–1970).

34. See Judge Rosalie Silberman Abella, *Equality in Employment: A Royal Commission Report,* (Ottawa: Supply and Services Canada, 1984): 7.

35. Canada, Public Service Commission, *Annual Report 1992,* (Ottawa: Supply and Services, 1993): 46.

36. Abella, *Equality in Employment,* (1984): 1.

37. Canada. Treasury Board of Canada Secretariat. *Employment Statistics for the Federal Public Service April 1, 1999–March 31, 2000.* Ottawa: Treasury Board Secretariat, 2000: 5. http://www.tbs-sct.gc.ca/pubs_pol/hrpubs/pse-fpe/es-se99-00-1_e.html

38. Martha Hynna, "Women in the Public Service—A Thirty-Year Perspective," *Canadian Public Administration,* 40, 4 (Winter, 1997): 619–620.

39. Canada. Treasury Board of Canada Secretariat. *Employment Statistics for the Federal Public Service April 1, 1999–March 31, 2000.* Ottawa: Treasury Board Secretariat, 2000: 5. http://www.tbs-sct.gc.ca/pubs_pol/hrpubs/pse-fpe/es-se99-00-1_e.html

40. See Susan D. Phillips, Brian R. Little and Laura A. Goodine, "Reconsidering Gender and Public Administration: Five Steps Beyond Conventional Research," *Canadian Public Administration,* 40, 4 (Winter, 1994): 576. See also Sandra Burt and Sonya Lynn Hardman, "The Case of the Disappearing Targets: The Liberals and Gender Equality," in Leslie A. Pal, ed. *How Ottawa Spends 2001–2002: Power in Transition,* (Toronto: Oxford University Press, 2001): 201–22.

41. Canada. Treasury Board of Canada Secretariat. *Employment Statistics for the Federal Public Service April 1, 1999–March 31, 2000.* Ottawa: Treasury Board Secretariat, 2000: 5. http://www.tbs-sct.gc.ca/pubs_pol/hrpubs/pse-fpe/es-se99-00-1_e.html

42. For a consideration of these themes in the context of women's careers in education, see Joan Williams, Shelagh Luka, Mary Elizabeth Luka, Greg Inwood and Nancy Bell, *Go For It! Barriers to Women's Promotion in Education,* (Toronto: The Federation of Women Teachers' Associations of Ontario, 1991).

43. Camilla Stivers, *Gender Images in Public Administration,* (Newbury Park, California: Sage, 1993): 4.

44. Hynna, "Women in the Public Service—A Thirty-Year Perspective," (1997): 618.

45. See Kenneth Kernaghan and Mohamed Charih, "The Challenge of Change: Emerging Issues in Contemporary Public Administration," *Canadian Public Administration,* 40, 2 (Summer, 1997): 227–228.

46. See Sid Noel, ed. *Revolution at Queen's Park: Essays on Governing Ontario,* (Toronto: Lorimer, 1997).

47. Douglas Booker, Natalie Dole, Stan Lee, Kathy Malizia, Daniel O'Connor and Rhonda Nause, *Demographic Study of the Visible Minority Community in the Federal Public Service,* (Ottawa: Public Service Commission of Canada, February, 2000): 3. http://www.psc-cfp.gc.ca/research/merit/merit_practices_e.htm

48. Leo Panitch and Donald Swartz, *The Assault on Trade Union Freedoms: From Wage Controls to Social Contract,* (Toronto: Garamond Press, 1993): 17.

49. See Miriam Smith, "The Canadian Labour Congress: From Continentalism to Economic Nationalism," *Studies in Political Economy,* 38 (Summer, 1992): 35–60.

50. Gene Swimmer, "Critical Issues in Public Sector Industrial Relations," in Amarjit S. Sethi, ed. *Collective Bargaining in Canada,* (Scarborough: Nelson, 1989): 401.

51. The following discussion is derived from P.K. Kuruvilla, "Collective Bargaining in the Canadian Public Service," in Kenneth Kernaghan, ed. *Public Administration in Canada: Selected Readings, Fifth Edition,* (Toronto: Methuen, 1985): 224–235.

52. See Audrey D. Doer, *The Machinery of Government in Canada,* (Toronto: Methuen, 1981): 63.

53. Canada, *Public Service 2000: The Renewal of the Public Service of Canada,* (Ottawa: Supply and Services, 1990): 63, 64.

54. Michael Mandel, *The Charter of Rights and the Legalization of Politics in Canada,* (Toronto: Thomson Educational Publishing, 1994): 294.

55. Canada, Public Service Commission, *Annual Reports 1997–1998, and 2000-2001,* (Ottawa: Minister of Public Works and Government Services Canada, 1998).

56. See Michael Cassidy, ed. *Democratic Rights and Electoral Reform in Canada,* (Toronto: Dundurn Press, for the Royal Commission on Electoral Reform and Party Financing, 1991).

57. For an early statement of this doctrine, see Kenneth Kernaghan, "Politics, Policy and Public Servants: Political Neutrality Revised," *Canadian Public Administration,* 21 (Fall, 1976) 432–456.

58. Canada, Public Service Commission of Canada, *Representativeness: An Integral Part of Merit,* (Ottawa: Public Service Commission of Canada, February, 2002). http://www.psc-cfp.gc.ca/cgi-bin/clf-upe/prn-impr.pl

59. Canada, Public Service Commission, *Annual Report 1997–1998,* (1998): 4.

60. Ralph Heintzman, "Introduction: Canada and Public Administration," in Jacques Bourgault, Maurice Demers and Cynthia Williams, eds. *Public Administration and Public Management: Experiences in Canada,* (Sainte-Foy, Quebec: Les Publications du Quebec, 1997): 5.

61. Cited in Alasdair Roberts, *So-Called Experts: How American Consultants Remade the Canadian Civil Service, 1918–21,* (Toronto: Institute of Public Administration of Canada, 1996): 3–4.

62. See Doug Owram, *The Government Generation: Canadian Intellectuals and the State 1900–1945,* (Toronto: University of Toronto Press, 1986).

63. See J.L. Granatstein, *The Ottawa Men: The Civil Service Mandarins, 1835–1957,* (Toronto: University of Toronto Press, 1982).

64. Bourgault and Carroll, "The Canadian Senior Public Service," (1997): 98

65. See John Porter, *The Vertical Mosaic: An Analysis of Social Class and Power in Canada,* (Toronto: University of Toronto Press, 1965).

66. See Canada, Royal Commission on Government Organization, *Report,* Five Volumes, (Ottawa: Queen's Printer, 1962–1963).

67. Bourgault and Carroll, "The Canadian Senior Public Service," (1997): 96.

68. Bourgault and Carroll, "The Canadian Senior Public Service," (1997): 97.

69. Ian D. Clark, "Restraint, Renewal, and the Treasury Board Secretariat," *Canadian Public Administration,* 37, 2 (Summer, 1994): 216.

70. James C. Simeon, "Canadian Public Administration and Government," in Randy Hoffman *et al. Public Administration: Canadian Materials, Third Edition,* (North York: Captus Press, 1998): 34.

71. Simeon, "Canadian Public Administration and Government," (1998): 35.

72. See Canada, Public Service Commission of Canada, *The Road Ahead: Recruitment and Retention Challenges for the Public Service,* (Ottawa: Public Service Commission of Canada, February, 2002).

73. Evert Lindquist, "Are Pubic Service Careers Changing? Images, Challenges, Strategies," Presentation to the *New Professionals Driving a New Public Service Conference,* (Toronto: October 22, 2001). http://www.newpublicservice.ca/en_indexframes.asp

74. See Canada, Public Service Commission of Canada, *Annual Report 2000–2001* (Ottawa: Public Service Commission of Canada, 2001) http://www.psc-cfp.gc.ca/centres/annual-annuel/2001/ann2001-e.pdf

75. Canada, Public Service Commission of Canada, *The Road Ahead: Recruitment and Retention Challenges for the Public Service,* (Ottawa: Public Service Commission of Canada, February, 2002): 26. For a sample of recruitment efforts aimed at post-secondary students, see Canada, Public Service Commission of Canada, *Jobs for Students and Graduates.* http://www.jobs.gc.ca/home_e.htm

76. Canada, Public Service Commission of Canada, *The Road Ahead: Recruitment and Retention Challenges for the Public Service,* (Ottawa: Public Service Commission of Canada, February, 2002): 26. For a sample of recruitment efforts aimed at post-secondary students, see Canada, Public Service Commission of Canada, *Jobs for Students and Graduates.* http://www.jobs.gc.ca/home_e.htm

77. Canada, Public Service Commission of Canada, *The Road Ahead: Recruitment and Retention Challenges for the Public Service,* (Ottawa: Public Service Commission of Canada, February, 2002): 26. For a sample of recruitment efforts aimed at post-secondary students, see Canada, Public Service Commission of Canada, *Jobs for Students and Graduates.* http://www.jobs.gc.ca/home_e.htm

78. Canada, Office of the Auditor-General of Canada, *Public Service Management Reform: Progress, Setbacks and Challenges,* (Ottawa: Minister of Public Works and Services, February, 2001).

KEY WORDS AND CONCEPTS

Civil Service Act 1908 (262)
Civil Service Act 1918 (262)
Civil Service Commission (262)
Public Service Commission (265)
representative (265)

employment equity (278)
affirmative action (278)
pay equity (284)
collective bargaining (287)
political neutrality (289)

REVIEW QUESTIONS

1. A Brief History of the Public Service: Who Works There, Anyway?
This section provided an overview of the composition of the public sector workforce and introduced some of the basic issues that have confronted the public service over time. It focused on merit and patronage and the tension between these. It asked the following: What is the public service? What historical developments

shaped the public service over the past 130 years? What issues have recently emerged, and how are they being addressed? How can the merit principle be reconciled with new developments?

2. The Public Service Today: An Overview

The public sector's response to the questions raised in the first section is evident in the many progressive changes it has pioneered in workplace. This section addressed some of those changes, as well as those produced by the attainment of collective bargaining rights by public servants. This section asked these questions: How large is the public service? How have equity issues come to the forefront within the public service? How has the public service changed recently? What is the significance of representativeness? How has unionization of the public service affected the union movement in Canada, the political rights of workers in the public service, and their relationship to the government?

Public servants clearly have a special relationship to the political system. Historically, their political rights were severely circumscribed. More recently, there has been a trend toward loosening the strictures against political activity. But the notion that the political rights of public servants are different from those of ordinary citizens has been difficult to overcome, running headlong, as it does, into principles such as the doctrine of political neutrality. As a result, this section asked, What grounds existed to limit the political rights of public servants? What is the doctrine of political neutrality? How has it affected the work that public servants do? What trends prevail in the relationship between public servants and the political system?

3. Human Resources Management

The issue of how the tens of thousands of public servants in the federal government are organized and managed was assessed from the perspective of the responsibilities of managers. To this end, this section asked these questions: How are systems of accountability established and maintained in the public service? What opportunities and constraints do managers have in the hiring and firing of personnel, and in setting pay levels and conditions of employment? How do merit and representativeness mesh or conflict with one another? What is being done around issues of recruitment, retention and succession planning?

FURTHER READING

1. A Brief History of the Public Service: Who Works There, Anyway?

Dwivedi, O.P., ed. *The Administrative State in Canada: Essays in Honour of J.E. Hodgetts.* Toronto: University of Toronto Press, 1981.

Johnson, A.W. *Reflections on Administrative Reform in the Government of Canada 1962–1991.* Ottawa: Office of the Auditor General, 1992.

Sutherland, Sharon L. and Bruce Doern. *Bureaucracy in Canada: Control and Reform.* Toronto: University of Toronto Press, 1985.

2. The Public Service Today: An Overview

Agocs, Carol. "Affirmative Action, Canadian Style: A Reconnaissance," *Canadian Public Policy,* 12 (March, 1986): 148–162.

Canada. Public Service Commission of Canada. *Representativeness: An Integral Part of Merit.* Ottawa: Public Service Commission of Canada, February, 2002. http://www.psc-cfp.gc.ca/cgi-bin/clf-upe/prn-impr.pl

Cassidy, Michael. "Political Rights for Public Servants: A Federal Perspective I," *Canadian Public Administration,* 29, (Winter, 1986): 653–654.

Pal, Leslie A. "The Federal Bureaucracy: Rethinking the Links Between State and Society," in Michael Whittington and Glen Williams, eds. *Canadian Politics in the 1990s. Fourth Edition.* Scarborough: Nelson, 1995: 276–291.

Ruemper, Fred. "Beyond Merit: The Representative Principle," in Randy Hoffman, *et al.*, *Public Administration: Canadian Materials. Third Edition.* Toronto: Captus Press, 1998: 252–271.

3. *Human Resources Management*

Agocs, Carol and Jack Roberts. "Is Employment Equity Fair and Necessary?" in Paul Barker and Mark Charlton, eds. *Crosscurrents: Contemporary Political Issues.* Scarborough: Nelson, 1991: 392–418.

Canada. *Beneath the Veneer: Report of the Task Force on Barriers to Women in the Public Service.* Four Volumes. Ottawa: Supply and Services, 1990.

Canada. Public Service Commission of Canada. *The Road Ahead: Recruitment and Retention Challenges for the Public Service.* Ottawa: Public Service Commission of Canada, February, 2002.

WEBLINKS

Public Service Commission of Canada—Career Recruitment
www.jobs.gc.ca/

Canadian Union of Public Employees
www.cupe.ca/

Public Service Alliance of Canada
www.psac.com/

Chapter 10

Public Administration, Management Reform *and* Financial Management

WHAT YOU WILL LEARN

Chapter 9 outlined some important features of the public service, and showed that the management of its human resources is a complex affair. In this chapter, we look at the complexity of managing other aspects of the public service. We'll examine what the managers of the public service do and how they do it. We'll also take another look, this time from a management perspective, at the major public sector reforms that were discussed in previous chapters.

Two central elements of public administration permit governments to do what they need to do. These are *money* and *personnel*. The management of these resources is an ongoing challenge. To begin with, governments need people to staff the institutions of the public sector, and those people must be managed. Historically, as we noted in Chapter 9, this was accomplished through the process of patronage: the practice of the governing party appointing its friends and supporters to key government positions. More recently, the principle of merit has been introduced into government hiring practices. The management of financial resources involves making decisions about how to divide the "pie" of government: Who gets what? Even in times when government coffers are full, this question is complicated, but in an era of diminishing revenues, it is hotly disputed. To resolve disputes over how financial resources are raised and spent, the government engages in complex and elaborate systems of budget-making. At their most general level, these involve figuring out who to tax and where to spend, but they also involve auditing and evaluation (as suggested in Chapter 8). Someone has to ensure that financial resources are being used wisely, and that every dollar of taxpayers' money can be accounted for. This, too, results in some of the most contentious political debate within government and society.

In their attempts to resolve disputes and create a transparent and fair system of budgeting, Canadian governments have experimented with a variety of budgeting models. But so far, no one system or model has been able to address all the issues surrounding the administration and management of government finances. This chapter examines issues related both to management reform and to financial management.

In reality, the two are often linked. So as a preface to our discussion of financial management, it will be useful to review several recent trends in reforming public service management. Hence, this chapter begins with an overview of contemporary reform efforts of the public service. The chapter is divided into the following sections:

1. *Restructuring the Public Service: The Management View*

Recent changes have altered the composition of the public service. Downsizing, reengineering, pay freezes, cutbacks, layoffs and firings were endemic throughout the 1990s. This section asks the following: What are the most important recent reforms to the management of the public service? How has restructuring affected the public service? What has it done to the morale of those remaining in the public service? How has it affected the delivery of services to the public? What are the implications of privatizing and contracting out? What does the future hold for those seeking a career in the Canadian public service?

2. *Financial Management*

The issues of power politics raised in Chapter 4 revolved around this question: Who gets what, when and how? We return to this by examining that most fundamental of issues related to government—money. Some observers of public administration have indeed concluded that to get anything done, governments need three things: money, money and money.[1] Canadian governments manage billions of dollars of taxpayers' money (that is, *your* money) every year. This fact alone raises a host of questions: How is that money managed? What budgeting systems have been established to ensure that probity, honesty, economy, efficiency and accountability are maintained? Who is ultimately responsible for the management of funds? What kinds of competitions do departments engage in to ensure that they get their share of the loot? What is the budgetary cycle?

Restructuring the Public Service: The Management View

The last decade of the 20th century was a difficult one for the public service in Canada. Recognizing the debilitating trends of low morale, cutbacks, wage freezes and the general disparagement aimed at public servants, managers have recently turned their attention to the vexing issue of how to rebuild a once-proud institution. Since 1999, public service renewal has again moved to the forefront of the agenda of many Canadian governments. At the federal level, a number of new initiatives have been launched, including: adoption of performance management measures; an increased focus on human resources planning, with emphasis on identifying and addressing retention and recruitment problems; exploration of other forms of partnerships such as employee takeovers; pension reform; and development of a new employment classification structure.[2] Before we explore the specifics of these issues, we need to review the depth and breadth of change in the public service over the years.

Imagine that it is 1970 and you're fresh out of university. You are attracted to the prospect of a career in the public service, because you have always understood that serving your country in this way is a lofty and honourable ambition. Your instructors in public administration courses have regaled you with tales of the proud and powerful mandarinate that dominated the halls of bureaucratic power in the post-war years, reconstructing the country after the war, building the great edifice known as the "social welfare state," and contributing in no small way to the greatest era of sustained prosperity in the history of the country. You are versed in the literature of Keynesian macro-economic management, as well as the latest systems approaches and modern social science management techniques. The world is your oyster, and you confidently accept your responsibility as a management trainee in an important federal department, content in the knowledge that your long and satisfying career will lead you, in no time, right to the deputy minister's office.

Now flash ahead to 2003. You have somehow survived the various purges that decimated the ranks of your colleagues in the 1980s and 1990s. You are a few short years from retirement, and are being pressured to leave early, even though it will adversely affect your pension and post-work lifestyle. The much-vaunted Keynesian management systems that you were taught have long been discredited by newfangled approaches known as monetarism and neoconservatism, the underlying premises of which are that you are a useless parasite sucking the lifeblood out of the nation. Successive prime ministers, from Trudeau to Campbell to Mulroney to Chrétien, have denigrated your work. The negative impression of the public service has been adopted by the public and the media, where you and your colleagues are regularly vilified. You are held responsible for everything from the national debt to the lack of competitiveness of Canadian industry to the sorry state of the health-care system to the rise in crime to the decline in morality, and on and on! And somewhere along the way, you found your march up the career ladder blocked by a huge cohort of your fellow public servants, all about your age and with the same ambitions. At some point, you realized that you had been "shelved."

What on earth happened in the intervening years?

Managing the public service has always been a challenging task. Notwithstanding the nostalgic recollections of the "glory years" after the Second World War, there have always been stresses and strains, conflicts and challenges for public service managers. But from the 1970s onward, the nature and set of issues and challenges seem to have both altered and intensified, and the management of the public service ran into serious—and heretofore largely unknown—difficulties. A variety of internal problems coincided with a change in societal views about the role and place of the public service. Just as the transition between the minimalist state and the Keynesian welfare state was difficult (the Great Depression of the 1930s), so, too, was the transformation from the Keynesian welfare state to the neoconservative state. (These terms, you will recall, were used in Chapter 1.)

Government deficits and debt, technological change, globalization and the rise of new social movements and interest groups, coupled with a more assertive and skeptical citizenry, have created new problems for public service managers. These have been exacerbated by two issues. First, managers' ability to respond to the forces of change has been hampered by inadequate internal systems and processes for the management of their departments. Second, widespread external criticism emerged that the bureaucracy had grown out of control and was incapable of doing its job. The first set of challenges was summarized by one former secretary of the Treasury Board:

The 1983 auditor general's report observed that "productive management" was constrained by "the impact of political priorities on the management process, the degree of administrative procedures with which managers have to cope, and the disincentives to productive management that are characteristic of the public service." The report noted that executives complained about excessive administrative regulations, incentives not to allow funds to lapse, inflexible contracting rules, too many requests for information from central agencies, unresponsive and costly common service agencies, as well as time-consuming classification, staffing, and related personnel procedures. The auditor general, while acknowledging that the public will always want constraints on public service managers and that control and accountability should not be sacrificed, called on the government to articulate a management philosophy, to delegate more authorities to departments, and rely more heavily on managers to address problems, to review the costs of internal regulation and reduce disincentives, and to identify pilot projects to test the viability of new management approaches.[3]

Moreover, the auditor general's infamous statement in 1976 that "Parliament—and indeed the government—had lost or was close to losing effective control of the public purse" shocked Canadians and galvanized the public sector.[4] In 1978, the auditor general reported that public servants had developed the attitude that the government was a bottomless pit of money, were engaged in empire-building, and had little regard for efficiency and economy, or the interests of the taxpayer.[5] Subsequent reports, while couched in more moderate language, frequently reinforced these negative impressions of government management.

Have these concerns been adequately addressed? In 2001, the auditor general identified four key areas where the management of the federal public service remains especially problematic:

·*The erosion of parliamentary control over how the government raises money and spends it. Canadians have the right to control how public funds are collected and used, and ultimately it is the members of Parliament we elect who carry out this control on our behalf. That is why I am concerned about recent examples of the erosion of parliamentary control, involving billions of dollars of revenue and expenditure.* **Strengthening fiscal and financial management.** *Over the last five years there has been a significant change in the federal government's fiscal position. The transparency and discipline that have yielded impressive results so far are critical to continued success. Steps have also been taken to improve financial management in departments and agencies. Money must be managed prudently in the interest of the public.* **The undermanagement of grant and contribution programs.** *The recent attention paid to grants and contributions has not yet translated into an overall improvement in the way they are managed across government. Government-wide problems require government-wide solutions.* **The internal health of the federal public service.** *The government has established an ambitious schedule for modernizing human resource management. Good government depends on the performance of the public service. I will be watching these modernization efforts closely.* [Emphasis added.][6]

It would seem that many of the same themes that animated the consternation of the auditors general 20 and 30 years ago persist.

The second set of challenges, derived from the widespread external criticism that the bureaucracy had grown out of control and was incapable of doing its job, has had a profound effect on the notion of the public service as a lofty and honourable calling, and has contributed to the strikingly low levels of morale in the public service. This impression was confirmed recently and forcefully by the clerk of the Privy Council's warnings of a "quiet crisis" in the public service (discussed in Chapter 9). The overall result has been confusion, insecurity, hopelessness, anger and frustration among many public servants. It has also meant that the management of the public sector has been undergoing a virtually continuous process of reform at least since former prime minister John Diefenbaker unleashed the Glassco Commission on the world of Canadian public administration in 1960, with its admonition to "let the managers manage." Al Johnson served in the government of Saskatchewan and federally at the senior-most level, and by his reckoning there have been reforms concerning the effective and efficient management of the public service about every two to five years since the Glassco Commission.[7] This is in itself a factor contributing to the ennui felt in this once-respected institution.

Reform is not a factor exclusive to the Canadian public sector, of course. Much has been written and noted about similar trends in countries such as New Zealand, Great Britain, and Australia.[8] Contemporary reforms include the following: borrowing "best practices" from the private sector; focusing on "clients" (instead of serving "citizens"); strategic alliances with the private sector and other levels of government; increased reliance on volunteer and nonprofit organizations for the delivery and development of services; the use of new technologies to improve service delivery and communication with Canadians. These have all become mantras of the new approaches to management of the public service.

In Canada, the preoccupation with renewal has brought continual attitudinal, institutional and structural changes throughout the 1980s and 1990s. Most recently, though, it is renewal within a new paradigm—one in which government is made to run more like business, and in which public servants are therefore expected to become more and more entrepreneurial in their work. And this renewal is taking place within a public service where managers are suffering "death by a thousand cuts." These "cuts" include: a lack of vision and leadership among senior managers and political executives; a lack of autonomy among frontline managers; a rapid turnover of senior managers (for example, deputy ministers rotate their positions on average every 22 months); a "vertical solitude" between senior and middle managers in which trust and respect is lacking; a stale organizational culture; severe financial cutbacks; and other related problems.[9] As well as PS2000 and La Relève, several other initiatives have been launched recently, with varying degrees of success, to address these serious problems.[10] We cannot review them all here, but will consider some of the more important ones over the past 20 years. These include the 1984 Productivity Improvement Program; the Ministerial Task Force on Program Review; and the Increased Ministerial Authority and Accountability Initiative. The point here is to give you a picture of the ongoing upheaval that has beset the public service, and that has in some ways only sustained the problems it was meant to address. The final outcome of this process may well be that "the patient died, but the operation was a success."

The Productivity Improvement Program

In the dying days of Pierre Trudeau's last government, an initiative called the **Productivity Improvement Program** was launched. Administered by the Treasury Board, it was a response to the Auditor General's complaint that red tape and procedures were hampering the efficient provision of government services and programs. The manner in which central agencies imposed controls on departments was investigated, and proposals were made to improve productivity by eliminating needless rules and regulations. However, the program was overtaken by events. The Mulroney Conservatives took office in September 1984, bringing with them an especially dismissive attitude toward the public service. Mulroney had boasted of providing public servants with "pink slips and running shoes" in the 1984 election campaign, and when he arrived in office he began his assault immediately. This new government had a significantly different ideological perspective from the one that had launched the Productivity Improvement Program. The Mulroney Conservatives quickly established two new approaches to public service reform. The first was a Ministerial Task Force on Program Review. The second was an initiative called Increased Ministerial Authority and Accountability.

The Ministerial Task Force on Program Review

The Mulroney Conservatives came to power suspicious of the federal bureaucracy, which, under the Trudeau Liberals, had grown immensely in size and power. So Mulroney set up the **Ministerial Task Force on Program Review** the very day after assuming office, to review existing programs and identify those no longer needed. The task force also sought to improve the remaining programs by focusing on the point at which the government met the citizen; in other words, the frontlines of service provision. With this in mind, the task force sought to make procedures simpler by cutting red tape and streamlining organizations. In addition, it was hoped that more businesslike practices could be introduced into the running of government. Mulroney put his no-nonsense deputy prime minister Eric Nielsen, a long-serving MP (and brother of film star Leslie Nielsen), in charge of the task force, and appointed to it three of the most senior ministers in the Cabinet. The four ministers' political weight, and especially Nielsen's well-known antipathy toward bureaucracy, signalled that this could be a significant initiative.

Nielsen established an 11-member private sector advisory group chaired by an accountant, and 19 study teams were created, composed of a mix of private sector and public sector people. They were given three months to complete the job of reviewing programs and making recommendations, and their reports were tabled on March 11, 1986.[11] Nielsen identified $500 million in potential savings through program eliminations and reforms, and recommended that the government adopt a comprehensive contracting-out policy (called "make or buy"). But Donald Savoie, a professor of public administration, observes that "notwithstanding its early support, the Mulroney government did not follow through on the great majority of the Nielsen recommendations. The government claims that $280 million in direct ongoing spending reductions and $215 million in tax expenditures can be attributed to the Nielsen task force.... [but] the great majority of programs reviewed are still in place and virtually intact."[12] From another perspective, it has been noted that bringing in "amateurish outsiders" (the private sector consultants on the task force) to examine federal government activities made them easy marks for the "well-informed insiders" who felt compelled to defend their work by sidetracking recommendations for reform wherever possible.[13]

Increased Ministerial Authority and Accountability

The next initiative was the **Increased Ministerial Authority and Accountability** exercise, set up in February 1986.[14] The Mulroney Conservatives launched this reform also, based mainly on work undertaken by the Treasury Board. It involved a two-step process. The first step consisted of a general review of the Treasury Board policies and procedures, with the goal of creating more flexibility for departments, and for ministers in their roles. The result was a decrease in the number of time-consuming reports that each department had to submit to the Treasury Board, and an an increase in the level beyond which expenses had to be authorized by the Treasury Board, giving departments more financial latitude. In effect, managers were given more authority and discretion regarding decision-making about their resources. The second step involved departments in voluntary negotiations with the Treasury Board to establish a management and accountability framework. This gave the departments increased flexibility in interpreting the Treasury Board instructions. In return, the Treasury Board would receive detailed accountability reports, performance indicators, and a major review from the departments every three years.[15] As one professor of public management concluded, "[T]he fact that, over a four-year period, only 10 departments (a third of the federal public service) reached an agreement with the Treasury Board shows that IMAA achieved a limited success. This seems to indicate that the government's approach in the area of devolution of authority lacked political leadership or strategic direction."[16]

PS2000

PS2000 followed on the heels of this exercise. Surveys of public sector managers in 1986 and 1988 by two Ottawa University professors revealed striking differences from the attitudes of private sector managers.[17] Low morale was endemic, and the further down the hierarchy, the lower it was. Thus, there was a disjunction between the attitudes of senior managers and their subordinates. Moreover, the scores obtained from rating various attitudes tended to be lower in the public service than in the private sector (see Box 10-1). The results of the surveys provided the impetus for PS2000, announced by the prime minister in December 1989. It was led by the clerk of the Privy Council, Paul Tellier, with the intent that the public service would engage in a thorough self-examination, and "heal itself."

Ten task forces were set up under the leadership of deputy ministers, who were charged with finding ways to further simplify personnel policies, to loosen central agency controls and increase the managerial freedom of department managers, and to increase efficiency and program delivery.[18] Thousands of public servants and others outside government were consulted, and a White Paper was issued, summarizing the findings of the exercise.

The white paper highlighted several challenges, including fast-paced economic and social changes, the growing complexity of policy issues, the need for a simpler and more transparent political process, the multiplication of controls, too many procedures hindering change, low morale among public servants, low public administration productivity, growing financial constraints, and the citizens' lack of confidence in the public service. These challenges begged for a more open relationship between Canadians and the public service, as well as for greater flexibility in government procedures. A change in bureaucratic culture was called for to pave the way to a culture based on consultation and service to the citizens.[19]

It was in PS2000 that the suggestion was made that each department should produce that '90s business-school contrivance, the *mission statement*. Managers would delineate specific service-oriented goals, and embrace notions of participatory management. PS2000 called for department managers to consult broadly, not only with their own employees but also with citizens, to establish service standards and a more service-oriented culture. And organizational reform was achieved by flattening structures such that no more than three executive levels existed under each deputy minister. (Recall our discussion of span of control in Chapter 3.) The goal here was to improve communication and to empower managers. Furthermore, it was suggested that the number of categories and levels within groups be reduced to simplify both personnel matters and decision-making procedures. Finally, the government decided to reinforce the importance of new organizational models of service delivery, called Special Operating Agencies (SOA), which had been introduced earlier by the Treasury Board.

Ian Clark called the budget reforms resulting from PS2000, which allowed managers more control over their funds, its most important recommendation. But as one observer of this process concludes, "[E]mpowerment of public servants

BOX 10-1

Morale in the Public Service

The following story documents the strained conditions and low morale currently commonplace in the federal public service.

Dan Murray loved his job in Canada's elite foreign service.

As a trade officer at the Canadian embassy in Seoul, he performed all sorts of jobs, from helping a small Canadian company sell computer software in South Korea to negotiating a big telecommunications agreement.

"It was fascinating work," he recalled. "The most fun career challenge I've ever had." But when his Seoul posting came to an end last year, he faced returning to Ottawa with a wife and three children on a salary of $35 000. That meant a rented two-bedroom apartment and no car.

It also meant standing in line for a handful of promotions—a wait that might take two years.

So when an old employer called to offer him a job, he had a tough decision to make. "I agonized for months," he said. "In the end I felt I had to do it."

Today, at 38, Mr. Murray is the president of a company that makes digital hearing-aid circuits. The company pays him more than three times what he got at Foreign Affairs, plus a healthy annual bonus. He has a nice house in Kitchener, Ontario, and he doesn't have to worry about a car: the company throws that in.

The story is far from unusual. Long considered the pinnacle of Canada's public service, the Department of Foreign Affairs is losing many of its best and brightest. Discouraged by low pay, scarce promotions and the hidebound attitudes of superiors, these people are leaving for top positions at banks, law firms and universities, and other government departments.

Thirty-four people have departed so far this year, and the grapevine is humming with rumours of others who may go soon.

Morale among some young officers is so low that they have set up an electronic-mail chat group called the E-whine, which they use to exchange complaints....

But the most crowded exits are those on the lower decks. Foreign Affairs says it now loses at least a quarter of its officers before they reach their seventh year on the job—a phenomenon that it calls the "seven-year itch." That's double the rate of a decade ago.

Source: Marcus Gee, "Inside a Head Hunter's Paradise," *Globe and Mail*, (Friday, August 28, 1998): A1

was the cornerstone of Public Service 2000."[20] Whether it worked or not is the subject of some dispute. The Auditor General concluded in his 1993 report that while some progress had been made, there was still a feeling of skepticism among public service managers.[21] Political scientist Peter Aucoin echoed this sentiment in his assessment of PS2000.[22] But even the head of the public service at the time, Paul Tellier, whose job it was to develop and implement PS2000, described it as a failure. He claimed his plan was defeated by the "culture of caution" that permeates the public service, especially among managers.[23] In any event, many middle-level managers regarded it as fiat passed down from above; an executive-level exercise removed from the real day-to-day concerns of the middle-level manager. To them, it lacked legitimacy. By the end of 1993, PS2000 had faded from view as a reform program, supplanted by other, newer reform attempts and unable to recover.

Program Review

When the Liberals came to power on the heels of the demise of PS2000, a major restructuring of government had already begun. Chrétien's predecessor, Conservative Kim Campbell, had reduced the number of government ministries from 32 to 23. This necessitated building new management structures and consolidating the activities and operations of the old departments into the fewer new ones. Chrétien opted for a similar streamlined government, and created 24 ministries. He also dedicated his government to three main tasks: renewing federalism, reviewing all government programs, and reforming the public service. Significantly, he designated one of his Cabinet members as minister for Public Sector Renewal. Marcel Massé was given this job, and proceeded to implement the new goals of public service management.[24]

Of these three goals, the one that most interests us here is the **Program Review** (raised in earlier chapters).[25] The driving force behind this round of reforms was deficit reduction. During the 1993 election campaign, the Liberals had promised to reduce the deficit to 3 percent of GDP by 1997–1998. Beyond this, according to two observers of the public administration process, Program Review involved

clarifying the core responsibilities of the federal government and rebalancing the division of labour among the different levels of government and the private and not-for-profit sectors in the Canadian governance system, and equipping the federal public service with the tools necessary to improve the efficiency of public sector management.[26]

In spring 1994, all government departments and government agencies were given expenditure targets, and were expected to reform their programs to fit these targets. Six "tests" of Program Review were instituted against which all programs were to be measured. As we noted in Chapter 3, these tests asked these questions: Was there a public interest at stake? Was there a legitimate role for government in the issue? Was the federal government the right level of government jurisdictionally? Could the activities of the program be transferred to the private or voluntary sector? How could efficiency be improved? And was the program in question affordable?[27] In his February 1995 budget, then Finance Minister Paul Martin called for reductions in program spending of $29 billion over a three-year period, as well as the elimination of 45 000 civil servant jobs (14 percent of the entire public service). Transfer payments to the provinces for health, welfare and post-secondary education were unilaterally reduced by $4.5 billion, although the provinces were given greater flexibility in how they were to spend whatever sums they did receive. Expenditure reductions varied across departments and agencies, with some having to cut as little as 5 percent from their budgets, and others having to cut as much as 60 percent. Only the Department of Indian Affairs and Northern Development was spared. As Figure 10.1 shows, the most deeply affected departments were Transport, Industry and Natural Resources.[28] A Program Review Secretariat was created within the Privy Council Office to oversee these developments.

FIGURE 10.1   Changes in Federal Departments' Spending 1997–98 Relative to 1994–95

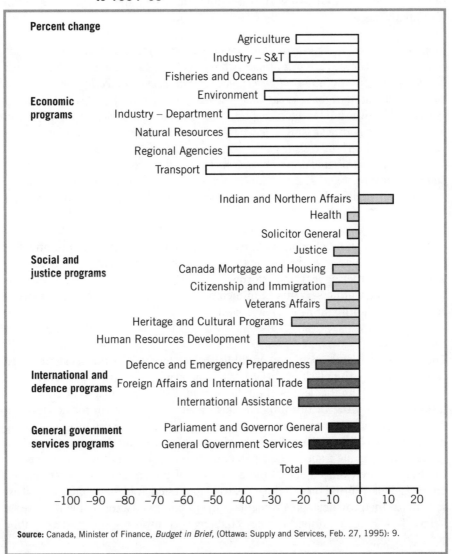

Source: Canada, Minister of Finance, *Budget in Brief,* (Ottawa: Supply and Services, Feb. 27, 1995): 9.

According to two analysts of Program Review, the exercise did not meet its expectations. "Our general diagnosis is that it has not been as effective as it might have been," they suggest. "It has undoubtedly triggered some expenditure reductions, and these are likely to continue." However, it did not fundamentally reform the governance of the system, which was a basic goal of Program Review.[29] Part of the problem lay in the fact that, as with PS2000, the Program Review was conducted largely by "insiders." And it was also a top-down process, for the most part. It should be obvious why it was difficult to get middle-level bureaucrats to embrace reform that was not based on consultation, especially when it might have adversely affected the very programs that they administered. Moreover, those people outside government who would be most affected by the program cutbacks resulting from expenditure cutbacks were not consulted either. In the end, the results of Program Review were assessed by a senior public servant as falling fall short of its ambitious goals:

From my perspective, the Federal Program Review, while producing dramatic results in terms of dollars or job cuts, was primarily a scramble for cash, and did not represent a "re-design" or "re-invention" of government as had been claimed by some. Federal Departments cut what could be cut, and little real attention was paid to the six starting criteria. There was little or no attempt made to examine the structure and process of government on a horizontal basis, to lessen the pressures which require departments to incur such enormous overhead costs (e.g., the massive impact of bloated Central Agencies and their multiple controls and demands on departments, the costs of the unwieldy, obsolete and ineffective personnel system—which every critic since Glassco has vainly tried to reform—and the unwieldy centralized and control-oriented financial and administrative systems).[30]

Yet another round of reforms ultimately failed to achieve the wide-scale and fundamental reorientation of the public service that seems to be called for by the various crises confronting it. These reforms may even have worsened the situation, as morale among public servants plummeted and the malaise noted earlier deepened with each brilliant new scheme launched.

La Relève

The culmination of the battering of public service morale was the declaration of a "quiet crisis" by the clerk of the Privy Council, who launched **La Relève** as a means of plumbing the depths of public servant dissatisfaction and of finding solutions to renew the institution. The term itself is an acronym for Leadership, Action, Renewal, Energy, Learning, Expertise, Values and Excellence. Beginning in January 1997, more than 15 000 public servants from all departments and regions were consulted about their perceptions of working in the public service. Conferences were staged across the country, and parliamentarians were briefed on the La Relève Task Force findings, as were interested academics, professional associations, the provincial governments, foreign countries and the media. The La Relève Task Force identified the key challenges confronting the modern public service as globalization, new information technologies, and changing attitudes toward traditional hierarchical institutions.

The "quiet crisis" resulted from a number of factors: "the loss of talent through many years of downsizing; a demographic skew after years of limited recruitment; constant criticism of the public sector which seriously affected morale; many years of pay freezes; and increasing interest by the private sector in acquiring the skills possessed by public servants."[31] It urged a more responsible and participatory role for managers at all levels, and a "democratization" of the decision-making process which emphasized leadership across the public service.

One result of La Relève has been the targeting of demographics, representativeness and recruitment as three important contemporary challenges to the public service. Student work programs and cooperative education programs have been instituted to address the demographic reality of a civil service in need of new blood. A concerted effort by departments and agencies has been made to renew the public service workforce through recruitment, training and development initiatives. As well, the high level of departures by senior managers has inspired an effort to renew the leadership cadre of the civil service. As we noted in Chapter 9, campaigns to recruit university graduates and professionals with specialized skills have been developed, along with ones to better train public servants and increase their mobility within the organization. This is a two-pronged approach, involving investing in experienced public servants and recruiting new ones. Career management planning, advisory services and support for continuous learning have been implemented across the public service. While there is still a long way to go, Box 10-2 reveals that some career public servants do retain a latent and powerful sense of pride.

The cumulative impact of all this public service navel-gazing has been to create a culture of self-(re)assessment and to alert management to the fact that serious structural problems persist. And now, the most recent embrace of New Public Management (NPM) approaches, as reflected in many of the reforms discussed above, seem to be giving way to yet another stage. Some observers argue that we have in fact entered a new era of the "post-bureaucratic organization."[32] They suggest that where policy and management culture, structure of organizations and orientation toward the free market are concerned, a significant number of changes have occurred. These changes are summarized in Table 10.1.

According to the President of the Canadian Centre for Management Development, the challenge for the contemporary public service over the next 10 years will be to evolve from the bureaucratic management model of the past to a public service learning-organizational model. She describes the difference between the two in the following way:

The bureaucratic management model is to the public service what the industrial management model has been to the private sector. It is based on clearly defined, repetitive tasks. Similar tasks are grouped in units, units in branches, and so on. The whole works like the well-oiled machines of the Industrial Age. A bureaucratic organization is expected to improve its performance constantly by doing more or less the same thing. It performs around predictable and pre-determined outcomes.

Box 10-2

At Your Service with Pride

The following article was written by a career public servant, Bob Chartier of Saskatoon, who works in the Department of Indian and Northern Affairs.

I am a public servant. In the 30 years of my career, there have been more times than I would care to admit when I was not very comfortable saying that out loud, much less in print. However, like everyone lately, my world has been rocked. The embassy bombings, the bombing of the federal building in Oklahoma City and the Sept. 11 images of public servants—police officers and firefighters—running towards the horror instead of away from it will stay with us forever. I have had to recognize that many terrorists target governments and, as we know, public servants are the front line of governance.

For years, public servants struggled with a "poor cousin" image in the workplace. It was insinuated that the brightest and the best would always go into the private sector. The rest of us, for many different reasons, made the decision to spend our lives teaching your kids, hooking up your intravenous, protecting your border, checking the maintenance record on the aircraft taking you to Cancun and responding to 911 calls.

Oh, we heard your snickers over the years.

We have heard your comments about road crews leaning on their shovels, striking nurses, mindless clerks processing paper, lazy teachers and cops in doughnut shops. And this was the tame stuff. I believe it's time to rethink our views on public service. First of all, understand that we do the things that no one else really wants to do and that there is no real money in it. Try to buy police services from a street vendor. What price would the market pay to find an illegal immigrant? Ask a major private-sector company to write a new fair-trade policy. Try to shop around for a good deal on a passport.

The private-enterprise capitalist system is fine by me. It is adept at doing those things it is supposed to do, but it can't do it all. When it comes to writing good policy on parole violations, we don't freelance the contract; we ask a public servant with a weighty academic background, a wealth of experience and an ear to the street to compose it. When we need protection, high standards in our goods, food and water, we again look to the public servant. Whoa, let's stop right there. On that water thing. You're right. We have Walkerton and North Battleford to consider. I grew up in North Battleford and, as a working government guy, I was appalled that, for decades, city workers there drew drinking water a kilometre downstream from the spot they dumped the sewage. Let's be honest. Public servants make mistakes. Big ones, little ones and some really stupid ones. But so does the private sector. Our trouble, as public servants, is that our mistakes can cause a lot more grief.

It is true, we are notorious for our red tape, our obsession with paper and our slowness. But we are working really hard. We can and will be just as fast, as effective and as quality-minded as the private sector, even more. We have many masters, however, and sometimes when we try to cut the red tape we get beat up for what is then called a lack of accountability. It's always hard for us to know whom we really serve—politicians or citizens. But I believe we can serve both and do it with accountability and effectiveness.

So what have we got here? Well, we have jobs that have no market value. We are under constant public scrutiny. We get paid what citizens, not the market, think we are worth and we provide always essential but often hidden services. And most of us really like our work. We love your kids, we fell for you in the intensive-care unit, we want to find the bad guys and we are driven to develop policy that reflects Canadian values.

Public servants may now feel even more like a target for evil, but they will go to work every day. They will be here for us, the first to run into the trouble and to lead in the rebuilding. The war on terrorism will not be fought in the market, it will be defended at the border, in policy-making decisions on privacy and in the day by day readiness of emergency workers. And that is why I serve the public, with pride.

Source: *Maclean's*, 115, 2 (January 14, 2002): 9.

A learning organization—public or private—is built around people, teams and networks. It is expected to innovate and to constantly explore new and better ways of achieving its mission. It is expected to anticipate and constantly adapt to change. Doing more of the same, even if it is done well, is no longer good enough. Reacting to change is too costly, too slow—too late.[33]

This changing landscape of public service management has led to several new trends. Four of the most significant, according to two close observers of the scene, are:

➤ *partnering* in policy-making, management, program development, and the delivery of goods and services within and across departmental and agency boundaries, between orders of government, and across sectors;

➤ the ongoing development of and commitment to a *service-to-the-public* focus as one critical factor of an effective public sector;

➤ the *shifting of responsibilities* from one authority to another, as evidenced by increased decentralization, deconcentration, devolution, and deregulation in favour of the market and self-regulation; and

TABLE 10.1   From the Bureaucratic to the Post-Bureaucratic Organization

Characteristics of the bureaucratic organization	Characteristics of the post-bureaucratic organization
Policy and Management Culture	
ORGANIZATION-CENTRED Emphasis on needs of the organization itself	CITIZEN-CENTRED Quality service to citizens (and clients/stakeholders)
POSITION POWER Control, command and compliance	PARTICIPATIVE LEADERSHIP Shared values and participative decision-making
RULE-CENTRED Rules, procedures and constraints	PEOPLE-CENTRED An empowering and caring milieu for employees
INDEPENDENT ACTION Little consultation, cooperation or coordination	COLLECTIVE ACTION Consultation, cooperation and coordination
STATUS-QUO-ORIENTED Avoiding risks and mistakes	CHANGE-ORIENTED Innovation, risk-taking and continuous improvement
PROCESS-ORIENTED Accountability for process	RESULTS-ORIENTED Accountability for results
Structure	
CENTRALIZED Hierarchy and central controls	DECENTRALIZED Decentralization of authority and control
DEPARTMENTAL FORM Most programs delivered by operating departments	NON-DEPARTMENTAL FORM Programs delivered by wide variety of mechanisms
Market Orientation	
BUDGET-DRIVEN Programs financed largely from appropriations	REVENUE-DRIVEN Programs financed as far as possible on cost-recovery basis
MONOPOLISTIC Government has monopoly on program delivery	COMPETITIVE Competition with private-sector program delivery

Source: Kenneth Kernaghan, Brian Marson and Sandford Borins, *The New Public Organization*. Toronto: Institute of Public Administration of Canada, 2000: 3

➤ the increased commitment to and dependency on *information technologies* in all aspects of governing, from political policy- and decision-making, to the management of programs, to the delivery of goods and services to clients, customers, and the general public.[34]

All of these management reforms need to be seen in the context of organizational theory as discussed in chapters 2 and 3. In particular, it is evident that NPM has had an important impact on the management of the public service. But we are already moving beyond NPM.

NPM may not have provided the answers needed to reinvigorate public service management. Its critics are legion, and it may indeed turn out to be simply the "flavour of the month" in a smorgasbord of management-school reforms.[35]

Still, the early results of the post–La Relève initiatives, informed by NPM or not, suggest that a corner may have been turned, and that the public service is emerging from its darkest days. What is less clear is whether this corner has been turned as a result of reforms associated with the NPM generally, and La Relève specifically, or because of the new fiscal realities of balanced budgets and reduced government debt. These questions are considered in more detail in Chapter 13. But for now it may be worth noting that in the absence of financial resources, public sector renewal appears to be a self-defeating exercise, since it mainly requires self-inflicted denigration of the institution in the face of hostile external attacks. However, if the rationale for public sector downsizing is fiscal constraint, and that rationale is removed, we can conclude that the future of the public service looks brighter now than it has for a long time. We turn now to a consideration of financial management.

Financial Management

Financial management of an enterprise that generates and spends billions of dollars of taxpayers' money is no small task. The complexities of budgeting have spawned an extensive literature dedicated to developing the best possible system for the management of the public's fiscal resources. We will consider these developments briefly in historical perspective before turning to the nuts-and-bolts of public sector financial management, as it is currently practised. Keep in mind, though, that financial management is mainly about "who gets what" from government and society.

The State and Economy

The rise of a new class of "mandarins" in the post-war years (as noted in Chapter 9) coincided with and made possible a huge expansion of the role of the state in Canada. While the state in Canada has always had some role in the economic life of the nation (see Chapter 1), in the 1930s and 1940s the federal government shifted its attention from such things as tariffs and transportation—the pillars of Canada's "national policy" of the late-19th century—to new responsibilities. Monetary policy and the construction of a new welfare state on the basis of Keynesian theory emerged as what one observer called a "new national policy." The federal government consequently expanded its role into areas where it had previously feared to tread. The crises of the Great Depression in the 1930s and the Second World War in the 1940s accelerated this process, with profound consequences for the management of the federal public service:

> *As a result, by 1945 the federal and civil service had swollen to 115 000 employees, compared to the 10 000 estimated in 1896. The wages alone for these government employees represented a sum five times larger than the total government budget 50 years earlier. The total 1945 budget was $5.25 billion, compared to $36 million in 1896. The range of federal government activities had expanded to include such responsibilities as old-age pensions, unemployment insurance, family allowances, subsidized housing and other social policies, as well as a new conception of the federal government's role in economic management.*[36]

The implications for the financial management of the government's business were huge. The result has been a dramatic growth in government spending until recently. Donald Savoie sums up the trend in the following way.[37] He points out that the total federal government budgetary spending in 1920–1921 was $476 million. This figure actually dropped in 1923–1924 to $352 million. But from then on it gradually climbed higher. In 1939, total expenditures were $533 million. By 1950–1951, it had risen to $2.4 billion; in 1960–1961, it reached $6.7 billion; in 1970–1971, it was $15.3 billion; in 1980–1981, it reached $62 billion; in 1983–1984, it was $96.6 billion; in 1987–1988, it reached $122.5 billion. Strikingly, after more than a decade of restructuring, total expenditures climbed to $175.2 billion by 2000–2001.

These numbers are difficult to contemplate; they are abstractions that are hard to conceptualize. So look at them this way. The total value of the goods and services produced by a country is referred to as its Gross Domestic Product (GDP). If we look at the percentage of GDP accounted for by government, we get another perspective on the growth of the state. In 1930–1931, federal government expenditures represented 6.8 percent of GDP. They represented 16 percent of GDP by 1940–1941, levelled off to 12.8 percent in 1950–1951, reached 17.6 percent in 1960–1961, 21 percent in 1976–1977, 23.6 percent in 1982–1983, and 23 percent in 1986–1987. In short, the federal government has always been a key player in the economy, and has, over time, increased the share of the economic pie accounted for by its activities.

Recently, though, this trend has abated somewhat. Figure 10.2 shows federal revenue, program spending and the deficit as a percentage of GDP from 1989–1990 to 1998–1999. This reveals that after nearly a decade of concerted effort, the federal government has turned the corner on the constant government expansion that marked the period from the post-war years up to the end of the 1980s. Still, it is clear from these figures that the government remains a major actor in the economy.

The issue of raising and spending money can usefully be conceptualized by thinking about some government departments as "savers" and others as "spenders." The key "savers" are the Department of Finance and the Treasury Board. The Privy Council Office also plays an important part. The spenders are all the other departments. The two types are engaged in a constant struggle. Each has its own set of clients, both within government and out in the broader society, pressuring the government to take action—or not to take action. Each has its champions and villains

FIGURE 10.2   Federal Revenue, Program Spending, and Deficit as Percentage of GDP 1989–90 to 1998–99

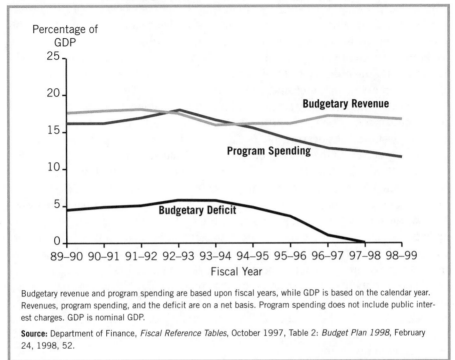

Budgetary revenue and program spending are based upon fiscal years, while GDP is based on the calendar year. Revenues, program spending, and the deficit are on a net basis. Program spending does not include public interest charges. GDP is nominal GDP.

Source: Department of Finance, *Fiscal Reference Tables*, October 1997, Table 2: *Budget Plan 1998*, February 24, 1998, 52.

within Cabinet, Parliament, interest groups, the media and the public. For example, the Ministry of Agriculture is a "spender" department. It wants government to dedicate sufficient resources to agricultural interests in Canada, to guarantee the ongoing viability and vitality of this sector of the economy. The ministry is pressured by the farming community, manufacturers of farm equipment, chemical, pesticide and herbicide makers, rural Canadians and others to make sure that agricultural ways of life are protected and promoted. The Finance Department, on the other hand, is chief among the "saver" departments. It has ultimate responsibility for the government's overall fiscal health, and keeps a firm hand on the purse strings. It is constantly pressured by "spender" departments, such as Agriculture, to reapportion the government pie. But it is simultaneously pressured by other actors, as well. For instance, the big business community might be asking for tax breaks; organized interests and think tanks might be producing studies showing the importance of reducing the deficit; the Auditor General may be demanding an end to the government's profligate ways. The Finance Department bears the brunt of all these and countless other pressures in managing the government's financial resources.

Overall, for many years it seemed as though the "spenders" were winning the battle, if not the war. But through the 1980s and 1990s, the "savers" launched a forceful counter-offensive. As a result, we have seen significant downsizing and a deliberate and concerted effort to wrestle the deficit to the ground. Moreover, there has been an increased emphasis on improving the various financial controls and reporting mechanisms used to oversee the entire government budgetary process. Now, however, the spenders are re-emerging in this new era of surpluses.[38] The key question remains, though, of how best to design and implement controls and mechanisms for financial management. As two observers put it, "[I]ndeed, the authorities granted to governments by legislatures to collect and expend public funds, and the obligations to report on the use of these funds, are at the heart of parliamentary governance and democracy."[39]

Budgeting involves many actors and institutions, making it a highly complex exercise. Parliament, Cabinet, departments, central agencies, and the Auditor General are key players within government. The media and interest groups have historically been keen observers of the process, often acting as watchdogs to uncover government malfeasance. Ordinary citizens are increasingly being consulted on the budget-making exercise that dominates the life of governments—an exercise that was once closed, secretive and exclusive to a handful of mandarins and the finance minister.

The most recent important reforms to the budgeting process can be summed up in three initiatives: the Expenditure Management System (EMS); departmental business plans; and improved reporting to Parliament. At the root of the system we are about to explore is one fundamental principle, which we briefly looked at in earlier chapters: responsible government. At the end of the day, the government is held responsible by Parliament for its actions to the citizens of the country. In particular, the government is held responsible for its handling of the taxpayers' money, and it can only hold power as long as it demonstrates that it has acted reasonably and responsibly in managing those monies.

Consider the organizational features of government financial management that underpin this theory. At Confederation in 1867, the statutory basis of financial management was established in the *BNA Act,* section 102, which gives Parliament the right to control public money, and which also calls for the creation of a single consolidated revenue fund to receive all money belonging to Canada. As well, authority to pay money out of the consolidated revenue fund is given to Parliament in section 106. Thus, it is Parliament that formally and constitutionally is responsible for approving the raising and spending of public money. Donald Savoie explains the importance of this point:

Several principles underpin Parliament's role in the budget process. The first is that the government—or the executive—can have no revenue which is not sanctioned by Parliament, and the second is that the government can make no expenditures except those approved by Parliament. In addition, Parliament does not grant a permanent right to spend, so that the government must submit a new budget every year. Thus funds allocated by Parliament but not spent must lapse. Detailed spending plans are submitted annually in the form of spending "estimates." The government must also account to Parliament for its management of public moneys, both revenues and expenditures.[40]

Once again, though, we should note that there is a disjuncture between theory and practice. In the real world of Canadian politics, control over the public purse is in the hands of the executive (that is, the Cabinet). Because of the practice of party discipline, the executive receives support for its budgetary plans virtually automatically. So in reality, the role played by Parliament is more one of "watchdog," "legitimating" the government's financial plans, rather than setting them.

Canadians are apprised of the state of their finances through four major reports that are made annually to Parliament. The most visible and politically significant of these is the budget by the minister of Finance, "which includes a comprehensive financial statement, including a forecast of financial requirements for government operations for the forthcoming year, and the ways and means proposed by the government to achieve its multiple objectives."[41] Second, the government annually provides Estimates to inform Parliament of its spending plans for the coming year. The Estimates provide the basis for the legislation that Parliament passes to authorize spending by the government. Third, every month in the *Canada Gazette,* a Statement of Financial Operations is published. This provides detailed information on financial transactions for the previous month, as well as a running total for the year. Finally, the government's annual audited financial statements are found in the Public Accounts of Canada. These are presented to Parliament by the president of the Treasury Board on behalf of the government, although they are prepared under the direction of the Treasury Board president and the minister of Finance by the Receiver General of Canada. The reports are also presented to the Auditor General, who reviews them and presents to Parliament his or her independent assessment of the management of Canada's finances. In turn, the Auditor General's Report becomes part of the Public Accounts of Canada. These are reviewed by a parliamentary committee called the Standing Committee on Public Accounts, which also reports to Parliament.

This brief sketch only scratches the surface of the process, which, as you can see, is complex and involves many important actors.. Before taking a more in-depth look at the process in the context of the annual budgetary timetable, it will be useful to review the major trends in reporting and control of the public purse. We briefly introduced the **Programming, Planning, Budgeting System (PPBS)** in Chapter 8. Here we expand on it and other subsequent budgeting systems that have come and gone over the years in Ottawa.

Managing Government Fiscal Resources

As with many recent reform developments, our discussion of financial control systems begins with the Glassco Commission. This set the stage for reform of financial management systems and improved reporting to Parliament; it continues to influence developments in this area to this day. Prior to Glassco, there was an emphasis on accountability in terms of ensuring accuracy and probity in raising and spending money. And this is still true. But less attention used to be paid to the budget as a tool of effective management, planning and evaluation. And the budget was not considered a tool of macro-economic management of the Canadian economy until after the rise of Keynesianism. Typically, control of the budget was in the hands of the Department of Finance. Other departments would negotiate with Finance over the increased dollars they would receive to run their programs after accounting for inflation or the establishment of new programs. The process was incremental, with a little bit added each year, and little attention being paid to the cumulative impact of the many decisions that went into the annual budget.

The key problem that Glassco identified in financial management was the practice of setting departmental (and hence governmental) budgets by approving transactions before they occurred. This meant that individual managers would offer their best "guesstimate" of how much money they would need to offer services and run programs for the upcoming fiscal year. This technique, besides not being particularly systematic, had the effect of putting upward pressure on the government's overall expenditures. Few managers would admit to needing fewer resources than in previous years, since this might imply that their program or service was of diminishing importance, and therefore disposable. Moreover, this system monopolized power over the government's overall financial resources, and managers had little opportunity to see the "big picture" of governmental budgeting.

So, in this context, Glassco's rallying cry of "let the managers manage" meant increasing the authority of managers as well as their responsibility and accountability. It suggested introducing methods by which the value and efficiency of expenditures could be measured (see Chapter 8). And it suggested introducing a five-year budgetary planning cycle. Shortly thereafter, in 1966, the Treasury Board was separated from the Department of Finance. It was given its own minister and department, and took over control of budget, personnel and administrative policy.

By the 1970s, after 30 years, economic growth had slowed. The new challenge was to figure out how to do more with less; that is, how to provide the same or even higher levels of service with less and less funding. Flattened tax revenues, a decline in business confidence and investment, new overseas competition in sectors of the economy that Canada had traditionally been strong in—all combined to exert pressure on the ability of the state to carry on "business as usual." As well, the tax burden had gradually shifted, so that corporations were now paying a smaller proportion of the overall burden, while individuals were paying a greater one. The government's extensive use of tax breaks and tax expenditures began to catch up with it. The positivist, activist vision of the Canadian state eroded as taxpayers increasingly came to see many government programs as wasteful, although this did not necessarily stop them from demanding that services still be provided.

As a result, and following from Glassco, a veritable alphabet soup of decision-making systems was introduced into financial management. The thrust of these systems was to introduce rationality, planning and advanced management techniques into the process. The first step along this path was to change the nature of expenditure requests by managers. In the past, such requests had been based on a rudimentary **line-item method of budgeting**. This technique simply involves listing the main objects of expenditure (e.g., How many paper clips does the department need? How much will be paid out in salaries? How much does it cost to rent office space?). Little or no attempt was made to evaluate the effectiveness of these expenditures. But henceforth, a manager would be expected to produce formal statements outlining his department's objectives, and how he planned to systematically evaluate the effectiveness of the programs the department administered.

The Programming, Planning, Budgeting System (PPBS) was the first attempt to reorganize financial management in this way.

PPBS was based on the budgeting techniques in vogue in the United States, and was adopted by the Treasury Board in 1969. It sought to provide a framework for budgeting that went beyond line-item budgeting to analyze new initiatives and develop longer-range plans to meet departmental and governmental objectives. This became known as **program budgeting**. There were also to be ongoing assessments of the impact of programs, and of whether they met the stated goals and objectives of the government in the most efficient way. Also, "an important objective was to improve policy analysis, program evaluation, and performance measurement throughout the public service in order to better hold department managers to account and to better inform decision-making and resource allocation."[42] PPBS introduced the idea of the "A" budget, the "B" budget, and the "X" budget into each department. Managers would design the "A" budget to cover the costs of ongoing programs. The "B" budget was intended for new or expanded programs. And the "X" budget was meant to cover low-priority items that might be reduced or eliminated.

But while the beauty of PPBS was its rational basis, its fatal flaw was the added bureaucracy required to administer it. Copious amounts of paperwork and reporting were necessary to keep it afloat, and gradually the Cabinet decision-making process it was supposed to support was swamped. Moreover, the introduction of PPBS coincided with a serious downturn in the Canadian economy, and the resulting mish-mash of financial management resulted in the commissioning of yet another royal commission to sort out the mess. The Lambert Commission (the Royal Commission on Financial Management and Accountability) was struck in 1976 to investigate standards for financial management and accountability. Even before the commission reported, however, the government created the position of Comptroller General to do just that. While most of the Lambert Commission's recommendations were initially ignored by the government, it did contribute to the general climate that suggested a need for improved financial management.

In fact, the next set of reforms actually resembled several of the suggestions put forth by Lambert. In 1979, the Conservative government of Joe Clark introduced a new system called the **Policy and Expenditure Management System (PEMS)**.[43] While Clark's government only lasted nine months in office, his innovations were adopted by the Trudeau administration. The goal of PEMS was similar to those of many earlier reforms: it improved ministerial control over financial management in the area of priority-setting, and allowed ministers to more easily appraise both the medium- and long-term picture of policy development and financial management. Moreover, it was meant to promote a more collegial decision-making process in Cabinet with respect to allocating fiscal resources across the government. An "envelope" system was introduced regarding expenditures, in which ministers were figuratively handed an envelope with a set amount of cash in it, and expected to make their department's spending fit the amount. Cabinet committees determined how much went into each departmental envelope.[44] To assist them in this work, departments were required to submit Strategic Overviews of their activities, as well as Multi-Year Operational Plans.

Through the 1980s, piecemeal changes were made to PEMS, including a shift away from the envelope system in favour of *reference levels* for departments, a more flexible way of apportioning resources. In addition, the delivery of the minister of Finance's annual budget was brought in line with the annual expenditure cycle (usually in February of each year). And consultations with groups outside government became a regular feature of the budgetary process, in contrast to the highly secretive methods of the past. Once again, however, the excessive bureaucratic and administrative work required to keep PEMS alive proved daunting. Gradually, it too fell into disrepute, particularly as the problems of growing deficits and debt continued to bedevil the government, notwithstanding the introduction of these rational planning and financial management techniques.[45] As a result, PEMS gave way to **EMS**—the **Expenditure Management System**—in January 1995.

Under EMS, there was a heavy emphasis on "getting government right," which had become the buzz-phrase of the day. Where budgeting was concerned, this meant focusing on efficiency, and EMS introduced the practice of having departments produce annual Business Plans. These were documents based on a private sector model of reporting that would replace the Multi-Year Operational Plans introduced under PEMS. Business Plans, delivered to the Treasury Board by each department in the fall of each year, are meant to show how departments planned to improve or restructure programs—increasingly referred to now as *lines of service*. The **Business Plans** are also intended to signal ways in which departments can adjust their activities to promote efficiencies and improvements in services to clients, as well as measure performance.[46]

An increased emphasis was also placed on "results-based" reporting and evaluation. To place these developments in the context of the overall budget system, it is necessary to go back to the observation above, that Parliament alone can authorize the spending and raising of money, which it does in the Estimates. The Estimates are the means by which the government seeks Parliament's permission to access the Consolidated Revenue Fund. The Estimates comprise three parts. Part I summarizes the government's expenditure plans for the year, while Part II shows the amounts that the government requires for specific votes (that is, for each department or agency). But it was Part III of the Estimates that contained the most detailed information regarding each department's expenditure requirements. Part III was added to the Estimates in 1981, as a result of the reforms made during the PEMS era, and was influenced in its design and presentation by the Office of the Comptroller General. Unfortunately, the Estimates were often so convoluted and difficult to read that they were of little use as accountability mechanisms for Parliament. Thus, they have been simplified through the Business Plan format to make it easier for Parliament to hold the government accountable. Concerted efforts have also been made to improve the reporting functions of departments, and to improve performance measurement and evaluation, through EMS.

Clearly, EMS—and the budgetary process in general—is a complex system that is a challenge to understand. Perhaps a look at the day-to-day process of budget-making and the various roles by the key actors in that process will help clarify this most important aspect of public administration. To this end, we now turn to an examination of the budgetary cycle as it unfolds within the EMS framework.

The Budgetary Cycle

It may appear that the central focus of the budget process is on the Minister of Finance when he delivers his budget speech to the House of Commons. And this is undoubtedly a key moment in the life of the government. But it is important to understand that the budget, and financial management in general, go on throughout the year, as Figure 10.3 reveals. The cycle and the key actors within EMS can be outlined in the following way.[47]

In the spring, from March to June, the Cabinet conducts strategy sessions that examine the results of the last budget, determining priorities largely on the basis of advice received from the Cabinet policy committees. Then, in the summer, Cabinet uses this information to guide the process of determining and defining

FIGURE 10.3   The Expenditure Management System

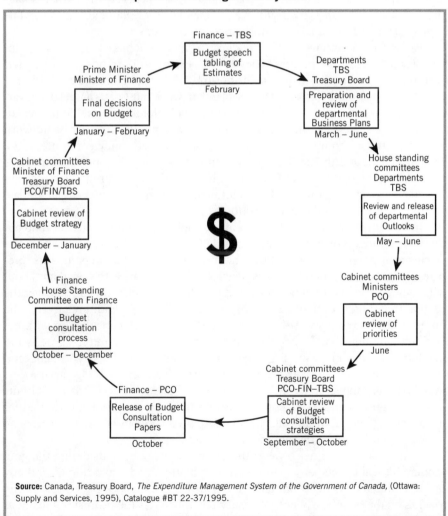

Source: Canada, Treasury Board, *The Expenditure Management System of the Government of Canada*, (Ottawa: Supply and Services, 1995), Catalogue #BT 22-37/1995.

reallocation and policy options for the consultation process that will take place in the fall.

The Cabinet policy committees oversee the design and implementation of new initiatives announced in the previous budget, and decide on new policy proposals in response to the strategic directions laid out by Cabinet. Meanwhile, departments and agencies prepare their multi-year Business Plans based on resources allocated in the previous budget. Their goal is to figure out how to match up their Business Plans and programs within available resources. At this time, departments also release documents called Outlooks on Program Priorities and Expenditures for review by the standing committees.

The Treasury Board reviews departmental Business Plans to ensure that departments are sticking to budget targets, and to assess the implications of these plans on the government overall. It also identifies areas where it feels intervention or support might be needed to ensure that departments adhere to their strategies and targets. The Treasury Board will also identify new reallocation options, while flagging areas that need more performance information.

Parliamentary committees use the departmental Outlooks as the starting point for their reviews of the process. They look at expenditure trends, priorities and performance, and report their conclusions to Parliament before the end of June.

During the summer, from June to September, while most of us are relaxing, various central agencies play an important part in the unfolding drama. In particular, the Privy Council Office, the Department of Finance and the Treasury Board work with departments to integrate the advice from Cabinet policy committees, the Treasury Board and the parliamentary committees. They then present strategies and options to the minister of Finance for his consideration during the budgetary consultation stage. Meanwhile, the Department of Finance also prepares an update on the general fiscal and economic outlook.

In the fall, from September to December, Cabinet as a whole considers and approves the budget consultation strategies devised by the minister of Finance. The Department of Finance, assisted by other central agencies and departments, prepares Budget Consultation Papers as the basis of discussions with Canadians about what ought to go into the upcoming budget. These Consultation Papers cover the economic and fiscal outlook, and prospective fiscal and expenditure targets. The minister of Finance releases these papers and then begins consultation with the Standing Committee on Finance, provincial finance ministers, interest groups and the public. Meanwhile, work is going on in the central agencies, departments and Cabinet policy committees to refine their contributions to the budgetary process in light of evolving circumstances. The Standing Committee on Finance submits its report at this time as well, commenting on the fiscal strategy being drafted for the upcoming budget. Meanwhile, the minister of Finance busily tries to incorporate all these inputs into the development of the budget.

In the winter, Cabinet reviews the budget strategy by considering the government's fiscal targets, any new spending initiatives and reallocations, and any proposed reductions in spending. The Department of Finance puts the finishing touches on the budget, while the Treasury Board finalizes the Estimates. Finally, as the country breathlessly awaits, the minister of Finance stands up in the House of Commons sometime around the end of February and delivers the budget, while the president of the Treasury Board tables the Estimates.

While this may appear to be the end of the story, it is in fact only the beginning... of the next round of budget preparation. For upon delivery of the budget by the minister of Finance, the departments go back to the task of preparing their Business Plans all over again. And the cycle continues.

As should be obvious, EMS involves a veritable army of actors playing a variety of important roles (see Figure 10.4). It is a complex process whose importance cannot be underestimated, since, once again, it is in the budget that the age-old political question of "Who gets what, when and how?" is answered.

FIGURE 10.4   Roles in the Expenditure Management System

Budget consultations

Cabinet
- Review Budget strategies, policy priorities and fiscal targets

Parliament
- House standing committees review and report on Estimates and departmental Outlooks
- Standing Committee on Finance reviews and reports on Budget Consultation Papers

The Public
- Provide input to individual ministers and the Minister of Finance on the Budget
- Comment on proposed spending plans to parliamentary standing committees

Cabinet decision-making process

Service to the public and value for money

Policy Committees of Cabinet
- Formulate strategic sector priorities for input into the Budget and expenditure planning processes
- Oversee the design and implementation of new programs
- Develop reallocation packages to fund any significant new initiatives

Expenditure Management System

Departments and Agencies
- Deliver effective and efficient programs and services
- Develop departmetnal Business Plans and release Outlooks that reflect Budget decisions
- Prepare departmental Estimates, including Part III

Privy Council Office
- Focus on overall government and prime ministerial priorities and the integrity and functioning of the system
- Provide support to Cabinet and its committees

Finance Minister/ Department
- Set the fiscal framework
- Focus on the economic outlook, macro-economic management, tax and fiscal policy, expenditure management at the macro level with primary emphasis on major statutory programs and debt management
- Prepare Budget Consultatiion Papers and the Budget documents

Treasury Board/ Secretariat
- Account for expenditures, including Main Estimates
- Help develop reallocation options
- Review departmental Business Plans
- Focus primarily on all expenditures other than major statutory expenditures and public debt and manage the Operating Reserve

Expenditure and Budget planning and coordination

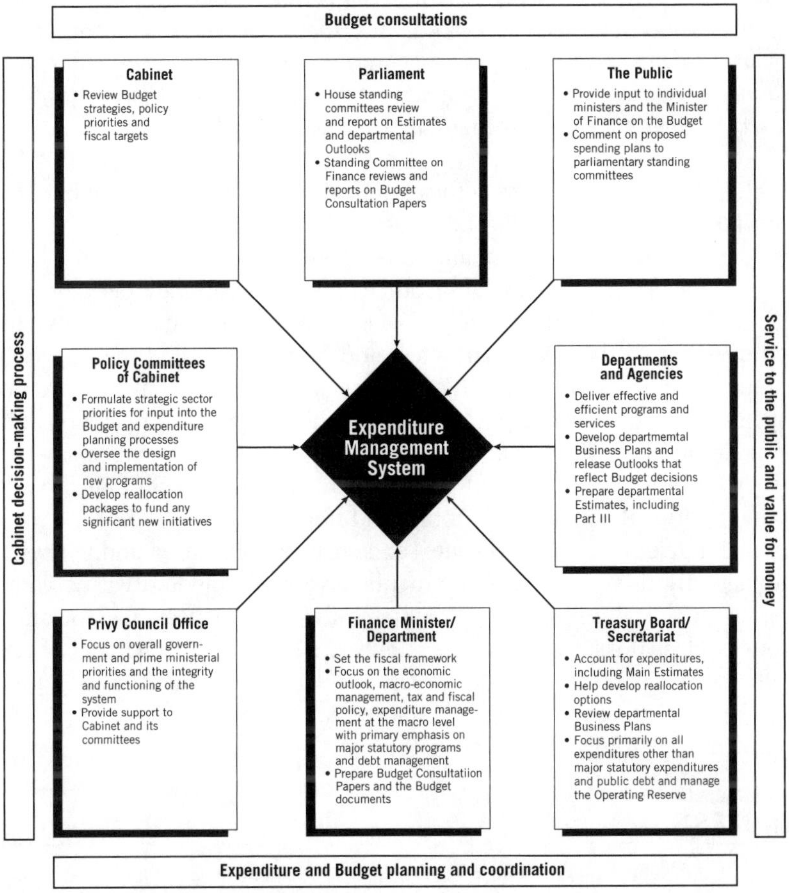

Source: Canada, Treasury Board, *The Expenditure Management System of the Government of Canada*, (Ottawa: Supply and Services, 1995), Catalogue #BT 22-37/1995.

WHAT YOU HAVE LEARNED

When new human resource or financial management systems are employed, public sector managers must ensure that the cure is not worse than the disease. There has been a lot of experimentation in pubic sector management, and the ultimate results may not be known for some time. The quantity and, more importantly, the quality of public services that Canadians have come to expect hang in the balance.[48]

Evert Lindquist, professor of public administration, summarized the changes in public service management in Canada over the past 20 years in the following way:

For those who work in Canada's public services, the last two decades have been remarkable. The 1980s can be characterized as a decade of government indecision, fiscal restraint, and mounting frustration for public servants, while the 1990s was a decade of decisive government action, significant downsizing, and great turmoil in most public bureaucracies. And, given demographic trends, continuing pressure to lower taxes and reduce public debt, the prospect of new regimes from negotiations between the federal government and provincial and aboriginal governments, and the opportunities presented by information technologies, the next decade promises to be just as dramatic for Canada's public services, but in new and perhaps unpredictable ways.[49]

In this chapter, we addressed the complexity of managing the public service. We considered what the managers of the public service do and how they do it, in the context of ongoing reform and in relation to money.

The management of financial resources involves elaborate decision-making systems dedicated to dividing the "pie" of government and answering the fundamental question, "Who gets what, when and how?" We noted the impact of diminishing revenues and other contemporary stresses and strains confronted by managers in the public service. And we noted the increased emphasis on auditing and evaluation (as suggested in Chapter 8), as well as performance assessment, efficiency and the importation of private sector business techniques to accompany the traditional concerns of probity and honesty.

In their attempt to resolve disputes and create a transparent and fair system of budgeting, various Canadian governments have experimented with a variety of budgeting models. But so far, no one system or model has been able to address all the hotly contested issues around the administration and management of government finances. Chapter 10 examined issues related to financial management by tracing the development of budgetary reform inspired by the Glassco Commission and actualized by PPBS, PEMS and EMS.

ENDNOTES

1. Robert F. Adie and Paul G. Thomas, *Canadian Public Administration: Problematical Perspectives, Second Edition,* (Scarborough: Prentice Hall, 1987): 252.
2. Canada. Treasury Board of Canada Secretariat. *Employment Statistics for the Federal Public Service April 1, 1999–March 31, 2000.* Ottawa: Treasury Board Secretariat, 2000: 1. http://www.tbs-sct.gc.ca/pubs_pol/hrpubs/pse-fpe/es-se99-00-1_e.html

3. Ian D. Clark, "Restraint, Renewal, and the Treasury Board Secretariat," *Canadian Public Administration,* 37, 2 (Summer, 1994): 213–214.

4. Canada, Auditor General, *Annual Report 1976,* (Ottawa: Supply and Services, 1976): 10.

5. Canada, Auditor General, *Annual Report 1978,* (Ottawa: Supply and Services, 1979).

6. Canada, Office of the Auditor General, *Report of the Auditor General of Canada—2001* (Ottawa: Office of the Auditor General, 2001). http://www.oag-bvg.gc.ca/domino/reports.nsf/html/01sice.html

7. See A.W. Johnson, *Reflections on Administrative Reform in the Government of Canada 1962–1991,* (Ottawa: Office of the Auditor General of Canada, 1992).

8. See Peter Aucoin, *The New Public Management: Canada in Comparative Perspective,* (Montreal: Institute for Research on Public Policy, 1995).

9. Gilles Paquet and Robert Shepherd, "The Program Review Process: A Deconstruction," in Gene Swimmer, ed. *How Ottawa Spends 1996–1997: Life Under the Knife,* (Ottawa: Carleton University Press, 1996): 42. The phrase "vertical solitude" is from D. Zussman and J. Jabes, *The Vertical Solitude: Managing in the Public Sector,* (Halifax: Institute for Research on Public Policy, 1989).

10. For an overview, see Michel Paquin, "Administrative Modernization Within the Canadian Government," in Jacques Bourgault, Maurice Demers and Cynthia Williams, eds. *Public Administration and Public Management: Experiences in Canada,* (Sainte-Foy, Quebec: Les Publications du Quebec, 1997): 144–154.

11. For Nielsen's own reflections on the work of his task force, see Eric Nielsen, *The House is Not a Home: An Autobiography,* (Toronto: Macmillian, 1989).

12. Donald J. Savoie, *Thatcher, Reagan, Mulroney: In Search of a New Bureaucracy,* (Pittsburgh: University of Pittsburgh Press, 1994): 130.

13. V.S. Wilson, "What Legacy? The Nielsen Task Force Program Review," in Katherine Graham, ed. *How Ottawa Spends 1988–1989: Conservatives Heading Into the Stretch,* (Ottawa: Carleton University Press, 1990): 23–47.

14. See Paquin, "Administrative Modernization Within the Canadian Government," (1997): 145.

15. See Clark, "Restraint, Renewal and the Treasury Board Secretariat," (1994): 215–216.

16. Paquin, "Administrative Modernization Within the Canadian Government," (1997): 216.

17. See Zussman and Jabes, *The Vertical Solitude,* (1989).

18. On the mandate of PS2000, see Government of Canada, *Public Service 2000: The Renewal of the Public Service of Canada,* (Ottawa: Supply and Services Canada, 1990): 3–4; and P.M. Tellier, "Public Service 2000: The Renewal of the Public Service," *Canadian Public Administration,* 33, 2 (Summer, 1990): 123–132.

19. Paquin, "Administrative Modernization Within the Canadian Government," (1997): 147.

20. Paquin, "Administrative Modernization Within the Canadian Government," (1997): 148.

21. Canada, Auditor General of Canada, *Auditor General's Report to the House of Commons,* (Ottawa: Ministry of Supply and Services, 1993).

22. See Peter Aucoin, *The New Public Management: Canada in Comparative Perspective,* (Montreal: Institute for Research on Public Policy, 1995).

23. Sandro Contenta, "A New Attack on Red Tape," *Toronto Star,* (Saturday, March 12, 1994): B4.

24. See Marcel Massé, "Getting Government 'Right': The Challenges of Governing Canada," in James John Guy, ed. *Expanding Our Political Horizons: Readings in Canadian Politics and Government,* (Toronto: Harcourt, Brace, 1997): 8–14.

25. See Paquin, "Administrative Modernization Within the Canadian Government," (1994): 152–153.

26. Gilles Paquet and Robert Shepherd, "The Program Review Process: A Deconstruction," in Gene Swimmer, ed. *How Ottawa Spends 1996–1997: Life Under the Knife,* (1996): 39–40.

27. See Canada, Privy Council Office, *Getting Government Right: A Progress Report,* (Ottawa: Minister of Supply and Services, 1996).

28. See Susan D. Phillips, "The Liberals' Mid-Life Crises: Aspirations Versus Achievements," in Susan D. Phillips, ed. *How Ottawa Spends 1995–1996: Mid-Life Crisis,* (Ottawa: Carleton University Press, 1995): 15.

29. Paquet and Shepherd, "The Program Review Process," (1996): 40.

30. Cited in Paquet and Shepherd, "The Program Review Process," (1996): 51–52.

31. Canada, *First Progress Report on La Relève: A Commitment to Action,* (Ottawa: La Relève Task Force, 1998): 2.

32. See Kenneth Kernaghan, Brian Marson and Sandford Borins, *The New Public Organization*, (Toronto: The Institute of Public Administration of Canada, 2000).

33. Jocelyne Bourgon, *Management Reform Agenda: 2001–2010,* Speech at the Association for Public Policy Analysis and Management, (Seattle, Washington, November 3, 2000): 3.

34. Anne Perkins and Robert P. Shepherd, "Managing in the Public Service: Some Implications for How We Are Governed," in Leslie A. Pal, ed. *How Ottawa Spends 2001–2002: Power in Transition*, (Toronto: Oxford University Press, 2001): 96–97. Jacques Bourgault and Barbara Wake Carroll, "The Canadian Senior Public Service: The Last Vestiges of the Whitehall Model?" in Jacques Bourgault, Maurice Demers and Cynthia Williams, eds. *Public Administration and Public Management: Experiences in Canada,* (Sainte-Foy, Quebec: Les Publications du Quebec, 1997): 93.

35. See John Shields and B. Mitchell Evans, *Shrinking the State: Globalization and Public Administration "Reform,"* (Halifax: Fernwood, 1998); and Peter Aucoin, *The New Public Management: Canada in Comparative Perspective,* (Montreal: Institute for Research on Public Policy, 1995).

36. Ralph Heintzman, "Introduction: Canada and Public Administration," in Jacques Bourgault, Maurice Demers and Cynthia Williams, eds. *Public Administration and Public Management: Experiences in Canada,* (Sainte-Foy, Quebec: Les Publications du Quebec, 1997): 8.

37. Donald J. Savoie, *The Politics of Public Spending in Canada,* (Toronto: University of Toronto Press, 1990): 4.

38. See Michael J. Prince, "Budegetary Trilogies: The Phases of Budget Reform in Canada," in Christopher Dunn, ed. *The Handbook of Canadian Public Administration*, (Toronto: Oxford Press, 2002).

39. Pater Harder and Evert Lindquist, "Expenditure Management and Reporting in the Government of Canada: Recent Developments and Backgrounds," in Jacques Bourgault, Maurice Demers and Cynthia Williams, eds. *Public Administration and Public Management: Experiences in Canada,* (Sainte-Foy, Quebec: Les Public Actions du Quebec, 1997): 72. The following discussion is partly derived from this source.

40. Savoie, *The Politics of Public Spending in Canada,* (1990): 26.

41. Harder and Lindquist, "Expenditure Management and Reporting in the Government of Canada," (1997): 73.

42. Harder and Lindquist, "Expenditure Management and Reporting in the Government of Canada," (1997): 76.

43. See Richard Van Loon, "The Policy and Expenditure Management System in the Federal Government: The First Three Years," *Canadian Public Administration,* 26 (Summer, 1983): 255–285.

44. See Ian D. Clark, "Recent Changes in the Cabinet Decision-Making System in Ottawa," *Canadian Public Administration,* 28, 2 (Summer, 1985): 185–201.

45. See Peter Aucoin, "Organizational Change in the Machinery of Canadian Government: From Rational Management to Brokerage Politics," *Canadian Journal of Political Science,* 19, 1 (March, 1986): 3–27.

46. See Evert A. Lindquist, "On the Cutting Edge: Program Review, Government Restructuring and the Treasury Board of Canada," in Gene Swimmer, ed. *How Ottawa Spends 1996–1997: Life Under the Knife,* (Ottawa: Carleton University Press, 1996): 205–252; and Harder and Lindquist, "Expenditure Management and Reporting in the Government of Canada," (1997): 85–86.

47. This description is derived from Canada, Treasury Board, *The Expenditure Management System of Canada,* (Ottawa: Minister of Supply and Services Canada, 1995).

48. See Peter Aucoin, "The Politics and Management of Restraint Budgeting," in André Blais and Stèphane Dion, eds. *The Budget-Maximizing Bureaucrat: Appraisals and Evidence,* (Pittsburgh: University of Pittsburgh Press, 1991): 119–141.

49. Evert A. Lindquist, "Government Restructuring and Career Public Service in Canada: Introduction and Overview," in Evert A. Lindquist, ed. *Government Restructuring and Career Public Services,* (Toronto: Institute of Public Administration of Canada, 2000): 1.

KEY WORDS AND CONCEPTS

Productivity Improvement Program (310)
Ministerial Task Force on Program Review (310)
Increased Ministerial Authority and
  Accountability (311)
PS2000 (312)
Program Review (314)
La Relève (316)

PPBS (325)
line-item budgeting (326)
program budgeting (327)
PEMS (327)
EMS (328)
Business Plans (328)

REVIEW QUESTIONS

1. Restructuring the Public Service: The Management View
Recent changes have altered the composition of the public service. Downsizing, reengineering, pay freezes, cutbacks, layoffs and firings have been endemic. This section asked the following: What are the most important recent reforms to the management of the public service? How has restructuring affected the public service? What has it done to the morale of those remaining in the public service? How has it affected the delivery of services to the public? What are the implications of privatizing and contracting out? What does the future hold for those seeking a career in the Canadian public service?

2. Financial Management
The fundamental questions of power politics raised in Chapter 4 revolved around the question of "Who gets what, when and how?" We returned here to this question by examining that most fundamental of issues related to government: money. The federal government manages billions of dollars of taxpayers' money (that is, *your* money) every year. This fact alone raises a host of questions: How is that money managed? What budgeting systems have been established to ensure that probity, honesty, economy, efficiency and accountability are maintained? Who is ultimately responsible for the management of funds? What kinds of competitions do departments engage in to ensure that they get their share of the loot? What is the budgetary cycle?

FURTHER READING

1. Restructuring the Public Service: The Management View

Albo, Gregory. "Democratic Citizenship and the Future of Public Management." In G. Albo, D. Langille and L. Panitch, eds. *A Different Kind of State? Popular Power and Democratic Administration.* Toronto: Oxford University Press, 1993.

Campbell, Colin and George Szablowski. *The Superbureaucrats: Structure and Behaviour in Central Agencies.* Toronto: Macmillan, 1979.

Canada. Public Service Commission of Canada. *A Timeline of the Public Service Commission of Canada.* Ottawa: Public Service Commission of Canada, 1998: 7–10. http://www.psc-cfp.gc.ca/research/timeline/psc_timeline_e.htm

Hodgetts, J.E., William McCloskey, Reginald Whitaker and V. Seymour Wilson. *The Biography of an Institution: The Civil Service of Canada, 1908–1967.* Montreal: McGill-Queen's University Press, 1972.

Kernaghan, Kenneth. "Empowerment and Public Administration: Revolutionary Advance or Passing Fancy." *Canadian Public Administration,* 35, 2. (Summer, 1992).

2. *Financial Management*

Hood, Christopher. "Emerging Issues in Public Administration," *Public Administration*, 73 (1995): 165–183.

Panitch, Leo. "A Different Kind of State?" In G. Albo, D. Langille and L. Panitch, eds. *A Different Kind of State? Popular Power and Democratic Administration*. Toronto: Oxford University Press, 1993.

Strick, John C. *The Public Sector in Canada: Programs, Finance and Policy*. Toronto: Thompson Educational Publishing, 1999.

 ## WEBLINKS

Department of Finance
www.fin.gc.ca/

Canadian Centre for Management Development
www.ccmd-ccg.gc.ca

Public Service Commission of Canada: Management Trainee Program
jobs.gc.ca/mtp-psg/index_e.htm

Chapter (11)

Public Administration *and* Ethics

One of the distinguishing features of public administration is that in the interests of accountability, public servants are subject to ethical guidelines that are often absent in the private sector. Although it is important to ensure the honesty and integrity of those dedicated to serving the public interest, the guidelines may impede efficiency in providing services. So, yet again, we encounter the difficulty of two core values—accountability and efficiency—clashing with one another in the workings of public administration.

This chapter assesses the issue of ethics in the public service. It considers how the behaviour of public servants is shaped and constrained in the context of several ethical dilemmas. It also considers measures that can be taken to ensure the highest standards of conduct by public servants. To this end, the chapter is divided into the following sections:

1. *Ethical Dilemmas in the Public Service*
   This section sketches out some of the broad controversies surrounding the ethical standards of behaviour in the public sector. It asks these questions: What behaviours are acceptable within the public sector, and what are not? Are standards of behaviour in the public sector significantly different from those in the private sector? What is the "public interest"? What is the importance of discretion, partisanship, public comment, conflict of interest, lying to the public, and public versus private-sector ethics?

2. *Codes of Conduct*
   Powerful arguments have been put forth to suggest that ethical behaviour can only be maintained if public sector employees are subject to written codes of conduct

that spell out both acceptable activities and penalties for failure to comply. Others have suggested that written codes are unsuitable and that education and role models are preferable means for ensuring ethical behaviour. This section addresses this debate and asks the following: What are ethical codes of conduct? How do they work, and are they effective? Why is it felt that codes of conduct are required? What other mechanisms can be used to ensure that the highest ethical standards are upheld? What alternative means exist to ensure the integrity of public servants?

Ethical Dilemmas in the Public Service

Ethical conduct among civil servants and their political masters is important. It has long been established that public officials must not use their offices for private gain. Nor may they disclose confidential information or place themselves in positions of conflict of interest. As a result of these and other considerations (discussed below), the strictures on the behaviour of public servants are considerable, as are the opportunities and temptations that present themselves. They are also unique, compared to the private sector. Public servants may find themselves in untenable situations as a result of their overriding need to behave in an ethical manner. To behave ethically requires a sense of personal integrity shaped in part by the standards of the profession, but also by personal socialization outside the workplace. Reconciling these two sources of ethical and moral principle can be tremendously difficult.

The issue of **ethics** in the public service is relatively new as a subject of study in Canadian public administration. It has also recently spawned new practices, institutions and behaviours. But questionable ethical behaviour has been a feature of Canadian political life since before Confederation. As two observers put it,

Scandals and rumours of scandals have been an ever-present curse within the Canadian political system from well before Confederation. Canadian history is replete with "horror stories" involving the Château Clique and the Family Compact, the Grand Trunk and the CPR, the Ross rifle and liquor licensing. Of more recent vintage, allegations and verified incidents of unethical political party financing arrangements, as well as conflicts of interest involving government contracting, influence-peddling, favoritism and nepotism have attracted attention on the federal and provincial stages.[1]

Moreover, the Civil Service reforms of 1918, while ushering in a meritocracy, said little or nothing about ethical behaviour.

One of the reasons ethics has garnered more attention as of late is the changing nature of public administration, much of which we documented in earlier chapters. In the days when government was small, a coterie of mandarins controlled the public service, and were able to infuse it with a set of shared values, attitudes and beliefs. Ethical norms and standards were derived largely from these role models at the apex of the bureaucracy. But as government grew and became more complex and unwieldy, and as scores of new recruits brought their own ethical "baggage" with them, the shared values of an earlier era gave way to new ones. Control, in the form of inculcating bureaucrats with the same values as the mandarins, eroded. As the public service grew, the chains of command lengthened; and as they lengthened, they loosened, making room for new interpretations of what constituted ethical behaviour.

Related to these developments is the fact that opportunities for bureaucratic **discretion** increased, and attitudes changed about the appropriate role of public servants. More and more, they were seen as agents of change, rather than simply as passive servants of the public will, and the old distinctions between politics and administration were increasingly challenged. Moreover, as morale in the public sector has plunged, the notion of a "career" public servant has undergone a metamorphosis, so the core values that used to characterize the career also have undergone change. In addition, the new climate of evaluation emerging in Canadian public administration meant taking a closer look, not just at management, but at the ethical and moral behaviour of public servants, and ways to evaluate it. Freedom of information and privacy acts and commissioners proliferated, as did ombuds offices. The practices of auditors general and comptrollers provided the templates for considering ways in which the ethical behaviour of public servants could be measured, and calls for establishing **ethics commissioners** emerged.[2]

In 1996, a groundbreaking report was published entitled *A Strong Foundation*[3] which provided in-depth discussion of values and ethics in the public service. Also known as the Tait Report after its author John Tait, it called for government bodies to identify core corporate values and standards of ethical conduct. The Tait Report looked at core values in the public service, such as democratic values (respect for elected officials, accountability, non-partisanship); professional values (innovation, resourcefulness); ethical values (probity, public interests); and people values (openness, fairness, courage). Following the Tait Report, in 1999 the Clerk of the Privy Council named two senior public servants as "co-champions" of a government-wide dialogue on ethics in the public service. They worked to impress upon the broader public service the centrality of values and ethics in the work of public servants, and contributed to the development of a comprehensive framework for values and ethics in the public service. Also in 1999, the Office of Values and Ethics was created to undertake public service-wide initiatives to promote values and ethics (see Box 11-1). It was also made responsible for the conflict of interest code for public servants and for developing an internal disclosure policy.[4]

Recent changes rooted in neoconservative approaches and the New Public Management have created a new orientation toward ethics. For instance, the trend toward "partnering" and contracting out, and toward merging public and private sector practices, has meant that the value systems of the two are increasingly bumping up against one another, posing new challenges.

Ethical behaviour in the public service is particularly important because it contributes to the public's perception of our political institutions. It promotes trust and efficacy. Since public servants and politicians are the guardians of the public's interests, there should be a special bond between the state and citizens,

Box 11-1

The Office of Values and Ethics

 Treasury Board of Canada
Secretariat

Secrétariat du Conseil du Trésor
du Canada

Dialogue on Public Service Values and Ethics

Working Definitions

Values—are enduring beliefs that influence opinions, actions and the choices and decisions we make.

Ethics—is that dimension of human thought and behaviour which is guided by standards and principles of right conduct. It involves a commitment to do the right thing.

An Ethical Dilemma—is a situation in which:
- You are unsure of the right thing to do.
- Two or more of our values may be in conflict.
- Some harm may be caused, no matter what you do.

How Do You Decide What To Do?

- You consider your obligation to act.
- You consider the options you have.
- You choose the best option that considers:

| **Authority to Act** | **Values** |
| **Consequences** | **Care for Others** |

- If unsure, talk to those you trust, to your ombudsman or ethics counsellor (if applicable) or to your supervisor. Someone is prepared to listen and help, anytime you have a concern or problem.

- You decide. You act. You accept responsibility for your actions.

expressed through the latter's belief that public officials can be depended upon to act in the best interests of Canadians. Lately, though, public confidence in government has diminished. Canadians are reported to be more cynical and disrespectful of public institutions. Not all of this can be blamed on the unethical behaviour of public officials, but a considerable amount of the public's perceptions are shaped by this factor. For example, the resignation of a half-dozen Cabinet ministers from the Mulroney government for a variety of offences, both real and perceived, and an unsavoury series of scandals in the Chrétien government con-

Office of Values and Ethics
www.tbs-sct.gc.ca/veo-bve *(613) 957-2458*
....

Public Service Values and Ethics
Extract from *A Summary* of the Tait Report (Feb 97)

The four families of core values:

The Democratic Values of:

Responsible government ● Rule of law ● Support for democracy ● Loyalty ● Respect for authority of elected office holders ●Neutrality/non-partisanship ● Accountability ● Due process ● Public interest/public good

The "Traditional" Professional Values of:

Neutrality ● Merit ● Excellence ● Effectiveness ● Economy ● Frankness ● Objectivity and impartiality in advice ● Speaking truth to power ● Balancing complexity ● Fidelity to the public trust

The "New" Professional Values of:

Quality ● Innovation ● Initiative ● Creativity ● Resourcefulness ● Service to clients/citizens ● Horizontality (collaboration) ● Teamwork

The Ethical Values of:

Integrity ● Honesty ● Probity ● Prudence ● Impartiality ● Equity ● Selflessness ● Discretion ● Public trust

The People Values of:

Respect ● Concern/caring ● Civility/courtesy ● Tolerance ● Openness ● Collegiality/participation ● Fairness ● Moderation ● Decency ● Reasonableness ● Humanity ● Courage

Canada

tributed heavily to the growing public disgust with politicians, who are increasingly seen as self-interested. Changing attitudes toward authority seem to be a part of the contemporary political culture, and they influence the public's attitude regarding the ethical standards that should be applied to public servants and their political masters. According to political scientist Neil Nevitte, there has recently been a marked decline in the public confidence in government institutions. For example, in 1981, about 36.9 percent surveyed claimed to have "high" confidence in government institutions in Canada. By 1990, this number had dropped to 29.4 percent.[5] More recent polling data shows that since the 1990s, the percentage of Canadians who have trust in the government has remained at about 30 percent.[6]

The concept of the public interest underscores the expectation of ethical behaviour in the public service. One of the early considerations of this issue was undertaken by E. Pendleton Herring in his 1936 book *Public Administration and the Public Interest.*[7] Herring was concerned with the tremendous growth in the scope of government activity, and in particular, the fact of growing bureaucratic discretion in decision-making. He noted that laws and regulations were often vague in their wording, and that, as such, bureaucrats were left to interpret what the politicians meant before actually implementing their instructions. This called into question who was really in charge, as we noted in Chapter 1—the bureaucrats or the politicians? More to the point, the bureaucrat may be required to make determinations about what constitutes the public interest. According to Herring, the most effective way this can be accomplished, while still remaining true to the spirit and intent of the legislation at hand, is for the bureaucrat to establish a sound working relationship with the societal interest most affected by the legislation, and "broker" differences between competing groups. An added concern, Herring points out, is that between the time a law is passed and the time an administrative agency is responsible for its implementation, societal conditions that inspired the law may well have changed. Thus, to implement the law as originally intended may actually run counter to the public interest as newly expressed.

Unfortunately, Herring also argues, the concept of the public interest that ought to guide public servants in these circumstances is an ambiguous one. It is defined in part by the subjective perceptions of the civil servant involved. Thus, the ethical standards of these individuals must be beyond reproach. But in any event, we rely tremendously on their discretion in the administrative process. We elaborate on the issue of discretion below.

The notion of the public interest is perhaps the single most important concept guiding the ethical dimension of administrative behaviour.[8] John Tait wrote:

The ideal of service is one of the deepest sources of public service motivation. In the heart of most public servants lies the conviction that service to the public, to the public good, or to the public interest is what makes their profession like no other. It is why they chose it, for the most part; and why they keep at it, with enthusiasm and conviction, despite difficulties and frustrations along the way. Service to the public and to the public interest is the vision of the public service, and it is a creative, essential and compelling vision.[9]

But developing a set of guidelines so that every decision can objectively be said to serve the public interest is impossible. There are too many variables involved. And the concept itself is too ambiguous. It changes over time and under different circumstances. And it often differs according to whether one is politician, bureaucrat or citizen. This does not mean, though, that we should throw our hands up in despair and declare that there is no ethical standard that can be used to determine the public interest.

How, then, is a standard arrived at? One answer is for various groups in society to mobilize themselves to influence government. Government, in turn, acts as a neutral referee between these groups, determining whose interests are met and whose are declined. In this scenario, the objective application of a set of guidelines is all that government requires in order to determine as fairly and honestly as possible who the winners and losers are. However, what this ignores is that not all the groups involved in this struggle have equal resources. Some are well-financed, sophisticated organizations with access to the halls of power. Others are relatively penniless, with little knowledge of how government works, and are shut out of the network. Under these circumstances, can we still say that the public interest is being served if some are able to get their views across to government and others aren't?

This raises ethical issues, because the objects of attention of these groups are politicians and public servants. The question that arises is this: Can we be sure that ethical values of fairness and honesty are being followed in circumstances in which some citizens seem able to achieve privileged access to decision-makers and others cannot? Indeed, what happens when decision-makers succumb to the blandishments of the well-organized? Do they override the broader public interest? More directly, what if some material reward is offered by those interests—the promise of a job after leaving office, for instance, or cash or services? Or, to consider the issue from a slightly different perspective, is the public servant who responds only to the voices she can hear doing a proper job? Or is the public servant who actively seeks out the marginalized, the dispossessed and the unorganized—that is, all interests related to a particular issue—doing the ethical thing? Is it the job of the public servant to solicit the views of societal interests, or merely to respond to them? To simply respond is to leave some citizens out. But if the public servant solicits views, she must invariably do so on the basis of her own personal value judgments about what groups should be heard. In other words, she is injecting her own ethical and moral value system into the process of public administration. Is it ethical to sit back and accept that the public interest is defined somewhere else, knowing that some societal interest will not get a fair hearing? Is it ethical to step forward and try to shape the "public interest" by injecting your own views into the struggle, even though this would seem to run counter to the job of public servant? The resolution of these conflicts is rooted in the debate over how to ensure ethical standards of behaviour among public servants. There are no easy answers to these questions.

"Administrative ethics," according to one observer, "involves the application of moral principles to the conduct of officials in organizations."[10] As you will recall from our discussion of organizational theory in chapters 2 and 3, understanding the behaviour of individuals in organizations is a challenging and complex undertaking. Even assuming you can understand their motives, it is still not certain that all the members of an organization subscribe to the same general moral code. In other words, it is not always clear what rights and duties individuals respect when they engage in activity that affects the public interest. At the root of the problem is the fact that moral behaviour in organizations requires individuals to assume an objective and disengaged perspective. It requires them, in other words, to separate their own self-interest from the interest of those they are serving, and to be as unbiased in the application of rules and procedures as is humanly possible. However, the complicating factor is that we are all humans, and we all carry biases with us. Moreover, finding common moral ground with others in the organization is a challenge for two reasons. First, questions need to be answered about who *may judge*; second, questions need to be answered about who *is to be judged*. The former raises the notion that bureaucrats are supposed to be neutral in fulfilling their duties; that is, they should not be guided by their own personal morality or principles, but by those of the organization. The latter suggests that responsibility for the decisions of the organization should rest not with the individuals, but with the organization itself (through its senior officers).

In an ideal organizational world, civil servants carry out the orders of their superiors and implement the policies of the government. In this scenario, they are ethically neutral vessels or instruments. They need not exercise independent moral judgment, and are not expected to act on moral principles that they may themselves hold. Instead, they simply act on the principles contained in the orders they are given and the policies they are to implement. Simply put, "They serve the organization so that the organization may serve society."[11]

This is not to deny that individual civil servants have moral and ethical belief systems of their own. Clearly they do. But the theory described above suggests that, in effect, they park those belief systems at the door when they arrive at work. Their goal is to understand what policy their political masters intend, and to faithfully enact it. If there is a conflict, they do not fall back on their own personal moral code, but rather look to whatever legal or constitutional guidelines exist that might apply in the given case. This view sees administrators as instruments serving the goals of the organization. If they find themselves in a position of unbearable moral or ethical conflict, they have the option to resign. Thus, it is argued, the organization is made capable of serving any social end, regardless of the personal views of those who hold office.

Is this a realistic view of the roles of individuals within organizations where ethical issues are concerned? It may seem as though it requires humans to become automatons—robotic in their behaviour. This criticism is not far off the mark. Requiring people to suspend their own morality to serve the greater ends of the organization seems like a hyper-Weberian recipe—geared solely toward efficiency at the expense of other more human values. And yet, consider an organization at the other end of the spectrum. Think of one in which all decisions and actions are subject to the moral and ethical belief systems of each and every individual concerned. Would anything get done? *Could* anything get done? Surely paralysis of the organization would result. Ideally, then, a smoothly functioning and responsible organization must somehow strike a balance between the strictures of pure neutrality described above, and the chaos of moral relativism that would result if each individual in the organization was left to inject her own personal morality into every decision and action.

The dilemmas posed by trying to strike that balance are many and varied. To illustrate, we will now turn to some particular examples, including the following issues: discretion, partisanship, public comment, conflict of interest, lying to the public, and the ethics of the public sector versus private sector.[12] In each of the following scenarios, imagine that you are a civil servant confronted with the ethical dilemma. How would you respond?

Discretion

The first issue concerns discretion, which means simply the power of free decision of choice within certain legal bounds. It reflects our abilities to exercise judgment and discriminate between courses of action. Public servants exercise a certain amount of power. As a result, they are frequently placed in situations where their own personal judgment of the integrity of their actions comes into play. So, public servants enjoy a high level of discretion in their conduct.

For example, a directive may come down the chain of command from the minister, through the deputy minister, to the assistant deputy minister, and so on down to you, working in the frontlines of a service-providing agency of the government. But by the time the directive gets to you, its instructions, while well-intentioned, bear little relation to the issues you face on a day-to-day basis. And they may even run counter in some ways to the expectations of citizens about the type of service you provide. For example, suppose you issue support payments to social assistance recipients. The rules from on high dictate that recipients must produce proof of residence before you can give them a cheque. Now suppose a regular client comes in and tells you that he has been kicked out of his apartment, but has a new place lined up for next week. Technically, without proof of residence, you cannot issue the cheque. But you have come to know this individual and some of the problems he is experiencing in trying to get his life in order. What do you do?

Your own personal sense of integrity and compassion suggest that issuing a cheque just this once will not hurt anyone, and will certainly benefit this individual who faces the prospect of a few nights in a shelter. But your institutional training warns you that issuing the cheque is a breach of rules. Clearly your own discretion comes into play in these circumstances.

Discretion in small cases may be acceptable, providing the law is not transgressed and no one is denied what they are entitled to from the government. But we enter a hazy area when discretion is applied too liberally or too frequently, so that the rules are made a mockery of, the law is broken, or citizens are denied their entitlements. When discretion is abused, we enter the realm of unethical conduct. Public servants enjoy a certain amount of discretion in fulfilling their duties, and there is scope for misconduct, for instance in the handling of confidential information. As with many of our examples, the issue often comes down to a question of whether the means justify the end. In other words, do the discretionary acts of public servants justify the outcome?

Partisanship

Partisanship is another pitfall of which public servants must be aware. This refers to the notion that bureaucrats should remain loyal to the government in the execution of their duties, and not to the political party that happens to hold power. In other words, they are to be politically neutral in discharging their duties. The Statement of Principles of the Institute of Public Administration of Canada puts it this way:

Public employees should be sensitive to the political process and knowledgable about the laws and traditions regarding political neutrality that are applicable to their spheres of employment.

It is the responsibility of public employees to provide forthright and objective advice to, and carry out the directions of, their political superiors.

Public employees have a duty to carry out government decisions loyally, irrespective of the party or persons in power and irrespective of their personal opinions.[13]

But consider this example: What if you, as a public servant, are ordered to conceal information that might affect the outcome of an election? In this instance, you are pulled in two directions at once. On the one hand, you have a duty to follow the orders of your superiors; on the other hand, you have a responsibility to serve the **public interest**. You are trained to be nonpartisan, yet by taking no action, you are perhaps tilting the balance of an election toward one party over another.

This dilemma is related to several features of public administration discussed earlier in this book. For instance, it reflects the associated problems of the politics-administration dichotomy; that is, politicians make the rules and bureaucrats implement them. It raises again the question of merit and patronage. Presumably, in an era of widespread patronage appointments, nonpartisanship was largely irrelevant—indeed, even antithetical—to the workings of government. But in a merit-based era, the opposite is true. And finally, it raises the issue of loyalty. Public servants are required to loyally serve the government, irrespective of their personal feelings about that government's policies. The reward for loyalty is tenure; public servants cannot be arbitrarily dismissed as long as they perform their jobs satisfactorily. But clearly, these principles are severely tested by the type of ethical issue alluded to above.

Public Comment

The notion of **public comment** reflects the idea that public servants should remain anonymous and stay out of the public limelight. But the temptation to go public with information may be hard to resist, if not doing so conflicts with an individual's personal integrity. Consider this example: You receive confidential ministry documents that suggest a possible coverup of government neglect regarding the discharge of toxic chemicals into the environment. Coincidentally, an old friend who works as a journalist calls you up and invites you for lunch. Do you reveal the information to her?

Or consider this example: You are a senior public servant in possession of facts which reveal that the government's policy in a certain area is marginally damaging to some Canadians, although overall the policy benefits those it was intended to help. You are required to appear before a parliamentary committee to testify about certain aspects of the legislation; however, you are not questioned directly on the material in your possession. Do you nonetheless explicitly criticize your minister and department by revealing the information publicly? It is worth noting that a recent trend in Canadian public administration has seen senior public servants being called into the public limelight more and more often to explain the actions of their departments. This would seem to undermine the principle of refraining from commenting publicly. We explore this development in more detail in Chapter 12, when we consider the changing nature of accountability.

Conflict of Interest

Conflicts of interest can bedevil public servants in large and small ways. For instance, is it a conflict of interest to accept a modest gift or a dinner from a corporation seeking a government contract? And should there be a "cooling-off period" after you, as a former high-level bureaucrat, leave a post to work in the private sector, before you can turn around and begin to lobby your former department? Or what if you are pressured from on high to award a contract to a particular firm, even though you know that firm did not present the best bid? What if you possess financial information concerning an upcoming budget and could profit from that information by playing the stock market? Should you tell your family or friends? Is it a conflict to "moonlight"—that is, to accept employment outside your regular public sector job?[14]

Conflict of interest is a common ethical dilemma in the public service. It arises when there is a possibility that public servants will materially benefit from activities related to their employment, or in situations where the objective performance of their job is interfered with. The Institute of Public Administration of Canada's Statement of Principles cites the following prohibitions concerning conflicts of interest:

Public employees should not engage in any business or transaction or have any financial or other personal interest that is, or may appear to be, incompatible with the performance of their official duties.

Public employees should not, in the performance of their official duties, seek personal or private gain by granting preferential treatment to any persons.

Public employees should not solicit nor, unless duly authorized, accept transfers of economic value from persons with whom they have contact in their official capacity.

Public employees should not use, or permit the use of, government property of any kind for activities not associated with the performance of their official duties, unless they are authorized to do so.

Public employees should not seek or obtain personal or private gain from the use of information acquired during the course of their official duties which is not generally available to the public.[15]

These are guidelines only, of course. But they indicate the scope of potential conflicts that the public servant is confronted with and which he must avoid. A complicating factor is that there are differences between real, apparent and potential conflicts of interest. In other words, appearances can be as important as reality. So conflict of interest is a slippery concept, but a significant one in the realm of the ethical conduct of civil servants.

Lying for the Public Good

Other sorts of ethical dilemmas confront public servants. Are there ever circumstances in which public servants ought to lie to the public? The issue of **lying for the public good** has been considered since the earliest of times. For instance,

"Plato, in *The Republic*, used the expression the 'noble lie' in presenting a fanciful story to persuade people to accept class distinctions and thereby safeguard social harmony; and Machiavelli's prince was most certainly encouraged to engage in deceit, if it was in his interest to do so."[16]

A recent case involved scientists in the Ministry of Agriculture allegedly being required to suppress information concerning the harmful effects on humans of drinking milk from cattle treated with a particular growth hormone. Allegations were made that senior bureaucrats ordered a coverup, and may have shredded sensitive documents that could have substantiated the claims of the scientists counselling caution. Millions of dollars in the Canadian agri-business sector were at stake, as was the livelihood of countless dairy farmers and their families. Is it possible that senior public servants, and perhaps even their political masters, were "captured" by the interests promoting the use of the hormone, prompting a web of deceit to descend over the issue? To put it more directly, if you were a public official in this case, would you withhold the entire truth about the harmful effects of the hormone if you knew so much was at stake? If there was 100-percent scientifically validated evidence that the hormone was harmful, probably not. But what if there was only a 50-percent chance? Or a 10-percent chance? Or a 1-percent chance?

It is conceivable that there are circumstances under which lying actually promotes the public good, and this fact complicates the search for ethical guidelines all the more. Consider these three examples, for instance.[17] First, imagine that you are confronted with an overwhelming national crisis wherein harm can only be averted by deceit. Second, consider the opposite case, where the effect of the lie is so harmless that it hardly seems to matter. Third, consider a situation in which the release of vital information invades the privacy of individuals whom you are sworn to protect. Is lying justifiable in any of these cases?

It is probably safe to say that most people abide by a personal moral code that tells them that lying is wrong. Yet in the public service, are there situations in which lies are justifiable? Is it ethically and morally wrong, for instance, to withhold the truth about national security issues? Is it wrong to withhold potentially damaging information about a government policy? Should public servants be guided by the admonition, "Don't do or say anything you don't want to read about in the papers"? Again, there are no easy answers to these questions; they indicate the depth of the ethical dilemma confronting public servants.

Public Sector versus Private Sector Ethics

Should you implement policies with which you disagree, or from which you can visualize damage resulting? In other words, do public servants owe their primary allegiance to the public, to their political masters, or to their own personal moral code and conscience? Can the rules be bent for particular cases, or must they be rigidly adhered to in all cases? Is the measure of acceptable behaviour the consequences of actions taken, or is there some other higher moral standard? These are questions that are wrestled with daily in the public service.

If we search for answers to them by comparing practices in the public sector to those in the private sector, we may be frustrated by what we find. It is sometimes argued that in their obligations to the public, civil servants have an additional, more rigorous set of standards and constraints than those found in the private sector. The former chairman and chief executive officer of Imperial Oil argued that "there is an added ethical dimension expected of those in the public service" due to the fact that they must uphold the public trust.[18] Many acceptable practices in the private sector are either forbidden or frowned upon in the public sector.

These include the following: accepting certain kinds of gifts; discussion of certain kinds of appointments; promises or threats of government action under certain circumstances; receiving or holding large amounts of cash; withholding information contrary to the public's need to know; leaking information that should be kept private. These activities underline the differences between the private and public sector where ethical behaviour is concerned—differences further illustrated by the following:

A democratic government is not a family business, dominated by its patriarch; nor is it a military battalion, or a political campaign headquarters. It is a producing organization which belongs to its members, and it is the only such organization whose members include all the citizens within its jurisdiction. Those who work for and are paid by the government are ultimately servants of the whole country, which owns and supports the government.[19]

Moreover, there is a regime of constitutional and administrative law that informs the actions of civil servants and that applies to their work in a more direct

FIGURE 11-1

Source: Theo Moudakis, *Toronto Star.*

manner than in the private sector. As a result, it is generally recognized that citizens expect higher standards of ethical conduct from public servants than they do from business persons. Finally, the two have different motivations. As we noted in Chapter 1, private sector activity is motivated by the bottom line, whereas the public sector has no such motivation. These qualitative differences should not be overlooked.

Now, however, we have entered an era in which governments are supposed to be run in a more businesslike fashion. Does this mean importing the ethics of the private sector along with its management practices? Moreover, the trend now is for governments to increasingly share responsibility with stakeholders, creating a new balance between the private and public worlds. As one observer puts it, "We are witnessing a shift from emphasis on the government as regulator to the government as co-regulator. Interdependency is what creates the new balance—and this has definite moral implications."[20] No longer will the government be the sole or most important watchdog of the public good under these conditions. But are private sector actors willing and able to assume this part of government's traditional role, along with the benefits accruing from these new partnerships? From an ethical point of view, is it appropriate to expect commercial associations, whose goal is profit maximization, to develop and implement policy, and to self-regulate? These questions have not yet been satisfactorily answered.

This is not a comprehensive list of all possible ethical dilemmas public servants face. But it should give you some sense of the complexity of the issues. There is unfortunately not always a straightforward "correct" answer to many of the situations cited above. This fact has led to the call for some sort of institutionalization of ethical conduct. It is argued that only by putting rules, regulations and guidelines on paper for all to see and read can the proper ethical standards needed in the public sector be understood and upheld. As a result, arguments for standardized "codes of ethics" have become increasingly common. But as we will see, this solution is not without its detractors.

Codes of Conduct

According to two professors of public administration, there are seven "commandments" to which the responsible public servant is expected to adhere. They are as follows:

[A]ct in the public interest; be politically neutral; do not disclose confidential information; protect the privacy of citizens and employees; provide efficient, effective and fair service to the public; avoid conflicts of interest; and be accountable.[21]

To ensure that the public retains confidence in the administrative machinery of the government, these issues must be managed sensitively. This explains the codes of conduct, regulations, guidelines and laws that have evolved over the past few decades. But clearly, some of the issues raised above defy easy resort to written or codified rules of conduct. Thus, the issue of codifying the ethical behaviour of civil servants is contentious. So, some believe that other means are needed to achieve the objectives intended by a code of conduct approach. This section will consider the pros and cons of codes of ethics, as well as two other techniques for reinforcing ethical behaviour: training and education, and role models.[22]

Do Codes of Conduct Work?

According to one view, responsible behaviour by public servants should be measured against the expectation that ethical behaviour in government should reinforce the democratic process. It should be ensured that officials respect the rights of citizens and uphold values seen by the broader society as essential to democracy. But it is not always easy to ensure that officials in public service are sensitive to these values. Nor is it obvious that they are sufficiently self-questioning about the bigger ethical concerns in their daily decision-making or execution of policies.[23]

Consequently, the drive toward codifying ethical behaviour has gained momentum. In the 1970s and 1980s, governments began to trip over themselves in issuing "codes of conduct" and "ethical guidelines to behaviour" and "conflict of interest regulations." A veritable explosion of interest developed in the issue of ethics. This was partly a response to major scandals such as Watergate in the United States during the 1970s, when U.S. president Richard Nixon was forced to resign after having been charged with unethical and illegal behaviour. It was also a response to the increasing role of the media in uncovering government malfeasance.[24] While many of these codes of conduct related primarily to political actors, concern spread to the actions of public servants too. The Canadian government jumped on the bandwagon and introduced a Conflict of Interest Code in 1985, after having staged a Task Force on Conflict of Interest the year before.[25]

More recently, in 1995, the Clerk of the Privy Council formed a Task Force on Public Service Values and Ethics, composed of Deputy Ministers, to investigate contemporary issues and developments in this area.[26] And, as noted above, an Office of Values and Ethics was created in 1999. The media has played a prominent role in placing these kinds of issues before the public. In so doing, it has played two roles simultaneously: as investigator, it uncovers malfeasance and brings it to light for the public; and as watchdog, it acts as a deterrent to public servants and politicians fearful of having their names splashed across the front pages of the newspaper. (See Box 11-2.)

Ultimately, it would seem that the effectiveness of codes of conduct depends upon ongoing scrutiny of the activities of public officials by their colleagues within the organization, by other organizations, by the media and by an attentive public. This, of course, depends on openness and accountability. But there is no sure-fire way of ensuring ethical behaviour that is consonant with the public interest. It ultimately depends on the individuals who aspire to public office, and the system of values into which they have been socialized. This, of course, creates a contemporary dilemma for governance, since public institutions are held in less regard than they once were. Thus, a vicious cycle has been set up in which the low quality of public servants attracts the scorn of the public, which feeds the perception that the public service is no longer a higher calling, which means "quality" people avoid making their careers there, which means that the scorn of the public is reinforced, and on and on. Recent attempts by schools of public administration,

Box 11-2

New Liberal Ethics Guidelines

Although this chapter is mainly concerned with the ethical behaviour of public servants, a good deal of attention has recently been paid to the behaviour of politicians as well. A series of damaging scandals prompted Prime Minister Chrétien to take action in the form of drafting guidelines for the behaviour of Cabinet ministers. Here are the guidelines, as summarized in the *Globe and Mail*:

Prime Minister Jean Chrétien's eight-point ethics plan yesterday aimed to patch up holes in rules that have opened up his government to allegations of patronage and favouritism. Here is an analysis of the specific measures:

1. **New leadership rules for ministers:** Leadership campaign activities by four current and former ministers—Paul Martin, Allan Rock, Sheila Copps and John Manley—have caused considerable headaches for the government. Problems came from all sides: Lobbyists working directly with departments headed by their leadership candidate; political aides using government funds to travel across the country for political purposes; fundraising activities giving rise to the appearance of conflict of interest; and one campaign member advising potential donors on a possible way to obtain an illegal tax credit on a contribution. Mr. Chrétien insisted yesterday that he will not allow cabinet ministers to engage in pre-leadership planning while he remains in office. Still, leadership contenders will be asked to reveal immediately funds currently in their war chests, with future activities allowed only after they receive the green light to organize: Ministers now have 30 days to disclose all donations that they have already received to their leadership campaigns. Future donations must be disclosed within 60 days or be placed in a blind trust for disclosure 30 days before a leadership convention. Ministers cannot give contracts to people who work on their leadership campaigns. Ministers cannot receive leadership support from lobbyists registered to lobby their department.

2. **Reforming the fundraising rules for political parties:** The Chrétien government has been embarrassed by revelations that generous donors to the Liberal Party of Canada obtained juicy government contracts. In particular, the government has been under attack over Liberal-friendly

Works Canada, with little work to show for it. In addition, government critics have pointed to loopholes in the party financing law that allow some contributions to riding associations to go unrecorded. Mr. Chrétien has long fought changes to the law, but said yesterday that reform is on its way. His proposals include: Putting a cap on maximum contributions; Using tax incentives and possibly increasing government financing to compensate for lower fundraising among companies and individual contributors.

3. **The public release of Mr. Chrétien's Guide for Ministers and Secretaries of State:** Mr. Chrétien has kept secret his recommendations to cabinet members since 1993, meaning Canadians were not aware of some of the rules governing the conduct of politicians. The first line of the guide makes it clear who is in charge: "Ministers of the Crown are chosen by the Prime Minister, who may ask for their resignation at any time." Here are other excerpts from the document, which aims to inform ministers of their duties and the internal functioning of government: On ethical behaviour: "Ministers must act with honesty and must uphold the highest ethical standards so that public confidence and trust in the integrity, objectivity and impartiality of government are maintained and enhanced.... This obligation is not fully discharged merely by acting within the law." On cabinet solidarity: "Policies presented to Parliament and to the public must be agreed policies of the cabinet. Ministers cannot dissociate themselves or repudiate the decisions of their cabinet colleagues unless they resign from cabinet." On ministerial responsibility: "When errors or wrongdoing are committed by officials under their direction, ministers are responsible for promptly taking the necessary remedial steps and for providing assurances to Parliament that appropriate corrective action has been taken to prevent reoccurrence."

4. **New rules governing the relationship between ministers and Crown corporations:** Mr. Chrétien and one of his former ministers, Alfonso Gagliano, came under pressure for pushing Crown firms to, respectively, award a loan to a constituent and to hire a political organizer. Under the new rules, "ministers should not personally promote the private interests of any individual, corporation or non-governmental organization, including a constituent, with any Crown corporation." Still, ministerial staff can keep dealing with Crown corporations.

5. **A new code of conduct for MPs and senators:** This was proposed in 1997 but quickly shelved. The government now says that all MPs must be policed by ethical rules that are enforced by an independent parliamentary officer. Rules need to be debated, but Mr. Chrétien said, among other things, parliamentarians would now have to disclose trips worth more than $250 paid by others.

6. **Toughening up the Lobbyist Registration Act:** Lobbyists have to register with the government in the name of transparency, but current rules are loosely defined and it is almost impossible to prosecute those who break them. New legislation will more clearly define lobbying and create stronger enforcement provisions.

7. **Increased independence for the ethics counselor:** The government's ethics counselor has come under fire because, contrary to a Liberal promise, he does not report to Parliament. From now on, the ethics counselor will be selected in consultation with the opposition and be appointed for a fixed five-year term. This will remove the Prime Minister's power to get rid of the ethics counselor arbitrarily.

8. **New accounting rules in the civil services:** Bureaucrats have come under fire for mishandling millions in contracts. The Treasury Board is working on new rules to enhance the accountability of civil servants in management of public funds.

Source: Daniel Leblanc, "New Liberal Ethics Guidelines," Globe and Mail, Wednesday, June 12, 2002, A4.

and by the public sector itself, have sought to break the cycle by placing more emphasis on public service ethics.

Written codes of ethics are one way of achieving this. Another is better training, and yet another is providing role models in the upper ranks of the public service who subscribe to and demonstrate the highest standards of ethical conduct (discussed below). According to one observer, interrelated objectives in seeking improved ethical standards in the public service include the following:

(1) to promote public trust and confidence in the ethical performance of public servants; (2) to decrease and, if possible, to eliminate, unethical practices by discouraging and punishing them; (3) to legitimate the imposition of sanctions for unethical behaviour; (4) to sensitize both current and aspiring public servants to the ethical and value dimensions of bureaucratic decisions; (5) to reduce uncertainty as to what constitutes ethical and unethical behaviour; (6) to develop skills in the analysis of ethical and value issues; (7) to assist public servants to resolve ethical and value dilemmas; and (8) to promote moral development.[27]

But are written codes of conduct the best way to ensure ethical behaviour in the public sector? Critics suggest that for a number of reasons, codes may not be as useful in promoting ethical behaviour as they seem.[28] First, the guidelines set out in codes are often difficult to apply in real-life situations. As the examples of ethical dilemmas above suggest, it would be impossible to develop a single code to comprehensively account for every situation that might arise in the course of a public servant's job. Related is the fact that codes of ethics are often difficult to enforce. Indeed, many codes contain no reference to how their provisions should be enforced. Third, given the complexity of modern governments, is it reasonable to assume that a generalized code of ethics can be drafted that applies to all government departments, regulatory bodies and agencies? Surely the differences in organization and structure, policy focus and activities mitigate against a sort of one-size-fits-all approach to codifying ethical behaviour. Fourth, codes of behaviour sometimes cast their nets so wide that innocents are caught up in them, as when public servants are required to disclose, not only their own personal financial interests, but those of immediate family members. Fifth, management of some ethical issues by reference to a code of ethics is inappropriate. For instance, no code can set out what level of risk to the public is acceptable in a given policy decision. The specificity of some ethical decisions belies the generality of codes of ethics. Finally, where widespread or systematic corruption commonly inform the actions and decisions of public servants, these will override the most elegantly and articulately formulated code.

Still, these criticisms assume, perhaps, that codes of ethics can do more than in reality they are intended to. It may well be the case that the existence of a code of ethics raises expectations about the standards of behaviour in the public service beyond that which can be reasonably expected. Thus, rather than throw the baby out with the bathwater by accepting all these criticisms as an indictment of codes of ethics, it is more advisable to acknowledge that no single code is going to "solve" all ethical dilemmas. What a code might do is contribute to an environment in which the highest standards of behaviour are aspired to by the organization and the individuals working therein.

Two other effective means of compelling bureaucrats to act ethically include training and education, and role models. We turn to these other methods now.

Training and Education

Arguments have been made that improved training is the key to improved ethics in the public service. By focusing on developing the ability to identify ethical issues in day-to-day work scenarios, public servants can be stimulated to recognize ethical dilemmas and, perhaps, solve them. This allows for a deepening of their comprehension of ethical issues, and provides them with some tools with which to engage in ethical analysis. By drawing attention to exemplary ethical behaviour, the hope is that public servants can be socialized into the highest ethical norms of the profession.[29]

The importance of training and education does not lie in the expectation that a previously amoral or unethical individual will, somehow, suddenly "find" morality or ethics. It is not argued that these things can be "taught" to an individual whose lifelong socialization has shaped him in ways that no course in ethical behaviour is going to undo. Instead, the expectation is that this kind of training will simply promote an awareness of ethical dilemmas confronted by public servants. The point is to sensitize public servants to the issues and assist them in developing the analytical skills and the practical means of dealing with the issues. It is further argued that this approach is most effective for those at the early stages of their public service career.[30]

Role Models

Finally, it is also argued that inculcating ethical standards of behaviour depends on the presence of ethical leadership at the top of the organization. It is often suggested, for instance, that codes of conduct fail to provide the "living, breathing" consequences of ethical behaviour. Senior public servants can create a climate and set examples to be emulated by their junior colleagues, who, studies show, are significantly influenced by the tone set by their superiors.

However, the examples that exist of senior public servants effectively socializing their charges into a regime of ethical behaviour and standards tend to have happened in the past, when government was smaller and relations between bureaucrats were more intimate. Today, government departments are so large that personal contact with the most senior administrators is rare for most public servants. As a result, it is more difficult for their influence to reach down through the organization, the way it did in the past. Thus, "it is unrealistic to argue that the role model provided by bureaucratic leaders can serve as the sole means of promoting ethical behaviour in the public service. Like a code of ethics, ethical leadership is necessary but insufficient."[31]

In any event, contemporary demographic realities within the public service are creating new challenges. As the Director of the Office of Values and Ethics reports:

We are about to witness a massive change in the demographics of the federal public service. The expected turnover in the next ten years, with 60-70% of employees eligible to retire, has two major implications for government. As many have said already, we will need to attract a huge influx of new recruits—our share of the best and brightest—who will need to acquire quickly a sense of "self" as a public servant. Less often noted is the need to capture and transfer the legacy of the public service that exists now—not only the "corporate memory" but the culture, the traditions and the values that will be the solid foundation for these young people as they grapple with their own new challenges.[32]

Moreover, the role and place of the public servant is constantly changing. It has been argued that governments are moving away from strict hierarchical accountability, which means that public servants continue to obey orders, of course, but that they do not *merely* obey orders. "Instead they take responsibility for the work they do. The stereotype of the timid, reactive and rule-bound official has become passé."[33] This point, again, raises the importance of discretion, which we discussed earlier.

Ultimately, it would seem that some combination of a code of ethics, training and education, and role models is required to ensure that a standard of ethical behaviour prevails in the public service (see Box 11-3). However, there is one other factor that is required: an attentive public.

An Attentive Public

It is only by being vigilant that citizens can realistically expect to receive public administration of the highest ethical calibre.

At the end of the day, ethics in public service is an issue of crucial importance. In the modern world much of life, both qualitatively and quantitatively, depends on government. Because government is now so big and deals with more than basic needs and elements of protection, the professionalism of public servants is even more important than in the past.

BOX 11-3

An Ethics Regime for Government

Professor of public administration Kenneth Kernaghan suggests the following items ought to be included as part of government's ethics regime:

1. The evaluation of ethical performance as a basis for appointing and promoting all members of the public service, but especially its leadership.
2. A statement of values, including ethical values, either as part of a strategic plan or as a separate document.
3. A code of ethics (or conduct), linked to a value statement (if one exists) that sets out general principles or ethical conduct.
4. Elaboration on the code, usually as commentary under each principle, which explains more fully the meaning of the principle and/or provides illustrations of violations of the principle.
5. Reference to the existence of ethics rules (statutes, regulations, etc.) related to the problem areas covered in the code and/or to problem areas covered elsewhere.
6. Elaboration on the code, either following each principle or in a separate part, which adapts the code's principles to the particular needs of individual organizations.
7. Provisions for administering the code, including publicity, penalties for violations and provisions for grievance.
8. An ethics counsellor to perform advisory and administrative functions for senior public servants across the government.
9. An ethics counsellor, ombudsman or committee to provide advice on ethics rules and ethics issues within a single department or agency.

10. Ethics education and training for public servants, beginning with the senior echelons and new employees.

Additional, less common, measures that may be adapted are these:

11. An ethics audit to evaluate the organization's policies and procedures for preserving and nurturing ethical behaviour.
12. The raising of ethical considerations in a deliberate and regular way at meetings and through other means of communication, such as newsletters.
13. The provision of a confidential hotline that public servants can use to discuss concerns about their personal ethical behaviour or that of others.
14. The inclusion of exit interviews (i.e., interviews with employees leaving the organization) to ask questions about the employee's view of the ethical culture of the organization.

Source: Kenneth Kernaghan, "Values, Ethics and Public Service," in Jacques Bourgault, Maurice Demers and Cynthia Williams, eds. *Public Administration and Public Management: Experiences in Canada.* Sainte-Foy, Quebec: Les Publications du Quebec, 1997: 101–111.

Consequently the qualities of individual public servants are also important. Public servants must be trusted to exercise judgements wisely, and they must be carefully selected for that trust. It is in their crucial work involving discretion and advice, as well as policy-making, that the ethical standards of public service are evident. Nevertheless, it remains the ultimate responsibility of citizens, through their governments, to ensure that all the structures and procedures of government are best suited to their purposes, in good working order, continuously reviewed, and positively supportive to public servants when they carry out their satisfying and demanding, but also very responsible work.[34]

WHAT YOU HAVE LEARNED

A distinguishing feature of public administration—a rigorous regime of ethical standards to which public servants are subject—makes already complicated work even more so. But at some level, the public interest must be served, and it cannot be served by nefarious, corrupt, self-serving scoundrels abusing the trust of the public (or their hard-earned dollars). This means that guidelines that are often absent in the private sector play a key role in shaping our expectations about the behaviour of public servants. It is of the utmost importance to ensure the honesty and integrity of those dedicated to serving the public interest. And while there are many ways to do this (e.g., codes of conduct, ethics commissioners, education and training, role models) it is ultimately up to the public to keep a watchful eye. In turn, this implies that accountability of public officials is also a significant factor in public administration. It is to an examination of the issue of accountability that we next turn in Chapter 12.

ENDNOTES

1. Warren R. Bailie and David Johnson, "Government Ethics and Ethics Agencies," *Canadian Public Administration,* 34, 1 (Spring, 1991): 158.

2. See Ian Greene, "Government Ethics Commissioners: The Way of the Future?" *Canadian Public Administration,* 34, 1 (Spring, 1991): 165–170.

3. See John Tait, "A Strong Foundation: The Report of the Task Force on Public Service Values and Ethics (the summary)," *Canadian Public Administration,* 40, 1 (Spring, 1997). See also Canada, Treasury Board of Canada Secretariat, *Building on a Strong Foundation—The Dialogue Continues Volume II: Further Case Studies on Values and Ethics in the Public Service,* (Ottawa: Canadian Centre for Management Development, 2001).

4. The recent history of the issue of values and ethics in the public service is outlined in: Canada, Treasury Board of Canada Secretariat, "Creating a Value Based Public Service: Remarks by Catherine MacQuarrie, Director, Office of Values and Ethics, Treasury Board Secretariat," (Ottawa: Treasury Board of Canada Secretariat, July 11, 2001).

5. Neil Nevitte, *The Decline of Deference: Canadian Value Change in Cross-National Perspective,* (Peterborough: Broadview Press, 1996): 56.

6. See Ekos Research Associates, "Rethinking Government: Exploring Changing Relationships Among Individuals, Governments and Business," (2001): 10. www.http://ekos.ca/studies/default.asp

7. E. Pendleton Herring, *Public Administration and the Public Interest,* (New York: McGraw-Hill, 1936).

8. See W.T. Stanbury, "Definitions of the Public Interest," in Douglas G. Hartle, *Public Policy Decision Making and Regulation,* (Montreal: Institute for Research on Public Policy, 1979): 213–218.

9. Tait, "A Strong Foundation," (1996): 32.

10. Dennis F. Thompson, "The Possibility of Administrative Ethics," in Jay M. Shafritz and Albert C. Hyde, eds. *Classics of Public Administration, Third Edition,* (Pacific Cove, California: Brooks/Cole Publishing, 1992): 523.

11. Thompson, "The Possibility of Administrative Ethics," (1992): 524.

12. The Canadian Centre for Management Development and the Treasury Board Secretariat have recently sponsored an ongoing series of discussions and case studies of ethics in the public service. See Canada, Treasury Board of Canada Secretariat, *Building on a Strong Foundation—The Dialogue Continues Volume II: Further Case Studies on Values and Ethics in the Public Service,* (Ottawa: Canadian Centre for Management Development, 2001).

13. Cited in Kenneth Kernaghan and John W. Langford, *The Responsible Public Servant,* (Halifax: The Institute for Research on Public Policy, 1990): 205.

14. See John W. Langford, "Moonlighting and Mobility," *Canadian Public Administration,* 34, 1 (Spring, 1991): 62–72.

15. Cited in Kernaghan and Langford, *The Responsible Public Servant,* (1990): 206.

16. Richard A. Chapman, "Ethics in Public Service," in Richard A. Chapman, ed. *Ethics in Public Service,* (Ottawa: Carleton University Press, 1993): 158–159.

17. See Sissela Bok, *Lying: Moral Choice in Public and Private Life,* (New York: Pantheon, 1978).

18. Arden R. Haynes, "The Ethical Dimension in Business and Government," *Canadian Public Administration,* 34, 1 (Spring, 1991): 18.

19. Frederick C. Mosher *et al. Watergate: Implications for Responsible Government,* (Washington, D.C.: National Academy of Public Administration, 1974). Cited in Jay M. Shafritz and Albert C. Hyde, eds. *Classics of Public Administration, Third Edition,* (1992): 416–417.

20. Elaine Todres, "The Ethical Dimension in Public Service," *Canadian Public Administration,* 34, 1 (Spring, 1991): 12.

21. Kernaghan and Langford, *The Responsible Public Servant,* (1990): 2.

22. See George Thomson, "Personal Morality in a Professional Context," *Canadian Public Administration,* 34, 1 (Spring, 1991).

23. Richard A. Chapman, "Introduction," in Richard A. Chapman, ed. *Ethics in Public Service,* (Ottawa: Carleton University Press, 1993): 2.

24. See Bailie and Johnson, "Governmental Ethics and Ethics Agencies," (1991): 159.

25. See Canada, Treasury Board, *Conflict of Interest and Post-Employment Code for the Public Service,* (Ottawa: Supply and Services, 1985).

26. See John Tait, "A Strong Foundation: The Report of the Task Force on Public Service Values and Ethics (the summary)," *Canadian Public Administration,* 40, 1 (Spring, 1997): 1–22. See also Peter Aucoin, "A Profession of Public Administration?: A Commentary on 'A Strong Foundation,'" *Canadian Public Administration* 40, 1 (Spring, 1997): 23–39.

27. Kenneth Kernaghan, "Promoting Public Service Ethics: The Codification Option," in Richard W. Chapman, ed. *Ethics in Public Service,* (Ottawa: Carleton University Press, 1993): 18.

28. The following reasons are derived from Kernaghan, "Promoting Public Service Ethics," (1993): 19.

29. See M.W. Jackson, "How Can Ethics be Taught?" in Richard A. Chapman, ed. *Ethics in Public Service,* (Ottawa: Carleton University Press, 1993): 31–42.

30. Kernaghan, "Promoting Public Service Ethics," (1993): 25–26.

31. Kernaghan, "Promoting Public Service Ethics," (1993): 25.

32. Canada, "Creating a Value Based Public Service" (2001): 3.

33. Todres, "The Ethical Dimension in Public Service," (1991): 15.

34. Chapman, "Ethics in Public Service," (1993): 170.

KEY WORDS AND CONCEPTS

ethics (338)	public interest (346)
discretion (339)	public comment (346)
ethics commissioners (339)	conflict of interest (347)
partisanship (345)	lying for the public good (347)

REVIEW QUESTIONS

1. Ethical Dilemmas in the Public Service

Some of the broad controversies surrounding the ethical standards of behaviour in the public sector were introduced in this section. It asked the following: What does the public expect of the behaviour of public servants? What dilemmas are posed for public servants in the course of their work? What is the "public interest," and how is it served?

2. Codes of Conduct

This section addressed the debate over whether written codes of conduct are useful tools in securing the highest ethical behaviour among public officials. It also suggested other ways that this might be achieved, and asked these questions: What are ethical codes of conduct, and how effective are they? What alternative measures can be taken to ensure the ethical conduct of public servants? In what way can training and education, and role models, supplement and complement codes of conduct? What role does the "attentive public" have to play?

FURTHER READING

1.   *Ethical Dilemmas in the Public Service*

Greene, Ian and David P. Shugarman. *Honest Politics: Seeking Integrity in Canadian Public Life*. Toronto: James Lorimer, 1997.

Hiebert, Janet. *Political Ethics: A Canadian Perspective*. Toronto: Dundurn Press, 1993.

Kernaghan, Kenneth, ed. *Do Unto Others: Proceedings of a Conference on Ethics in Government and Business*. Toronto: Institute of Public Administration of Canada, 1991.

Rohr, John A. *Ethics for Bureaucrats: An Essay on Law and Values, Second Edition*. New York: Marcel Dekker, 1989.

2.   *Codes of Conduct*

Canada, Report of the Auditor General. *Values and Ethics in the Federal Public Service*. Ottawa: Supply and Services, 2000.

Canada, Task Force on Conflict of Interest. *Ethical Conduct in the Public Sector*. Ottawa: Supply and Services Canada, 1984.

Greene, Ian. "Conflicts of Interest and the Canadian Constitution: An Analysis of Conflict of Interest Rules for Canadian Cabinet Ministers." *Canadian Journal of Political Science*, 23, 2 (June, 1990): 233–256.

WEBLINKS

The Institute for Global Ethics
www.globalethics.org/

The Office of Values and Ethics
www.tbs-sct.gc.ca/veo-bve

Chapter (12)

Public Administration *and* Accountability

WHAT YOU WILL LEARN

Many references have been made throughout this book to the important concept of accountability, which simply means being required to explain one's actions by answering to someone else. It is a central feature of public administration as practised in the Canadian political system. At this point, though, it is necessary to explain in more detail exactly why this is so. The concept of accountability informs every step of the public service decision-making process, from top to bottom. As such, it manifests itself in several different ways, each of which is elaborated in the following sections. In short, you will learn who is accountable to whom, for what and under what circumstances. To achieve this, the chapter is divided into the following sections.

1. — *Accountability and Democracy*

This section reviews the central principle of responsible government first raised in Chapter 4. It then establishes the link between accountability and democracy by asking the following: What is the significance of the principle of responsible government? How does it work in theory and in practice in the Canadian setting?

2. — *Ministerial Responsibility*

The principle of responsible government depends in part on the doctrine of ministerial responsibility. This doctrine sets the parameters of ministerial action, and the guidelines that establish how government can be held to account. This section explains the pure theory of ministerial responsibility, and reveals how it has been altered by contemporary developments, by asking these questions: What is the theory of ministerial responsibility? What is individual ministerial responsibility? What is collective ministerial responsibility?

What is the doctrine of answerability? How has the traditional expectation about how responsibility is realized in the political system changed over time? What does the doctrine look like now?

3. — *Accountability and Public Servants*

The traditional doctrine of ministerial authority combines with the politics-administration dichotomy to set the expectations of public servant accountability. But recent changes to the concept of accountability have left public servants on unfamiliar ground. This section addresses both the traditional role of public servants and the recently emerging role, and asks the following: How have public servants been held accountable for their actions? How has the concept of ministerial responsibility and the politics-administration dichotomy influenced the way public servants do their jobs? How have changes to these doctrines altered the role of public servants in terms of accountability?

4. — *Accountability in Action: The Role of the Office of the Auditor General*

There are many links in the chain of accountability. One of the most significant is the Office of the Auditor General. Here we review briefly the role of this important actor in terms of its contribution to the accountability process by asking these questions: How does the government get objective, unbiased assessment of its policies? What role does the Office of the Auditor General play in this process? If the auditor general watches over government, who, in turn, watches over the auditor general?

5. — *Contemporary Issues of Accountability and Control*

Recent developments have seen some of the traditional precepts of accountability change. The traditional notions of ministerial responsibility and the role of public servants have altered as new organizational norms and systems, such as the New Public Management, come into play. This section asks the following: What impact has reform of public administration had on traditional notions of accountability? How has the New Public Management altered the usual relationships within government where responsibility is concerned?

Accountability and Democracy

Central to any democracy is the ability of the people to hold their elected officials **accountable** for their actions. This point has been made several times in this book. The most general sense in which this is exercised is through the ballot box. If citizens do not believe their representatives have been doing a good job, or believe the representatives have failed to account properly for their actions, they can "throw the rascals out." It is, after all, power that the citizens are vesting in their elected officials. But if that power is abused or poorly exercised, the people have the right to take it back and give it to someone else. Therefore, the government of the day ought to act in a **responsible** manner and be accountable to the people, or it may lose control over the reins of power.

While this generally describes the conditions pertaining in democratic societies, it was not always thus. Imagine a time before the rise of democracy. As Weber tells us, the basis of the right to rule was often either divine intervention or the charisma of individual leaders. But consider what this meant in terms of accountability. Generally, it meant that the masses dared not question their leaders, for to do so would anger the gods, and invite divine retribution and whatever punishment this might bring in the afterlife (that is, to question the king was to question the deity that anointed the king). To question the charismatic leader was to invite scorn, ostracism, and perhaps imprisonment or death. It was only when societies began to move toward systems of government in which the people could choose their leaders and remove them at will that the modern notion of accountability came into play. As one observer reports, "It took several centuries in the tortuous evolution of the modern nation state to develop a coherent, binding, respected ideology of public accountability, together with efficient means of enforcement that would permit the peaceful transfer of power and the voluntary ceding of public office."[1] It was only when the absolute rule of a single leader was replaced by the rule of representative legislative assemblies overseen by an appointed executive, which could be held collectively and individually responsible for running the affairs of the state, that we could begin to see accountability emerge in its modern guise.

This is the basis of the principle of **responsible government** (see Box 12-1), which was achieved in Canada in the 1840s.[2] It was first adopted by Nova Scotia and the Province of Canada (now Quebec and Ontario) in 1848, Prince Edward Island in 1851, New Brunswick in 1854 and Newfoundland in 1855. Its origins can be found in the earlier development of responsible government in the British political system, the model from which the Canadian system is largely derived.[3] The British Crown had been bound by the principle of seeking the consent of the Lords before it could tax them. This was incorporated in the *Magna Carta* in the 12th century. But it was not until the 17th century that the king's obligation to consult the elected representatives of the people (and this eventually meant the House of Commons) was established. At the time, however, the king's ministers were not also members of the House of Commons. But with the growing importance of the House, it gradually dawned on people that ministers ought to be members of parliament, and in that way their responsibility and accountability as representatives of the people would be more direct, and could be better managed. The next step in this evolutionary process saw the rise of organized political parties in the 18th century, and it was largely this model that emerged in Canada as well.

You might ask yourself why the achievement of responsible government was a significant development in the evolution of the Canadian political system, and what bearing it has on public administration today. To approach these questions, consider the motivations behind vesting power in the hands of the people's representative and making the government (that is, the Cabinet) responsible to them. You might come up with two strikingly different perspectives: one arguing that

BOX 12-1

Definitions of Responsible Government

In order to govern... the Prime Minister and the Cabinet require the confidence of the elected House of Commons. This constitutional principle is called responsible government. If a government loses the confidence of the House—this would be either through a defeat on an important piece of legislation or on a motion of no confidence proposed by an opposition party—it loses the right to govern.

* * *

The term "responsible government" defines the relationship of Cabinet ministers to the House, the Crown, and to each other. Collectively, the Cabinet is responsible to the House of Commons in that the government must maintain the support of a majority of MPs if it is to continue in office. If Cabinet loses the "confidence" of the House through a specific "want of confidence" or non-confidence vote, or through the defeat of a major government bill, unwritten constitutional convention calls for the government to tender its resignation. In practice the prime minister would usually ask the Governor General for the "dissolution" of Parliament, and would go to the people in a general election.

* * *

Responsible government means that the political executive is not able to act without the support of a majority in the legislature (the chamber of representatives).

* * *

The democratic principle is that all public officials are accountable to the people and can rule only by their consent.

Sources: 1. Stephen Brooks, *Canadian Democracy: An Introduction, Second Edition*, (Toronto: Oxford University Press, 1996): 99. 2. Roger Gibbins, *Conflict and Unity: An Introduction to Canadian Political Life, Second Edition*, (Scarborough: Nelson, 1990): 30. 3. Larry Johnston, *Politics: An Introduction to the Modern Democratic State*, (Peterborough: Broadview Press, 1997): 120. 4. Leonard T. Hobhouse, *Liberalism*, (New York: Oxford University Press, 1911). Cited in James John Guy, *People, Politics and Government: A Canadian Perspective, Fourth Edition*, (Scarborough: Prentice Hall, 1998): 80.

responsible government is a bulwark of democracy; the other suggesting that it is an elaborate system to actually check the power of the people, and protect the privileged position of the elite.

The first argument—that responsibility is meant to democratize government by giving more power to the people (or, in the context of the 1800s, less power to the Crown)—was supported by those who saw in responsible government the opportunity to transfer power from an unaccountable sovereign (as represented by the governor general and his appointees in Cabinet) to the people through their representatives in Parliament. We will call the people who supported this view **democrats**. The underlying assumption of the democrats is that power rightly belongs to the people and that, short of involving every citizen in the direct governance of the country (recall our discussion of direct democracy in Chapter 4), it is sufficient to maximize ordinary citizens' power by giving their representatives real power.

Ironically, the opposite viewpoint also supported the concept of responsible government, but for a different set of reasons. Assuming that society was naturally divided into the *ruled* and the *rulers,* this group of people—which we will call the **conservatives**—saw in responsible government an opportunity to shelter the exercise of power from the direct interference of the "great unwashed," that is, the people. The conservatives were inherently suspicious of democracy as we understand it today, because they saw rule by the people as destabilizing and dangerous. The mass of the citizenry were seen as too uneducated, too prone to fall under the sway of demagogues, and too likely to ignore the rights of minorities to be trusted with power.[4] But by establishing institutions such as responsible government, power would be transferred, not to the people, but to their representatives, who tend always to come from the class of society deserving to rule. In any event, if certain undesirable democrats managed to get themselves elected, they could always be checked in their unsavory ambitions to further democratize government by the countervailing weight of the executive branch of government (that is, the Cabinet) and the Upper House in Parliament (the Senate), whose members are appointed by the Crown. Thus, the drive to responsible government was supported by these two groups, but for quite different reasons.[5]

Whichever perspective you find most compelling, the conventional notion has developed that accountability is enforced primarily through the ballot box. Of course, responsible government is made up of several other components, too, through which this underlying principle is reinforced. For instance, the institutions of parliamentary government have a number of mechanisms through which the government is held to account, such as the daily Question Period in the House of Commons, and the actions of the opposition parties. Outside Parliament, the media and interest groups also play an important part in holding the government to account. The judiciary, of course, also forces the government to be accountable, as when a citizen, interest group, corporation or other government challenges a government's actions in a court of law. It is noteworthy that the emergence of modern democratic government was accompanied by the proscription that no one—not even the leaders of the government—was beyond the law. As a result, accountability is reinforced by the judicial system through constitutional and administrative law as well. Thus, "The law would further reduce official discretion by prescribing the precise arrangements whereby public business was to be conducted, arrangements that included the structure of the machinery of government, the number and tenure of public officials, the handling of public property and monies, the code of conduct governing official behaviour, and methods for handling citizens and aliens."[6] All of these institutions are meant to support democratic governance. But it is ultimately elections that allow the people to pass judgment on a government.

For public administration, this means that at some level, everything public officials do should in some way relate to the *will of the people* as expressed through their selection of representatives in Parliament. As a result, the focus of policy formulation, implementation and evaluation, is Parliament. It receives advice from public servants, it instructs them, and it evaluates their work, all in the name of the people. In other words, Parliament is the sun around which the planets and stars in the constellation of public administration revolve. In turn, this also contributes to the uniqueness of the public service compared to the private sector:

Public service exists to satisfy certain needs of the community. Its existence depends upon the trust, confidence and support (both financial, through taxation, and legal, through obedience to laws and regulations enforced by public servants) it derives from the public through their representatives. Unlike the private sector, it cannot (as expected) become too self-seeking and obscure. Its every action and inaction is subject to thorough scrutiny. The community expects public servants to be fair, ethical and dedicated in administering public policies and programs. And public trust and confidence is assured when public servants are found managing public programs soundly, and are found to be held accountable for their actions.[7]

But note also that the concept of accountability is an empty shell unless it is connected to a system of rewards and punishments. If there is no tangible benefit from acting in an accountable manner, can people be counted on to act responsibly? Not always. Similarly, if there are no punishments or sanctions for failing to act responsibly, can people be relied upon to do so? Again, not always. As a result, a complex system of rewards and punishments has evolved to ensure compliance with measures designed to promote accountability and responsibility. At the most general level, failure of the government overall to act responsibly will result in its losing power at the next election. Moving to a more specific level, failure of a Cabinet minister or member of Parliament to act responsibly could result in a range of sanctions—from a reprimand from the prime minister, to dismissal from Cabinet, to being passed over for plum positions, to being kicked out of the political party. For public servants, the motivation to act responsibly is tied to the system of job-related rewards (raises, promotions, status, etc.) and punishments (reprimand, suspension, dismissal, etc.). At a more extreme level, legal sanctions can be invoked against either politicians or public servants in the event of criminal abuses of power. Together, this package of rewards and punishments serves to reinforce and remind public officials that their primary duty is not to themselves, but to the public interest. Compliance with the rules and regulations meant to support accountability will bring rewards, but any breach of trust or failure to act responsibly will be dealt with in a serious manner.

Society cannot allow public servants to simply act on their own whims and fancies. Public servants must be answerable to somebody. We can think of the institutions that enforce the answerability as the political, legal and administrative arrangements that seek to ensure that the power of the rulers is controlled ultimately by the ruled. The trick is to balance the requirement for some constraints with the need to be able to act. As one observer put it, "Too much independence and too few constraints have allowed too much wrongdoing. Too many controls and too little trust have stultified government and prevented rapid, flexible action."[8]

Further complicating our understanding of accountability and democracy is the idea that we can subdivide accountability by looking at both administrative responsibility and political responsibility. This will remind us of the admonition from the politics-administration dichotomy that politicians lead and public servants follow. Thus, it is conceptually useful to try to distinguish when and where purely political actions and decisions can be separated from purely administrative ones. For example, the decision to build a bridge in one riding and not another is a political decision. The decision to locate that bridge at what engineers say is the safest and most accessible point on the river, where it will serve the greatest amount of traffic in the most efficient manner possible, is an administrative decision. If the public is outraged because the bridge is built in a particular riding solely to create jobs so that the local member of Parliament might more easily get reelected, there may be a political price to pay. But if the bridge falls down because of poor construction or technical miscalculations about the strength of the riverbank to support the pylons, there are administrative and legal sanctions. Of course, in the real world, the neat division over responsibilities is less clear-cut than this. For instance, the decision to award a particular firm the contract to construct the pylons may have been influenced by that firm's financial support of the party in power, in which case the political and administrative boundaries over responsibility are blurred. It is exactly this type of scenario that makes it challenging to analyze and apply doctrines of accountability in a precise manner. (See Box 12-2.)

Box 12-2

How Specs Live Forever

It is sometimes difficult to figure out the origins of a particular policy, and thus who should be accountable for it. Consider the following example that has been making the rounds in various incarnations on the Internet and via e-mail.

Can a horse's back-end be responsible for modern-day U.S. railroad specifications? Yes—sort of. The U.S. Standard railroad gauge—the distance between the rails—is four feet, eight and a half inches. Many early U.S. railway lines were designed to accommodate British-built standard gauge locomotives. These locomotives were in turn based on northern English tramway lines used for transporting coal. These tramways used a four-foot-eight gauge.

The four-foot-eight gauge was derived from wagon wheel ruts that were most commonly spaced at five feet. Why five feet? Five feet allowed for the wagons to comfortably fit behind a team of two draft animals. Adjusting for two two-inch wide rails (with a half-inch leeway) resulted in a four-foot-eight gauge. Therefore, 21st century engineers designing high-speed locomotives are still bound by specifications that began on mud-covered paths a thousand years ago.

Source: Cecil Adams, "Was Standard Railroad Gauge (4'8") Determined by Roman Chariot Ruts?" http://www.straightdope.com/columns/000218.html (8 October, 2002)

According to political scientist Paul Thomas, accountability consists of "an obligation to explain and justify how one discharges responsibilities, the origins of which may be political, constitutional, statutory, hierarchical, or contractual. Different origins give rise to several variants of accountability, which in turn differ in the degree of direct control and public disclosure involved."[9] He goes on to suggest that there are four components in any accountability relationship. The first is an assignment of responsibilities related to agreed-upon goals. The second is an obligation to answer for the fulfilling of those responsibilities. The third is evaluation of performance to make sure that instructions have been complied with. And the fourth is sanctions or penalties for nonperformance, as well as rewards for good performance. Together, assignment, obligation, evaluation, and sanctions and rewards constitute a framework within which we can assess any accountability regime.

To further refine our thinking about these complex matters, we can look at accountability in another way. It is useful to think of the issues we have been exploring so far in terms of three interrelated key elements: responsibility, accountability and liability.

To be responsible is to have the authority to act, power to control, freedom to decide, the ability to distinguish (as between right and wrong) and to behave rationally and reliably and with consistency and trustworthiness in exercising internal judgement. To be accountable is to answer for one's responsibilities, to report, to explain, to give reasons, to respond, to assume obligations, to render a reckoning and to submit to an outside or external judgement. To be liable is to assume the duty of making good, to restore, to compensate, to recompense for wrongdoing or poor judgement.[10]

The mechanisms for ensuring the realization of these three interrelated goals have been surveyed in earlier chapters. But we now return to some of the features of public administration outlined earlier, to assess their usefulness in meeting these goals.

Ministerial Responsibility

One problematic aspect of accountability is the question of who is directly and personally responsible when the government screws something up. As you now know, the theory of **ministerial responsibility** tells us that individual Cabinet ministers are ultimately responsible for all the actions of their departments, and must answer for them when they make a mistake. If the mistake is significant enough, and the mistake is the result of actions that can be attributed personally and directly to the minister involved, the minister may have to resign her position as a sign that she has taken responsibility. No minister in Canada has ever resigned because of a mistake made directly by a subordinate in her ministry, unless the minister has been seen to be personally responsible. "If one of the minister's officials makes a mistake, the requirements of ministerial responsibility are satisfied when the minister answers to the House for the mistake and implements the necessary remedial action."[11] This is sometimes referred to as the **doctrine of answerability**, and is regarded as a somewhat watered-down version of the doctrine of individual ministerial responsibility.[12]

The other aspect of ministerial responsibility is that the Cabinet acts collectively in every government decision, and therefore must accept **collective responsibility** for any errors. This convention of government is tested when votes are held in the House of Commons. When a majority supports the government by voting in favour of its policies, it is signalling confidence in the ability of the government to carry on. But if a majority votes against the government, it must resign, signalling that it collectively takes responsibility for its actions. In this way accountability is realized.

The doctrine of collective ministerial responsibility is also important in terms of maintaining government stability and confidentiality.[13] It requires ministers to support Cabinet decisions publicly, the main advantage of which is to promote consensus and, as a result, political stability. This is closely linked to the notion of Cabinet confidentiality; even when individual ministers disagree with decisions taken at the Cabinet table, they keep their disagreements to themselves. Confidentiality of discussions within Cabinet promotes consensus, as it encourages open debate and a frank assessment of all alternatives in the privacy of the Cabinet, and leaves ministers secure in the knowledge that divisions within government will not be publicly aired.

Box 12-3

A Guide for Ministers and Secretaries of State

In June 2002, Prime Minister Chrétien released guidelines for Cabinet ministers which spelled out the extent of their responsibility.[14] Chrétien wrote, in part:

A Guide for Ministers and Secretaries of State A Message to Ministers and Secretaries of State

I believe it is essential to maintain the integrity of elected public office and, more generally, of public life in Canada. The members of the Ministry represent many cultures and perspectives, and our activities must be guided by trust, integrity and respect. Consistent with the demands and expectations of Canadians, I hold you, as Ministers and Secretaries of State, accountable for maintaining the highest standards of conduct for all your ministerial and personal actions.

Public confidence in our government institutions is vital to democracy. *A Guide for Ministers and Secretaries of State* explains the principles of ministerial responsibility and actions that are intended to guide you in undertaking your official duties. The conduct of Ministers and Secretaries of State is to be guided by the following principles:

➤ Ministers and Secretaries of State must act with honesty. They must uphold the highest ethical standards so that public confidence and trust in the integrity, objectivity and impartiality of government are conserved and enhanced. Ministers and Secretaries of State, in particular, have an obligation to perform their official duties and arrange their private affairs in a manner that bears the closest public scrutiny. This obligation is not fully discharged merely by acting within the law.

➤ Ministers are responsible for preserving public confidence in the integrity of management and operations within their departments. They must carry out the powers, duties and functions of their portfolios in accordance with the constraints provided by statute and convention.

➤ Ministers are accountable to Parliament for the use of powers vested in them by statute. This requires their presence in Parliament to answer questions about the use of those powers. They must accept the responsibilities that flow from those powers. It is of paramount importance for Ministers to give honest, accurate and truthful information to Parliament. They must take steps to correct any inadvertent error at the earliest opportunity.

➤ Ministers and Secretaries of State are bound by their oath as Privy Councillors. This oath requires them to uphold the rules and confidentiality of Cabinet decision-making and to share equally in the collective responsibility for their actions.

➤ Ministers and Secretaries of State must respect the non-partisan nature of the Public Service of Canada. They can rely on it to provide the support they need to fulfil their ministerial functions and mandate without regard to political partisanship.

A Guide for Ministers and Secretaries of State will assist you in fulfilling your commitment to the Canadian public to perform your duties in an open and ethical manner that will withstand public scrutiny and maintain a culture of integrity.

Jean Chrétien
Prime Minister of Canada
June 2002

One Privy Council Office official sums up the doctrines of both individual and collective ministerial responsibility this way:

As a general rule, ministerial responsibility, both collective and individual, is a "guarantee" that the political executive's decision-making power will be exercised responsibly, that is, in accordance with the will of the people. Collective responsibility enables the House of Commons, and therefore the people of Canada, to hold the Cabinet accountable for its collective decisions. As for individual responsibility, it enables the House of Commons to exercise control over the public service through the responsible ministers.[15]

The problem with the theory, of course, is that it rarely works this way in the real world due to the convention of **party discipline**, which dictates that the members of a party will always support their leader in votes in the House of Commons. Party discipline is an important convention, it is argued, because without it, government would be inherently unstable. If ordinary members of Parliament could shift their support from one party to the next on each vote, it would be tremendously difficult for anyone to command the support of the majority for any length of time. Consequently, governments would be falling all the time, forcing Canadians to go to the polls for elections with alarming frequency.[16]

What exactly are ministers responsible for in the real world of government?[17] There are currently more than 135 organizations that are accountable through ministers to Parliament. These include 23 departments, 37 Crown corporations, 26 tribunals and quasi-judicial bodies, and at least 48 service organizations of various kinds. All told, about 370 000 full-time employees labour in these institutions of government. As an illustration of the extent of ministerial involvement, one study indicated that in one year the Ministry of Industry, Trade and Commerce took about 4700 decisions. And while only 190 of these decisions were kept under the minister's direct control, they accounted for well over half of the department's expenditures.[18] Ministers are responsible for each of these types of organizations, although the exact number and type of each varies by ministry. There are diminishing levels of direct ministerial oversight as you move from departments to service agencies to Crown corporations to tribunals and quasi-judicial bodies. For example, departments are under direct ministerial control, and ministers can and do intervene on any departmental matters, as they wish. Service agencies, which are established by law to deliver services within an established policy and legal framework, are also closely controlled by the minister responsible. Crown corporations are less directly in the minister's purview. Generally, the minister responsible simply approves the corporation's business plans and the presentation of annual reports to Parliament. Finally, administrative tribunals and quasi-judicial bodies are subject to the least direct ministerial control. They generally require an arm's-length relationship with the minister responsible for them, so as to be able to do their work without fear of political interference or reprisal. Still, the minister has responsibility for them, and plays an important role in terms of allocating their financial resources. Still other organizations, such as the Office of the Auditor General, report directly to Parliament, and effectively, for the most part, bypass direct ministerial control. In short, the levels of ministerial responsibility are many and complex, and indicate different degrees of responsibility. The ability to successfully juggle these different degrees of responsibility is a feat in itself, but must be managed if the underlying principles of responsible government are to be upheld.

Recently, there has been a trend toward a form of accountability that undermines the theory of ministerial responsibility. Bureaucrats traditionally toil anonymously behind the scenes, allowing the elected representatives (their bosses) to take

both the credit and blame for government actions. But there is now a strong movement towards holding civil servants publicly accountable for the results achieved
by their departments. This reflects the fact that Cabinet ministers cannot realistically be expected to be on top of every single development within their ministries,
which may employ thousands of people and run hundreds of distinct programs.
A case in point is the so-called Al-Mashat Affair, in which Iraq's former ambassador to the United States entered Canada as a landed immigrant only a month after
applying to get in to Canada. He and his family thereby jumped the immigration
queue and bypassed the usual long, drawn-out process that most immigrants must
go through. The Mulroney government pinned the blame for this mistake directly
on the senior bureaucrats involved, rather than having the minister accept responsibility[19] (see Box 12-4).

Another difficulty with ministerial accountability relates to the politics-
administration dichotomy. As we have seen in earlier chapters, at the top of the public service sits a cadre of senior managers who generally are career civil servants specially trained in the art of public sector administration. They are extremely powerful
because of their knowledge of the workings of government. Some people regard this
as problematic, in that these individuals may be able to challenge their political masters (Cabinet ministers) in setting public policy, by virtue of their greater knowledge of government administration. In theory, at least, the elected representatives

BOX 12-4

The Al-Mashat Affair

According to political scientist Sharon Sutherland, the so-called Al-Mashat Affair severely tested the doctrine of ministerial responsibility, and found it wanting:

*Through May and June of 1991... the federal government handled a public relations
disaster that had the potential to become a scandal, the Al-Mashat affair, by denying that ministers are necessarily responsible for decisions taken in the departments of government....*

*On March 30, 1991, Iraq's former ambassador to the United States entered Canada
as a landed immigrant.... He and his wife disembarked in Canada as ordinary
landed immigrants in the retired class. The process from Mr. Al-Mashat's first inquiries
in Vienna to his arrival in his new country had taken less than a calendar month.*

*When Al-Mashat's presence in Canada became known a week after his entry, the
government claimed that the whole immigration process had been seen through
by officials from start to finish, without the hand on it of even one minister: this apparently meant to the government that its responsibility had not been engaged at
the time the decision had been taken. Nor had ministerial responsibility been sig-
nified by the silent compliance of ministers, because all ministers were now on
record as regretting the admission. Despite the unusual features of the case, such*

as the fact that the Canadian Security Intelligence Service go-ahead was provided within a day, the government also declared that it was satisfied that there were no legal or technical flaws in the decision that could lead to its reversal. In short, there was only one difficulty in the processing of the case, ministers said. That was that officials had acted autonomously, without any personal consultation with any minister.

After an internal investigation into process lasting a weekend, one that did not extend to ministers or their offices, the government named two men in the Department of External Affairs as the parties at fault. It was said that they had jointly failed to alert the Secretary of State for External Affairs, in whose foreign and security establishments the decision to admit Mr. Al-Mashat had taken place. This strategy meant that the problem in political terms was not Mr. Al-Mashat's new status, nor the quality of the assessment of his file, but simply the failure of an official and a political aide to make certain that the Secretary of State for External Affairs, then Mr. Joe Clark, had become personally aware of the file. The assiduity of officials in the immigration department was not challenged. Mr. Clark was the only judge of whether or not he had been aware, and thereby of whether he was responsible as the minister. Here was an action of the crown, with the ministers on whose jurisdictions it touched washing their hands of it, at the same time as they acknowledged it as a fait accompli, yet still refusing to take ownership from this point forward for any purpose except to claim the right to allocate blame.

The persons named were Mr. Raymond Chrétien, a career public servant and Associate Under-Secretary of State for External Affairs, and Mr. David Daubney, the minister's chief of staff, a political rather than a career appointment.... Mr. Daubney, a lawyer, had once served as a public servant in the Department of Justice, but was more recently known as a Conservative Member of Parliament from 1984 to 1988. While an MP, he had served as chairman of the Standing Committee of Justice. Mr. Chrétien had had a professional career of twenty-five years in the public service. Although at this point it may seem inappropriate to note it of a public servant of such long standing, Mr. Chrétien is the nephew of [Prime Minister Jean Chrétien]....

[T]he Al-Mashat case is important and in a class by itself because a full [parliamentary] committee inquiry into the comportment of a departmental official was supported by the government, as a substitute for ministerial answerability. The inquiry also put the seal of approval of the Clerk of the Privy Council on this major premise of the inquiry: that it is appropriate to hold officials to account for their actions in purely political, public forums, where they have no status and thus no rights or protection. The inquiry thus constitutes a revision of the conventions that allocate political responsibility under the constitution, the duty of the government's ministers to answer in the assembly of which they are members.

Source: S.L. Sutherland, "The Al-Mashat Affair: Administrative Accountability in Parliamentary Institutions," *Canadian Public Administration*, 34, 4 (Winter, 1991): 573–577.

are supposed to direct government, while the appointed officials simply assist. But if the senior managers have knowledge, expertise and experience, and the elected politicians lack these traits, it is possible that the traditional relationship between politicians and bureaucrats is turned on its head. Moreover, Cabinet ministers are not only responsible for the running of their ministries; they also perform a variety of other roles that take them away from their departments. For instance, they must attend Question Period in the House of Commons, and perform other legislative duties; they must respond to the demands of the constituents in their ridings; they are party members with responsibilities to their political party and caucus, and so on.

But most importantly, most Cabinet ministers are not "experts" in the field over which they are given responsibility. Long-serving senior bureaucrats, such as deputy ministers, assistant deputy ministers, heads of regulatory bodies and Crown corporations, and senior managerial staff—all can become major actors in the formulation, implementation and evaluation of policy, because they are the ones with greater expertise. This problem reflects a weakness in the politics-administration dichotomy theory, which says that ministers should be "on top," while bureaucrats should be "on tap."[20] But ministers who must rely extensively on the expertise of their appointed aides may be at a disadvantage and become overly dependent. This implies that there is a grey area where accountability is concerned.

This reality is widely recognized within public administration, and various reforms have been implemented over the years to try to ensure that the proper relationship between politicians and senior bureaucrats is maintained. The aforementioned central agencies (Finance Department, Privy Council Office, Prime Minister's Office and Treasury Board Secretariat) were developed in part to give the ministers sources of information and guidance apart from their own departmental officials. Attempts to limit the influence and power of the bureaucrats can also be seen in the complex Cabinet committee systems that have been developed. This is an institutional reform designed to allow ministers in related policy fields to come together on a formal basis to exchange information and advice regarding policy. Whether these innovations have actually promoted democratic government is a matter of some contention. Some people argue that while these reforms do provide ministers with countervailing sources of information and advice, they also immensely increase the bureaucratization of decision-making, and that, in any case, ministers are simply substituting one set of bureaucratic advisors for another.[21]

A relatively new twist to the accountability issue is derived from the recent trend toward restructuring of the public service. Ministers are increasingly seeking advice from outside consultants, given the cutbacks in their own ministries, with the result that the chain of accountability is broken, since outsiders have no relationship to the traditional structures of decision-making in government. And just as problematic is the trend toward calling public servants onto the carpet for the mistakes of these outside consultants, as has been the case with the spate of advertising contract scandals that have beleaguered the Chrétien government in the early 2000s.[22]

Accountability thus consists of a number of aspects. But it ultimately comes down to the notion that in a democratic society, elected officials must accept responsibility for the actions of their public servants and the government on behalf of the people. One former Cabinet minister in British Columbia, who had previously been a poultry farmer, put it this way:

Eggs have to be candled to check the interior quality as well as examining the exterior. I did not lay the eggs, but if a customer complained to me about the quality of one of those eggs that I was selling him, there was no point in me blaming the chicken, finding out which hen laid it and saying that she was to blame. I was responsible. I was the proprietor and it was my responsibility.[23]

Where wrongdoing has occurred, the doctrine of ministerial responsibility suggests that the minister ought to resign if the offence is a serious enough one. Of course, the definition of "serious" here is open to considerable debate, and largely depends on whether you happen to sit on the government side of the House of Commons, or on the opposition benches. But most would agree that no one individual minister can possibly be held personally liable for all the actions of his department. Thus, one of the ongoing struggles of governing involves trying to determine where the line can be drawn between minor breaches of responsibility, and more serious ones requiring the resignation of a minister. This question, already complex in itself, has become even more so with the latest developments in public administration associated with the New Public Management. We will turn our attention below to the set of issues this has raised. But for now, we will explain more fully what the concept of accountability means to public servants.

Accountability and Public Servants

There are five overlapping contexts within which accountability is applied to public servants:

➤ accountability to a superior

➤ accountability to elected officials

➤ accountability under the law

➤ accountability to professional norms and institutions

➤ accountability to the public[24]

These various levels of accountability are depicted in Table 12.1.

The first context in which accountability is applied is derived from the Weberian notion of bureaucracies as hierarchical organizations defined by a chain of command. Each employee is responsible to a superior, and each office in the hierarchy is sanctioned by and established through administrative procedures and law. The organization charts of government departments in Chapter 5 reflect these points. Rewards and penalties are prescribed for both observing accountability

TABLE 12.1   Accountability Streams for Public Servants

Superiors	Politicians	The Law	Professions	The Public
Deputy ministers	Legislature	Acts	Ethics	Individual citizens
Assistant deputy ministers	Ministers	Regulations	Codes	Citizen groups
Directors			Standards	Service quality
Managers				
Supervisors				

Source: Adapted from R.L. Gagne, "Accountability and Public Administration," *Canadian Public Administration*, 9, 2 (Summer, 1996): 215.

and transgressing it. In some parts of the organization, accountability crosses from administrative lines (say, from a manager to a director) to political lines (from a deputy minister to her minister). In this way, the entire organization is held accountable to elected officials.

In addition, the strictures of accountability are derived from the public servant's responsibility to uphold the law in the course of administering programs and policies. Thus, the various acts and regulations passed by government are (hopefully) dutifully observed and upheld by responsible, conscientious bureaucrats. This extends throughout the entire organization, from the most senior officers to the lowest clerk. But it is the senior-most officer—the deputy minister—who, under the *Financial Administration Act,* is given particular financial responsibilities for the department, and for personnel responsibilities under delegated authority from the Treasury Board and Public Service Commission.

In addition, though, there is another context of accountability that may be less obvious than those we have identified so far. This relates to the fact that since government is such a large and complex system, it requires the services of a variety of skilled and specially trained individuals to deliver services to the public. For instance, legions of scientists, engineers, doctors, nurses, lawyers, accountants, teachers and professors, surveyors, geologists, architects, real estate agents, urban planners, and countless other professionals work either directly or indirectly for the government. In many cases, these individuals have a responsibility, not just to the government, but also to the norms and standards of their profession as well. Various professions have their own codes of conduct, professional criteria, standards of behaviour, conflict of interest regulations, and so on, to which their members must be responsible. Even the right to practise in a given field may be determined by the professional body that oversees the field. Public servants who work in careers that have professional organizations overseeing them are, in effect, doubly accountable: once to the government, and once to their professional organization.

Finally, of course, there is accountability to the public, a point we have emphasized elsewhere. Suffice it to say that accountability to the public is something of a professional ethos for public servants. While there is no firm basis in law or administration for this context of accountability, there is nonetheless a powerful convention derived from the subjective responsibility felt by public servants toward the public. This is reinforced by the expectation on the part of the public that public servants will behave in a responsible manner toward them.

These contexts can be expressed in a slightly different way.[25] We can think about *administrative accountability* in terms of superior-subordinate relationships; *legal accountability* in terms of the mandates of departments, reporting requirements for public servants and contractual requirements; *constitutional accountability*, including ministerial responsibility, in terms of the approval of taxing and spending by Parliament; *professional accountability*, which refers to the need to adhere to professional standards and norms; and *political accountability*, which refers to competitive elections, and the relationship between representatives and their constituents and other societal interests. These categories roughly coincide with the five contexts above, but provide a slightly different perspective on accountability.

These five contexts and categories for accountability are not unconnected. Indeed, there is a considerable amount of overlap among them, conceptually and in practice, prompting one public administration practitioner to comment that "public servants sometimes feel like flies trapped in a spider's web of accountabilities."[26] In some cases the duty to one form of accountability comes into conflict with another. For instance, the professional duty of a doctor to observe the Hippocratic Oath may conflict with instructions from the minister to fudge scientific evidence regarding a particular health risk.

Perhaps more interestingly, there is also an apparent division within the public service itself over the relative importance of the various contexts of accountability. The higher the public servant is on the hierarchy ladder, the more inclined she is to feel responsible primarily to the minister and the government of the day. The lower down on the hierarchy, the more inclined bureaucrats are to feel responsible to the public, and especially to the clients they serve directly.[27] This creates tensions within the public service, some of which manifested themselves when exercises such as PS2000 and La Relève (discussed in chapters 9 and 10) provoked complaints that senior civil servants were out of touch with the concerns of their subordinates.

Finally, the recent erosion of the pure doctrine of ministerial responsibility, and its evolution into the doctrine of answerability, has created a new conundrum for public servants. Increasingly, as part of this process, public servants are being called on the carpet to answer for their actions. But this betrays the traditional precepts of anonymity, neutrality and tenure of service that should characterize the public service. You will recall that public servants "are appointed on the basis of merit, they provide frank and objective advice to ministers in private, they do not express their personal views in public or engage in partisan activities, they execute policies faithfully and to the best of their abilities, and in return for their support and loyalty they are protected from being personally named for mistakes and enjoy reactive job security based upon satisfactory performance."[28]

A couple of noteworthy developments are altering the traditional concept of ministerial responsibility where public servants are concerned. For instance, public servants are, more and more, being required to appear before parliamentary committees. These are very public fora, and this development means that the anonymity of public servants is being eroded. As Paul Thomas reports, public servants theoretically appear before these committees simply to provide background information to members of Parliament. However, "the rules to govern the interactions between public servants and politicians in what are essentially partisan areas are unwritten or vague at best. This new procedure means that public servants must be cautious and agile in order to avoid being drawn into partisan controversies."[29] An episode of the British sitcom *Yes, Prime Minister* depicts the Cabinet secretary being called before a parliamentary committee which questions him on certain improprieties committed by the government. "That is a political matter, and therefore only the prime minister can answer your questions," he sniffs. In the next scene, the prime minister is before the committee, to which he suggests that the matters under consideration "really are administrative matters" and therefore should be answered by his Cabinet secretary. Moreover, the increased emphasis on public-private partnerships and consultations with interest groups also exposes public servants to the light of day in fora that are very public in nature. This undermines the tradition of confidentiality between ministers and their public servants, since more information is being shared in ever wider circles.

The evolving role of the media has also had an impact on the traditional accountability of public servants. Increased coverage of government activities, as well as a more investigative and adversarial media (perhaps copying their U.S. cousins), has also shifted the spotlight such that it focuses more on public servants. The media has also become very savvy at using access-to-information legislation to see documents that previously might have stayed under lock and key. "These trends have not brought us to the point where public servants are recognizable household names," according to Thomas, "but they are better known in the sense that parliamentarians, pressure group representatives, and interested members of the public are better able today to identify the occupants of important positions within the bureaucracy, and may even feel confident in attributing certain policy perspectives to such individuals."[30]

The recent alterations to the doctrine of ministerial responsibility suggest two things about this traditional view of the role of public servants. First, if ministers do not take responsibility, and public servants are not *supposed to* or are not *expected to* take responsibility, then who does? The public has both the right and the need to know who is responsible for government action (or inaction). So who will now step forward? The answer seems to be that increasingly, public servants are being exposed as the culprits when things go awry in government.

But surely if this trend is allowed to persist, it will adversely affect the work that public servants do. They may react by being overly cautious in their recommendations to their political masters. Or they may slow the process down for fear of supplying advice that could later be used against them if a policy mistake emerges. This was the result, for instance, after the Human Resources and Development Canada

(HRDC) scandal which broke in 1999. Subsequently, HRDC staff adopted a "do-it-by-the-book" mentality, involving scrupulous attention to paperwork and risk avoidance. The result was delays of several weeks in the processing of services, as public servants sought to ensure a complete and thorough paper-trail accompanied every action.[31] It is one of the great ironies of public administration that this new emphasis on accountability can actually promote dysfunctions in government. Accountability is seen largely as being about assigning blame when things go wrong. But no one likes to accept blame, especially if it might curtail their career ambitions.. As a result, it has been observed that one of the impediments to accountability is that the emphasis on blame may lead to more "buckpassing and scapegoating by both politicians and appointed officials. In other words, because of its potential negative consequences, accountability may become something to be avoided at all costs."[32] Overall, the jury is still out on these developments. But so far, it is hard to see much benefit from them.

Accountability in Action: The Role of the Office of the Auditor General

Much of the discussion about accountability thus far may seem abstract and disconnected from the real world. Thus, it might be useful to briefly examine at least one mechanism through which accountability is realized. There are many links in the chain of accountability, including—besides Parliament and Cabinet—several specialized agencies and offices, such as the Information and Privacy Commission, the Commissioner of Official Languages, and the Human Rights Commission. Rather than survey all these bodies, we will now turn our attention to the Office of the Auditor General, which stands out for both its unique status (as an independent, arm's-length body) and its reporting function (it reports directly to Parliament, not to a minister). This body is one of the most significant institutions directly engaged in holding the government to account.[33]

As we pointed out earlier in this chapter, the public wants and needs to know that government is managing public monies effectively and efficiently, and that this management is based on the public trust. Confidence in democracy and government are reinforced when public funds are raised carefully and spent wisely; in short, when there is value for money spent. Parliament is the institution which has primary responsibility for this important task, and which acts on behalf of the people. The government cannot raise or spend a single penny without the authorization of Parliament to do so, and must explain to Parliament both the reasons for expending public money, and the results of the expenditures. To maintain accountability in this process, the government must report on its performance by submitting spending plans (Estimates) for each department, and reports of the previous year's activities. As well, it must produce annual financial statements showing all spending, borrowing and taxing, known as the Public Accounts of Canada. The result is that Parliament is inundated with information with which to hold the government to account. But also needed is independent assessment of all that information, so that members of Parliament can effectively assess the government's performance while feeling comfortable that the information upon which they are basing their assessment is unbiased and objective. This is where the Auditor General comes into play.

The Auditor General audits government operations and provides Parliament with the information it needs to hold the government to account. The position and office of an independent auditor general was established in 1878. Early reports to Parliament listed every single transaction government undertook, as well as reporting on whether public money had been spent by government in the way Parliament intended. The contemporary Office of the Auditor General began to take shape in the 1950s, but ran into some controversy when it began to overstep the bounds of its mandate by pronouncing on the quality of the government's policy choices. Later, the 1977 *Auditor General Act* gave it a broader mandate and clarified that the office does not comment on policy choices by the government (that is, it does not pronounce this policy "bad," and that policy "good"), but rather focuses on how those policies were implemented. More recently, in 1995, amendments to the Act established the position of Commissioner of the Environment and Sustainable Development within the Office of the Auditor General, reflecting contemporary concerns with these issues and the role of government therein. The vision and mission of the Office of the Auditor General is provided in Box 12-5.

The Auditor General is independent of the government of the day, and is appointed for a 10-year term to help reinforce the objectivity needed to support that independence. The 1977 *Auditor General Act* provided three questions to which the Auditor General must address himself or herself. These are as follows:

➤ Is the government keeping proper accounts and records and presenting its financial information accurately?

➤ Did the government collect or spend the authorized amount of money, and for the purposes intended by Parliament?

➤ Were programs run economically and efficiently? And does the government have the means to measure their effectiveness?

Each question corresponds to a particular type of audit that must be carried out by the Auditor General. The first question calls for *attest* auditing, which simply means that the auditor attests to or verifies the accuracy of financial statements. The second question calls for *compliance* auditing, in which the Auditor General reveals whether the government has complied with Parliament's wishes. The third question calls for *value-for-money* auditing, sometimes called *performance* auditing, in which the Auditor General investigates whether or not taxpayers got value for their tax dollars. In short, the accountability function of the Auditor General is a thorough one, contained in a broad framework intended to allow for a penetrating examination of the government's activities.

Public awareness about the activities of government is a key aspect of the Auditor General's work. To publicize what government has and has not done, the Auditor General issues an annual report to the House of Commons. As of 1994, with

BOX 12-5

Vision and Mission of the Office of the Auditor General of Canada

Vision: We are committed to making a difference for the Canadian people by promoting, in all our work for Parliament, answerable, honest and productive government.

Mission: The Office of the Auditor General of Canada conducts independent audits and examinations that provide objective information, advice and assurance to Parliament. We promote accountability and best practices in government operations.

Elaboration of Mission: In achieving our mission, we want to make a difference by promoting

➤ a fair and frank accounting of government's stewardship of financial and other resources

➤ efficiency and productivity in the public service

➤ cost effectiveness of government activities

➤ collection of revenues owed to the Crown.

Other effects we want to produce through our work are

➤ objective assurance on matters found to be satisfactory and unsatisfactory

➤ compliance with authority

➤ deterrence of fraud and dishonesty.

Source: Canada, Office of the Auditor General, *Auditing for Parliament*, (Ottawa: Minister of Public Works and Government Services Canada, 1997).

amendment of the *Auditor General Act,* as many as three reports are now produced each year. These reports contain the results of comprehensive audits of federal departments and agencies; government-wide audits; follow-up reports concerning previous audits; and audit observations, which are important matters not covered in any of the other reports. Other forms of reporting take place in regard to Crown corporations through the minister responsible, or in some cases directly to the boards of directors; through the Public Accounts every autumn; and through special audits ordered by Cabinet and not included in the regular reporting process. In addition, audits of the governments of the Yukon, Nunavut and Northwest Territories are reported annually to their legislative assemblies.

Finally, with all this reporting going on, it is reasonable to wonder who reports on the Office of the Auditor General. What mechanisms exist to ensure that the government "watcher" is adequately "watched"? This is accomplished by an external auditor annually appointed by the Treasury Board. This report is presented to the Treasury Board and tabled in the House of Commons. As well, the Auditor General's work is the focus of 15 different parliamentary committees, and its own spending is subject to review and inspection by the Public Accounts Committee of Parliament, and to the scrutiny of the Official Languages Commissioner on language issues, the Public Service Commission on staffing and classification practices, and the Privacy Commissioner through the *Privacy Act*.

In short, as this brief overview reveals, multiple and reinforcing sources of accountability ripple throughout the organization of government. The process is complex and convoluted, and in part explains why government business sometimes takes so long to be completed. The multiple checks within the system may seem overly bureaucratic, time-consuming and inefficient. But the alternative may be even less palatable to citizens who have every right to expect their tax dollars to be used wisely. Recent developments have introduced new issues and problems where accountability is concerned, resulting in the need for ongoing review of the functions and roles of bodies such as the Auditor General, and indeed more broadly of government itself. We now turn our attention to some of these developments.

Contemporary Issues of Accountability and Control

The advent of the **New Public Management (NPM)** and the general trend toward making government more businesslike has had important implications for accountability. The concept and practice of accountability are different in the private sector than in the public sector. So what happens when you begin to import the practices of the former into the latter? This final section addresses this issue, bearing as it does directly on the future of public administration in Canada.

One observer suggests that the accountability regime under which public servants served in the past has changed:

Management principles like decentralization, achieving measurable results, and empowerment (key features of "managerialism") imply that public-sector managers are to be held accountable for performance results rather than for adhering to due process and to the equitable treatment of individuals. In addition, if the federal experience is any guide, individual public servants may now be held directly accountable for their own actions or those of their subordinates by parliamentary committees or their surrogates in provincial legislatures or on municipal councils (as the Al-Mashat Affair demonstrated), to say nothing of the potential for damages resulting from the increasing tendency for the public to file civil suits against particular public servants.[34]

These developments imply that our traditional understanding of who should be held to account for government action or inaction needs to be rethought. Factors such as downsizing and privatization have had significant impacts on accountability, as has an increasing tendency to resort to private sector management techniques focusing on improved efficiency and client service. For example, when a government downloads to the private sector its responsibility to provide a particular service, or indeed privatizes that service, who is accountable when things go awry? The answer to this question is not as clear-cut as you might assume.

Take the issue of responsibility for roads, for instance. Increasingly, governments in Canada are considering "selling" highways to private sector corporations, who would assume responsibility for their upkeep and maintenance by collecting tolls. But what if the roads fall into disrepair, and the corporations find it less and less profitable to maintain them? They could raise the tolls, but they would risk losing customers, which would translate into a loss of revenue to use for road repair. In the worst-case scenario, suppose a company abrogates its responsibilities altogether, perhaps by claiming that revenues cannot keep up with expenses, and that the company has no choice but to declare bankruptcy. The state is left to assume responsibility, using taxpayers' dollars, for the lack of accountability inherent in the original arrangement.

Or consider another emerging trend. Introducing private sector management techniques into the public service often involves "letting the managers manage," that is, decentralizing control over the actions of subordinates, giving them more flexibility in their roles, and permitting them to make more decisions regarding the provision of services to clients, i.e., citizens. These attempts to empower public servants and make them more responsive to Canadians may seem laudable. But surely at some level they conflict with certain traditional values of accountability. Emphasizing efficiency and responsiveness substitutes the private sector's value system for the public sector's. This may mean that in the pursuit of efficiency, due process will have to be sacrificed. As professor of public administration Donald Savoie suggests, incorporating private-sector management practices into the public sector "means rejecting traditional public-administration concerns with accountability and control, and giving way to the business-management emphasis on productivity, performance, and service to clients."[35] The overriding concern is that public servants operate in a political environment involving the public trust, whereas business operates in a different environment altogether. As Savoie also says, "In business it does not much matter if you get it wrong 10 percent of the time as long as you turn a profit at the end of the year. In government, it does not much matter if you get it right 90 percent of the time because the focus will be on the 10 percent of the time you got it wrong."[36] Another view, however, is that if "managerialism enables objectives to be expressed more clearly and encourages better measurement of results, it can actually make control more meaningful and provide better information to ministers, thereby enhancing, not diminishing, their ability to account for the use they make of public funds."[37]

A variety of organizational models have been introduced into public administration recently that test the traditional doctrine of ministerial responsibility and the concept of accountability in general. Greater decentralization and more autonomy for civil servants seem to be recurring themes in these models, and practices in other countries have been noted by the Canadian government. In Great Britain, for instance, the concept of *executive agencies* has been introduced. These are bodies that are delegated a certain amount of responsibility by the minister concerned. The chief executives of these agencies are accountable to the minister through certain performance contracts rather than through traditional hierarchical channels. This model leaves responsibility for overall policy-making in the hands of the minister, but it transfers responsibility for operations to the chief executives. New Zealand has introduced something called the *state-owned enterprise,* in which a higher level of independence is granted to these enterprises than is traditionally the case with the older Crown corporation model. In Canada, a number of similar initiatives are under way. For instance, as a result of Program Review, the air navigation system under the auspices of Transport Canada began operating on a commercial basis in November 1996. The Translation Bureau in the Department of Public Works and Government Services became a Special Operating Agency (SOA) around the same time. New agencies are under development in areas such as parks management, food inspection, revenue and securities, some of which add another layer of complication to the responsibility issue, since they cross over from federal into provincial jurisdiction. These examples and others developing elsewhere implicitly strain the conventional understanding of accountability, leaving some observers to conclude that "the question of ministerial responsibility and the structures within which the new service delivery agencies are to be held accountable to Parliament must be seriously examined." Moreover, "to fail to do so would jeopardize the doctrine of ministerial responsibility, which could in turn undermine an important part of the Canadian democratic system."[38]

As an example of the changing nature of accountability brought on by NPM, consider the idea of empowerment of public servants through more decentralized decision-making and the encouragement of risk-taking.[39] These developments potentially conflict with traditional notions of accountability. In the first place, existing strictures and institutions (like central agencies) tend to constrain empowerment and risk-taking, and so new strictures and approaches need to be developed. In the second place, public sector managers, unlike their private-sector counterparts, are typically risk-averse, fearing that mistakes will attract the attention of the media, interest groups and opposition parties, thus curtailing their career potential. Third, and related, notions of neutrality and anonymity are compromised, as public servants employing their increased decision-making powers come to be more and more identified with government initiatives.

Still, governments are increasingly redefining accountability, through the lens of empowerment and other precepts of the NPM, to place greater emphasis on *results* rather than *process*. As some observers suggest, "governments are more aware that holding public servants accountable through a variety of formal controls is a necessary but insufficient means of ensuring responsible administrative conduct." Further, "empowerment envisages increased emphasis on psychological or personal responsibility, in the sense of loyalty to, or identification with, organizational and program goals."[40] But again, we bump up against a potential conflict between a sense of personal responsibility on the part of individual public servants, and the larger framework of ministerial responsibility. Unless ministers are willing to broaden their conception of ministerial responsibility to include a defense of risk-taking by public servants, and of the mistakes that inevitably will be made, there seems little chance that the tensions between old and new forms of accountability will dissipate.

Political scientist Paul Thomas identifies a clear trend in relation to the erosion of the tradition of the anonymous career public servant. He suggests that "under the sway of NPM ideas there is a growing insistence that public servants be personally accountable for results through, for example, the development and publication of performance indicators."[41] As political scientist J.E. Hodgetts foresaw in the early 1990s:

if the inevitable drift of public management into the political realm of governance itself... is to be the path of the future, then we must be prepared to see senior managers assume the role of scapegoats for the failures of others who, in our system of responsible cabinet government, have hitherto been elected to bear that direct responsibility.[42]

Flushing public servants out from the shadows where they traditionally reside is problematic, if for no other reason than that there is no one else, other than their own superiors within the hierarchical chain of command, to whom they are required to answer directly. The recent use of parliamentary committees (as in the Al-Mashat Affair) to roast public servants on the open fires of Parliament is inappropriate, since they were intended as accountability mechanisms that ministers—not their bureaucrats—answer to. In any event, only ministers can impose penalties or sanctions for errors committed by public servants; parliamentary committees do not possess that right. But, at the same time, public servants' reputations and careers can be severely damaged in the partisan arena of Parliament, leading Thomas to conclude that "placing public servants before parliamentary committees creates risks in terms of inappropriate and unfair questions by politicians, and not just from those on the opposition benches."[43]

Thomas cites some other concerns with these developments. He suggests, "The NPM literature tends to denigrate existing approaches to accountability as mistaking adherence to procedures for the achievement of results, stifling creativity and initiative and adding to the costs of running government. Control is seen only in negative terms of adding to red tape."[44] Yet control through accountability measures may actually improve efficiency and effectiveness by preventing abuses that lead to waste. Thus, while the NPM is dismissive of traditional mechanisms and systems of accountability (see Box 12-6), it tends to ignore the fact that the bureaucracy of accountability actually fosters the values NPM supports. Moreover, as another critic of NPM points out, "Those who argue that the principle of ministerial responsibility is dated have a responsibility to outline a new regime and to detail how it is to work. This has never been done."[45]

The implications of many of the contemporary developments related to accountability can be traced right back to our discussion of constitutional and administrative law in Chapter 6. The Constitution, you will recall, sets out the relationship between individuals and the state, and relationships among the different institutions of government. It does this in order to promote the rule of law, the premise of which is that no one in society—not even the most politically, economically or socially powerful—is above the law. This includes, of course, the government itself and those who work in it. In this sense, the courts have played

BOX 12-6

Accountability Mechanisms

The mechanisms that now exist to promote accountability include the following:

➤ new systems to strengthen collective decision-making in Cabinet

➤ a more prominent role for central agencies

➤ new budgetary systems to merge policy determination with expenditure allocation

➤ mandatory requirements for the periodic and systematic evaluation of programs

➤ clarification of the responsibilities of the deputy minister

➤ new accountability frameworks for nondepartmental bodies such as Crown corporations and regulatory agencies

➤ greater scrutiny of the bureaucracy by parliamentary committees through estimates, the review of order-in-council appointments, and general investigations

➤ a strengthened role for the Auditor General to practise comprehensive auditing

➤ the passage of access-to-information and privacy laws

➤ the adoption of legislation to register lobbyists and to publicize their activities

➤ the passage of conflict-of interest guidelines, codes of conduct, and the appointment of an ethics commissioner

➤ development of numerous consultative mechanisms: discussion papers, task forces, partnerships, and so on

➤ extension of judicial review as a form of supervision over the exercise of discretionary authority.

Source: Paul G. Thomas, "The Changing Nature of Accountability," in B. Guy Peters and Donald J. Savoie, eds. *Taking Stock: Assessing Public Sector Reforms,* (Montreal: McGill–Queen's University Press, 1998): 385.

a prominent role in accountability, being a primary mechanism by which penalties are imposed for transgressions. The courts uphold the rule of law, and hence the Constitution, in ensuring that politicians and public servants do not overstep the bounds of accountability imposed upon them by the myriad rules and institutions we have surveyed above. However, the NPM may be changing the role and impact of the rule of law, as well as the courts, in maintaining accountability. The NPM draws for its inspiration on the literature and language of private management. Traditional public administration, in contrast, draws on the literature and language of law and political science. Clearly the latter is more directly concerned with issues of justice and legality, the Constitution, the rule of law, and related matters. The former is more concerned with management techniques that promote efficiency, effectiveness and economy. Yet again, we see another manifestation of the conflicting-values problem in public administration, this time related to the issue of accountability.

The various controversies currently swirling around the issue of accountability are unlikely to be resolved anytime soon. It is not as though they have a single easy answer. Instead, what is called for is gradual change through reforms and experimentation, new initiatives and careful consideration and analysis of existing systems of accountability. But remember that accountability is based on the underlying principle of responsible government. This fundamental democratic premise of the Canadian system of government should drive all attempts at coordinating the actors, institutions, ideas, and formal and informal systems and processes that animate the regime of accountability. Failure to focus on this basic point means that citizens will be ill-served, since both politicians and bureaucrats may be less inclined to "pay attention to their respective assigned and accepted responsibilities [and] to understand that it does matter."[46]

WHAT YOU HAVE LEARNED

The concept of accountability embraces several different aspects of public administration. It is vital to democratic government, yet it is not always clearly understood. When modern society created democratic systems of government, the convention developed that public office was a matter of public trust, that the powers associated with public office should be used for the betterment of society (and not just the office-holder's personal gain), and that in pursuing this goal, office-holders were expected to act with integrity, honesty and responsibility. Moreover, they were to constantly account for their actions and for the exercise of power entrusted to them. This meant that they would have to report regularly on their activities in a public and visible way; that they would make themselves available to public scrutiny and be able to justify all their actions and decisions; that they would follow constitutional and administrative law in so doing; and that they would ultimately work toward improved provision of public services. Moreover, they would assume liability if they misused office. It is often suggested that public administration, in this conception, was not the administration *of* the public, but administration *for* the public. In short, notwithstanding the new trends in Canadian public administration, the responsibilities of the public servant were unlike those of an individual in private business, wherein the regime of accountability is less comprehensive, more limited, and different in orientation.

ENDNOTES

1.   Gerald E. Caiden, "The Problem of Ensuring the Public Accountability of Public Officials," in Joseph G. Jabbra and O.P. Dwivedi, eds. *Public Service Accountability,* (West Hartford, Connecticut: Kumarian Press, 1988): 19.

2.   See J.R. Mallory, *The Structure of Canadian Government,* (Toronto: Gage, 1971).

3. See Canada, Privy Council Office, *Responsibility in the Constitution*, (Ottawa: Minister of Supply and Services, 1993): 11–27.

4. James John Guy, *How We Are Governed: The Basics of Canadian Politics and Government*, (Toronto: Harcourt Brace and Company, 1995): 35.

5. See Keith Archer *et al.*, *Parameters of Power: Canada's Political Institutions*, (Scarborough: Nelson, 1995): 72.

6. Caiden, "The Problem of Ensuring the Public Accountability of Public Officials," (1988): 20.

7. O.P. Dwivedi, "The Issue of Accountability in the Public Service of Canada," in Joseph G. Jabbra and O.P. Dwivedi, eds. *Public Service Accountability: A Comparative Perspective*, (West Hartford, Connecticut: Kumarian Press, 1988): 86.

8. Caiden, "The Problem of Ensuring the Public Accountability of Public Officials," (1988): 17.

9. Paul G. Thomas, "The Changing Nature of Accountability," in B. Guy Peters and Donald J. Savoie, eds. *Taking Stock: Assessing Public Sector Reforms*, (Montreal: McGill–Queen's University Press, 1998): 352.

10. Caiden, "The Problem of Ensuring the Public Accountability of Public Officials," (1988): 25.

11. Nicole Jauvin, "Government, Ministers, Macro-Organization Chart and Networks," in Jacques Bourgault, Maurice Demers and Cynthia Williams, eds. *Public Administration and Public Management: Experiences in Canada*, (St. Foy, Quebec: Les Publications du Quebec, 1997): 49.

12. Thomas, "The Changing Nature of Accountability," (1998): 359.

13. See Jauvin, "Government, Ministers, Macro-Organization Chart and Networks," (1997): 48.

14. Canada, Privy Council Office, *A Guide for Ministers and Secretaries of State*, (Ottawa: Privy Council Office, 2002): 2–3.

15. Jauvin, "Government, Ministers, Macro-Organization Chart and Networks," (1997): 49.

16. David Kilgour, John Kirsner and Kenneth McConnell, "Discipline Versus Democracy: Party Discipline in Canadian Politics," and Robert J. Jackson and Paul Conlin, "Imperative of Party Discipline in the Canadian Political System," in Mark Charlton and Paul Barker, eds. *Crosscurrents: Contemporary Political Issues, Second Edition*, (Scarborough: Nelson, 1994): 192–208.

17. The following section is derived largely from Jauvin, "Government, Ministers, Macro-Organization Chart and Networks," (1997): 55–56.

18. Ian Clark, "A 'Back to Basics' Look at the Government Decision-Making Process," unpublished paper, (November 4, 1983): 13. Cited in Robert J. Jackson and Doreen Jackson, *Politics in Canada: Culture, Institutions, Behaviour and Public Policy, Fourth Edition*, (Scarborough: Prentice Hall, 1998): 273.

19. See S.L. Sutherland, "The Al-Mashat Affair: Administrative Accountability in Parliamentary Institutions," *Canadian Public Administration*, 34, 4 (Winter, 1991): 573–603.

20. See Flora MacDonald, "Who is on Top? The Minister or the Mandarins?" and Mitchell Sharp, "A Reply From a Former Minister and Mandarin," in Paul W. Fox and Graham White, eds. *Politics Canada, Eighth Edition*, (Toronto: McGraw-Hill, 1995): 448–456.

21. See Richard J. Van Loon and Michael S. Whittington, *The Canadian Political System, Fourth Edition*, (Toronto: McGraw-Hill Ryerson, 1987): chapters 15 and 17; and Evert A. Lindquist, "Has Federal Cabinet Decision-Making Come Full Circle?" in Paul W. Fox and Graham White, eds. *Politics Canada, Eighth Edition*, (Toronto: McGraw-Hill, 1995): 544–552.

22. See Graham Fraser, "Civil Service a Victim in Sponsorship Scandals," *Toronto Star* (June 16, 2002).

23. Cited in Sutherland, "The Al-Mashat Affair," (1991): 582.

24. See R.L. Gagne, "Accountability and Public Administration," *Canadian Public Administration*, 39, 2 (Summer, 1996): 214.

25. See Thomas, "The Changing Nature of Accountability," (1998): 356.

26. J. David Wright, "Exposing the Chameleon: Response to 'Accountability and Public Administration,'" *Canadian Public Administration*, 39, 2 (Summer, 1996): 229.

27. Donald J. Savoie, *Thatcher, Reagan, Mulroney: In Search of a New Bureaucracy*, (Pittsburgh: University of Pittsburgh Press, 1994): 216–217.

28. Thomas, "The Changing Nature of Accountability, (1998): 360.

29. Thomas, "The Changing Nature of Accountability," (1998): 360–361.

30. Thomas, "The Changing Nature of Accountability," (1998): 361.

31. See Graham Fraser, "Scandal Leaves Ottawa Swamped in Paperwork," *Toronto Star*, (December 13, 2000): A23. The HRDC scandal is reviewed in Canada, Treasury Board of Canada Secretariat, *Building on a Strong Foundation—The Dialogue Continues Volume II: Further Case Studies on Values and Ethics in the Public Service*, (Ottawa: Canadian Centre for Management Development, 2001): 41–48. See also Sharon L. Sutherland, "'Biggest Scandal in Canadian History': HRDC Audit Starts Probity War," (Kingston: Queen's University Working Paper 23, August, 2001).

32. Thomas, "The Changing Nature of Accountability," (1998): 353.

33. The following description of the auditor general's role is derived from Canada, Office of the Auditor General, *Auditing for Parliament,* (Ottawa: Minister of Public Works and Government Services Canada, 1997). For a critical review of the work of the Auditor-General during the HRDC scandal, see Sharon L. Sutherland, "'Biggest Scandal in Canadian History': HRDC Audit Starts Probity War," (Kingston: Queen's University Working Paper 23, August, 2001).

34. Gagne, "Accountability and Public Administration," (1996): 220.

35. Savoie, *Thatcher, Reagan, Mulroney,* (1994): 283.

36. Donald J. Savoie, "What is Wrong With the New Public Management?" *Canadian Public Administration,* 38, 1 (Spring, 1995): 115.

37. Wright, "Exposing the Chameleon," (1996): 232.

38. Jauvin, "Government, Ministers, Macro-Organization Chart and Networks," (1997): 58.

39. See Kenneth Kernaghan, Brian Marson and Sandford Borins, *The New Public Organization*, (Toronto: Institute of Public Administration of Canada, 2000): 175–177.

40. Kernaghan, Marson and Borins, *The New Public Organization*, (2000): 176.

41. Paul G. Thomas, "The Changing Nature of Accountability," (1998): 382.

42. J.E. Hodgetts, *Public Management: Emblem of Reform for the Canadian Public Service*, (Ottawa: Canadian Centre for Management Development, 1991): 13. Cited in O.P. Dwivedi and James Iain Gow, *From Bureaucracy to Public Management: The Administrative Culture of the Government of Canada*, (Peterborough: Broadview Press, 1999): 176.

43. Thomas, "The Changing Nature of Accountability," (1998): 382.

44. Thomas, "The Changing Nature of Accountability," (1998): 383.

45. Donald J. Savoie, "What is Wrong With the New Public Management?" (1996): 112–121.

46. Canada, Royal Commission on Financial Management and Accountability, *Final Report,* (Ottawa: Supply and Services, 1979): 9.

KEY WORDS AND CONCEPTS

accountable (364)	ministerial responsibility (370)
responsible (365)	doctrine of answerability (371)
responsible government (365)	collective responsibility (371)
democrats (367)	party discipline (373)
conservatives (367)	New Public Management (NPM) (384)

REVIEW QUESTIONS

1. Accountability and Democracy

The central principle of responsible government first raised in Chapter 4 was the focus of discussion here. This principle lies at the root of the accountability issue.

The link between accountability and democracy was explained, and the following questions were addressed: How is the principle of responsible government significant where accountability is concerned? How does the principle work in theory and in practice in the context of Canadian public administration?

2. Ministerial Responsibility

Responsible government, we determined, depends in part on the doctrine of ministerial responsibility, which sets the boundaries of ministerial action. It also establishes the guidelines that state how government can be held to account. This section explained the pure theory of ministerial responsibility, and showed how contemporary trends and developments have affected the original theory, by asking these questions: What is the theory of ministerial responsibility? What is individual ministerial responsibility? What is collective ministerial responsibility? How has the doctrine of answerability modified the accountability of ministers? How has the traditional approach to ministerial responsibility in the political system changed over time? What does this mean for the concept of accountability now?

3. Accountability and Public Servants

Where the traditional doctrine of ministerial authority meets the politics-administration dichotomy, certain expectations about the role and behaviour of public servants emerge. But recent changes to the concept of accountability have altered the conventional set of expectations, leaving bureaucrats on unfamiliar ground. This section addressed both the traditional role of public servants and the newly emerging one, by asking the following: In what ways have public servants traditionally been held accountable for their actions? How have the concepts of ministerial responsibility and the politics-administration dichotomy affected the position and work of public servants in terms of accountability? What problems do public servants face in trying to live up to the accountability regime? How do public servants respond to the multiple demands of executives, legislatures, judiciary, interest groups, professional associations, regulatory boards, the media, clients, and citizens when responsibility demands conflict? Which take precedence?

4. Accountability in Action: The Role of the Office of the Auditor General

The Office of the Auditor General is one of the most important links in the chain of accountability. We briefly reviewed the role of this important actor in terms of how it contributes to the accountability process, by asking the following: What role does the Office of the Auditor General play in the process promoting accountability by providing the government with objective, unbiased assessments of its work? If the Auditor General watches over government, who, in turn, watches over the Auditor General?

5. Contemporary Issues of Accountability and Control

This section revealed that the accountability regime is in flux. Recent developments have altered the traditional understanding of who is responsible to whom for what. Traditional notions of ministerial responsibility and the role of public servants have altered due to the emergence of new organizational norms, and systems such as the New Public Management. The drive to put government on a more businesslike footing is behind a large number of these changes. This section asked these questions: How have traditional notions of accountability been altered under the influence of new developments in Canadian public administration? What impact has the New Public Management had on the usual relationships within government where responsibility is concerned? Are these developments helpful or hurtful to the accountability regime?

FURTHER READING

1. Accountability and Democracy

Johnson, David. *Thinking Government: Public Sector Management in Canada.* Peterborough: Broadview Press, 2002: chapter 12.

Mosher, Frederick C. *Democracy and the Public Service.* New York: Oxford University Press, 1968.

Sutherland, Sharon L. and G. Bruce Doern. *Bureaucracy in Canada: Control and Reform.* Toronto: University of Toronto Press, 1985.

2. Ministerial Responsibility

Denton, T.M. "Ministerial Responsibility: A Contemporary Perspective," in Richard Shultz, Orest M. Kruhlak and John C. Terry, eds. *The Canadian Political Process: A Reader, Third Edition.* Toronto: Holt, Rinehart and Winston, 1979: 344–362.

Sutherland, S.L. "Responsible Government and Ministerial Responsibility," *Canadian Journal of Political Science,* 24, 1 (March, 1991): 91–120.

3. Accountability and Public Servants

Cameron, D.M. "Power and Responsibility in the Public Service: Summary of Discussions," *Canadian Public Administration,* 21, 3 (Autumn, 1978): 358–372.

Finer, Herman. "Administrative Responsibility in Democratic Government," *Public Administration Review,* 1, 4 (1941): 335–350.

Friedrich, Carl J. "Public Policy and the Nature of Administrative Responsibility," in Carl J. Friedrich and Edward S. Mason, eds. *Public Policy.* Cambridge: Harvard University Press, 1940: 3–24.

Kernaghan, Kenneth and John Langford. *The Responsible Public Servant.* Halifax: Institute for Research on Public Policy, 1990.

Osbaldeston, Gordon. *Keeping Deputy Ministers Accountable.* Toronto: McGraw-Hill Ryerson, 1989.

Thomas, Paul C. "Parliament and the Public Service," in Christopher Dunn, ed. *The Handbook of Canadian Public Administration.* Toronto: Oxford Univerity Press, 2002: 341–68.

4. Accountability in Action: The Role of the Auditor General's Office

Sutherland, Sharon L. "The Politics of Audit: The Federal Office of the Auditor General in Comparative Perspective," *Canadian Public Administration,* 29, 1 (Spring, 1986): 118–148.

5. Contemporary Issues of Accountability and Control

Aucoin, Peter. "The Design of Public Organizations for the 21st Century: Why Bureaucracy Will Survive in Public Management," *Canadian Public Administration,* 40, 2 (Summer, 1997): 290–306.

Aucoin, Peter. *The New Public Management: Canada in Comparative Perspective.* Montreal: Institute for Research on Public Policy, 1995.

Carroll, Barbara Wake and David I. Dewar. "Performance Management: Panacea or Fools' Gold?" in Christopher Dunn, ed. *The Handbook of Canadian Public Administration.* Toronto: Oxford Univerity Press, 2002: 413–29.

Jabbra, Joseph G. and O.P. Dwivedi. *Public Service Accountability: A Comparative Perspective.* West Hartford, Connecticut: Kumarian Press, 1988.

Panet, Philip de. L. and Michael J. Trebilcock. "Contracting Out Social Services." *Canadian Public Administration*, 41, 1 (Spring, 1998): 21–50.

Seidle, F. Leslie. *Rethinking the Delivery of Public Services to Citizens.* Montreal: Institute for Research on Public Policy, 1995.

 ## WEBLINKS

Privacy Commissioner of Canada
www.privcom.gc.ca

Treasury Board, "Getting Government Right: Improving Results Measurement and Accountability"
www.tbs-sct.gc.ca/rma/communic/prr96/PRR96.e.htm

Auditor General of Canada
www.oag-bvg.gc.ca/

Chapter (13)

Public Administration *and* the Post-Deficit World: Surpluses *and* Security

WHAT YOU WILL LEARN

In his budget speech on February 24, 1998, Finance Minister Paul Martin announced the following:

What I am about to say is something no Canadian government has been able to say for almost fifty years. We will balance the budget next year. We will balance the budget the year after that. And, Mr. Speaker, we will balance the budget this year... it is clear that a new era lies ahead.[1]

A dramatic shift has taken place in the world of public administration as a result of this pronouncement. What we are interested in pursuing about this shift is the following question: If deficits have been the rationale for much of the reshaping of public administration since the 1980s, what happens when that rationale is removed? In other words, if the premise of most contemporary developments in public administration has been that governments must do more with less, what happens when governments suddenly have more?

This chapter will address these questions with an admittedly speculative look at the future of Canadian public administration. This exercise will require accepting certain assumptions, primary among them that "dollars" matter in public administration. What this means is that fiscal concerns create both opportunities and constraints for government, and that while focusing solely on the ledger of government cannot explain everything, it does go a long way toward explaining many things about public administration. So this chapter will focus on what it might mean to the world of Canadian public administration to be moving into an era of balanced budgets. It will do so in relation to the several issues that have been flagged in this book as being vital to practising and understanding public administration. The chapter is divided into the following sections:

(1. — *The Politics of Deficits*

This section looks at the prevailing ideas that have shaped public administration recently. It specifically considers how the issue of deficits and balanced budgets has changed over time, resulting in changes to the course of public policy-making and governance generally. It asks the following: What views prevailed in the past about deficits and balanced budgets? What views prevail currently? How and why did these views change over time? What policy and organizational consequences flowed from these changes? Why is this important to Canadian public administration?

(2. — *Toward a Post-Deficit Future and the New Security Agenda*

This section considers what public administration will look like in the future if current projections for budgetary surpluses unfold according to expectations. It considers the broader societal struggles that are even now emerging over what to do with the "fiscal and social dividend" expected to result from deficit elimination. It asks, What is the fiscal and social dividend? What groups in Canadian society are agitating about how it should be handled? What course of action—tax cuts, social spending, debt reduction, etc.—are on the table? What policy responses are the government open to? How does the debate over the post-deficit future of Canada affect public administration? How do the events of September 11, 2001, affect public administration? What is the security agenda?

The Politics of Deficits

Public administration is about finding the answers to certain questions. The set of questions is constantly changing, though, and this is what makes both the study and practice of public administration so challenging. Five or 10 years ago, for instance, the set of questions revolved largely around the following issue: What can be done to get the deficit under control? As one commentator put it, "The dominant talk these days is about deficit reductions and shrinking the state or at least retooling it so as to be more efficient and thus, presumably, save money. To borrow a phrase, going public is out. Going private is in."[2]

This question of what can be done about the deficit can, in turn, be broken down into two further sets of questions. The first would deal with institutional changes to government that would help realize this goal. For instance, what combination of changes to the machinery of government would help realize the goal of preventing the return of the deficit? Cutbacks? Freezes? Layoffs? Restructuring the ministries? A smaller Cabinet? A new budgetary system? Reformed responsibilities for the central agencies? A new Cabinet committee structure? Privatization? Deregulation? The second set of questions would deal with policies and programs. Which ones are worth saving? Terminating? Expanding? Shrinking? Are there new ones that ought to be introduced?

The answers to these questions are still unfolding. But to the extent that they have been addressed, they have been the focus of an intense struggle in Canadian society and within the state. The public, interest groups and the media have all offered, in varying degrees, their perceptions of the problem and how it might best be handled. Considerable controversy has been generated among the public about whether the government's fixation on the deficit was a matter of misplaced priorities, or of cutting too far too fast, or too slow, or not enough, or too much, and so on. Within government, the ongoing struggle between "saver" and "spender" departments has played itself out against the backdrop of the deficit issue, often with dramatic results. These include the following: the firing of 45 000 federal civil servants; the reorganization of the federal Cabinet from about 40 portfolios to 23; the reemergence of the Finance Department as the key institutional actor in Ottawa (representing the ascendance of the "saver" departments); the introduction of the New Public Management; Program Review, La Relève and other similar reforms of the public service; and so on. In one way or another, all of these steps can be traced back to the fundamental question of how to get the deficit under control.

Yet, if you went back another 20 years or so, these questions would seem entirely inappropriate, since a whole other set of concerns dominated the public agenda. The concerns then were more with the redistributive capacity of government; that is, with the ability of government to design an ever-expanding array of social programs to serve the varied and changing needs of Canadian society. Citizens were clamouring for new and improved services, and the dramatic post-war expansion of the **social welfare state** had conditioned them to expect no less. Within government, "spender" departments were on the rise, and it seemed, for a while at least, that no good program or policy could be refused simply because there was insufficient money.

Each successive reorganization of the bureaucracy resulted in an increased number of ministries, Crown corporations and regulatory bodies. The policy responses of the era were based on Keynesian macro-economic management, as we noted earlier in the book. This meant, in part, that there was a built-in expectation that governments would run deficits during at least part of the business cycle to help stimulate the economy during downturns. Deficits were thus seen not as evil incarnate, but rather as a policy tool that could be manipulated to help manage the overall economy. Nonetheless, as one observer suggests, "By the early 1980s, politicians realized that less and less was big government held in high esteem. The need to control government spending and the deficit came to dominate the political agenda, perhaps as much as the need to expand economic and social programs had done in the 1960s."[3] As a result, the focus and tone of the debate in Canada was altogether different from the one that has emerged recently.

The 1960s and 1970s generated a whole different set of questions than did the era of deficit obsession. And they prompt a whole different set of responses. Consider, for example, the set of values with which each era is predominantly concerned. The deficit era is foremost concerned with the three Es of efficiency, effectiveness and economy. The earlier era was more interested in democracy and social justice. As a result, the questions that were asked and answered in each era, in terms of the requisites of public administration, were significantly different. The deficit era saw a concerted effort to make government more businesslike in its internal operations, and to drastically cut back the role of the state in society. The earlier era implicitly and explicitly acknowledged that government was

different from business, and that it was thus folly to run it along the same organizational lines. Moreover, it was a period of higher levels of state intervention—
a phenomenon that was understood as beneficial, and indeed necessary, to the
construction of a just society.

But we are now apparently turning another corner, as the above quote from
Paul Martin attests. In the 2001 budget, Martin proclaimed that "the federal government recorded a budgetary surplus of $17.1 billion in 2000–01. This is the
largest annual surplus since Confederation and the fourth consecutive annual
surplus, following surpluses of $3.5 billion in 1997–98, $2.9 billion in 1998–99
and $12.3 billion in 1999–2000."[4] Concerns about getting the deficit under con-
trol are abating. There is a consensus emerging that government is getting its fiscal house in order, and, as a result, new public policy options are opening up
before us. So what questions are vitally important today for practitioners and
students of public administration? The questions for the new millennium are increasingly focusing on what it means to have a solvent government with a balanced
budget. According to professor of social policy Michael Prince, then, the following line of questions seems to be emerging:

*What do balanced budgets symbolize in political and policy terms at the end of the 1990s?
Are the years of social policy cuts really over? Is salvation-by-surplus at hand, or is it a
myth, as many have argued, as death-by-deficit was in recent times? How large could the
fiscal dividend become and how long might federal surpluses last? Does it make sense
yet to talk of a post-deficit era? What should be done with a fiscal dividend? Who should
get what? When? How? Will federal budget surpluses lead to shifts in power relations
among different groups? Will we see a substantially more activist and assertive Ottawa
in the second mandate of the Chrétien Liberals? Will "social" Liberals successfully assert
themselves against "business" Liberals?[5]*

To this list of questions could be added: How have the events of September 11,
2001, and the emergence of a new security agenda impacted upon the era of the
fiscal dividend? The answers will not—and indeed cannot—be provided here.
Rather, they are raised to provide a framework for our concluding thoughts on
the theory and practice of public administration, in the hope that it will enrich
our understanding to have something concrete to contemplate along with the
more philosophical approach of this concluding chapter.

We are going to focus, then, on the notion that understanding contemporary
public administration requires a recognition of the struggles that play themselves
out through the state and society. As we move forward, the central issue of money
has emerged in a forceful way, and this provides us with a convenient hook on
which to hang our thoughts. Let us imagine for just a moment that we could reduce the complexities of public administration to a single variable or cause. We cannot really do this, of course, because doing so results in an overly deterministic
approach—essentially reducing complex phenomena to a single cause or reason.
Unfortunately, the world is rarely so neat and tidy. But let us put this concern
aside for just a moment and assume that for argument's sake, we can understand
public administration best by looking at the financial imperatives that underlie

it. Doing so leads us to focus on the kinds of questions cited above, and raises some interesting possibilities in terms of trying to project what future public administration might look like. In so doing, let us sketch the implications and meaning of a **post-deficit** public administration in Canada.

In the first place, we need to understand the politics of deficits.[6] The term **deficit** simply refers to the amount by which government spending exceeds revenues in one year, while the **debt** is the accumulation of deficits over the years. The basic problem confronting Canadian government since about 1970 is that it has spent more than it has taken in (see Figure 13.1). The cumulative impact of running

FIGURE 13.1   Fourth Consecutive Budgetary Surplus

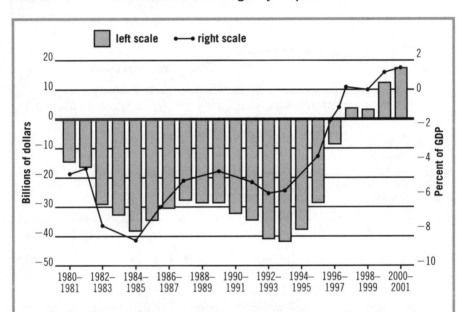

- There was a record surplus of $17.1 billion in 2000–01. The federal government has now achieved four consecutive annual *surpluses*, including *surpluses* of $3.5 billion in 1997–98, $2.9 billion in 1998–99 and $12.3 billion in 1999–2000.

- As a percentage of *GDP*, the budgetary balance improved from a deficit of 5.8 percent in 1993–94 to a surplus of 1.6 percent in 2000–01, the largest surplus, as a percentage of the *GDP*, since 1948–49.

- The four annual surpluses—totalling $35.8 billion since 1997–98—have been applied to reducing the net public debt.

- This achievement reverses a trend of more than a quarter of a century of uninterrupted government *deficits*. Four consecutive surpluses have not been recorded since 1951–52.

- In a span of seven years the *federal budget* balance has improved by $59.1 billion, from a $42-billion *deficit* in 1993–94 to a $17.1-billion surplus in 2000–01.

Source: Canada, Department of Finance, *The Budget Plan 2001*, (Ottawa: Department of Finance, 2001): 2.
http://www.fin.gc.ca/budget01/bp/bpch3e.htm

**FIGURE 13.2   Federal Revenue, Expenditures and the Deficit
1990–91 to 1999–2000**

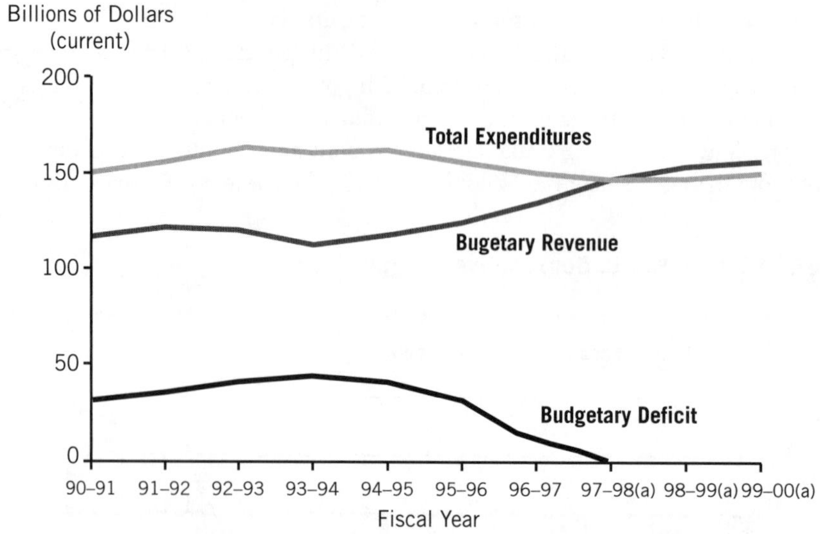

(a) Figures for these years are estimates. Total expenditures include program spending and public interest charges on the debt.

Sources: Department of Finance, *Fiscal Reference Tables*, October 1997, Table 1 and 2; Department of Finance, *The Budget Plan 1998*, February 24, 1998, Table 3.1; *Public Accounts of Canada*, Statement of Revenues and Expenditures, various years.

a deficit in each year means that as of 1997–1998, Canadian federal government debt stood at about $700 billion. Put another way, the debt was equal to about 70 percent of Canada's Gross Domestic Product (GDP), which is the total value of all goods and services produced in the country. The debt became so large that the interest payments on it were a major drain on the government's spending. About 35 cents of every dollar spent by the government in 1996–1997 went to service the debt. (See Figure 13.2.) The situation is further complicated, though, by the fact that about 45 percent of the country's debt is held outside Canada. This means that we are susceptible to the perceptions that foreign bond-holders have of the stability of our country, economically and otherwise. If they decide Canada is a risky investment, they can simply withdraw their money, which forces interest rates up and negatively affects the dollar. This raises questions about the sovereignty of the Canadian nation-state in an increasingly globalized economy. At the very least, it suggests there is some virtue in reducing the debt now that the deficit has been dealt with, an issue we will return to later.

But focusing on the deficit and the debt means making political choices that tend to favour some groups and individuals in Canadian society over others. The argument has been forcefully made that Canada has been living beyond its means and must therefore cut back. But who do the cutbacks favour, and who do they hurt? Clearly the deficit-mania of the recent past has been driven by the concerns of the business community, which sees government spending on social programs as a luxury that it is no longer willing to help fund through its taxes. This view has been distilled and refined through the ideology of neoconservatism, a perspective shared by much of the business community in Canada, the economics profession, and several corporate-funded think tanks, such as the C.D. Howe Institute and the Fraser Institute.[7] The right-wing governments of Ralph Klein in Alberta, Mike Harris in Ontario, Gordon Campbell in British Columbia, and Brian Mulroney and Jean Chrétien in Ottawa exemplify this approach. Opponents to this approach argue that the deficit fight has been waged on the backs of the poor and the dispossessed. Not only are these groups most adversely affected by the cuts to social programs, but they are least able to organize themselves to fight back against the forces favouring those cutbacks. They rely most on a strong state to protect their interests. But according to this view, in many ways the "fight against the deficit" is code name for the fight to roll back the state.

From about 1975 to the early 1990s, Canadian federal governments have paid lip service to deficit reduction. The issue has generally been couched in terms of out-of-control expenditures, particularly in the area of social policy. This is a caricature of the situation, of course, since the reality is that it was not simply or mainly increased social spending that caused the deficit to rise so high. The reality is far more complex. Rather, it was a combination of decreasing revenues generated by lower corporate tax rates, combined with high interest-rate policies by the federal government that increased borrowing costs and thus spending on the debt. Thus, declining revenues rather than increased social spending has actually been the culprit.

Whatever the cause, the issue of the deficit took on a life of its own. It came to be blamed for everything from a bloated state, to market failure, to the inability of Canada to remain competitive on the global stage, to runaway inflation, to high interest rates. It has been strongly argued in some quarters that we were mortgaging the well-being of future generations of Canadians by saddling them with unmanageable debt. An assistant deputy minister of Finance imperiously announced to a class of undergraduates shortly after the 1984 election that the vote did not matter, because whoever won would not be able to pursue any set of policies that did not have deficit reduction as its guiding light. Perhaps the low point of the entire debate came in New Zealand, where it was actually suggested that a baby hippopotamus at a zoo would have to be shot because the government was in such perilous financial straits that it could no longer afford to feed it![8] Hindsight shows what the wise knew at the time: these claims were often wildly exaggerated. Nonetheless, they played an important role in raising public consciousness about the deficit, and prompting it to put pressure on politicians to do something about this modern-day plague on the body politic.

In any event, an "ideology" of deficit reduction gripped the major political parties, the bureaucracy, the business community, and significant segments of the public. In the ensuing years, a series of policy recommendations resulted, many of which

FIGURE 13.3   Have a Nice Day

Source: Reprinted by permission, Gable, *The Globe and Mail.*

have been explored in earlier chapters. They included government restructuring, program cutbacks, downsizing the public service, privatization and deregulation. Meanwhile, new policy initiatives were shelved, while old ones were expected to make do with less. The national government promised a new national child-care program, but never delivered. It withdrew from several fields, including social housing. It severely cut transfer payments to the provinces. Payments for health, post-secondary education and welfare were lumped into one block fund called the Canada Health and Social Transfer (CHST).[9] This gave the provinces more flexibility in designing programs in these areas, but the catch was that they had some $4.5 billion less with which to be flexible! In effect, then, the federal government passed its deficit problems down the line to the provinces. In turn, many provinces have passed them on to their municipal governments. The phenomenon of deficit *offloading* was born, and became a key feature of public administration in the 1990s. Federal-provincial tensions rose as a result, further poisoning an already strained relationship. Increasingly, governments began to take drastic measures in an arbitrary manner without consulting citizens or stake-holders (notwithstanding the claims of the New Public Management to better serve clients). A powerful new form of deficit politics came to dominate, reshaping public administration in countless ways.

Perhaps the symbolic apotheosis of deficit obsession was the Ontario government's "Common Sense Revolution," in which the Conservative Party under

Mike Harris adopted the position of shrinking the state and reducing taxes.[10] But much of the poularity of this approach was lost with the Walkerton water tragedy of 2000 (see Box 13-1). Seven people died in this small Ontario town, and another 2300 became ill after drinking water contaminated with E. coli bacteria. This disaster came on the heels of the provincial government's decision in 1996 to privatize water treatment and testing, coupled with draconian budget and personnel cuts to the Ministry of the Environment which crippled its monitoring and inspection functions. Many of those functions were downloaded to municipal officials in the Walkerton Public Utilities Commission (PUC), who lacked the training and expertise to perform them. It was furthermore revealed that those same PUC officials had been following incorrect procedures, but due to the cutbacks at the Ministry of the Environment, they had not been properly monitored.

The driving force behind these policy decisions, the obsession of premier Mike Harris with reducing the deficit, apparently at any cost, was forcefully repudiated by the events in Walkerton. Notably, Harris's successor, Ernie Eves, quickly abandoned the hard line taken by Harris, and began his new administration with a budget that postponed tax cuts and increased government spending. Eves also cancelled the planned privatization of Hydro One (the transmission arm

FIGURE 13.4   Remain Calm—Your Water is Safe

Source: Patrick Corrigan, *Toronto Star.*

Box 13-1

The Walkerton Water Tragedy

The most serious case of water contamination in Canadian history could have been prevented by proper chlorination of drinking water, a judicial inquiry reported about Walkerton, Ontario's fatal E. coli outbreak.

Justice Dennis O'Connor's report also points to the region's public utilities managers and Ontario government cutbacks as contributors to the tragedy.

Seven people died and 2300 became ill after Walkerton's water supply became contaminated with manure spread on a farm near the town, the report concludes.

The report, released in two parts over the winter and spring of 2002, contains hundreds of findings and recommendations.

From part one of the report issued January, 2002:

➤ Up to 400 illnesses could have been prevented if water manager Stan Koebel had monitored the chlorine levels daily and had notified authorities right away that the water was contaminated.

➤ The Ontario government failed to make reporting of positive tests for contamination mandatory when water testing was privatized in 1996.

➤ Government cuts at the province's Environment Ministry made it less capable of identifying and dealing with problems at Walkerton's water utility.

➤ The local health unit was quick to respond to the crisis with a boil-water advisory, but it should have been more widespread. Many Walkerton residents were not aware of the warning.

This is how Justice Dennis O'Connor summarizes the inquiry's findings:

➤ Seven people died, and more than 2300 became ill. Some people, particularly children, may endure lasting effects.

➤ The contaminants, largely E. coli O157:H7 and Campylobacter jejuni, entered the Walkerton system through Well 5 on or shortly after May 12, 2000.

➤ The primary, if not the only, source of the contamination was manure that had been spread on a farm near Well 5. The owner of this farm followed proper practices and should not be faulted.

➤ The outbreak would have been prevented by the use of continuous chlorine residual and turbidity monitors at Well 5.

➤ The failure to use continuous monitors at Well 5 resulted from shortcomings in the approvals and inspections programs of the Ministry of the Environment (MOE). The Walkerton Public Utilities Commission (PUC) operators lacked the training and expertise necessary to identify either the vulnerability of Well 5 to surface contamination or the resulting need for continuous chlorine residual and turbidity monitors.

➤ The scope of the outbreak would very likely have been substantially reduced if the Walkerton PUC operators had measured chlorine residuals at Well 5 daily, as they should have, during the critical period when contamination was entering the system.

➤ For years, the PUC operators engaged in a host of improper operating practices, including failing to use adequate doses of chlorine, failing to monitor chlorine residuals daily, making false entries about residuals in daily operating records, and misstating the locations at which microbiological samples were taken. The operators knew that these practices were unacceptable and contrary to MOE guidelines and directives.

➤ The MOE's inspections program should have detected the Walkerton PUC's improper treatment and monitoring practices and ensured that those practices were corrected.

➤ The PUC commissioners were not aware of the improper treatment and monitoring practices of the PUC operators. However, those who were commissioners in 1998 failed to properly respond to an MOE inspection report that set out significant concerns about water quality and that identified several operating deficiencies at the PUC.

➤ On Friday, May 19, 2000, and on the days following, the PUC's general manager concealed from the Bruce-Grey-Owen Sound Health Unit and others the adverse test results from water samples taken on May 15 and the fact that Well 7 had operated without a chlorinator during that week and earlier that month. Had he disclosed either of these facts, the health unit would have issued a boil water advisory on May 19, and 300 to 400 illnesses would have been avoided.

➤ In responding to the outbreak, the health unit acted diligently and should not be faulted for failing to issue the boil water advisory before Sunday, May 21. However, some residents of Walkerton did not become aware of the boil water advisory on May 21. The advisory should have been more broadly disseminated.

➤ The provincial government's budget reductions led to the discontinuation of government laboratory testing services for municipalities in 1996. In implementing this decision, the government should have enacted a regulation mandating that testing laboratories immediately and directly notify both the MOE and the Medical Officer of Health of adverse results. Had the government done this, the boil water advisory would have been issued by May 19 at the latest, thereby preventing hundreds of illnesses.

➤ The provincial government's budget reductions made it less likely that the MOE would have identified both the need for continuous monitors at Well 5 and the improper operating practices of the Walkerton PUC.

of the public power utility). Whether this new direction is sustained remains to be seen, but does signal a realization at some level that the pendulum had perhaps swung too far in the direction of denigrating government and the public service.

It now appears that the era of deficit obsession is drawing to a close (although it should be noted that a few provincial governments have not yet balanced their books, and British Columbia in particular has recently enacted a series of neo-conservative policies). (See Table 13.1.) But overall, a new politics seems to be arising in which the focus is on debt reduction and the fiscal dividend generated by balanced budgets and surpluses. The events of September 11, 2001, however, sharply refocused the attention of governments and society on the emergent "security agenda," which we will consider below along with the implications of a *post-deficit* public administration.

Toward a Post-Deficit Future and the New Security Agenda

If the government were suddenly flush with financial resources, what would you *expect* it to do? What would you *want* it to do? Should the government return to the days (characterized somewhat inaccurately) of high spending, borrowing and taxing? Should it maintain the current draconian practices of fiscal restraint? Or should it find some middle ground?

Generally, the choices confronting government today fall into three broad categories. The first is that government might cut taxes. The second is that it could create new social programs or reinvest in existing ones. The third is that it could pay down the national debt. Clearly, each choice carries certain opportunities and certain risks; each is surrounded by a set of administrative and political questions and controversies. Debate as to what is to be done has already emerged within the government, within the governing party and the opposition parties, between Ottawa and the provinces, and among interest groups, the media and citizens.

For its part, the federal government announced in 1997 that it planned to exercise what it called "fiscal prudence" in allocating the fiscal dividend expected from the reduction of the deficit. It argued that it would allocate half the fiscal surplus to a combination of reducing taxes and reducing the national debt, while the other half would go toward social and economic needs through program expenditures. But this 50-50 formula is itself the subject of considerable controversy, since it does not address the allocation of the surplus in any detail.

Again, looking at these proposals from the viewpoint of who wins and who loses is instructive. The degree of controversy around the reduction of the deficit can be seen by examining the perspectives of different political actors. According to Prince,

For the Liberal government, for instance, a budget surplus stands for its prudent fiscal management; the powerful role of Finance Minister Paul Martin and the Finance Department in Ottawa; and the triumph in the first mandate of fiscal Liberals, but a

TABLE 13.1   Federal Government Deficits, Debt and Financial Requirements

Fiscal Year	Forecast Deficit ($billion)	Actual Deficit ($billion)	Deficit/ GDP Ratio (%)	Net Public Debt/ GDP Ratio (%)	Financial Require- ments ($billion)	Financial Require- ments/ GDP Ratio (%)
1984–85	29.6	38.4	8.6	46.8	29.8	6.7
1985–86	33.8	34.6	7.2	50.8	30.5	6.4
1986–87	29.5	30.7	6.1	54.1	22.9	4.5
1987–88	29.3	27.8	5.0	54.6	18.8	3.4
1988–89	28.9	28.8	4.7	54.4	22.4	3.7
1989–90	30.5	28.9	4.4	55.1	20.5	3.2
1990–91	28.5	32.0	4.8	58.4	24.5	3.7
1991–92	30.5	34.4	5.1	62.9	31.8	4.7
1992–93	27.5	41.0	5.9	67.6	34.5	5.0
1993–94	32.6	42.0	5.8	70.2	29.8	4.1
1994–95	39.7	37.5	4.9	71.6	25.8	3.4
1995–96	32.7	28.6	3.6	71.9	17.2	2.2
1996–97	24.3	8.9	1.1	71.1	-1.3	-0.2
1997–98	17.0	0.0	0.0	68.1	-12.0	-1.4
1998–99	0.0	n/a	0.0	65.4	-6.0	-0.7
1999–2000	0.0	n/a	0.0	62.9	-9.0	-1.0

Notes:
(a) Figures for fiscal years after 1996–97 are based on forecasts.
(b) The "Forecast Deficit" is the forecast made near the beginning of the fiscal year in the Budget Speech.
(c) The "Actual Deficit" for 1997–98 is the estimate presented in the February 1998 Budget. It is not final.
(d) Ratios for deficit, net public debt, and financial requirements to GDP are derived from the "Actual Deficit" up to 1997–98, and the "Forecast Deficit" subsequently.
(e) Financial requirements exclude foreign exchange requirements.

Sources: Michael Prince, "New Mandate, New Money, New Politics: Federal Budgeting in the Post-Deficit Era," in Leslie A. Pal, ed. *How Ottawa Spends 1998–1999: Balancing Act: The Post-Deficit Mandate.* Don Mills: Oxford University Press, 1998: 35; Canada, Department of Finance, Fiscal Reference Tables (Ottawa, October 1997); Paul Martin, Minister of Finance, Budget Plan (Ottawa: Public Works and Government Services Canada, 1998).

chance in the second mandate to be social policy leaders again. For Progressive Conservatives, a surplus will reflect in part the foundational work of finance ministers Michael Wilson and Don Mazankowski in the Mulroney governments, when the public was not as receptive to deficit reduction. For Conservative and [Canadian Alliance] Party members alike, the disappearing deficit symbolizes overtaxation of Canadians, while for New Democrats it symbolizes less compassionate politics and cuts to health care, social programs, and other essential public services. For provincialists and Quebec sovereignists, a balanced budget in Ottawa has been achieved by dumping costs and responsibilities onto the provinces and territories. For federalists, a fiscal dividend signifies the restoration of the Canadian government, so that it is once again able to promote the national interest and present a more positive image of federalism, particularly within Quebec, and more generally across the country.[11]

Thus, the old adage "Where you stand depends on where you sit" seems to apply here. The issue is not one of simply having more money to spend, and then spending it. Rather, in the world of public administration there are countless interests whose points of view need to be accounted for before action can be taken. The fiscal dividend is not simply a numerical indicator of the fiscal health of the nation; it is a loaded political symbol, the disposal of which says much about whose interests are served by government. It is a fundamental indicator, for public administration students and practitioners, of where power resides and how it is exercised. Expectations have been raised already among the public that we will turn away from belt-tightening and move toward looser purse strings. As a result, we can expect the tenor and focus of political debate in Canada to undergo a metamorphosis in the coming years, as various actors and interests position themselves to take advantage of the new fiscal realities.

Fundamentally, the debate over the fiscal dividend, like the debate over the deficit, and the debates over political-economic management of the country in general, revolve around the issue of the appropriate size and role of the government in our lives. This is a theme raised in several places in this book already, but it bears reiteration. In the recent past, it would have been foolhardy to expect proposals for new social programs to be taken seriously, given the overwhelming prerogative of shrinking the state to get the deficit under control, and the climate under which this view developed. Now, however, the queue is already forming outside the door of the minister of Finance, as social policy initiatives, such as pharmacare, home care, student financial assistance, enhanced child tax benefits and other issues and demands, are resurfacing on the political agenda. The provinces have already stated their preferences for a "new social union," based partly on Ottawa's diminished presence in providing and designing social programs, coupled with its expanded financial support of the same.[12] Corporate Canada is beating the drum of tax cuts and debt reduction. Social movements are arguing for a strengthened social safety net.

Moreover, the arsenal of policy instruments is once again expanding rather than contracting. That is to say, the government is now able to select from a broader array of tools to enact its policies, given the rosier financial picture that is emerging. Prime Minister Chrétien, for instance, has been quoted as suggesting that the days of program cuts are over. A veritable flurry of federal initiatives has been launched, indicating a new assertiveness and willingness to reclaim the dominant position enjoyed by the federal government in the past *vis-à-vis* the provinces.

One line of argument suggests that this is long overdue. "The rush to devolve, disentangle and dismantle social programs in the name of 'less government is good government' has not been good for Canadians," according to this view. "A strong federal presence is required to reinforce Ottawa's crucial redistributive role and ensure strategic investment in high-priority areas such as employment, child poverty, health care and targeted tax relief."[13]

It seems unlikely that a return to Keynesian principles is in the cards. The idea of running government deficits during economic downturns to boost growth does not have much credence in governing circles, the business community, or the broader public. In any event, steps have been taken recently that appear to allow the federal government to have a "kitty" to draw on, should a rainy day occur. These include a massive surplus in the Employment Insurance account (resulting from drastically cutting benefits to unemployed workers and tightening up eligibility by increasing the amount of time one must work before qualifying), and a Contingency Reserve Fund. Moreover, the federal government has limited its commitments to transfer payments to the provinces. Thus, the next time there is a serious economic downturn and social assistance caseloads rise in the provinces, federal transfer payments will not rise in a corresponding manner.

More generally, the battle against the deficit has seen the state withdraw from many of the functions that it assumed in the post-war years. Will the emergence of the fiscal dividend mean a return of the state to those traditional roles? As we have seen, many of its functions have been passed on to the private sector. The emphasis of recent organizational theory on running government more like a business—the use of business plans and performance reports, for instance, coupled with the wholesale takeover of certain government functions by the private sector, the introduction of user fees and cost-recovery systems, Special Operating Agencies, and a resurgence of the voluntary and nonprofit sector—means that a return to the *status quo ante* seems a remote possibility. A number of obstacles would need to be overcome, reforms would have to be turned back, and a new/old set of ideas would have to resurface. However, it should be noted that maintenance of the current situation also seems unlikely.

The philosophy of public finance that is emerging is one in which the prevailing priority is to keep the fiscal house in order, and live within our means. The Expenditure Management System (EMS) introduced in 1995 is biased toward the saver departments over the spender departments. Unlike previous budgetary systems, it does not provide ministers with fat little envelopes full of money for new program spending. Instead, it emphasizes making do with what is already there, and cutting existing expenditures to make room for new growth. The miserly approach fostered by EMS encouraged ministers to keep their own fiscal bailiwicks in order, as well as to negotiate collectively about the priorities of government overall. Now, however, with the prospect of new money, will the pent-up frustration of ministers with good ideas for new programs burst forth?

Meanwhile, public opinion has gradually been shifting. It has moved from a position of abiding concern about the deficit to one of heightened expectation mixed with caution about policies that will permit the deficit to rear its ugly head again. The general impression is that "the federal government cut too far, too fast" through initiatives such as Program Review. But the public is leery about the possibility of returning to the high-spending ways of the past, too. The results of several public opinion surveys suggest that

among the electorate there is widespread belief that new major programs would be ineffective and wasteful—a belief that reflects reduced confidence in government and less deference toward political elites. The public is interested in accountability, efficiency and effectiveness in public services. Government deficits are to be avoided, and much of federal spending should continue to be strictly controlled.... Canadians favour debt reduction foremost, followed by tax relief, and then new spending on programs.[14]

Strikingly, these sentiments generally seem to reflect the preferences of the saver departments in government over the spenders. As usual, the political struggle within Cabinet as it emerges will be one in which some note of public opinion will have to be taken, lest the government is seen as too out of step. Still, the view that the government can and should act as an agent of social change is also reemerging and being given some credence—particularly among new **social movements**—after years of being discredited.

A lot can be learned about a society by examining the way in which its resources are allocated or shared, whether by markets or by governments.[15] As we have seen, there are two mechanisms that are responsible for making decisions about the allocation of resources—or who gets what, when and how. These are the **state** and the **market**. The former belongs to the political realm; the latter, to the economic realm. But both are core concepts to the study and practice of public administration. The way in which a society is organized will, to a large extent, relate to the role and importance it gives to the state and the market in allocating goods and services. Some societies rely heavily on the state to perform this function; others do just the opposite, and leave it up to the market as much as possible. In many ways, the recent debate in Canadian society about the deficit can be characterized as a fight about the primacy of markets over the state.

Why is it important to know whether a society relies on the state or the market to organize the distribution of resources and goods? Simply because different people benefit in different ways from the mix of state and market forces in a society. There are biases in the structure and activity of both the state and the market. Both function systematically to the benefit of certain groups within society; they are not neutral. For example, normally, the unfettered functioning of the market tends to benefit owners of firms more than it does workers, and so it is not unusual to hear business owners clamouring for less state intervention in their economic affairs. But less state intervention means that workers are susceptible to greater control and exploitation, and so they naturally look to the state for greater protection. Seen from another perspective, the level of state intervention helps determine the distribution of wealth within a society. Simply put, as we have noted, a dollar that goes to the state in taxes from a corporation cannot also go toward profit. Thus, a struggle ensues to determine whether that dollar will stay in private hands or be given over to the state for public purposes. This, in turn, generates political conflict.

Where does this conflict come from? It arises from disagreements over the allocation and distribution of scarce resources in society. In any given society, there is never enough of anything to go around, and so conflict arises over who gets what, when and how. In addition, markets invariably lead to an unequal distribution of these resources and goods, and of wealth; this, in turn, manifests itself in unequal relations between individuals within society. It is this inequality that forms the basis for the political conflict that public administration addresses.

You will recall from Chapter 4 that authority is the fundamental concept underlying our understanding of what the state is and what it can do. The state is the only institution in society that is vested with the legitimate authority to compel individuals to act in a particular manner, and to back up that compulsion by resorting, if necessary, to the use of force. In other words, the state enjoys a monopoly on the legitimate use of force, and is the only institution in society that can command obedience from its citizens. Thus, the state can determine how goods and resources in society are distributed and allocated by choosing what gets produced, how much of it gets produced, to whom it is sold, how land labour and capital is disposed of, and so on. These are great and far-reaching powers. Indeed, the state is the most powerful societal institution in existence.

But there are important constraints on this apparently impressive power, the most significant of which is societal resistance contesting the legitimacy of the state's authority to act. In particular, when a state begins to act in such a way that societal benefits are conferred on one group and costs on another, the aggrieved group may well organize resistance to the actions of the state, and may undermine the legitimacy of the state. It is arguable that this is what happened over the past 10 or 20 years around the issue of the deficit. As state spending increased over this period, and its sources of revenue declined, it borrowed money. But to do so meant incurring a deficit. The business community in Canada looked at one side of the ledger, saw increased taxes to support increased social programs, and decided to launch an all-out assault on government. As a result of a well-organized and executed campaign, it convinced not only governments, but much of the citizenry, that the deficit was public enemy number one. And so the state aimed its considerable power at eliminating the deficit, even to the point of increasing the misery and poverty of thousands of ordinary Canadians. Thus, we must keep in mind the powers of the state, which are formidable, but also the potential and real constraints on that power, particularly in a market-based society.

The market does not enjoy the luxury of having any authority over society in the way that the state does. Rather, it relies on the mechanism of exchange to carry out the production and allocation of societal resources. A market is simply an arena where people carry out the exchange of land, labour, capital goods and services. The market cannot rely on coercion or force to back up its desires, as the state does. Rather, exchange is voluntary, and can take various forms (through barter, through the medium of money, for labour, etc.). The rules of supply and demand form the basis of market exchange. In this configuration, production is determined by the individual producers, responding to the demands of individual consumers, who make their decisions as to what they want or need according to a rational calculation based on the recognition that the purchase of one good or service leaves less money for the purchase of something else. Meanwhile, producers produce goods and services in a quantity and quality such that they will secure the highest profit possible.

However, this relatively simple scenario, although it has conveyed benefits in terms of the progress of civilization and society, is not without problems. For instance, although it is based on a notion of voluntary exchange, there are obvious circumstances in which individuals are compelled to enter into the exchange process. One example is the starving worker who must exchange her skills and labour for subsistence wages; another is the person who possesses a valuable instrument of exchange, namely property, which gives him an advantage over those who do not. Thus, the initial distribution of property (including cash) is crucial to market activities, and is usually accompanied by conflict. There is, therefore, a built-in inequality that severely strains the extent to which we can say the exchange process is purely voluntary. Some view the state as a key agent in mitigating this inequality.

It is largely the interaction of states and markets that shapes public administration, and, in fact, both are intimately and inextricably intertwined and mutually dependent. States and markets need one another. Each can perform functions that are necessary to the operation and survival of the modern society, but which the other cannot perform. The state needs the market because of the market's efficiency in responding to consumer demand and coordinating production. Markets need the state because they need a body that can legitimately, and with all the authority of society, enforce property rights and private contracts. Ultimately, it is the task of students and practitioners of public administration to try to figure out this complex interrelationship between the state and markets.

The development of democracy in the modern age has had important ramifications for the state, markets and capitalism, as we also noted in Chapter 4. The gradual expansion of the franchise and democratic entitlements and rights over the years has meant that those who were denied the privilege of ownership of property or wealth in the capitalist system could use their numerical superiority over the capitalists to pressure governments to use state authority to mitigate the worst excesses of the capitalist system. Democracy, by requiring governments to be elected, permits some degree of control over the state by those not privileged as members of the elite. This, in turn, permits some control over the functioning of the market, because ordinary citizens, when mobilized, can persuade and entice the state to use its legitimate authority to regulate and control the market.

Somewhere in the complex interplay of states, markets, democracy and capitalism, we hope to find the answers to the key questions of public administration. By briefly examining its intellectual roots, as we did in chapters 1 and 2, we can see where the interplay of these ideas is realized through the organizations that have developed in recent times, both in the public and private realm, each influencing the other in myriad ways.

The debates about the post-deficit world of Canadian administration are by no means simply academic ones. They are germane to the lives of all Canadians. The outcome is going to have a direct impact on the future of the lives we all live. But what will that future look like? Conflicting visions of Canadian society abound.

Consider that the United Nations Human Development Index rated Canada first in the world in terms of purchasing power, life expectancy, literacy and educational attainment four times in seven years. (And notice that many of these criteria are dependent upon a well-developed state.)[16] Yet simultaneously, food banks are commonplace, the streets of urban centres are filled with the homeless, one in four Canadian children lives in poverty, and much of the Aboriginal community is subsisting at Third World levels. Moreover, recent studies indicate that the gap between the rich and poor is growing, and that women still earn less on average than men for work of equal value. Any sociological profile of Canadian society is bound to produce these apparently contradictory images.

Consider as well the state of the Canadian economy. It seems to oscillate between crises, recession, high unemployment, instability, on the one hand, and growth, wealth production, low inflation and high productivity, on the other hand. Why is this the case? And what can be done to alleviate the problems currently faced by this country? Where do we look for solutions to the current economic crises? Some suggest that we must allow the market to be left alone to determine what goods and services are produced, in what quantities, and at what prices, and that only by doing so can we overcome the current difficulties. Others argue that only governments can solve the current problems, by taking a greater role in the economic life of the country through regulating and monitoring the market, or perhaps even replacing it through public agencies and Crown corporations.

For public administration, the issue is how to reconcile these images through a constructive set of policies that seeks to mitigate the worst effects of markets, while promoting the best use of the state. That today this means a revised role for the state seems clear. But in what direction? More or less government intervention? We return to the question posed at the outset. If the rationale for reducing the role of government is taken away—that is, if the deficit/debt issue is dealt with—is it logical to continue down that path?

A caveat is in order here. Answering these questions by looking exclusively at current trends in public administration can be misleading, since, as religious leader and author William Ralph Inge once said in another context, "He who marries the spirit of his age will be a widower in the next." In other words, we need to place the most recent trends in public administration management in historical context, which is what we have tried to do in this book. This, it is hoped, leads to an awareness that the preferred school of thought in today's public administration may not occupy such a privileged position tomorrow. One observer puts it this way:

Veteran observers of management fashion will note how quickly these fashions enter and depart the world of management discourse. Like the fashion industry, new products have to be trotted out. Politicians looking for something to sell, in order to say they are doing their all to run a tight ship and save the taxpayers money, watch the runway for newly fashioned models—Program Planning Budgeting System (PPBS), Zero-Based Budgeting (ZBB), Management by Objective (MBO), and Total Quality Management (TQM)—to name a few.[17]

Add to this list the NPM, which emphasizes markets and clients and erases the lines between public and private sector management. Accountability, in this latest swing of the management pendulum, is given short shrift.[18] Moreover, the traditional role of the civil servant "is undergoing a shift from protector of the integrity and regularity of public transactions to that of management scientist."[19] As political scientist Bert Rockman concludes,

In sum, should the new management paradigm persist, it will reflect the retreat of tra-
ditional conceptions of the role of the state and of the civil service. Like other modern
organizations, governments may get remade to be managerially adaptive. This is apt to
mean fewer rules and more discretion, less predictability and more risk-taking. It also sug-
gests there will be fewer state-run services and more contracting out and privatization.
The state is surely not shrinking financially (though its rate of growth is), but its corpus
of rules and regulations and procedures may well shrink. While all of this is in some
measure speculative and remains to be seen, should it come to pass, it would in fact con-
stitute a revolution truly spelling the end of the dominance of the Weberian paradigm. There
is, of course, always the possibility that a new public management will displace the New
Public Management.[20]

All the various reforms of recent times—privatization, contracting out, empowerment, deregulation, new operating agencies, downsizing, delayering of management levels, a focus on clients rather than citizens—aimed at modernizing
government by making it more businesslike, have influenced the institutions of government. But it would be a mistake to assume that today's paradigms of public
administration will provide us with all tomorrow's answers.

The point is that current fashions in public administration come and go in
response to broader socioeconomic and political forces in society. The current
mania for businesslike solutions may turn out to be a passing fancy. Now that
conditions are changing again, new schools of thought will invariably arise as to how
to practise public administration. And it is this constant dynamism and change
that makes the study of public administration so engaging.

Occasionally in the life of a nation, a single event or series of events can come
to completely dominate the public agenda. War, revolution, depression, natural disaster and other similar developments can cause a nation to focus virtually exclusively on the issue at hand and marshal all of its resources to overcome it. We can
add to this list terrorist attacks. The events of September 11, 2001, so forcefully in-
truded upon the societal and state consciousness that in the blink of an eye a new
"security agenda" arrived full blown upon the ledger of Canadian (and global)
concerns. Moreover, given Canada's primary continental relationship, "the indirect effects of US policy priorities and decisions on Canada were increased to an unprecedented degree."[21] Thus the post-deficit politics era, which should have given
way to the fiscal dividend era, was transformed instead into the security era, dominated to a large extent by the responses emanating from Washington.

How long-lasting and profound this new reality will be remains to be seen. But
it does illustrate that speculating on the future of public administration can be a very
imprecise exercise. For example, the federal government commissioned a deputy
minister task force to look into the future of the public service in Canada. In its 1997
Report, the task force cited three broad future scenarios, none of which came anywhere near predicting the magnitude and impact of a September-11-type crisis.[22]
Nonetheless, for the short-to-medium term, it instantly reshaped and refocused the
attentions of those concerned with public administration. Suddenly it became
necessary to mobilize and expand the vast resources of the state to respond to the

threat of terrorism while simultaneously paying more attention than ever to the continental imperative. We will briefly consider here how this has become the case.

When Martin rose to introduce the federal government's budget on December 10, 2001, he noted two interrelated factors that set the context for the country's economic performance. To begin with, "for the first time in 25 years, we find ourselves in the midst of a global economic slowdown," a reality which, he acknowledged was "made worse by the September 11 terrorist attacks on the U.S."[23] The global economic downturn caused federal revenues to decline while some social policy expenditures rose. This, in turn, forced the government to temper its prognostications about the projected surplus.[24] Then, the unthinkable began to be thought—should the government be prepared to stimulate the economy and, if necessary, return to the practice of deficit financing to do so? Indeed, as political scientist Geoffrey Hale notes, "if Martin had not used a variety of accounting tricks in his December 2001 budget, the use of previous planning frameworks would have resulted in a projected $5.5 billion deficit for the 2002/3 fiscal year."[25]

As it turned out, of course, the American economy reignited after a period of slowdown in the wake of September 11, and the Canadian economy could not help but follow suit. Deficit financing was not necessary. Nonetheless, the 2001 budget was the "largest 'spending increase' budget" of Martin's nine years as finance minister[26]—this after a long period in which spending decreases and tax cuts primarily shaped the agenda of the federal (and many provincial) government. As it turned out, by June 2002, following a strong economic recovery, the government was projecting a surplus of between $6 billion and $7.5 billion.[27]

Still, there was the aftermath of September 11 to deal with. The reassertion of the role of the Canadian state which resulted raised interesting questions for Canadians. The package of responses from the federal government included a range of mildly to deeply interventionist policies: new anti-terrorism legislation; reforms to immigration law; the allocation of new resources for the Department of National Defense, Canadian Security Intelligence Service, and police and emergency services forces; new directives aimed at helping Health Canada prepare for anthrax and other bio-terrorism threats; enhanced airport security measures; and a plan to deal with the sorry state of the Canadian airline industry.[28] Meanwhile, external pressures mounted, particularly from our continental partner, to assert our position as ally in the fight against terrorism, by committing ground troops to the war in Afghanistan, cooperating in the development of a North American security perimeter, and participating in the further integration of North American defense.

But to realize all or any of these initiatives required the state to commit the resources to support them. To that end, the government committed itself to spending $7.6 billion on security matters (see Table 13.2), including:

➤ Intelligence and Policing, $1.6 billion

➤ Screening of Entrants to Canada, $1 billion

➤ Emergency Preparedness and Military Deployment, $1.6 billion

➤ A New Approach to Air Security, $2.2 billion (including a new federal air security authority), funded by a new Air Traveller's Security Charge

➤ Border Security and Facilitation, $1.2 billion[29]

TABLE 13.2 Security Initiatives in the 2001 Federal Budget

Expenditures (millions)

	2001–2002	2002–2003	2003–2004	2004–2005	2005–2006	2006–2007	Total
SECURITY[1]							
Intelligence and policing							
Equipping and deploying more intelligence and police officers	235	182	189	193	190	188	1,177
Improving co-ordination and information sharing	7	10	15	15	15	15	76
Enhanced marine security	5	12	13	10	10	10	60
Cutting off terrorist finances	10	15	10	10	10	10	63
Other initiatives	16	25	29	31	31	31	163
Contingency	–	10	20	20	20	25	95
Subtotal	273	253	276	279	275	278	1,634
Screening of entrants to Canada							
Better and more accurate screening	89	61	61	61	61	61	395
More resources for detentions, removals and refugee determination	30	42	42	32	32	32	210
Fraud-resistant documents	25	73	61	44	42	42	287
Contingency	–	10	20	20	30	30	110
Subtotal	143	186	184	157	165	165	1,001
Emergency preparedness and military deployment							
Supporting Canada's military	400	110	–	–	–	–	510
Expanded anti-terrorist capacity	44	15	15	15	15	15	119
Chemical, biological, radiological and nuclear threats	62	110	95	92	77	77	513

Emergency preparedness	30	71	74	74	75	75	396
Contingency	–	10	20	20	25	25	100
Subtotal	**535**	**316**	**204**	**201**	**192**	**192**	**1,638**
A NEW APPROACH TO AIR SECURITY	**115**	**462**	**573**	**367**	**366**	**306**	**2,189**
Total security initiatives	**1,067**	**1,217**	**1,236**	**1,003**	**998**	**941**	**6,462**
A SECURE, OPEN AND EFFICIENT BORDER							
Border security and facilitation							
Expediting pre-approved travellers	–	15	15	12	8	8	58
Better tools for risk assessment and detection	6	17	12	11	10	10	67
Better equipment for detecting dangerous shipments	3	52	15	14	12	12	107
Integrated Border Enforcement Teams	10	25	25	25	25	25	135
Better service to small business	–	5	5	2	2	2	14
Other initiatives	52	37	34	34	34	34	226
Contingency	–	5	5	10	10	10	40
Subtotal	**72**	**156**	**110**	**107**	**101**	**101**	**646**
Border infrastructure	–	150	150	150	100	50	600
Total border initiatives	**72**	**306**	**260**	**257**	**201**	**151**	**1,246**
Total	**1,139**	**1,523**	**1,496**	**1,260**	**1,199**	**1,092**	**7,708**
REVENUES							
Air Travellers Security Charge[2]	–	430	445	445	445	445	2,210
Other	–	50	50	30	25	25	180
Total revenues	**–**	**480**	**495**	**475**	**470**	**470**	**2,390**

Note: Totals may not add up due to rounding.
[1] This includes $1.2 billion for the Department of National Defence and its agencies.
[2] Figures include net *goods and services tax (GST)*.

But financial concerns were not the only issue on the mind of the government. The institutions of governing were targeted for quick reform as well. Thus the prime minister appointed an ad hoc Cabinet committee under the direction of the foreign minister to coordinate government-wide efforts with regard to the war on terrorism, improving domestic security requirements, and addressing concerns over the Canada–United States border. Departments, Crown corporations, agencies, boards and commissions all found themselves engaged in the formulation of new plans, strictures and policies to confront the possibility of future terrorist activity.

Interestingly, the need to respond to the new security agenda came into sharp conflict with the need to carry on with business as usual, in terms of cross-border commercial relations with the United States. As two observers note, "faced by an angry United States determined to do what was necessary to strengthen its homeland security, and an anxious Canadian business community fearful of what tighter border administration would mean for Canadian trade and prosperity, the government took steps in both legislative change and in the Budget speech of 10 December to bring its agenda into line with the new reality."[30] As political scientist Bruce Doern put it, "Any reluctance the Chrétien Liberals may have felt about the new border regime as a security package was undoubtedly overcome by their larger concerns about ensuring continued cross-border trade and smooth and speedy flow of goods and services. Long lines at the border in the autumn of 2001 led to the mobilization of Canadian business lobbies to ensure that *free* trade did not become *slow and secure* trade."[31]

Overall, the September 11 crisis mobilized the state in ways not seen in decades. Suddenly, it seemed, going public was back in again. This brings us back to a consideration raised earlier about the appropriate role for the state. The politics of the deficit dictated a diminished role for governments; the politics of the surplus presented us with a set of choices not yet fully acted on; the security agenda, however, has forced the hand of government and society. It has dictated that there are simply some things that civil society requires of the state rather than markets. Consider, for instance, the whole area of public sector management reform. While we alluded to the point earlier that the NPM, with its orientation toward business practices, was already being superceded by new approaches, it is possible that the events of September 11 have greatly accelerated its demise. Two experts on the American scene, whose observations are relevant to the Canadian experience where public sector reform is concerned, drew these conclusions:

The events of Fall 2001 have changed the context and priorities for reform. Faith in government has suddenly rebounded, and fiscal constraints have been loosened. Some of the dangers of a preoccupation with lean administration or client satisfaction have become more evident. Ambivalence about the private provision of key services has become more pronounced. The critical importance of interagency and intergovernmental collaboration has been emphasized. This is not a complete turnabout in reform priorities. Nevertheless, the new security agenda seems likely to be less hesitant about asserting a role for government, and on preferring direct public provision; more careful about balancing client satisfaction with enforcement functions; and attentive to the challenges of coordination.[32]

They point out as well that there are basic functions of the state which remain profoundly important, a realization that was driven home by September 11. These include national security and the maintenance of and domestic peace and order, for instance. Moreover, public opinion polling in the United States shows trust in government rebounding dramatically. A *Washington Post* poll in October 2001 revealed that 64 percent of Americans trusted government to do what is right most or all of the time, a figure not seen since the 1960s.[33]

In Canada, levels of trust toward government have not shown so dramatic an increase.[34] But clearly there is the post–September 11 expectation that government needs to be seen to be doing more. Interventionism is now a viable option once again. Indeed, some of the less palatable impacts of decades of cutbacks have come home to roost—for instance the Canadian Armed Forces proved woefully understaffed and ill-equipped for the jobs it is now being asked to do. Public dissatisfaction with this state of affairs is in part driving governments to rethink the trajectory they have been following for many years now.

All of this is not to say that the landscape is unalterably and irrevocably changed; nor is it to say that the outline of future trends in public administration are clear. It is important to note that certain traditional and long-standing concerns of public administration which were highlighted throughout this book remain prominent among the concerns of both practitioners and academics. Thus, the lens through which the issues are viewed has been fogged-over. But the core concerns persist. For the foreseeable future, underlying future developments in public administration will be: the nature of state-market relations; the tensions between democracy and efficiency; the relative weight of public versus private sector values; the politics-administration dichotomy; the proper organizational form for government; the relationship between public administration and law; the enhancement of public policy formulation, implementation and evaluation; the challenges of human and financial resource management; the evolution of the ethical regime in the public service; and other related matters. As students of public administration, we all can look forward to the myriad challenges and opportunities inherent in this most vital and fascinating of human endeavours.

WHAT YOU HAVE LEARNED

Finance Minister Paul Martin's dramatic announcement in February 1998, that the federal government would henceforth produce balanced budgets, altered the terrain upon which public administration had settled over the previous 10 to 15 years. The drama lay in the fact that his words threw into question the very rationale of the major restructuring of public administration that had been going on for several years. What was less clear, though, was whether the reforms would remain appropriate to the emerging era of post-deficit public administration. The question of what happens when that premise is removed is central to the set of challenges that lies ahead for students and practitioners of public administration in Canada.

This chapter has attempted to offer some speculative observations on the future of public administration, based on the broad assumption that "dollars" matter. Both opportunities and constraints are in store for government and society, and while focusing solely on the government ledger cannot explain everything, it does permit us to formulate certain plausible scenarios. Therefore, in relation to several main issues that have been explored in this book, this chapter has addressed what an era of balanced budgets might mean to the world of Canadian public administration.

ENDNOTES

1. Canada, Department of Finance, *The Budget Speech 1998,* (Ottawa: Department of Finance Canada, February 24, 1998): 4.

2. Bert A. Rockman, "The Changing Role of the State," in B. Guy Peters and Donald J. Savoie, eds. *Taking Stock: Assessing Public Sector Reforms,* (Montreal: McGill–Queen's University Press, 1998): 20.

3. Donald J. Savoie, *The Politics of Public Spending in Canada,* (Toronto: University of Toronto Press, 1990): 16.

4. Canada, Department of Finance, *Budget 2001: Canada's Fiscal Progress Through 2000–2001,* (Ottawa: Department of Finance, 2001): 5.

5. Michael J. Prince, "New Mandate, New Money, New Politics: Federal Budgeting in the Post-Deficit Era," in Leslie A. Pal, ed. *How Ottawa Spends 1998–1999: Balancing Act: The Post-Deficit Mandate,* (Don Mills: Oxford University Press, 1998): 32.

6. See, for example, David A. Wolfe, "The Politics of the Deficit," in G. Bruce Doern, ed. *The Politics of Economic Policy,* (Toronto: University of Toronto Press, 1985): 111–162.

7. See Tom Walkom, "Tory Talk: How the Conservative Captured the English Language," *This Magazine,* 18, 6 (February, 1985): 5–8.

8. See Linda McQuaig, *Shooting the Hippo: Death by Deficit and Other Canadian Myths,* (Toronto: Penguin Books, 1995).

9. See Thomas J. Courchene, *Celebrating Flexibility: An Interpretive Essay on the Evolution of Canadian Federalism,* (Toronto: C.D. Howe Institute, 1995).

10. See Michelle Weinroth, "Deficitism and Neo-Conservatism in Ontario," in Diana Ralph, Andre Regimbald and Neree St.-Amand, *Open for Business, Closed to People: Mike Harris's Ontario,* (Halifax: Fernwood Press, 1997): 54–67; Sid Noel, ed. *Revolution at Queen's Park: Essays on Governing Ontario,* (Toronto: Lorimer, 1997); John Ibbitson, *Promised Land: Inside the Mike Harris Revolution,* (Scarborough: Prentice Hall, 1997); and John Ibbitson, *Loyal No More: Ontario's Struggle for a Separate Identity,* (Toronto: HarperCollins, 2001): chapter 6.

11. Prince, "New Mandate, New Money, New Politics," (1998): 43.

12. See Provincial/Territorial Council on Social Policy Renewal, *Progress Report to Premiers,* (August 1998).

13. Ken Battle, Sherri Torjman and Michael Mendelson, "Reinvest the Fiscal Dividend," *Policy Options,* 19, 1 (January–February, 1998): 22.

14. Prince, "New Mandate, New Money, New Politics," (1998): 50.

15. The following discussion is based in part on Michael Howlett and M. Ramesh, *The Political Economy of Canada: An Introduction,* (Toronto: McClelland and Stewart, 1992): chapter 1.

16. United Nations, *Human Development Report 1996,* (New York: Oxford University Press, 1996).

17. Rockman, "The Changing Role of the State," (1998): 30.

18. See Peter Aucoin, "Administrative Reform in Public Management," *Governance,* 3 (1990): 115–137.

19. Rockman, The Changing Role of the State," (1998): 37.

20. Rockman, "The Changing Role of the State," (1998): 37.

21. Michael Hart and Brian Tomlin, "Inside the Perimeter: The US Policy Agenda and its Implications for Canada," in G. Bruce Doern, ed. *How Ottawa Spends 2002–2003: The Security Aftermath and National Priorities,* (Toronto: Oxford University Press, 2002): 59.

22. See Canada, Privy Council Office, *Deputy Ministers Task Force on the Future of the Public Service*, (Ottawa: Privy Council Office, 1997). http://www.ccmd-ccg.gc.ca/documents/dmtf/intromtf.htm. See also Canada, Office of the Auditor General, *Public Service Management Reform: Progress, Setbacks and Challenges*, (Ottawa: Office of the Auditor General, 2001).

23. Canada, Department of Finance, *Budget 2001: Enhancing Security for Canadians*, (Ottawa: Department of Finance): 1.

24. See G. Bruce Doern, "The Chretien Liberals' Third Mandate: The Security Aftermath and National Priorities," in G. Bruce Doern, ed. *How Ottawa Spends 2002–2003: The Security Aftermath and National Priorities*, (Toronto: Oxford University Press, 2002): 5.

25. Geoffrey Hale, "Innovation and Inclusion: Budgetary Policy, the Skills Agenda, and the Politics of the New Economy," in G. Bruce Doern, ed. *How Ottawa Spends 2002–2003: The Security Aftermath and National Priorities*, (Toronto: Oxford University Press, 2002): 41.

26. See Hale, "Innovation and Inclusion," (2002).

27. Heather Scoffield, "Surplus Fuels PM's Big Plans," *Globe and Mail*, (Tuesday, June 21, 2002): A1.

28. For a discussion of these measures, see Doern, "The Chrétien Liberals' Third Mandate," (2002): 8–9.

29. Canada, Department of Finance, *Budget 2001: Enhancing Security for Canadians*, (Ottawa: Department of Finance, 2001): 2–4.

30. Hart and Tomlin, "Inside the Perimeter" (2002): 61.

31. Doern, "The Chrétien Liberals' Third Mandate," (2002): 8.

32. Donald P. Moynihan and Alasdair Roberts, "Public Service Reform and the New Security Agenda," Paper presented to the Symposium on Governance and Public Security, Campbell Public Affairs Institute, Syracuse University, (January 18, 2002): 131. See also William T. Gormley Jr., "Reflections on Terrorism and Public Management," Paper presented to the Symposium on Governance and Public Security, Campbell Public Affairs Institute, Syracuse University, (January 18, 2002). Both papers available online at: http://www.maxwell.syr.edu/campbell/Goverance_Symposium/security.htm

33. Cited in Moynihan and Roberts, "Public Service Reform and the New Security Agenda," (2002): 132. http://www.maxwell.syr.edu/campbell/Goverance_Symposium/security.htm

34. See Kim Lunman, "Poll Finds Distrust of Government Higher in Canada," *Globe and Mail*, (Friday, June 21, 2002): A4.

KEY WORDS AND CONCEPTS

social welfare state (397)

post-deficit era (399)

deficit (399)

debt (399)

social movements (410)

state (410)

market (410)

REVIEW QUESTIONS

1. The Politics of Deficits

The prevailing ideas that have shaped public administration recently—namely, the issues of deficits and balanced budgets—have profoundly affected both the institutions and the practices of public administration. Several dramatic changes have resulted to public policy-making and governance generally. This chapter addressed those changes in the context of the politics of deficits by asking the following: What past attitudes prevailed about deficits and balanced budgets? What views are currently in vogue, and what explains the change? What consequences have these changes had, and why is this important to Canadian public administration?

2. Toward a Post-Deficit Future and the New Security Agenda

If current projections for deficit elimination unfold according to expectations, the future world of Canadian public administration will be quite different from the one we now know. At the very least, we know that a variety of societal struggles are even now emerging over what to do with the "fiscal and social dividend" expected to result from deficit elimination. In considering these developments in the context of the respective roles of states and markets, this section asked, What is the fiscal and social dividend? What groups in Canadian society are agitating about how it should be handled? What course of action—tax cuts, social spending, debt reduction, for example—are on the table? What policy responses is the government open to? How does the debate over the post-deficit future of Canada affect public administration? How do the events of September 11, 2001, affect public administration? What is the "security agenda"?

FURTHER READING

1. The Politics of Deficits

Peters, B. Guy and Donald J. Savoie, eds. *Governance in a Changing Environment.* Montreal: McGill–Queen's University Press, 1995.

Rockman, Bert A. " 'Honey, I Shrank the State'—On the Brave New World of Public Administration," in Ali Farazmand, ed. *Politics and Bureaucrats in Modern Systems of Governance.* Newport Beach, California: Sage, 1997: 275–294.

Savoie, Donald J. *The Politics of Public Spending in Canada.* Toronto: University of Toronto Press, 1990.

2. Toward a Post-Deficit Future and the New Security Agenda

Hoberg, George, ed. *Capacity for Choice: Canada in a New North America.* Toronto: University of Toronto Press, 2002.

Pal, Leslie A., ed. *How Ottawa Spends 1998–1999: Balancing Act: The Post-Deficit Mandate.* Ottawa: Carleton University Press, 1998.

Scarth, William. "A Long-Term Debt Reduction Strategy for Ottawa." *Policy Options,* 19, 1 (January–February, 1998): 10–12.

Trebilcock, Michael. *Prospects for Reinventing Government.* Toronto: C.D. Howe Institute, 1994.

 WEBLINK

Department of Finance, Economic and Fiscal Info
www.fin.gc.ca/access/ecfisce.html

Glossary

accountability—a fundamental principle of democratic government which states that those who hold governmental power must be answerable and responsive to the people for the way in which that power is exercised. *See also* administrative responsibility.

accountable—*see* accountability.

accumulation—a concept employed in neo-Marxist theory referring to the need for capital to generate (accumulate) profits and for government to formulate policies that foster the conditions to make profitability possible.

administrative evaluation—the examination of the efficiency of delivery of government services, in order to determine if the best value for money is being realized within the framework of democracy and justice, using technical methodologies involving the compilation and analysis of data on program costs and benefits. *See also* policy evaluation.

administrative law—that part of the law which is concerned with the legal limitations on the actions of government officials and the remedies available to anyone affected by a transgression of these limits.

administrative responsibility—the requirement that public servants be answerable and accountable in fulfilling their duties as authorized by a superior.

advisory board—an organization composed of citizens, created by the government, but outside of the normal bureaucracy, to provide independent advice to a minister.

affirmative action—*see* employment equity.

alienation—a concept used in Marxist analysis to describe the condition in which the bureaucracy and/or state is seen as a distant, impersonal and oppressive force by citizens.

amending formula—a procedure introduced in the *Constitution Act*, 1982, used to formally change the Constitution. Generally, the amending formula requires the agreement of Ottawa, and seven out of ten provinces, representing at least 50% of the population. Some constitutional amendments, however, require the unanimous agreement of all 11 governments.

audit—a process of examining government accounts to see that they are correct. *See also* comprehensive audit.

Auditor General—responsible directly to Parliament, the Auditor General is the financial "watchdog" who performs an audit each year of the Public Accounts and prepares an annual report on the financial management of the government. The results of these audits are released to the public.

authority—the basis of state rule, in which the right to rule others and to legitimately compel obedience in the behaviour of citizens is held by state officials.

autonomy—freedom of action. This term is used by Marxists in connection with the freedom of state officials to formulate policies independently of the control or influence of capital.

budget—an annual statement of the government's revenues and expenditures.

bureaucracy—a form of organization characterized by hierarchy, a division of labour and a system of hiring and promotion based on merit, and management by detailed but impersonal rules.

bureaucratic discretion—the degree of freedom of judgement and action that bureaucrats have in implementing public policies.

bureaucratic pathology—a phenomenon in which the strict adherence to rigid rules and regulations supplants the real goals of a bureaucratic organization.

bureaucratization—the organization of human behaviour into formal organizations and structures for the purposes of efficiency and control.

business planning—*see* business plans.

business plans—a private sector managerial technique increasingly adopted by the public sector as part of the New Public Management movement. These are detailed plans of the multi-year objectives of line departments and their strategies for achieving the best possible service delivery at the least possible cost.

central agency—a coordinating agency of government with the authority to intervene and direct the affairs of other government departments. Currently, there are four central agencies in the federal government: the Prime Minister's Office; the Privy Council Office; the Department of Finance; and the Treasury Board.

charismatic legitimacy—a form of legitimacy outlined by Max Weber in which citizens accept that an individual has the right to rule over them by virtue of his or her personal characteristics and strength of personality. *See also* legal-rational legitimacy and traditional legitimacy.

Charter of Rights and Freedoms—added to the Canadian Constitution in 1982, the Charter protects Canadians' fundamental freedoms, democratic rights, mobility rights, legal rights, equality rights, language rights and Aboriginal rights.

Civil Service Acts, **1908 and 1918**—reforms to the federal civil service which eliminated patronage as the basis of hiring in the public service and set in motion the movement toward a merit-based, professional public service.

Civil Service Commission—*see* Public Service Commission.

class conflict—a central premise of Marxist theory, which argues that capitalist societies are divided into mutually antagonistic classes whose fundamental interests are ultimately irreconcilable.

code of ethics—a written set of regulations setting out the boundaries of acceptable and unacceptable behaviour for public servants and promoting the highest ethical conduct and standards required of public servants. Codes of ethics generally govern such matters as conflicts of interest, moonlighting, non-partisanship, confidentiality, lying to the public and similar issues.

collective bargaining—a means of determining wages, hours and working conditions through negotiation between an employer and union.

collective ministerial responsibility—the principle that members of the Cabinet (the executive branch of government) are collectively responsible for the policies and management of the government as a whole. *See also* individual ministerial responsibility.

common law—the rules developed by the courts and based on the principle of *stare decisis* (that is, established legal precedents guide current judgements).

comprehensive audit—an audit of a program focusing on its economy, efficiency and effectiveness.

conflict of interest—a circumstance in which a politician or public servant has a personal interest in a policy or program such that his or her professional position and role is compromised.

conservatism—in Canada, traditionally an ideology which values hierarchy, order and security above individual freedom and advocates a certain level of state intervention to restrain personal freedom for the greater good of the community.

conservative—*see* conservatism.

constitution—the supreme law of the land. Constitutions delineate the relationship between the state and citizens, between the parts of the state (executive, legislative and judicial) and, in a federal system, between levels of government (national and provincial).

constitutional convention—the unwritten part of the constitution which is derived from habit, tradition and past practices. Although not legally enforceable, constitutional conventions carry important political weight.

constitutional law—that part of the constitution composed of written documents and the common law, and which is enforceable through the courts.

contracting out—the practice by government of employing the private sector to deliver services in order to save money.

Crown corporation—a corporation which the state owns wholly or in part in order to promote the national interest, but which operates at arm's length from direct government control. Crown corporations are part of the arsenal of governing instruments available to the state.

debt—the accumulation of deficits over the years.

deficit—the amount by which government expenditures exceed revenues during a specified period of time (usually one year).

department—an organizational unit of government headed by a minister.

deputy minister—the administrative head of a government department appointed by the prime minister.

deregulation—the process of removing government regulations over an industry or sector of the economy, so that it may operate according to the dictates of the free market.

direct democracy—a form of government by the people in which citizens make all important community decisions as a whole, usually in some form of public assembly. This stands in contrast to a system of representative democracy, in which citizens choose representatives to make decisions on their behalf.

disallowance—section 56 of the *Constitution Act*, 1867 (formerly the *British North America Act*, 1867) which permits the federal government to disallow provincial legislation.

discretion—*see* bureaucratic discretion.

division of labour—a principle of organization in which specialization in the organization of work is imposed in order to narrow the range of tasks each person is responsible for. The goal is to improve the overall efficiency of the organization and thus boost productivity.

division of powers—those sections of the constitution which set out the jurisdictional responsibilities of each level of government. In general, federal powers are spelled out in section 91 and provincial powers in section 92 of the Canadian Constitution.

doctrine of answerability—a watered-down version of the principle of ministerial responsibility in which the minister of a department is required simply to explain the errors of her subordinates, but not actually resign as a result of those actions.

elite—a small group of people who exercise considerable power in society—politically, economically, socially and/or bureaucratically.

employment equity—a set of programs and policies aimed at removing systemic barriers to employment and promotion among groups historically underrepresented in the public service. *See also* representativeness.

estimates—the government's annual request to Parliament for an appropriation of funds to support its programs.

ethics—rules and codes of morality guiding human behaviour.

ethics commissioners—officials appointed by government to oversee ethical rules and codes governing the behaviour of public servants.

evaluation—*see* policy evaluation.

executive branch of government—composed of the monarch and governor general at the formal (or symbolic) level, and the prime minister, Cabinet and bureaucracy at the po-

litical level, the executive is the organizational centre of power in the political system.

Expenditure Management System (EMS)—the system of budgeting introduced by the Chrétien government to promote greater control over government expenditures.

federalism—a system of governing in which the activities of government are divided in a written constitution between a national and regional governments, each of which is coordinate with but independent of the other in its own jurisdictional areas.

Financial Administration Act—the statute that governs financial accountability for federal departments, agencies and Crown corporations, and which defines the responsibilities of the Treasury Board and the Department of Finance in the area of financial management.

formulation—part of the policy cycle involving the development of public policy. *See also* public policy and policy cycle.

Free Trade Agreement (FTA)—the Free Trade Agreement between Canada and the United States was passed by the Conservative government of Brian Mulroney in 1988 and took effect in 1989. It created a tariff-free border while institutionalizing the Canada–U.S. relationship to an unprecedented degree. *See also* North American Free Trade Agreement.

governing instruments—the array of tools available to government to realize its policy goals, ranging from the privatization of conflict to direct government intervention.

Governor General—the representative of the monarch in Canada, appointed by the monarch on the recommendation of the prime minister. The legal and constitutional powers of the Governor General are impressive on paper, but are almost entirely symbolic in practice.

Hawthorne experiments—experiments conducted by industrial psychologists at the Hawthorne Works plant of Western Electric (near Chicago), beginning in 1924, to determine how physical conditions of work could be adjusted to improve productivity. The experiments are generally regarded as the origin of the human relations school of organizational theory. *See also* humanist theories.

hierarchy—the ordering of individuals or groups within an organization and their relationships of power and control.

hierarchy of human needs—a theory developed by Abraham Maslow that argues that humans are motivated by the satisfaction of a variety of needs ranging from basic physical requirements (food, shelter, clothing) to self-actualization. As lower level needs are realized, people move on to fulfill higher level ones.

homogeneity—the principle that asserts that similar activities ought to be grouped together in the same unit under a single supervisor and a single plan. Thus in public administration, things related to health care ought to be grouped in one department, those related to education in another, and so on. Moreover, within departments, there is a further division of labour, with scientists grouped in one unit, policy analysts in another, clerical staff in another, and so on, for the purposes of job function, promotion and wages. Also referred to as unity of direction.

humanist theories—a school of thought about organizing and managing workplaces which focuses on the inherent worth of individual workers *and* their needs. It originated with the Hawthorne studies on workplace organization in the 1920s and 1930s.

implementation—the part of the policy cycle involving the realization of public policy. *See also* public policy and policy cycle.

Increased Ministerial Authority and Accountability—the 1986 reform by the Mulroney government intended to allow for more flexibility in the roles and functions of ministers and their departments relative to their control by central agencies.

incrementalism—an approach to policy-making in which small, incremental changes are made to the status quo.

individual ministerial responsibility—the principle which states that individual ministers are responsible for the actions of their departments, and accountable for their departments to Parliament and the Canadian people. *See also* collective ministerial responsibility.

informal group—term used to describe the phenomenon discovered by the Hawthorne experiment researchers that the dominant factor in employee productivity was workers' membership in casual associations of fellow-employees, who together motivated each other to perform at certain levels by influencing values and attitudes and establishing social norms of behaviour in the workplace. *See also* Hawthorne experiments.

intra vires—a legal phrase which describes a federal or provincial statute as being within the constitutional jurisdiction of that level of government, as determined through judicial review of the *Constitution Act*.

interest group—an organized association that attempts to influence the government to pursue policies favourable to its own interests.

judicial branch of government—the Supreme Court and justices and all the other courts and justices below it. The judiciary in Canada is appointed rather than elected, and is separate from and independent of the other two branches of government (the executive and legislative branches).

Judicial Committee of the Privy Council—the British law Lords who acted as the court of final appeal for Canadians until 1949, when the Supreme Court of Canada was made the final arbiter of Canadian legal cases.

judicial evaluation—concerned with the legal issues arising out of administrative actions, judicial evaluation is a facet of administrative and constitutional law that involves the judges and the courts passing judgment on the behaviour and practices of the public service. *See also* judicial review.

judicial review—the power of the court to determine if the actions of other branches of the government are constitutional or not.

Keynesian welfare state—a broad term used to encompass the social welfare state constructed in the post-Second World War years on the basis of a theoretical model developed by British economist John Meynard Keynes, which promoted an activist role for government in the macroeconomic management of the economy.

La Relève—the internal review of the public service launched by the Clerk of the Privy Council in 1996 to deal with the "quiet crisis" within the federal bureaucracy.

legal-rational legitimacy—a form of legitimacy outlined by Max Weber in which citizens accept that an individual has the right to rule over them by virtue of the law. *See also* charismatic legitimacy and traditional legitimacy.

legislative branch of government—that branch of government charged with making and amending laws. In Canada it is composed of the Parliament, which is made up of the elected House of Commons and the appointed Senate.

legitimation—a concept employed in neo-Marxist theory referring to the need for the state to pass policies that legitimate capitalism in the eyes of those oppressed by it. Thus, social policies like welfare and unemployment insurance are seen as policies which legitimate the system for the working class, so that they do not rise up and overthrow it.

line-item budgeting—a rudimentary system of budgeting emphasizing the objects of expenditures (e.g., how many paper clips are needed, how much office space must be rented, etc.) rather than the purpose of expenditures.

Management by Objectives (MBO)—a management system associated with the work of Peter Drucker and others which focuses on cooperation between managers and workers in the establishment of broad-based annual goals and objectives for the organization.

market—an arena in which the organization of the economy and society for the production and distribution of goods and services takes place through the mechanism of exchange predicated on the voluntary actions of individuals. The human and social costs of relying on self-regulating markets have been so great that governments have been forced over time to step in and limit or regulate certain market excesses.

Marx, Karl—influential German philosopher (1818–1883) and founder of the political philosophy of Communism. *See* Marxist analysis and neo-Marxist theory.

Marxist analysis—a broad school of thought premised on the idea that modern capitalist societies are based on class conflict, and positing that the role of the state is to promote policies of accumulation for the capitalist class and policies of legitimation for the working class. *See also* neo-Marxist theory.

merit principle—the principle that all citizens should have an equal opportunity to be considered for employment in the public service based on their qualifications and skills, and should be promoted on the basis of their abilities and talents.

minimalist state—term used to describe the relatively minor role played by the Canadian state in the social and economic affairs of Canadians from the Confederation period to the 1930s.

minister—the political head of a department of government, appointed by the prime minister.

ministerial responsibility—*see* collective ministerial responsibility and individual ministerial responsibility.

Ministerial Task Force on Program Review—task force set up in 1984 by the Mulroney government under the leadership of Deputy Prime Minister Eric Nielsen to conduct a government-wide review of programs, with the goal of cutting waste and inefficiencies.

ministry—*see* department.

mixed-scanning—a theoretical approach to explaining policy-making which suggests that policy-makers combine rationality and incrementalism in the process of determining what action (or inaction) to take. *See also* incrementalism and rational-comprehensive theory.

mobilization of bias—term derived from pluralist theory to describe policy formulation as the result of a process of interest groups acting to influence government decision-makers.

neoconservative state—term used to describe contemporary governments that focus on reducing the size and intrusiveness of government through policies of deregulation, privatization, reducing taxes, reducing public services and reducing spending. It is premised on an ideological world-view which favours the free market over the state.

neo-Marxist theory—a broad school of thought that reconceptualizes the original theories about the capitalist state put forward by Karl Marx. *See also* Marxist analysis.

New Public Management (NPM)—a school of thought originating in Margaret Thatcher's Britain, advocating changes to organizational design and managerial practices consistent with neoconservative ideas. It is broadly aimed at making the state more responsive to political direction and to citizens, and at introducing more private sector practices into the public sector.

North American Free Trade Agreement (NAFTA)—the extension in 1994 of the Free Trade Agreement between Canada and the U.S. to include Mexico.

Office of the Comptroller General—created in 1978, this body has authority over administrative practices and controls in the areas of financial management and procedures for program evaluation.

organization development—a team-based approach to management decision-making and problem solving.

participatory management—a management style which incorporates the views of workers in the decision-making process.

partisanship—the degree of loyalty members of a political party feel towards one another.

party discipline—a key pillar of responsible government, party discipline means that party members support their leaders and act in unison in the legislature. It is supported by a system of rewards and punishments.

patronage—the awarding of contracts and the appointment of individuals to government positions on the basis of partisan support for, or contributions to, the governing party, rather than of merit.

pay equity—a shorthand term for equal pay for work of equal value, in which comparisons are made between different jobs for the same employer.

performance budgeting—a system of budgeting in which expenditures are related to specific activities to determine the costs of providing services.

Planning, Programming, Budgeting System (PPBS)—a broad-based budgeting system introduced in Canada in the 1960s and 1970s in an effort to impose greater rationality over the budget process. It was premised on the view that expenditure requests should be presented in terms of the objective of spending rather than in terms of input costs and particular functions, but ultimately fell out of favour due to the layers of complexity it added to the process.

pluralist theory—the view that power in society is widely dispersed between diverse groups which vie to influence government to produce policies favourable to their own interests.

Policy and Expenditure Management System (PEMS)—a system involving the use of Cabinet committees to coordinate, plan and integrate government budgeting and policy-making. It was introduced in 1979 by the Joe Clark government to improve ministerial control over financial management in the areas of priority-setting and to allow ministers to see the longer-range view of government policy development and financial activities.

policy cycle—the theoretical construction that suggests that public policy can best be understood as a process of formulation, implementation and evaluation. *See also* public policy; policy formulation; policy implementation; and policy evaluation.

policy evaluation—the part of the policy cycle involving the determination of needed policy or administrative changes through a process of in-depth analysis of institutions, programs and policies. *See also* public policy and policy cycle.

policy formulation—the part of the policy cycle involving the development of public policy. *See also* public policy and policy cycle.

policy implementation—the part of the policy cycle involving the realization of public policy. *See also* public policy and policy cycle.

political culture—the broad pattern of beliefs, values and attitudes citizens hold toward politics and the political system.

political evaluation—the ongoing process by which the electorate determines the worth of government policy by supporting or opposing the governing party in elections or through the expression of views in royal commissions, task forces, parliamentary committees, or to Cabinet, central agencies or line departments through the actions of citizens, interest groups, the media and so on. *See also* policy evaluation.

political neutrality—the principle that public servants must not engage in partisan politics but should rather remain politically impartial and neutral, serving the government of the day, not the political party which happens to hold power.

politics-administration dichotomy—the notion that there is a distinction between the duties and responsibilities of politicians who make public policy, and their public servants, who faithfully execute it.

POSDCORB—an acronym defining the administrative process by classifying the functions of top executives in an organization as planning, organizing, staffing, directing, coordinating, reporting and budgeting. It was devised by Luther Gulick.

post-deficit era—the period in which governments balance their budgets, eliminate their deficits and move toward debt reduction, opening up new possibilities for public spending on social and other programs.

power—the ability to influence or coerce others to conform to one's own goals and values.

pressure groups—*see* interest group.

Prime Minister's Office—a central agency of government staffed by appointees of the prime minister to provide partisan advice and monitor political developments for the prime minister.

private sector—that part of the economy not under government control.

privatization—the act of selling or turning over Crown corporations to the private sector.

Privy Council—a largely ceremonial body composed of current and former ministers of the Crown and other individuals recommended by the prime minister and appointed for life by the governor general.

Privy Council Office—a central agency which provides policy advice and administrative support to the Cabinet and its committees. It is the main organization responsible for developing and coordinating government policy.

Productivity Improvement Program—a set of reforms introduced in the dying days of the last Trudeau government to cut red tape and procedures hampering the efficient provision of government services through initiatives undertaken by the Treasury Board.

program budgeting—a system of budgeting that seeks to measure the impact of expenditures on the goals of the organization.

Program Review—a wide-reaching initiative introduced by the Chrétien government in 1994 to review all government programs, with the goal of identifying potential cost savings. The Review was driven by the government's desire to eliminate the deficit.

province building—the process of aggressive and assertive provincial premiers and governments seeking enhanced powers and responsibilities, while also seeking to diminish the role of the federal government.

PS2000—a review of the public service meant to address the low morale and disjunction between the senior and lower levels of public servants. Launched in late 1989, it was organized around 10 task forces headed by deputy ministers charged with finding ways to simplify personnel policies, loosen central agency controls, increase the managerial freedom of department managers, and increase program efficiency.

public administration—the ways in which governments conduct themselves through bureaucratic processes. This includes the norms and values of government officials, the organization of the bureaucracy, the accountability of public servants, the relationship between politicians and bureaucrats, and the decision-making systems used to formulate, implement and evaluate public policy.

public choice theory—a theoretical approach derived from classical economics which is premised on the notion that individuals act on the basis of a rational calculation of self-interest.

public comment—an aspect of the doctrine of political neutrality through which public servants are expected not to express publicly their personal views on government policy or administration. *See also* political neutrality.

public policy—what governments choose to do or not to do.

public sector—the collective term used to describe the institutions and personnel of the state.

Public Service Commission—called the Civil Service Commission until 1967, this independent agency is responsible for recruiting employees through competitive examinations and interviews, and for staffing and promotion using the merit principle.

Public Service Employment Act—passed in 1967, this Act granted the Public Service Commission the exclusive authority to appoint persons to and within the public service according to the merit principle, and to administer appeals, layoffs and dismissals. As well, it liberalized the restrictions on political activities by public servants.

Public Service Staff Relations Act—passed in 1967, this Act sets out the responsibilities of the quasi-judicial Public Service Staff Relations Board and provides for the structure and operation of the collective bargaining process in the public service. It also oversees the resolution of disputes and grievances, and conducts research on matters relevant to contract negotiations such as rates of pay, benefits and working conditions.

rational-comprehensive theory—a theoretical model that seeks to explain public policy decision-making as the product of a reasoned and thorough consideration of all the available options and their consequences.

recall—the procedure by which an elected official is removed from office by a vote of the electorate.

referendum—a means by which a particular question is put directly to the total electorate rather than to the elected representatives of the people.

regulatory agency—a government body which administers economic, environmental, social or other activities in the public interest according to guidelines and regulations established by government.

representative democracy—*see* representative government.

representative government—a political system with an elected legislature.

representativeness—the notion that the public service should reflect the social composition of the population it serves.

reservation—section 57 of the *Constitution Act*, 1867 (formerly the *British North America Act*, 1867) which permits the lieutenant governor of a province to withhold assent to a piece of provincial legislation pending review by the federal Cabinet.

responsible government—a system of government in which the executive branch of government requires the support and confidence of the legislative branch (and through it, the people) in order to govern.

rule of law—the principle that both the ruled and the rulers are answerable to the law.

scientific management—generally associated with the work of Frederick Winslow Taylor, scientific management is a management style that emphasized finding the "one best way" of accomplishing a task. It introduced the use of time and motion studies into the workplace with the goal of improving productivity by increasing efficiency.

social movements—informal networks of groups of citizens with shared values and identities oriented toward influencing the government on various social policies and issues through social and/or political struggle. *See also* interest group.

social welfare state—the term used to describe the interventionist state in post-war western industrialized countries, wherein governments took on an ever-expanding set of responsibilities in the areas of social welfare policy, health care, education, housing, pensions, unemployment insurance, etc.

span of control—an organizational mechanism indicating the number of subordinates reporting to a particular supervisor.

spending power—the power of the federal government to spend money on programs even if they are within provincial jurisdiction. This power is nowhere written in the Constitution, but is nonetheless a powerful federal tool in intergovernmental relations.

state—a form of political organization encompassing governmental institutions and personnel which are capable of maintaining order and implementing rules and laws over a given population within a given territory.

structuralist theory—the school of organization theory which is premised on a view of workers as little more than interchangeable parts in a machine. The goal of structuralist organization theory is to devise structures within which the work of individuals could be maximized through rigid rules and regulations so as to increase the efficiency of the organization. Little regard is paid to the needs or views of individual workers.

Supreme Court of Canada—composed of nine justices appointed by the prime minister, the Supreme Court is Canada's highest court for civil, criminal and constitutional cases.

three E's—the three E's are efficiency, effectiveness and economy. They represent a particular set of values underlying reforms to improve the functioning of organizations within the private sector, but they have increasingly been adopted in the public sector as well, where they compete with other values such as democracy, justice and accountability.

time and motion studies—an innovation introduced by Frederick Winslow Taylor, father of scientific management, in his effort to discover the "one best way" of routinizing workplace functions. Taylor used a stopwatch to record the time it took to complete every motion in a particular piece of work, allegedly to improve efficiency by eliminating unnecessary motions.

traditional legitimacy—a form of legitimacy outlined by Max Weber in which citizens accept that an individual has the right to rule over them by virtue of divine right; that is, that the gods anointed an individual as leader. *See also* charismatic legitimacy and legal-rational legitimacy.

Treasury Board—a Cabinet committee composed of six Cabinet ministers (including the President of the Treasury Board and the Minister of Finance) responsible for the preparation of the expenditure budget and for administrative management of government departments.

Treasury Board Secretariat—a central agency that supports the Treasury Board.

ultra vires—a legal phrase which describes a federal or provincial statute as beyond the constitutional jurisdiction of that level of government, as determined through judicial review of the *Constitution Act*.

unity of direction—*see* homogeneity.

user fees—the practice by governments of charging fees to citizens for services previously provided free or for a nominal charge, to cover the cost of providing the service, as a strategy for fighting deficits. User fees are a regressive form of taxation.

Weber, Max—German sociologist (1864–1920) generally regarded as the most influential writer on the subject of bureaucracy.

Index

A

Abella, Rosalie, 280
Aboriginal peoples, 284
accountability
    in action, 381–384
    administrative, 379
    Al-Mashat Affair, 374, 375
    anonymity, loss of, 374, 387
    attest auditing, 382
    best practices in, 250
    and bureaucracy, 8, 12–13
    compliance auditing, 382
    conservatives, 367
    contemporary issues, 384–389
    contexts of, in public service, 377–379
    and democracy, 364–370
    and democrats, 367
    doctrine of answerability, 371, 379
    hierarchical, movement away from, 356
    key elements of, 370
    legal, 379
    mechanisms, 388
    media, evolving role of, 380
    ministerial responsibility. *See* ministerial
        responsibility
    and New Public Management (NPM),
        384–387
    Office of the Auditor General, 381–384
    organization models and, 386
    performance auditing, 382
    and policy evaluation, 245
    political, 379
    professional, 379
    to the public, 379
    and public servants, 377–381
    redefining, 386
    reinforcement of, 367
    responsible government, 99, 365, 366
    rewards and punishment system, 368
    subdividing, 369
    value-for-money auditing, 382
    will of the people, 368
accumulation (of capital), 32, 217
Adie, Robert F., 34, 149
administrative, 379
administrative coordinative departments,
    129
administrative evaluation, 239
administrative law
    audi alteram partem, 190
        certiorari, 193
        concerns of, 188
        and constitutional law, 189
        courts' role in review of administrative
            practice, 189
        delegation, limitation on, 189, 190–191
        development of, 190
        discretion, 190
        habeas corpus, 193
        judicial review, 191–192
        mandamus, 193
        prohibition, 193
        quo warranto, 193
        remedies, 193
        Roncararelli v. Duplessis, 192
        ultra vires, 191
advisory body, 121
affirmative action, 280
Agrarian Socialism (Lipset), 37
Aitken, Hugh G.J., 150
Al-Mashat Affair, 374, 375
alienation, 28, 30
Allison, Graham, 11
Almond, Gabriel, 87, 92
alternative service delivery (ASD), 137–139
amending formula, 171
Anderson, James, 210
anomie, 52, 56
anonymity, 142, 374, 387
answerability, doctrine of, 371, 379
Anti-Inflation Act (1975), 181
attentive public, 356–357
attest auditing, 382
Aucoin, Peter, 70, 71, 73, 314
Auditor General, 241, 381–384
Auditor General Act, 383
audits, 239
authoritative, 82
authority, 34, 78, 91
autonomy, 30

B

Barnard, Chester, 51
Baxter-Moore, Nicolas, 223
Bennett, Bill, 19
Bennett, R.B., 180
Blake, Sara, 187

Board of Commerce Act and Combines and Fair Prices Act, Re, 180
Borden, Sir Robert, 15, 292
Bougon, Jocelyn, 267, 270–272
Bradford, Neil, 117
Brandeis, Louis D., 43
British North America Act (1867), 102, 163, 169–170
    see also Constitution Act (1867)
Brittain, Donald, 261
Brooks, Stephen, 90, 200, 204
budget, 325, 331
Budget Consultation Papers, 330
budget deficits. *See* deficits
budget process, 324
budget surplus. *See* post-deficit public administration
budgetary cycle, 329–332
bureaucracy
    accountability, 8
    client behaviour, 39
    conventions of behaviour, 8
    defined, 7
    and democracy, underlying tension between, 126
    described, 7
    dysfunctions in, 37–38
    elements of, 7
    formal rules, 8
    and oppression of women, 82
    and passion, role of, 40
    tension between politicians and bureaucrats, 37
    traditional bureaucratic organizations, 72
bureaucratic organization
    perspectives on, 28
    theories of. *See* theories of public administration
    ubiquitous nature of, 28
bureaucratic pathologies, 37–38, 41
"Bureaucratic Structure and Personality" (Merton), 38
bureaucrats
    attitudes towards, 261
    rule by officials, fear of, 125
    self-interest *vs.* organizational interest, 38, 125
Business Planning process, 252
Business Plans, 328, 330

C
the Cabinet, 105, 106, 122
Cabinet decision-making, 130
cabinet-parliamentary government
    executive branch, 119, 121
    judicial branch, 119, 122–123
    legislative branch, 119, 122

"myth and reality," 121
    and organizational structure, 119–123
    power, exercise of, 121
Calgary Accord, 185, 186
Campbell, Gordon, 19, 147, 314, 401
Campbell, Kim, 127
Canada
    continentalism, 95
    demography, 94
    direct democracy, 85–86
    diverse roles of the state, 147
    economic ties with U.S., 100
    founding cultures, 94–95
    geography, 94
    political culture in, 92–101
    political fragmentation, 98
    public ownership in, 147
    regionalism, 98–100
    scope of governments in Canada, 203
    state involvement in economy, 89
Canada Act, 171
Canada Customs and Revenue Agency, 270
Canada Health Act, 220
Canada Health and Social Transfer (CHST), 402
Canada Temperance Act, 178
Canadian Association of Programs in Public Administration (CAPPA), 5
Canadian Broadcast Corporation (CBC), 149
Canadian Centre for Management Development (CCMD), 5, 295, 317–319
Canadian Constitution. *See* the Constitution
Canadian public administration
    New Public Management (NPM), 73
    organization theory, impact of, 64–66
    Ottawa, power in, 80
    participatory management in, 69
    Program Review, 71
Canadian Wheat Board, 151
capital strike, 216
capitalist democracy, 116–117
Cappe, Mel, 269, 270
central agencies
    defined, 133
    Finance Department, 133–134
    horizontal coordination, 133
    Prime Minister's Office (PMO), 135
    Privy Council Office (PCO), 134–135
    Treasury Board Secretariat (TBS), 134
certiorari, 193
Chaplin, Charlie, 47
Charest, Jean, 123
charismatic legitimacy, 80

Charlottetown Accord, 173, 174
Charter of Rights and Freedoms
   creation and adoption of, 171
   employment of, 201
   entrenchment of rights, 122, 174
   human rights legislation, constitutionality of,
      107
   implementation of public policy, 222
   issues concerning judicial role, 102
   political culture, reflection of, 102
   violation of, as ground of unconstitutionality,
      163
Chartier, Bob, 318–319
Chrétien, Jean, 19, 127, 173, 262, 266, 272,
      314, 351–353, 371–372, 408
Chrétien, Raymond, 375
Citizen's Insurance v. Parsons, 181
The Civic Culture (Almond and Verba), 87
civil law, 165
Civil Service Act (1961), 265, 287
Civil Service Acts (1908 and 1918), 262
Civil Service Commission, 262, 265
Clark, Ian, 314
Clark, Joe, 127, 327
class conflict, 28
classic federalism, 175–177
classic theorists
   criticism of Marxist theory, 32
   criticisms of Weberian model, 35–41
   impact on Canadian public administration, 64
   Marxist theory, 28–31
   neo-Marxists, 32
   Weberian model, 33–35
classifications of organizations, 58
client behaviour, 39
Co-operative Commonwealth Government
      (CCF), 37
codes of ethics, 350–355
collective bargaining, 287–288, 291
collective responsibility, 371
"Common Sense Revolution," 403–406
communism, 31
compact theory, 177–178
"Comparative Political Systems" (Almond), 92
compliance auditing, 382
Confederation, 14, 18, 102, 119, 177
conflict of interest, 346–347
Conflict of Interest Code, 351
conflict resolution, and politics, 82
consent, 91
Conservative Party, 108
conservatives, 367

the Constitution
   ambiguous language, 118
   amending formula, 171
   Charlottetown Accord, 173, 174
   Charter of Rights and Freedoms. See Charter of
      Rights and Freedoms
   constitutional conventions, 168
   described, 101–103
   disallowance, power of, 176
   division of powers, 103–104, 119
   elements of, 167
   federal government powers, 119
   federal *vs.* provincial rights, 177–178
   and federalism, 174–177
   history of, 168–174
   the law and the courts, 166
   Meech Lake Accord, 171, 172–173
   peace, order and good government, 165,
      178–181
   provincial government powers, 118, 119
   Quebec, 171–173
   reservation, power of, 176
Constitution Act (1867), 104, 163
   see also British North America Act (1867)
Constitution Act (1982), 171
constitutional conventions, 168
constitutional law
   and administrative law, 189
   Board of Commerce Act and Combines and Fair
      Prices Act, Re, 180
   Citizen's Insurance v. Parsons, 181
   compact theory, 177–178
   contract theory, 177–178
   defined, 168
   division of powers, 178
   Employment and Social Service Act Reference, 182
   federal-provincial bargaining, 181–182
   Fort Frances Pulp and Power Company v. the
      Manitoba Free Press, 180
   Local Prohibition case, 178
   Patriation Reference, 182
   Public Service Board v. Dionne, 182
   Russell v. The Queen, 178
   Toronto Electric Commissioners v. Snider, 180
   unilateral secession by province, 182
constitutions, 166–187
contemporary evaluation practices, 247–255
Continental Divide (Lipset), 96
continentalism, 95, 209
Contingency Reserve Fund, 409
contingency theory, 57
continuity, 33
contract theory, 177–178
contracting out, 70, 339

Copps, Sheila, 352
the courts, 164–166
Critique of Hegel's Philosophy of Right (Marx), 31
Crown corporations, 149–153
"culture of the mandarinate," 294–295
cybernetics, 57

D

Daubney, David, 375
Dawson, R. MacGregor, 5
De Villars, Ann S., 191
debt, 400
decentralization, 66, 70
decision-making models
    basic model, 208
    development of, 208
    incremental theory, 212–213
    Marxist analysis, 215–217
    micro-level approach, 210
    mixed-scanning theory, 214
    pluralism, 214–215
    public choice theory, 217–218
    rational-comprehensive theory, 210–212
deficit financing, 415
deficits
    blame on, 401
    debt, 400
    defined, 400
    neoconservatism, 401
    new set of questions, 398
    off-loading, 402
    past perspectives on, 397–398
    politics of, 400–406
    reduction, obsession on, 396–397, 401–406
delegation, 189, 190–191
Demings, W. Edwards, 69
democracy
    and accountability, 364–370
    capitalist democracy, 116–117
    definitions of, 84
    direct democracy, 84–85, 85–86
    economic democracy, 87–88
    plebiscite, 85
    and political culture, interplay of, 101–107
    political democracy, 86–87
    referenda, 85
    representative democracy, 84, 85–86
    tyranny of the majority, 86
democratic administration, 62
democratic society, 6
democrats, 367
demography, 94
department, 118

Department of Finance, 133–134
Department of Foreign Affairs and
        International Trade, 131, 312–313
departmental organizations
    administrative coordinative departments, 129
    and Cabinet decision-making, 130
    central agencies, 133–135
    deputy minister (DM), 140–144
    generic model, 133
    gradual growth in, 127
    line departments, 133
    ministerial responsibility, 140
    ministries, 127
    policy coordinative departments, 130
    span of control, 130–131
    statutory bodies, 127
    vertical constituency departments, 129
deputy minister (DM), 140–144, 293,
        294–295
deregulation, 70, 146–148
Dickson, William, 51
direct democracy, 84–85, 85–86
disallowance, power of, 176
discretion, 190, 339, 344–345
discrimination, 276
dispute resolution, 104
distribution of power, 209
division of labour, 47
division of powers, 103–104, 119
        see also constitutional law
Dobuzinskis, Laurent, 263, 264–265
doctrine of answerability, 371, 379
Doern, G. Bruce, 223
downsizing, 70
Drucker, Peter, 67
Duplessis, Maurice, 192
Durkheim, Emile, 52
Dwivedi, O.P., 355
Dye, Thomas, 200

E

Easton, David, 82
economic democracy, 87–88
economics, and Canadian political culture,
        101
the economy, 321–325
economy (three Es), 13–14, 71
education, and ethics, 355
effectiveness, 13–14, 71
efficiency, 13–14, 71
elected representatives, 6
elitist view, 209

Employment and Social Service Act Reference, 182
employment equity, 280–284
Employment Equity Act, 284
Employment Insurance, 409
Englebert, Ernest A., 355
entrance exam, 276
environmental factors, 208–209
equity, and representativeness, 280–286
Estimates, 325, 328
ethics
    codes of ethics, 350–355
    conflict of interest, 346–347
    defined, 17
    discretion, 339, 344–345
    enforcement of ethical behaviour, 17
    ethical dilemmas in the public service, 338–350
    guidelines, development of, 342
    history of, in Canadian political life, 338
    Liberal ethics guidelines, 351–353
    lying for the public good, 347–348
    new orientation towards, 339
    partisanship, 345
    public comment, 346
    and public interest, 341
    and public perception, 341
    public sector *vs.* private sector, 348–350
    role models, 356
    training and education, 355
    vigilant citizens, 356–357
ethics commissioners, 339
ethics regime, 357–358
Etzioni, Amitai, 214
evaluation
    accountability, 245
    administrative, 239
    basic questions of, 242
    Business Planning process, 252
    case studies, 253
    contemporary evaluation practices, 247–255
    defined, 237
    described, 206, 229–230
    development of, 237–243
    financial management, 253
    indicators, 244
    judicial, 239
    lack of resources for, 245
    management, education of, 250
    managing for results, 254
    methodological problems, 244
    NPM and, 252
    Office of the Comptroller General, 240, 243
    political, 240
    in practice, 246–247

problems of, 243–245
    Program Review, 71, 248, 252
    results reporting and access, 250
    six factors, 246–247
Evans, B. Mitchell, 146
Eves, Ernie, 406
exchange process, 412
the executive, 105–106
executive agencies, 386
executive branch, 119, 121
executive federalism, 184–185
Expenditure Management System (EMS), 324, 328, 329, 331, 409
expenditure reduction initiatives, 70
expertise, 33
external auditor, 384
extra-parliamentary actors
    defined, 105
    interest groups, 108–109
    media, 109–110
    political parties, 108

F
Federal Court of Canada, 165
federal government
    alternative service delivery (ASD), 137–139
    central agencies, 133–135
    Crown corporations, 149–153
    departmental organizations, 126–133
    deputy minister (DM), 140–144
    disallowance, power of, 176
    division of powers, 103–104, 119
    ministerial responsibility, 140
    ministers, 119
    powers of, 119
    regulatory agencies, 144–149
    reservation, power of, 176
    spending power, 178
    taxation powers, 176
federal-provincial bargaining, 181–185
Federal-Provincial Relations Office (FPRO), 133
federalism
    in Canada, 103–104
    classic federalism, 175–177
    and the Constitution, 174–177
    Constitution, function of, 167
    and division of powers, 118–119
    executive federalism, 184–185
    and organizational structure, 118–119
Finance Department, 133–134
Financial Administration Act, 127, 288, 378
financial management

budget, 325, 331
Budget Consultation Papers, 330
budgetary cycle, 329–332
budgeting, 324
Business Plans, 328, 330
deficits. *See* deficits
departmental "savers" and "spenders," 323–324
Estimates, 325, 328
Expenditure Management System (EMS), 328, 329, 331
Glassco Commission recommendations, 326
government fiscal resources, 325–328
line item budgeting, 327
lines of service, 328
organizational features of, 324
Outlooks on Program Priorities and Expenditures, 330
Policy and Expenditure Management System (PEMS), 327–328
post-war government spending, 322
program budgeting, 327
Programming, Planning, Budgeting System (PPBS), 327
Public Accounts of Canada, 325
the state and economy, 321–325
Statement of Financial Operations, 325
fiscal dividend, 408, 409
Ford, Henry, 47
Foreign Affairs. *See* Department of Foreign Affairs and International Trade
formative events, 96
formulation of public policy
decision-making models, 210–214
distribution of power, 209
environmental factors, 208–209
incremental theory, 212–213
institutional structure, 210
Marxist analysis, 215–217
mixed-scanning theory, 214
pluralism, 214–215
procedural factors, 210
public choice theory, 217–218
rational-comprehensive theory, 210–212
responsibility of, 206
social attitudes and ideas, 209
Fort Frances Pulp and Power Company v. the Manitoba Free Press, 180
The Founding of New Societies (Hartz), 96
Fox, Francis, 123
Fraser, John, 140
Free Trade Agreement (FTA), 100, 245
FTA, 100
Fulton-Favreau formula, 171
The Functions of the Executive (Barnard), 51
future of Canadian society, 412–414

G
Gaebler, Ted, 70
Gagliano, Alfonso, 353
geography, 94
"Getting Government Right: A Progress Report," 228
Gladden, E.N., 3
Glassco Commission, 16, 66, 241, 294, 326
goal displacement, 38
goals of public administration, 11
Goodnow, Frank J., 40
Goudlner, Alvin, 39–40
governing instruments, 202, 222–227
government
as agent of social change, 410
bureaucracy, 7
ethics, 17
ethics regime, 357–358
expenditures and revenues, changes in, 20–21
fiscal resources, 325–328
personnel, 8
policy instruments, 8
professionalism, 14–17
and public administration, 5–17
public *vs.* private sectors, 9–10
spending power, 118
vs. the state, 89–91
Great Depression, 18, 322
Great Shelf Principle, 40
Gross Domestic Product (GDP), 20–21, 322
group, 62
Guide for Ministers and Secretaries of State, 371–372
Gulick, Luther, 46
Guy, James John, 14

H
habeas corpus, 193
Hale, Geoffrey, 415
Harris, Mike, 19, 147, 284, 401, 403–406
Hartz, Louis, 96
Hawthorne Experiments, 49–50
Hegel, G.W.F., 28, 30
Herring, E. Pendleton, 341
hierarchical accountability, 356
hierarchy, 30, 33
hierarchy of human needs, 53
Hobbes, Thomas, 151
Hodgetts, J.E., 127
horizontal coordination, 133
Horowitz, Gad, 26, 151
House of Commons, 106, 127

Howlett, Michael, 145–159
Human Development Index, 272
human relations approach
    criticisms of, 54–56
    democratic administration, 62
    described, 48–54
    the group, 62
    Hawthorne Experiments, 49–51
    hierarchy of human needs, 53
    impact on Canadian public administration, 66
    informal group, 50
    management-centred approach, 56
    Mayo's philosophy, 52–53
    participatory management, 67–69
    recruitment programs, 277
    rewards, 52
    sanctions, 52
    social norms, 52
    supervision, 53
human resource management
    career patterns of deputy ministers, 294–295
    collective bargaining and, 291
    "culture of the mandarinate," 294–295
    debates in, 290–291
    development of, 292
    discipline, 297
    entrance exam, 276
    firing decisions, 296
    major issues, 274, 294
    origins of, 291–292
    Performance Review and Appraisal Report, 296
    in post-war years, 294
    problems, 11
    recruitment, 297–298
    reevaluation of, 295
    reforms, 292, 293
    representativeness, 276–288
    retention, 297
    senior bureaucrats, 293
    specialized training, necessity of, 295
Human Resources and Development Canada, 381
human rights legislation, 107, 284
humanist theories, 42, 48–56

I
ideal-type, 36
impersonality, 33
implementation of public policy
    external forces, 221
    frontline worker and, 220
    governing instruments, choice of, 222–227
    New Public Management (NPM), impact of, 227, 228
    political feasibility, 220
    process, 218–222
    public spending, 225
    recent developments, 227–229
    regulation, selection of, 226
    resistance within bureaucracy, 219
    responsibility of, 206
Increased Ministerial Authority and Accountability, 311
incremental theory, 212–213
informal group, 50
information technologies, 321
Inge, William Ralph, 413
Innis, Harold Adams, 97
Institute of Public Administration of Canada. See Statement of Principles of the Institute of Public Administration of Canada
institutional structure, 210
institutions
    basic institutions of Canadian government, 120
    Canadian Constitution, 101–103
    democracy and political culture, interplay of, 101–107
    described, 9
    the executive, 105–106
    extra-parliamentary actors, 105, 108–110
    federalism, 103–104
    interest groups, 108–109
    judiciary, 104, 107
    the legislature, 106–107
    media, 109–110
    North American Free Trade Agreement, 103
    parliamentary actors, 104–107
    political parties, 108
interest groups, 108–109, 214
intergovernmental negotiations, 183
intra vires, 107, 122
intrusiveness of policy instruments, 223

J
Jackson, Doreen, 140, 210, 278
Jackson, Robert J., 140, 210, 278
job structure, influence of, 55
Johnson, David, 21
Johnston, Larry, 81
Jones, David P., 191
judicial branch, 119, 122–123
judicial evaluation, 239
judicial review, 191–192
judiciary, 104, 107
jurisdictional issues. See constitutional law

K

Katz, Robert, 56
Kernaghan, Kenneth, 357–358
Kerr, Clark, 55
Kesey, Ken, 37
Keynes, John Meynard, 209
Keynesian principles, 409
Keynesian welfare state, 18–19
Khan, Daniel, 56
Klein, Ralph, 147, 401

L

La Relève, 268, 316–321
Labour Code, 152
Lambert Commission, 327
Lang, Fritz, 47
language, and representativeness, 278
Laswell, Harold, 82
the law
    administrative law. *See* administrative law
    civil law, 165
    constitutional law. *See* constitutional law
    and the courts, 164–166
    function of, 165
    rule of law, 165
Leadbeater, Alan, 187
learning organization, 319
legal accountability, 379
legal-rational legitimacy, 80–81
legislative branch, 119, 122
the legislature, 106–107
legitimacy, 80, 91
legitimation, 32, 217
Lévesque, René, 171
Liberal ethics guidelines, 351–353
Liberal Party, 108
Lindquist, Evert, 297, 332
line departments, 133
line item budgeting, 327
lines of service, 328
linguistic duality, 100
Lipset, Seymour Martin, 37, 96
Local Prohibition case, 178
Locke, John, 151
Loranger, T.J.J., 177
Lowi, Theodore, 223
loyalty, 143
lying for the public good, 347–348
Lyon, Sterling, 19

M

MacDonald, Flora, 141
Macdonald, Sir John A., 14, 18, 106, 127, 150, 175, 183, 263
Macdonnell, J.J., 243
Mackenzie King, William Lyon, 180
macro-level approach, 210
Magna Carta, 365
Mallory, J.R., 166
Management and the Workers (Roethlisberger and Dickson), 51
Management by Objectives (MBO), 67–68
management reform
    challenges of, 308–309
    Increased Ministerial Authority and Accountability, 311
    information technologies, 321
    key problem areas, 308–309
    La Relève, 316–321
    Ministerial Task Force on Program Review, 310–311
    mission statement, 312
    and NPM, 317
    partnering, 319
    and preoccupation with renewal, 310
    Productivity Improvement Program, 310
    Program Review. *See* Program Review
    PS2000. *See* PS2000
    service-to-the-public focus, 319
    shifting of responsibilities, 319
    Special Operating Agencies (SOA), 312
    trends, 319–321
managing for results, 254
mandamus, 193
mandarinate, culture of, 294–295
mandate of public administration, 11
Mandel, Michael, 289
Manley, John, 352
the market, 410, 411
Martin, Paul, 352, 395, 398, 415
Marx, Karl, 28–31, 32, 82
    see also Marxist theory
Marxist theory
    alienation, 28, 30
    capitalism, and class division, 88
    class conflict, 28
    criticisms of, 32
    critique of Hegel, 31
    decision-making, 215–217
    described, 28–31
    impact on Canadian public administration, 64
    neo-Marxists, 32
    the state, 90

Maslove, Alan, 244
Maslow, Abraham, 53
Mayo, Elton, 51, 52
Mazmanian, Daniel, 222
McCall-Newman, Christina, 80
McRoberts, Kenneth, 177
means of public policy, 203–204
media, 109–110, 380
Meech Lake Accord, 171, 172–173, 184–185
Mercier, Honoré, 177
Merton, Robert K., 38–39
Metropolis (Lang), 47
micro-level approach, 210
Miliband, Ralph, 32, 90
minimalist state, 18
ministerial responsibility
    Al-Mashat Affair, 374, 375
    anonymity, doctrine of, 142, 374
    answerability, doctrine of, 371
    changes in traditional concept of, 380–381
    collective responsibility, 371
    described, 140
    extent of ministerial involvement, 373
    Guide for Ministers and Secretaries of State,
        371–372
    and non-experts, 376
    and outside consultants, 376
    party discipline, 373
    and politics-administration dichotomy, 376
    resignation of minister, 377
Ministerial Task Force on Program Review,
    310–311
ministers, 119
ministries, 127
Ministry of Agriculture, 347
Ministry of Canadian Heritage, 270
mission statement, 312
mixed-scanning theory, 214
mobilization of bias, 205
Model Forest Program, 250
Modern Times (Chaplin), 47
morale, 312, 313
Morgan, Gareth, 58
Morgan, Nicole, 264
Mowat, Oliver, 176, 177, 183
Mulroney, Brian, 19, 93, 127, 171, 173, 184,
    262, 266, 310, 311, 341

N
NAFTA. *See* North American Free Trade
    Agreement
national dimensions, 180

National policy (1878), 18
National Transportation Act, 147
Natural Resources Canada, 250
neo-Marxists, 32
neoconservatism, 401
neoconservative state, 19–21
neutrality, 142
New Democratic Party (NDP), 37, 108
New Public Management (NPM)
    and accountability, 384–387
    assumptions of, 70
    contracting out, 70
    critics of, 73
    decentralization, 70
    deregulation, 70
    downsizing, 70
    evaluation and, 252
    expenditure reduction initiatives, 70
    impact on Canadian public administration, 73
    and management reform, 317
    origin of, 69
    policy implementation, impact on, 227, 228
    private sector values, 71
    privatization, 70
    reinventing government, 70
    three Es, 71
    user fees, 70
Nielsen, Eric, 311
Nixon, Richard, 351
North American Free Trade Agreement, 100,
    103, 245

O
Office of the Auditor General, 12, 13,
    381–384
Office of the Comptroller General, 13, 240,
    243
Office of Values and Ethics, 339
Official Languages Act, 278
On the Art of Cutting Metal (Taylor), 44
One Flew Over the Cuckoo's Nest (Kesey), 37
Organization Development (OD), 68
organization theories. *See* theories of public
    administration
organizational structure
    alternative service delivery (ASD), 137–139
    cabinet-parliamentary government, 119–123
    capitalist democracy, 116–117
    central agencies, 133–135
    Crown corporations, 149–153
    departmental organizations, 126–133
    factors influencing, 116–125
    federalism, 118–119

ministerial responsibility, 140
   regulatory agencies, 144–149
Osborne, David, 70
Ottawa, power in, 80
Outlooks on Program Priorities and
   Expenditures, 330
overload thesis, 202

P

Pal, Leslie, 204
"Papers on the Science of Administration"
   (Gulick and Urwick), 46
Parks Canada, 270
parliamentary actors
   defined, 105
   the executive, 105–106
   judiciary, 107
   the legislature, 106–107
participatory management
   impact on Canadian public administration, 69
   Management by Objectives (MBO), 67–68
   Organization Development (OD), 68
   Total Quality Management (TQM), 69
partisanship, 345
partnering, 319, 339
party discipline, 99, 373
passion, role of, 40
Patriation Reference, 182
patronage, 15, 262–263, 292
pay equity, 284–285
peace, order and good government, 165,
   178–181
Pearson, Lester, 127, 147, 288
performance auditing, 382
Performance Review and Appraisal Report, 296
persons with disabilities, 284
Peter Principle, 40
Phidd, Richard W., 223
plebiscite, 85
pluralism, 214–215
pluralist view, 209
P.O.G.G. *See* peace, order and good
   government
Policy and Expenditure Management System
   (PEMS), 327–328
policy capacity, 204
policy coordinative departments, 130
policy cycle, 206
policy implementation. *See* implementation
   of public policy
policy instruments, 8
political accountability, 379

political-administrative relationships,
   125–126
political culture in Canada
   continentalism, 95
   and democracy, interplay of, 101–107
   demography, 94
   described, 92–94
   distinctiveness, 101
   economics, 101
   elites and, 97
   formative events, 96
   founding cultures, 94–95
   geography, 94
   Hartzian approach, 96
   interpretations of, 95–101
   linguistic duality, 100
   long-range historical perspective, 98
   party discipline, 99
   political fragmentation, 98
   and political parties, 108
   regionalism, 98–100
   staples approach, 97
   U.S. penetration of Canada, 100
political democracy, 86–87
political evaluation, 240
political neutrality, 289–290
political parties
   party discipline, 99, 373
   and political culture, 108
political trust, 101
politics
   conflict and competition over limited
      resources, 81
   of deficits, 400–406
   definitions, 82
   existence of, 81
   and power, 78–82
   vs. private sphere, 82
   and public servants, 288–290
politics-administration dichotomy, 6, 40,
   143, 376
Politics and Administration (Goodnow), 40
population ecology theory, 58
Porter, John, 32, 97, 293
POSDCORB, 46
post-deficit public administration
   broader array of tools, 408
   choices in, 406
   and distribution of resources, 410
   fiscal dividend, 408
   future of Canadian society, 412–414
   implication and meaning of, 399
   Keynesian principles, unlikelihood of
      returning to, 409
   living within our means, 409

public opinion, 409–410
security agenda, 414–419
September 11, 2001, impact of, 414–419
state and market, 410–412
transfer payments, limited commitment to, 409
Poulantzas, Nicos, 32
power
and authority, 78
charismatic legitimacy, 80
distribution of, 209
legal-rational legitimacy, 80–81
in Ottawa, 80
and pluralism, 215
and politics, 78–82
traditional legitimacy, 80
Preparatory Committee on Collective
Bargaining in the Public Service, 288
Pressman, Jeffrey, 219
Prime Minister, 105, 106, 127, 141
Prime Minister's Office (PMO), 135
Prince, Michael, 398, 406–408
Principles of Scientific Management (Taylor),
43, 45
private sector
efficiency and service, 13–14
ethics in, 348–350
mandate and goals, 10–13
vs. public sector, 9–10
privatization, 70, 153
privatization of conflict, 225, 227
Privy Council Office (PCO), 134–135
procedural attitudes, 209
procedural factors, 210
Productivity Improvement Program, 310
professional accountability, 379
professionalism, 14–17
program budgeting, 327
Program Review, 71, 248, 252, 314–316
Programming, Planning, Budgeting System
(PPBS), 242, 243, 264, 325, 327
prohibition, 193
"proverbs of administration," 40
province-building, 183
Provincial Rights movement, 177
PS2000, 16–17, 228, 248, 268, 288–289,
312–314
public, 78
Public Accounts of Canada, 325
public administration
American influence, 4
vs. business administration, 9–10
in Canada. *see* Canadian public administration
defined, 2–5

and democratic government, 5–7
perspectives, 3
study of, in Canada, 5
theories of organization. *See* theories of public
administration
Public Administration and the Public Interest
(Herring), 341
public choice theory, 217–218
public comment, 346
public goods, 12
public interest, 341, 345
public policy
conscious government choices, 201
costs, 204
decision-making models, 210–214
defining, 200–206
distribution of power, 209
environmental factors, 208–209
evaluation stage. *See* evaluation
formulation stage, 207–218
goals of, 204
governing instruments, 202, 222–227
implementation stage, 206, 218–230
incremental theory, 212–213
institutional structure, 210
Marxist analysis, 215–217
means, 203–204
mixed-scanning theory, 214
mobilization of bias, 205
overload thesis, 202
pluralism, 214–215
policy capacity, 204
policy cycle, 206
procedural factors, 210
process of implementation, 218–222
public choice theory, 217–218
rational-comprehensive theory, 210–212
resources, 205
scope, 202
social attitudes and ideas, 209
symbolic resources, 205
value problems, 204, 205
public sector
changes in, 270, 307
in Confederation times, 262–263
efficiency and service, 13–14
employment trends, 271
ethics. *See* ethics
evolution of, 18–21
history of, 260–272
institutional changes, 270
mandate and goals, 10–13
morale in, 312, 313
neoconservative arguments, 266–267
in 1950s, 264

in 1960s and 1970s, 264–265
in 1980s and 1990s, 266
overview, 272–276
patronage, 262–263
patronage-based, 15
political neutrality, 289–290
post-war efforts, 270–272
vs. private sector, 9–10
"quiet crisis," 267, 317
reform, 262
renewal of, 294, 310
representative of society, failure to be, 265
representativeness, 276–288
restructuring, 18–21
service provision and, 261
societal changes, effect of, 265
unionization, 286–288
upper ranks, recruitment to, 293
women in, 281–282
public servants
and accountability, 377–381
and politics, 288–290
public service. See public sector
Public Service Board v. Dionne, 182
Public Service Commission, 263, 269, 284,
288, 295
Public Service Employment Act, 16, 127, 265,
276, 288, 289
Public Service Reform Act, 268
Public Service Staff Relations Act, 152, 265,
270, 288, 295
public spending, 225, 322

Q
Quality Service Initiative, 73
Quebec
Charlottetown Accord, 173, 174
and the Constitution, 171–173
electoral system and, 87
Meech Lake Accord, 171, 172–173
sovereignty association referendum, 173
"quiet crisis," 267, 317
quo warranto, 193
quota laws, 284

R
Rae, Bob, 216
Ramesh, M., 145–159
rational-comprehensive theory, 210–212
Reagan, Ronald, 266
recruitment challenges, 297–298
recruitment programs, 275
reelection, 14

referenda, 85
reform. See management reform
region, and representativeness, 277
regional economic development, 151
regionalism, 98–100
regulation
under NPM, 144–149
when to select, as policy instrument, 226
regulatory agencies, 144–149
regulatory bodies, 144–149
regulatory reform, 148
Reinventing Government (Osborne and
Gaebler), 70
remedies, 193
Report to the Prime Minister on the Public
Service of Canada (Bourgon), 267
representative, 265
representative democracy, 84, 85–86
representativeness
Aboriginal peoples, 284
and equity, 280–286
language, 278
pay equity, 284–285
persons with disabilities, 284
in public service, 276–288
region, 277
theoretical arguments, 277
visible minorities, 284, 286
women, 281–282
reservation, power of, 176
resources for policy-making, 205
responsible government, 99, 365, 366
see also accountability; ministerial responsibility
Revenue Canada, 270
reverse discrimination, 284
rewards, 52
Rist, Ray, 229
Rock, Allan, 352
Rockman, Bert, 413–414
Roethlisberger, F.J., 51
role models, 356
Roncararelli v. Duplessis, 192
Royal Commission on Bilingualism and
Biculturalism, 278
Royal Commission on Financial Management
and Accountability, 327
Royal Commission on Government
Organization. See Glassco
Commission
rule of law, 165
Russell, Peter, 119
Russell v. The Queen, 178

S

Sabatier, Paul, 222
sanctions, 52
"savers," 323–324
Savoie, Donald, 71, 242, 322, 324, 385
Sayre, Wallace, 10, 73
Schattschneider, E.E., 215
scientific management
    criticisms of, 47–48
    described, 42–47
    division of labour, 47
    Frederick Winslow Taylor, 43–44, 45
    impact on Canadian public administration,
        65–66
    POSDCORB, 46
    time and motion studies, 44
    universal principles of administration, 46
    worker-management cooperation, assumption
        of, 46
scope of public policy, 202
Scott, Frank, 189
scrutiny of public sector, 12
Second World War, 322
security agenda, 414–419
self-interest vs. organizational interest, 38
the Senate, 106
seniors' pensions, 93
September 11, 2001, 414–419
service, 13–14
service-to-the-public focus, 319
Sharp, Mitchell, 141
Shields, John, 146
shifting of responsibilities, 319
Siegel, Abraham, 55
Simeon, James, 296–297
Simeon, Richard, 208, 209
Simon, Herbert, 40
slate-owned enterprise, 386
social attitudes and ideas, 209
social equality, 88
social movements, 410
social norms, 52
The Social Psychology of Organizations
        (Katz and Khan), 56
social welfare state, 397
span of control, 40, 41, 130–131
Special Operating Agencies (SOA), 312, 386
"spenders," 323–324
spending power, 118, 178
Spry, Graham, 150
staples approach, 97
the state

allocation of resources, 410–411
and financial management, 321–325
vs. government, 89–91
importance of, 90
Keynesian welfare state, 18–19
legitimacy, 91
meaning of, 89
minimalist state, 18
neoconservative state, 19–21
role of, 18–21, 89
social welfare state, 399
welfare state, 201–202
Statement of Financial Operations, 325
Statement of Principles of the Institute of
        Public Administration of Canada, 345,
        346–347
Statistics Canada, 249, 250
statutory bodies, 127
Stevenson, Garth, 263
Stivers, Camilla, 82
Strick, John, 148
A Strong Foundation (Tait), 339
structuralist theories, 42, 48
SUFA, 185
supervision, 53
Sutherland, Sharon, 374–375
symbolic gesture or response, 223
systems theory, 56–57

T

Tait, John, 341, 341–342
Tait Report, 339
Task Force on Conflict of Interest, 351
Task Force on Public Service Values and
        Ethics, 351
taxation powers, 176
Taylor, Frederick Winslow, 43–44, 45
Teeple, Gary, 147–148
Tellier, Paul, 312, 314
Thatcher, Margaret, 69, 70, 266
theories of public administration
    classic theorists, 28–41
    contemporary developments, 67–74
    contingency theory, 57
    cybernetics, 57
    history of development of, 28
    human relations approach, 48–56
    humanist theories, 42, 48–56
    impact on Canadian public administration,
        64–66
    Management by Objectives (MBO), 67–68
    New Public Management (NPM), 69–74
    Organization Development (OD), 68

participatory management, 67–69
population ecology theory, 58
scientific management, 42–48
structuralist theories, 42, 48
systems theory, 56–57
Total Quality Management (TQM), 69
theory of representativeness. *See* representativeness
"third sector," 19
Thomas, Paul G., 34, 149, 370, 387
Thompson, Victor, 39–40
three Es, 13–14, 71
time and motion studies, 44
Toronto Electric Commissioners v. Snider, 180
Total Quality Management (TQM), 69
traditional bureaucratic organizations, 72
traditional legitimacy, 80
trained incapacity, 38
training, and ethics, 355–356
transfer payments, 409
Treasury Board, 254, 265, 270, 274–275, 326, 384
Treasury Board Secretariat (TBS), 134
triple-E model, 106
Trotsky, Leon, 89
Trudeau, Pierre Elliot, 57, 127, 147, 171, 200, 262, 278, 310
Turner, John, 127
tyranny of the majority, 86

U
ultra vires, 107, 122, 191
unionization, 286–288
United Nations, 272
Urwick, Lyndall, 46
user fees, 70

V
value-for-money auditing, 382
value problems, 204, 205

Vander Zalm, Bill, 19
Verba, Sidney, 87
vertical constituency departments, 129
The Vertical Mosaic (Porter), 97, 293
Veteran's Independence Program, 250
Victoria Charter, 171
vigilant citizens, 356–357
visible minorities, 284, 286

W
Walkerton water tragedy, 403, 404–405
Watertown Arsenal, 45
Weber, Max
organization theory, 33–35
power, 80
the state, 89
Weberian model of organization theory
continuity, 33
criticisms of, 35–41
described, 33–35
expertise, 33
hierarchy, 33
ideal-type, 36
impact on Canadian public administration, 64
impersonality, 33
welfare officers, Merton's observations on, 38–39
welfare state, 201–202
Wheare, K.C., 118
Whitaker, Reginald, 15
Wildavsky, Aaron, 219
will of the people, 368
Wilson, Michael, 266
Wilson, Woodrow, 4, 10, 263
women
employment equity, 280–282
oppression of, 82
pay equity, 284–285
in public service, 281–282